CAPITAL THEORY, EQUILIBRIUM ANALYSIS AND RECURSIVE UTILITY

CAPITAL THEORY

EQUILIBRIUM ANALYSIS AND

RECURSIVE UTILITY

ROBERT A. BECKER

JOHN H. BOYD III

First published 1997

Blackwell Publishers Inc.
350 Main Street
Malden, Massachusetts 02148, USA

Blackwell Publishers Ltd
108 Cowley Road
Oxford OX4 1JF
UK

Library of Congress Cataloging in Publication Data
Becker, Robert A.
    Capital theory, equilibrium analysis, and recursive utility /
Robert A. Becker and John H. Boyd III
        p.   cm.
    Includes bibliographical references and index.
    ISBN 1–55786–413–6 (alk. paper)
    1. Equilibrium (Economics) 2. Statics and dynamics (Social sciences)
3. Capital. 4. Utility theory. 5. Economic development.
I. Boyd, John A., III. II. Title.
HB145.B385   1997
339.5—dc20   96–41656
                                                                  CIP

British Library Cataloguing in Publication Data
A CIP catalogue record for this book is available from the British Library

ISBN 1557864136

Typeset by AMS-TeX

This book is printed on acid-free paper

To Adam and Karen:

—RAB

To my parents:

—JHB

Contents

List of Examples

Chapter 8

Preface

Capital theory provides the foundation for economic dynamics. Even a casual glance at the modern literature on macroeconomic dynamics and growth theory shows the ways in which dynamic optimization and equilibrium principles rooted in capital theory provide the theoretical underpinnings for those theories.

Much work in capital theory, growth theory, macroeconomic dynamics, and resource economics derives from Ramsey's classic paper on optimal growth. Such models typically specify a planner's objective which is time additive separable (TAS). Properties of these models, or their equilibrium counterparts, are then found by exploiting this additional structural assumption. The additive separability hypothesis has long been recognized as special, but has been regarded as relatively harmless in the optimal growth context. The TAS model was preferred primarily for its technical convenience over Fisher's theory of interest. He assumed the rate of impatience depended on the underlying consumption stream, even in a steady state. In the TAS case the steady state rate of impatience is independent of the consumption profile.

The Walrasian theory of competitive equilibrium has influenced the structure of capital theoretic models ever since the publication of von Neumann's seminal paper on balanced growth in a multisector economy. Not only did his model and the methods used to demonstrate the existence of a solution foreshadow many of the developments of modern general equilibrium theory, but they also exerted a profound influence on the development of capital theory. Hicks's program of replacing static equilibrium with dynamic equilibrium served to further intensify the linkage between capital theory and Walrasian equilibrium theory.

The Hicksian program, marrying capital theory and equilibrium analysis, has been extraordinarily fruitful. In spite of this success, it suffers from a fundamental weakness. The restrictions imposed by additive separability are an obstacle to the proper analysis of long-run phenomena, and to the analysis of economies where different agents evaluate the future differently.

Koopmans's theory of recursive utility, first formulated in the early 1960s, provides a way out of this dilemma. Koopmans suggested that we broaden the class of dynamic preferences by relaxing the separability requirement, allowing more general specifications of intertemporal preferences. The resulting recursive utility functions enjoy a time consistency property that still permits a dynamic programming analysis of optimal growth. They also allow the steady state rate of impatience to vary with the consumption level. This permits enough flexibility to avoid the long-run and heterogeneity problems of additive separable dynamic equilibrium models. Moreover, recursive utility permits relatively comprehensive analytical and computational analysis of dynamic models.

The development of both recursive utility theory and equilibrium analysis has now reached the point where they can be joined on Hicksian lines. Our book presents a synthesis of capital theory and equilibrium analysis within a recursive utility framework.

Our goal is to combine the ideas of Fisher, Ramsey, and Koopmans with those of Walras, von Neumann, and Hicks. We have integrated related research by others into our framework, and drawn on our own previously published and unpublished work as well as that of our students. The theory we present is cast in a unified framework where infinitely lived agents act out their economic decisions in a discrete time setting devoid of any uncertainty.

We chose the deterministic discrete time setup in part because its technical demands seemed to intrude less on the economic arguments than would otherwise be the case. This choice also allows us to present our topics in a common framework, and address a greater variety of issues.

This book is intended as both a research monograph and an overview of capital theory. It can be used by researchers, or as a textbook in graduate courses on growth theory, general equilibrium theory, or economic dynamics. In addition, the book may be of interest to mathematicians seeking applications of functional analysis and Riesz spaces.

We weave existing theory together within a unified framework. In doing so we show how the pieces fit together. This process yielded a number of connections between different literatures. The knowledgeable reader will notice these scattered throughout the text. For instance, we relate biconvergence and myopia in Chapter 3, and treat the overtaking criterion as a variety of recursive utility. We reworked results from the literature, as in our presentation of turnpike theory in Chapter 5. We also found significant gaps in the published record. To fill these gaps, we worked out multisector results for the existence and characterization of optima in Chapter 4 and built Chapter 8 upon recent developments in infinite dimensional general equilibrium analysis.

The numerous examples throughout the book are an essential element of our presentation. They help provide intuition, delineate the scope of the results, clarify the role of the assumptions, and illustrate the type of models that our work encompasses. Besides the 84 named and numbered examples, the reader will discover many other small examples tucked away in the text.

Our treatment begins with an introductory chapter that illustrates some of the problems that occur with additive utility, and shows how they may be resolved by using recursive models. It also contains a number of examples illustrating the variety of different models that a general theory of dynamic economics should encompass.

The basic tools we use are drawn from functional analysis, dynamical systems theory, and lattice programming. The deterministic discrete time framework is based on sequences of vectors of capital, consumption and prices. Chapter 2 provides most of the necessary functional analytic background, including the theory of ordered vector spaces, for examining optimal growth and equilibrium models based on such sequences.

Chapter 3 focuses on preferences and recursive utility. We examine recursive preferences from three vantage points. The first, in the spirit of Koopmans's original work, seeks to axiomatically characterize recursive preferences. The second viewpoint asks about attitudes toward the future, how much patience or impatience do preferences exhibit? The final vantage point sees intertemporal preferences as deriving from Fisherian preferences over present consumption and future utility. It focuses on the construction of recursive preference orderings from these Fisherian primitives.

Questions of existence and characterization of optimal paths take center stage in Chapter 4. We start with one-sector TAS models in order to illustrate the basic principles of existence theory, with and without discounting. These ideas are used in showing existence and continuity of optimal paths in multisector recursive models. Dynamic programming gives us another perspective on these issues. It also provides some key information for showing the necessity of the transversality condition. We end the chapter by completely characterizing optimal paths via Euler equations and a transversality condition.

Once paths are characterized, we are ready to start studying their dynamics in Chapter 5. Monotonicity of optimal paths, existence of steady states, convergence to steady states, and the presence of cycles and chaos are all examined here. Much more could be written about the dynamics of optimal paths. To do it justice would probably require another volume, and we have confined our attention to a few key results and tools.

Chapter 6 takes a first stab at dynamic equilibrium theory. We focus on representative agent economies, and show the interrelationship between optimal growth theories and their equilibrium counterparts when each agent has recursive preferences. Under a wide range of conditions, equilibria of representative agent economies correspond to optimal growth problems, and vice versa. This connection even holds in certain economies with tax distortions, where the equilibrium solves an artificially constructed optimal growth problem.

This equivalence between equilibria and optimal paths facilitates the study of comparative dynamics in Chapter 7. The economy is subjected to a parametric change, resulting in a new optimal path. This section draws heavily on recent developments in lattice programming, and we have included the necessary background material.

Chapter 8 ties together threads from the previous chapters. It considers dynamic equilibria when agents are heterogeneous. We show the existence of equilibria, prove the welfare theorems, examine the equivalence between welfare maxima and equilibria, and provide a core equivalence theorem.

Neither uncertainly nor continuous time are examined here. We have excluded them because they require significantly more technical prerequisites, and because each would require an additional volume if treated on an equal footing with the discrete time deterministic models. The literature in both cases is voluminous and our references contain only a few key citations that fit into our current treatment's scope.

Most of the notation is introduced as needed. Many of the more specialized symbols also appear at the start of the index, or indexed under "spaces." Section numbers have the form chapter.section or chapter.section.subsection. Examples, theorems, etc. are numbered consecutively within each chapter. We refer to them by number within their chapter. When the reference is in another chapter, we prepend the chapter number, e.g., Example 4.2 is in Chapter 4. The named and numbered examples are set off within starting (▶) and ending (◀) triangles. The ends of proofs are denoted by □.

As usual, we have accumulated a long list of debts to our colleagues, collaborators, and peers. We would like to single out Buz Brock, Edwin Burmeister, Lionel McKenzie, and the late Trout Rader for their intellectual inspiration, and Ciprian Foias, Lionel McKenzie, and Mukul Majumdar for the joint work that underlies portions of the book. Thanks go to the following for their encouragement and comments during this long process: Roko Aliprantis, Buz Brock, Subir Chakrabarti, Fwu-Ranq Chang, Roy Gardner, Michael Kaganovich, Tom Kniesner, and Itzhak Zilcha, with special thanks to Nick Spulber for first suggesting we write this book and providing his usual insightful comments on our manuscript, and to Robert Lucas for stressing the advantages of a unified technical framework. Robert Becker thanks Dean Morton Lowengrub and Jay Wilson, former chairman of the economics department, for making various resources available that helped us complete the manuscript. John Boyd also thanks Academic Press for permission to utilize portions of papers he previously published in the *Journal of Economic Theory* (Boyd, 1990a; 1996).

This book has its immediate origins in our survey (Becker and Boyd,

1990; 1993) and our lectures on capital theory at Indiana University and the University of Rochester. We would like to thank the various generations of capital theory students at Indiana and Rochester who have suffered through many preliminary versions of portions of this book. Among the current and former students, special thanks go to Hajime Kubota, Eiichi Miyagawa, Tomoichi Shinotsuka, and Danyang Xie (all Rochester) for their helpful comments on recent drafts. Although they are implicitly thanked in the references, we also explicitly thank those former students whose dissertations and later work is used in our text: James Dolmas, Chrisophe Faugère, Alejandro Hernández D., Mark Hertzendorf, and Tomoichi Shinotsuka (all Rochester) and Sumit Joshi (Indiana).

We would also like to thank Donald E. Knuth for creating the mathematical typesetting program TEX, Eberhard Mattes for his excellent OS/2 implementation, emTEX, and the American Mathematical Society for the use of their $\mathcal{AMS}$-TEX macros.

Finally, Robert Becker thanks his family, Karen and Adam, for their encouragement and support.

CHAPTER 1

The Recursive Utility Approach

1.1 Introduction

Most of the literature on capital theory and optimal growth proceeds on the assumption that preferences are represented by a functional which is additive over time and discounts future rewards at a constant rate. This assumption is unnecessarily restrictive. Research in the study of preference orders and utility functions has led to advances in intertemporal allocation theory on the basis of weaker hypotheses. The class of recursive utility functions has been proposed as a generalization of the additive utility family. A large body of theory has now been developed for recursive utility. The recursive utility functions share many of the important characteristics of the additive class. Notably, recursive utility functions enjoy a time consistency property that permits dynamic programming analysis of optimal growth and competitive equilibrium models. We focus on the discrete time theory of recursive utility functions and on their applications in dynamic economics.

Recursive utility involves flexible time preference. In contrast, the rigid time preference of the common additively separable utility functions may yield results that seem strange in ordinary circumstances. A consumer facing a fixed interest rate will try either to save without limit, or to borrow without limit, except in the knife-edge case where the rate of impatience equals the interest rate. This problem is especially severe when there are heterogeneous households. Unless all of the households have the same discount factor, the most patient household ends up with all the capital in the long run, while all other households consume nothing, using their labor income to service their debt. The constant discount rate hypothesis also creates problems for the calculation of welfare losses arising from capital income taxation. The after-tax return to capital is always the pure rate of time preference. The capital tax is therefore completely shifted to labor in the long run. As a result, the welfare cost of the tax is higher than it would be if some adjustment of the after-tax rate of return could occur.

Recursive utility escapes these dilemmas by allowing impatience to depend on the path of consumption. The assumptions made on utility allowing for variable time preference imply a weak separability between present and future consumption. This leads to a representation of the utility function in terms of an aggregator function expressing current utility of a consumption path as a function of current consumption and the future utility derived from the remaining periods' consumption. In this way, recursive utility recalls the two-period model of Fisher (1930).

Time additive separable utility has dominated research in economic dynamics owing to the mathematical simplification derived from that functional form. The economic plausibility of additive utility was pushed aside in the interest of obtaining insights and directions for further research. The body of work in this book focuses on dynamic optimization models with intertemporally dependent preferences as embodied in the recursive utility hypothesis. The foundations of recursive utility theory were set by Koopmans and his collaborators during the 1960s and early 1970s, and the theory has undergone substantial development since. We re-examine this work in light of further advances in general equilibrium theory involving infinite dimensional commodity spaces. We concentrate on the optimal growth model and its equilibrium twin as the paradigm for dynamic models in order to illustrate the methods used to analyze the implications of a recursive utility specification of preferences.

1.2 What Is a Recursive Utility Function?

A common practice in dynamic economic models of infinite horizon decision making is to postulate that the preference order over non-negative real-valued sequences of consumption bundles may be represented by the utility function

$$U(\mathbf{c}) = \sum_{t=1}^{\infty} \delta^{t-1} u(c_t), \qquad (1)$$

with $0 < \delta < 1$ and u bounded, strictly increasing, and strictly concave on $\mathbb{R}_+ = [0, \infty)$.[1] The parameter δ is called the *discount factor* and $\delta^{-1} - 1 = \varrho$ is called the *pure rate of time preference*. The function u is known as the *one-period reward* or *felicity* function.[2] We use the notational convention that $\mathbf{c}$ denotes the real-valued sequence with terms c_t, $t = 1, 2, \ldots$; this is also written $\mathbf{c} = \{c_t\}_{t=1}^{\infty}$. Consumption sequences are understood to be non-negative in the sense that $c_t \geq 0$ for all t. In order to guarantee convergence in the series (1), we temporarily assume u is bounded. The function defined in (1) is known as the *time additive separable* (TAS) utility function. It is the familiar welfare criterion in

---

[1] As usual, $\mathbb{R}$ denotes the real numbers and $\mathbb{R}^m$ denotes m-dimensional Euclidean space.

[2] The felicity function u is usually assumed to be twice continuously differentiable on $\mathbb{R}_{++} = (0, \infty)$.

optimal growth theory and is commonly found in applied models of the dynamic consequences of various tax policies as well as in the literature on macrodynamics.[3]

The TAS form has two interesting properties. First, the marginal rate of substitution between any pair of adjacent dates depends only on consumption at those dates. Formally,

$$\text{MRS}_{t,t+1}(\mathbf{c}) = \frac{u'(c_t)}{\delta u'(c_{t+1})}.$$

In particular, for constant consumption profiles denoted by $\mathbf{c} = \mathbf{c}_{con}$ ($c_t = c$ for all t),

$$\text{MRS}_{t,t+1}(\mathbf{c}_{con}) = \delta^{-1},$$

which is independent of $\mathbf{c}_{con}$.

The second property is that U is *recursive*. The behavior embodied in the TAS specification of U has a self-referential property: namely, the behavior of the planner over the infinite time horizon $t = 1, 2, \ldots$ is guided by the behavior of that agent over the tail horizon $t = T + 1, T + 2, \ldots$ (for each T) hidden inside the original horizon.[4] For the TAS functional, recursivity means the objective from time $T + 1$ to $+\infty$ has the same form as the objective starting at $T = 0$ (except for some time shifts in consumption dates). Formally, (1) may be rewritten as

$$\sum_{t=1}^{\infty} \delta^{t-1} u(c_t) = \sum_{t=1}^{T} \delta^{t-1} u(c_t) + \delta^T \sum_{t=1}^{\infty} \delta^{t-1} u(c_{t+T}). \tag{2}$$

The last sum in (2) is the utility of $(c_{T+1}, c_{T+2}, \ldots)$.

An important implication of the recursive structure found in the TAS utility specification is that intertemporal planning in a stationary environment is time consistent in the sense first used by Strotz (1955). If the planner is given the opportunity to revise his decisions at some time $T > 0$, he will choose to stick with his original choice. This happens if his decisions at T depend on the past only through accumulated assets, rather than depending *directly* on past consumption patterns. It is this weak separability of the past from the present and future that makes dynamic programming possible. Recursive utility preserves this separation. Indeed, recursive utility is the intertemporal analogue of weak separa-

---

[3] Stokey and Lucas with Prescott (1989), Sargent (1987), and Cooley (1995) are good sources of examples of models with TAS utility specifications.

[4] We are adapting Gleick's (1987, p. 179) characterization of recursive structures to our economic context.

bility of future consumption from present consumption as formulated in standard finite horizon demand theory.[5]

▶ Example 1: The Ramsey problem. Ramsey (1928) proposed the optimal growth problem in a seminal paper. The case where the planner discounts future utilities can be illustrated with a simple example. The planner's utility function is $U(\mathbf{c}) = \sum_{t=1}^{\infty} \delta^{t-1} \log c_t$ where $0 < \delta < 1$ is the discount factor. Production takes place in a single sector and is described by the production function $f(k) = k^\rho$ where $0 < \rho < 1$ and k represents the current capital input. The output good is a composite consumption/capital good. At each time t the planner chooses how to split the output between current consumption c_t and next period's input capital k_t. Previous capital k_{t-1} is used as input, so $c_t + k_t = k_{t-1}^\rho$. Of course, we require c_t, $k_t \geq 0$. The economy starts with an initial endowment of capital k_0.

Formally, the planner chooses sequences $\mathbf{c}$ and $\mathbf{k}$ to solve

$$\sup \sum_{t=1}^{\infty} \delta^{t-1} \log c_t$$
$$\text{s.t. } c_t + k_t \leq k_{t-1}^\rho, \ c_t, k_t \geq 0 \ (t = 1, \dots)$$

given $k_0 > 0$. This Ramsey problem is solved explicitly in Section 5.1. The solution is described by the *consumption policy function* $g(k) = (1 - \delta\rho)k^\rho$ and the *capital policy function* $h(k) = \delta\rho k^\rho$. These functions make intuitive sense. We would expect that the marginal rate of intertemporal substitution $(\text{MRS}_{t,t+1})$ would equal the marginal product $(f'(k_t))$ at the optimum. The solutions must satisfy these *Euler equations*, and they do. Since $\text{MRS}_{t,t+1} = c_{t+1}/\delta c_t$, we can substitute the policy functions to obtain:

$$\text{MRS}_{t,t+1} = \frac{(1 - \delta\rho)k_t^\rho}{\delta(1 - \delta\rho)k_{t-1}^\rho} = \frac{k_t^\rho}{\delta k_{t-1}^\rho} = \frac{\rho k_t^\rho}{k_t} = \rho k_t^{\rho-1} = f'(k_t)$$

At each date, the policy functions tell the planner how much to consume and how much to save given the current level of capital stock k. The optimal consumption and capital sequences are found by iterating the policy functions starting with initial capital k_0. For example, the optimal capital sequence $\mathbf{k}(k_0)$ is calculated from h by setting $k_t(k_0) = h(k_{t-1}(k_0))$ for $t = 1, \dots$ and $k_0(k_0) = k_0$. Carrying out the iteration yields the explicit solution $k_t(k_0) = (\delta\rho)^{\rho^{t-1} + \dots + 1} k_0^{\rho^t}$.

The optimal policy functions do not depend on calendar time. The planner's optimal action at any date depends only on the current level

---

[5] Consult Blackorby, Primont, and Russell (1978) for details on finite horizon discrete time demand theory. Also, see the discussion in Section 4.3.

of the capital stock. This is the time consistency feature of the optimal solution. The planner need know neither the history of the economy's capital accumulation process nor past consumption patterns.

The qualitative features of the optimal solution also follow from the policy functions' properties. The fixed points of h, points where $h(k) = k$, play a special role. For any δ, h has a unique positive fixed point $k^\delta = (\delta\rho)^{1/(1-\rho)}$. The stock k^δ is called the *modified golden-rule capital stock*. If the planner's initial stock is k^δ, it will be optimal to choose current consumption $c^\delta = (1 - \delta\rho)(k^\delta)^\rho = f(k^\delta) - k^\delta$, maintaining the stock k^δ. The planner thereby enjoys the consumption level c^δ in every period since the next period's capital stock is again k^δ.

The capital policy function is also increasing in k. This implies that the optimal capital sequence is monotonic. Since that sequence is bounded, it has a limit. The limit is k^δ, as can be seen by inspecting the explicit solution above. Similar properties hold for the consumption policy function. The observation that the optimal capital and consumption sequences converge to their modified golden-rule levels is call the *Turnpike Theorem*. ◄

One of the major themes in this book concerns the generality of the qualitative properties of this one-sector Ramsey model. Do properties such as monotonicity and the Turnpike Theorem apply in more general models? What happens if the technology is not convex, or includes multiple sectors or types of capital goods? What happens if the objective does not have the TAS form?

There is reason to question the use of the TAS objective. The TAS functional has been criticized by various authors, dating back to Fisher (1930). They argue that the pure rate of time preference should not be independent of the size and shape of the consumption profile. When preferences are time additive, this independence is a direct consequence of the strong separability property embodied in (1). Hicks (1965, p. 261) criticized the TAS formulation on grounds that successive consumption units should be strong complements. Hicks argued that the amount of consumption in period 1 the planner would be willing to give up to increase consumption in period T should also depend in some way on the planned consumption in adjacent periods (e.g., periods $T - 1$ and $T + 1$). The additivity hypothesis denies this connection. In essence, Hicks maintained that the potential for smoothing consumption in the presence of complementarity between periods is lost in the acceptance that felicities are independent as found in the TAS specification of utility. Lucas and Stokey (1984) argued that the only basis for studying the TAS case is its analytic tractability. Indeed, the TAS form is the favored specification in much of the literature on theoretical and applied dynamic economic models with explicitly optimizing agents. This dominance of the TAS form is due to the relative ease of obtaining results and the perception that alternative formulations of utility may either have insufficient structure to obtain sharp conclusions or pose difficult analytical barriers.[6]

Koopmans (1960) laid the foundation for eliminating both deficiencies of the TAS functional via recursive preferences. The recursive utility class is designed to introduce a degree of generality that is consistent with Fisher's time preference views, offers time consistent optimal planning, and preserves much of the analytical convenience of the TAS case. The following examples are designed to illustrate the range of recursive utility structures.

The first example of a non-TAS recursive utility functional is based on an uncertain lifetime model.

▶ Example 2: Endogenous uncertain lifetimes. Let $e^{-v(c)}$ with $v \geq 0$ denote the probability that the agent survives given current consumption level c. For example, nutritional levels can affect survival prospects.[7] Similar considerations arise in fishery models (e.g., Clemhout and Wan, 1986). Let $U_0 = U(0)$ be the utility level of the agent if dead. We assume the agent receives utility $u(c)$ from current consumption, and does not discount the future. It follows that today's expected utility is

$$EU(\mathbf{c}) = u(c_1) + e^{-v(c_1)}EU(S\mathbf{c}) + [1 - e^{-v(c_1)}]U_0,$$

where $S\mathbf{c} \equiv (c_2, c_3, \dots)$ denotes the *shift operator* applied to the profile $\mathbf{c}$.

Now suppose $U_0 = 0$, which requires $u(0) = 0$. Then expected utility has the simpler form

$$EU(\mathbf{c}) = u(c_1) + e^{-v(c_1)}EU(S\mathbf{c}). \tag{3}$$

Since the expectation enters linearly in (3), we can find a von Neumann-Morgenstern utility index obeying recursion (3).[8] Expected utility has the *Uzawa-Epstein-Hynes* (UEH) form

$$EU(\mathbf{c}) = \sum_{t=1}^{\infty} u(c_t) \exp\left(-\sum_{\tau=1}^{t-1} v(c_\tau)\right).$$

Since the only uncertainty concerns the time of death, no expectation appears in the right-hand side. We have converted the uncertain lifetime problem's objective to an equivalent deterministic payoff functional.

---

[6] The recent use of computer simulations in the macroeconomic literature portends a move toward more general formulations of preferences and technology.

[7] McKeown (1976) provides evidence on this. Ray and Streufert (1993) examine some of the theoretical implications.

[8] Epstein (1983) discusses this utility function in a stochastic framework.

The UEH utility function is a member of the recursive class. Indeed, following the derivation of (2) in the UEH case leads to

$$\sum_{t=1}^{\infty} u(c_t) \exp\left(-\sum_{\tau=1}^{t-1} v(c_\tau)\right) = \sum_{t=1}^{T} u(c_t) \exp\left(-\sum_{\tau=1}^{t-1} v(c_\tau)\right)$$
$$+ \exp\left(-\sum_{\tau=1}^{T} v(c_\tau)\right) \sum_{t=T+1}^{\infty} u(c_t) \exp\left(-\sum_{\tau=T+1}^{\infty} v(c_\tau)\right).$$

The UEH utility from $(c_{T+1}, c_{T+2}, \dots)$ appears in the last term.

If $u' > 0$, $v' \leq 0$, and $v > 0$, the utility function is increasing. One special case arises when $v(c) = \log \delta^{-1}$ is constant. Then expected utility reduces to the TAS functional $U(\mathbf{c}) = \sum_{t=1}^{\infty} \delta^{t-1} u(c_t)$.

Another special case arises when $U_0 = -e^{-v(0)}/(1 - e^{-v(0)}) < 0$ and $u(c) = (e^{-v(0)} - e^{-v(c)})/(1 - e^{-v(0)})$. Then expected utility obeys $EU(\mathbf{c}) = (-1 + EU(S\mathbf{c})) e^{-v(c)}$ and is given by the *Epstein-Hynes* (EH) form

$$EU(\mathbf{c}) = -\sum_{t=1}^{\infty} \exp\left(-\sum_{\tau=1}^{t} v(c_\tau)\right). \tag{4}$$

In this case, $v' > 0$ implies utility is increasing.[9] ◄

The TAS functional represents the utilitarian objective since lifetime welfare is the sum of one-period rewards, weighted according to their probability of occurrence. The UEH utility function is based on a weaker notion of additivity over time—lifetime utility is the sum over t of functions depending on histories of consumption of length t. A non-additive alternative to the TAS and UEH criteria may be founded on the notion that programs might be ranked according to the lowest realized consumption level. The result is the maximin criterion.

► Example 3: The Rawls maximin utility function. The maximin functional introduced by Rawls (1971) is defined by

$$U(\mathbf{c}) = \inf_t c_t.$$

Clearly,

$$U(\mathbf{c}) = \inf_t c_t = \inf\{c_1, \inf_{t \geq 2} c_t\} = \inf\{c_1, c_2, \dots, c_T, \inf_{t \geq T+1} c_t\}.$$

This computation shows the maximin functional also enjoys a recursive structure in common with the TAS and EH cases. The maximin utility function is extremely conservative. In savings–investment problems a

---

[9] See Epstein and Hynes (1983) for a deterministic account of this functional in continuous time.

maximin decision maker never sacrifices current consumption by saving to obtain a higher future consumption. ◀

Let $\mathcal{X}$ denote a commodity space of positive consumption sequences and let $\succsim$ denote the planning agent's preference order over commodities. Given a preference order $\succsim$ on $\mathcal{X}$, a utility representation, U, of $\succsim$ is a *recursive utility function* if there is a real-valued function u defined on $X \subset \mathbb{R}_+$ and a real-valued function W defined on $u(X) \times U(\mathcal{X})$ such that[10]

$$U(\mathbf{c}) = W(u(c_1), U(S\mathbf{c})). \tag{5}$$

The function W is called the *aggregator* and equation (5) is called *Koopmans's equation*. We refer to u as the *felicity* function. A recursive utility function expresses the weak separability of the future from the present. Fisher's two-period conception of an agent contemplating current consumption and future utility may be modeled by recursive utility functions.

The examples introduced above fall under the recursive utility definition. For the TAS case, the aggregator is $W(c, y) = u(c) + \delta y$. The EH functional has $W(c, y) = -(1 + y)\exp(-v(c))$ as an aggregator, while $W(c, y) = u(c) + e^{-v(c)}y$ for the related UEH functional. The maximin aggregator is $W(c, y) = \min\{c, y\}$. These and other recursive utility functions form the class of objective functionals that will be systematically investigated in this book. However, there are interesting utility functions which do not belong to the recursive family.

▶ Example 4: Majumdar's example. Given $T > 0$, define

$$U(\mathbf{c}) = w(c_1, c_2, \ldots, c_T) + \sum_{t=1}^{\infty} \delta(t)v_t(c_1, c_2, \ldots, c_t),$$

over non-negative, bounded real-valued sequences of consumption where $\delta(t) \geq 0$ for all t, $\sum \delta(t) = 1$, $w \colon \mathbb{R}_+^T \to \mathbb{R}_+$ is continuous, quasi-concave, non-decreasing in each argument, and $\{v_t\}$ is a sequence of quasi-concave, continuous functions from $\mathbb{R}_+^t$ to $\mathbb{R}_+$, with each v_t strictly increasing in all its arguments and with the sequence uniformly bounded above. There is special significance accorded to consumption in periods $1, \ldots, T$ as measured by the w function. Moreover, history counts since the felicity given by c_t at time t depends on the consumption enjoyed in all previous periods. This U is not recursive when w is non-trivial and $v_t(c_1, \ldots, c_t) = v(c_t)$ and $\delta(t) = (1-\delta)\delta^{t-1}$.[11] We refer to this utility function as the *Majumdar*

---

[10] We require $S\mathcal{X} \subset \mathcal{X}$ to ensure that the definition makes sense.

[11] The factor $(1 - \delta)$ arises in order for $\{\delta(t)\}$ to satisfy the normalization $\sum \delta(t) = 1$. In this case, the marginal rate of substitution between consumption in adjacent time periods is not constant along constant paths, while recursive utility would require the MRS be constant.

utility functional after the example introduced by Majumdar (1975). If w vanishes, v_t is a stationary function only of c_t, and $\{\delta(t)\}$ is not a geometric progression, then U reduces to the utility function studied by Strotz (1955) in his discussion of time inconsistent optimal planning models. ◄

Many other examples of recursive and non-recursive utility functions will be discussed in the following chapters. One of the important points to be developed concerns the ways in which recursive utility functions may be recovered by postulating only the form of the aggregator function. This will offer an enormous simplification of the definition of recursive utility functions. More importantly, assumptions on the aggregator may be motivated by economic intuition derived from the Fisherian two-period intertemporal consumption model. The study of the aggregator foundation of recursive utility will lead us to a detailed analysis of Koopmans's equation.

1.3 Why Study Recursive Utility?

Why should one model household or planner behavior on a recursive utility foundation, instead of using the more restrictive time additive separable objective? The best way to answer this question is to give examples where the time additive separability assumption leads to a strong conclusion that depends on a fixed time preference rate. We then show that the recursive utility specification broadens the scope of the analysis leading to a different conclusion that merits economic attention. For this purpose we have selected two illustrations of the limits of TAS models.

1.3.1 The Long-Run Incidence of Capital Taxation

We begin by introducing a model of capital taxation and address the question of long-run incidence of a capital income tax.

The Tax Model

We consider a perfect foresight model of capital income taxation in a stylized one-sector neoclassical model of capital accumulation. There is a representative consumer perfectly anticipating future returns to capital and labor. Capital income is taxed at a constant rate; the tax revenue is rebated as a lump sum at each time. Labor is supplied inelastically. This simplifies the analysis and isolates the effects of the capital tax. The household maximizes lifetime utility subject to a sequence of budget constraints reflecting the anticipated profile of factor returns and government transfer payments. Lifetime utility is given by a recursive utility function. The household accumulates capital and provides for consumption at each time from disposable income. Income is derived from the rental of capital, supply of labor, and government transfer payments. Since the current price of capital is always one, there are no capital gains to include in current income. Hence, capital income coincides with net rental income. A perfect foresight equilibrium rules whenever the household's planned accumulation program agrees with static profit maximization in the production sector. The production sector's decision is myopic and uses the pre-tax return to capital to calculate desired capital demand at each time. The capital income tax places a wedge between the cost of capital in the production sector and the return to capital observed by the household sector.[12]

Assume that a single commodity is available for consumption or capital accumulation. Let the private sector consist of a representative household and producer. The household owns the production process. Also, the household inelastically supplies one unit of labor at each time; the residual payment made to the household is identified as the wage rate. The public sector collects the capital tax income revenue and returns the revenue in a lump-sum manner to the household. In this way, the analysis is conducted for a compensated tax.

The household forecasts non-negative, non-zero sequences $\{r_t, w_t, g_t\}$ given the initial value of capital holdings k and the tax rate τ, where r_t is the after-tax or net rate of return per unit of capital, w_t is the wage rate, and g_t is the lump-sum transfer at time t. All prices and transfers are denominated in units of the consumption good of date t. The initial capital stock is assumed to be positive. The tax rate τ is independent of calendar time with $0 \leq \tau \leq 1$. The net return to capital reflects the tax rate as $r_t = (1 - \tau)R_t$, with R_t the before-tax or gross rate of return to capital per unit. In the absence of taxation, the total return to capital per unit would be $1 + R_t$ signifying the payment of principal plus interest. In the case of a capital income tax, the after-tax total return is given by $1 + (1 - \tau)R_t$.

A non-negative sequence $\{(c_t, x_{t-1})\} \equiv (\mathbf{c}, \mathbf{x})$ is *attainable* provided $x_0 = k$ and

$$c_t + x_t \leq w_t + (1 + r_t)x_{t-1} + g_t, \text{ for } t = 1, 2, \ldots. \qquad (6)$$

The household confronts a sequence of budget constraints—one for each time. Attainable sequences satisfy those constraints given the anticipated profile $\{r_t, w_t, g_t\}$ and the starting value of capital. The household seeks to maximize lifetime utility $U(\mathbf{c})$ by choice of an attainable sequence. Lifetime utility obeys Koopmans's equation (5).

---

[12] This model is a discrete time version of Chamley's (1981) perfect foresight model. A variant of this model also appears in Becker (1985a) where the capital tax is designed to place a wedge between the total gross (principal plus interest) and net total returns. The latter model is examined in Chapters 6 and 7.

The production sector is modeled by the sequence of one-period problems

$$\sup_x [f(x) - (1 + R_t)x], \text{ for } t = 1, 2, \ldots \tag{7}$$

by choice of $x \geq 0$ given the non-negative gross return to capital R_t at each time. The production function is f. Capital is compensated with a one-period lag. Therefore the solution to (7) yields the production sector's desired demand for capital services carried from period $t - 1$ to produce output available during period t. The production sector is assumed to maximize static profits in each period as all consumption–savings decisions are in the household domain. Hence the myopic structure of problem (7).

The production function, f, is assumed to be derived from a neoclassical positively homogeneous of degree one production function, F, with $f(x) = F(1, x)$ and $l = 1$ the fixed labor input. Furthermore, f is assumed to be non-negative, $f(0) = 0$, strictly concave, strictly increasing, and twice continuously differentiable on $\mathbb{R}_{++}$ with the *Inada properties*

$$\lim_{x \to 0} f'(x) = +\infty; \quad \lim_{x \to \infty} f'(x) < 1. \tag{8}$$

The first property in (8) eliminates corner solutions to (7). The second property in (8) implies there is a *maximum sustainable stock*, k^M, with $f(k^M) = k^M > 0$. In the sequel it is understood that $0 < k < k^M$.

Sequences $\{\bar{r}_t, \bar{w}_t, \bar{g}_t, \bar{R}_t, \bar{c}_t, \bar{x}_t\}$ constitute a τ-*perfect foresight competitive equilibrium* (τ-PFCE) if, for all t,

$$\bar{r}_t = (1 - \tau)\bar{R}_t; \tag{9}$$

$$1 + \bar{R}_t = f'(\bar{x}_{t-1}); \tag{10}$$

$$\bar{w}_t = f(\bar{x}_{t-1}) - (1 + \bar{R}_t)\bar{x}_{t-1}; \tag{11}$$

$$\bar{g}_t = \tau \bar{R}_t \bar{x}_{t-1}; \tag{12}$$

and, given a sequence $\{\bar{r}_t, \bar{w}_t, \bar{g}_t\}$ of interest rates, wages, and transfers,

$$\{\bar{c}_t, \bar{x}_{t-1}\} \text{ maximizes } U(\mathbf{c}) \text{ subject to (6) and } \bar{x}_0 = k. \tag{13}$$

A 0-PFCE corresponds to the no-distortion case and is simply abbreviated as PFCE. Equilibrium condition (9) states that the after-tax rate of return per unit of capital equals the gross rate of return per unit less the tax payment per unit. Condition (10) supplies the profit maximization requirement for (7) while (11) gives the residual wage payment. Condition (12) says the government has a balanced budget at each time. Condition (13) is the requirement of household utility maximization given the forecast sequences of factor returns and lump-sum transfers. The sequences $\{\bar{r}_t, \bar{w}_t, \bar{g}_t, \bar{R}_t\}$ are self-justifying in equilibrium. The household's optimal program and the solution to the producer's optimum problems are such that combining (9)–(13) with (6) results in

$$\bar{c}_t + \bar{x}_t \leq f(\bar{x}_{t-1}) \; (t = 1, 2, \ldots)$$

and $\bar{x}_0 = k$. Thus, planned supply of output equals or exceeds planned demand for capital and planned demand for consumption. Moreover, if $u' > 0$, the consumer's budget constraint must hold with equality, and planned demand and supply of output must be equal. This definition of τ-PFCE anticipates the interiority of equilibrium programs as well as the underlying constant returns to scale technology.

Tax Incidence with TAS Utility

We now specialize to the case where $U(\mathbf{c})$ has the TAS form (1). The felicity function, u, is assumed to be twice continuously differentiable on $\mathbb{R}_{++}$, strictly concave, strictly increasing, and with the property

$$\lim_{c \to 0} u'(c) = +\infty.$$

The last condition is designed to eliminate corner solutions with zero consumption whenever the household's income is positive.

The long-run incidence of a capital income tax may be examined by calculating the steady-state τ-PFCE equilibrium constellation. In a stationary equilibrium the household will equate its pure rate of time preference $\varrho \equiv \delta^{-1} - 1$ to the after-tax rate of return, i.e., $\varrho = r$ where r is the steady-state net rate of return on capital. This result is a consequence of the form of the objective functional (1) as will be seen below. The implication is that the capital income tax is shifted to the labor income component in the long run whereas capital bears the entire burden of the tax in the short run.

The Kuhn-Tucker necessary conditions for the household's optimal program take the form of a *no-arbitrage condition* for each t:

$$\delta(1 + \bar{r}_{t+1})u'(\bar{c}_{t+1}) = u'(\bar{c}_t). \tag{14}$$

Equation (14) may be derived from the following intuitive argument. Assume an interior equilibrium program so that $\bar{c}_t > 0$ for all t; note $\bar{x}_{t-1} > 0$ must also hold on every date. Suppose the household contemplates a change in its consumption–asset decision at time t. One option is to invest in an additional unit of capital at time t and receive a net return r_{t+1} in period $t+1$ after payment of the capital income tax. The household reverses its position at time $t+1$, enjoying a receipt of $u'(\bar{c}_{t+1})$ utils per unit of capital from the reconversion of capital into consumption.[13] Thus, the

---

[13] This is allowed in the one-sector model since the capital and consumption goods are physically the same and at any date one may be freely transformed into the other.

marginal benefit from this trade realized at time $t+1$ is $u'(\bar{c}_{t+1})(1+\bar{r}_{t+1})$ in units of utility at time $t+1$. Multiplying by the discount factor converts this into the marginal benefit with focal date t, i.e.,

$$\text{MB}_t \equiv \delta u'(\bar{c}_{t+1})(1+\bar{r}_{t+1}).$$

The marginal cost of this transaction is measured at time t by the expression

$$\text{MC}_t \equiv u'(\bar{c}_t),$$

since an extra unit of capital costs one unit of consumption on the margin. A necessary condition for a household's optimal choice (as well as for an equilibrium profile) is that $\text{MB}_t \leq \text{MC}_t$ hold at every date. Since capital is positive at each time in equilibrium, the opposite transaction may be considered by the agent yielding the reverse inequality. These two inequalities are equivalent to (14) in equilibrium.[14]

A stationary τ-PFCE is a τ-PFCE which is independent of calendar time. Thus a stationary τ-PFCE occurs when

$$\delta(1+\bar{r}) \equiv \delta[1+(1-\tau)(f'(\bar{x})-1)] = 1.$$

Rearranging this equation yields the expression

$$(1-\tau)[f'(\bar{x})-1] = \varrho. \tag{15}$$

The steady-state after-tax rate of return to capital is independent of the tax rate. The capital income tax is completely shifted to the untaxed labor factor which is in inelastic supply. This shifting of the tax does *not* mean that long-run total capital income is the same with and without the tax. Capital does receive the same after-tax net rate of return in both cases, but the long-run stock of capital is smaller given the tax as compared to the 0-PFCE steady-state capital stock. Moreover, the felicity function u does not affect the long-run steady state and the pure rate of time preference is independent of the consumption profile, so (15) is determined by the properties of f as well as the magnitudes of the parameters ϱ and τ. It is in this sense that the form of the household's objective function (1) is responsible for the full shifting of the capital tax onto the labor factor.

Tax Incidence with Epstein-Hynes Utility
A recursive utility objective function in the household sector may change the long-run incidence of the capital income tax. The full shifting result

---

[14] The arbitrage argument here uses the so-called *one-period reversed arbitrage*. For a detailed discussion see Section 4.6. We also provide an interpretation of the transversality condition $\lim_{t\to\infty} \delta^{t-1} u'(\bar{c}_t)\bar{x}_t = 0$ as a no-arbitrage condition for open-ended or *unreversed arbitrages*.

derived from the TAS utility model is due to capital being in perfectly elastic long-run supply. Flexible time preference may be used to modify the elasticity of the long-run supply schedule for capital and thereby alter the conclusion of the TAS model that the tax is fully shifted from capital to labor. The exact long-run incidence will depend on the specific functional forms taken by the economic primitives governing preferences and technology. For illustrative purposes, assume that the household's preference ranking may be represented by an Epstein-Hynes functional, given by equation (4).[15]

The model is identical to the TAS τ-PFCE model except for the change in the form of the utility function. The no-arbitrage necessary conditions for an equilibrium are as before where

$$U_{t+1}(\bar{c})[1 + (1 - \tau)(f'(\bar{x}_t) - 1)] = U_t(\bar{c}), \tag{16}$$

with U_t denoting the partial derivative of U with respect to c_t. For the EH utility function, evaluated in a steady state, equation (16) reduces to

$$[1 + (1 - \tau)(f'(\bar{x}) - 1)] = 1/\exp(-v(\bar{c})),$$

where $\bar{c}$ and $\bar{x}$ denote the steady-state consumption and capital levels. Clearly the steady-state capital and consumption levels are determined as the solution to the equation

$$[1 + (1 - \tau)(f'(x) - 1)] = \exp v(c(x)), \tag{17}$$

where $c(x) = f(x) - x$. We can think of the left-hand side as long-run capital demand $D(x) \equiv [1 + (1 - \tau)(f'(x) - 1)]$, and the right-hand side as long-run capital supply $S(x) \equiv \exp v(c(x))$. Now $\exp v(c) \geq 1$ as $v \geq 0$, so the solution must be in the range where $f'(x) \geq 1$. A routine computation shows that the demand price is decreasing in x for each τ and decreasing in τ for each x over this range. Moreover, the Inada conditions show the demand price is infinite at zero and drops below 1 for x large. The supply price is increasing over the range $f'(x) \geq 1$. Hence for each τ there is a unique solution to (17) denoted by $x(\tau)$, as illustrated in Figure 1.

An increase in the capital tax to τ' shifts the demand curve downward to D', and so decreases the steady-state capital stock as in Figure 2. Further, an increase in the capital tax rate decreases the steady-state stocks less with the EH utility specification than would arise with the TAS objective.[16] Thus flexible time preference lessens the long-run impact of the tax on the economy's capital stock: the loss in steady-state consumption

---

[15] We adapt the continuous time model used by Epstein and Hynes (1983, pp. 622–624).
[16] In the TAS case long-run capital supply is perfectly elastic at price $1 + \varrho$. It is clear from the diagram that capital would decrease more in the perfectly elastic case.

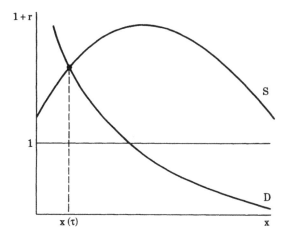

Figure 1: Given a tax rate τ, the steady-state capital stock $x(\tau)$ is determined by the intersection of long-run capital supply $S(x) = \exp v(c(x))$ and demand $D(x) = [1 + (1 - \tau)(f'(x) - 1)]$.

compared to the no-tax case is smaller with flexible time preference than with a constant rate of impatience.[17] Moreover, it is clear from Figure 2 that the after-tax steady-state rate of return on capital falls in the long run.

The importance of flexible time preference is that the long-run capital stock is no longer perfectly elastically supplied in contrast to the case of the TAS model. In both models the short-run impact of a change in the capital tax is the same as capital is in perfectly inelastic supply. The additional flexibility of the time preference pattern in the EH case opens the possibility that the magnitude of the long-run impact of a tax change might be settled as an empirical matter whereas this is precluded *by assumption* in the TAS framework. It is this additional degree of freedom possessed by the EH functional that is indicative of the broader range of outcomes possible with a recursive utility function model. The results found with the TAS specification become important examples in a more general theory. Thus, our goal with recursive utility models is to generate a theory which contains the findings of the constant time preference models and opens the range of theoretical results in order to see what is special in the TAS case as well as what is robust.

---

[17] Of course, this comparison is meaningful only when both specifications yield the same steady state in the zero-tax case: just set $1 + \varrho = \exp(v(c^*))$ where c^* is the no-tax level of steady-state consumption in the EH specification.

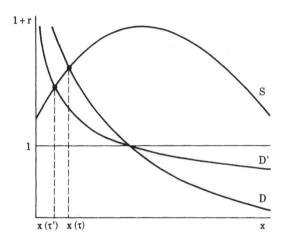

Figure 2: An increase in the capital income tax rate from τ to τ' shifts the long-run capital demand curve $D(x)$ to $D'(x)$. The steady-state capital stock declines from $x(\tau)$ to $x(\tau')$.

1.3.2 The Impatience Problem

For the second example, set the tax rate to zero. The *Equivalence Principle* (discussed in Chapter 6) implies that a PFCE is a solution to the following optimum growth problem and vice versa. We use a TAS utility objective, and define the *Ramsey optimum growth problem*, or simply *Ramsey problem*, as the problem:

$$\sup_{\mathbf{c},\mathbf{x}} \sum_{t=1}^{\infty} \delta^{t-1} u(c_t)$$
$$\text{s.t.} \quad c_t + x_t \le f(x_{t-1}), \ t = 1, 2, \ldots;$$
$$c_t \ge 0, \ x_t \ge 0, \ \text{and} \ x_0 \le k,$$

where k is the starting value of capital and all functions have the same meaning as in the tax model. The properties of u and f are also as before. Example 1 now arises as a special case of this model. Optimal growth models provide an important class of dynamic models that appear in various guises in capital theory.

Suppose instead that the one-sector production function is linear in capital, i.e., $f(x) = \beta x$ where $\beta > 1$. The parameter β is the constant marginal (average) product of capital; the production function exhibits constant returns to scale. We call this the *linear Ramsey model* to distinguish the model from the classical case exhibiting diminishing marginal returns to capital, as in Example 1.[18]

The linear Ramsey model arises naturally in the theory of intertemporal consumer demand. Consider the household demand problem in the τ-PFCE model. In the case where the net return to capital is a constant, the tax rate is zero, and wages and lump-sum transfers are zero, then the consumer demand problem is the same as a linear Ramsey model.

The linear Ramsey model may be used to illustrate the *impatience problem*. If $\delta\beta = 1$, then the no-arbitrage equations show that $\varrho = \beta - 1$ is required for a stationary optimal program. This is a program offering a constant consumption profile equal to $(\beta-1)x$ at each time by maintaining capital stocks at the level x. Indeed, if $\varrho = \beta - 1$ it will always be optimal to remain at the initial stock, regardless of what it may be. If $\varrho \neq \beta - 1$ it will never be optimal to hold a fixed amount of capital. In fact, an optimal program must be monotonic in this model and cannot converge to a steady state if $\beta - 1 > \varrho$ and converges to zero if $\beta - 1 < \varrho$.[19] The difficulty is the same as with the long-run tax incidence question: the long-run supply of capital is perfectly elastic when the net rate of return to capital equals ϱ. This fact causes serious problems when constructing equilibrium models. Suppose there are many households. Unless all of the households have the same discount factor, the most patient household (the one having the lowest ϱ) ends up with all the capital in the long-run, while all other households consume nothing, using any other income they have to service their debt.[20] Similar considerations apply in models of international trade where there are many small open economies, each described by an infinitely lived representative agent.[21] The impatience problem is another reason to have models that accommodate flexible time preference. One such alternative is recursive utility.

---

[18] Ramsey considered a linear model in his 1928 paper. This linear model was further examined by Samuelson in several 1949 RAND Corporation memoranda. He used it to exposit the von Neumann model, explore balanced growth, and characterize dynamic efficiency. These papers were later incorporated into Chapters 11 and 12 of Dorfman, Samuelson, and Solow (1958) and subsequently published in volume II of his *Collected Works* (1966). Rebelo's (1991) reinterpretation of this model appears in the endogenous growth literature (e.g., Barro and Sala-i-Martin, 1995) as the AK model.

[19] We demonstrate this in Example 5.6 as the consequence of the Non-Optimality Lemma.

[20] This problem has been noted in various forms dating to the work of John Rae (1834). Ramsey (1928) gave the first formulation of this distribution question. See Becker (1980) for a more recent setup of this problem that introduces borrowing constraints allowing the relatively impatient agents to consume at least their wages (assuming f exhibits diminishing marginal returns to capital and there is a fixed labor supply).

[21] Obstfeld (1990) examines recursive models applicable to small open economies. There is also a brief discussion in Obstfeld and Rogoff (1996, pp. 722–726).

The Impatience Problem with Epstein-Hynes Utility

Flexible time preference adds a degree of freedom to the economic model that resolves the impatience problem in some circumstances. The necessary condition for a stationary optimal program with an Epstein-Hynes utility function and linear technology is

$$\beta = \exp v(c(x)), \tag{18}$$

where $c(x) = (\beta - 1)x$ denotes steady-state consumption in terms of a stationary capital stock. If $v(0) < \log \beta < v(\infty)$, then (18) has a unique solution (in the variable x) giving the steady-state capital stock denoted by k. Time preference is flexible in the sense that the steady-state rate of impatience depends on the underlying consumption stream. The solution to (18) exists assuming only a mild restriction on the "discounting" function v. The flexibility of the rate of time preference in the EH contrasts sharply with the rigid TAS case.

Now suppose there are two households with EH utility functions satisfying $v_1 \le v_2$ and $v_h(0) < \log \beta < v_h(\infty)$ for $h = 1, 2$.[22] The first household is more patient than the second. A stationary Pareto optimal allocation will satisfy (18) for each agent's utility function. Since the analogue of (18) holds for each agent separately and is independent of the other agent's choices (by linearity of f), there are unique stationary consumption levels c_1 and c_2 such that

$$\beta = \exp v_h(c_h), \text{ for } h = 1, 2.$$

Since v_h is strictly increasing and $v_1 \le v_2$, the steady-state consumption distribution satisfies $c_1 \ge c_2$ and both agents may hold positive capital stocks. Inequality of consumption is still possible with the EH utility functions. In this case, the more patient household has more income and wealth than the less patient household. However, the extreme solution of at most one agent enjoying a positive consumption level may be avoided, depending on the form of the v_h functions.

1.4 Recursive Utility and Commodity Spaces

A recursive utility function is a representation of a preference order over the commodity space. The choice of the domain of recursive utility is equivalent to the definition of a commodity. What are appropriate commodity spaces? A tentative answer may be given following consideration

---

[22] This is the discrete time analogy of an example in the Epstein and Hynes (1983) paper.

of some examples motivated by optimal growth theory and the "new" endogenous growth literature. Indeed, the accommodation of technologies consistent with persistent growth in consumption levels as found in Kaldor's (1961) six "stylized facts" of growth theory will necessitate consideration of commodity spaces with unbounded consumption profiles.[23]

An infinite horizon is a crucial feature of all the models considered in this book. The infinite horizon may arise in at least two ways. The first simply follows from the observation that the economic problem has no obvious end, even though the world as we know it will end in finite time. The second and related way is to recognize explicitly that the planning horizon is finite, but of uncertain duration, as in the discussion of the Epstein-Hynes functional. In some situations, this random stopping problem is equivalent to a deterministic model cast with an infinite horizon. Both approaches yield the same outcome: there are an infinite number of dates on which consumption may take place. The standard practice in equilibrium theory of distinguishing commodities by physical characteristics and date of delivery leads to the treatment of a consumption profile as an element of an infinite dimensional vector space.[24] The assumption that time may be taken as occurring in discrete periods leads us to consider alternative sequence spaces as models for commodity spaces. Those spaces have many structural features that will be exploited throughout the text. For example, many spaces admit a partial order relation. Order structures on the commodity space also play a fundamental role in the formulation of axioms governing preferences underlying recursive utility functions. Moreover, many important features of commodity spaces possessing an order structure have interesting economic interpretations. Many properties of those spaces are reviewed in the next chapter. The current problem is to motivate the interest in discussing alternative sequence spaces.

1.4.1 Diminishing Returns and Bounded Growth

Consider the Ramsey optimal growth model where f is subject to diminishing marginal returns. Define the *path of pure accumulation* as the feasible program satisfying the constraints with zero consumption at each time and having

$$x_t = f(x_{t-1}), \tag{19}$$

---

[23] Romer (1989) gives a thorough review of those traditional "facts" as well as arguments for several new candidates based on empirical regularities uncovered with the Maddison (1982) and Summers and Heston (1984) data sets.

[24] The vector space requirement for a commodity space is common in equilibrium analysis and is maintained here without further discussion. Hence the divisibility and additivity properties of commodity bundles are taken as given and represent a good approximation for the economic problems under discussion.

where $x_0 = k$. Clearly this path is found by iterating the difference equation (19). Denote the solution by $\{x_t(k)\}_{t=1}^{\infty}$. Every consumption profile that is feasible for the Ramsey problem is bounded from above by the path of pure accumulation in the sense that the planner can never consume more than $x_t(k)$ at time t. Thus feasible consumption bundles satisfy the relation $0 \leq c_t \leq x_t(k)$ for each time t. The assumption that f is subject to diminishing returns together with the Inada conditions implies that there is a maximum sustainable stock, $k^M > 0$, having $f(k^M) = k^M$. The path of pure accumulation starting from positive initial stocks always converges to k^M as t tends to infinity. Since consumption is necessarily bounded by k^M, a sustained positive growth rate of consumption is impossible. Thus diminishing returns bounds the sequences of attainable consumption. The same argument also implies that capital sequences are bounded from above by the maximum sustainable stock.[25]

The implication that every attainable consumption profile forms a non-negative bounded sequence suggests that the appropriate commodity space is ℓ_+^{∞}, the positive cone of the space of all bounded real-valued sequences, ℓ^{∞}. Recall that $\mathbf{x} \in \ell^{\infty}$ if and only if $\|\mathbf{x}\|_{\infty} < \infty$ where $\|\mathbf{x}\|_{\infty} = \sup_t |x_t|$ is the *sup norm*. The choice of the positive cone of ℓ^{∞} as the commodity space reflects the notion that negative consumption is not economically meaningful. This commodity space is a natural choice when there are diminishing returns. However, problems arising in the design of PFCE and the so-called "new" growth theory models suggest that spaces containing ℓ^{∞} are more appropriate in many applications of deterministic capital theory. Other applications may require commodity spaces whose consumption profiles form a subspace of ℓ^{∞}.

▶ Example 5: The cake-eating problem. The problem of intertemporal allocation with exhaustible resources uses the *cake-eating model* introduced by Gale (1967) as a basic parable. Suppose there is a fixed cake of unit size. The planner is assigned the problem of dividing the cake and consuming it over the infinite horizon. Formally, the problem is for a given optimality criterion to choose a non-negative consumption sequence $\mathbf{c}$ having the property

$$\sum_{t=1}^{\infty} c_t \leq 1.$$

The consumption sequence is summable and hence lies in the positive cone of the space ℓ^1 of all sequences $\mathbf{x}$ such that $\sum_{t=1}^{\infty} |x_t| < \infty$; note $\ell^1 \subset \ell^{\infty}$. ◀

---

[25] Assume $0 < k < k^M$.

1.4.2 Non-Decreasing Returns and Sustained Growth

The potential for unbounded consumption sequences can be seen by examining the constant returns to scale, or linear, version of the Ramsey problem. The corresponding path of pure accumulation is found by iterating $x_t = \beta x_{t-1}$ with $x_0 = k$ and yields solution $x_t(k) = \beta^t k$. The planner can obtain arbitrarily large consumption by following the path of pure accumulation for a sufficiently long time and then consuming all the output. Consumption profiles are bounded from above at each t by $\beta^t k$, but this bound moves upwards as time increases. Bounded as well as unbounded consumption profiles are obtainable within the constraints for a fixed starting value of the capital stock. The commodity space can no longer be restricted to ℓ_+^∞ but must contain all sequences of consumption that grow at the rate $\beta - 1 > 0$. Commodity bundles are non-negative vectors contained in the space s^1 of all real-valued sequences. The positive cone of this space will be denoted by s_+^1. On the other hand, feasibility according to the constraints for the linear Ramsey problem precludes using all of s_+^1 for the commodity space. We will model this type of situation later by making the commodity space a principal ideal of the space s^1. This construction will use the fact that there is a natural vector partial order on s^1 which is reflected in the definition of the positive cone s_+^1.

A similar argument holds for a competitive equilibrium, where wages and lump-sum transfers may be present. The consumer faces a sequence of affine budget constraints. Again, unbounded consumption profiles may arise that are feasible according to the budget constraints. A space "larger" than ℓ_+^∞ *must* be used to frame the basic household savings–consumption decisions, *even if* the technologically feasible set is contained in ℓ_+^∞.

Growth and Exogenous Technical Progress

Traditional neoclassical growth theory derived from Solow's (1956) article, as well as the optimum theory based on Ramsey's seminal (1928) paper, makes exogenous technical change the engine driving sustainable growth. In the absence of exogenous technical change, the presence of diminishing returns to capital accumulation drives the long-run growth rate of the economy to zero when labor is essential for production. This is inconsistent with the "stylized facts" of growth theory first put forward by Kaldor.

Exogenous technical change may be grafted onto the Ramsey optimal growth model by defining a sequence of production functions, $f_t(x_{t-1}) = A_t f(x_{t-1})$, with the coefficients A_t representing the exogenous technical change process. For instance, if $f(x) = x^\rho$, then A_t could be interpreted as an exogenous change in the total factor productivity coefficient of a Cobb-Douglas production function over capital and labor, holding the latter input constant. Total factor productivity grows geometrically in the Hicks neutral case $A_t = Ag^t$ for $g > 1$ and $A > 0$ given parameters. Arguments analogous to those in the previous two subsections lead to the conclusion once again that ℓ_+^∞ will be an inadequate choice for the commodity space.

In the absence of international trade, the Turnpike Theorem for the standard neoclassical growth model with exogenous technical change predicts convergence of the growth of per capita income to a level independent of the starting value of the capital stock. Let us note for now that the growth theory interpretation of the turnpike result is that in the long run, both poor economies and rich economies tend to grow at the same rate and have the same capital/labor ratio. This implies that poor countries, which currently have low capital/labor ratios, initially grow faster than the better endowed economies. Barro and Sala-i-Martin (1992) estimated a growth model using US data covering the 48 contiguous states to study this convergence hypothesis. They found that in order to match their quantitative estimates of the key parameters it was necessary to calibrate the model to imply diminishing returns to capital set in "slowly." Thus the construction of theoretical models designed to investigate the scope of the convergence hypothesis will probably have to accommodate unbounded consumption spaces.[26]

Endogenous Growth Models

Several models have been advanced by growth theorists under the heading of *endogenous growth models* that attempt to find an engine for growth which is a structural component of the model rather than an exogenous appendage. The idea is to restore capital accumulation as the basis for growth rather than resorting to the device of assuming growth arises outside the model.[27] Two different types of endogenous growth models are introduced below as examples of that literature. In each case, the space of consumption sequences must be taken as a subset of s_+^1 strictly containing ℓ_+^∞.

▶ Example 6: A convex model of endogenous growth. In the traditional Ramsey-Solow model, diminishing returns arise from the presence of a fixed level of the labor input. That input is *essential* in the sense that output is zero if labor is not utilized in a positive amount. One hypothesis in the "new" growth theory is that sustained growth may be possible with a concave production function when there is an *inessential* fixed input. The canonical example of a concave production function with the desired

---

[26] See Barro and Sala-i-Martin (1995) for a more thorough survey of the convergence hypothesis.

[27] See Romer (1989) and Barro and Sala-i-Martin (1995) for a full discussion.

properties is specified by

$$f(x) = \beta x + x^\rho, \tag{20}$$

where $\beta > 1$ and $0 < \rho < 1$. This model is a blend of the standard neoclassical model and the linear model.[28] The model is said to be *convex* since the production set generated by the production function f is a convex set; strictly increasing marginal returns are not admissible in this framework. Calculation of the path of pure accumulation yields the conclusion that arbitrarily large consumption is attainable (in at least one time period); the attainable consumption profiles do not form a bounded set. ◄

▶ Example 7: Human capital and endogenous growth. Many endogenous growth models introduce increasing returns and external spillover effects to build a foundation for sustainable growth. One way to do this is through the explicit consideration of the role played by human capital and technical know-how in the accumulation-growth process. An influential model due to Lucas (1988) combines physical and human capital in a two-sector setup. As in the convex technology growth models, the human capital sector is assumed to be unconstrained by any essential fixed factors. Diminishing returns to capital accumulation exist for fixed levels of human capital and any other fixed factor (e.g., land), but a positive sustainable growth rate may arise from increasing returns at the social level provided the level of human capital can grow at a geometric rate. Let h_t denote the stock of human capital at time t. Let h_{1t} be the human capital devoted to producing physical output goods at time t and h_{2t} the human capital allocation to the knowledge accumulation sector. Obviously the two uses of human capital must add to the total at each time t, that is $h_{1t} + h_{2t} = h_t$ must hold at every t. The planner controls the share of human capital devoted to output producing activities, denoted by $\eta_t \in [0,1]$. Evidently $1 - \eta_t$ is the proportion of the capital stock placed in the knowledge accumulation sector. The first key assumption is there are constant returns to scale in human capital accumulation with the equation of evolution of the human capital stock given by

$$h_{t+1} = \mu(1 - \eta_t)h_t, \tag{21}$$

where $h_0 > 0$ is given and μ is the constant marginal product of human capital in the production of human capital. Human capital grows whenever $\mu(1 - \eta_t) > 1$. We assume $\mu > 1$ so that growth is possible. Output

---

[28] Production functions of type (20) satisfy Gale and Sutherland's (1968) strong productivity condition. They examined the existence of optimal programs and supporting prices in such models. Jones and Manuelli (1990) utilized such production functions in their theory of endogenous growth which is the role model for our discussion in this example.

is produced via a constant returns to scale technology. The inputs are human capital h_{1t}, physical capital x_{t-1}, and labor L_t. Output is divided between consumption and physical capital, and evolves according to the equation

$$c_t + x_t = (x_{t-1})^\alpha (h_{1t})^{1-\alpha-\beta} (L_t)^\beta, \qquad (22)$$

where $1 - \alpha - \beta > 0$ and $\alpha, \beta \in (0,1)$ with $L_t = 1$ at each date t. Assume the planner adopts a TAS criterion. The optimal growth problem is to find non-negative sequences $(\mathbf{c}, \mathbf{x}, \mathbf{h})$ satisfying the constraints (21) and (22) starting with $x_0 = k$ and achieving a maximum discounted sum of one-period felicities according to (1). One of the control variables is $\eta_t \in [0,1]$ in this maximization problem. The feasible consumption sequences for this model do not lie in a bounded subspace of s^1_+, just as with the other models allowing sustained rate of growth in consumption. This can be seen by considering a special feasible program with fixed share $\eta \in (0,1)$, $\mu(1 - \eta) > 1$ and savings rate at the level $s \in (0,1)$. Solve (21) for the human capital sequence $h_t = [\mu(1-\eta)]^t h_0$ (for $t = 1, 2, \dots$), which grows at rate $[\mu(1-\eta)] - 1$. Substitute it into the evolution equation, along with $h_{1t} = \eta h_t$, obtaining

$$x_t = s(x_{t-1})^\alpha (\eta h_{1t})^{1-\alpha-\beta} = s h_0^{1-\alpha-\beta} [\mu(1-\eta)]^{(1-\alpha-\beta)t} (x_{t-1})^\alpha.$$

Observe that the capital stock sequence grows monotonically and tends to infinity as t tends to infinity. The corresponding consumption sequence also grows without bound. The commodity space must be chosen to allow for unbounded consumption profiles. ◄

The variety of examples discussed above illustrates the scope of models that we will accommodate in our construction of a domain for recursive utility functions. The space of consumption goods is a subset of s^1_+, and is frequently the positive cone of a linear space in its own right. Bounded and unbounded consumption profiles arise in applications. The general theory of recursive utility functions will be built on commodity spaces that abstract the properties found in the examples. The goal is to provide a unified structure to support the analysis of several theoretical and applied models. We will present the mathematical background necessary to follow our arguments in Chapter 2. The lesson to be noted for later reference is that the specification of the domain of a recursive utility function will be connected to the technology via the growth rate for the path of pure accumulation. Preferences and technology are not specified independently as commonly practiced in finite dimensional equilibrium analysis. The infinite dimensional structure of the commodity space will necessitate the formulation of some joint conditions on preference orders and the properties of the technology.

1.4.3 Order Structures

There are two important precedence relations in the construction of dynamic models. The first comes about through the order induced by the passage of time: there is the present (today) and the future (tomorrow). Inputs precede outputs and consumption today occurs before consumption tomorrow. The timing of production and consumption decisions lies at the heart of dynamic choice problems and intertemporal resource allocation theory. The second order relation comes about through the requirement that consumption be measured as a non-negative number at each time. This leads to a pointwise order relation on consumption profiles of the form: $c \geq c'$ if and only if $c_t \geq c_t'$ for each time t. The relation $\geq$ is a partial order on the elements of the commodity space. Hence the vector space structure of the commodity space is supplemented by an order relation.

Weak Separability of the Future from the Present

The unidirectional arrow of time plays a fundamental role in the axioms governing preference orders with recursive utility representations. Discussions of separability and functional structure in demand theory with a finite number of commodities makes a clear distinction between *symmetric separability* and *asymmetric separability*—the latter defined as separability of one group of commodities from another relative to an *ordered* partition of the commodity list.[29] Recursive structures are derived in the asymmetric separability case. This can be seen briefly in the condition that recursive utility functions reflect the weak separability of the future consumption stream from the present consumption bundle. The time index set is $\{1, 2, \ldots, t, \ldots\}$ with the ordering of the natural numbers. In the case of a single consumption good this index set coincides with the list of commodities. Koopmans's axioms for recursive utility act on an ordered partition of this index set into two disjoint subsets $\{1\}$ and $\{2, 3, \ldots\}$ corresponding to the present and future respectively. The key axiom, called *limited independence* by Koopmans, asserts that the preference order has the property that the future goods form a commodity group that is weakly separable from the current consumption good. This separability axiom is not in general taken to be symmetric in the sense that the present consumption good need not be weakly separable from the future consumption profile. Indeed, a strengthening of the weak separability of the present from the future in conjunction with Koopmans's other postulates leads to an additive utility representation: TAS utility then becomes a special case of recursive utility.[30] The role of the *stationarity*

---

[29] This is discussed exhaustively in Blackorby, Primont, and Russell (1978).

[30] The axiom expressing this property is called *extended independence*.

axiom is to make the weak separability property independent of calendar time: for any date t the future commodity group corresponding to the ordered set $\{t+1, t+2, \dots\}$ is weakly separable from the past history given by the ordered list $\{1, 2, \dots, t\}$; W is also the aggregator in this case. The important time consistency property of decisions taken by recursive utility maximizers is a consequence of the limited independence and stationarity axioms. We will take up the analysis of Koopmans's axioms in Chapter 2. The essential point is that recursive structures reflect an underlying order property based on the fact that consumption and production take place over time.

Partial Orders on the Commodity Space

The combination of the vector space and order structures yields several important economic and mathematical properties for the underlying commodity space. On the economic front, nonsatiation may be expressed in terms of the notion that "more is better" by assuming that $\mathbf{c} > \mathbf{c}'$ (in the sense that $c_t > c'_t$ for all t) implies $\mathbf{c} \succ \mathbf{c}'$ where $\succ$ denotes the strict preference relation.[31] The mathematical advantage is that the theory of ordered vector spaces may be used to define the domain of recursive utility. For example, the domain of a recursive utility function must certainly include all the consumption sequences that could be attained from the given starting stocks allowing for the technological constraints. This will lead us to the consideration of commodity spaces, called *principal ideals*, that capture all the economically relevant programs. These sets contain all the programs that cannot grow faster than the path of pure accumulation. In some cases the combination of an order structure with a linear topology will yield an important mathematical structure (e.g., when the commodity space is a Banach lattice). In turn, this may have an effect on the structure of price systems that can arise as equilibria.[32] We will return to this issue in Chapters 2 and 8.

The examples given above take the positive cone of a vector space as the consumption set. This specification is not always adequate for economies with production activities.[33] Consumption sets with a finite lower bound may be shown to be equivalent to assuming the positive cone contains the consumption set. A consumption set which contains its infimum has

---

[31] There is a notion of nonsatiation that is not dependent on the algebraic or order structures of the commodity space. A profile $\mathbf{c}^*$ is a point of *saturation* if $\mathbf{c}^* \succsim \mathbf{c}$ for all $\mathbf{c}$ in the commodity space. Nonsatiation can be formalized as the assumption that the preference order has no points of saturation. The monotonicity form of the nonsatiation axiom cannot be expressed without an explicit order relation defined on the commodity space.

[32] See Becker (1991a; 1991b) for a discussion of this in the context of the fundamental welfare theorems.

[33] We follow the discussion here in Boyd and McKenzie (1993).

two major inadequacies. First, it does not allow for trade in personal services, even when production is absent. In particular, it does not allow for the use of differentiated labor services in production, unless each consumer can only supply one type of labor. This is an important restriction for models allowing agents a consumption–leisure choice. Second, it does not allow substitution between goods on the subsistence boundary of the possible consumption sets. The specification of an agent's trading set necessarily involves positive and negative coordinates according to the standard convention of treating negative commodities as supplies in the household sector and inputs in the production sector. However, the existence of a partial order on the underlying commodity space is still used in an essential way just to define the distinction between inputs and outputs and include personal services and labor supply in the model. The equilibrium theory presented in Chapter 8 will use the commodity space's order structure to accommodate trading sets that do not contain their infima.

1.5 Conclusion

The Dutch graphic artist M.C. Escher wrote in an essay on infinity that "man is incapable of imagining that time could ever stop."[34] Escher went on to describe his efforts to arrive at a satisfactory plane representation of infinity displaying continuity, one-way direction, and unity of color in each row. The sequence of woodcuts in the *Circle Limit* series were the result of his attempt to imagine infinity. Each picture on a "unit" disk displays a motif with the pattern drawn at successively smaller scales as the boundary of the disk is approached—much in the way that the Mandelbrot set contains itself on smaller and smaller scales. The choice of a disk as the domain is designed to allow a glimpse of infinity within a finite area.

The problem of representing preference orders over infinite sequences of consumption raises many problems analogous to those encountered by Escher during his search for a graphic portrayal of infinity. The notion of a recursive utility function is an economic answer to this representation problem. The consideration of preference orders that will give rise to a recursive utility function embody a mathematical notion of continuity that will link impatience, the one-way passage of time (present versus future), and time consistency of decision making (analogous to Escher's unity of color in each line). Discounting of the future realization of consumption gives the appearance of the same level of physical consumption at a future date as having less and less satisfaction from the vantage point of the

---

[34] See M. C. Escher, "Approaches to infinity," in Escher and J. L. Locher (1984, p. 15).

present. Just as Escher uses the same pattern over and over, recursive utility uses the same pattern of preferences over and over into the future. The final result is the representation of the recursive utility function in the form of an aggregator over current consumption and prospective future utility. The stationarity of the preference order is combined with the other mentioned properties to decompose the utility of an infinite sequence into a function of today's consumption and future utility. Infinity is grasped by an agent governed by recursive utility through the reduction of the infinite stage consumption prospect to a two-stage (and hence finite) picture of the present versus the future prospects.

The remaining chapters in this book are devoted to the exploration of the behavioral implications of hypothesizing that economic agent's objectives are modeled as recursive utility functions. The first task is to formalize the construction of suitable commodity spaces and lay out the structure of preferences giving rise to recursive utility functions. This is the goal of Chapters 2 and 3. Optimum growth models are the focus of Chapters 4 and 5. The connection between optimal growth and competitive equilibrium programs is made in Chapter 6. Comparative dynamics of optimal programs and equilibrium profiles are studied in Chapter 7. The order structure of the commodity space is shown via lattice programming techniques to yield many interesting sensitivity results. Chapter 8 examines the theory of competitive equilibrium, the core, and welfare economics in light of our development of recursive utility theory.

CHAPTER 2

Commodity and Price Spaces

2.1 Introduction

A characteristic feature of capital theoretic models is the absence of a definite termination date. Since goods delivered at different dates are different goods, this forces the consideration of an infinite set of goods. Many models of market equilibrium allow delivery to take place on one date. If the infinity of goods were for delivery on a single date, it may be reasonable to presume they belong to a compact space, and may be adequately approximated by a finite set of goods. In this case, the infinite horizon assumption precludes this possibility of approximating the commodity space by a finite set of goods. It was a major contribution of *Value and Capital* (Hicks, 1946) to provide a full-scale analysis of an economy in which this fact is recognized. An infinite horizon implies the number of goods is infinite, even when deliveries are scheduled at discrete intervals. The infinity of goods must be dealt with simultaneously since the market is analyzed as though all contracts are executed at the beginning of time. This is a limiting form of Hicks's futures economy.

The infinite horizon assumption implies that commodity spaces are infinite dimensional. Functional analytic techniques form the language and methods underlying the analysis of markets with an infinite number of commodities. The typical market model is based on a dual pair of linear commodity and price spaces as first proposed by Debreu (1954a).[1] The relevant functional analysis material will be exposited in this chapter. The properties of the various sequence spaces that arise are collected here.

2.2 Commodity Spaces

The development of dynamic models with a recursive utility representation of an intertemporal preference order is most easily cast in a world with

---

[1] The dual pairing approach applies to complete market models. This setup may not be appropriate in incomplete market settings. See Becker, Boyd, and Foias (1991) for an incomplete markets model where the price system is not an element of the dual space.

a countable infinity of time periods, $t = 1, 2, \ldots, T, \ldots$[2] Let $c_t \in \mathbb{R}^m$ denote the consumption vector in period t. We will denote the components of consumption at time t by c_{it} where $i = 1, \ldots, m$. The sequence of consumption bundles $\mathbf{c} = \{c_t\}_{t=1}^{\infty}$ is an element of s^m, the space of all sequences in $\mathbb{R}^m$.

The commodity space $\mathbf{E}$ is a subspace of s^m. Elements of $\mathbf{E}$ are denoted by lower-case boldface letters, e.g., $\mathbf{c} = \{c_t\}_{t=1}^{\infty}$. The space $\mathbf{E}$ may be chosen as a proper subspace of s^m. The case $\mathbf{E} = \ell^{\infty} \subset s^1$, the space of all bounded real-valued sequences, is typically used for the one-sector growth model.

As usual, we assume commodity bundles are both divisible and additive. Bundles can be added and multiplied by a scalar. We use the general equilibrium convention that positive components of a consumer's consumption bundle represent demands; the negative components represent supplies. Similarly, positive components of a producer's input–output vector are outputs; negative components are inputs. As a result, we model our commodity space as a vector space over the reals.[3]

Recall that a *vector space* or *linear space* is a set $\mathbf{E}$ with two special operations. These are *vector addition*, a map from $\mathbf{E} \times \mathbf{E} \to \mathbf{E}$ taking $(\mathbf{x}, \mathbf{y})$ to $\mathbf{x} + \mathbf{y}$, and *scalar multiplication*, mapping $\mathbb{R} \times \mathbf{E} \to \mathbf{E}$ by taking $(\lambda, \mathbf{x})$ to $\lambda \mathbf{x}$. These operations must obey certain conditions:

Vector Space. A vector space (linear space) over the real numbers is a triple $(\mathbf{E}, +, \cdot)$ such that, for all $\mathbf{x}, \mathbf{y}, \mathbf{z} \in \mathbf{E}$ and $\lambda, \mu \in \mathbb{R}$:

(1) $\mathbf{x} + \mathbf{y} = \mathbf{y} + \mathbf{x}$ (addition is commutative);
(2) $\mathbf{x} + (\mathbf{y} + \mathbf{z}) = (\mathbf{x} + \mathbf{y}) + \mathbf{z}$ (addition is associative);
(3) There exists a unique zero element $(\mathbf{0})$ with $\mathbf{x} + \mathbf{0} = \mathbf{x}$;
(4) For every $\mathbf{x}$ there exists an additive inverse $-\mathbf{x}$ with $-\mathbf{x} + \mathbf{x} = \mathbf{0}$;
(5) $\lambda(\mathbf{x} + \mathbf{y}) = \lambda\mathbf{x} + \lambda\mathbf{y}$ (right distributive law);
(6) $(\lambda + \mu)\mathbf{x} = \lambda\mathbf{x} + \mu\mathbf{x}$ (left distributive law);
(7) $\lambda(\mu\mathbf{x}) = (\lambda\mu)\mathbf{x}$ (multiplication is associative);
(8) $1\mathbf{x} = \mathbf{x}$ (multiplicative identity).

Given arbitrary vector spaces $\mathbf{E}$ and $\mathbf{F}$, a *linear mapping* from $\mathbf{E}$ to $\mathbf{F}$ is a function $f\colon \mathbf{E} \to \mathbf{F}$ that obeys $f(\lambda\mathbf{x} + \mu\mathbf{y}) = \lambda f(\mathbf{x}) + \mu f(\mathbf{y})$. Two vector spaces $\mathbf{E}$ and $\mathbf{F}$ are *isomorphic* if there is a one-to-one linear mapping from $\mathbf{E}$ onto $\mathbf{F}$. In that case, the inverse mapping exists and is linear from $\mathbf{F}$ onto $\mathbf{E}$. Isomorphic vector spaces are identical as far as their vector space properties are concerned, although they may differ in other attributes. A *vector subspace* of $\mathbf{E}$ is a set $\mathbf{F} \subset \mathbf{E}$ such that $\lambda\mathbf{x} + \mu\mathbf{y} \in \mathbf{F}$ whenever

---

[2] A set is *countable* if it can be indexed by a subset of the positive integers.

[3] For technical reasons we will sometimes need to use a vector space over the complex numbers. In that case, substitute the complex numbers for the real numbers in the definition of vector space.

$x, y \in F$ and $\lambda, \mu \in \mathbb{R}$. Of course, a vector subspace is a vector space in its own right. A *linear variety* is a translate of a vector subspace.

2.2.1 Order Properties

The space s^m has a natural order property. One consumption vector is larger than another if it yields more consumption of each good at every point in time. More precisely, for elements $\mathbf{x}$ and $\mathbf{y}$ of s^m, define $\geq$ by $\mathbf{x} \geq \mathbf{y}$ if and only if $x_{it} \geq y_{it}$ for all $i = 1, \ldots, m$ and $t = 1, 2, \ldots$. The relation $\geq$ may be used to define the *positive cone* (positive orthant) of s^m, denoted s^m_+, by $s^m_+ = \{\mathbf{x} \in s^m : \mathbf{x} \geq \mathbf{0}\}$, where $\mathbf{0} = \{0\}_{t=1}^{\infty}$ is the zero vector. The subspace $\mathbf{E}$ inherits the order structure determined by the relation $\geq$; $\mathbf{E}_+$ (or sometimes $\mathbf{E}^+$) denotes the positive cone of $\mathbf{E}$. The relation $\geq$ is a partial order, and we refer to it as the *usual order* on s^m.

Partial Order. A binary relation $\leq$ on a set X is a partial order if:

(1) $x \leq x$ for all $x \in X$ (reflexive);
(2) $x \leq y$ and $y \leq x$ implies $x = y$ (anti-symmetric);
(3) $x \leq y$ and $y \leq z$ implies $x \leq z$ (transitive).

We will usually refer to a partial order as an order. An order is a *total order* if any two elements of X can be compared: if either $x \leq y$ or $x \geq y$ for all $x, y \in X$. A totally ordered set is sometimes called a *chain*. The partial order on s^m is compatible with the vector space structure. If we add the same vector to $\mathbf{x}$ and $\mathbf{y}$, or if we multiply by a positive scalar, it does not change their order. This natural order turns s^m into an ordered vector space.

Ordered Vector Space. A vector space $\mathbf{E}$ equipped with a partial order $\leq$ is an ordered vector space if:

(1) $\mathbf{x} \leq \mathbf{y}$ implies $\mathbf{x} + \mathbf{z} \leq \mathbf{y} + \mathbf{z}$ for all $\mathbf{x}, \mathbf{y}, \mathbf{z} \in \mathbf{E}$;
(2) $\mathbf{x} \leq \mathbf{y}$ implies $\lambda \mathbf{x} \leq \lambda \mathbf{y}$ for all $\mathbf{x}, \mathbf{y} \in \mathbf{E}$ and $\lambda \geq 0$.

It is easy to see that the positive orthant of any ordered vector space obeys $\mathbf{E}_+ + \mathbf{E}_+ \subset \mathbf{E}_+$, $\lambda \mathbf{E}_+ \subset \mathbf{E}_+$ for $\lambda > 0$, and $\mathbf{E}_+ \cap (-\mathbf{E}_+) = \{\mathbf{0}\}$. In fact, any set $C \subset \mathbf{E}$ obeying these properties would induce an order on $\mathbf{E}$ that makes $\mathbf{E}$ an ordered vector space by defining $\mathbf{x} \leq \mathbf{y}$ if $\mathbf{y} - \mathbf{x} \in C$. Given an ordering, we define the *order interval* $[\mathbf{x}, \mathbf{y}] = \{\mathbf{z} \in \mathbf{E} : \mathbf{x} \leq \mathbf{z} \leq \mathbf{y}\}$. A set is *order bounded* if it is contained in an order interval.

The space s^m has a further useful order property. It is a *lattice*. For every pair of vectors $\mathbf{x}$ and $\mathbf{y}$, the supremum (least upper bound) and infimum (greatest lower bound) of the set $\{\mathbf{x}, \mathbf{y}\}$ exist in s^m. In fact, these are just the coordinatewise maximum and minimum of $\mathbf{x}$ and $\mathbf{y}$. Using standard lattice notation, $\mathbf{x} \vee \mathbf{y} = \sup\{\mathbf{x}, \mathbf{y}\}$ and $\mathbf{x} \wedge \mathbf{y} = \inf\{\mathbf{x}, \mathbf{y}\}$.[4] An

---

[4] Additional material on lattices, relevant to comparative dynamics analysis, may be

order is *Archimedean* if $\mathbf{x} \leq \mathbf{0}$ whenever $n\mathbf{x} \leq \mathbf{y}$ for all positive integers n. The usual order on the real numbers is Archimedean, as is the usual order on s^m. The lexicographic order on $\mathbb{R}^2$ is an example of a non-Archimedean order which is total.

The space s^m is an example of a *Riesz space* (or *vector lattice*).[5] We will require $\mathbf{E}$ to be a Riesz subspace of s^m, that is, whenever $\mathbf{x}$ and $\mathbf{y} \in \mathbf{E}$, the elements $\mathbf{x} \vee \mathbf{y}$ and $\mathbf{x} \wedge \mathbf{y}$ both belong to $\mathbf{E}$. We define the *absolute value* of $\mathbf{x} \in \mathbf{E}$ by $|\mathbf{x}| = \mathbf{x} \vee (-\mathbf{x})$ and the positive and negative parts by $\mathbf{x}^+ = \mathbf{x} \vee \mathbf{0}$ and $\mathbf{x}^- = (-\mathbf{x}) \vee \mathbf{0}$. The next lemma follows easily from the definitions.[6]

Lemma 1. *If* $\mathbf{E}$ *is a Riesz space, the following identities hold for all* $\mathbf{x}, \mathbf{y} \in \mathbf{E}$ *and* $\lambda \in \mathbb{R}$:

(1) $\mathbf{x} + \mathbf{y} = \mathbf{x} \vee \mathbf{y} + \mathbf{x} \wedge \mathbf{y}$;
(2) $|\lambda \mathbf{x}| = |\lambda|\,|\mathbf{x}|$;
(3) $|\mathbf{x} + \mathbf{y}| \leq |\mathbf{x}| + |\mathbf{y}|$;
(4) $|\mathbf{x}^+ - \mathbf{y}^+| \leq |\mathbf{x} - \mathbf{y}|$;
(5) $\mathbf{x} = \mathbf{x}^+ - \mathbf{x}^-$;
(6) $|\mathbf{x}| = \mathbf{x}^+ + \mathbf{x}^-$.

Free Disposal

Free disposal is assumed in many economic applications. Thus, we turn our attention to Riesz subspaces of $\mathbf{E}$ that permit *free disposal*: if $\mathbf{x} \in \mathbf{E}$ and $\mathbf{x} \geq \mathbf{y} \geq \mathbf{0}$, then $\mathbf{y} \in \mathbf{E}$. Now if $\mathbf{x} \in \mathbf{E}$, $\mathbf{0} \leq \mathbf{x}^+ = \mathbf{x} \vee \mathbf{0} \in \mathbf{E}$, and similarly $\mathbf{x}^- \in \mathbf{E}$. But then $|\mathbf{x}| = \mathbf{x}^+ + \mathbf{x}^- \in \mathbf{E}$. Moreover, if $|\mathbf{x}| \in \mathbf{E}$, $\mathbf{x}^+$ and $\mathbf{x}^- \in \mathbf{E}$ by the same argument, so $\mathbf{x} = \mathbf{x}^+ - \mathbf{x}^- \in \mathbf{E}$. It follows that any subspace which permits free disposal must be *solid*: $|\mathbf{y}| \leq |\mathbf{x}|$ and $\mathbf{x} \in A$ imply $\mathbf{y} \in A$. Solid Riesz subspaces are referred to as *Riesz ideals*. The combination of additivity, divisibility, and free disposal virtually forces us to restrict our attention to Riesz ideals.

An important class of commodity spaces is the class of ideals that are generated by a single element of s^m. Given a vector $\omega = (\omega_1, \omega_2, \dots) \in s^m$ let

$$A_\omega = \{\mathbf{x} \in s^m : |\mathbf{x}| \leq \lambda|\omega| \text{ for some } \lambda \geq 0\},$$

where λ is a scalar. The set A_ω is the *principal Riesz ideal* generated by ω. Of course, A_ω is a Riesz ideal of s^m and it is easily verified that it is the smallest Riesz ideal containing ω. Notice that for $\omega = (1, 1, \dots) \in s^1$,

---

found in Chapter 7.

[5] For a general discussion of Riesz spaces with economic applications, see Aliprantis, Brown, and Burkinshaw (1989). The books by Aliprantis and Burkinshaw (1978; 1985) and Aliprantis and Border (1994) contain more detail on Riesz spaces.

[6] See Aliprantis and Burkinshaw (1978, p. 3).

$A_\omega = \ell^\infty$. In applications of recursive utility models, the natural commodity space will typically be a principal ideal. The particular application will determine the choice of ω. For instance, in an exchange economy, ω would be the aggregate or social endowment vector. The commodity space must contain the endowment, and all vectors that can be obtained from it by free disposal. The smallest Riesz subspace of s^m that contains all these vectors is precisely A_ω. In the Ramsey optimal growth setting, ω would be the path of pure accumulation generated by iteration of the production function with seed k. All feasible capital and consumption paths would be no larger than ω. Here A_ω is the smallest Riesz ideal of s^m containing all feasible consumption (or capital) vectors.

2.2.2 Topological Properties

Being able to distinguish more from less is not the only property we require of our commodity space. Commodity bundles that are physically close should be close in terms of preference. We need to be able to tell when vectors are close together, and when they are far apart; when a sequence converges, and when it does not. For this, we require a topology.[7] Let X be a set.

Topology. A collection τ of subsets of X is a topology on X if:

(1) The union of any subcollection of τ is in τ;
(2) The intersection of any finite subcollection of τ is in τ;
(3) Both the entire space and the empty set are in τ.

The members of τ are called *open sets*, and the pair (X, τ) is referred to as a *topological space*. If we have two distinct topologies, σ and τ, on X, we say σ is *weaker* (*coarser*) than τ (or that τ is *stronger* or *finer* than σ) if $\sigma \subset \tau$. The collection of all subsets of X is a topology, the *discrete topology*. A second possible topology on X, the *trivial topology*, consists of $\{X, \emptyset\}$. The discrete and trivial topologies are the strongest and weakest possible topologies, respectively.

For any $x \in X$, we say $V \subset X$ is a *neighborhood* of x if there is an open set U, $x \in U \subset V$. If $A \subset X$ contains a neighborhood of x, we say that x is an *interior point* of A. The set of all interior points of A, the *interior* of A, is denoted int A. Let $\mathcal{U}_x = \{$neighborhoods of $x\}$. The collection $\mathcal{U}_x$ then forms a neighborhood system.

Neighborhood System. The collection $\mathcal{U}_x$ of subsets of X is a neighborhood system at x if:

(1) $x \in U$ for all $U \in \mathcal{U}_x$;

---

[7] Good references on basic topology are Kelley (1955), Willard (1970), and the first part of Simmons (1963). Proofs of the lemmas and theorems in this section are standard and can be found in any of these.

(2) If $U \in \mathcal{U}_x$ and $V \in \mathcal{U}_x$ then $U \cap V \in \mathcal{U}_x$;

(3) If $U \in \mathcal{U}_x$ and $U \subset V$ then $V \in \mathcal{U}_x$;

(4) If $U \in \mathcal{U}_x$, there is some $V \in \mathcal{U}_x$ with $U \in \mathcal{U}_y$ for all $y \in V$.

Knowing the neighborhood system at each point is equivalent to knowing the topology. If we have a neighborhood system at each point, and define a set to be open if it contains a neighborhood of each of its points, we obtain a topology having that neighborhood system. It is fairly easy to generate neighborhood systems. This is usually done by using a neighborhood base.

Neighborhood Base. A neighborhood base is a non-empty collection of sets $\mathcal{B}_x$ for each point in X that obeys:

(1) If $U \in \mathcal{B}_x$ then $x \in U$;

(2) If $U, V \in \mathcal{B}_x$, then there is some $W \in \mathcal{B}_x$ with $W \subset U \cap V$;

(3) If $U \in \mathcal{B}_x$, there is some $V \in \mathcal{B}_x$ such that for every $y \in V$ there is a $W \in \mathcal{B}_y$ with $W \subset V$.

A set is open if and only if it contains a basic neighborhood of each of its points. If we have a neighborhood base $\mathcal{B}_x$, we define the associated neighborhood system $\mathcal{U}_x$ by $U \in \mathcal{U}_x$ if and only if there is a $V \in \mathcal{B}_x$ with $V \subset U$. Similarly, we can define a base for the entire topology τ. A collection $\mathcal{B}$ is a *base* for τ if $\tau = \{\cup \, \mathcal{C} : \mathcal{C} \subset \mathcal{B}\}$.[8] This implies that every element of $\mathcal{B}$ is in τ, and hence $\mathcal{B}$ is a collection of open sets.

Topological Base. A collection $\mathcal{B}$ is a base for a topology on X if and only if:

(1) $X = \cup \, \mathcal{B}$;

(2) Whenever $U, V \in \mathcal{B}$ with $x \in U \cap V$, there is a $W \in \mathcal{B}$ with $x \in W \subset U \cap V$.

The associated topology is given by $\tau = \{\cup \, \mathcal{C} : \mathcal{C} \subset \mathcal{B}\}$. The main difference between a base for a topology and the totality of the neighborhood bases is that sets in the neighborhood bases need not be open. However, if we have a base $\mathcal{B}$, and define $\mathcal{B}_x = \{U \in \mathcal{B} : x \in U\}$, we obtain a neighborhood base of open sets. Conversely, if we have an open neighborhood base at each point, we can obtain a base for the topology by setting $\mathcal{B} = \cup_{x \in X} \mathcal{B}_x$.

The size of the collection used to define a topology τ can be further reduced by defining a subbase. A collection $\mathcal{C}$ of subsets of X is a *subbase* (or *subbasis*) for τ if the collection of finite intersections of elements of $\mathcal{C}$ forms a base for τ. Thus any open set can be expressed as a union of finite intersections of members of $\mathcal{C}$. The family of sets having either the form

---

[8] The notation $\cup \, \mathcal{C}$ means $\cup \{C : C \in \mathcal{C}\}$.

$(-\infty, a)$ or (b, ∞) is a subbase for the usual topology on $\mathbb{R}$. One reason for the interest in subbases is that any collection of subsets of X can be regarded as a subbase for some topology on X. This makes subbases a particularly flexible tool for describing topologies.

We call $A \subset X$ *closed* if its complement is open. The intersection of any collection of closed sets is closed; the union of finitely many closed sets is closed; the entire space and the empty set are closed. A point x is called a *limit point* of A if every neighborhood of x intersects A in a point other than x. The set A, together with its limit points, is a closed set denoted cl A. This is the smallest closed set that contains A and is referred to as the *closure* of A.

If $A \subset X$, the *relative topology* on A is $A \cap \tau$, i.e., it is the collection of sets $A \cap U$ with $U \in \tau$. The two topologies on $A \subset X$ do differ. If $B \subset A$, B may have limit points as a subset of X that are not limit points in the relative topology as a subset of A because the would-be limit points are not in A. This can occur in the unit interval $[0, 1]$. Let $X = [0, 1]$, $A = (0, 1)$ and $B = (0, 1/2)$. As a subset of X, B has closure $[0, 1/2]$, while as a subset of A, B has closure $(0, 1/2]$.

The definition of closed set implies (via De Morgan's laws) that any result concerning open sets in a topological space may be translated into a result about closed sets by replacing "open" and "closed" and interchanging unions and intersections.[9] For example, we may define a *closed subbase* as a collection of sets $\mathcal{D}$ such that every closed set may be written as an intersection of finite unions of members of $\mathcal{D}$. The family of sets having either the form $(-\infty, a]$ or $[b, \infty)$ is a closed subbase for the usual topology on $\mathbb{R}$.[10]

A set $A \subset X$ is *dense* if cl $A = X$. A space X is *separable* if it has a countable dense subset.

A *Hausdorff topological space* is a topological space where any two distinct points have disjoint neighborhoods. This implies that the closure of $\{x\}$ is $\{x\}$. Singletons are closed in Hausdorff spaces. Roughly speaking, non-Hausdorff topologies have trouble distinguishing points. This is undesirable in economic applications, and we will focus on the Hausdorff topologies.

Metric Spaces
One way to get a Hausdorff topology is to use a metric or norm. Either one gives us a numerical measure of distance.

---

[9] Recall that *De Morgan's Laws* say that the complement of an intersection of sets is the union of their complements, and that the complement of a union of sets is the intersection of their complements.

[10] This specification of a closed subbasis underlies the description of the order interval topology discussed in Section 7.3.1.

Metric. A metric is a function $d\colon X \times X \to \mathbb{R}_+$ such that:

(1) $d(x,y) \geq 0$ and $d(x,y) = 0$ if and only if $x = y$ (positive definite);
(2) $d(x,y) = d(y,x)$ (symmetric);
(3) $d(x,y) \leq d(x,z) + d(z,y)$ (triangle inequality)

for all $x, y, z \in X$.

The pair (X, d) is called a *metric space*. Given a metric, define the *ball* of radius ϵ about x by $B_\epsilon(x) = \{y \in X : d(x,y) < \epsilon\}$. A neighborhood of x is a set that contains some ball about x, and an open set is a set that contains a ball about each of its points. The set of balls about x (or even the balls with rational radii) is a neighborhood base at x. Note that different metrics can lead to the same topology. If they do, the metrics are called *equivalent*. The d-topology is coarser than the ρ-topology if there is an $\alpha > 0$ with $\alpha\rho(x,y) \leq d(x,y)$, and d and ρ are equivalent if there are $\alpha \geq \beta > 0$ with $\beta\rho(x,y) \leq d(x,y) \leq \alpha\rho(x,y)$.

▶ **Example 1: Equivalent metrics.** In fact, any metric is equivalent to a bounded metric. Define $\rho(x,y) = d(x,y)/[1 + d(x,y)]$. This is clearly bounded, positive definite, and symmetric. We need only verify the triangle inequality to show it is a metric.

Since d obeys the triangle inequality, we need only show that if $a, b, c \geq 0$ with $a \leq b + c$, then $a/(1+a) \leq b/(1+b) + c/(1+c)$ (take $a = d(x,y)$, $b = d(x,z)$, and $c = d(z,y)$). Now $a \leq b + c \leq b + bc + c + bc + abc$, so

$$a(1 + b)(1 + c) = a + ab + ac + abc$$
$$\leq b + ab + bc + abc + c + ac + bc + abc$$
$$= b(1 + a)(1 + c) + c(1 + a)(1 + b).$$

Dividing by $(1 + a)(1 + b)(1 + c)$ shows $a/(1+a) \leq b/(1+b) + c/(1+c)$.

Finally, the ϵ-ball for d is the same as the $\epsilon/(1 + \epsilon)$-ball for ρ, so any ρ-neighborhood contains a d-neighborhood and vice versa. ◀

In the case of vector spaces, a metric will often be derived from a norm.

Norm and Seminorm. A seminorm is a function $\|\cdot\|$ from $\mathbf{E}$ to $\mathbb{R}_+$ that satisfies the following properties for all $\mathbf{x}, \mathbf{y} \in \mathbf{E}$:

(1) $\|\mathbf{x}\| \geq 0$;
(2) $\|\lambda\mathbf{x}\| = |\lambda| \, \|\mathbf{x}\|$ for all scalars λ;
(3) $\|\mathbf{x} + \mathbf{y}\| \leq \|\mathbf{x}\| + \|\mathbf{y}\|$.

A seminorm is a norm if $\|\mathbf{x}\| = 0$ implies $\mathbf{x} = \mathbf{0}$.

▶ **Example 2: ℓ^p-spaces.** The family of ℓ^p-norms gives us a set of examples. For $1 \leq p < \infty$, define $\|\mathbf{x}\|_p = \left(\sum_{t=1}^\infty \sum_{i=1}^m |x_{it}|^p\right)^{1/p}$. Note that the sum converges to a non-negative number or to $+\infty$. When $p = \infty$, we define $\|\mathbf{x}\|_\infty = \sup\{|x_{it}| : i = 1, \ldots, m; \ t = 1, 2, \ldots\}$. Now define $\ell^p = \{\mathbf{x} \in$

$s^m : \|\mathbf{x}\|_p < \infty\}$. The p-norm $\|\cdot\|_p$ is a norm on ℓ^p. Moreover, ℓ^p is a Riesz space. However, although the ℓ^p for $p < \infty$ are Riesz ideals of s^m, they are not principal ideals. The space ℓ^∞ is a principal Riesz ideal of s^m, and is generated by the vector $\mathbf{e}$ defined by $e_{it} = 1$. Two Riesz ideals that are contained in all of the ℓ^p are $c_0 = \{\mathbf{x} \in s^m : \lim_t x_{it} = 0\}$ and $c_{00} = \{\mathbf{x} \in s^m : \text{there is a } T \text{ with } x_{it} = 0 \text{ for } t > T\}$. Both c_0 and c_{00} are ℓ^p-dense subsets of ℓ^p for $p < \infty$. Moreover, the elements of c_{00} with rational components form a countable dense subset of ℓ^p for $p < \infty$; thus ℓ^p is separable for $p < \infty$.

However, neither c_0 nor c_{00} is ℓ^∞-dense in ℓ^∞. In fact, c_0 is a closed subset of ℓ^∞. These sets cannot be used to show ℓ^∞ is separable. There is a good reason for this. The space ℓ^∞ is not separable.

Whenever A is a subset of the positive integers, we can regard its characteristic function χ_A as a vector in ℓ^∞, by setting $(\chi_A)_t$ to 0 when $t \notin A$ and 1 when $t \in A$. Note that $\|\chi_A - \chi_B\|_\infty = 1$ if $A \neq B$. Now suppose ℓ^∞ has a countable dense subset X. For each subset A of the positive integers, we could find an element of X within 1/3 of χ_A. Since each element of X would then be associated with at most one subset A, this would imply that there are only countably many subsets of the positive integers. But there are an uncountable number of subsets of the positive integers, and so ℓ^∞ cannot have a countable dense subset.

We can also consider the ℓ^p-norms on $\mathbb{R}^m$, e.g., $\|\mathbf{x}\| = \left(\sum_{i=1}^m |x_i|^p\right)^{1/p}$. On $\mathbb{R}^m$, all of the ℓ^p-norms are equivalent. This follows because $\|\mathbf{x}\|_\infty \leq \|\mathbf{x}\|_p \leq m^{1/p}\|\mathbf{x}\|_\infty$ for $1 \leq p < \infty$. ◄

A (semi-)norm on a Riesz space is a *lattice* or *Riesz (semi-)norm* if $|\mathbf{x}| \leq |\mathbf{y}|$ implies $\|\mathbf{x}\| \leq \|\mathbf{y}\|$. The ℓ^p-norms are lattice norms. Any principal ideal A_ω of a Riesz space has a natural lattice seminorm defined by $\|\mathbf{x}\| = \inf\{\lambda > 0 : |\mathbf{x}| \leq \lambda|\omega|\}$. If the order is Archimedean, the seminorm is actually a norm. Taking $m = 1$ and setting $\omega = (1, 1, \ldots)$, we find that $A_\omega = \ell^\infty$ and the natural norm coincides with the ℓ^∞-norm. More generally, by setting $\omega_{it} = \beta^t$ we obtain the weighted ℓ^∞-space $\ell^\infty(\beta) = \{\mathbf{x} \in s^m : \|\mathbf{x}\|_\beta = \sup_{i,t}\{|x_{it}|/\beta^t\} < \infty\}$. The norm $\|\mathbf{x}\|_\beta = \sup_{i,t}\{|x_{it}|/\beta^t\}$ is called the β-*norm*. These norms can be thought of as having the discount factor $1/\beta$ built in.[11] The sets $\ell_+^\infty(\beta)$ play an important role throughout this book.

We may define a metric on any normed vector space by $d(\mathbf{x}, \mathbf{y}) = \|\mathbf{x} - \mathbf{y}\|$. Two normed vector spaces are *(isometrically) isomorphic* if there is an isomorphism f between them with $\|\mathbf{x}\| = \|f(\mathbf{x})\|$. Such normed spaces are identical as far as their normed space properties are concerned.[12]

---

[11] Topologies of this type have been used by Chichilnisky and Kalman (1980), Dechert and Nishimura (1980) and Boyd (1990a) to study optimal paths.

[12] They may seem quite distinct when other properties are considered. For example,

If $\{\rho_n\}_{n=1}^{\infty}$ is a family of seminorms such that $\rho_n(\mathbf{x}) = 0$ for all n implies $\mathbf{x} = 0$, we may define a metric by

$$d(\mathbf{x}, \mathbf{y}) = \sum_{n=1}^{\infty} 2^{-n} \frac{\rho_n(\mathbf{x} - \mathbf{y})}{1 + \rho_n(\mathbf{x} - \mathbf{y})}.$$

Note that the nth term is less than 2^{-n}, so the sum is convergent and is less than 1. Properties (1) and (2) are again both clear, and the triangle inequality follows as in Example 1. In particular, this construction applies to s^m with seminorms $\rho_t(\mathbf{x}) = |x_t| = \max_i |x_{it}|$. The topology induced by this metric coincides with the topology s^m has when regarded as a product of countably many copies of $\mathbb{R}^m$. We refer to this as the *product topology* on s^m.[13] Since the spaces $\ell^{\infty}(\beta)$ are subsets of s^m, we now have two topologies on these spaces. In fact, $\ell^{\infty}(\alpha) \subset \ell^{\infty}(\beta)$ for $\alpha < \beta$, so we have many topologies (even norm topologies) on any $\ell^{\infty}(\beta)$.

Continuity

Given topologies on X and Y, a function $f: X \to Y$ is *continuous at x* if for each neighborhood V in Y of $f(x)$ there is a neighborhood U in X with $f(U) \subset V$. The function is *continuous* if it is continuous at each point of X. In fact, we could replace "neighborhood" with "basic neighborhood" and the definition would be unchanged. In the case of metric spaces, this tells us that for each neighborhood $B_\epsilon(f(x))$ there is a neighborhood $B_\delta(x)$ with $f(B_\delta(x)) \subset B_\epsilon(f(x))$. When $f: X \to \mathbb{R}$, this says that for every $x \in X$ and $\epsilon > 0$ there is a $\delta > 0$ with $|f(x) - f(y)| < \epsilon$ whenever $d(x, y) < \delta$, which is the familiar ϵ–δ definition. One standard result on continuity is:

Theorem 1. *When $f: X \to Y$, the following are equivalent:*

(1) *f is continuous;*
(2) *For every open set U in Y, $f^{-1}(U)$ is open in X;*
(3) *For every closed set F in Y, $f^{-1}(F)$ is closed in X.*

In metric spaces we can also characterize continuity using sequences. However, sequences are inadequate to describe the topology in general topological spaces, including some of those we will need to use. Sequences are only adequate to describe the topology of metric or metrizable spaces. Fortunately, the notion of sequence can be generalized so that it does work on general spaces.

$L^2(0, 1)$ and ℓ^2 are isometrically isomorphic.

[13] We will see in Section 2.2.3, in conjunction with the Minkowski functional, that s^m is not a normed space.

Directed Set. A set Λ is a directed set if there is a relation $\leq$ on Λ that satisfies:

(1) $\lambda \leq \lambda$ for all $\lambda \in \Lambda$ (reflexive);
(2) If $\lambda \leq \mu$ and $\mu \leq \nu$, then $\lambda \leq \nu$ (transitive);
(3) If $\lambda, \mu \in \Lambda$ there is a $\nu \in \Lambda$ with $\lambda \leq \nu$ and $\mu \leq \nu$.

The relation $\leq$ is sometimes referred to as a *direction* on Λ. One example of a directed set is the positive integers with the usual order. Another example of a directed set is the neighborhood base at x, $\mathcal{B}_x$, ordered by reverse inclusion. That is, $U \leq V$ if and only if $U \supset V$.

Net and Subnet. A net is a function $n\colon \Lambda \to X$. A subnet is a composition $n \circ \lambda$ where λ is a function from a directed set M to Λ such that:

(1) $\lambda(\mu_1) \leq \lambda(\mu_2)$ whenever $\mu_1 \leq \mu_2$;
(2) For each $\lambda_0 \in \Lambda$, there is a $\mu \in M$ with $\lambda_0 \leq \lambda(\mu)$.

The point $n(\lambda)$ is usually denoted x^λ, and $n(\lambda(\mu))$ is denoted $x^{\lambda(\mu)}$ or x^{λ_μ}. A sequence is a net based on the positive integers, and a subsequence is a subnet that is also based on the positive integers. If x is a limit point of A, we may define a net based on the neighborhood base $\mathcal{B}_x$ as follows: for each $U \in \mathcal{B}_x$, take $x^U \in U \cap A$ with $x^U \neq x$.

We say $\{x^\lambda\}_{\lambda \in \Lambda}$ *converges* to x if for each neighborhood U of x, there is a $\lambda_0 \in \Lambda$ with $x^\lambda \in U$ for $\lambda \geq \lambda_0$. The point x is referred to as the *limit* of x^λ, written $x^\lambda \to x$ or $\lim x^\lambda = x$. One useful property of Hausdorff spaces is that a convergent net has a unique limit. When x is a limit point of A, our net x^U above converges to x since if V is a neighborhood of x, $x^U \in V$ for $U \geq V$ ($U \subset V$). It follows that if x is in the closure of A, then there is a net in A that converges to it. The converse is also true: if there is a net in A converging to x, then $x \in \operatorname{cl} A$.[14] We can use this fact to recharacterize continuity in terms of nets.

Theorem 2. *Let $f\colon X \to Y$. Then f is continuous at $x \in X$ if and only if $x^\lambda \to x$ implies $f(x^\lambda) \to f(x)$. If X is metric, the same holds for sequences.*

Compactness and Product Spaces

Given a collection of spaces X_α for $\alpha \in A$, the *Cartesian product* $\prod_{\alpha \in A} X_\alpha$ is $\{\mathbf{x}\colon A \to \cup_{\alpha \in A} X_\alpha : \mathbf{x}(\alpha) \in X_\alpha \text{ for each } \alpha \in A\}$. The value $x(\alpha)$ is usually denoted x_α, and we will write $\mathbf{x} = (x_\alpha)_{\alpha \in A}$. The *product topology* has as base the sets $\prod_{\alpha \in A} U_\alpha$ where U_α is open in X_α for all $\alpha \in A$ and $U_\alpha = X_\alpha$ for all but finitely many α. The product topology has a simpler description using nets. A net $\{\mathbf{x}^\lambda\}$ converges to $\mathbf{x}$ if and only if $x_\alpha^\lambda \to x_\alpha$ for each α. We denote product convergence by $\mathbf{x}^\lambda \xrightarrow{p} \mathbf{x}$.

---

[14] In a metric space, $\{B_{1/n}(x)\}_{n=1}^\infty$ is a neighborhood base at x, so there is actually a sequence converging to any limit point of a closed set, and vice versa.

Theorem 3. *Suppose $\prod_{\alpha \in A} X_\alpha$ has the product topology. A net $\mathbf{x}^\lambda \xrightarrow{p} \mathbf{x}$ if and only if $x_\alpha^\lambda \to x_\alpha$ for each $\alpha \in A$.*

▶ Example 3: The product topology on s^m. When $A = \{1, 2, \dots\}$ and $X_\alpha = \mathbb{R}^m$ for each α, we obtain the sequence space s^m. The product topology τ coincides with the topology given by the Fréchet metric $d_F(\mathbf{x}, \mathbf{y}) = \sum_{\alpha=1}^\infty 2^{-\alpha} |x_\alpha - y_\alpha| / (1 + |x_\alpha - y_\alpha|)$ where $|x_\alpha|$ denotes $\max_i |x_{i\alpha}|$. Suppose $\mathbf{x}^\lambda \xrightarrow{p} \mathbf{x}$ in the product topology and $\epsilon > 0$. Choose N large enough that $\sum_{\alpha=N+1}^\infty 2^{-\alpha} < \epsilon/2$. Now consider the product neighborhood U with $U_\alpha = B_{\epsilon/2}(x_\alpha)$ for $\alpha = 1, \dots, N$ and $U_\alpha = X_\alpha$ otherwise. Clearly $d_F(\mathbf{x}, \mathbf{y}) < \epsilon$ whenever $\mathbf{y} \in U$. Since $\mathbf{x}^\lambda \xrightarrow{p} \mathbf{x}$, there is a λ_0 with $\mathbf{x}^\lambda \in U$ for $\lambda \geq \lambda_0$. Thus $d_F(\mathbf{x}^\lambda, \mathbf{x}) < \epsilon$ for $\lambda \geq \lambda_0$, and the net converges in (s^m, d).

Now suppose $\mathbf{x}^\lambda \to \mathbf{x}$ in d_F. Let U be a basic neighborhood in s^m. Choose N large enough that $U_\alpha = X_\alpha$ for $\alpha > N$. Then choose ϵ_α so that $B_{\epsilon_\alpha}(x_\alpha) \subset U_\alpha$ for $\alpha \leq N$. Let $\epsilon = \min\{2^{-\alpha} \epsilon_\alpha / (1 + \epsilon_\alpha) : \alpha = 1, \dots, N\}$. Then $B_\epsilon(\mathbf{x}) \subset U$. Now there is a λ_0 with $\mathbf{x}^\lambda \in B_\epsilon(\mathbf{x}) \subset U$ for $\lambda \geq \lambda_0$. Thus $\mathbf{x}^\lambda \xrightarrow{p} \mathbf{x}$ in the product topology. Since convergence is equivalent in both topologies, the closed sets must be the same. But then the open sets, and hence the topologies, must also be identical.

We can also define an alternative base for the sequence space, instead of using balls. Let $G(\mathbf{x}, \epsilon, N) = \{\mathbf{y} \in s^m : |x_t - y_t| < \epsilon \text{ for } t = 1, \dots, N\}$. Now for $\mathbf{y} \in G(\mathbf{x}, \epsilon, N)$, $d_F(\mathbf{x}, \mathbf{y}) < \max\{\epsilon, 1/2^N\}$. Thus $G(\mathbf{x}, \epsilon, N)$ is contained in the ball of radius $\max\{\epsilon, 1/2^N\}$ about $\mathbf{x}$. Furthermore, given $\epsilon > 0$, we can take N with $1/2^N < \epsilon$. In that case, $B_\epsilon(\mathbf{x}) \subset G(\mathbf{x}, \epsilon, N)$. Since any ball contains one of the Gs, and is contained by one of the Gs, the collection of $G(\mathbf{x}, \epsilon, N)$ forms a base for the product topology. ◀

Let $A \subset X$. A collection $\mathcal{C}$ of open sets is an *open cover* of A if $A \subset \cup \mathcal{C}$. A set A is *compact* if whenever $\mathcal{C}$ is an open cover of A, there is a finite subcollection of $\mathcal{C}$ which also covers A. We record some standard facts about compact sets.

Theorem 4.

(1) *The continuous image of a compact set is compact.*

(2) *A closed subset of a compact set is compact.*

(3) *A set A is compact if and only if every net in A has a subnet that converges to a point of A.*

(4) *A set A in a metric space is compact if and only if every sequence in A has a subsequence that converges to a point of A.*

(5) *A compact subset of a Hausdorff space is closed.*

(6) *A subset of $\mathbb{R}^m$ is compact if and only if it is closed and bounded (Heine-Borel Theorem).*

One theorem that is extremely useful for our purposes is the Tychonoff

Theorem.[15]

Tychonoff Theorem. *The product of compact sets is compact in the product topology.*

Corollary 1. *Order intervals are compact in the product topology of s^m.*

Proof. The order interval $[\mathbf{a}, \mathbf{b}]$ is the product $\prod_{t=1}^{\infty}[a_t, b_t]$. $\square$

This will be an essential component in showing that optimal paths exist in capital accumulation models in Chapter 4 where it will imply that the feasible set is compact. Note that order intervals need not be compact in arbitrary topologies.

▶ Example 4: Non-compact order interval. Consider the order interval $[\mathbf{0}, \mathbf{e}]$ $\subset \ell^\infty \subset s^1$ under the sup-norm topology. The vectors $\mathbf{x}^n = \{x_t^n\}$ defined by $x_n^n = 1$ and $x_t^n = 0$ for $t \neq n$ are elements of $[\mathbf{0}, \mathbf{e}]$. The sequence $\{\mathbf{x}^n\}$ does not have any subsequence converging in the sup norm topology. Indeed, if $\{\mathbf{x}^n\}$ did have any sup norm convergent subsequence, then that subsequence would converge in the product topology. But $\mathbf{x}^n \xrightarrow{P} \mathbf{0}$, so any subsequence would also have to converge to $\mathbf{0}$ in the sup norm topology. However, this is impossible as $\|\mathbf{x}^n - \mathbf{0}\|_\infty = 1$ for each n.[16] This example also shows that sup-closed and bounded subsets of ℓ^∞ need not be sup-compact. ◀

Connectedness

A topological space (X, τ) is *disconnected* if there are disjoint non-empty open sets U and V with $X = U \cup V$. A space is *connected* if it is not disconnected. We extend the definition to subsets of X by using the relative topology.

▶ Example 5: $[0, 1]$ is connected. Suppose there is a disconnection U, V for $[0, 1]$. Label the sets so that $1 \in V$. Because V is open, it contains some interval $(a, 1]$, so $b \equiv \sup U \leq a < 1$. As U is non-empty and open, $b > 0$. If b were in U, there would be an open interval about b contained in U, contradicting the fact that $b = \sup U$. Thus $b \in V$. But then, some interval $(b - \epsilon, b + \epsilon) \subset V$. This implies $b - \epsilon/2$ is a upper bound for U, contradicting the definition of b. It follows that $[0, 1]$ cannot be disconnected. ◀

Theorem 5. *The continuous image of a connected set is connected.*

Proof. If the image is disconnected by U, V, then the original set is disconnected by the inverse images of U and V. $\square$

Theorem 5 also implies that the continuous image of an interval is always connected. One implication of this fact is the Intermediate Value Theorem.

---

[15] See Kelley (1955, p. 143), Simmons (1963, p. 119), or Willard (1970, p. 120).

[16] Majumdar (1975) presents a similar example.

Intermediate Value Theorem. *Let $f \colon \mathbb{R} \to \mathbb{R}$ be continuous. Then whenever y is between $f(a)$ and $f(b)$, there is an x between a and b with $f(x) = y$.*

Proof. Label points so that $a < b$. The image of $[a, b]$ is connected. If there were a y between $f(a)$ and $f(b)$ that was not in the range of f, the sets $U = f([a, b]) \cap \{z : z < y\}$ and $V = f([a, b]) \cap \{z : z > y\}$ would disconnect the connected set $f([a, b])$. As this is impossible, there must be $x \in [a, b]$ with $f(x) = y$. $\square$

The observation that continuous images of intervals are connected is the basis for another definition. A space (X, τ) is *path-connected* if, for any pair of points $a, b \in X$, there is a continuous function $f \colon [0, 1] \to X$ such that $f(0) = a$ and $f(1) = b$. The function f is referred to as a *path*. Under the usual topology, any convex set in $\mathbb{R}^m$ is path-connected, as the path $f(t) = (1 - t)a + tb$ shows.

Theorem 6. *Any path-connected space is connected.*

Proof. Suppose U and V disconnect X. Take $a \in U$ and $b \in V$. Because X is path-connected, there is a path f from a to b. But then $f^{-1}(U)$, $f^{-1}(V)$ disconnects $[0, 1]$. This is impossible as $[0, 1]$ is connected. Thus X must be connected. $\square$

As a corollary, any convex subset of $\mathbb{R}^m$ is connected. Looking ahead to the next section, any convex set in a topological vector space will also be connected.

2.2.3 Linear Topologies

Consider a vector space that has a topological structure consistent with its linear structure. If vectors are close together, they should still be close together when we add to them vectors that are themselves close, or multiply by scalars that are close.[17]

Topological Vector Space (TVS). A topological vector space is a vector space $(\mathbf{E}, \times, \cdot)$ with a topology τ where vector addition and scalar multiplication are continuous.

▶ Example 6: Normed spaces. Suppose $\mathbf{E}$ has norm $\| \cdot \|$. As we have a metric, we need only consider sequences. Suppose $(\mathbf{x}_n, \mathbf{y}_n) \to (\mathbf{x}, \mathbf{y})$. Now $\|\mathbf{x} + \mathbf{y} - \mathbf{x}_n - \mathbf{y}_n\| \leq \|\mathbf{x} - \mathbf{x}_n\| + \|\mathbf{y} - \mathbf{y}_n\|$. Since the latter converges to zero, $\mathbf{x}_n + \mathbf{y}_n \to \mathbf{x} + \mathbf{y}$. Now suppose $(\lambda_n, \mathbf{x}_n) \to (\lambda, \mathbf{x})$. Then

$$\|\lambda_n \mathbf{x}_n - \lambda \mathbf{x}\| \leq |\lambda_n| \|\mathbf{x}_n - \mathbf{x}\| + |\lambda - \lambda_n| \|\mathbf{x}\|. \tag{1}$$

---

[17] Robertson and Robertson (1973) is a good introduction to topological vector spaces. Schaefer (1966) is a more advanced introduction.

Let $\epsilon > 0$ and choose N so that $|\lambda_n| \leq |\lambda| + 1$ for $n \geq N$. Then choose $N' \geq N$ with $\|\mathbf{x}_n - \mathbf{x}\| < \epsilon/2(1+|\lambda|)$ and $|\lambda_n - \lambda| < \epsilon/2\|\mathbf{x}\|$.[18] For $n \geq N'$, $\|\lambda_n\mathbf{x}_n - \lambda\mathbf{x}\| < \epsilon$, so $\lambda_n\mathbf{x}_n \to \lambda\mathbf{x}$. Since both operations are continuous, any normed space is a topological vector space. ◄

▶ Example 7: Convergence in s^m. Convergence reduces to convergence in each factor space $\mathbb{R}^m$. Now each factor space is normed, so the vector operations are continuous there. It follows that they are continuous in the product topology. ◄

The continuity of vector addition means that we can characterize the topology via a neighborhood base at zero. By adding $\mathbf{x}$, we obtain a neighborhood base at $\mathbf{x}$. A set U is a neighborhood of $\mathbf{x}$ if and only if $U - \mathbf{x}$ is a neighborhood of $\mathbf{0}$.

A set A in a vector space is *balanced* if $\mathbf{x} \in A$ and $|\lambda| \leq 1$ implies $\lambda\mathbf{x} \in A$; *convex* if $\mathbf{x}, \mathbf{y} \in A$ and $0 \leq \lambda \leq 1$ implies $\lambda\mathbf{x} + (1 - \lambda)\mathbf{y} \in A$; *absolutely convex* if it is balanced and convex. A TVS is a *locally convex space* (LCS) if it has a base consisting of absolutely convex sets. Since the balls of a normed space are balanced and convex, any normed space is an LCS; clearly s^m is also an LCS.

We call a set A *absorbing* if, for every $\mathbf{x} \in \mathbf{E}$, there is a λ with $\mathbf{x} \in \mu A$ for all μ with $|\mu| \geq \lambda$. If U is a balanced neighborhood of zero, there is some $\epsilon > 0$ with $\lambda\mathbf{x} \in U$ for $|\lambda| \leq \epsilon$ because scalar multiplication is continuous. But then $\mathbf{x} \in \mu U$ for $|\mu| \geq 1/\epsilon$, so U is absorbing.

Each neighborhood of zero, indeed, each absolutely convex absorbing set, gives rise to a seminorm in a natural way. Given a neighborhood U of zero, define the *Minkowski functional* or *gauge* of U by $p_U(x) = \inf\{\lambda > 0 : \mathbf{x} \in \lambda U\}$. It is easily verified that the Minkowski functional is a seminorm, and that $\{\mathbf{x} : p_U(\mathbf{x}) < 1\} \subset U \subset \{\mathbf{x} : p_U(\mathbf{x}) \leq 1\}$. Moreover, p_U is continuous if and only if U is a neighborhood of zero. The topology in an LCS can be described in terms of its continuous seminorms.

Theorem 7.

(1) *In an LCS* $\mathbf{E}$, *a seminorm* p *is continuous if and only if it is continuous at zero.*

(2) *If* p *is the gauge of the absolutely convex absorbing set* U, p *is continuous if and only if* U *is a neighborhood. In this case* $\{\mathbf{x} : p(\mathbf{x}) < 1\}$ *is the interior of* U *and* $\{\mathbf{x} : p(\mathbf{x}) \leq 1\}$ *is the closure of* U.[19]

We have already encountered a Minkowski functional. We previously defined a norm on any principal Riesz ideal A_ω by $\|\mathbf{x}\| = \inf\{\lambda > 0 : |\mathbf{x}| \leq$

---

[18] We need not worry about the second term in equation (1) if $\mathbf{x} = 0$.

[19] See Robertson and Robertson (1973, p. 14).

$\lambda|\boldsymbol{\omega}|\}$. This is the Minkowski functional for the neighborhood $\{\mathbf{x} : |\mathbf{x}| \leq |\boldsymbol{\omega}|\}$.

A set is *bounded* if it is absorbed by every neighborhood of zero. In a normed space, every ball is bounded. Thus there is a base of bounded neighborhoods. Moreover, any bounded U yields a Minkowski functional that is equivalent to the norm. In fact, normed spaces are precisely those LCS spaces where there is a bounded absolutely convex neighborhood of zero. Its Minkowski functional is a norm, and the topology can be described solely in terms of that norm.

It is not generally the case that Minkowski functionals are norms. Consider s^1. If A is bounded, it is absorbed by the neighborhood $[-1,1] \times \mathbb{R} \times \mathbb{R} \times \cdots$. Thus there is a λ_1 with $-\lambda_1 \leq x_1 \leq \lambda_1$ for all $\mathbf{x} \in A$. Similarly, there are λ_n with $-\lambda_n \leq x_n \leq \lambda_n$, so $A \subset [-\lambda_1, \lambda_1] \times [-\lambda_2, \lambda_2] \times \cdots$. However, no such set can contain any basic neighborhood $U = \prod_{n=1}^{\infty} U_n$ since $U_n = \mathbb{R}$ for all but finitely many n. Incidentally, this shows that the product topology on s^1 cannot be generated by a norm, even though it is a metric topology.

There is one other useful topological property we will often require of our linear spaces—completeness. A net $\{\mathbf{x}^\lambda\}$ in an LCS space is a *Cauchy net* if for every neighborhood U of zero, there is a λ_0 with $\mathbf{x}^\lambda - \mathbf{x}^\mu \in U$ for all $\lambda, \mu \geq \lambda_0$. A set A is *complete* if every Cauchy net in A converges to a point of A. A complete normed space is called a *Banach space* and a complete metric LCS is called a *Fréchet space*. A *Banach lattice* is a Banach space that is also a Riesz space; a *Fréchet lattice* is a Fréchet space that is also a Riesz space. The spaces $\ell^\infty(\beta)$, ℓ^p, and c_0 are Banach lattices while s^m is a Fréchet lattice that is not a Banach lattice. We note that:[20]

Theorem 8.

(1) *Closed subsets of complete sets are complete.*

(2) *In a metric space, compact sets are complete.*

Order Convergence

Subsets of s^m also inherit a notion of convergence derived from the usual order. A net $\{\mathbf{x}^\lambda\}$ is *decreasing (increasing)* if $\lambda \geq \mu$ implies $\mathbf{x}^\lambda \leq \mathbf{x}^\mu$ ($\mathbf{x}^\lambda \geq \mathbf{x}^\mu$). We write $\mathbf{x}^\lambda \downarrow \mathbf{x}$ to indicate $\{\mathbf{x}^\lambda\}$ is decreasing with $\inf_\lambda \mathbf{x}^\lambda = \mathbf{x}$; $\mathbf{x}^\lambda \uparrow \mathbf{x}$ to indicate $\{\mathbf{x}^\lambda\}$ is increasing with $\sup_\lambda \mathbf{x}^\lambda = \mathbf{x}$. A Riesz space is *Dedekind complete* if every non-empty subset that is bounded above has a supremum (equivalently, every non-empty subset that is bounded below has an infimum). The spaces s^m with the product topology and $\ell^\infty(\beta)$ with the β-topology are Dedekind complete.

---

[20] See Simmons (1963, pp. 73, 125).

Order Convergence. A net $\mathbf{x}^\lambda$ is order convergent to $\mathbf{x}$ (denoted $\mathbf{x}^\lambda \xrightarrow{o} \mathbf{x}$) if there is a net $\mathbf{y}^\lambda \downarrow \mathbf{0}$ with $|\mathbf{x}^\lambda - \mathbf{x}| \leq \mathbf{y}^\lambda$.

A set is *order closed* if it contains all of its order limits. An order closed ideal is called a *band*. The smallest band that contains a set A is referred to as the band generated by A. If $\omega \in s^m$ has strictly positive components, the band generated by ω is all of s^m. For $\mathbf{x} \in s^m$, simply replacing x_t by 0 for $t \geq T$ gives a sequence in A_ω that converges in order to $\mathbf{x}$ as $T \to \infty$. More generally, the band generated by ω is $B_\omega = \{\mathbf{x} \in \mathbf{E} : |\mathbf{x}| \wedge n|\omega| \uparrow |\mathbf{x}|\}$. A function $f \colon \mathbf{E} \to \mathbb{R}$ is *order continuous* if $f(\mathbf{x}^\lambda) \to f(\mathbf{x})$ whenever $\mathbf{x}^\lambda \xrightarrow{o} \mathbf{x}$.

Order convergence on s^m and its subsets is easily related to the product topology.

Theorem 9. *In s^m, an order convergence net is product convergent and a product convergent sequence is order convergent.*

Proof. Suppose $\mathbf{x}^\lambda \xrightarrow{o} \mathbf{x}$. Then there are $\mathbf{y}^\lambda \downarrow \mathbf{0}$ with $|\mathbf{x}^\lambda - \mathbf{x}| \leq \mathbf{y}^\lambda$. Fix t. Then $|x_t^\lambda - x_t| \leq y_t^\lambda$. Now $y_t^\lambda \downarrow 0$ because $\mathbf{y}^\lambda \downarrow \mathbf{0}$. It follows that $x_t^\lambda \to x_t$ for each t. Thus $\mathbf{x}^\lambda \xrightarrow{p} \mathbf{x}$.

Now suppose $\mathbf{x}^n \xrightarrow{p} \mathbf{x}$. For each t, there is an n_0 with $|x_t^n - x_t| < 1$ for $n \geq n_0$. The sequence $\{|x_t^n - x_t|\}$ is then bounded, and we can define $\mathbf{y}^n = \sup_{q \geq n} |\mathbf{x}^q - \mathbf{x}|$. Clearly $\mathbf{y}^n \geq |\mathbf{x}^n - \mathbf{x}|$, and $\mathbf{y}^n$ is decreasing. Finally, for each ϵ and t there is an n_1 with $|x_t^n - x_t| < \epsilon$ for $n \geq n_1$, so $y_t^{n_1} \leq \epsilon$. As ϵ was arbitrary, $\inf \mathbf{y}^n = \mathbf{0}$, which shows $\mathbf{x}^n \xrightarrow{o} \mathbf{x}$. $\square$

Since sequences characterize the product topology on s^m, we can show that product and order continuity are equivalent.

Corollary 2. *A function $f \colon s^m \to \mathbb{R}$ is order continuous if and only if it is product continuous.*

Proof. Suppose f is order continuous and the sequence $\{\mathbf{x}^n\}$ product converges to $\mathbf{x}$. By the theorem, $\mathbf{x}^n \xrightarrow{o} \mathbf{x}$, and by order continuity $f(\mathbf{x}^n) \to f(\mathbf{x})$.

Now suppose f is product continuous and the net $\{\mathbf{x}^\lambda\}$ order converges to $\mathbf{x}$. By the theorem, $\mathbf{x}^\lambda \xrightarrow{p} \mathbf{x}$, and by product continuity $f(\mathbf{x}^\lambda) \to f(\mathbf{x})$. $\square$

It is not true that a product convergent net is necessarily order convergent. Let $\Lambda = \{(n, s) : n \text{ and } s \text{ are positive integers}\}$ and order Λ in the usual way. For $\lambda = (n, s)$, define $x_t^\lambda = 0$ for $t \leq n$ and $x_t^\lambda = s$ for $t > n$. For $\lambda \geq (T, 1)$, $d(\mathbf{x}^\lambda, \mathbf{0}) < 1/2^T$, so $\mathbf{x}^\lambda \xrightarrow{p} \mathbf{0}$. But $\mathbf{x}^\lambda$ is not order convergent. The sequence $\mathbf{x}^\lambda$ cannot be majorized by a decreasing net since $\sup_{\lambda \geq \lambda_0} \mathbf{x}^\lambda$ does not exist.

A vector $\mathbf{e} \in \mathbf{E}_+$ is an *order unit* if for any $\mathbf{x} \in \mathbf{E}$, there is a $\lambda > 0$ with $\mathbf{x} \leq \lambda \mathbf{e}$. In ℓ^∞, any vector with $\inf_{it} x_{it} > 0$ is a unit. In the case of a Banach lattice, the existence of an order unit implies that norm $\|\mathbf{x}\| = \inf\{\lambda > 0 : |\mathbf{x}| \leq \lambda\mathbf{e}\}$ is equivalent to the original norm, and that the unit ball under this norm is the interval $[-\mathbf{e}, \mathbf{e}]$. A normed Riesz space where $\|\mathbf{x} + \mathbf{y}\| = \max\{\|\mathbf{x}\|, \|\mathbf{y}\|\}$ whenever $\mathbf{x} \wedge \mathbf{y} = \mathbf{0}$ is called an *M-space*. A Banach lattice that is an M-space is called an *AM-space* or abstract M-space. The spaces $\ell^\infty(\beta)$ are AM-spaces with units.

Semicontinuity

Define the *extended real numbers* by $\mathbb{R}^* = [-\infty, \infty]$. The usual order on $\mathbb{R}$ is extended in the obvious way to $\mathbb{R}^*$. We can use the order structure on $\mathbb{R}^*$ to define a pair of topologies on $\mathbb{R}^*$. The *upper order topology* has closed subbase $\{[-\infty, a] : a \in \mathbb{R}^*\}$, while the *lower order topology* has subbase $\{[a, +\infty] : a \in \mathbb{R}^*\}$.[21]

Let f be a function taking values in $\mathbb{R}^*$. The function f is *upper semicontinuous* if it is a continuous map into $\mathbb{R}^*$ with the lower order topology, i.e., if $\{x : f(x) \geq \lambda\} = f^{-1}[\lambda, +\infty]$ is closed for every $\lambda \in \mathbb{R}^*$.[22] This is equivalent to $\{x : f(x) < \lambda\} = f^{-1}[-\infty, \lambda)$ is open. Conversely, call f *lower semicontinuous* if it is a continuous map into $\mathbb{R}^*$ with the upper order topology, i.e., if $f^{-1}[-\infty, \lambda]$ is closed (equivalently, $f^{-1}(\lambda, \infty]$ is open) for all $\lambda \in \mathbb{R}^*$. Of course, f is upper semicontinuous if and only if $-f$ is lower semicontinuous.

Examples of upper semicontinuous functions include the characteristic function of a closed set, the function defined by $u(x) = \sqrt{x}$ for $x \geq 0$ and $-\infty$ otherwise, and $u(x) = \log x$ for $x > 0$ and $-\infty$ otherwise.

Proposition 1. *The infimum of any collection of upper semicontinuous functions is upper semicontinuous. The supremum of any collection of lower semicontinuous functions is lower semicontinuous.*

Proof. Let $\{f_\alpha\}$ be a collection of upper semicontinuous functions and define f by $f(x) = \inf_\alpha f_\alpha(x)$. Suppose $x^\nu \to x$ and $f(x^\nu) \geq \lambda$. Then $f_\alpha(x^\nu) \geq \lambda$ for all α. Since each f_α is upper semicontinuous, $f_\alpha(x) \geq \lambda$. But then $f(x) = \inf_\alpha f_\alpha(x) \geq \lambda$, and $f^{-1}([\lambda, \infty))$ is closed. Apply this to $-f$ to obtain the result on lower semicontinuity. $\square$

This proposition allows upper semicontinuous functions to arise naturally through a limiting process. For example, consider the partial sums defined by $S_T(\mathbf{c}) = \sum_{t=1}^{T} \delta^{t-1} u(c_t)$ where $\delta < 1$. For $u \leq 0$ and upper

---

[21] There are also upper and lower order topologies for collections of sets, which are closely related to upper and lower semicontinuity for correspondences. See Klein and Thompson (1984).

[22] It is unfortunate that these concepts are named as they are, but there is no easy way out. The topological terminology came much later, and was chosen for consistency with the theory of correspondences, which means it is the opposite of the notation for functions.

semicontinuous, the S_T form a non-increasing sequence of upper semicontinuous functions. Thus $U(\mathbf{c}) = \lim_{T\to\infty} S_T(\mathbf{c}) = \inf_T S_T(\mathbf{c})$ is upper semicontinuous by Proposition 1. Alternatively, we could have considered $c_t(\mathbf{k}) = f(k_{t-1}) - k_t$; note $c_t(\mathbf{k}) \geq 0$ for all feasible $\mathbf{k}$. Define $g_t(\mathbf{k}) = u(c_t(\mathbf{k}))$; the same argument shows that $V(\mathbf{k}) = \sum_{t=1}^{\infty} \delta^{t-1} g_t(c_t(\mathbf{k}))$ is an upper semicontinuous function of $\mathbf{k}$. Another application of the proposition shows the maximin utility function is upper semicontinuous: $U(\mathbf{c}) = \inf_t c_t$ is the pointwise infimum of product continuous functions.[23]

Proposition 2. *A function f is upper semicontinuous if and only if $f(x^*) \geq \limsup_{\nu\to\infty} f(x^\nu)$ whenever $x^\nu \to x^*$.*

Proof. Let f be upper semicontinuous. Set $f^* = \limsup_{\nu\to\infty} f(x^\nu)$. Consider the set $A_\epsilon = \{x : f(x) \geq f^* - \epsilon\}$ for $\epsilon > 0$. The set A_ϵ is closed by upper semicontinuity. Further, $x^\nu \in A_\epsilon$ for ν large. It follows that $x^* \in A_\epsilon$; that $f(x^*) \geq f^* - \epsilon$. Letting $\epsilon \to 0$ we see $f(x^*) \geq f^*$.

Now suppose $f(x^*) \geq \limsup f(x^\nu)$ whenever $x^\nu \to x^*$. Take arbitrary α and consider $A = \{x : f(x) \geq \alpha\}$. If x^* is a limit point of A, there are $x^\nu \in A$ with $\lim x^\nu = x^*$. Then $f(x^*) \geq \limsup f(x^\nu) \geq \alpha$, so $x^* \in A$. Because A contains its limit points, it is closed. Therefore f is upper semicontinuous. □

Contraction Mapping Theorems

One extremely useful result for complete metric spaces is the Contraction Mapping Theorem. Let (X, d) be a metric space. We call a mapping $T: X \to X$ a *strict contraction* if there is a $\theta < 1$ with $d(Tx, Ty) \leq \theta d(x, y)$ for every $x, y \in X$.[24]

Contraction Mapping Theorem. *Let T be a strict contraction on a complete metric space (X, d). Then there is a unique $x \in X$ with $Tx = x$.*

Proof. Let $x_0 \in X$ and define x_n inductively by $x_{n+1} = Tx_n$. Now for $k > 0$, $d(x_{n+k}, x_n) \leq d(x_{n+k}, x_{n+k-1}) + \cdots + d(x_{n+1}, x_n)$ by the triangle inequality. Moreover, $x_n = T^n x_0$, so $d(x_{n+1}, x_n) \leq \theta^n d(x_1, x_0)$. Thus $d(x_{n+k}, x_n) \leq (\theta^{n+k-1} + \cdots + \theta^n) d(x_1, x_0) \leq \theta^n d(x_1, x_0)/(1 - \theta)$. Thus for $n \leq m$, $d(x_n, x_m) \leq \theta^n d(x_1, x_0)/(1 - \theta)$. Given $\epsilon > 0$, we may now choose N large enough that $m \geq n \geq N$ implies $d(x_n, x_m) < \epsilon$. Thus $\{x_n\}$ is Cauchy, and so converges. Moreover, $Tx = T \lim x_n = \lim Tx_n = \lim x_{n+1} = x$.

Finally, if $Tx = x$ and $Ty = y$, $d(x, y) = d(Tx, Ty) \leq \theta d(x, y)$, which requires $d(x, y) = 0$. Therefore, $x = y$, and the fixed point is unique. □

In principal Riesz ideals with their associated lattice norm, the following monotone form of the Contraction Mapping Theorem, which general-

---

[23] The function c_t is the projection of $\mathbf{c}$ onto the tth factor space and is continuous by the definition of the weak topology on the space of real-valued sequences.

[24] A contraction merely requires $\theta \leq 1$.

izes Blackwell (1965), is extremely useful.

Monotone Contraction Mapping Theorem for Ideals. *Let A_ω be a principal Riesz ideal of the Riesz space $\mathbf{E}$ that is complete in the associated lattice norm. Suppose $T: A_\omega \to \mathbf{E}$ obeys:*

   (1) $T\mathbf{x} \le T\mathbf{y}$ *whenever* $\mathbf{x} \le \mathbf{y}$;
   (2) $T\mathbf{0} \in A_\omega$;
   (3) $T(\mathbf{x} + \alpha\omega) \le T\mathbf{x} + \alpha\theta\omega$ *with* $0 \le \theta < 1$.

Then T is a strict contraction and has a unique fixed point.

Proof. For all $\mathbf{x}, \mathbf{y} \in A_\omega$, $|\mathbf{x} - \mathbf{y}| \le \|\mathbf{x} - \mathbf{y}\|\omega$. So, $\mathbf{x} \le \mathbf{y} + \|\mathbf{x} - \mathbf{y}\|\omega$ and $\mathbf{y} \le \mathbf{x} + \|\mathbf{x} - \mathbf{y}\|\omega$. Properties (1) and (3) yield $T\mathbf{x} \le T\mathbf{y} + \theta\|\mathbf{x} - \mathbf{y}\|\omega$ and $T\mathbf{y} \le T\mathbf{x} + \theta\|\mathbf{x} - \mathbf{y}\|\omega$. Thus $\|T\mathbf{x} - T\mathbf{y}\| \le \theta\|\mathbf{x} - \mathbf{y}\|$.

Setting $\mathbf{y} = 0$, we have $\|T\mathbf{x} - T(0)\| \le \theta\|\mathbf{x}\|$, and so $\|T\mathbf{x}\| \le \theta\|\mathbf{x}\| + \|T(0)\| < \infty$ by property (2). Hence $T: A_\omega \to A_\omega$. As $\theta < 1$, T is a strict contraction on A_ω. By the Contraction Mapping Theorem, it has a unique fixed point. $\quad\square$

These theorems will assume particular importance when $\mathbf{E}$ is a space of continuous functions. Given a Hausdorff space X and normed space Y, let $\mathcal{C}(X;Y)$ denote the continuous functions from X to Y, and let $\mathcal{C}_b(X;Y)$ be the set of bounded continuous functions. Define $\|f\| = \sup\{|f(x)| : x \in X\}$ where $|\cdot|$ denotes the norm on Y (which is not necessarily absolute value). The norm on $\mathcal{C}_b$ is referred to as the *supremum* or *uniform norm*. If Y is a normed lattice, $\mathcal{C}_b(X;Y)$ is a vector lattice. If Y is complete, so is $\mathcal{C}_b(X;Y)$.

Theorem 10. *Let Y be a closed subset of a complete normed space. Then $\mathcal{C}_b(X;Y)$ is a Banach space.*

Proof. Suppose $\{f_n\}$ is a Cauchy sequence. Then $|f_n(x) - f_m(x)| \le \|f_n - f_m\|$, so $\{f_n(x)\}$ is Cauchy for each x. As Y is complete, $\{f_n(x)\}$ has a limit $f(x)$.

Let $\epsilon > 0$. There is an N with $|f_n(x) - f_m(x)| \le \|f_n - f_m\| < \epsilon$ for all x whenever $n, m \ge N$. Letting $m \to \infty$, we see $|f_n(x) - f(x)| \le \epsilon$ for $n \ge N$. Thus $\|f_n - f\| \le \epsilon$ for $n \ge N$, and $f_n \to f$ in sup norm. Moreover, $|f(x)| \le \epsilon + |f_N(x)|$. Thus f is bounded because f_N is bounded. The only remaining step is to show that f is continuous. This is accomplished in the following lemma. $\quad\square$

Lemma 2. *Suppose $f_n \in \mathcal{C}_b(X;Y)$ where Y is a subset of a normed space, and $f_n \to f$ uniformly. Then f is continuous.*

Proof. The proof uses the standard "3-ϵ" argument. Let $\epsilon > 0$. Consider $|f(x) - f(y)| \le |f(x) - f_n(x)| + |f_n(x) - f_n(y)| + |f_n(y) - f(y)|$. Choose n large enough that $\|f_n - f\| < \epsilon$. Then $|f(x) - f(y)| < 2\epsilon + |f_n(x) - f_n(y)|$. Because f_n is continuous, we can choose a neighborhood U of x so that

$|f_n(x) - f_n(y)| < \epsilon$ for $y \in U$. But then $|f(x) - f(y)| < 3\epsilon$ for all $y \in U$, which means f is continuous. $\square$

Now let $\varphi > 0$ be a continuous real-valued function on X. Define

$$C_\varphi(X;Y) = \{f \in C(X;Y) : \sup_{x \in X} |f(x)|/\varphi(x) < \infty\}$$

and the *weighted supremum norm* by $\|f\|_\varphi = \sup_{x \in X}\{|f(x)|/\varphi(x)\}$. Consider the mapping $V: C_\varphi \to C_b$ defined by $Vf = f/\varphi$. Note that $\|f\|_\varphi = \|Vf\|$, and that V is invertible. Since C_b is a Banach space, so is C_φ. Moreover, when Y is a Riesz space with order unit $\mathbf{e}$, we can regard C_φ as the principal ideal generated by $\varphi\mathbf{e}$. We immediately have the following corollary to the Monotone Contraction Mapping Theorem for Ideals.

Weighted Contraction Mapping Theorem. *Let Y be a subset of a Riesz space with order unit $\mathbf{e}$. Suppose $T: C_\varphi(X;Y) \to C(X;Y)$ such that:*

(1) *T is non-decreasing;*
(2) *$T(0) \in C_\varphi$;*
(3) *$T(\xi + A\varphi\mathbf{e}) \leq T\xi + A\theta\varphi\mathbf{e}$ for some constant $\theta < 1$ and all $A > 0$.*

Then T has a unique fixed point.

Of course, if $Y \subset \mathbb{R}$, then $\mathbf{e} = 1$, and the theorem reduces to the analogous theorem in Boyd (1990a).

2.3 Commodity Price Dualities

What do we need of a price system in a competitive economic model? The price system must assign a dollar value to each commodity bundle. In a perfectly competitive model, the price of each unit does not depend on the number of units bought. There are no quantity discounts or surcharges. If we take two bundles and add them together, their combined price is the sum of their individual prices. If we scale a bundle, its price scales. This describes a *linear form*—a linear mapping from the commodity space $\mathbf{E}$ to the real numbers. We denote the space of linear forms on $\mathbf{E}$ by $\mathbf{E}^*$. We will further require that bundles that are close together have prices that are close together. The linear form must be continuous. Continuous linear forms are referred to as *linear functionals*. The space of linear functionals is called the *dual space*, and is denoted $\mathbf{E}'$, or $\mathbf{E}'_\tau$ when we need to emphasize the topology τ.

The open-ended horizon characteristic of dynamic economic models means that there are generally several Hausdorff linear topologies available for $\mathbf{E}$. This stands in contrast to the finite horizon case where there can be only one such topology. Thus several dual spaces may also be available in the infinite horizon framework. The choice of a topology for $\mathbf{E}$ as well as a selection of the dual space has important economic consequences. Koopmans (1960) first observed that the continuity hypothesis maintained on an agent's preference order contained an implicit behavioral assumption about myopia. The topology chosen determines which bundles are close together, both topologically and in terms of preferences. The properties of the dual space show up in the representation of prices realized in a perfect foresight equilibrium or in support of an optimum allocation. The representation of the price system links to questions about the possibility of bubbles in an equilibrium configuration.[25]

When $\mathbf{p} \in \mathbf{E}'$ and $\mathbf{x} \in \mathbf{E}$, the value of $\mathbf{p}$ at $\mathbf{x}$ is commonly denoted by any of $\mathbf{p}(\mathbf{x})$, $(\mathbf{p}, \mathbf{x})$, $\langle \mathbf{p}, \mathbf{x} \rangle$, $\mathbf{px}$, or $\mathbf{p} \cdot \mathbf{x}$. The dual space is itself a vector space. Define $\langle \alpha \mathbf{p} + \beta \mathbf{q}, \mathbf{x} \rangle = \alpha \langle \mathbf{p}, \mathbf{x} \rangle + \beta \langle \mathbf{q}, \mathbf{x} \rangle$. The zero element is defined by $\langle \mathbf{0}, \mathbf{x} \rangle = 0$. The vector axioms are then easily verified.

Theorem 11. *Let* $\mathbf{E}$ *and* $\mathbf{F}$ *be topological vector spaces and* $f : \mathbf{E} \to \mathbf{F}$ *be linear. Then* f *is continuous if and only if it is continuous at zero.*

Proof. The "only if" part is clear, so suppose f is continuous at $\mathbf{0}$, and V is a neighborhood of $f(\mathbf{x})$ in $\mathbf{F}$. Now $V' = V - f(\mathbf{x})$ is a neighborhood of $\mathbf{0}$. Thus there is a neighborhood U' of $\mathbf{0}$ in $\mathbf{E}$ with $f(U') \subset V'$. As $U = U' + \mathbf{x}$ is a neighborhood of $\mathbf{x}$, we have found the required neighborhood of $\mathbf{x}$ with $f(U) \subset V$. $\square$

Theorem 12. *Let* $\mathbf{E}$ *be an LCS,* $\mathbf{F}$ *be normed and* $f : \mathbf{E} \to \mathbf{F}$ *be linear. Then* f *is continuous if and only if there is an absolutely convex neighborhood* U *of zero and* $\alpha > 0$ *with* $\|f(\mathbf{x})\| \leq \alpha p_U(\mathbf{x})$.

Proof. By the preceding theorem, we need only consider continuity at zero. Suppose such α and U exist and let $\epsilon > 0$. Then if $\mathbf{x} \in (\epsilon / \alpha) U$, $\|f(\mathbf{x})\| \leq \epsilon$, so f is continuous.

Now suppose f is continuous. There exists a neighborhood U with $\|f(\mathbf{x})\| \leq 1$ whenever $\mathbf{x} \in U$. For $\mathbf{x} \in \mathbf{E}$, $p_U(\mathbf{x}/2p_U(\mathbf{x})) < 1$, so $\mathbf{x}/2p_U(\mathbf{x}) \in U$. Thus $\|f(\mathbf{x})/2p_U(\mathbf{x})\| \leq 1$, which implies $\|f(\mathbf{x})\| \leq 2p_U(\mathbf{x})$. $\square$

Corollary 3. *If* $\mathbf{E}$ *and* $\mathbf{F}$ *are normed spaces and* $f : \mathbf{E} \to \mathbf{F}$ *is linear, then* f *is continuous if and only if there is an* α *with* $\|f(\mathbf{x})\| \leq \alpha \|\mathbf{x}\|$ *for all* $\mathbf{x} \in \mathbf{E}$.

A linear mapping between normed spaces is called *bounded* if there is an α with $\|f(\mathbf{x})\| \leq \alpha \|\mathbf{x}\|$. We can define a norm on the space of continuous linear mappings from $\mathbf{E}$ to $\mathbf{F}$ (denoted $\mathcal{B}(\mathbf{E}, \mathbf{F})$) by $\|f\| = \sup\{\|f(\mathbf{x})\| : \|\mathbf{x}\| \leq 1\}$. If $\mathbf{F}$ is complete, so is $\mathcal{B}(\mathbf{E}, \mathbf{F})$. When $\mathbf{F} = \mathbb{R}$, $\mathcal{B}(\mathbf{E}, \mathbf{F}) = \mathbf{E}'$. Thus the dual space of any normed space is a Banach space.

▶ Example 8: The dual of ℓ^1 is ℓ^∞. We first show that any element of ℓ^∞

---

[25] See Gilles (1989) and Gilles and LeRoy (1992).

is in $(\ell^1)'$. For $\mathbf{p} \in \ell^\infty$ and $\mathbf{x} \in \ell^1$, define

$$\langle \mathbf{p}, \mathbf{x} \rangle = \sum_{t=1}^\infty \sum_{i=1}^m p_{it} x_{it}. \qquad (2)$$

Since $|p_{it}| \leq \|\mathbf{p}\|_\infty$, $|\langle \mathbf{p}, \mathbf{x} \rangle| \leq \|\mathbf{p}\|_\infty \sum_{t=1}^\infty \sum_{i=1}^m |x_{it}| \leq \|\mathbf{p}\|_\infty \|\mathbf{x}\|_1$. Thus, the sum defining $\langle \mathbf{p}, \mathbf{x} \rangle$ converges, and $\|\mathbf{p}\| \leq \|\mathbf{p}\|_\infty$. Now define the unit vector $\mathbf{e}^{it}$ by $e_{it}^{it} = 1$ and $e_{js}^{it} = 0$ otherwise. Because $\|\mathbf{e}_{it}\|_1 = 1$, $|p_{it}| = |\langle \mathbf{p}, \mathbf{e}_{it} \rangle| \leq \|\mathbf{p}\|$. Taking the supremum over i and t we find $\|\mathbf{p}\|_\infty \leq \|\mathbf{p}\|$ so $\|\mathbf{p}\| = \|\mathbf{p}\|_\infty$. This establishes that ℓ^∞ can be regarded as a subset of $(\ell^1)'$.

Now suppose $\mathbf{p} \in (\ell^1)'$. We associate a sequence $\mathbf{q}$ with $\mathbf{p}$ as follows. Define $q_{it} = \langle \mathbf{p}, \mathbf{e}_{it} \rangle$. Now $|q_{it}| \leq \|\mathbf{p}\|$, so $\mathbf{q} \in \ell^\infty$, and $\|\mathbf{q}\|_\infty = \|\mathbf{p}\|$. Let $\mathbf{q}_T = (q_1, \ldots, q_T, 0, \ldots)$. Consider $\mathbf{x} \in \ell^1$ and define $\mathbf{x}_T = (x_1, \ldots, x_T, 0, 0, \ldots)$. Since $\mathbf{x}_T$ can be written as a linear combination of the $\mathbf{e}_{it}$, $\langle \mathbf{p}, \mathbf{x}_T \rangle = \sum_{t=1}^T \sum_{i=1}^m p_{it} x_{it} = \langle \mathbf{q}_T, \mathbf{x} \rangle$. Now $|\langle \mathbf{p}, \mathbf{x} \rangle - \langle \mathbf{q}_T, \mathbf{x} \rangle| = |\langle \mathbf{p}, \mathbf{x} - \mathbf{x}_T \rangle| \leq \|\mathbf{p}\| \|\mathbf{x} - \mathbf{x}_T\|_1$. But $\|\mathbf{x} - \mathbf{x}_T\|_1 \to 0$, so $\langle \mathbf{p}, \mathbf{x} \rangle = \lim \langle \mathbf{q}_T, \mathbf{x} \rangle = \langle \mathbf{q}, \mathbf{x} \rangle$ for all $\mathbf{x} \in \ell^1$, which means $\mathbf{p} = \mathbf{q}$. ◄

More generally, for $1 \leq p < \infty$, the normed space ℓ^p has dual ℓ^q where $p^{-1} + q^{-1} = 1$. The proof of this is similar to above, using Hölder's inequality $|\langle \mathbf{p}, \mathbf{x} \rangle| \leq \|\mathbf{p}\|_q \|\mathbf{x}\|_p$.[26] One consequence is that any ℓ^p for $p > 1$ is a dual space. In fact, when $1 < p < \infty$, $\ell^p = (\ell^q)' = (\ell^p)''$. Such a space, which is its own second dual, is called *reflexive*. What about ℓ^1? Although we may regard elements of ℓ^1 as elements of $(\ell^\infty)'$, they do not exhaust $(\ell^\infty)'$. Rather, ℓ^1 is the dual of a subspace of ℓ^∞, c_0.

► Example 9: The dual of c_0 is ℓ^1. The basic argument here follows the previous example. The only difference is that $\|\mathbf{x} - \mathbf{x}_T\|_\infty \to 0$ follows from the fact that $x_{it} \to 0$ as $t \to \infty$ because $\mathbf{x} \in c_0$. As this would not follow for $\mathbf{x} \in \ell^\infty$, there is the possibility that $(\ell^\infty)'$ contains elements that are not in ℓ^1. We will return to this point in Example 12. ◄

► Example 10: The dual of s^m is c_{00}. Again, the sum (2) converges, in fact has only finitely many non-zero terms, for any $\mathbf{p} \in c_{00}$ and $\mathbf{x} \in s^m$. Continuity requires a different argument. Choose T with $p_{it} = 0$ for $t > T$. Then $\langle \mathbf{p}, \mathbf{x} \rangle = \sum_{t=1}^T \sum_{i=1}^m p_{it} x_{it}$ for all $\mathbf{x} \in s^m$. Now suppose $\mathbf{x}^n \xrightarrow{p} \mathbf{x}$, so $x_{it}^n \to x_{it}$ for all i and t. The finite sum defining $\langle \mathbf{p}, \mathbf{x} \rangle$ is clearly continuous in x_{it} for $t \leq T$, so $\mathbf{p}$ is a continuous linear functional on s^m.

Now suppose $\mathbf{p} \in (s^m)'$. Define q_{it} as before. If $q_{it} \neq 0$ for infinitely many pairs (i, t), define $x_{it} = 1/q_{it}$ for $p_{it} \neq 0$ and $x_{it} = 0$ otherwise. Again $\mathbf{x}_T \to \mathbf{x}$, so $\langle \mathbf{q}_T, \mathbf{x} \rangle = \langle \mathbf{q}, \mathbf{x}_T \rangle \to \langle \mathbf{p}, \mathbf{x} \rangle$. But $\langle \mathbf{p}, \mathbf{x}_T \rangle$ gives the

---

[26] Simmons sketches a proof for the finite dimensional case (1963, p. 218). Taking the limit yields the ℓ^p case.

number of non-zero terms of $\mathbf{x}_T$, which converges to ∞, not $\langle \mathbf{p}, \mathbf{x} \rangle < \infty$. This contradiction establishes that $\mathbf{q} \in c_{00}$. Since $\langle \mathbf{q}_T, \mathbf{x} \rangle$ also converges to $\langle \mathbf{q}, \mathbf{x} \rangle$, $\mathbf{q} = \mathbf{p}$ and we are done. ◀

▶ **Example 11:** α-norm on $\ell^\infty(\beta)$. Consider the set $\ell^\infty(\beta)$ but give it the topology from the α-norm for $\alpha > \beta$, denoted $\ell_\alpha^\infty(\beta)$. The mapping $T\mathbf{x}$ defined by $(T\mathbf{x})_{it} = x_{it}/\alpha^t$ is a linear isometric mapping from $\ell_\alpha^\infty(\beta)$ into c_0. In fact, since the image of $\ell_\alpha^\infty(\beta)$ contains c_{00}, $X = T(\ell_\alpha^\infty(\beta))$ is sup-dense in c_0.

We can use the linear isomorphism between $\ell_\alpha^\infty(\beta)$ and X to generate linear functionals on c_0 from linear functionals on $\ell_\alpha^\infty(\beta)$. For $\mathbf{p} \in (\ell_\alpha^\infty(\beta))'$, define $\mathbf{q}: X \to \mathbb{R}$ by $\langle \mathbf{q}, \mathbf{x} \rangle = \langle \mathbf{p}, T(\mathbf{x}) \rangle$. Note that $\|\mathbf{q}\| = \|\mathbf{p}\|$ because T is isometric. Given $\mathbf{x} \in c_0$, take $\mathbf{x}^n \in X$ with $\mathbf{x}^n \to \mathbf{x}$. Now $\{\mathbf{x}^n\}$ is Cauchy and $|\langle \mathbf{q}, \mathbf{x}^n \rangle - \langle \mathbf{q}, \mathbf{x}^m \rangle| \le \|\mathbf{p}\| \|\mathbf{x}^n - \mathbf{x}^m\|$, so $\{\langle \mathbf{q}, \mathbf{x}^n \rangle\}$ is also Cauchy and has a limit. Define $\langle \mathbf{q}, \mathbf{x} \rangle = \lim \langle \mathbf{q}, \mathbf{x}^n \rangle$. It is easy to see that this definition is independent of the choice of $\mathbf{x}^n \to \mathbf{x}$, and that it defines a linear functional on c_0 with norm $\|\mathbf{p}\|$. Now $\mathbf{q}$ can be represented by an element of ℓ^1. Working through, we find that for $\mathbf{p} \in \ell^1$, $\langle \mathbf{p}, T(\mathbf{x}) \rangle = \sum_{t=1}^\infty \sum_{i=1}^m p_{it} x_{it}/\alpha^t$, so $q_{it} = p_{it}/\alpha^t$. Thus we can represent elements of the dual of $\ell_\alpha^\infty(\beta)$ as sequences $\mathbf{q}$ with $\sum_{t=1}^\infty \sum_{i=1}^m |q_{it}|\alpha^t < \infty$. The dual is a weighted ℓ^1-space, $\ell^1(1/\alpha)$. ◀

2.3.1 Duals and Hyperplanes

Elements of the dual $\mathbf{E}'$ can also be regarded as hyperplanes in $\mathbf{E}$. A *hyperplane through the origin (hyperplane about zero)* is a maximal vector subspace of $\mathbf{E}$. That is, it is a set $M \subset \mathbf{E}$ where $\mathbf{x}, \mathbf{y} \in M$ implies $\alpha\mathbf{x} + \mathbf{y} \in M$ (a subspace), and is maximal in the sense that any other subspace containing M is either the whole space $\mathbf{E}$ or M itself. A *hyperplane* is a translate of a hyperplane through zero. Hyperplanes come in two flavors—closed and dense.

Lemma 3. *In a TVS, a hyperplane is either closed or dense.*

Proof. Let M be a hyperplane. We can write M as $x + H$ where H is a hyperplane through zero. Clearly $\mathrm{cl}\, M = x + \mathrm{cl}\, H$. As $\mathrm{cl}\, H$ is a linear subspace, either $\mathrm{cl}\, H = H$ or $\mathrm{cl}\, M = \mathbf{E}$. In the first case M is closed, in the second M is dense. □

Hyperplanes are the level sets of linear forms, and closed hyperplanes are the level sets of continuous linear forms, as shown in the following theorems.

Theorem 13. *A subset H of a vector space $\mathbf{E}$ is a hyperplane if and only if there is a $\mathbf{p} \in \mathbf{E}^*$ and $\alpha \in \mathbb{R}$ with $H = \{\mathbf{x} : \mathbf{p}(\mathbf{x}) = \alpha\}$.*

Proof. First, let $H = \{\mathbf{x} : \mathbf{p}(\mathbf{x}) = \alpha\}$. Take $\mathbf{x}_0 \in H$ with $\mathbf{p}(\mathbf{x}_0) = \alpha$. Then $H = \mathbf{x}_0 + M$ where $M = \{\mathbf{x} : \mathbf{p}(\mathbf{x}) = 0\}$. Let V be a subspace with

$M \subset V$. If $V \neq M$, there is an $\mathbf{x} \in V$ which is not in M, so $\mathbf{p}(\mathbf{x}) \neq 0$. We can assume $\mathbf{p}(\mathbf{x}) = 1$. For any $\mathbf{y} \in \mathbf{E}$, $\mathbf{p}(\mathbf{y} - (\mathbf{p}(\mathbf{y}))\mathbf{x}) = 0$. Since $\mathbf{y} - (\mathbf{p}(\mathbf{y}))\mathbf{x} \in M \subset V$ and $\mathbf{x} \in V$, $\mathbf{y} \in V$. Thus $V = \mathbf{E}$ and M is maximal. It follows that H is a hyperplane.

Next, assume H is a hyperplane, so $H = \mathbf{x}_0 + M$ for some $\mathbf{x}_0 \in \mathbf{E}$ and maximal subspace M. If $\mathbf{E} = M$ set $\mathbf{p} = 0$. Take $\mathbf{x}_1 \notin M$ and consider the set of linear combinations of $\mathbf{x}$ and elements of M. This is a vector subspace that properly contains M, so it must be the whole space. Any element of $\mathbf{E}$ can be written $\mathbf{x} = \beta \mathbf{x}_1 + \mathbf{y}$ with $\mathbf{y} \in M$. Define $\mathbf{p}(\mathbf{x}) = \beta$. This is well defined, and $M = \{\mathbf{x} : \mathbf{p}(\mathbf{x}) = 0\}$. Setting $\alpha = \mathbf{p}(\mathbf{x}_0)$ gives the desired representation of H. $\square$

Theorem 14. *A linear form is continuous if and only if* $M = \{\mathbf{x} : \mathbf{p}(\mathbf{x}) = 0\}$ *is closed.*

Proof. The "only if" part is clear since M is the inverse image of a closed set under a continuous map.

There is nothing to show if $\mathbf{p} = 0$, so assume $\mathbf{p} \neq 0$. If M is closed, there is an $\mathbf{x}$ with $\mathbf{p}(\mathbf{x}) = 1$ since $\mathbf{p}$ is not zero. As the complement of M is open, we may choose a neighborhood W' of $\mathbf{x}$ which does not intersect M. Translate to the origin by setting $W = W' - \mathbf{x}$. Since $(\alpha, \mathbf{x}) \to \alpha \mathbf{x}$ is continuous, there is an ϵ and a neighborhood U of zero with $\alpha \mathbf{y}$ in W whenever $|\alpha| < \epsilon$ and $\mathbf{y} \in U$. Consider the open set $V = \cup \{\mu U : |\mu| \leq \epsilon\} \subset W$. Note that $|\lambda| \leq 1$ implies $\lambda V \subset V$ (V is balanced). Suppose $\mathbf{z} \in V$. If $|\mathbf{p}(\mathbf{z})| \geq 1$, then $-\mathbf{z}/\mathbf{p}(\mathbf{z}) \in V$ as V is balanced. Now $\mathbf{p}(\mathbf{x} - \mathbf{z}/\mathbf{p}(\mathbf{z})) = 1 - 1 = 0$. But this is impossible as $\mathbf{x} - \mathbf{z}/\mathbf{p}(\mathbf{z}) \in W'$. It follows that $|\mathbf{p}(\mathbf{z})| < 1$ for all $\mathbf{z} \in V$. Thus $\mathbf{p}$ is bounded, and therefore continuous. $\square$

2.3.2 Hahn-Banach Theorems

So far, we have examined several dual spaces. In general, we know that the dual is non-empty as $\mathbf{0} \in \mathbf{E}'$. However, we have not yet ruled out the possibility that $\mathbf{0}$ is the only element of $\mathbf{E}'$. In fact, LCSs are richly endowed with dual vectors. That is one of the consequences of the Hahn-Banach Theorems. Roughly speaking, these theorems say that linear functionals defined on a subspace may be extended to the whole space.[27]

Hahn-Banach Extension Theorem. *Suppose that p is a seminorm on the vector space $\mathbf{E}$ and that f is a linear form on M with $|f(\mathbf{x})| \leq p(\mathbf{x})$ for all $\mathbf{x} \in M$. Then there is a $g \in \mathbf{E}^*$ extending f and obeying $|g(\mathbf{x})| \leq p(\mathbf{x})$ for all $\mathbf{x} \in \mathbf{E}$.*

---

[27] These Hahn-Banach theorems are covered in Robertson and Robertson (1973, pp. 24–31).

Corollary 4. *Any continuous linear form defined on a vector subspace M of an LCS* **E** *has a continuous extension to* **E**.

Proof. There is an absolutely convex neighborhood of zero, U, with $|f(\mathbf{x})| \le 1$ on $U \cap M$. Thus $|f(\mathbf{x})| \le p_U(\mathbf{x})$ on M. Then apply the Hahn-Banach Extension Theorem. $\square$

Corollary 5. *If* $\mathbf{a} \in \mathbf{E}$ *and* p *is a seminorm on* **E**, *there is a linear form on* **E** *with* $|f(\mathbf{x})| \le p(\mathbf{x})$ *and* $f(\mathbf{a}) = p(\mathbf{a})$.

Proof. Take M as the subspace of scalar multiples of $\mathbf{a}$, and define f on M by $f(\lambda \mathbf{a}) = \lambda p(\mathbf{a})$. Then apply the Extension Theorem. $\square$

Corollary 6. *Let* **E** *be an LCS. If* $f(\mathbf{a}) = 0$ *for all* $f \in \mathbf{E}'$, *then* $\mathbf{a} = \mathbf{0}$.

Proof. Suppose $\mathbf{a} \ne \mathbf{0}$. Then there is a neighborhood U of $\mathbf{0}$ with $\mathbf{a} \notin U$, so $p_U(\mathbf{a}) > 0$. Then apply Corollary 5 to obtain an $f \in \mathbf{E}'$ with $f(\mathbf{a}) = p_U(\mathbf{a}) > 0$. This contradicts the hypothesis. Therefore $\mathbf{a} = \mathbf{0}$. $\square$

This last corollary tells us that $\mathbf{E}'$ has enough elements to *separate points* of **E**. That is, if $\langle \mathbf{p}, \mathbf{x} \rangle = \langle \mathbf{p}, \mathbf{y} \rangle$ for all $\mathbf{p} \in \mathbf{E}'$, then $\mathbf{x} = \mathbf{y}$. There is also a geometric form of the Hahn-Banach Theorem that relates hyperplanes and convex sets rather than linear functionals and seminorms.

Geometric Hahn-Banach Theorem. *Let* C *be a convex set with nonempty interior, and suppose* V *is a linear variety which does not intersect the interior of* C. *Then there is a closed hyperplane* H *which contains* V *and does not intersect the interior of* C; *i.e., there is* $\mathbf{p} \in \mathbf{E}'$ *and* $\alpha \in \mathbb{R}$ *with* $\mathbf{p}(\mathbf{x}) = \alpha$ *for all* $\mathbf{x} \in V$ *and* $\mathbf{p}(\mathbf{y}) < \alpha$ *for all* $\mathbf{y} \in \operatorname{int} C$.

Proof. By translation, we may assume that $\mathbf{0} \in \operatorname{int} C$. Let M be the smallest subspace of **E** that contains V. Of course $M = \cup_\lambda \lambda V$. Note that V is a hyperplane in M which does not contain $\mathbf{0}$, so there is a linear form f on M with $V = f^{-1}(1)$.

Let p be the Minkowski functional of C. Since V contains no interior points of C, $f(\mathbf{x}) = 1 \le p(\mathbf{x})$ for $\mathbf{x} \in V$. By homogeneity, $f(\alpha \mathbf{x}) = \alpha \le p(\alpha \mathbf{x})$ for any $\mathbf{x} \in V$ and $\alpha > 0$. For $\alpha < 0$, $f(\alpha \mathbf{x}) \le 0 \le p(\alpha \mathbf{x})$ for $\mathbf{x} \in V$. Thus $f(\mathbf{x}) \le p(\mathbf{x})$ for all $\mathbf{x} \in M$. By the Hahn-Banach Extension Theorem, we can extend f to all of **E**. Since C has an interior, p is continuous. It follows that the extension of f is continuous. Denote the extension $\mathbf{p}$. Now $H = \mathbf{p}^{-1}(1)$ is the desired hyperplane containing V. Since $p(\mathbf{x}) < 1$ on $\operatorname{int} C$, H does not contain any interior points of C. $\square$

The Geometric Hahn-Banach Theorem immediately leads to another form that is very useful in economics.

Hahn-Banach Separation Theorem. *Let* **E** *be an LCS. Suppose that* A *and* B *are disjoint non-empty convex sets and that* A *is open. Then there is a* $\mathbf{p} \in \mathbf{E}'$ *and* $\alpha \in \mathbb{R}$ *such that* $\langle \mathbf{p}, \mathbf{x} \rangle > \alpha$ *for* $\mathbf{x} \in A$ *and* $\langle \mathbf{p}, \mathbf{x} \rangle \le \alpha$ *for* $\mathbf{x} \in B$.

Proof. Let $C = A - B$. Since A and B are disjoint, $\mathbf{0} \notin C$. Set $V = \{\mathbf{0}\}$ and apply the Geometric Hahn-Banach Theorem. $\square$

This is the form that yields supporting prices for preferred sets and for production sets. It is also useful for obtaining a general form of the Kuhn-Tucker Theorem, and for building the theory of concave optimization. It can also help us investigate the dual of ℓ^∞ a bit further by constructing Banach limits. First, recall the shift operator S on s^m defined in Chapter 1 by $S\mathbf{x} = (x_2, x_3, \ldots)$.

Banach Limit. A Banach limit is a linear functional Λ on $\ell^\infty \subset s^1$ such that:

(1) $\Lambda(\mathbf{x}) \geq 0$ if $\mathbf{x} \geq \mathbf{0}$;
(2) $\Lambda(\mathbf{x}) = \Lambda(S^N \mathbf{x})$ for $N = 1, 2, \ldots$;
(3) $\liminf_t x_t \leq \Lambda(\mathbf{x}) \leq \limsup_t x_t$.

▶ **Example 12: Banach limits.** Define $\Lambda_n(\mathbf{x}) = (x_1 + \cdots + x_n)/n$, let $p(\mathbf{x}) = \limsup_n |\Lambda_n(\mathbf{x})|$, and set $M = \{\mathbf{x} \in \ell^\infty : \Lambda(\mathbf{x}) = \lim_n \Lambda_n(\mathbf{x})$ exists$\}$. Clearly Λ is a linear form on M, and $p(\mathbf{x})$ is a seminorm on ℓ^∞ with $|\Lambda(\mathbf{x})| \leq p(\mathbf{x})$ for all $\mathbf{x} \in M$. Apply the Hahn-Banach Extension Theorem to extend Λ to all of ℓ^∞. Then Λ is continuous because $p(\mathbf{x}) \leq \|\mathbf{x}\|_\infty$. Moreover, $p(\mathbf{x}) = \limsup_n |\Lambda_n(\mathbf{x})| \leq \max\{\limsup_n x_n, -\liminf_n x_n\}$, so $|\Lambda(\mathbf{x})| \leq \limsup_n x_n$ and $|\Lambda(\mathbf{x})| \leq -\liminf_n x_n$. Combining these yields (3), and this implies (1). For (2), note that $\Lambda_n(\mathbf{x} - S\mathbf{x}) = (x_1 - x_{n+1})/n$, so $|\Lambda_n(\mathbf{x} - S\mathbf{x})| \leq 2\|\mathbf{x}\|_\infty/n$. Thus $p(\mathbf{x} - S\mathbf{x}) = 0$ for all $\mathbf{x} \in \ell^\infty$. Iterating, we obtain (2).

A Banach limit cannot be represented by an element of ℓ^1. In fact, $\Lambda(\mathbf{e}^{it}) = 0$ by (2), so the associated ℓ^1-vector is $\mathbf{0}$. Moreover, $\Lambda(\mathbf{x}) = 0$ for any $\mathbf{x} \in c_0$. This fact makes it difficult to interpret Banach limits (and many other elements of $(\ell^\infty)'$) as price systems.[28] ◀

2.3.3 Dual Pairs and Weak Topologies

Our investigation of the dual of ℓ^∞ has revealed something rather curious. We have a Banach space, $\ell^1 \subset (\ell^\infty)'$, which is not the entire dual of ℓ^∞, even though it separates points of ℓ^∞ (and vice versa), and has a nice interpretation as a price system. The space ℓ^1 acts like a dual to ℓ^∞. With this in mind, we say a pair of LCSs $\langle \mathbf{E}, \mathbf{F} \rangle$ is a *dual pair* if we have a bilinear mapping $\langle \cdot, \cdot \rangle : \mathbf{E} \times \mathbf{F} \to \mathbb{R}$ such that $\mathbf{E}$ separates points of $\mathbf{F}$ and $\mathbf{F}$ separates points of $\mathbf{E}$. We can regard $\mathbf{F}$ as a linear subspace of $\mathbf{E}^*$, and vice versa. The pair $\langle \ell^\infty, \ell^1 \rangle$ qualifies with $\langle \mathbf{p}, \mathbf{x} \rangle$ defined by equation (2), as does $\langle \mathbf{E}, \mathbf{E}' \rangle$ for any LCS $\mathbf{E}$.

---

[28] But see Gilles (1989) and Gilles and LeRoy (1992) for a dissenting view. We return to this question of interpretation when we consider the price support properties of optimal programs and competitive equilibria in Chapter 8.

Given a dual pair $\langle \mathbf{E}, \mathbf{F} \rangle$, we define a *weak topology* on $\mathbf{E}$ by taking as a base at $\mathbf{0}$ all sets of the form $\{\mathbf{x} \in \mathbf{E} : \sup_{1 \leq i \leq n} |\langle \mathbf{x}, \mathbf{p}_i \rangle| \leq 1\}$ for every finite collection of vectors in $\mathbf{F}$.[29] We denote this topology by $\sigma(\mathbf{E}, \mathbf{F})$. We have already met such a topology before. The product topology is the $\sigma(s^m, c_{00})$-topology. We can now topologize c_{00} with the $\sigma(c_{00}, s^m)$-topology.[30] When $\mathbf{E}$ is a Banach space with norm dual $\mathbf{E}'$, we refer to $\sigma(\mathbf{E}', \mathbf{E})$ as the *weak topology* on $\mathbf{E}'$, and $\sigma(\mathbf{E}, \mathbf{E}')$ as the *weak* topology* on $\mathbf{E}$.[31]

Any dual space $\mathbf{E}'$ has both a weak (i.e., $\sigma(\mathbf{E}', \mathbf{E}'')$) and a weak* (i.e., $\sigma(\mathbf{E}', \mathbf{E})$) topology. In general, the weak topology is stronger than the weak* topology. If $\mathbf{E}$ is reflexive, the topologies will be the same. Thus the weak and weak* topologies coincide on ℓ^p for $1 < p < \infty$. However, these topologies are quite different on $\ell^\infty = (\ell^1)'$. Consider the sequence $\mathbf{x}^n$ defined by $x_t^n = 0$ for $t < n$ and $x_t^n = 1$ for $t \geq n$. For $\mathbf{p} \in \ell^1$, $\mathbf{p}(\mathbf{x}^n) = \sum_{t=n}^\infty p_t \to 0$, so $\mathbf{x}^n \to \mathbf{0}$ in the weak* topology. However, if $\mathbf{p}$ is a Banach limit $\mathbf{p}(\mathbf{x}^n) = 1$, so $\mathbf{x}^n$ does not weakly converge to $\mathbf{0}$; hence $\mathbf{x}^n$ does not converge in the weak topology.

Theorem 15. *Let $\langle \mathbf{E}, \mathbf{F} \rangle$ be a dual pair and give $\mathbf{E}$ the $\sigma(\mathbf{E}, \mathbf{F})$-topology. The space of linear functionals on $\mathbf{E}$ is $\mathbf{F}$.*

So there are at least two spaces that deserve to be called the dual of ℓ^∞: the norm dual, and ℓ^1. For $1 < p < \infty$, the weak ($\sigma(\ell^p, \ell^q)$) and norm duals are the same. The space ℓ^1 also has at least two legitimate duals, ℓ^∞ and c_0 (from the $\langle \ell^1, c_0 \rangle$ duality). This phenomenon of multiple duals cannot occur in finite dimensional vector spaces. They have only one LCS topology, which is given by any of the ℓ^p-norms on $\mathbb{R}^m$.

Further complexities arise in ℓ^p. There can also be a number of distinct topologies that yield the same dual. This happens on ℓ^p for $1 < p < \infty$. The norm dual is ℓ^q with $p^{-1} + q^{-1} = 1$. This is also the dual under the weak topology $\sigma(\ell^p, \ell^q)$. These topologies are distinct since the sequence $\mathbf{e}^t$ does not converge in norm, but converges to $\mathbf{0}$ weakly because $\langle \mathbf{e}^t, \mathbf{p} \rangle = p_t \to 0$.

We call τ a *topology of the dual pair* $\langle \mathbf{E}, \mathbf{F} \rangle$ if $\mathbf{E}'_\tau = \mathbf{F}$. Topologies of a dual pair have the same closed convex sets.[32]

Theorem 16. *Suppose $A \subset \mathbf{E}$ is convex and τ is a topology of the dual pair $\langle \mathbf{E}, \mathbf{F}' \rangle$. Then $\mathrm{cl}_\tau A = \mathrm{cl}_\sigma A$ where $\sigma = \sigma(\mathbf{E}, \mathbf{E}')$.*

---

[29] This is the unit ball of the seminorm $p(\mathbf{x}) = \sup_{1 \leq i \leq n} |\langle \mathbf{x}, \mathbf{y}_i \rangle|$.

[30] This topology on c_{00} is also an example of a strict inductive limit topology. The dual of a countably seminormed space, such as s^m, is always a strict inductive limit. See Robertson and Robertson (1973, Chapter 5) for details.

[31] See Robertson and Robertson (1973, p. 33).

[32] See Robertson and Robertson (1973, p. 34).

Corollary 7. *A convex set in a Banach space is norm closed if and only if it is weak* closed.*

We use the notion of a polar topology to try to bring some order to this situation. Let $\langle \mathbf{E}, \mathbf{F} \rangle$ be a dual pair and $A \subset \mathbf{E}$. Define the *polar* of A, A°, by $A^\circ = \{\mathbf{p} : \sup_{\mathbf{x} \in A} |\langle \mathbf{x}, \mathbf{p} \rangle| \leq 1\}$. It is easy to see A° is absolutely convex and $\sigma(\mathbf{F}, \mathbf{E})$-closed. Moreover, if A is $\sigma(\mathbf{E}, \mathbf{F})$-bounded, A° is absorbing and $p'_A(\mathbf{p}) = \sup_{\mathbf{x} \in A} |\langle \mathbf{x}, \mathbf{p} \rangle|$ is a seminorm with unit ball A°. Our first big fact about polars is:[33]

Alaoglu-Bourbaki Theorem. *If U is a neighborhood of the origin, then $U^\circ \subset \mathbf{E}'$ is $\sigma(\mathbf{E}', \mathbf{E})$-compact.*

Alaoglu's Theorem. *The closed unit ball in the dual of a normed space is weak* compact.*

Since order intervals in A_ω are contained in some ball, we have:

Corollary 8. *Order intervals in any A_ω are weak* compact.*

If $\mathcal{A}$ is a collection of $\sigma(\mathbf{E}, \mathbf{F})$-bounded sets, there is a weakest topology where all of the A° for $A \in \mathcal{A}$ are neighborhoods. A base for the topology is given by all scalar multiples of finite intersections of polars of sets of $\mathcal{A}$. This is the *polar topology* of $\mathcal{A}$ or *topology of uniform convergence* on $\mathcal{A}$. When $\mathcal{A}$ is the collection of finite subsets of $\mathbf{E}$, this polar topology is the weak topology $\sigma(\mathbf{F}, \mathbf{E})$. It is the weakest polar topology. The strongest polar topology takes $\mathcal{A}$ as the collection of all weakly bounded subsets of $\mathbf{E}$. This is the *strong topology* $\beta(\mathbf{E}, \mathbf{F})$. When $\mathbf{E}$ is a normed space, $\beta(\mathbf{E}', \mathbf{E})$ is the norm topology on $\mathbf{E}'$. Finally, we define the *Mackey topology*, $\tau(\mathbf{E}, \mathbf{F})$, by taking $\mathcal{A}$ as all absolutely convex $\sigma(\mathbf{F}, \mathbf{E})$-compact subsets of $\mathbf{F}$. Since these include all finite subsets, $\sigma \subset \tau \subset \beta$. The following sharpens the relation between these topologies.[34]

Mackey-Arens Theorem. *Suppose that $\mathbf{E}$ is an LCS with topology ξ and dual $\mathbf{F}$. Then $\sigma(\mathbf{E}, \mathbf{F}) \subset \xi \subset \tau(\mathbf{E}, \mathbf{F})$.*

This tells us that the Mackey topology is the strongest topology with dual $\mathbf{F}$. In particular, the Mackey and norm (strong) topologies coincide on ℓ^p for $1 < p < \infty$. Our last result concerning weak topologies relates weak and norm convergence.

Mazur's Theorem. *Let $\mathbf{E}$ be a normed linear space. Suppose a sequence $\mathbf{x}^n$ converges weakly to $\mathbf{x}$. Then, for any $\epsilon > 0$, there exist n and $\lambda_i \geq 0$ with $\sum_{i=1}^n \lambda_i = 1$ such that $\|\mathbf{x} - \sum_{i=1}^n \lambda_i \mathbf{x}^i\| < \epsilon$.*

Proof. By subtracting $\mathbf{x}^1$ from the $\mathbf{x}^i$ and $\mathbf{x}$, we may assume that $\mathbf{x}^1 = \mathbf{0}$ without loss of generality. Let M be the set of finite convex combinations

---

[33] See Robertson and Robertson (1973, p. 62) or Schaefer (1966, pp. 84, 125).

[34] The theorem is actually a corollary to the usual Mackey-Arens Theorem. See Robertson and Robertson (1973, p. 62) or Schaefer (1966, p. 131) for details.

of the $\mathbf{x}^i$. Note $\mathbf{0} = \mathbf{x}^1 \in M$. Suppose that $\|\mathbf{y} - \mathbf{x}\| \geq \epsilon$ for every $\mathbf{y} \in M$. The set $U = \{\mathbf{z} \in \mathbf{E} : \|\mathbf{z} - \mathbf{y}\| \leq \epsilon/2$ for some $\mathbf{y} \in M\}$ is a convex neighborhood of zero, and $\|\mathbf{z} - \mathbf{x}\| \geq \epsilon/2$ for all $\mathbf{z} \in U$. Let p be the Minkowski gauge of U. Note that $p(\mathbf{x}) > 1$, and set $\mathbf{y} = \mathbf{x}/p(\mathbf{x})$. Consider the linear subspace N of multiples of $\mathbf{y}$, and define $f(\lambda\mathbf{y}) = \lambda$ on N. Note that $|f(\lambda\mathbf{y})| = p(\lambda\mathbf{y})$. By the Hahn-Banach Extension Theorem, this extends to a real linear form, also denoted f, defined on $\mathbf{E}$ with $|f(\mathbf{z})| \leq p(\mathbf{z})$ for all $\mathbf{z} \in \mathbf{E}$. Since U is a neighborhood of zero, f is continuous. Moreover, $\sup_{\mathbf{z} \in M} f(\mathbf{z}) \leq \sup_{\mathbf{z} \in U} f(\mathbf{z}) \leq \sup_{\mathbf{z} \in U} p(\mathbf{z}) = 1 < p(\mathbf{x}) = f(\mathbf{x})$. Thus $\lim f(\mathbf{x}^i) \leq 1 < f(\mathbf{x})$, which contradicts the weak convergence of the $\mathbf{x}^i$ to $\mathbf{x}$.[35] □

Corollary 9. *Let* $\mathbf{E}$ *be a normed linear space with* $\mathbf{x}^n$ *converging weakly to* $\mathbf{x}$. *Then there is a sequence of convex combinations of the* $\mathbf{x}^n$ *that converges in norm to* $\mathbf{x}$.

When applied to measure spaces, this yields even more since a subsequence of the norm convergent sequence then converges pointwise.[36]

Mazur's Theorem can sometimes be combined with Alaoglu's Theorem. Alaoglu's Theorem is used to obtain a weak* convergent subsequence. When the space is reflexive (e.g., ℓ^2), this sequence is also weakly convergent and Mazur's Theorem applies. When working with a space of measurable functions, the norm convergent sequence obtained from Mazur's Theorem has a pointwise convergent subsequence. This property can be very useful.

Unfortunately, this type of argument does not work on ℓ^∞ or L^∞. However, when μ is a finite measure, there is a trick that can be used on $L^\infty(\mu)$.

▶ Example 13: L^∞ *duality trickery.* If f^n converges to f in the weak* topology, it means that $\int f^n g \, d\mu \to \int f g \, d\mu$ for all $g \in L^1$. Since μ is finite, $L^1 \supset L^\infty$; so $f^n, f \in L^1$. Thus for any $g \in L^\infty \subset L^1, \int f^n g \, d\mu \to \int f g \, d\mu$. That is, $f^n \to f$ in $\sigma(L^1, L^\infty)$ follows from the fact that $f^n \to f$ in $\sigma(L^\infty, L^1)$. In other words, weak* convergence in L^∞ implies weak convergence in L^1. Mazur's Theorem does apply after all, but in L^1 rather than L^∞. ◀

2.3.4 Order Duals

So far, we have looked at price systems from the standpoint of topology and regarded them as continuous linear functionals. But we have ignored the economically natural order structure that our vector spaces possess in addition to their topological structure(s). An economically sensible price

---

[35] This proof was based on that in Yosida (1974, p. 120).
[36] See Romer (1986) for an application to continuous time models.

system would require that consumption bundles of goods (not bads!) have non-negative values. Unambiguously larger bundles of goods should cost more.

The order structure should also be compatible with the topology. This may restrict the number of economically interesting locally convex Hausdorff topologies available on $\mathbf{E}$. In the case of s^m, this will leave us with only one appropriate topology—the product topology.

Let $\mathbf{E}$ be a Riesz space. We say $\mathbf{p} \in \mathbf{E}^*$ is *order bounded* if it maps order bounded subsets of $\mathbf{E}$ into bounded subsets of $\mathbb{R}$. The order bounded functionals form a linear space, which we denote $\mathbf{E}^\sim$. We define a partial order on $\mathbf{E}^\sim$ by $\mathbf{p} \geq \mathbf{q}$ if and only if $\langle \mathbf{p}, \mathbf{x} \rangle \geq \langle \mathbf{q}, \mathbf{x} \rangle$ for all $\mathbf{x} \in \mathbf{E}$. Note that any positive element of $\mathbf{E}^*$ is automatically order bounded since $\langle \mathbf{p}, \mathbf{a} \rangle \leq \langle \mathbf{p}, \mathbf{x} \rangle \leq \langle \mathbf{p}, \mathbf{b} \rangle$ for all $\mathbf{x} \in [\mathbf{a}, \mathbf{b}]$. If $\mathbf{E}$ has a Riesz norm, order bounded sets are bounded, and so $\mathbf{E}^\sim = \mathbf{E}'$. In this case, requiring that prices of non-negative bundles be non-negative automatically restricts our attention to the dual. The space $\mathbf{E}^\sim$ is actually a Riesz space.[37]

Theorem 17. *If $\mathbf{E}$ is a Riesz space, then $\mathbf{E}^\sim$ is a Dedekind complete Riesz space. Moreover,*

(1) $\mathbf{p} \vee \mathbf{q}(\mathbf{x}) = \sup\{\mathbf{p}(\mathbf{y}) + \mathbf{q}(\mathbf{z}) : \mathbf{y}, \mathbf{z} \in \mathbf{E}^+ \text{ and } \mathbf{y} + \mathbf{z} = \mathbf{x}\}$;
(2) $\mathbf{p} \wedge \mathbf{q}(\mathbf{x}) = \inf\{\mathbf{p}(\mathbf{y}) + \mathbf{q}(\mathbf{z}) : \mathbf{y}, \mathbf{z} \in \mathbf{E}^+ \text{ and } \mathbf{y} + \mathbf{z} = \mathbf{x}\}$

for all $\mathbf{p}, \mathbf{q} \in \mathbf{E}^\sim$, $\mathbf{x} \in \mathbf{E}^+$. In addition $\mathbf{p}^\alpha \downarrow \mathbf{0}$ is equivalent to $\mathbf{p}^\alpha(\mathbf{x}) \downarrow 0$ for each $\mathbf{x} \in \mathbf{E}^+$.

Given a band B in $\mathbf{E}$, define its *disjoint complement* B^d by $B^d = \{\mathbf{x} \in \mathbf{E} : |\mathbf{x}| \wedge |\mathbf{y}| = \mathbf{0} \text{ for all } \mathbf{y} \in B\}$. The following theorem will be useful in characterizing $(\ell^\infty)'$.[38] Recall a vector space $\mathbf{G}$ is the *direct sum* of two vector spaces $\mathbf{E}$ and $\mathbf{F}$ (denoted by $\mathbf{G} = \mathbf{E} \oplus \mathbf{F}$) if each $\mathbf{x} \in \mathbf{G}$ has a unique representation $\mathbf{x} = \mathbf{y} + \mathbf{z}$ for $\mathbf{y} \in \mathbf{E}$ and $\mathbf{z} \in \mathbf{F}$.

Theorem 18. *If B is a band in a Dedekind complete Riesz space $\mathbf{E}$, then $\mathbf{E} = B \oplus B^d$.*

Denote the set of order continuous linear functionals by $\mathbf{E}_n^\sim$. This is a band in $\mathbf{E}^\sim$, so $\mathbf{E}^\sim = \mathbf{E}_n^\sim \oplus (\mathbf{E}_n^\sim)^d$. We call $\mathbf{E}_\sigma^\sim = (\mathbf{E}_n^\sim)^d$ the space of *singular functionals*. For some spaces, $\mathbf{E}_\sigma^\sim = \{\mathbf{0}\}$.

We will now equip $\mathbf{E}$ with a linear topology τ compatible with both the linear and the lattice structures of the space. This requires a *locally convex-solid topology*, a locally convex topology with a base at zero consisting of sets that are absolutely convex and solid.[39]

Riesz Dual System. A dual pair of linear spaces $\langle \mathbf{E}, \mathbf{E}' \rangle$ is a Riesz dual

---

[37] Aliprantis and Burkinshaw (1985, p. 12).
[38] See Aliprantis and Burkinshaw (1985, p. 33).
[39] Note that any solid set is automatically balanced.

system if:

(1) $\mathbf{E}$ is a Riesz space;

(2) $\mathbf{E}'$ is an ideal of the order dual $\mathbf{E}^\sim$ separating the points of $\mathbf{E}$;

(3) the duality function $\langle\cdot,\cdot\rangle$ is the natural one given by the evaluation $\langle\mathbf{p},\mathbf{x}\rangle = \mathbf{p}(\mathbf{x}) \equiv \mathbf{px}$ for all $\mathbf{x}\in\mathbf{E}$ and all $\mathbf{p}\in\mathbf{E}'$.

All of the dual pairs we have studied in this chapter are Riesz dual systems. The assumption that $(\mathbf{E},\tau)$ is a locally convex-solid topology implies the dual system $\langle\mathbf{E},\mathbf{E}'\rangle$ is a Riesz dual system where $\mathbf{E}'$ is the τ-dual of $\mathbf{E}$.[40] The Riesz dual system $\langle\mathbf{E},\mathbf{E}'\rangle$ is *symmetric* whenever every order interval of $\mathbf{E}$ is $\sigma(\mathbf{E},\mathbf{E}')$-compact.[41] By Alaoglu's Theorem, the pairs $\langle\ell^p,\ell^q\rangle$ for $1 < p \le \infty$ constitute symmetric Riesz dual systems, as does the pair $\langle c_0,\ell^1\rangle$. By Tychonoff's Theorem, $\langle s^m,c_{00}\rangle$ is also a symmetric Riesz dual system. In the case of s^m there is only one (Hausdorff) locally convex-solid topology, the product topology.[42]

2.3.5 The Dual of ℓ^∞

We are now ready to finish our examination of the space ℓ^∞ and its dual. This space is worth extra attention as our commodity spaces will typically be contained in some $\ell^\infty(\beta)$, which is isometrically isomorphic to ℓ^∞. There are no less than four distinct topologies worthy of consideration, yielding two different duals. Besides the weak and norm topologies, ℓ^∞ has a weak* topology as the dual of ℓ^1. Moreover, the Mackey $(\tau(\ell^\infty,\ell^1))$ topology has also been used in economic applications (e.g., Bewley, 1972). The Mackey topology has a particularly simple characterization due to Conway (1967). It is equivalent to the *strict topology* defined by seminorms of the form

$$\|\mathbf{x}\|_\gamma = \sup_t |x_t\gamma_t|,$$

where $\lim_t \gamma_t = 0$. The Mackey neighborhoods are trumpet-shaped; they flare out at infinity. The Mackey topology on ℓ^∞ is finer than the β-topology since the β-norm is one of the seminorms used to define the Mackey topology. Of course, the dual of ℓ^∞ under the weak* or Mackey topologies will be ℓ^1.

We now turn our attention to the norm dual, which we denote ba. This can be regarded as a space of "measures" that are bounded and finitely additive, but are not necessarily countably additive. If A is a subset

---

[40] See Aliprantis, Brown, and Burkinshaw (1989, pp. 99, 101).

[41] There are several equivalent properties for symmetric Riesz dual systems. See Aliprantis, Brown, and Burkinshaw (1989, p. 102).

[42] See Aliprantis and Border (1994, p. 431).

of the positive integers, we can regard its characteristic function χ_A as a vector in ℓ^∞, by setting $(\chi_A)_t$ to 0 when $t \notin A$ and 1 when $t \in A$. Then $\mathbf{p} \in ba$ assigns "measure" $\langle \mathbf{p}, \chi_A \rangle$ to A. If $A_1, \ldots, A_N$ are disjoint and $A = \cup_{n=1}^N A_n$, then $\chi_A = \sum_{n=1}^N \chi_{A_n}$. Linearity then implies that the associated "measure" is finitely additive because $\langle \mathbf{p}, \chi_A \rangle = \sum_{n=1}^N \langle \mathbf{p}, \omega_{A_n} \rangle$. Such bounded (finitely) additive "measures" are sometimes called *charges*. However, it is not necessarily the case that $\sum_{n=1}^\infty \chi_{A_n}$ converges in ℓ^∞ for disjoint A_n. As a result, the "measure" need not be countably additive. Defining the integral in the usual way, we can represent ba as this collection of finitely additive measures on the positive integers.[43] When we want to emphasize the measure aspect of ba, we will write

$$\langle \pi, \mathbf{x} \rangle = \int \mathbf{x}(t) \, d\pi.$$

Now any element of ba can be written uniquely as the sum of an order continuous functional, and a functional that is orthogonal to the order continuous functionals. The order continuous functionals are easy to characterize.

Lemma 4. *A* $\mathbf{p} \in ba$ *is order continuous if and only if* $\mathbf{p} \in \ell^1$.

Proof. That $\mathbf{p} \in \ell^1$ is order continuous is trivial. We consider the case $\mathbf{p} \in ba$. Define $p_t = \langle \mathbf{p}, \mathbf{e}_t \rangle$. Note that $\sum_{t=1}^T (\operatorname{sgn} p_t) \mathbf{e}_t \xrightarrow{o} \mathbf{x}$ with $x_t = \operatorname{sgn} p_t$. Thus $\|\mathbf{p}\| \geq \sum_{t=1}^\infty |p_t| = \|\mathbf{p}\|_1$, so $(p_1, p_2, \ldots) \in \ell^1$. For $\mathbf{x} \in \ell^\infty$, $(x_1, \ldots, x_T, 0, \ldots) \xrightarrow{o} \mathbf{x}$, so $\mathbf{p} = (p_1, p_2, \ldots)$. $\square$

The order continuous (countably additive) elements of ba have natural price interpretations. However, there are continuous linear functionals on $(\ell^\infty, \| \cdot \|_\infty)$, such as Banach limits, which are not identifiable with price systems in this fashion. In fact, Banach limits are singular functionals.

Since ℓ^1 coincides with the band of order continuous functionals, we can now decompose ba into the direct sum $\ell^1 \oplus (\ell^1)^d$. Since ba contains elements that are not in ℓ^1, such as Banach limits, $(\ell^1)^d$ is non-trivial. We denote $(\ell^1)^d$ by pfa or pch, and refer to its elements as *purely finitely additive measures* or *pure charges*.

Yosida-Hewitt Theorem. *Any* $\mathbf{p} \in ba$ *can be uniquely written as a sum* $\mathbf{p} = \mathbf{p}_1 + \mathbf{p}_f$ *with* $\mathbf{p}_1 \in \ell^1$ *and* $\mathbf{p}_f \in pch$.[44]

Elements of pch must take the value zero on c_0. To see that, consider $\mathbf{p} \in pch$. Then $|\mathbf{p}| \wedge |\mathbf{e}_t| = 0$ since $\mathbf{e}_t \in \ell^1$. Now $0 = |\mathbf{p}| \wedge |\mathbf{e}_t|(\mathbf{e}_t) = \inf\{|\mathbf{p}(\lambda \mathbf{e}_t)| + \mathbf{e}_t((1-\lambda)\mathbf{e}_t) : 0 \leq \lambda \leq 1\}$ by Theorem 17. The infimum

---

[43] See Dunford and Schwartz (1957, pp. 160–168) or Bhaskara Rao and Bhaskara Rao (1983) for details.

[44] This is a special case of the Yosida-Hewitt Decomposition Theorem (Yosida and Hewitt, 1952; Bhaskara Rao and Bhaskara Rao, 1983, p. 241).

occurs when $\lambda = 1$, so $|\langle \mathbf{p}, \mathbf{e}_t \rangle| = 0$. By linearity, $\langle \mathbf{p}, \mathbf{x} \rangle = 0$ for all $\mathbf{x} \in c_{00}$. Finally, the facts that $\mathbf{p}$ is continuous and c_{00} is dense in c_0 imply $\langle \mathbf{p}, \mathbf{x} \rangle = 0$ for all $\mathbf{x} \in c_0$.

2.4 Conclusion

A distinguishing feature of Western music is its emphasis on harmony. The use of multiple melodies that harmonize well (polyphony or counterpoint) started in the Middle Ages. A simple example of counterpoint is a round, such as "Row, Row, Row Your Boat." The melody enters in a single voice. After a brief interval, a second voice starts another version of the melody while the first voice continues on with new material. Then a third voice enters with the original melody. A round just goes round and round like this (yielding a so-called contrapuntal canon). In principle, it can go on forever. The notes in a round must play dual roles. They not only carry the tune, but harmonize with it as well.

Like rounds, canons have a theme that harmonizes with itself. However, rather than merely repeating the first voice, other mappings between the first and other voices are permitted. The canons in J.S. Bach's *Musical Offering* and *The Art of Fugue* contain a variety of examples. Bach inverts themes, plays them backwards, alters their speeds, and otherwise transforms them, all the while maintaining harmony. Three of the canons are even puzzle canons. Bach gives enough information to recover the other parts from the theme, just as we can recover a utility function from an expenditure function. More recent developments have freed the harmonic parts from such close dependence on the melody. An extreme example is Charlie Parker's "Ko Ko," which puts an entirely different melody on top of the harmonic structure of the song "Cherokee."

Like harmony, duality plays a key role in modern economics. Consumer theory, general equilibrium, public finance, and the real theory of trade all use it heavily. Even when market prices are absent, shadow prices shed new light on the optimum, just as harmonic structures enhance our appreciation of a melody. In this chapter, we have developed the basic framework of commodity spaces and their dual price spaces. One interesting aspect of duality in infinite dimensional spaces is that a space may take part in several dual relations. In particular, the important commodity space ℓ^∞ can have either ℓ^1 or ba as dual, just as the same underlying harmonic structure can support two entirely different melodies.

CHAPTER 3

Representation of Recursive Preferences

3.1 Introduction

The properties of an agent's preference order on an infinite dimensional commodity space provide the economic primitives governing tastes in intertemporal choice models. Recursive preferences emerge as a further specialization of the axioms governing intertemporal preference orders. A better appreciation of the postulates giving rise to recursive utility functions may be grounded on a thorough development of basic preference and utility theory in an infinite dimensional framework. This exposes the limitations and range of the properties used to strengthen the underlying preference structure yielding recursive utility. Moreover, the use of a unified utility framework facilitates the classification of various objectives proposed in optimal growth theory into membership in the recursive or non-recursive class.

An important economic difference arises between finite and infinite dimensional commodity spaces in the specification of axioms governing choice. The differences in the two cases derive in part from important differences in the mathematical structure of the commodity spaces. For example, a finite dimensional vector space admits only one Hausdorff linear topology—all norms are topologically equivalent. An arbitrary infinite dimensional vector space admits many linear Hausdorff topologies—some of those topologies need not even be metrizable. The potential for multiple Hausdorff topologies to be associated with an arbitrary space is responsible for the emergence of subtle behavioral restrictions implied by the continuity axiom, which requires the closure of the upper and lower contour sets belonging to a preference order. In the infinite dimensional setting, the continuity of preference order assumption implies a behavioral restriction that may be interpreted as a form of impatience or myopia. The type of myopia exhibited by continuous preferences depends on the topology used. By reexamining the structural features of the preference order within a unified framework we hope to clarify the variety of forms of impatience that follow from the continuity postulate.

There are two approaches to the construction of recursive utility functions. The first is *axiomatic* and proceeds by specializing the basic postulates on intertemporal preference relations. The axiomatic approach leads to a representation of the utility function in the form of an aggregator over current consumption and prospective future utility. The axiomatic approach emphasizes structural properties of the preference order through the property requiring weak separability of future consumption goods from the current consumption good. The uniqueness of the resulting aggregator function may also be investigated. The alternative *aggregator model* treats the aggregator as the primitive concept and recovers utility from assumed properties of the aggregator. Postulating the aggregator as the economic primitive is analogous to the practice of specifying alternative foundations for standard consumer choice theory. Duality methods (expenditure and indirect utility functions) are commonly used in finite dimensional commodity space models as the economic primitive representing tastes. These traditional models utilize prices to axiomatize preferences and recover all the information in the preference order. The aggregator model avoids duality notions which are more subtle in the infinite dimensional case compared to static finite dimensional theory. We develop both the axiomatic and aggregator approaches in this chapter. The question of the uniqueness of the utility function is investigated for the aggregator model. The axiomatic method was initiated by Koopmans (1960) whereas the aggregator model was first proposed by Lucas and Stokey (1984).

One advantage of taking the aggregator as the foundational building block is that economic intuition gained from studying a two-dimensional commodity space may more readily give insights into the interpretation of specific preference notions. Aggregators may also be easily written down and translated into computer code. There are examples of aggregators where the corresponding functional form for the utility function remains unknown. The general theory may be invoked to show that the proposed aggregator is consistent with some utility function.

3.2 Preference Orders and Utility Theory

Preference orders are defined over a fixed commodity space, $\mathbf{E}$. The space $\mathbf{E}$ is usually assigned a linear Hausdorff topology denoted by τ. The real-valued τ-continuous linear functionals on $\mathbf{E}$ constitute price systems. Following the seminal work of Debreu (1954a) we choose a dual pair $\langle \mathbf{E}, \mathbf{E}' \rangle$ for the commodity-price duality. We require $\langle \mathbf{E}, \mathbf{E}' \rangle$ to be a Riesz dual system with $\mathbf{E}$ a Riesz subspace of s^m. The preference relation of the planning agent is denoted by $\succsim$. The planning agent might be a central planner as in optimal growth theory or an infinitely lived household in an intertemporal market setup. We assume the following preference axioms.

Preference Axioms.

(P1) $\succsim$ is a preference order: it is a reflexive, complete, and transitive binary relation.

(P2) $\succsim$ is a monotone relation: $\mathbf{x} \geq \mathbf{y}$ in $\mathbf{E}_+$ implies $\mathbf{x} \succsim \mathbf{y}$.

(P3) $\succsim$ is a convex relation: the set $\{\mathbf{y} \in \mathbf{E}_+ : \mathbf{y} \succsim \mathbf{x}\}$ is convex for each $\mathbf{x} \in \mathbf{E}_+$.

A stronger version of the monotonicity axiom (P2) is used in many applications.

Strict Monotonicity.

(P2′) $\succsim$ is a strictly monotone relation: $\mathbf{x}, \mathbf{y} \in \mathbf{E}_+$ with $\mathbf{x} \geq \mathbf{y}$ and $\mathbf{x} \neq \mathbf{y}$ implies $\mathbf{x} \succ \mathbf{y}$.

Properties (P1)–(P3) of the preference relation are based on the algebraic and order structures of $\mathbf{E}$. Topological considerations will be introduced shortly in the form of continuity hypotheses. The derived strict preference relation $\succ$ is defined by $\mathbf{x} \succ \mathbf{y}$ if $\mathbf{x} \succsim \mathbf{y}$ and not $\mathbf{y} \succsim \mathbf{x}$. The indifference relation $\sim$ is defined by $\mathbf{x} \sim \mathbf{y}$ if $\mathbf{x} \succsim \mathbf{y}$ and $\mathbf{y} \succsim \mathbf{x}$ hold.

Endow $\mathbf{E}$ with a linear topology τ. Continuity of the preference relation says roughly that programs that are close to one another are ranked similarly with respect to other profiles. More formally:

Continuous Preferences.

(P4) $\succsim$ is a continuous relation: the sets $\{\mathbf{x} \in \mathbf{E}_+ : \mathbf{y} \succsim \mathbf{x}\}$ and $\{\mathbf{x} \in \mathbf{E}_+ : \mathbf{x} \succsim \mathbf{y}\}$ are τ-closed.

The continuity hypothesis is fundamental. The variety of alternative topologies for $\mathbf{E}$ raises the question of whether or not there are behavioral implications implicit in the choice of a particular topology for $\mathbf{E}$. We will take up many of these issues in Section 3.4.

It is worth noting that there are examples of preference orders which fail the continuity test on all of s^m. Time additive separable utility functions need not be continuous, or even defined, on all of s^m.

▶ Example 1: Continuity and TAS preferences. Consider the following relation on $\ell_+^\infty(\alpha) \subset s_+^1$:

$$\mathbf{x} \succsim \mathbf{y} \text{ if and only if } \sum_{t=1}^\infty \delta^{t-1} x_t^\rho \geq \sum_{t=1}^\infty \delta^{t-1} y_t^\rho,$$

where $\delta, \rho \in (0,1)$ and $\delta\alpha^\rho < 1$. In this example, α is a parameter representing the growth rate of capital in the optimal accumulation model or the growth rate of the endowment in an exchange economy. Note that this utility function does not even make sense on all of s_+^1 (e.g., $x_t = \delta^{-t/\rho}$

yields a divergent sum). However, it does converge on the positive orthant of the principal ideal $\ell^\infty(\alpha)$ since if $\mathbf{x} \in \ell^\infty_+(\alpha)$, $0 \le x_t \le a\alpha^t$ for some a. This implies $0 \le \delta^{t-1}x_t^\rho \le (a\alpha)^\rho(\delta\alpha^\rho)^{t-1}$ and the utility sum converges because $(\delta\alpha^\rho)^{t-1}$ is a convergent series for $\delta\alpha^\rho < 1$. This is a typical occurrence, and a major motivation for our interest in the principal ideals A_ω.

Beals and Koopmans (1969) showed this preference relation is not continuous at the origin of $\ell^\infty_+(\alpha)$ in the Fréchet metric d_F. However, it will turn out that this relation is continuous on a subset of the commodity space consistent with the feasible allocations. The continuity failure results from the upper contour set at many vectors $\mathbf{y}$ failing to be d_F-closed. Consider the vector $\mathbf{y} = (1, 0, \dots)$, and let $x_t^n = 0$ for $t \ne n$ and $x_t^n = \delta^{(1-n)/\rho}$ for $t = n$. Then $\mathbf{x}^n \succsim \mathbf{y}$. Now $\mathbf{x}^n \to \mathbf{0}$ in the d_F-topology. If the upper contour set $\{\mathbf{x} \in \ell^\infty_+(\alpha) : \mathbf{x} \succsim \mathbf{y}\}$ were d_F-closed, we could conclude $\mathbf{0} \succsim \mathbf{y}$. But $\mathbf{0} \prec \mathbf{y}$, and so the upper contour set cannot be closed. ◄

▶ **Example 2: The maximin criterion.** Consider the dual pairing $\langle s^1, c_{00} \rangle$ where s^1 has the Fréchet metric topology. The Rawls maximin preference order is defined by

$$\mathbf{x} \succsim \mathbf{y} \text{ if and only if } \inf_t x_t \ge \inf_t y_t.$$

It is not continuous in the Fréchet distance, although $\{\mathbf{y} \in \mathbf{E}_+ : \mathbf{y} \succsim \mathbf{x}\}$ is d_F-closed. The problem is that $\{\mathbf{y} \in \mathbf{E}_+ : \mathbf{x} \succsim \mathbf{y}\}$ need not be a d_F-closed set, as the sequence $\mathbf{y}^n$ defined by $y_t^n = 1$ for $t = 1, \dots, n$; $y_t^n = 0$ for $t = n+1, \dots$ shows for $\mathbf{x} = \mathbf{0}$. ◄

A *utilitarian criterion* adds the felicities for a sequence of one-period rewards in order to evaluate a prospective program. The strongest statement of the utilitarian objective in capital theory is found in Ramsey's (1928) seminal paper on optimal saving. He argued the planner should not discount future utility. His model corresponds to the TAS case with $\delta = 1$. One obvious difficulty is that the sequence of partial felicity sums, $\{\sum_{t=1}^T u(c_t)\}_{T=1}^\infty$, need not converge. Ramsey rescaled the utility functional to induce convergence by shifting the origin of the felicity function to the *bliss level*; intertemporal utility according to the utilitarian criterion is defined for a subset of feasible programs. Modern researchers beginning with von Weizsäcker (1965) have formulated the planner's preference order in the undiscounted case using an overtaking criterion.[1] This formulation of the preference criterion does not depend on convergence of

---

[1] The overtaking criterion is an example of an *extended utilitarian objective*. The adjective "extended" means the summation of felicities in the utilitarian criterion has been modified for infinite horizon planning problems.

the felicity sums since comparisons are only made over initial segments. The golden rule is used in place of bliss to define a renormalized utility function. The trick is to use the golden rule as the new zero value of the felicity function. This transformation of the felicity function preserves the ordering of programs according to the overtaking criterion. The importance of overtaking criteria in the optimal growth literature is reason enough to include this order in our example catalog.[2]

▶ Example 3: The overtaking criterion and the golden rule. A profile c' *overtakes* c if

$$\liminf_{T \to \infty} \sum_{t=1}^{T} [u(c'_t) - u(c_t)] > 0.$$

An easy calculation shows that c' is eventually better than c by some strictly positive amount.[3] Program c' is better than c if c' overtakes c.

There is an obvious way to form a weak preference relation by using a weak inequality. Define c' *weakly overtakes* c if

$$\liminf_{T \to \infty} \sum_{t=1}^{T} [u(c'_t) - u(c_t)] \geq 0.$$

This fails to define a complete ordering as the utility sums may alternate in sign. This occurs if we try to compare the paths

$$(1, 0, 0, 1, 1, 0, 0, \ldots) \text{ and}$$
$$(0, 1, 1, 0, 0, 1, 1, \ldots).$$

Let f denote the one-sector neoclassical production function assumed to obey standard concavity assumptions and exhibit a positive maximum sustainable stock. If there is a k that maximizes $f(k) - k$ (thus 1 is a supergradient of f at k), then k is called the *golden-rule stock* and denoted by k_g.[4] When f is strictly concave, there is at most one such k. Assume that f is strictly concave and a positive golden-rule stock exists. There is an associated positive *golden-rule consumption* level $c_g = f(k_g) - k_g$. This is the maximum possible steady-state consumption.

The overtaking criterion can be simplified on the feasible set by comparing each feasible program to the golden rule. A profile c is said to be a *good program* if there is an $M > -\infty$ with $\sum_{t=1}^{T} [u(c_t) - u(c_g)] \geq M$ for all

---

[2] The overtaking criterion is also prominent in the theory of repeated games. See Rubinstein (1979).

[3] See Hieber (1981) for a thorough discussion of various overtaking criteria. Brock (1970a) gives an axiomatic characterization of the overtaking criterion.

[4] We say that p is a *supergradient of f* at a if $f(x) \leq f(a) + p(x - a)$. When f is differentiable at a and concave, $p = f'(a)$ is the only supergradient.

T. It follows that a program is good if and only if it is not infinitely worse than the golden rule, that is, $\liminf_{T \to \infty} \sum_{t=1}^{T}[u(c_t) - u(c_g)] > -\infty$. Programs that are not good are called *bad programs*. Goodness fits in well with the overtaking criterion. Anything that overtakes a good program is also good. More precisely, if $\mathbf{c}'$ overtakes $\mathbf{c}$, and $\mathbf{c}$ is good, then a routine calculation shows $\mathbf{c}'$ is also good.

When both u and f are strictly concave, good programs must converge to the golden rule. To see this, first note that $u(c_t) - u(c_g) \leq p(c_t - c_g) = p(f(k_{t-1}) - k_t - f(k_g) + k_g)$ where p is a supergradient of u at c_g. Equality holds only when $c_t = c_g$. Now $f(k_{t-1}) \leq f(k_g) + (k_{t-1} - k_g)$ with equality only when $k_{t-1} = k_g$ since f is strictly concave and 1 is a supergradient of f at k_g. Thus the *value loss* $L(k_{t-1}, k_t) \equiv p(k_{t-1} - k_t) - u(c_t) + u(c_g)$ is non-negative, and is zero only when $k_{t-1} = k_g$ and $c_t = c_g$ (equivalently, $k_{t-1} = k_t = k_g$). Because consumption at time t is the output produced with k_{t-1} that is not devoted to capital k_t intended for production in the next period, we could write the value loss as

$$L(k_{t-1}, k_t) = p(k_{t-1} - k_t) - u(f(k_{t-1}) - k_t) + u(c_g).$$

Intuitively, the value loss is comprised of three parts, all involving comparisons with the golden rule: the direct utility loss, $u(c_g) - u(c_t)$, the lost value of capital goods to be used in next period's production (valued at the golden rule utility price of capital p) $p(k_g - k_t)$, and finally, the loss from using excessive inputs (valued at the golden rule price p, multiplied by the marginal product $f'(k_g) = 1$ of last period's capital stock), $p(k_{t-1} - k_g)$. Although the total loss is non-negative, individual pieces of it may be negative, indicating a gain compared to the golden rule.

The definition of L implies

$$\sum_{t=1}^{T}[u(c_t) - u(c_g)] = pk - pk_T - \sum_{t=1}^{T} L(k_{t-1}, k_t),$$

where k is the initial capital stock. Since $k_T \geq 0$, it follows that $L(k_{t-1}, k_t) \to 0$ for good programs. By convexity of L, and the fact that $L(k_{t-1}, k_t) = 0$ only at $k_{t-1} = k_t = k_g$, this implies $k_t \to k_g$ (the *turnpike property*).

By comparing programs to the golden rule we can define the *renormalized utility function* by

$$U_R(\mathbf{c}) = p(k - k_g) - \sum_{t=1}^{\infty} L(k_{t-1}, k_t).$$

Clearly $U_R(\mathbf{c}) = \sum_{t=1}^{\infty}[u(c_t) - u(c_g)]$ for good programs. As the infimum of upper semicontinuous functions, the renormalized utility function is upper semicontinuous. Further, whenever $U_R(\mathbf{c})$ is finite, the value loss converges to zero, and the turnpike property holds. It follows from the above calculations that $U_R(\mathbf{c}) = \sum_{t=1}^{\infty}[u(c_t) - u(c_g)]$ and $\mathbf{c}$ is good whenever $U_R(\mathbf{c})$ is finite. Thus, a profile $\mathbf{c}' \succsim \mathbf{c}$ according to the overtaking criterion if and only if $U_R(\mathbf{c}') \geq U_R(\mathbf{c})$. ◀

The importance of the golden rule in defining a renormalized utility function to represent the overtaking order is illustrated in the next example.

▶ Example 4: Cake-eating and utility values. Suppose utility has the undiscounted form $U(\mathbf{c}) = \lim_{T \to \infty} \sum_{t=1}^{T} u(c_t)$. The cake-eating technology is $f(k) = k$. With this technology, a path $\mathbf{c} \geq \mathbf{0}$ is feasible when $\sum_{t=1}^{\infty} c_t \leq k_0$ holds where k_0 is the given amount of the cake (initial capital). We start with a fixed amount of cake and eat it over time. If $u(c) = -1/c$, then $c_t \to 0$ implies $u(c_t) \to -\infty$ and so $U(\mathbf{c}) = -\infty$ for every feasible path. Overtaking cannot help us here. Although any capital stock is a golden rule, the corresponding consumption $c_g = 0$ yields felicity $u(c_g) = -\infty$. Thus good programs cannot be defined. ◀

Continuity of the preference relation is important for establishing the existence of optimal allocations. Clearly, only the set $\{\mathbf{y} \in \mathbf{E}_+ : \mathbf{y} \succsim \mathbf{x}\}$ need be τ-closed for the existence of optimal allocations in the presence of a τ-compact constraint set. This is equivalent to upper semicontinuity of the utility function. The preference orders generated by Examples 2 and 3 have only upper semicontinuous utility functions. The existence of optimal programs according to various criteria will be discussed in Chapter 4.

Continuity of $\succsim$ also is critical in demonstrating the existence of a utility function which carries the properties of the preference relation in a convenient analytical format. Since most of optimal growth theory is cast in the framework of a utility representation of the planner's preference order, it is natural to present conditions sufficient for the existence of a continuous representation of $\succsim$.

A function $U: \mathcal{X} \to \mathbb{R}$ is a *utility function representing* $\succsim$ on a set $\mathcal{X} \subset \mathbf{E}_+$ provided

$$\mathbf{x} \succsim \mathbf{y} \text{ if and only if } U(\mathbf{x}) \geq U(\mathbf{y}).$$

Many preference orders in economic dynamics are defined in terms of utility functions or have obvious representations in terms of utility functions. The additive separable function in Example 1 and maximin preference order in Example 2 are formulated using a function defined on the commodity space. The overtaking order in Example 3 is represented by the renormalized utility function. More generally, it is desirable to have sufficient conditions on a preference order to represent it as a utility function.

The following theorem of Debreu (1954b; 1959) gives one answer to this representation problem.

Separable Representation Theorem. *Suppose $\succsim$ is a continuous preference relation ((P1) and (P4) hold) on a separable connected set $\mathcal{X}$. Then $\succsim$ is represented by a continuous utility function U.*

The Separable Representation Theorem applies to preference orders on $\mathcal{X} = s_+^m$ where $\mathcal{X}$ is given the relative product topology inherited from s^m. As s^m is a separable space, a continuous utility function exists given (P1) and (P4). Another application occurs in the case $\mathcal{X} = \ell^\infty(\alpha)$ equipped with the β-topology ($\beta > \alpha$), which is also a separable normed space. In fact, it is isomorphic to a dense subspace of c_0.

As a topological space, $(\ell^\infty, \|\cdot\|_\infty)$ is not separable. Thus, even if $\succsim$ is $\|\cdot\|_\infty$-continuous on ℓ^∞, we cannot apply the Separable Representation Theorem in order to represent $\succsim$ by a continuous utility function. However, Mas-Colell (1986) exploited the order structure of $\mathbf{E}$ and the monotonicity axiom (P2) in the manner of Kannai (1970) to deduce the existence of a continuous utility representation of $\succsim$ on a portion of the program space.

Monotone Representation Theorem. *Suppose $\succsim$ is a continuous monotonic preference relation ((P1), (P2), and (P4) hold) on a non-empty order interval $\mathcal{X} \subset \mathbf{E}_+$. Then there is a continuous utility function $U \colon \mathcal{X} \to [0,1]$ representing the preference relation $\succsim$.*[5]

Proof. Let $\mathcal{X} = [\mathbf{a}, \mathbf{b}]$ where $\mathbf{a}, \mathbf{b} \in \mathbf{E}_+$. Since $\mathbf{b} \geq \mathbf{a}$, (P2) implies $\mathbf{b} \succsim \mathbf{a}$. If $\mathbf{a} \succsim \mathbf{b}$, there is nothing to prove. So, let $\mathbf{b} \succ \mathbf{a}$. Consider the set

$$J = \{\theta\mathbf{a} + (1 - \theta)\mathbf{b} : 0 \leq \theta \leq 1\}.$$

Since J is topologically a segment, Debreu's Separable Representation Theorem yields a continuous $f \colon J \to [0,1]$ such that $f(\mathbf{a}) = 0$, $f(\mathbf{b}) = 1$, and $f(\mathbf{x}) \geq f(\mathbf{y})$ whenever $\mathbf{x}, \mathbf{y} \in J$ and $\mathbf{x} \succsim \mathbf{y}$. For any $\mathbf{x} \in \mathcal{X}$ let $v(\mathbf{x})$ be such that $v(\mathbf{x}) \in J$ and $v(\mathbf{x}) \sim \mathbf{x}$. Because J is connected and can be written as the union of the non-empty closed sets $\{\mathbf{y} \in J : \mathbf{y} \succsim \mathbf{x}\}$ and $\{\mathbf{y} \in J : \mathbf{x} \succsim \mathbf{y}\}$, such a $v(\mathbf{x})$ must exist. Now set $U(\mathbf{x}) = f(v(\mathbf{x}))$. Obviously, U is a well-defined utility function. Since U is onto $[0,1]$, given any $t \in [0,1]$, there exists an $\mathbf{x} \in \mathcal{X}$ such that $U(\mathbf{x}) = t$. The sets

$$U^{-1}[t, \infty) = \{\mathbf{y} : \mathbf{y} \succsim \mathbf{x}\};$$
$$U^{-1}(-\infty, t] = \{\mathbf{y} : \mathbf{x} \succsim \mathbf{y}\}$$

are closed by (P4). Therefore U is continuous. $\square$

---

[5] The proof is a slight repackaging of Mas-Colell (1986, p. 1044).

The Monotone Representation Theorem applies to Beals and Koopmans's example (Example 1) when $\mathcal{X} = [0, 1]$ and ℓ^∞ has the sup-norm topology. In the optimal growth model, define an order interval by taking ω to be the path of pure accumulation with seed k_0. If there is a maximum sustainable stock $k^M > 0$ and the production function is stationary, then the order interval $[0, \omega]$ with $\omega_t = k^M$ works. Growth can also be captured using $\ell^\infty(\alpha)$ with $\alpha > 1$. The Monotone Representation Theorem implies that a preference order defined over $\mathbf{E}_+$ may only admit a continuous utility function on $[0, \omega]$. This order interval is sufficiently "large" to contain *all* economically relevant consumption programs. Paths offering consumption $\mathbf{c} \notin [0, \omega]$ cannot be realized by any feasible plan of accumulation given the initial stocks. As such, those programs may be ignored for the theory developed to analyze the existence and characterization of optimal allocations. Finally, we remark that the order property of $\mathbf{E}$ was the critical structural feature of the choice space used to obtain the representation of the preference relation.

3.3 Recursive Utility: the Koopmans Axioms

Theories of intertemporal decision making further specialize the axiom system (P1)–(P4) to capture the essential role of time in the preference order. The purpose of this section is to investigate the axiomatic basis of a recursive representation of $\succsim$. Let $\mathcal{X} \subset s^m$ with $S\mathcal{X} \subset \mathcal{X}$, and set $X = \pi\mathcal{X}$ where π is the *projection* defined by $\pi\mathbf{x} = x_1$. Given a preference order $\succsim$ on $\mathcal{X}$, a utility representation U of $\succsim$ is a *recursive utility function* if there is a function $u \colon X \to \mathbb{R}$ and a real-valued function W defined on $u(X) \times U(\mathcal{X})$ such that

$$U(\mathbf{c}) = W(u(c_1), U(S\mathbf{c})). \tag{1}$$

The function W is called the *aggregator* and equation (1) is called *Koopmans's equation*. We refer to u as the *felicity function*. A recursive utility function expresses the weak separability of the future from the present. Fisher's two-period conception of an agent contemplating current consumption and future utility may be modeled by recursive utility functions.

Many examples previously introduced in Chapter 1 fall under the recursive utility definition. For the TAS case, the aggregator is $W(c, y) = u(c) + \delta y$ with utility function $U(\mathbf{c}) = \sum_{t=1}^\infty \delta^{t-1} u(c_t)$. The EH functional has $W(c, y) = (-1 + y)\exp(-v(c))$ as an aggregator and utility given by $U(\mathbf{c}) = -\sum_{t=1}^\infty \exp{-[\sum_{\tau=1}^t v(c_\tau)]}$. The maximin aggregator is $W(c, y) = \min\{c, y\}$ with $U(\mathbf{c}) = \inf_t c_t$.

3.3.1 The Axioms

We start by describing sufficient conditions for $\succsim$ to exhibit a recursive utility representation. The axiom system employed differs slightly from that in Koopmans (1960). Let $\mathcal{X}$ be a path-connected subspace of $\mathbf{E}_+$ with $S\mathcal{X} \subset \mathcal{X}$. The notation $(z, \mathbf{x})$ denotes the sequence $(z, x_1, x_2, \ldots)$. We assume the shift operator S defined on $\mathbf{E}$ is continuous as is the embedding $z \mapsto (z, \mathbf{x})$ of $\mathbf{x}$ into $\mathbf{E}$ for each $\mathbf{x}$. The projection of $\mathbf{E}_+$ onto the first coordinate subspace is denoted $\pi\mathbf{E}_+$.

Koopmans's Axioms. Koopmans's axioms are:

- (K1) $\succsim$ is a stationary relation: $(z, \mathbf{x}) \succsim (z, \mathbf{x}')$ for all $z \in \pi\mathcal{X}$ if and only if $\mathbf{x} \succsim \mathbf{x}'$.
- (K2) $\succsim$ exhibits limited independence: for all $z, z' \in \pi\mathcal{X}$ and $\mathbf{x}, \mathbf{x}' \in \mathcal{X}$, $(z, \mathbf{x}) \succsim (z', \mathbf{x})$ if and only if $(z, \mathbf{x}') \succsim (z', \mathbf{x}')$.
- (K3) $\succsim$ is a sensitive relation: there is an $\mathbf{x} \in \mathcal{X}$ and a $z, z' \in \pi\mathcal{X}$ with $(z', \mathbf{x}) \succ (z, \mathbf{x})$.

Axiom (K1) states that preferences over future consumption streams are independent of the level of current consumption. This makes the preference order independent of calendar time. Merely postponing a decision between two programs will not alter their rank order. The time inconsistency problem raised by Strotz (1955) does not arise when preferences are stationary. Axiom (K2) says that preferences between present consumption alternatives are independent of future consumption. Under (K2) we may evaluate consumption today without knowing what we will consume in the future. Whatever we do consume will not alter our preferences toward consumption today. Axiom (K3) rules out complete indifference between levels of current consumption. It ensures that the preference order is non-trivial. Note that sensitivity follows from strict monotonicity (P2').

Obviously, Koopmans's equation implies (K1)–(K3) for recursive utility functions. Koopmans's (1960) result is that (K1)–(K3) are sufficient for $\succsim$ to have a recursive utility representation. In such cases, we say that the preference order is *recursively separable*.

Recursive Representation Theorem. *Suppose a preference relation $\succsim$ satisfies axioms (P1)–(P4) and the Koopmans axioms (K1)–(K3) on a path-connected set $\mathcal{X} \subset \mathbf{E}$. If $\succsim$ has a continuous utility representation U, then there are continuous functions $u \colon \mathcal{X} \to \mathbb{R}$ and $W \colon \mathbb{R}^2 \to \mathbb{R}$ with $U(\mathbf{c}) = W(u(\pi\mathbf{c}), U(S\mathbf{c}))$. Further, W is non-decreasing in each of its arguments.*

Proof. Take $\mathbf{c}_0 \in \mathcal{X}$ and define $u(z) = U(z, \mathbf{c}_0)$. Note that $u(z) = u(y)$ is equivalent to $U(z, \mathbf{c}_0) = U(y, \mathbf{c}_0)$ which is in turn equivalent to

$U(z, \mathbf{c}) = U(y, \mathbf{c})$ for all $\mathbf{c}$ by (K2). Since U depends only on $u(z)$, there is a function F with $U(z, \mathbf{c}) = F(u(z), \mathbf{c})$.

Now if $U(\mathbf{c}) = U(\mathbf{c}'), U(z, \mathbf{c}) = U(z, \mathbf{c}')$ for all z by (K1). Thus F depends on $\mathbf{c}$ only through $U(\mathbf{c})$, so there is a function W with $U(z, \mathbf{c}) = W(u(z), U(\mathbf{c}))$.

To show W is non-decreasing, consider z and z' with $u = u(z) \geq u(z') = u'$. Then $U(z, \mathbf{c}_0) \geq U(z', \mathbf{c}_0)$ so $U(z, \mathbf{c}) \geq U(z', \mathbf{c})$ for all $\mathbf{c}$. Applying the definitions to the last inequality yields $W(u, U(\mathbf{c})) \geq W(u', U(\mathbf{c}))$. A similar argument shows that W is non-decreasing in U. Continuity follows from the following lemma.[6] □

Lemma 1. *If U is continuous, then u and W are continuous.*

Proof. Since $u(z) = U(z, \mathbf{c}_0)$, u is continuous.

We next show W is separately continuous in u and U. Fix $u = u(z)$ and let $U_n \uparrow U$. Take $\mathbf{c}_1$ and $\mathbf{c}$ with $U(\mathbf{c}_1) = U_1$ and $U(\mathbf{c}) = U$. Since $\mathcal{X}$ is a path-connected space we can take a path $\{\mathbf{c}(t)\}$ in $\mathcal{X}$ from $\mathbf{c}_1$ to $\mathbf{c}$. Clearly $U(\{\mathbf{c}(t)\}) \supset [U_1, U]$ since $U(\{\mathbf{c}(t)\})$ is connected and contains both $U(\mathbf{c}_1)$ and $U(\mathbf{c})$. Take t_n with $U(\mathbf{c}(t_n)) = U_n$. Let t^* be any cluster point of $\{t_n\}$. As $\mathbf{c}(t_n) \rightarrow \mathbf{c}(t^*)$, we have $W(u, U_n) = U(z, \mathbf{c}(t_n)) \rightarrow U(z, \mathbf{c}(t^*)) = W(z, U)$. This also applies to $U_n \downarrow U$, so W is continuous in U for fixed u. Similarly, W is continuous in u for fixed U.

Finally, we combine separate continuity with monotonicity to obtain joint continuity. Let $(u_n, U_n) \rightarrow (u, U)$. Define $v_n = \sup_{m \geq n} u_m$, $V_n = \sup_{m \geq n} U_m$, $y_n = \inf_{m \geq n} u_m$, and $Y_n = \inf_{m \geq n} U_m$. Then $(y_n, Y_n) \leq (u_n, U_n) \leq (v_n, V_n)$, so

$$W(y_n, Y_n) \leq W(u_n, U_n) \leq W(v_n, V_n).$$

Fix m, then for $n \geq m$:

$$W(v_m, V_n) \geq W(v_n, V_n) \geq W(u, U)$$

because $(v_n, V_n) \geq (u, U)$ and $v_m \geq v_n$. By letting $n \rightarrow \infty$ and using the continuity of W in U, we see that

$$W(v_m, U) \geq \lim_n W(v_n, V_n) \geq W(u, U).$$

Now let $m \rightarrow \infty$ to see $\lim_n W(v_n, V_n) = W(u, U)$. Using a similar argument on (y_n, Y_n) shows $\lim_n W(y_n, Y_n) = W(u, U)$. Finally, the fact that $\lim_n W(u_n, U_n)$ is squeezed between these limits completes the proof. □

Remark. If monotonicity axiom (P2) is strengthened to (P2′), then W is strictly increasing in future utility.

---

[6] Note that continuity was not required to obtain either u or W.

Remark. When $\mathcal{X} \subset s^1$, we can incorporate u into W without loss of generality, writing $U(\mathbf{c}) = W(c_1, U(S\mathbf{c}))$. This would be a mistake in s^m for $m > 1$ as a utility function could then obey Koopmans's equation but fail limited independence. This would happen if the marginal rate of substitution between two types of current consumption depended on future utility.

Koopmans (1960) and Koopmans, Diamond, and Williamson (1964) assume $\succsim$ is continuous with respect to the sup-norm topology. However, as noted subsequently in Koopmans (1972b), this type of uniform continuity is not required for the Recursive Representation Theorem.

The Recursive Representation Theorem assumes $\succsim$ has a continuous utility representation. If $\mathcal{X}$ is an order interval and (P2) is strengthened to (P2'), then the Monotone Representation Theorem implies utility is recursive.

Corollary 1. *If $\mathcal{X}$ is an order interval in $\mathbf{E}_+$ and (P1), (P2'), (P3), (P4), and (K1)–(K3) hold for a preference order $\succsim$, then $\succsim$ has a recursive utility representation.*

If $\mathcal{X}$ is a separable space, then this also holds by the Separable Representation Theorem. For example, consider the space $\ell^\infty(\alpha)$ endowed with the $\|\cdot\|_\beta$-norm, and having $\beta > \alpha$. This is a separable space and pathwise-connected normed linear space. Therefore, any preference order on $\ell^\infty(\alpha)$ which is β-continuous, stationary, and obeys the limited independence and sensitivity axioms must have a recursive representation.

Note that the aggregator depends on the utility representation we use. A monotonic transformation of utility would change the aggregator. In fact, if we apply the monotonic transformation φ, the new utility function $\varphi \circ U$ has aggregator $V(u, y) = \varphi \circ W(u, \varphi^{-1} \circ y)$. For example, raising U to the γ power transforms W to $V(u, y) = [W(u, y^{1/\gamma})]^\gamma$. In deterministic models, we are free to pick the form that is most convenient to work with. In stochastic models, such transformations alter risk aversion. This fact has been exploited by Epstein and Zin (1989), who use it to generate a form of non-expected utility.

The role of Koopmans's sensitivity axiom is to ensure a non-trivial representation of U in terms of the aggregator. If sensitivity fails, then utility functions such as $U(\mathbf{c}) = \Lambda(\mathbf{c})$ on $\mathcal{X} = \ell^\infty_+(\alpha)$ are admissible where Λ is a Banach limit. Recalling the definition from Chapter 2:

Banach Limit. A Banach limit is a linear functional such that:

   (1) $\Lambda(\mathbf{c}) \geq 0$ if $\mathbf{c} \geq \mathbf{0}$;
   (2) $\Lambda(\mathbf{c}) = \Lambda(S^N\mathbf{c})$ for $N = 1, 2, \ldots$;
   (3) $\liminf_t c_t \leq \Lambda(\mathbf{c}) \leq \limsup_t c_t$.

Given a Banach limit Λ, a preference order is induced on $\ell^\infty_+(\alpha)$ with the sup-norm topology by defining $\mathbf{x} \succsim \mathbf{y}$ if and only if $\Lambda(\mathbf{x}) \geq \Lambda(\mathbf{y})$. Note that (1) implies (P2): if $\mathbf{x} \geq \mathbf{y}$, then $\mathbf{x} - \mathbf{y} \geq \mathbf{0}$ and (2) implies $\Lambda(\mathbf{x} - \mathbf{y}) \geq 0$, hence $\Lambda(\mathbf{x}) \geq \Lambda(\mathbf{y})$. Banach limit utility functions obey the aggregator $W(u, y) = y$ by property (2) and are not properly represented by the aggregator since every Banach limit has this same aggregator. If utility is given by a Banach limit, $U(\mathbf{c}) = \Lambda(\mathbf{c})$, then $\Lambda(\mathbf{c}) = \Lambda(c_1, S\mathbf{c}) = \Lambda(S\mathbf{c})$ by (2). Thus, if W is any aggregator satisfying the recursive relation $W(c_1, U(S\mathbf{c})) = U(\mathbf{c})$, then $\Lambda(\mathbf{c}) = W(c_1, \Lambda(S\mathbf{c})) = W(c_1, \Lambda(\mathbf{c})) = \Lambda(\mathbf{c}) = U(\mathbf{c})$, and $W(u, y) = y$ is the only aggregator that works with Banach limits.[7]

▶ Example 5: Long-run average criterion and Banach limits. The long-run average criterion is a variant of the utilitarian criterion based upon averaging the felicity sums over time.[8] The average consumption function is clearly a special case of the long-run average criterion; utility according to this objective functional is defined by the formula

$$U(\mathbf{c}) = \lim_{T \to \infty} \frac{1}{T} \sum_{t=1}^{T} c_t,$$

where $\mathbf{c} \in \{\mathbf{x} \in \ell^{\infty} : \lim_{T \to \infty} \frac{1}{T} \sum_{t=1}^{T} x_t < \infty\}$. The Hahn-Banach Theorem implies that $U(\mathbf{c})$ can be extended to a Banach limit on ℓ_+^{∞}, and that the extension is not unique. Thus, the long-run average criterion does not generate a utility function which is uniquely represented by an aggregator. ◀

3.3.2 Biconvergence

Koopmans's Recursive Representation Theorem says that a recursively separable utility function determines a unique recursive aggregator W. Streufert (1990) investigated the converse: does W uniquely determine U?[9] This uniqueness problem can be cast as an investigation of the uniqueness of a solution U to Koopmans's equation given W. Streufert introduces the notions of biconvergence and tail sensitivity to provide an

---

[7] Looking ahead to Section 3.5, a Banach limit utility function has $\delta \beta^\rho = 1$ whereas we require $\delta \beta^\rho < 1$ for the aggregator framework.

[8] There is a general belief that the long-run average criterion reflects the behavior of a discounted felicity criterion as the discount factor goes to one. This idea is explored in more depth by Dutta (1991). This intuition (and the technical convenience of the average criterion) have played an important role in the theory of repeated games. See the seminal papers by Aumann and Shapley (1994) and Rubinstein (1994).

[9] The aggregator was first taken as a primitive for preferences on ℓ_+^{∞} in Lucas and Stokey (1984). The subsequent analysis of Boyd (1990a) extended their results to larger sequence spaces. Lucas and Stokey as well as Boyd attacked the uniqueness problem. Their approach is the heart of Section 3.5.

affirmative answer to this issue.[10] Biconvergence of U is defined for a fixed order interval $[0, \omega] \subset \mathbf{E}_+$, where ω has strictly positive components. Biconvergence requires both that a "poor" consumption profile cannot be preferred to a program eventually offering a "tail" of ω (upper convergence) and that a "good" consumption profile cannot be inferior to another eventually offering zero consumption in the tail (lower convergence). The biconvergence property of U is invariant to continuous monotonic transformations of U. The basic intuition for tail insensitivity is similar. The difference between the two concepts is that tail sensitivity is an ordinal property of the utility scale. Streufert proved that under the biconvergence hypothesis, U is the unique "admissible" solution to Koopmans's equation in W. His converse proposition says that if U is not biconvergent, then Koopmans's equation has multiple "admissible" solutions. In this sense, biconvergence is the weakest condition delivering a unique solution to the Koopmans's equation in W.

Fix an order interval $[0, \omega] \subset \mathbf{E}_+$. We assume $\omega_t \gg 0$ for each t, and $\omega \succ \mathbf{0}$.[11] A utility function U is said to be *upper convergent* over $[0, \omega]$ if for every $\mathbf{c} \in [0, \omega]$

$$\lim_{T \to \infty} U(\pi_T \mathbf{c}, S^T \omega) = U(\mathbf{c}),$$

where $\pi_T \mathbf{c} = (c_1, \ldots, c_T)$. The limit always exists since U is monotone and $(\pi_T \mathbf{c}, S^T \omega) \geq (\pi_{T+1} \mathbf{c}, S^{T+1} \omega)$. The function U is said to be *lower convergent* over $[0, \omega]$ if for every $\mathbf{c} \in [0, \omega]$

$$\lim_{T \to \infty} U(\pi_T \mathbf{c}, \mathbf{0}) = U(\mathbf{c}).$$

Again, the limit always exists because U is monotone and $(\pi_T \mathbf{c}, \mathbf{0}) \leq (\pi_{T+1} \mathbf{c}, \mathbf{0})$.

The function U is said to be *biconvergent* over $[0, \omega]$ if it is both upper and lower convergent over $[0, \omega]$. Notice that if U is a Banach limit, it is not lower convergent: let $\mathbf{c} = (1, 1, \ldots)$, then $\Lambda(\pi_T \mathbf{c}, \mathbf{0}) = 0$ for each T and $\Lambda(\mathbf{c}) = 1$. We also notice here that $\mathbf{0}$ has a special role in the definition of biconvergence. In particular, the TAS form with log felicity cannot be lower convergent on $[0, \omega]$.

Let $U_1 : \mathbf{E}_+ \to [0, \infty]$ denote a utility representation of $\succsim$. The function U_1 need not be monotonic or stationary, hence it does not have to equal U—the primitive in Koopmans's Recursive Representation Theorem. Such a function U_1 is a *general solution* to Koopmans's equation (here $u(z) = z$) if there exists a sequence of *subutility* functions

---

[10] Kreps (1977) independently proposed related upper and lower convergence concepts.
[11] The notation $x \gg y$ means $x_i > y_i$ for all i.

$(U_2, U_3, \ldots)$ such that for all $\mathbf{c} \in \mathbf{E}_+$ and for all $t \geq 0$:

$$U_t(S^{t-1}\mathbf{c}) = W(c_t, U_{t+1}(S^t\mathbf{c})).$$

A general solution U_1 is *admissible* if for all $\mathbf{c} \in [\mathbf{0}, \boldsymbol{\omega}], U(\mathbf{0}) \leq U_1(\mathbf{c}) \leq U(\boldsymbol{\omega})$.

▶ Example 6: Admissibility. The following example drawn from Streufert (1990) illustrates the need for the admissibility qualification. Let $\boldsymbol{\omega} = (1, 1, \ldots)$ and U have the TAS form

$$U(\mathbf{c}) = \sum_{t=1}^{\infty} \delta^{t-1} c_t.$$

U is biconvergent over $[\mathbf{0}, \boldsymbol{\omega}]$. The aggregator $W(c, y) = c + \delta y$ has the *inadmissible* solution defined by

$$U_t(S^{t-1}\mathbf{c}) = U(S^{t-1}\mathbf{c}) + \delta^{-t}$$

when $S^{t-1}\mathbf{c} \in c_{00}$, and

$$U_t(S^{t-1}\mathbf{c}) = U(S^{t-1}\mathbf{c})$$

otherwise. This is inadmissible as $U_1(\pi_t\boldsymbol{\omega}, \mathbf{0}) = (1 - \delta)^{-1}(\delta^{-1} - \delta^t) > (1 - \delta)^{-1} = U(\boldsymbol{\omega})$ for large t. Moreover, U_1 is not lower convergent at $\boldsymbol{\omega}$. ◀

Streufert's first theorem is:[12]

Biconvergence Theorem. *If U is biconvergent over $[\mathbf{0}, \boldsymbol{\omega}]$, and $\succsim$ satisfies (P2'), then for any admissible general solution U_1 to Koopmans's equation, $U_1 = U$ over $[\mathbf{0}, \boldsymbol{\omega}]$.*[13]

Proof. Choose $\mathbf{c} \in [\mathbf{0}, \boldsymbol{\omega}]$. Admissibility implies for each $t \geq 1$ that $U_{t+1}(S^t\mathbf{c}) \geq U(\mathbf{0})$, otherwise W strictly increasing in future utility would imply

$$U_1(\pi_t\mathbf{0}, S^t\mathbf{c}) = W(0, \ldots W(0, U_{t+1}(S^t\mathbf{c})) \cdots)$$
$$< W(0, \ldots W(0, U(0, 0, \ldots)) \cdots) = U(\mathbf{0}),$$

---

[12] Streufert (1990, p. 81) notes the aggregator is strictly increasing in future utility if utility is weakly increasing, after-period-1 separable, and stationary. The maximin utility function generates an aggregator that is only non-decreasing in future utility. We use a weaker form of limited independence than Streufert. For this reason we require (P2') instead of (P2).

[13] After Streufert (1990, pp. 83–84). He has continued this work at a more abstract level in Streufert (1992; 1997).

which would contradict admissibility. Similarly, admissibility implies that for each t,

$$U_{t+1}(S^t\mathbf{c}) \leq U(S^t\omega).$$

These two bounds on $U_{t+1}(S^t\mathbf{c})$ imply for each t that:

$$\begin{aligned}
U(\pi_t\mathbf{c}, S^t\omega) &= W(c_1, \ldots W(c_t, U(S^t\omega)) \cdots) \\
&\geq W(c_1, \ldots W(c_t, U_{t+1}(S^t\mathbf{c})) \cdots) = U_1(\mathbf{c}) \\
&\geq W(c_1, \ldots W(c_t, U(\mathbf{0})) \cdots) = U(\pi_t\mathbf{c}, \mathbf{0}).
\end{aligned}$$

Biconvergence implies these upper and lower bounds on $U_1(\mathbf{c})$ both converge to $U(\mathbf{c})$. Therefore U and U_1 agree on $[\mathbf{0}, \omega]$. □

Streufert also proved a converse to the Biconvergence Theorem.

Non-Biconvergence Theorem. *Suppose that for every* $\mathbf{c} \in [\mathbf{0}, \omega]$ *and every period* $t \geq 1$, $U(\pi_t\mathbf{c}, [\mathbf{0}, S^t\omega])$ *is an interval. Then if* U *is not biconvergent over* $[\mathbf{0}, \omega]$, *there exists an admissible solution* U_1 *to Koopmans's equation in* W *such that* $U_1 \neq U$ *over* $[\mathbf{0}, \omega]$.

Proof. See Streufert (1990, Theorem B). □

Banach limits provide a family of non-biconvergent utility function examples. Any TAS utility function which is not bounded below on $[\mathbf{0}, \omega]$ is not lower convergent, hence it also must fail to enjoy the biconvergence property. The aggregator for these utility functions cannot uniquely determine U over $[\mathbf{0}, \omega]$. The difficulty is that $\mathbf{0}$ is an element of the order interval. The Upper Semicontinuous Existence Theorem in Section 3.5 provides a uniqueness result for aggregators unbounded from below on a region of the program space excluding commodities "close" to $\mathbf{0}$. The question of uniqueness is further discussed in Section 3.5 where the focus is on the aggregator as the primitive concept.

3.3.3 Recursive Preferences and Additivity

Koopmans (1972a; 1972b; 1985) explored the existence of a recursive utility representation of a preference order. He showed that under a slight strengthening of (K2), so that *all* complementarities between consumption in adjacent periods could be excluded, utility must be additive across time periods. Given the stationarity axiom, he concluded that utility took the TAS form. The key to the additive representation is the following axiom:

Extended Independence.

(K2') For all $z, w, z', w', \mathbf{x}$, and $\mathbf{x}'$: $(z, w, \mathbf{x}) \succsim (z', w', \mathbf{x})$ if and only if $(z, w, \mathbf{x}') \succsim (z', w', \mathbf{x}')$.

Extended independence says that preferences over the first two period's consumption are independent of consumption from period 3 onwards. Extended independence implies that the commodity group given by the first two periods' consumption is weakly separable from the future consumption profile commodity group. The axiom responsible for the TAS representation is:

Complete Independence.

(K2*) Axioms (K2) and (K2') both hold.

The complete independence axiom is also known as the *independence axiom*. This axiom implies additivity arises when the future consumption stream is weakly separable from the present consumption level and the first two periods' consumption bundles are a commodity group which is weakly separable from the future consumption stream. Notice that additivity results from combining two different asymmetric separability axioms on the relations between the commodity groups $\{1\}$ and $\{2, 3, \ldots\}$ and $\{1, 2\}$ and $\{3, 4, \ldots\}$.

The next axiom, *K-monotonicity*, is used to show the factor $\delta < 1$. Consider a program $\mathbf{y}$ and define $\mathbf{x}^N = \mathbf{y} + (\pi_N \mathbf{z}, \mathbf{0})$ for a fixed profile $\mathbf{z} \geq \mathbf{0}$. This adds the first N components of $\mathbf{z}$ to $\mathbf{y}$. The standard monotonicity property (P2) implies $\mathbf{x}^N \succsim \mathbf{y}$ for each N. Further, the program $\mathbf{x} = \mathbf{y} + \mathbf{z} \succsim \mathbf{y}$ also follows from monotonicity. Notice $\mathbf{x}$ is the end result of an infinite number of improvements of $\mathbf{y}$ taken one at a time. However, other periodwise improvements in $\mathbf{y}$ are possible. The next postulate is designed to include those paths as well as the ones found by application of the basic monotonicity property. The K-monotonicity axiom says that a program $\mathbf{x}$ which is the end result of an infinite sequence of improvements starting from $\mathbf{y}$ is itself an improvement over $\mathbf{y}$.

K-Monotonicity.

(K4) For every pair $\mathbf{x}, \mathbf{y} \in \mathbf{E}_+$: if $(\pi_N \mathbf{x}, S^N \mathbf{y}) \succsim (\pi_{N-1} \mathbf{x}, S^{N-1} \mathbf{y})$ for $N = 1, 2, \ldots$, then $\mathbf{x} \succsim \mathbf{y}$.

K-monotonicity automatically holds when $\mathbf{x}$ is obtained from $\mathbf{y}$ by improving consumption in a finite number of periods. Consider the case of an improvement that occurs only in the first two periods. Let $\mathbf{x}, \mathbf{y} \in \mathbf{E}_+$ with $S^2 \mathbf{x} = S^2 \mathbf{y}$. By the "if" part of (K4), $\mathbf{x} = (\pi_2 \mathbf{x}, S^2 \mathbf{y}) \succsim (\pi_1 \mathbf{x}, S \mathbf{y}) \succsim (\pi_0 \mathbf{x}, \mathbf{y}) = \mathbf{y}$. Transitivity of the preference relation implies $\mathbf{x} \succsim \mathbf{y}$. This argument can be continued for any improvements in $\mathbf{y}$ over a finite number of periods. The improvements need not be strictly larger than the corresponding components of the $\mathbf{y}$ program—tradeoffs can occur between periods in a finite segment of consumption periods. K-monotonicity is introduced to express that the limiting form of these improvements of $\mathbf{y}$ results in a program no worse than $\mathbf{y}$.

Koopmans's Additive Representation Theorem. *Let $\mathbf{E} = A_\omega$ for some constant sequence $\omega = \omega_{con} \gg \mathbf{0}$. Endow $\mathbf{E}$ with the topology induced* *by the lattice norm. Assume $\succsim$ satisfies axioms (P1)–(P4), (K1), (K2*), (K3), and (K4) on $\mathbf{E}_+$. Then there is a continuous TAS utility function U representing $\succsim$ on $\mathbf{E}_+$. Moreover, U is unique up to a positive linear transformation.*

The proof of Koopmans's Additive Representation Theorem is lengthy. However, the essential idea is to construct U in several steps. First, define a utility function U_T on the set of all programs $\mathbf{c} \in \mathbf{E}_+$ having $S^T \mathbf{c} = (z_{T+1}, z_{T+2}, \ldots)$ where $\mathbf{z}$ is a fixed reference program. Consumption paths restricted to this subspace may be ranked by an induced preference order on a subset of $\mathbb{R}_+^T$; standard utility representation theorems for independent factor spaces may be invoked to yield an additive utility function on this subspace.[14] Stationarity implies that utility on $\mathbb{R}_+^T$ has the form

$$U_T(c_1, c_2, \ldots, c_T) = \sum_{t=1}^{T} \delta^{t-1} u(c_t).$$

Koopmans then extends U_T to the subspace of programs which are eventually constant, i.e., $S^T \mathbf{c} = (c, c, \ldots)$ for some T. Let $\mathcal{X}_{con}$ denote the space of all eventually constant programs. The tail of any program $\mathbf{c} \in \mathcal{X}_{con}$ is shown to contribute an amount $\delta^T u(c)/(1-\delta)$ to the utility of a program. Thus $\mathbf{c} \in \mathcal{X}_{con}$ implies

$$U(\mathbf{c}) = U(c_1, \ldots, c_T, S^{T-1}\mathbf{c})$$

$$= u(c_1) + \delta u(c_2) + \cdots + \delta^{T-1} u(c_T) + \frac{\delta^T u(c)}{1-\delta}.$$

The function U is unique up to a positive linear transformation. The final step is to show that U may be extended to $\mathbf{E}_+$.[15] An application of the Additive Representation Theorem occurs for the case $\omega_{con} = (1, 1, \ldots)$ where $A_\omega = \ell^\infty$.

An interesting problem is to show the Additive Representation Theorem can be extended to cases of growth in ω as would occur if $\omega = (\alpha \mathbf{e}, \alpha^2 \mathbf{e}, \ldots)$ and $\alpha > 1$. However, additional restrictions on preference orders will be necessary for this extension. A positive result can be obtained when the preference relation is *homothetic*: that is, $\mathbf{x} \succsim \mathbf{y}$ implies $\lambda \mathbf{x} \succsim \lambda \mathbf{y}$ for all $\lambda > 0$. The isomorphism between $(A_\omega, \|\cdot\|_\alpha)$ and ℓ^∞ yields a TAS representation as an application of the Additive Representation Theorem. This observation is due to Dolmas (1995). Previously,

---

[14] See Gorman (1968a; 1968b), Koopmans (1972a), Debreu (1960), and Fishburn (1970).

[15] A careful reading of Koopmans's Proposition 3 (1972a, pp. 89–91) shows that his requirement that $\mathbf{c}$ be bounded in utility is equivalent to $\mathbf{0} \leq \mathbf{c} \leq \lambda \omega_{con}$ for some $\lambda > 0$. This holds here since $\mathbf{E}$ is the principal ideal generated by ω_{con}. The lattice norm topology coincides with the sup-norm topology utilized by Koopmans.

Rader (1981) proved homotheticity combined with continuity of the preference relation over s_+^1 implied additivity and the felicity function u is homogeneous or logarithmic. The homogeneous case was also conjectured by Hicks (1965).

Rader's Theorem. *If a function $U(\mathbf{c}) = \sum_{t=1}^{\infty} u_t(c_t)$ is stationary, monotonic, quasi-concave, and homothetic in $\mathbf{c}$, the u_t are continuous, and at least two u_t are non-constant, then there is a concave linear homogeneous function v, $\alpha > 0$, $1 \geq \rho \neq 0$, and $0 < \delta < 1$, such that, up to an additive constant, either $u_t(x) = \alpha \delta^t v(x_t)^\rho$ or $u_t(x) = \alpha \delta^{t-1} \log v(x)$.*

Proof. This follows immediately from Rader's (1981) Theorems 2 and 3. □

Corollary 2. *Suppose the preference relation satisfies the assumptions of the Additive Representation Theorem on $A_\omega^+ \subset s^m$ where $S\omega = \alpha\omega$ with $\alpha > 1$ and $\omega \gg 0$. If the preference relation is homothetic, then there is a continuous TAS utility function U representing it on A_ω^+. Moreover, the additive utility function has homogeneous or log homogeneous felicity.*

Proof. Apply the mapping $\varphi \colon A_\omega^+ \to \ell_+^\infty$ defined by $(\varphi(\mathbf{x}))_t = x_t/\alpha^t$ to induce an order on ℓ_+^∞ by $\mathbf{x} \succsim_\varphi \mathbf{y}$ if and only if $\varphi^{-1}(\mathbf{x}) \succsim \varphi^{-1}(\mathbf{y})$. The relation $\succsim_\varphi$ satisfies all the assumptions of the Additive Representation Theorem given $\succsim$ satisfies them over A_ω^+—homotheticity is used only to verify stationarity. Therefore, Koopmans's Theorem applied to $\succsim_\varphi$ yields a sup-norm continuous utility function U representing $\succsim_\varphi$ on ℓ_+^∞. The composition $U \circ \varphi$ defined by $U(\varphi(\mathbf{x}))$ represents $\succsim$ on A_ω^+. The remainder follows from Rader's Theorem. □

Homothetic preference orders can be given a special representation.

Lemma 2. *If a homothetic preference order obeys (P1), (P2'), and (P4) on A_ω^+, then it has a continuous utility representation that is homogeneous of degree 1.*

Proof. Define $U(\lambda\omega) = \lambda$ for $\lambda \geq 0$. For any $\mathbf{c} \in A_\omega^+$, we have $0 \leq \mathbf{c} \leq \|\mathbf{c}\|\omega$ where $\|\cdot\|$ is the lattice norm. Thus $0 \precsim \mathbf{c} \precsim \|\mathbf{c}\|\omega$. It follows that both $\{0 \leq \lambda \leq \|\mathbf{c}\| : \mathbf{c} \precsim \lambda\omega\}$ and $\{0 \leq \lambda \leq \|\mathbf{c}\| : \mathbf{c} \succsim \lambda\omega\}$ are non-empty. They are also closed by (P4). Since $[0, \|\mathbf{c}\|]$ is connected, there must be a λ with $\mathbf{c} \sim \lambda\omega$. Moreover, that λ is unique by (P1) and (P2'). Define $U(\mathbf{c}) = \lambda$. This U is clearly homogeneous of degree 1, and continuous by (P4). □

Of course, any other utility representation of a homothetic preference order must be a monotonic transformation of the homogeneous function given by the lemma. Those that are themselves homogeneous are of special interest, and the homogeneity of the utility function results in a special type of aggregator.

Lemma 3. *If U is a recursive utility function that is homogeneous of degree γ, then its aggregator obeys $W(u(\lambda c), \lambda^\gamma y) = \lambda^\gamma W(u(c), y)$.*

Proof. This follows from the fact that for all $\mathbf{c} \in \mathcal{X}$, $\lambda^\gamma W(c_1, U(S\mathbf{c}))$ $= \lambda^\gamma U(\mathbf{c}) = U(\lambda \mathbf{c}) = W(u(\lambda c_1), U(\lambda S\mathbf{c})) = W(u(\lambda c_1), \lambda^\gamma U(S\mathbf{c}))$. $\square$

A converse will be given later. If the preference order is not homothetic, then an additive representation on A_ω^+ may not exist.

▶ Example 7: The TAS extension problem. We continue with the commodity space $\ell_+^\infty(\alpha) \subset s^1$ allowing for geometric growth paths. Define a preference order on this space by $\mathbf{x} \succsim \mathbf{y}$ if and only if $U(\mathbf{x}) \geq U(\mathbf{y})$ where

$$U(\mathbf{x}) = \limsup_t |x_t/\alpha^t| + \arctan\left(\liminf_T \sum_{t=1}^T \delta^{t-1} x_t\right),$$

for $\delta\alpha > 1$ and $\delta \in (0, 1)$. If $\mathbf{x} \in \ell_+^\infty$, then $\sum_{t=1}^T \delta^{t-1} x_t \to \sum_{t=1}^\infty \delta^{t-1} x_t < \infty$ and $\limsup_t |x_t/\alpha^t| = 0$. Hence $U(\mathbf{x}) = \arctan\left(\sum_{t=1}^\infty \delta^{t-1} x_t\right)$. The preference relation has a TAS representation on the subspace ℓ_+^∞ since the arctan function is increasing: $V(\mathbf{x}) = \arctan^{-1} U(\mathbf{x})$ is ordinally equivalent to U on ℓ_+^∞. Can this additive representation be extended to the entire commodity space? The answer is no. Suppose $\sum_{t=1}^T \delta^{t-1} x_t \to \infty$, then $U(\mathbf{x}) = \limsup_t |x_t/\alpha^t| + \pi/2$ and U is not ordinally equivalent to a TAS function over $\ell_+^\infty(\alpha)$. ◀

The implication of this example is additional hypotheses are required to obtain a TAS function when consumption may grow at a geometric rate. Since assuming a homothetic preference order imposes very strong properties on utility, we will look for other structural axioms yielding additivity.

The search for a new property for the preference order can be motivated further using the functions in the previous example. Notice the program $\mathbf{x} = \lambda\omega = (\lambda\alpha, \lambda\alpha^2, \dots)$ for $\lambda > 0$ takes the value $U(\lambda\omega) = \lambda + \pi/2$. We will argue that this preference relation does not exhibit a sufficient degree of impatience along growing paths such as $\lambda\omega$ even though those programs receive a finite utility value. Suppose N is a very large natural number. Define the profile $\mathbf{x}^N = (\mu\pi_N(\lambda\omega), S^N \mathbf{z})$ where $\mu > 0$ may be chosen later and $\mathbf{z} \in \ell_+^\infty(\alpha)$ is a constant program: that is, $z_t = z_{t+1} = z$ for all t; the choice $\mathbf{z} = \mathbf{0}$ is admissible. The program $\mathbf{x}^N$ provides utility $U(\mathbf{x}^N) < \pi/2$; thus $U(\mathbf{x}^N) < U(\lambda\omega)$ and this inequality is valid no matter how large N and μ are taken. Hence, it is impossible to compensate the agent for an eventual consumption decline ($\lambda\omega_t = \lambda\alpha^t > z$ for t large enough as $\alpha > 1$) with a possibly very large increase in consumption over the first N periods by choosing a large μ value: the comparison $\mathbf{x}^N \succ \lambda\omega$ simply does not hold. Put differently, the growing path $\lambda\omega$ dominates any finite improvement of the program $\lambda\omega$ acquired at the eventual expense of a lower constant consumption profile. In this sense, this preference order does not exhibit enough impatience to yield an additive utility representation. The next axiom states an impatience requirement that implicitly discounts future consumption growth.

Dolmas's Impatience Assumption.

(K5) For all $\mathbf{x} \in A_\omega^+$ there is a $\mu > 0$, a constant program $\mathbf{z}$ and an integer N such that $(\mu\pi_n\mathbf{x}, S^n\mathbf{z}) \succsim \mathbf{x}$ for all $n \geq N$.

Dolmas (1995) added (K5) to the other axioms in the Additive Representation Theorem in order to obtain a TAS utility representation of a preference relation defined on A_ω^+.

Dolmas's Representation Theorem. *Let* $\mathbf{E} = A_\omega$ *where* $S\omega = \alpha\omega$ *with* $\alpha > 1$ *and* $\omega \gg 0$. *Endow* $\mathbf{E}$ *with the topology induced by the lattice norm. Assume* $\succsim$ *satisfies axioms (P1)–(P4), (K1), (K2*), and (K3)–(K5) on* $\mathbf{E}_+$. *Then there is a continuous TAS utility function* U *representing* $\succsim$ *on* $\mathbf{E}_+$. *Moreover,* U *is unique up to a positive linear transformation.*

Dolmas proved this result by following the same basic steps used by Koopmans. First, the preference order is restricted to a space of paths whose tails coincide after T periods. This commodity space is equivalent to considering finite horizon bundles in $\mathbb{R}^{T+1}$. Standard utility representation theorems apply as before to yield a TAS functional form with a constant discount factor following from stationarity and (K4). Dolmas then extends this representation to programs which are constant after time T. The main step in his construction is to demonstrate programs growing like $\omega = (\alpha, \alpha^2, \dots)$ beyond date T may be incorporated into the utility representation. This means paths $\mathbf{x}$ satisfying $S^T\mathbf{x} = \lambda S^T\omega$ for $\lambda > 0$ must be shown to have a TAS representation. The impatience axiom (K5) is used at this stage to show the utility contribution of the tail of such a program is given by $\sum_{t=T+1}^{\infty} \delta^{t-1}u(\lambda\omega_t)$. He then proves the utility sum $\sum_{t=1}^{\infty} \delta^{t-1}u(\lambda\omega_t)$ exists implying $U(\mathbf{x}) = \sum_{t=1}^{\infty} \delta^{t-1}u(x_t)$ exists for all $\mathbf{x} \in A_\omega^+$. Thus, the preference order has a TAS representation.[16]

Variations on the recursive axiom system (K1)–(K3) are possible. Epstein (1986) introduces the class of implicitly additive utility functions as an alternative to the additive class based on the independence axiom. In his setup, the independence axiom states that the marginal rate of substitution between period t and t' consumption depends on the entire con-

---

[16] Streufert (1995) discusses abstract additive representation theorems with applications to intertemporal orders. He requires his commodity space to be the Cartesian copy of arcwise-connected spaces and assumes continuity of the preference relation in the product topology. For the case of s^1 his result agrees with Rader's Theorem.

sumption path but only through the value of its lifetime utility $U(\mathbf{c})$.[17] In Epstein's formulation, there is scope for a limited degree of complementarity between adjacent periods' consumption. He also weakens the stationarity postulate in order to express the idea that the passage of time does not have an effect on marginal rates of substitution so long as lifetime utility is kept constant. This means that we defer consumption by first consuming a level c with $U(c, \mathbf{c}) = U(\mathbf{c})$ where $(c, \mathbf{c}) \equiv \mathbf{c}'$ is the program defined by $c_1' = c$, $c_t' = c_{t-1}$ $(t \geq 2)$. The resulting utility function has the form

$$U(\mathbf{c}) = \sum_{t=1}^{\infty} (\delta(u))^{t-1} g(c_t, u),$$

where $u \equiv U(\mathbf{c})$, $\delta(u) \in (0, 1)$, $g(\cdot, u) \colon \mathbb{R}_+ \to \mathbb{R}$ is strictly concave, continuously differentiable with a positive derivative, and $g(0, u) = 0$.

Several writers have explored the consequences of eliminating the independence axiom. The Majumdar functional introduced in Chapter 1 is expressed by the equation

$$U(\mathbf{c}) = w(c_1, c_2, \ldots, c_T) + \sum_{t=1}^{\infty} \delta(t) v_t(c_1, c_2, \ldots, c_t),$$

defined on ℓ^{∞} where $\delta(t) \geq 0$ for all t, $\sum \delta(t) = 1$, $w \colon \mathbb{R}_+^T \to \mathbb{R}_+$ is continuous, quasi-concave, non-decreasing in each argument, and $\{v_t\}$ is a sequence of quasi-concave, continuous functions from $\mathbb{R}_+^t$ to $\mathbb{R}_+$, each v_t being strictly increasing in all its arguments and the sequence being uniformly bounded above. Clearly, this U is not representable by an aggregator when w is non-trivial, $v_t = v$, and $\delta(t) = (1 - \delta)\delta^{t-1}$. The presence of a finite memory violates independence and thereby excludes this functional from the recursive class.

3.4 Impatience, Discounting, and Myopia

An impatient consumer or planner prefers earlier rather than later consumption. The question of discounting versus non-discounting of future consumption as a property of a *planner's* preference order has been a central theme in capital theory dating to the seminal paper of Ramsey (1928). He argued (p. 543) that discounting was a "practice which is ethically indefensible and arises merely from the weakness of the imagination." It should be recalled that Ramsey also investigated the implications

---

[17] Epstein defines the marginal rate of substitution in terms of the Gâteaux derivatives of U in each coordinate direction. We return to this approach in the next section on impatience.

of discounting in his model. Indeed, his heterogeneous agent model operated with different agents distinguished by differences in their subjective discount rates. Ramsey seemed to distinguish the property of discounting for a social planner from the presumption of discounting on the part of private agents. Ramsey's view of impatience was in tune with classical perspectives in capital theory. Various writers (e.g., Böhm-Bawerk, 1912; Fisher, 1930; and Rae, 1834) advanced the impatience hypothesis. Modern research workers have distinguished several forms of impatience.[18] The terms discounting, time perspective, and myopia have been used in slightly different senses in the literature.

The infinite horizon structure of the choice problem raises problems regarding the presence, degree, and forms taken by impatience. We will focus on three aspects of these questions, successively interpreting impatience in terms of timing of consumption, continuity, and marginal trade-offs. We begin with a discussion of Koopmans's notions of impatience and time perspective. Next, we examine the linkage between continuity of the preference order and myopia. Finally, we turn to the concept of marginal impatience along a consumption profile.

3.4.1 Impatience and Time Perspective

We start with the naive notion of impatience, that *people* prefer earlier consumption to later consumption. We work in s_+^1, and consider consumption in time periods s and t with $s < t$. Let's interchange consumption in those two periods. Define a permutation $\Pi_{s,t}$ by setting $(\Pi_{s,t}\mathbf{c})_\tau = c_\tau$ for $\tau \neq s, t$, $(\Pi_{s,t}\mathbf{c})_s = c_t$, and $(\Pi_{s,t}\mathbf{c})_t = c_s$. The naive notion of impatience says that we prefer $\mathbf{c}$ to $\Pi_{s,t}\mathbf{c}$ if our consumption occurs sooner on $\mathbf{c}$. This happens if $c_s > c_t$, so we get more consumption sooner on the unpermuted path. We formalize this by saying that a consumer exhibits *positive absolute time preference* if $\mathbf{c} \succ \Pi_{s,t}\mathbf{c}$ whenever $c_s > c_t$. *Negative absolute time preference* then refers to the case where delayed consumption is better, where $\mathbf{c} \prec \Pi_{s,t}\mathbf{c}$.

The idea of absolute time preference can be extended to cases with many consumption goods at each time by using the usual order on $\mathbb{R}^m$. The fact that the usual order is incomplete limits the application of absolute time preference in such cases. When preferences obey Koopmans's axioms, a complete extension of the naive idea of impatience is possible, and was put forth by Koopmans (1960). Given a recursive utility function U with aggregator W and felicity u, a program $\mathbf{c}$ meets the *Koopmans's impatience condition* if $u(c_1) > u(c_2)$ implies

$$W(u(c_1), W(u(c_2), U(S^2\mathbf{c}))) > W(u(c_2), W(u(c_1), U(S^2\mathbf{c}))).$$

---

[18] See Epstein (1987b) for an excellent discussion of impatience.

Reversing the timing of first and second period felicity from consumption lowers lifetime utility if it places the second (smaller) felicity in the first period. This is impatience over one period; it can be easily extended to any initial segment of the horizon. Koopmans's definition of impatience is a form of *eventual impatience* in the sense that it reflects changes in consumption levels over a finite number of periods.

The standard TAS form of the utility function satisfies this impatience property as $\delta \in (0,1)$. Koopmans went on to demonstrate that the postulates (P1)–(P4) and (K1)–(K3) imply the existence of "zones of impatience" in the three-dimensional payoff space $(u_1, u_2, U \circ S^2)$, where $U \circ S^2(\mathbf{c}) = U(S^2 \mathbf{c})$. Koopmans found that the limit of the utility of a sequence of programs defined by shifting an arbitrary reference program and the repeated insertion of a fixed N-period consumption segment equals the utility of the program consisting of the infinite repetition of the N-period consumption vector. Koopmans (1960, p. 115) expressed surprise that his notion of impatience arose as an implication of his axiom system since the presumption in the literature dating back at least to Böhm-Bawerk (1912) was that impatience was a psychological characteristic of economic agents.[19]

Koopmans, Diamond, and Williamson (1964) explored another notion of time preference which they called *time perspective*. In words, a recursive utility function exhibits weak (strong) time perspective if the difference in the utility levels achieved by two programs does not increase (decreases) if the programs are delayed one period and a common first period consumption is inserted. The use of utility differences in the definition meant that this was a cardinal property of utility whereas the impatience concept was ordinal. However, they did demonstrate the existence of an ordinally equivalent representation of U satisfying the axioms (P1)–(P4) and (K1)–(K3), labelled U^*, such that U^* exhibited the weak time perspective property.

3.4.2 Myopia and the Continuity Axiom

The basic intuition underlying the linkage between continuity and impatience may be seen by looking at the definition of continuity for a utility function $U \colon s_+^1 \to \mathbb{R}$ where s^1 has the product topology. The function U is continuous in the product topology at $\mathbf{c} \in s_+^1$ if $U(\mathbf{c}^\nu) \to U(\mathbf{c})$ for all sequences $\{\mathbf{c}^\nu\}$ with $c_t^\nu \to c_t$ for all t. Equivalently, U is product continuous at $\mathbf{c}$ if for every $\epsilon > 0$ there are $\delta, N > 0$ such that the relation $\mathbf{c}' \in G(\mathbf{c}, \delta, N)$ implies $|U(\mathbf{c}') - U(\mathbf{c})| < \epsilon$ where $G(\mathbf{c}, \delta, N) = \{\mathbf{c}' : |c_t' - c_t| < \delta$ for $t = 1, \ldots, N\}$. As the latter formulation makes clear, if U is continuous at $\mathbf{c}$ in this topology, then U is not sensitive to variations in

---

[19] Recall, the utility function is $\| \cdot \|_\infty$-continuous in this setup.

consumption c_t for t sufficiently large. This is a strong impatience idea: utility is sensitive to changes over finite segments of the planning horizon. For t sufficiently large, the variations in consumption are "discounted" to yield no significant incremental contribution to utility. Total utility is dominated by what happens in only a finite number of periods.

The product topology is not the only topology that can be related to impatience. Bewley (1972) suggested an explicit link between the Mackey topology and impatience. Brown and Lewis (1981), Stroyan (1983), Boyd (1986) and Raut (1986) formalized myopia concepts as continuity requirements. Their ideas were later subsumed in a general framework offered by Aliprantis, Brown, and Burkinshaw (1989). They define myopia in terms of the order structure of the commodity space. We will pursue their approach in order to connect it to preference orders and utility functions typically encountered in capital theory.

Brown and Lewis (1981) focused on the space ℓ^∞. They called $\succsim$ *strongly myopic* if for all $\mathbf{x}$, $\mathbf{y}$, and $\mathbf{z} \in \mathbf{E}_+$, $\mathbf{x} \succ \mathbf{y}$ implied $\mathbf{x} \succ \mathbf{y} + (\pi_N \mathbf{0}, S^N \mathbf{z})$ for all N sufficiently large.[20] In words, if $\mathbf{z}$ is pushed far enough into the future, adding it to $\mathbf{y}$ does not change the preference for $\mathbf{x}$ over $\mathbf{y}$. This type of myopia follows from continuity in the product topology. However, there is also an order theoretic property that is hidden in the definition of a strongly myopic preference relation. The sequence of consumption programs $\{(\pi_N \mathbf{0}, S^N \mathbf{z})\}_{N=1}^\infty$ is decreasing: $(\pi_N \mathbf{0}, S^N \mathbf{z}) \downarrow \mathbf{0}$. The sequence $\mathbf{y}^N = (\mathbf{y} + (\pi_N \mathbf{0}, S^N \mathbf{z}))$ is also a decreasing sequence: $\mathbf{y}^N \downarrow \mathbf{y}$. It follows that $|\mathbf{y}^N - \mathbf{y}| = |(\pi_N \mathbf{0}, S^N \mathbf{z})| \downarrow \mathbf{0}$ as $N \to \infty$. But this is an example of an order convergent sequence. Brown and Lewis's strong myopia idea can be recast as stating $\mathbf{x} \succ \mathbf{y}$ implies $\mathbf{x} \succ \mathbf{y}^N$ for N sufficiently large when $\mathbf{y}^N$ is order convergent to $\mathbf{y}$ (written $\mathbf{y}^N \overset{o}{\to} \mathbf{y}$).[21]

Sawyer (1988) considers *upward* and *downward myopia*. Upward myopia coincides with Brown and Lewis's definition of strong myopia. Downward myopia occurs whenever $\mathbf{x} \succ \mathbf{y}$ implies for all $\mathbf{z}$ there exists an N such that $(\pi_N \mathbf{x}, S^N \mathbf{z}) \succ \mathbf{y}$. Downward myopia says that if $\mathbf{z}$ is pushed far enough into the future, then eventually switching plans from $\mathbf{x}$ to $\mathbf{z}$ does not change the preference for $\mathbf{x}$ over $\mathbf{y}$. In particular, if $\mathbf{z}$ offers a lower consumption than $\mathbf{x}$ in the distant future, then the preference for $\mathbf{x}$ over $\mathbf{y}$ is not reversed since the reductions in consumption are sufficiently postponed. Downward myopia also implies the truncation condition proposed by Prescott and Lucas (1972, p. 417). Their condition follows from downward myopia if $\mathbf{z} = \mathbf{0}$. The maximin order clearly fails to satisfy

---

[20] Brown and Lewis (1981) also studied a form of *weak myopia* where the vector $\mathbf{z}$ is a constant sequence in the strong myopia definition.

[21] Recall that a net $\{\mathbf{x}^\alpha\}$ in a Riesz space $\mathbf{E}$ is *order convergent* to an element $\mathbf{x}$, denoted $\mathbf{x}^\alpha \overset{o}{\to} \mathbf{x}$, whenever there exists another net $\{\mathbf{y}^\alpha\}$ with the same indexed set such that $\mathbf{y}^\alpha \downarrow \mathbf{0}$ and $|\mathbf{x}^\alpha - \mathbf{x}| \leq \mathbf{y}^\alpha$ holds for each α.

the downward myopia hypotheses of either Sawyer or Prescott and Lucas. Sawyer calls a preference order *fully myopic* if it is both upward and downward myopic. Clearly downward myopia also contains an order convergent property along the same lines as the Brown and Lewis strong myopia condition. Sawyer ultimately rejects the downward myopia property on grounds that it is implausible. He argues that downward myopia implies *all* future consumption beyond some date would be exchanged for an arbitrarily small first period consumption followed by no consumption into the indefinite future. Sawyer (1988) also linked his myopia concept to naive impatience along the lines initiated by Koopmans. He showed the existence of a class of stationary recursive utility functions which are not downwardly myopic but nevertheless exhibit zones of impatience analogous to those found by Koopmans.

The fundamental insight of Aliprantis, Brown, and Burkinshaw (1989) is to take order continuity of a utility function as the defining characteristic of myopia. One advantage of this approach is to free myopia from direct topological considerations by basing it solely on the lattice structure of the commodity space. It also extends the myopia idea, which is based on the unidirectional time flow where one consumption period precedes another. For example, the order convergent sequence $|(\pi_N \mathbf{0}, S^N \mathbf{z})| \downarrow \mathbf{0}$ as $N \to \infty$ adjusts consumption from each time N onward, and corresponds to the Brown and Lewis myopia conception. The order properties in the strong myopia definition encompass the order induced by the passage of time. The use of lattice properties of the commodity space yields a systematic way of abstracting these properties into a general concept of myopic preferences and utility.

A utility function U is *order continuous* whenever a net $\{\mathbf{x}^\alpha\} \xrightarrow{o} \mathbf{x}$ in $\mathbf{E}_+$ implies $U(\mathbf{x}^\alpha) \to U(\mathbf{x})$. An order continuous utility function is said to be *myopic* or *order myopic*. An order continuous utility function is taken as the abstraction of the myopia properties introduced by Brown and Lewis (1981) and their followers. We say U is τ-*myopic* if U is τ-continuous. In general, there exist myopic utility functions which are not τ-myopic on a space $\mathbf{E}$ and there are τ-myopic utility functions which are not myopic.[22]

▶ Example 8: Banach limit utility and myopia. Suppose that the utility function U defined on ℓ^∞_+ with the sup-norm topology is a Banach limit. Then U is not myopic. Let $\mathbf{x}^n$ be the commodity bundle which is zero in the first n entries and one thereafter. Clearly $\mathbf{x}^n \downarrow \mathbf{0}$ but $U(\mathbf{x}^n) = 1$ for all n. Notice that U is sup-norm continuous on the commodity space since it is a continuous linear functional. Thus, this is an example of a τ-myopic utility function which fails to be myopic.

---

[22] Aliprantis, Brown, and Burkinshaw (1989, pp. 121–122).

The failure of U to be myopic is not a surprise given that the utility of a profile depends on the tail of the sequence and not upon what is consumed in any initial finite segment of the planning horizon. This is especially clear in the case of a Banach limit extending the long-run average criterion embodied in the average consumption function: the averaging process smooths consumption variation over the planning horizon so that loading of consumption early in the program with lower consumption later may yield the same average consumption as a program with a small initial consumption and larger future consumption sequence. Such a functional does not capture any notion of impatience, discounting, or myopia. ◄

By Corollary 2.2, order continuity and product continuity are identical.

Proposition 1. *A utility function* $U: A_\omega^+ \to \mathbb{R}$ *is myopic if and only if it is* d_F-*myopic.*

Proposition 1 implies that the maximin utility function is not myopic on s_+^1 since it is not lower semicontinuous. This agrees with economic intuition. The utility functional U_R representing the overtaking partial order is not myopic because it is not d_F-myopic. Myopic utility functions enjoy a strong continuity property on ℓ^∞ (or any A_ω).

Proposition 2. *If* $U: \ell_+^\infty \to \mathbb{R}$ *is a myopic utility function, then* U *is* $\|\cdot\|_\infty$-*myopic.*

Proof. If $\mathbf{x}^n \to \mathbf{x}$ in ℓ^∞, it also converges in the relative product topology, and hence in order. Then $U(\mathbf{x}^n) \to U(\mathbf{x})$ by myopia, so U is also $\|\cdot\|_\infty$-myopic. □

Proposition 2 implies that every myopic utility function on ℓ_+^∞ is sup-norm continuous. A myopic utility function on ℓ_+^∞ implies the underlying preference order satisfies the strong myopia condition proposed by Brown and Lewis (1981). The definition of myopia requires that $U(\mathbf{x}^\alpha) \xrightarrow{o} U(\mathbf{x})$ for any net $\{\mathbf{x}^\alpha\} \xrightarrow{o} \mathbf{x}$. The Brown and Lewis strong myopia property only demands order convergence for a specially chosen sequence.

A similar comment applies to Streufert's biconvergence criterion for utility functions on $[0, \omega]$. It is clear that myopia implies biconvergence. However, myopia also implies the utility function is separately continuous, which is not part of biconvergence.[23] When preferences are monotonic, that is the only difference.

Proposition 3. *Suppose a utility function on* $[0, \omega]$ *is monotonic, biconvergent, and continuous at each time. Then it is myopic.*

Proof. Let U be the utility function. Let $\mathbf{x}^\alpha \xrightarrow{o} \mathbf{x}$, so there are $\mathbf{y}^\alpha \downarrow \mathbf{0}$

---

[23] Streufert (1990, p. 83) argues that biconvergence of U is equivalent to product continuity on the space $[0, \omega_1] \times [0, \omega_2] \times \cdots$ where each factor space has the discrete topology.

with $|\mathbf{x}^\alpha - \mathbf{x}| \leq \mathbf{y}^\alpha$. Then

$$\mathbf{w}^\alpha = (\mathbf{x} - \mathbf{y}^\alpha) \vee \mathbf{0} \leq \mathbf{x}^\alpha \leq (\mathbf{x} + \mathbf{y}^\alpha) \wedge \boldsymbol{\omega} = \mathbf{z}^\alpha.$$

By monotonicity, it is enough to show $U(\mathbf{w}^\alpha) \uparrow U(\mathbf{x})$ and $U(\mathbf{z}^\alpha) \downarrow U(\mathbf{x})$.
Let $\epsilon > 0$ and choose T large enough that

$$U(\mathbf{x}) > U(x_1, \ldots, x_T, \omega_{T+1}, \ldots) - \epsilon.$$

Define $\mathbf{z}_T^\alpha = (z_1^\alpha, \ldots, z_T^\alpha, \omega_{T+1}, \ldots)$. As in Lemma 1, monotonicity combined with separate continuity yields joint continuity in the first T time periods. Thus $U(\mathbf{z}_T^\alpha) \to U(x_1, \ldots, x_T, \omega_{T+1}, \ldots)$, so for α large enough, $U(\mathbf{x}) > U(\mathbf{z}_T^\alpha) - \epsilon/2 \geq U(\mathbf{z}^\alpha) - \epsilon/2$. Thus $U(\mathbf{z}^\alpha) \downarrow U(\mathbf{x})$. The case $U(\mathbf{w}^\alpha) \uparrow U(\mathbf{x})$ is similar. $\square$

Streufert (1990) drew an analogy between time perspective and biconvergence: the utility levels realized in the future from following the paths ω and $\mathbf{0}$ respectively appear to the observing agent at the beginning of the horizon as though they converge as time passes, just as the rails of railroad tracks appear to converge at the horizon.

Myopia also relates to Koopmans's K-monotonicity postulate (K4), and to Dolmas's impatience postulate (K5). A preference order defined by a myopic monotonic utility function automatically satisfies K-monotonicity (K4), and will satisfy impatience (K5) as well, unless there is an $\mathbf{x}$ with $\mu\mathbf{x} \sim \mathbf{x}$ for all $\mu \geq 1$. Thus, stationarity, complete independence, strict monotonicity (in the usual sense), and myopia imply the existence of an additive utility representation on the positive cone of any principal ideal of s^1.

Continuity of U (or the underlying preference order) in the product topology on $\mathbf{E}_+ = s_+^1$ has important economic consequences. We recall Diamond's (1965) Impossibility Theorem. A utility function U is *equitable* if for each $\mathbf{c}$, $\mathbf{c}' \in \mathbf{E}_+$, $U(\mathbf{c}) \geq U(\mathbf{c}')$ if and only if $U(\Pi\mathbf{c}) \geq U(\Pi\mathbf{c}')$ where Π is the permutation operator mapping $\mathbf{E}$ into $\mathbf{E}$ acting on finitely many components of a vector. An equitable utility function would meet Ramsey's standard. Diamond proved that there did not exist an equitable and strictly monotone utility function that is continuous in the product topology. In other words, equity is incompatible with product continuity.[24] You cannot treat all periods equally if you have product continuous preferences. Epstein (1987b) argues that the correct interpretation of Diamond's impossibility result is that the choice of the product topology has strong ethical significance given it precludes the possibility of an equitable preference order. The demands placed by the continuity axiom

---

[24] If (P2) is employed instead of (P2′), then the maximin functional is an equitable utility function. However, it is not lower semicontinuous in the product topology.

are sufficiently stringent to exclude the overtaking preference order: the renormalized utility function U_R is equitable and upper semicontinuous in the d_F-topology; it fails the lower semicontinuity test.

Proposition 2 yields a corollary to Diamond's Impossibility Theorem: there are no equitable and strictly monotone myopic utility functions on s_+^1. Shinotsuka (1997) has recently shown that Diamond's result can be considerably strengthened. Even on ℓ_+^∞ there are no non-trivial equitable myopic utility functions.

In spite of these impossibility results, there are topologies where continuity is compatible with equity. Svensson (1980) gives a disconnected metric topology for ℓ^∞ and exhibits a preference ordering that is continuous in it. This preference order is monotonic and equitable. His ordering is based on a generalization of the overtaking criterion, and cannot be represented by a utility function. Campbell (1985) also explored the equity question by introducing a stronger topology than the product topology. His aim was to construct a topology suitable for application of the classical Weierstrass Theorem promising the existence of maximal elements of a utility function which is upper semicontinuous over a compact constraint set. His topology is a metric topology but it does not turn the commodity space into a topological vector space. He also demonstrates an impossibility theorem: a preference relation $\succsim$ satisfying (P1) is continuous in Campbell's topology if and only if $\mathbf{x} \sim \mathbf{y}$ for all programs $\mathbf{x}, \mathbf{y}$. In his setup, continuity is inconsistent with *any* form of the monotonicity axiom.

Diamond's Impossibility Theorem shows how extending the continuity axiom on $\succsim$ from the finite time horizon to the infinite horizon carries strong behavioral implications. Mathematically speaking, the problem is that the topologies utilized in intertemporal analysis are not identical when there is an open-ended horizon. A finite dimensional vector space admits only one (up to equivalence) Hausdorff linear topology whereas the sequence spaces under consideration here admit several Hausdorff linear topologies. For instance, in the case of ℓ^∞, convergence of a sequence in the sup-norm topology implies convergence in the Mackey topology and Mackey convergence implies convergence in the relative product topology inherited from s^1. The converse is false: there exist sequences convergent in the product topology which are not convergent in the Mackey topology. Similarly, there exist Mackey convergent sequences which are not convergent in the sup-norm topology. Economically speaking, the continuity axiom (P4) takes on a different meaning depending on the choice of a topology for a given commodity space. In the ℓ^∞ case, a product continuous $\succsim$ is Mackey continuous and a Mackey continuous $\succsim$ is sup-norm continuous. As before, the converse implications are false. In the product topology case, only finitely many periods really count in determining whether or not two sequences are close to one another. In the Mackey case, there are restrictions on infinitely many coordinates in order to test if two sequences are close to one another.[25]

3.4.3 The Norm of Marginal Impatience Conditions

Any two distinct TAS utility functions which are d_F-continuous on s_+^1 are myopic by Proposition 1. Suppose U_1 and U_2 are TAS functions with identical bounded felicity functions but have $\delta_1 > \delta_2$. Both have identical myopia properties but the first has a higher discount factor than the second. Intuition suggests that U_1 discounts the future less than U_2. Put differently, U_2 is more impatient than U_1. This suggests that the myopia idea can be refined. One way to do this is to examine the tradeoff between consumption today and consumption tomorrow—the marginal rate of substitution. We can ask how much consumption we are willing to sacrifice tomorrow in order to obtain an extra unit of consumption today.

Of course, direct use of the marginal rate of substitution is too fine a concept. Each preference ordering is distinguished by it. We need a coarser concept in order to draw general conclusions. One such concept is the (upper) norm of marginal impatience, which was introduced by Becker, Boyd, and Foias (1991) as a refinement of the myopia idea. They were motivated to consider this sharper notion of impatience in order to demonstrate an equilibrium existence theorem for a model with heterogeneous agents having utility functions drawn from the recursive class as well as allowing some non-recursive elements. We present two additional axioms below in order to develop the norms of marginal impatience. The axioms are placed directly on the utility function, and facilitate use of the marginal rate of substitution. For simplicity, we only consider the case $U: s_+^1 \to \mathbb{R}$ for U d_F-continuous. We note that a utility function satisfying (P1)–(P4) is quasi-concave. For the remainder of this section we use the stronger monotonicity axiom (P2′) without further mention.

Concave Utility.

(P5) U is a concave function.

One implication of property (P5) is that the left- and right-hand partial (Gâteaux) derivatives of the utility function exist. These derivatives are denoted by $U_t^-(\mathbf{c})$ and $U_t^+(\mathbf{c})$ respectively. The right-hand directional derivative of U at $\mathbf{c}$ in the direction of $\mathbf{e}_t = (0, 0, \ldots, 0, 1, 0, \ldots)$, where 1 is in the tth place, is defined as

$$U_t^+(\mathbf{c}) = \lim_{\epsilon \to 0+} \frac{U(\mathbf{c} + \epsilon \mathbf{e}_t) - U(\mathbf{c})}{\epsilon}.$$

---

[25] A program $\mathbf{y}$ is in a Mackey neighborhood of $\mathbf{x}$ if there is an $\epsilon > 0$ and $\Gamma^k = \{\gamma_{tk}\}_{t=1}^{\infty} \in c_0$ with $k = 1, \ldots, K$ such that $\sup_k \{\sup_t |\gamma_{tk}(y_t - x_t)|\} \leq \epsilon$.

The left-hand partial derivative is defined by substituting $\epsilon \to 0^-$ in the limit. The concavity of U implies $U_t^+(\mathbf{c}) \le U_t^-(\mathbf{c})$. If equality holds, we write $U_t(\mathbf{c})$ for the common value and call this the partial derivative of U at $\mathbf{c}$ with respect to the tth coordinate. For technical reasons, we also require the following axiom:

Differentiable Utility.

(P6) The partial derivative U_t of U exists for every t.

We start developing the upper norm of marginal impatience by fixing a reference program ω which is strictly positive. The order interval $[\mathbf{0}, \omega]$ plays a crucial role in the following. We view $[\mathbf{0}, \omega]$ as the relevant domain of U in the sense that $[\mathbf{0}, \omega]$ strictly contains all feasible allocations. We assume that U is a recursive utility function. If U has a C^1 aggregator, then U_t exists and is found by the formula

$$U_t(\mathbf{c}) = W_2(c_1, U(S^1\mathbf{c}))W_2(c_2, U(S^2\mathbf{c})) \times$$
$$\cdots \times W_2(c_{t-1}, U(S^{t-1}\mathbf{c}))W_1(c_t, U(S^t\mathbf{c})), \quad (2)$$

where W_1 and W_2 are the partial derivatives of W with respect to the first and second coordinates.

The next condition restricts the marginal rates of impatience between adjacent time periods over a portion of the program space. Given $t, t+1$, we define the *marginal rate of impatience at* $\mathbf{c}$, $R_{t,t+1}(\mathbf{c})$, by the relation[26]

$$1 + R_{t,t+1}(\mathbf{c}) = \frac{U_t(\mathbf{c})}{U_{t+1}(\mathbf{c})}.$$

This definition yields the usual measure of the marginal rate of substitution in adjacent periods along a fixed utility contour. When R is 0, we will trade consumption today for consumption tomorrow on an equal basis. When R is positive, we demand more goods tomorrow than we give up today, and when R is negative, we are willing to take fewer goods tomorrow than we give up today.

In the differentiable aggregator case we use (2) to obtain

$$\frac{U_t}{U_{t+1}} = \frac{W_1(c_t, U(S^t\mathbf{c}))}{W_2(c_t, U(S^t\mathbf{c}))W_1(c_{t+1}, U(S^{t+1}\mathbf{c}))}.$$

Note that $R_{t,t+1}(\mathbf{c}) = R_{1,2}(S^{t-1}\mathbf{c})$. We will denote $R_{1,2}$ by R. Since $S^2\mathbf{c}$ only affects $R_{1,2}$ through $U(S^2\mathbf{c})$, R can alternatively be regarded as a function of c_1, c_2, and future utility $U(S^2\mathbf{c})$. The specific condition we impose on utility is given below.

---

[26] The concavity and strict monotonicity properties of U imply $U_t > 0$. Notice that the Rawlsian utility function $V(\mathbf{c}) = \inf\{c_t : t = 1, 2, \dots\}$ violates the strict monotonicity axiom and V_t can be 0.

Upper Norm of Marginal Impatience Condition. There is a $\bar{\varrho} > 0$ such that

$$\bar{\varrho} = \sup_{t=1,2,\ldots} \{R_{t,t+1}(\mathbf{c}) : \mathbf{c} \in \prod_{\tau=1}^{\infty} [\mathbf{0}, \omega_\tau], c_{t+1} = c_t\}.$$

The supremum of the $R_{t,t+1}$, which depends only on the ordinal properties of U, is called the *upper norm of marginal impatience*. We require the marginal rate of impatience to be uniformly bounded above on a subset of the program space containing, in particular, all feasible consumption programs with identical consumption at t and $t + 1$. The TAS case is easily seen to satisfy this condition: the upper norm of marginal impatience (which here coincides with the lower norm) is $\bar{\varrho} = \delta^{-1} - 1$ where δ is the discount factor.

Notice that the upper norm of marginal impatience restricts the marginal rate of substitution in a different way than properness.[27] Typically, uniformly proper preferences cannot satisfy the Inada condition at 0 (Back, 1988) whereas a bounded norm of marginal impatience is compatible with Inada conditions.

Many aggregators also satisfy $0 < \underline{\delta} \leq W_2 \leq \bar{\delta} < 1$, a strong version of Koopmans's time perspective axiom. In this case, we also have

$$\frac{U_t}{U_{t+1}} \leq \frac{W_1(z, U(S^t \mathbf{c}))}{\underline{\delta} W_1(z, U(S^{t+1} \mathbf{c}))} \tag{3}$$

when $c_t = c_{t+1} = z$. If $\mathbf{c}$ is a constant program, then the marginal rate of impatience at $\mathbf{c}$ is bounded from above by $1/\underline{\delta} - 1$. But other sequences are admitted in the upper norm of marginal impatience condition. Suppose ω is a constant sequence with $\omega_t = w$. The ratio on the right-hand side of (3) can blow up only as $z \to 0^+$ since $z \leq w$. This does not happen if there is a number M such that

$$\lim_{z \to 0+} \frac{W_1(z, y)}{W_1(z, y')} \leq M \tag{4}$$

for y and y' in the range of the corresponding utility function U. The commonly used aggregators satisfy (4). For the TAS class, $M = 1$ will do. The EH utility function and corresponding aggregator satisfy (4). Consequently, the EH utility function satisfies the upper norm of marginal impatience condition.[28] Thus two EH utility functions may be consistent with the same myopia property and possess different upper norms of marginal impatience.

---

[27] Properness is another commonly used restriction on the marginal rate of substitution. See Chichilnisky and Kalman, 1980; Mas-Colell, 1986; Chichilnisky, 1993).

[28] In Section 3.5, the aggregator is taken as primitive. Many other aggregators satisfy (4). For example, the KDW aggregator of Example 9 will satisfy this restriction.

One implication of the upper norm of marginal impatience condition is recorded below. This result says that the rate of marginal impatience is bounded above by $\bar{\varrho}$ over a portion of the program space. One consequence exploited by Becker, Boyd, and Foias is that consumption must increase when marginal productivity exceeds $1 + \bar{\varrho}$.

Proposition 4. *Let U be a utility function satisfying the upper norm of marginal impatience condition. Then*

$$\sup_{t=1,2,\ldots} \{R_{t,t+1}(\mathbf{c}) : \mathbf{c} \in \prod_{\tau=1}^{\infty} [\mathbf{0}, \omega_\tau], c_{t+1} \le c_t\} = \bar{\varrho}.$$

Proof. Let $\mathbf{c} \in [\mathbf{0}, \omega]$ with $c_{t+1} \le c_t$. Consider

$$\varphi(x, y) = u(c_1, c_2, \ldots, c_{t-1}, x, y, c_{t+2}, \ldots).$$

Notice there exists $\alpha \in [c_{t+1}, c_t]$ such that $\varphi(\alpha, \alpha) = u(\mathbf{c}) = \varphi(c_t, c_{t+1})$. Introduce the indifference curve $y = \psi(x)$ such that $\varphi(x, \psi(x)) = u(\mathbf{c})$. It is easy to show $-\psi'(x) = \varphi_x(x, y)/\varphi_y(x, y) \equiv \theta(x, y)$ for $y = \psi(x)$ and thus $\theta(x, \psi(x))$ is non-increasing in x. For $\alpha = \psi(\alpha)$ and $c_t \ge \alpha$ we have $\theta(c_t, c_{t+1}) = \theta(c_t, \psi(c_t)) \le \theta(\alpha, \psi(\alpha)) \le 1/\delta$. □

Similar definitions and results hold for the *lower norm of marginal impatience*, which guarantees that consumption decreases if productivity is very low.

Lower Norm of Marginal Impatience Condition. There is a $\underline{\varrho} > 0$ such that

$$\underline{\varrho} = \inf_{t=1,2,\ldots} \{R_{t,t+1}(\mathbf{c}) : \mathbf{c} \in \prod_{\tau=1}^{\infty} [\mathbf{0}, \omega_\rho], c_{t+1} = c_t\}.$$

Proposition 5. *Let U be a utility function satisfying the lower norm of marginal impatience condition. Then*

$$\inf_{t=1,2,\ldots} \{R_{t,t+1}(\mathbf{c}) : \mathbf{c} \in \prod_{\tau=1}^{\infty} [\mathbf{0}, \omega_\tau], c_{t+1} \ge c_t\} = \underline{\varrho}.$$

Steady-state impatience may be defined by considering the marginal rate of substitution along constant programs. We defer discussion of steady-state impatience to Chapter 5 on optimal growth dynamics, where we explore the connection between steady-state impatience and stability of optimal paths.

3.5 Recursive Utility: the Aggregator

In Section 3.3 we saw that recursive preferences give rise to an aggregator function that combines present consumption (or felicity from present consumption) and future utility to obtain present utility. This section utilizes the converse approach: the aggregator is postulated as the primitive concept and utility is recovered through a recursion operation. Since the utility function obeys Koopmans's equation (1), the preference order satisfies (K1) and (K2). Under mild additional conditions it will also obey (K3).

There is a pre-Koopmans literature on recursive utility that uses the aggregator exclusively. An early example is Fisher (1930). Much of Fisher's analysis is carried out using a two-good model. Utility depends on both current and future income. Early in the book, he explains that income is ideally thought of in utility terms; thus we should really think of current felicity and future utility combining to yield overall utility. This is precisely what the aggregator function does. Hayek (1941) also took the aggregator as a primitive, and even addressed stability issues in this framework.

The first modern paper to take the aggregator as primitive was Lucas and Stokey (1984). They started with an aggregator function W, which they assumed bounded, and showed how a recursive utility function could be constructed from W. They then characterized equilibria and examined stability when consumers have recursive preferences. We return to this equilibrium characterization problem in Chapters 5 and 6 on stability and the Equivalence Principle.

Taking the aggregator as the fundamental expression of tastes provides detailed information about preferences in a compact form. First, it is a lot easier to specify an aggregator than a recursive utility function. Koopmans, Diamond, and Williamson (1964) found an aggregator that had a specific property (increasing marginal impatience), but the corresponding utility function cannot be explicitly computed. It does not have a closed-form expression. Second, the aggregator, with its sharp distinction between current and future consumption, often makes it easier to incorporate hypotheses about intertemporal behavior. It can be quite difficult to translate axioms into usable conditions on the utility function. The normality conditions used by Lucas and Stokey (1984), Benhabib, Jafarey, and Nishimura (1988), Benhabib, Majumdar, and Nishimura (1987), and Jafarey (1988) to study equilibrium dynamics are most easily imposed directly on the aggregator.[29] We can derive a homothetic order by im-

---

[29] Epstein (1987a) has discovered conditions on the utility function that imply a similar

posing an appropriate condition on the aggregator, even in cases without a closed-form utility function. Finally, if we impose behavioral conditions as axioms, there is the question of their consistency. With aggregators, this is never a problem. Once the utility function exists, consistency is automatic.

Of course, the use of the aggregator does partially obscure the actual utility function and its properties. Fortunately, the aggregator usually contains all the information required to construct the utility function. Lucas and Stokey (1984) made the aggregator approach feasible when they showed that the utility function could be reconstructed when the aggregator is bounded. Boyd (1990a) introduced a refinement of the Contraction Mapping Theorem, the Weighted Contraction Theorem, which applies to a much broader class of utility functions that includes many standard examples. For many aggregators, this is enough to recover the utility function. Aggregators that allow $-\infty$ as a value require further treatment. Boyd combined the weighted contraction with a "partial sum" technique to construct the utility functions.

We will follow Boyd's (1990a) treatment to find the utility function. We begin by examining the basic properties required of the aggregator. A general existence and uniqueness theorem for the corresponding utility function when the aggregator is bounded below follows along with illustrative applications. Boyd's "partial sum" technique is deployed to obtain existence for general aggregators including the TAS examples which are unbounded from below.

3.5.1 Basic Properties of the Aggregator

We start with an aggregator V and associated subutility u. Now consider $W(c, y) = V(u(c), y)$. The aggregator W maps $\mathcal{X} \times \mathcal{Y}$ to $\mathcal{Y}$, where $\mathcal{X}$ is a subset of $\mathbb{R}_+^m$ and $\mathcal{Y}$ is a subset of $\mathbb{R}$. Aggregators will appear in the second argument, so W must take values in $\mathcal{Y}$. Recall the projection π and shift S are given by $\pi c = c_1$ and $Sc = (c_2, c_3, \dots)$ for $c \in s^m$.

The key property that makes a utility function U recursive with aggregator W is that it obeys Koopmans's equation $U(c) = W(\pi c, U(Sc))$. Any non-trivial solutions to Koopmans's equation for W will be recursive utility functions.[30] Intuitively, we can find U by recursively substituting it

---

normality condition in models with continuous time recursive utility.

[30] It is important here that $W(c, y) = V(u(c), y)$, else solutions to Koopmans's equations for W would not necessarily satisfy Koopmans's limited independence axiom (K2). Some non-trivial aggregators may also yield trivial utility functions, violating the sensitivity axiom (K3). Buckholtz and Hartwick (1989) note this phenomenon with the aggregator $W(c, y) = 1 - e^{-v(c)} + e^{-v(c)}y$, with $v > 0$ and $v' > 0$. Then $y = 1$ is the only solution to Koopmans's equation. By subtracting 1 from utility, we find that this aggregator is ordinally equivalent to the purely multiplicative aggregator

in this equation. This substitution is performed by the recursion operator T_W defined by $(T_W U)(\mathbf{c}) = W(\pi\mathbf{c}, U(S\mathbf{c}))$. Thus

$$(T_W^N 0)(\mathbf{c}) = W(c_1, W(c_2, \ldots, W(c_N, 0) \cdots)).$$

The recursive utility function is the unique fixed point of T_W.

The most familiar aggregator is $W(c, y) = u(c) + \delta y$, which yields the additively separable utility function $U(\mathbf{c}) = \sum_{t=1}^{\infty} \delta^{t-1} u(c_t)$. Obviously, $U(\mathbf{c}) = u(c_1) + \delta U(S\mathbf{c})$. Another aggregator is the modified Uzawa (1968) aggregator $W(c, y) = (-1 + y) \exp[-v(c)]$ used by Epstein and Hynes (1983). This aggregator yields the utility function[31]

$$U(\mathbf{c}) = -\sum_{t=1}^{\infty} \exp[-\sum_{\tau=1}^{t} v(c_\tau)]$$

from Chapter 1 since

$$\left(1 - \sum_{t=2}^{\infty} \exp[-\sum_{\tau=2}^{t} v(c_\tau)]\right) \exp[-v(c_1)] = -\sum_{t=1}^{\infty} \exp[-\sum_{\tau=1}^{t} v(c_\tau)].$$

This form is particularly intriguing since consumption only affects discounting, but does not seem to yield direct utility. Epstein (1983) considers a discrete time formulation that permits uncertainty. His generalized Uzawa aggregator is $W(c, y) = (u(c) + y)e^{-v(c)}$. The Epstein-Hynes form is the special case $u(c) = -1$.

▶ Example 9: The KDW aggregator. The KDW (Koopmans, Diamond, and Williamson, 1964) aggregator is defined by $W(c, y) = (\delta/d) \log(1 + ac^b + dy)$ where $a, b, d, \delta > 0$ and $b, \delta < 1$. There is no closed-form expression for the KDW utility function. However, the Continuous Existence Theorem below will show that Koopmans's equation has a unique solution for the KDW aggregator. Moreover, the utility function may be numerically calculated to any desired degree of accuracy for a given path. ◀

Without loss of generality, we may assume $0 \in \mathcal{Y}$. In fact, if there is a unique $y \in \mathcal{Y}$ with $W(0, y) = y$, we may even assume $W(0, 0) = 0$. If $W(0, y) = y$, then $U(\mathbf{0}) = y$. Now consider the utility function $\hat{U}(\mathbf{c}) = U(\mathbf{c}) - U(\mathbf{0})$. This transformation of the utility function induces a transformation of the aggregator. The new aggregator, $\hat{W}(c, y) = W(c, y + U(\mathbf{0})) - U(\mathbf{0})$, yields the transformed utility function since $\hat{W}(c_1, \hat{U}(S\mathbf{c})) = W(c_1, U(S\mathbf{c})) - U(\mathbf{0}) = U(\mathbf{c}) - U(\mathbf{0}) = \hat{U}(\mathbf{c})$. Both aggregators generate equivalent utility functions, and $\hat{W}(0, 0) = 0$.

$V(c, y) = e^{-v(c)} y$.

[31] Epstein and Hynes actually work in continuous time, but this is obviously a discrete version of their utility function.

When applied to the Epstein-Hynes (EH) aggregator, this yields

$$U(\mathbf{0}) = W(0, U(\mathbf{0})) = (-1 + U(\mathbf{0}))e^{-v(0)},$$

so $U(\mathbf{0}) = 1/(1 - e^{v(0)})$. The adjusted aggregator is then $\hat{W}(c, y) = [y - e^{v(0)}/(1 - e^{v(0)})]e^{-v(c)} - 1/(1 - e^{v(0)})$. Curiously, the new utility function can be written

$$\hat{U}(\mathbf{c}) = \sum_{t=1}^{\infty} e^{-tv(0)} \left[1 - \exp\left(-\sum_{\tau=1}^{t} [v(c_\tau) - v(0)] \right) \right],$$

which is the discounted sum of functions depending on *past* consumption. Note the contrast with the original form of the utility function where consumption seemed to only affect discounting. This form also shows us that even though recursive utility is forward-looking, the functional form may superficially appear to be backward-looking.

More formally:

Aggregator. A function $W: \mathcal{X} \times \mathcal{Y} \to \mathcal{Y}$ is an aggregator if:

(W1) W is continuous on $\mathcal{X} \times \mathcal{Y}$ and increasing in both c and y.

(W2) W obeys a Lipschitz condition of order one: there exists $\delta > 0$ such that $|W(c, y) - W(c, y')| \leq \delta|y - y'|$ for all c in $\mathcal{X}$ and y, y' in $\mathcal{Y}$.

(W3) $(T_W^N y)(\mathbf{c})$ is concave in $\mathbf{c}$ for all N and all constants $y \in \mathcal{Y}$.

When W is differentiable the Lipschitz bound in (W2) is given by $\delta = \sup W_2(c, y)$. This uniformly bounded time perspective is similar to the time perspective studied axiomatically by Koopmans (1960) and Koopmans, Diamond, and Williamson (1964). It ensures that future utility is discounted by at least δ. In the additively separable case, W_2 is the discount factor. In the EH case, the fact that W is increasing in c implies $v' \geq 0$ since $W \leq 0$. The Lipschitz bound then becomes $e^{v(0)}$. We do not yet impose $\delta < 1$ since we may want to consider undiscounted or even upcounted models.

The sole purpose of condition (W3) is to guarantee concavity of the utility function. It is not required for the existence results. Curiously, the aggregator need not be jointly concave in c and y for the associated utility function to be concave. Although the EH aggregator is not concave, the corresponding utility function $U(\mathbf{c}) = -\sum_{t=1}^{\infty} \exp[-\sum_{\tau=1}^{t} v(c_\tau)]$ is concave. Epstein previously (1983) gave sufficient conditions for the concavity of generalized Uzawa utility functions. In the EH case, $v'' < 0$ is sufficient. More generally, when the utility function is the limit of the functions $(T_W^N 0)(\mathbf{c})$, (W3) ensures concavity is inherited by U. Thus,

Lemma 4. *Suppose (W3) holds and $(T_W^N 0)(\mathbf{c}) \to U(\mathbf{c})$. Then U is concave on its domain. If, in addition, W is strictly concave in c and strictly increasing in y, then U is strictly concave. Conversely, if U is concave, condition (W3) holds for all y in the range of U.*

3.5.2 The Existence of Recursive Utility

When trying to construct the utility function, the first problem we confront is what domain to use. Obviously, the utility function will live on a subset of s_+^m. The question is, which subset? Since one of the motivations for studying recursive utility is to admit non-degenerate equilibria, we must use subsets that are appropriate for equilibrium problems—linear spaces.[32]

Even in the additively separable case for $m = 1$, it is unreasonable to expect the utility function to be defined on all of s^1. Consider the additively separable aggregator $\sqrt{c} + \delta y$ where $\delta < 1$. The utility function only makes sense when $\sum_{t=1}^{\infty} \delta^{t-1} \sqrt{c_t}$ converges. This will not happen for all vectors in s_+^1. For example, the sum does not converge when $c_t = \delta^{-2t}$. This is where the weighted ℓ^∞-spaces $\ell^\infty(\beta)$ come in. In this case, the utility function will only exist on $\ell_+^\infty(\beta)$ for $\beta < \delta^{-2}$. Our strategy will be to find a β so that the utility function exists and is β-continuous on $\ell_+^\infty(\beta)$.

Let $\mathcal{A} \subset s^m$ with $S\mathcal{A} \subset \mathcal{A}$ and $\pi\mathcal{A} \subset \mathbb{R}_+^m$.[33] Both the shift S and projection π are continuous in any topology on $\mathcal{A}$ that is stronger than the relative product topology, as are the β-topologies. Given a positive function φ, continuous on $\mathcal{A}$, let $\mathcal{C}$ be the space of continuous functions from $\mathcal{A}$ to $\mathcal{Y}$, and $\mathcal{C}_\varphi$ be the corresponding space of φ-bounded functions.[34] Since all the functions involved are continuous, $T_W : \mathcal{C}_\varphi \to \mathcal{C}$.

Continuous Existence Theorem. *Suppose the topology on $\mathcal{A}$ is stronger than the relative product topology, $W : \mathcal{X} \times \mathcal{Y} \to \mathcal{Y}$ obeys (W1) and (W2), φ is continuous, $W(\pi\mathbf{c}, 0)$ is φ-bounded, and $\delta\|\varphi \circ S\|_\varphi < 1$. Then there exists a unique $U \in \mathcal{C}_\varphi$ such that $W(\pi\mathbf{c}, U(S\mathbf{c})) = U(\mathbf{c})$. Moreover, $(T_W^N 0)(\mathbf{c}) \to U(\mathbf{c})$ in $\mathcal{C}_\varphi$.*

Proof. Since W is increasing in y, the recursion operator T_W is increasing. Now

$$|T_W(0)|/\varphi(\mathbf{c}) = |W(c_1, 0)|/\varphi(\mathbf{c}) < \infty$$

---

[32] An alternative, as used by Streufert (1990), is to focus purely on capital accumulation problems. This allows him to further restrict the size of the subsets, and thus expand the range of aggregators he can use.

[33] This ensures that the recursion operator always makes sense on $\mathcal{C}(\mathcal{A}; \mathcal{Y})$.

[34] See Chapter 2 for details.

because $W(\pi\mathbf{c}, 0)$ is φ-bounded. Finally,

$$T_W(\xi + A\varphi) = W(c_1, \xi(S\mathbf{c}) + A\varphi(S\mathbf{c}))$$
$$\leq W(c_1, \xi(S\mathbf{c})) + A\delta\varphi(S\mathbf{c}) \leq T_W\xi + A\delta\|\varphi \circ S\|_\varphi \varphi(\mathbf{c}).$$

The Weighted Contraction Mapping Theorem (see Section 2.2.3), with $\theta = \delta\|\varphi \circ S\|_\varphi < 1$, shows that T_W is a contraction, and has a unique fixed point U.

Now consider $\|U(\mathbf{c}) - (T_W^N 0)(\mathbf{c})\|_\varphi \leq \delta^N \|U(S^N\mathbf{c})\|_\varphi \leq \|U\|_\varphi (\delta\|\varphi \circ S\|_\varphi)^N$. As the last term converges to zero, $(T_W^N 0)(\mathbf{c}) \to U(\mathbf{c})$. $\square$

In fact, the full force of (W1) was not employed in the proof. The aggregator need not be increasing in c for the theorem to hold.

Corollary 3. *Suppose W as above obeys $W(\lambda c, \lambda^\gamma U) = \lambda^\gamma W(c, U)$. Then U is homogeneous of degree γ.*

Proof. In this case T_W maps homogeneous of degree γ functions to homogeneous of degree γ functions. Thus $(T_W^N 0)$ is homogeneous of degree γ, as is its limit U. $\square$

3.5.3 Aggregators Bounded from Below

The easiest application of the Continuous Existence Theorem is to a bounded aggregator with $\delta < 1$ and $\mathcal{A} = \ell_+^\infty$. Take φ as the constant 1, and use the product topology. As in Lucas and Stokey (1984), this yields a recursive utility function that is not only β-myopic for all $\beta \geq 1$, but also continuous in the relative product topology on ℓ_+^∞. This argument also applies when there are m goods available at each time.

We can also take $\varphi = 1$ when $\mathcal{A} = \ell_+^\infty$ and W is an Epstein-Hynes aggregator with $v(0) > 0$. Then $\delta = \sup W_2 = \sup e^{-v(c)} = e^{-v(0)}$ because $v' > 0$, and so $\delta < 1$.

Bounds on $W(c, 0)$ are obviously important in applications of the Continuous Existence Theorem. One way to obtain a bound is to exploit concavity. Whenever W is concave in c, we can bound $W(c, 0)$. For example, $W(c, 0) \leq W(1, 0) + \alpha(c - 1)$ for some supergradient α (if differentiable, $\alpha = W_1(1, 0)$). Thus we may set $\varphi(\mathbf{c}) = 1 + \|\mathbf{c}\|_\beta$ for a β-myopic utility function when the aggregator is concave in c with $\delta\beta < 1$.

Sharper bounds are sometimes possible. Brock and Gale (1969) gave two closely related measures of growth, the asymptotic exponent and the asymptotic elasticity of marginal utility. For a function $f: \mathbb{R}_+ \to \mathbb{R}_+$, define the *exponent* of f at x by

$$e_f(x) = \frac{\log f(x)}{\log x}.$$

The *upper asymptotic exponent* of f is

$$\bar{e}_f = \limsup_{x \to \infty} e_f(x).$$

Similarly, we may define the *upper asymptotic elasticity* as

$$\bar{E}_f = \limsup_{x \to \infty} \frac{x f'(x)}{f(x)}.$$

Now if $\bar{e}_f < \rho$ or $\bar{E}_f < \rho$, then $f(x) < A(1 + x^\rho)$ for some $A > 0$.

When $0 \leq W(c,0) \leq A(1 + c^\rho)$, as in the case where $W(c,0)$ has asymptotic exponent or asymptotic elasticity of marginal felicity less than $\rho > 0$, we can apply the Continuous Existence Theorem provided $\delta\beta^\rho < 1$. In this case, take $A = \ell_+^\infty(\beta)$ and $\varphi(\mathbf{c}) = 1 + \|\mathbf{c}\|_\beta^\rho$. Then $\|\varphi \circ S\|_\varphi = \beta^\rho$, and the recursive utility function is β-myopic. This applies to the aggregator $W(c,y) = c^\rho + \delta y$. The utility function $\sum_{t=1}^\infty \delta^{t-1} c_t^\rho$ is continuous on each $\ell_+^\infty(\beta)$ for $\delta\beta^\rho < 1$.

When $0 \leq W(c,0) \leq A(1 + \log(1 + c))$, as happens in the KDW case, a similar argument shows that U is β-myopic for all $\beta < \infty$. Take $\gamma > 0$ such that $\delta(\gamma + \log\beta)/\gamma < 1$ and set $\varphi(c) = \gamma + \log(1 + c)$. Then

$$\begin{aligned}
\delta\varphi(\|S\mathbf{c}\|_\beta) &= \delta\gamma + \delta\log(1 + \|S\mathbf{c}\|_\beta) \\
&\leq \delta\gamma + \delta\log(1 + \beta\|\mathbf{c}\|_\beta) \\
&\leq \delta\gamma + \delta\log\beta(1 + \|\mathbf{c}\|_\beta) \\
&\leq \delta\gamma + \delta\log\beta + \delta\log(1 + \|\mathbf{c}\|_\beta) \\
&\leq \gamma + \delta\log(1 + \|\mathbf{c}\|_\beta) \leq \varphi(\|\mathbf{c}\|_\beta).
\end{aligned}$$

Alternatively, we could have noted that the asymptotic exponent is 0 in this case, and so for any $\rho > 0$ find an $A > 0$ with $W(c,0) \leq A(1 + c^\rho)$. Given $\beta \geq 1$, we can make $\delta\beta^\rho < 1$ by taking $\rho > 0$ sufficiently small. Either way, the Continuous Existence Theorem yields a continuous utility function on $\ell_+^\infty(\beta)$ for any $\beta \geq 1$. In particular, this shows that the KDW utility of Example 9 can be generated from its aggregator, even though we are unable to find a closed-form representation.

The choice of $\mathcal{Y}$ is sometimes delicate. Take the aggregator $W(c,y) = c + \sqrt{y}$, with $\mathcal{X} = \mathbb{R}_+$. Although $\mathcal{Y} = \mathbb{R}_+$ is an obvious choice, it yields $\delta = +\infty$. But consider $\Phi(c) = U(c,c,\ldots)$. This obeys $\Phi(c) = c + \sqrt{\Phi(c)}$. The solutions are $\Phi(c) = (1 \pm \sqrt{1 + 4c})/2$. Discarding the decreasing case, we find $\Phi(c) = (1 + \sqrt{1 + 4c})/2$, so $\Phi(0) = 1$. This suggests setting $\mathcal{Y} = [1, \infty)$, which means $\delta = 1/2$. This new choice of $\mathcal{Y}$ allows us to apply the Continuous Existence Theorem on $\ell^\infty(\beta)$ for $\beta < 2$. The increase in discounting as utility gets larger suggests that results might be obtained for $\beta \geq 2$. Streufert (1990) takes advantage of the increased discounting by using an asymptotic measure of discounting. In this case, translating his results into our setup yields existence and product continuity of the utility function on β-bounded sets for any $\beta \geq 1$.

In spite of the success of Streufert's method when discounting decreases asymptotically, relaxing the condition $\delta\beta^\rho < 1$ does risk losing existence on $\ell_+^\infty(\beta)$. Again, the additively separable case makes this clear. Let $W(c, y) = c^\rho + \delta y$ and take $\beta = \delta^{-1/\rho}$. The utility function cannot be defined when $\mathbf{c}$ is given by $c_t = \beta^t$. No utility function can be constructed from the aggregator on $\ell_+^\infty(\beta)$. A smaller space must be used.

One last example comes from the non-additive homogeneous recursive utility functions discovered by Dolmas (1996a). Let u be homogeneous of degree γ and set $W(c, y) = u(c)w(y/u(c))$.[35] It is easy to see that $W(\lambda c, \lambda^\gamma y) = \lambda^\gamma W(c, y)$. Now specialize to the case $w(y) = [1 + \delta y]^\rho/\rho$ where $0 < \delta, \rho < 1$ and $u(c) = c^\gamma$. Then $W_2 = \delta[1 + \delta y]^{\rho-1} \leq \delta$ and $W(c, 0) = c^\gamma$, so the Continuous Existence Theorem applies on $\ell_+^\infty(\beta)$ whenever $\beta^\gamma\delta < 1$. Moreover, Corollary 3 applies and U is homogeneous of degree γ. It is easy to see this is not equivalent to any additive utility on $\ell_+^\infty(\beta)$ since the marginal rates of substitution between consumption at t and $t+1$ depend on future utility as well as c_t and c_{t+1}.

3.5.4 Unbounded Aggregators

The Continuous Existence Theorem can also be used indirectly to deal with aggregators that are not bounded below, such as $W(c, y) = \log c + \delta y$. These obey:

Assumption.

(W1′) W is increasing in both c and y, upper semicontinuous on $\mathcal{X} \times \mathcal{Y}$, continuous when $c > 0$ and $y > -\infty$, and obeys $W(c, -\infty) = W(0, y) = -\infty$ for all $c \in \mathcal{X}$ and $y \in \mathcal{Y}$.

For aggregators satisfying (W1′), paths that are near 0 can pose problems for the Continuous Existence Theorem. When $W(c, y) = \log c + \delta y$ these problems result in a utility function that is upper semicontinuous but not lower semicontinuous. However, they are not severe enough to preclude existence of the utility function.

To circumvent the problems posed by paths that are too close to zero, Boyd (1990a) considers a region that excludes them as the set $\mathcal{A}$. More precisely, choose $\gamma \leq \beta < \infty$, and set $_\gamma\|\mathbf{c}\| = \inf |c_t/\gamma^{t-1}|$ if $0 < \gamma$ and $_0\|\mathbf{c}\| = \infty$.[36] Then take $\mathcal{A} = \ell_+^\infty(\beta, \gamma) = \{\mathbf{c} \in s_+^m : 0 < {}_\gamma\|\mathbf{c}\|$ and $\|\mathbf{c}\|_\beta < \infty\}$. This is the set of paths that have a growth rate between γ and β. Thus $\ell_+^\infty(\beta, 0)$ is just our old friend $\ell_+^\infty(\beta)$.

---

[35] This works for s^m as well as s^1.
[36] When $\mathcal{A} \subset s^m$, $|c_t|$ denotes $\max\{|c_{it}| : i = 1, \ldots, m\}$.

To make this clear, consider the logarithmic case. For any such path, $_\gamma\|\mathbf{c}\|\gamma^{t-1} \le c_t \le \|\mathbf{c}\|_\beta \beta^{t-1}$. Thus

$$\sum_{t=1}^\infty \delta^{t-1}[(t-1)\log\gamma + \log{}_\gamma\|\mathbf{c}\|] \le \sum_{t=1}^\infty \delta^{t-1}\log c_t$$

$$\le \sum_{t=1}^\infty \delta^{t-1}[(t-1)\log\beta + \log\|\mathbf{c}\|_\beta].$$

Since $\sum_{t=1}^\infty \delta^{t-1}\log c_t$ is squeezed between convergent series, it converges. However, the limit need not be continuous since the convergence is not uniform. We can get β-upper semicontinuity. It is enough to show this for each ball $\{\mathbf{c} \in \ell_+^\infty(\beta) : \|\mathbf{c}\|_\beta \le \kappa\}$. On this ball, $\sum_{t=1}^T \delta^{t-1}(\log c_t - (t-1)\log\beta - \log\kappa)$ has non-positive terms. Each of the partial sums is upper semicontinuous, and so is the limit. Since the limit differs from the original utility function by a constant, the utility function is upper semicontinuous too. In fact, we have escaped the lower bound on consumption by taking partial sums. Some sequences may even have utility $-\infty$. Nonetheless, the logarithmic case is well behaved.

We are now forced to admit $-\infty$ as a possible value for utility. This causes some unpleasantness. The obvious solution to Koopmans's equation is not the only one. Amazingly, $U(\mathbf{c}) = -\infty$ satisfies the recursion too. Fortunately, we can restrict our attention to $\ell_+^\infty(\beta, \gamma)$ and see that this is not a reasonable solution.

The general case is similar. Intuitively, we expect to obtain the utility function by recursive substitution, as the limit of

$$(T_W^N u)(\mathbf{c}) = W(c_1, W(c_2, \ldots, W(c_N, y) \cdots))$$

with y constant. In fact, under appropriate conditions, the Continuous Existence Theorem applies on $\ell_+^\infty(\beta, \gamma)$, yielding a unique φ-bounded utility function Ψ. Of course, the iterates $T_W^N u$ converge to Ψ on $\ell_+^\infty(\beta, \gamma)$.

By using a process analogous to partial summation, Ψ can be extended to a utility function on all of $\ell_+^\infty(\beta)$. This extension is upper semicontinuous and recursive. Further, it is the *only* recursive upper semicontinuous extension of Ψ to $\ell_+^\infty(\beta)$.

Upper Semicontinuous Existence Theorem. *Suppose $W : \mathcal{X} \times \mathcal{Y} \to \mathcal{Y}$ obeys (W1'), the Lipschitz condition (W2) holds whenever W is finite, and there are increasing functions g and h with $g(c) \le W(c, 0) \le h(c)$. Set $\varphi(\mathbf{c}) = \max\{h(\|\mathbf{c}\|_\beta), -g(_\gamma\|\mathbf{c}\|)\}$ and suppose $\varphi > 0$ with $\delta\|\varphi \circ S\|_\varphi < 1$ for some $\beta > \gamma > 0$ with $\beta \ge 1$. Then there exists a unique U that is φ-bounded on $\ell_+^\infty(\beta, \gamma)$, obeys $W(\pi\mathbf{c}, U(S\mathbf{c})) = U(\mathbf{c})$, and is β-upper semicontinuous on $\ell_+^\infty(\beta)$.*

Proof. First, temporarily give $\mathcal{A} = \ell_+^\infty(\beta, \gamma)$ the discrete topology. As all functions are continuous there, and $W(c, 0)$ is clearly φ-bounded, the Continuous Existence Theorem applies, yielding a unique φ-bounded recursive utility function $\Psi \colon \ell_+^\infty(\beta, \gamma) \to \mathbb{R}$.

Second, let $\mathbf{z}$ be an arbitrary element of $\ell_+^\infty(\beta, \gamma)$ and define the "partial sums" on all of $\ell_+^\infty(\beta)$ by

$$\Psi_N(\mathbf{c}; \mathbf{z}) = [(T_W^N \Psi)(S^N \mathbf{z})](\mathbf{c})$$
$$= W(c_1, W(c_2, \ldots, W(c_N, \Psi(S^N \mathbf{z})) \cdots)).$$

Now for $\mathbf{z}, \mathbf{z}' \in \ell_+^\infty(\beta)$,

$$|\Psi_N(\mathbf{c}; \mathbf{z}) - \Psi_N(\mathbf{c}; \mathbf{z}')| \leq \delta^N |\Psi(S^N \mathbf{z}) - \Psi(S^N \mathbf{z}')|$$
$$\leq \delta^N M[\varphi(S^N \mathbf{z}) + \varphi(S^N \mathbf{z}')]$$
$$\leq M'(\delta \|\varphi \circ S\|_\varphi)^N$$

for some M'. The first step uses the Lipschitz bound (W2), the second uses the φ-boundedness of Ψ on $\ell_+^\infty(\beta, \gamma)$, and the third uses the fact that $\varphi(S^N \mathbf{z}) \leq (\|\varphi \circ S\|_\varphi)^N \varphi(\mathbf{z})$ for any $\mathbf{z} \in \ell_+^\infty(\beta, \gamma)$. It follows that if $\lim_{N \to \infty} \Psi_N(\mathbf{c}; \mathbf{z})$ exists, it must be independent of $\mathbf{z}$. Note that for $\mathbf{c} \in \ell_+^\infty(\beta, \gamma)$, $\Psi_N(\mathbf{c}; \mathbf{c}) = \Psi(\mathbf{c})$, so $\lim_{N \to \infty} \Psi_N(\mathbf{c}; \mathbf{z})$ exists on $\ell_+^\infty(\beta, \gamma)$ and is equal to Ψ there.

The third step is to show $U(\mathbf{c}) = \lim_{N \to \infty} \Psi_N(\mathbf{c}; \mathbf{z})$ exists and is β-upper semicontinuous on all of $\ell_+^\infty(\beta)$. For κ arbitrary, take $\mathbf{c} \in \ell_+^\infty(\beta)$ with $\|\mathbf{c}\|_\beta \leq \kappa$ and set $z_t = \kappa \beta^{t-1}$. Since $c_t \leq z_t$, $\Psi_N(\mathbf{c}; \mathbf{z})$ is a decreasing sequence. Its limit $U(\mathbf{c})$, which is also its infimum, must exist. Further, each of the Ψ_N is the composition of non-decreasing β-upper semicontinuous functions, so their infimum $U(\mathbf{c})$ is also β-upper semicontinuous on $\{\mathbf{c} : \|\mathbf{c}\|_\beta \leq \kappa\}$. Since upper semicontinuity is a local property, U is β-upper semicontinuous on all of $\ell_+^\infty(\beta)$.

The next step is to show that U is recursive. If $\pi \mathbf{c} = 0$ or if $U(S\mathbf{c}) = -\infty$, (W1$'$) implies $W(\pi \mathbf{c}, U(S\mathbf{c})) = -\infty = U(\mathbf{c})$. Otherwise, we have

$$W(\pi \mathbf{c}, U(S\mathbf{c})) = W(\pi \mathbf{c}, \lim_{N \to \infty} \Psi_N(S\mathbf{c}; S\mathbf{z}))$$
$$= \lim_{N \to \infty} W(\pi \mathbf{c}, \Psi_N(S\mathbf{c}; S\mathbf{z}))$$
$$= \lim_{N \to \infty} \Psi_{N+1}(\mathbf{c}; \mathbf{z}) = U(\mathbf{c}).$$

Therefore $W(\pi \mathbf{c}, U(S\mathbf{c})) = U(\mathbf{c})$ for all $\mathbf{c} \in \ell_+^\infty(\beta)$.

The last step is uniqueness. Let Φ be a β-upper semicontinuous recursive utility function that is φ-bounded on $\ell_+^\infty(\beta, \gamma)$. Since Ψ is unique, Φ, Ψ, and U agree on $\ell_+^\infty(\beta, \gamma)$. When $z_t = \|\mathbf{c}\|_\beta \beta^{t-1}$, $\mathbf{c} \leq \mathbf{z}$ and so

$\Phi(\mathbf{c}) \leq \Psi_N(\mathbf{c}; \mathbf{z})$. Thus $\Phi(\mathbf{c}) \leq \lim_{N \to \infty} \Psi_N(\mathbf{c}; \mathbf{z}) = U(\mathbf{c})$. If $c_t = 0$ for some t, $U(\mathbf{c}) = -\infty = \Phi(\mathbf{c})$. If $c_t > 0$ for all t, set $z_t = \gamma^{t-1}$ and consider the sequence $\mathbf{c}^n = (c_1, \ldots, c_n, z_{n+1}, z_{n+2}, \cdots)$. By construction, $\Phi(\mathbf{c}^n) = \Psi_n(\mathbf{c}; \mathbf{z})$. Since $\gamma < \beta$, $\mathbf{c}^n \to \mathbf{c}$ in the β-topology. By upper semicontinuity of Φ, $\Phi(\mathbf{c}) \geq \lim_{n \to \infty} \Psi_n(\mathbf{c}; \mathbf{z}) = U(\mathbf{c})$. It follows that $\Phi(\mathbf{c}) = U(\mathbf{c})$, and thus U is the unique such function. $\square$

Aggregators with $-1 + \min\{0, \log c\} \leq W(c, 0) \leq \alpha + \log(1 + c)$ fall into this framework when $m = 1$. Given $\delta < 1$ and $\beta \geq 1$, the constant α may be assumed large enough that $\delta(\alpha + \log \beta)/\alpha < 1$. Take $\alpha = 1$ and let $\varphi(\mathbf{c}) = \max\{\alpha + \log(1 + \|\mathbf{c}\|_\beta), 1 - \min\{0, \log_1\|\mathbf{c}\|\}\}$. As $\delta\varphi(S\mathbf{c})/\varphi(\mathbf{c}) \leq \delta(\alpha + \log \beta)/\alpha < 1$ since $_1\|\mathbf{c}\| \leq {_1}\|S\mathbf{c}\|$ and $\|S\mathbf{c}\|_\beta \leq \beta\|\mathbf{c}\|_\beta$, the utility function exists on $\ell_+^\infty(\beta, 1)$ for any β.

In other cases, upcounting ($\delta > 1$) may be allowed. When $-c^\rho \leq W(c, 0) \leq 0$ with $\rho < 0$, we set $\varphi(\mathbf{c}) = {_\gamma}\|\mathbf{c}\|^\rho$ so $\delta\varphi(S\mathbf{c})/\varphi(\mathbf{c}) \leq \delta\beta^\rho \leq \delta\gamma^\rho < 1$. As $\rho < 0$, $\beta^\rho < 1$ and there are γ that permit $\delta > 1$. The Upper Semicontinuous Existence Theorem applies to these examples.

▶ **Example 10: "Partial sums".** As Boyd (1990a) notes, the "partial sum" approach works on a wider range of aggregators than considered in the theorem. If there is a function $v(c)$ with $v(c) = W(c, v(c))$, then "partial sums" can be defined on $\{\mathbf{c} : \|\mathbf{c}\|_1 \leq \kappa\}$ by $[T_W^N v(\kappa)](\mathbf{c})$. These form a decreasing sequence, so their limit is an upper semicontinuous function $U(\mathbf{c})$. As $W(c_1, U(S\mathbf{c})) = \lim[T_W^{N+1} v(\kappa)](\mathbf{c}) = U(\mathbf{c})$, this yields a recursive utility function. This recursive utility function may fail to be lower semicontinuous. One such example is $W(c, y) = -1 + e^{-c}y$ so that $v(c) = -1/(1 - e^{-c})$ and utility is $U(\mathbf{c}) = -\sum_{t=1}^\infty \exp(-\sum_{\tau=0}^t c_\tau)$. Consideration of the sequence $\mathbf{c}^n = (c_1, \ldots, c_n, 0, \ldots)$, where $c_t = 2\log(t + 1)/t$, shows that this utility function is not lower semicontinuous since $U(\mathbf{c}^n) = -\infty$ but $U(\mathbf{c}) > -\infty$. Note that $\delta = 1$ in this example. Yet another class of aggregators amenable to "partial summation" appears in Section 5.3.2. ◀

▶ **Example 11: Overtaking and recursive utility.** The renormalized utility function U_R defined for the overtaking criterion is a recursive utility function provided $-\infty$ is admitted as a possible utility value. Utility is finite for good programs and $U_R(\mathbf{c}) = -\infty$ otherwise. If $\mathbf{c}$ is a good profile, then $U_R(\mathbf{c}) = v(c_1) + U_R(S\mathbf{c})$ when $v(c) \equiv u(c) - u(c_g)$. Define $W(c, y) = v(c) + y$ for $c \geq 0$ and $y \in \mathbb{R} \cup \{-\infty\}$. The function v may be chosen so that W satisfies $(W1')$.[37] If $\mathbf{c}$ is a good program, then

$$W(\pi\mathbf{c}, U_R(S\mathbf{c})) = W(\pi\mathbf{c}, W(\pi_2\mathbf{c}, \ldots, W(\pi_n\mathbf{c}, U_R(S^n\mathbf{c})) \cdots))$$

$$= \sum_{t=1}^n v(c_t) + U_R(S^n\mathbf{c}).$$

---

[37] The critical requirement is $W(c, -\infty) = -\infty$.

But $U_R(S^n c) \to 0$ as $n \to \infty$ since c is a good path. Hence

$$W(\pi c, U_R(Sc)) = \sum_{t=1}^{\infty} v(c_t) = U_R(c).$$

If c is not good, then $U_R(c) = -\infty = W(\pi c, -\infty)$. It follows that U_R is recursive.

The iterates of the recursion operator T_W^N do not converge to U_R for *arbitrary* initial seeds (chosen as constant functions as above). Indeed, $(T_W^N u)(c) = \sum_{t=1}^{n} v(c_t) + u$ does not converge to $U_R(c)$ on good programs unless $u = 0$.

Not surprisingly, the Upper Semicontinuous Existence Theorem fails to hold here. There are two problems. First, the domain $\ell_+^{\infty}(1, \gamma)$ defined for $0 < \gamma < 1$ contains many bad programs (we may choose $\beta = 1$ as there is a maximum sustainable stock). This can be seen by mimicking the calculations for the logarithmic example above. If $c \in \ell_+^{\infty}(1, \gamma)$, then $\gamma \|c\| \gamma^{t-1} \leq c_t \leq \|c\|_1$ implies $v(\gamma \|c\| \gamma^{t-1}) \leq v(c_t) \leq v(\|c\|_1)$. However, the programs defined by setting $c_t = \gamma \|c\| \gamma^{t-1}$ and $c_t^0 = \|c\|_1$ for all t are in general bad programs.[38] Therefore, calculating the utility sums as above will not squeeze the sum $\sum_{t=1}^{\infty} v(c_t)$ between two convergent series. In fact, for a good program c the inequality $\sum_{t=1}^{\infty} v(\gamma \|c\| \gamma^{t-1}) \leq \sum_{t=1}^{\infty} v(c_t) \leq \sum_{t=1}^{\infty} v(\|c\|_1)$ fails. The domain $\ell_+^{\infty}(1, \gamma)$ is not sufficiently restricted to apply to the overtaking criterion.

Second, the contraction hypothesis made in the Upper Semicontinuous Existence Theorem is also questionable in the overtaking case. There $\delta = 1$ and hence $\delta \|\varphi \circ S\|_{\varphi} < 1$ can hold only if $\|\varphi \circ S\|_{\varphi} < 1$. However, this clearly cannot generally hold: just take the case of the optimal program c starting from the given initial stocks for the case $u(0) = 0$. Then let $g(c) \equiv -u_g \leq W(c, 0) \leq v(c) \equiv h(c)$ and observe $\varphi(c) = \max\{v(\|c\|), u_g\}$. But it is known that when the initial capital stocks are below the golden-rule starting stocks, the optimal consumption program increases to the steady-state level. Hence, $\|c\| = c_g$, and $\varphi(c) = u_g$ for this case. This implies $\|\varphi \circ S\|_{\varphi} = 1$. In short, the contraction property cannot hold. Thus, although the renormalized overtaking criterion utility function is recursive, it cannot generally be computed strictly from information contained in the aggregator. Additional information on whether or not a program is good is necessary to choose the right value for the constant in the recursion operation. ◀

Many general results in capital theory have been obtained for the reduced-form model where consumption within the period is "maximized

---

[38] The exceptional case is $c_t^0 = c_g$ for all t.

out" and subutility functions are defined over capital stocks at the beginning and end of the period.[39] The additive discounted model takes the form of maximizing $\sum_{t=1}^{\infty} \delta^{t-1} v(k_{t-1}, k_t)$ by choice of the sequence $\{k_t\}_{t=1}^{\infty}$, $k_t \in \mathbb{R}_+^m$, $(k_{t-1}, k_t) \in T \subset \mathbb{R}^{2m}$ for all t, and $k_0 \leq k$ where k is the given initial starting stock vector. The set T is the technology set; it is typically taken to be a convex set and v is assumed concave with discount factor $\delta \in (0, 1)$. Sorger (1992a) extended the basic aggregator framework to reduced-form models of capital accumulation by adapting Boyd's methods. The reduced-form utility function $U(\mathbf{k})$ is defined for a capital sequence $\mathbf{k} = (k_0, k_1, \ldots)$ and has the domain $\mathcal{F} \subset \ell_+^{\infty}(\beta)$ for some $\beta \geq 1$. As usual, $\mathcal{F}$ contains all paths feasible given technology set $T \subset \mathbb{R}_+^{2m}$ and initial stock k. A reduced-form utility function is *recursive* if there is an aggregator $W : T \times \mathbb{R} \to \mathbb{R}$ such that

$$U(\mathbf{k}) = W((k_0, k_1), U(S\mathbf{k})).$$

For example, the additive framework is generated by the aggregator

$$W((k, k'), y) = v(k, k') + \delta y,$$

where k is the vector of capital stocks at the beginning of the period, k' is the vector of terminal capital stocks for that period, $v : T \to \mathbb{R}$ is a concave "subutility" function defined over the convex technology set T, and y is the proxy for future utility. Analogues of the Uzawa aggregator and KDW aggregators may be constructed along similar lines. Sorger also develops a maximum rate of impatience measure analogous to our upper norm of marginal impatience.

3.6 Conclusion

An important theme in impressionist and post-impressionist art is exploration of the limits of linear perspective in the projection of objects from three-dimensional space onto the two-dimensional world of the canvas. The rules of drawing or painting with perspective produced clear distortions of the painter's position relative to the object under study when translated onto the canvas. Degas flattened space while Caillebotte found sharp recessions in Haussmann's new Parisian boulevards. Matisse compressed space in his *Study in Red* to the point that the subject appeared to originate in a modern version of flatland.[40] The artist's rendering of spatial distortion represents the subjective view of an observable

---

[39] McKenzie (1986) surveys these models. We will use the reduced form in Chapter 5.
[40] See Varnedoe (1990) for more.

scene forced by the constraint of portraying three dimensions in a two-dimensional space. Differences in the visions of artists painting the same or similar subjects exposed the implications of linear perspective and the importance of the subjective element in representing the same or similar objects.

Like an artist's view of a scene, an agent's intertemporal preference relation is subjective. The evaluation of a consumption stream reflects that agent's desire for consumption smoothing over time or willingness to strike a balance between present and future consumption. The desire to smooth consumption flattens the time profile of consumption events while the willingness to trade consumption today for consumption tomorrow leads to the possibility of other time profiles as most desirable given the constraints. Two different agents may evaluate the same consumption profile differently depending on their attitudes towards the timing of consumption. Thus, the next important task is the exploration of how alternative criteria imply different consumption profiles along optimal programs given the constraints. Indeed, the very existence of a best course of action must be addressed in order to find out if an agent can have any vision of the most preferred decision. Once an optimum is constructed, or at least shown to exist, then the analysis can be focused on characterizing the outcome and calculating the responses to changes in the environment. The existence question is best addressed in as general a setting as possible in order to have a reasonably automatic theory for applications to recursive and non-recursive utility functions. Characterization results relying on the stronger recursive structures can be distinguished from general properties valid for an arbitrary τ-myopic or order myopic utility function.

CHAPTER 4

Existence and Characterization of Optimal Paths

4.1 Introduction

An intertemporal optimization problem is defined by a set of possible programs available within a given technology, a set of attainable programs limited to possible paths consistent with a starting value for the capital stock, and a welfare criterion. The interpretation of the abstract programming problem is flexible; it may represent a Ramsey-style central planner, a single household facing an intertemporal budget constraint given by market opportunities, the planning problem faced by a single firm in a market economy, or a welfare maximization problem that yields a competitive equilibrium allocation. For the purposes of defining the basic framework, we adopt a central planning interpretation of the optimization problem. We will use this problem in order to pose questions in Chapter 6 about the possibility of achieving a decentralized optimum.

The analysis of an intertemporal choice problem forms the basic questions of optimal growth. At the most fundamental level, we are interested in establishing the existence of optima. A negative answer would imply the stated objective was not sensible in light of the constraints. Koopmans (1967) calls this *mathematical screening* of an objective function. Objectives failing the basic existence test are to be eliminated from further consideration. Once the existence problem is affirmatively answered it is possible to derive properties of the model. First we ask if there is a unique optimal plan. Multiple solutions signal a problem: the stated criterion is not a complete guide to optimal growth since a metacriterion would be needed for the completion of the description of what a planner *should* choose. Non-uniqueness would also create problems for deriving the laws of change or comparative dynamics implications of the model. The famous "Cambridge controversies" are based in part on the possibility of multiple steady-state solutions in some models.

The description of the properties enjoyed by an optimum is called the *characterization problem*. In general, we seek a *complete characterization* of an optimal program. The goal is to find necessary and sufficient conditions for an optimum in terms of shadow prices which support an optimal allocation. In the context of a centrally planned model, we are led to question the possibility of achieving the optimum by a decentralized mechanism. This usually comes down to showing a social optimum is a competitive market allocation. We are also interested in the converse: does a decentralized market solution achieve an optimal allocation of resources in the intertemporal economy?

Once the characterization conditions have been found, they are subjected to further analysis in order to deduce the properties exhibited by an optimal path of capital accumulation and the corresponding path of consumption. We also use them to derive the laws of change which describe the response of the optimum to shifts in the various economically important parameters or the initial data (the initial capital stock). This is the problem of *comparative dynamics*. In practice, these different analytical levels are often interconnected rather than taken up in sequence. We will illustrate the types of questions we find interesting in the later parts of the book.

The focus of this chapter is on the existence, uniqueness, and complete characterization of the optimum. Our goal is to provide a reasonably automatic existence theory applicable to a wide range of technologies and preferences. The goal is always to solve the dynamic optimization problem. If one thinks of this as an exercise in detective work, then necessary conditions for an optimum provide the usual suspects. In the absence of an adequate existence theory, proofs of the necessary conditions' validity do not aid in convicting any suspect. This view of necessary conditions may seem extreme, but it is at heart a comment on the role played by existence and sufficiency theorems in obtaining a solution to a dynamic optimization problem.[1] For this reason we cast existence questions at the forefront of the analysis and develop a sufficiency theory for our problems that combined with the necessary conditions completely characterizes the solution of an optimal growth problem.

The commodity space, $\mathbf{E}$, is a subspace of s^m as specified in Chapter 2. This space is assigned a topology and the planner's preference order is a binary relation $\succsim$ defined on $\mathbf{E}_+ \times \mathbf{E}_+$. In most applications of the theory, the relation $\succsim$ is described by specifying a utility function or passing to a utility representation by application of the results in Chapter 3. Once we have a utility function, we can ask whether optimal paths exist. In the recursive case, the same conditions that guarantee existence of the utility function will also yield optimal paths, and a value function that satisfies Bellman's equation. Our next task is to characterize these paths via Euler equations and a transversality condition, and then investigate their properties. Are optimal paths monotonic? Do they enjoy a turnpike

---

[1] Young (1969) is the most forceful proponent of this view of necessary conditions.

property? The latter two properties are studied at length in Chapter 5.

We begin with a background discussion of the building blocks used in existence arguments. We frame the discussion within a basic one-sector model in Section 4.2. This section explores the classical existence results for TAS objectives in order to show the ways in which the basic methods apply in a concrete setting. Section 4.3 extends the basic existence theory to include multisectoral models with recursive utility functions. In Section 4.4, we show optimal paths exist and are continuous in an appropriate topology. The latter result is a sensitivity theorem. Section 4.5 shows how dynamic programming may be used on recursive utility, and that the value function is the unique continuous solution to Bellman's equation. The Euler and transversality conditions are taken up in Section 4.6 in order to provide a set of necessary and sufficient conditions for an optimal program. Concluding remarks are found in Section 4.7.

4.2 Fundamentals of Existence Theory

The nuts and bolts of existence arguments are covered in this section. We begin by defining the existence issues in the concrete setting of the classical discounted Ramsey model with the planner's objective defined by a TAS utility function. We set up the basic model in Section 4.2.1. More general versions will be considered in Section 4.4. Section 4.2.2 introduces the key tool for existence arguments—the Weierstrass Theorem. This is applied in Section 4.2.3 to obtain the existence of optimal paths in the discounted Ramsey model. Section 4.2.4 uses similar arguments to establish existence in undiscounted Ramsey models.

4.2.1 A Simple Capital Accumulation Model

The traditional one-sector growth model (Ramsey model) has one all-purpose good available at each point in time. This good is used both for consumption, and as an input to production in the next period. Production proceeds under conditions of diminishing returns to scale, and is described by a production function. The planner starts with an initial capital stock, and maximizes a TAS utility functional over all feasible consumption paths.

Let c_t denote consumption in time period t and let k_t denote the capital stock accumulated during period t, used for production in period $t + 1$. The initial capital stock is k_0. Consider the sequences of consumption levels, $\mathbf{c} = \{c_t\}_{t=1}^\infty$, and capital stocks, $\mathbf{k} = \{k_t\}_{t=1}^\infty$. Both $\mathbf{c}$ and $\mathbf{k}$ are elements of s_+^1, the positive cone of the set of all real-valued sequences.

Let f be a non-decreasing continuous *production function* such that $f(0) \geq 0$. In each time period, income $y_t = f(k_{t-1})$ is freely divided between consumption c_t and capital k_t. Any income that is not accumulated as capital may be consumed.[2] A pair of sequences $(\mathbf{c}, \mathbf{k})$ is *feasible* from k if $c_t, k_t \geq 0$ and $0 \leq k_t + c_t \leq f(k_{t-1})$ for $t = 1, 2, \ldots$. The *feasible set* is $\mathbf{Y}(k_0) = \{(\mathbf{c}, \mathbf{k}) : (\mathbf{c}, \mathbf{k})$ is feasible from $k\}$. The sets of feasible capital and consumption programs are $\mathbf{F}(k_0) = \{\mathbf{k} : (\mathbf{c}, \mathbf{k}) \in \mathbf{Y}(k_0)$ for some $\mathbf{c}\}$ and $\mathbf{B}(k_0) = \{\mathbf{c} : (\mathbf{c}, \mathbf{k}) \in \mathbf{Y}(k_0)$ for some $\mathbf{k}\}$, respectively. Feasible consumption paths obey $0 \leq c_t \leq f(k_{t-1}) - k_t$, and $\mathbf{B}(k_0)$ is referred to as the *budget set*.

Utility U is a TAS functional derived from a *felicity function* (one-period utility function or subutility function) u and a *discount factor* δ. The felicity function $u \colon \mathbb{R}_+ \to \mathbb{R} \cup \{-\infty\}$ is assumed to be upper semicontinuous and strictly increasing. As such, it can take the value $-\infty$ only at 0. The above assumptions on felicity and production will be referred to as the *basic assumptions*. When both u and f are concave, we have a *convex model*. If both are differentiable on $\mathbb{R}_{++}$, we say the model is *differentiable*. Given the utility function U and feasible set $\mathbf{Y}(k_0)$, we call a pair $(\mathbf{c}, \mathbf{k}) \in \mathbf{Y}(k_0)$ *optimal* if $U(\mathbf{c}) \geq U(\mathbf{c}')$ for all $\mathbf{c}' \in \mathbf{B}(k_0)$.

Now that the model is set up, we can investigate some of the potential problems. Consider the production function $f(k) = 2k$, and felicity function $u(c) = c$. For any $\beta < 2$, there are feasible paths of the form $c_t = \bar{c}\beta^t$ with utility $\bar{c}\beta \sum_{t=1}^{\infty} (\delta\beta)^{t-1}$. When $\delta\beta < 1$, such paths have finite utility, but if $\delta\beta \geq 1$, these paths will have infinite utility. When $\delta < \frac{1}{2}$, all such paths will have finite utility. In fact, the theory we develop in this chapter will guarantee the existence of optimal paths. However, if $\delta > \frac{1}{2}$, there will be feasible paths with infinite utility. Our utility function is incapable of properly comparing these paths.

One attempted fix is to use an overtaking criterion. One path is eventually better than another if $\sum_{t=1}^{T} \delta^{t-1} c_t$ is larger for all large T. However, this too runs into problems. Although it can compare some paths with infinite utility, we can always improve on any feasible path. This is illustrated by the paths that grow at a constant rate. A path that grows at a higher rate will eventually be better than a path that grows at a lower rate, no matter how small the starting level of the fast path is taken. Since it is possible to show this economy cannot grow at the rate $\beta = 2$, any such path can be improved on! Thus, existence issues in the basic model are fundamental and must be satisfactorily addressed by one or more techniques before we can continue.

There are two fundamentally different approaches to obtaining the existence of an optimal growth solution. The first technique is the *direct method* grounded on Weierstrass's Theorem. This method is followed

---

[2] We can interpret this as 100 percent depreciation. An alternative interpretation is that f denotes output net of depreciation and investment is reversible.

through the remainder of this section. It also forms the basis for our more general existence results for recursive utility objectives in Section 4.4. The direct approach begins from the position that an optimal growth problem may be cast as a programming problem defined on an infinite dimensional commodity space. Formally, the problem is to find a feasible consumption sequence achieving the optimal value U^* defined by $U^* = \sup\{U(\mathbf{c}) : \mathbf{c} \in \mathbf{B}(k_0)\}$. The number U^* always exists, although it may be either $+\infty$ or $-\infty$.

The second technique for proving existence is *dynamic programming*. Existence theory founded on dynamic programming exploits the multistage characteristics of the intertemporal optimization problem. The recursive structure of production and preferences is heavily utilized in an effort to solve the optimization problem via dynamic programming. We defer our dynamic programming discussion to Section 4.5.

4.2.2 The Weierstrass Theorem

We examine the original one-sector infinite horizon problem cast as a mathematical programming problem on an infinite dimensional space. With some work, the existence of optimal paths will follow from the classical Weierstrass Theorem, which we prove in this section.

Recall that a function u is upper semicontinuous if and only if it obeys $\limsup_{n\to\infty} u(c^n) \leq u(c)$ whenever $c^n \to c$. This fact is important for showing the existence of an optimum by a direct argument based on Weierstrass's Theorem. This classic result says that an upper semicontinuous function achieves its maximum value over any compact set.[3] We will use this fact to establish the existence of an optimal path in the basic model and its generalizations to accommodate recursive utility.

Weierstrass Theorem. *Let* **B** *be a feasible set and* U *a utility function on* **B**. *If* **B** *is compact and* U *is upper semicontinuous, there exists a* $\mathbf{c}^* \in \mathbf{B}$ *that maximizes* U *on* **B**.

Proof. Let $U^* = \sup\{U(\mathbf{c}) : \mathbf{c} \in \mathbf{B}\} \leq \infty$ and choose a sequence $\{\mathbf{c}^\nu\}_{\nu=1}^\infty$ with $U(\mathbf{c}^\nu) \to U^*$. Compactness of **B** implies $\{\mathbf{c}^\nu\}$ has a convergent subsequence $\{\mathbf{c}^{\nu_j}\}_{j=1}^\infty$. Call the limit of this sequence $\mathbf{c}^*$, where $\mathbf{c}^* \in \mathbf{B}$ and $U(\mathbf{c}^*) \leq U^*$. Then upper semicontinuity of U implies $U(\mathbf{c}^*) = U(\lim_{j\to\infty} \mathbf{c}^{\nu_j}) \geq \lim_{j\to\infty} U(\mathbf{c}^{\nu_j}) = U^*$. It follows that $U(\mathbf{c}^*) = U^*$. $\square$

The proof of the Weierstrass Theorem provides a procedure for proving the existence of optima in any programming problem. This so-called *direct method* calls for constructing a sequence $\{\mathbf{c}^\nu\}$ such that $U(\mathbf{c}^\nu) \to U^*$;

---

[3] Recall that a subset of a metric space is *compact* if and only if any sequence has a convergent subsequence. In finite dimensional Euclidean spaces a set is compact if and only if it is closed and bounded.

this sequence is called a *maximizing sequence* and it always exists by the definition of the supremum. The existence proof is completed by extracting a convergent subsequence whose limit point is feasible (via compactness) and achieves the optimal value U^* (which is well defined whether or not an optimal solution exists). The last step is demonstrated by appealing to the upper semicontinuity of the objective. The application of the Weierstrass Theorem therefore requires objective functions enjoy the semicontinuity property in the same topology in which the constraint set is compact. In many optimization problems cast in an infinite dimensional space setting this compatibility requirement is delicate. The choice of a weak topology usually ensures compactness but may make proving continuity of the objective more difficult. Conversely, strengthening the topology may result in the loss of compactness while providing a suitable topology for the continuity of welfare criterion to obtain. In many of the applications in this book, the product (order) topology on the space of all real-valued sequences has an easily checked compactness property (Tychonoff's Theorem) and upper semicontinuity of the objective also holds for this topology.

4.2.3 One-Sector TAS Existence Theory

We complete the existence proof for the basic Ramsey model in this section. The existence argument for the basic model proceeds in two steps. We first show that $\mathbf{F}(k)$ and $\mathbf{B}(k)$ are compact in a suitable topology. The key to this is Tychonoff's Theorem. We combine conditions on preferences and technology to show that the utility function is upper semicontinuous on the budget set, after which Weierstrass's Theorem yields the existence of an optimum. The Tychonoff and Weierstrass Theorems are instrumental in proving the existence of optimal paths and capture the essence of most existence proofs.[4]

With the machinery in hand, the proof that feasible sets are compact is easy.

Proposition 1. *Both* $\mathbf{B}(k_0)$ *and* $\mathbf{F}(k_0)$ *are compact in the product topology.*

Proof. Define the tth iterate of f, f^t, inductively by $f^1(x) = f(x)$, $f^t(x) = f(f^{t-1}(x))$. As f is increasing, $c_t, k_t \leq f^t(k_0)$, and so both $\mathbf{B}(k_0)$ and $\mathbf{F}(k_0)$ are contained in $\prod_{t=1}^{\infty}[0, f^t(k_0)]$. This set is compact by Tychonoff's Theorem.

Take feasible $\mathbf{k}^\nu$ with $\mathbf{k}^\nu \to \mathbf{k}$. Then $0 \leq k_t^\nu \leq f(k_{t-1}^\nu)$. Taking the limit shows $0 \leq k_t \leq f(k_{t-1})$. Thus $\mathbf{F}(k_0)$ is closed. As a closed subset of a compact set, $\mathbf{F}(k_0)$ is compact.

---

[4] Brock and Gale (1969) is a typical example of discrete time existence arguments.

Now suppose $\mathbf{c}^\nu \in \mathbf{B}(k_0)$ with $\mathbf{c}^\nu \to \mathbf{c}$. Consider the associated $\mathbf{k}^\nu \in \mathbf{F}(k_0)$. Take a convergent subsequence with limit $\mathbf{k}$. Retaining notation, we denote it $\mathbf{k}^\nu$. Then $0 \le k_t^\nu + c_t^\nu \le f(k_{t-1}^\nu)$. Taking the limit in the feasibility constraints, we find $\mathbf{c} \in \mathbf{B}(k_0)$. As a closed subset of a compact set, $\mathbf{B}(k_0)$ is also compact. $\square$

▶ Example 1: Existence of an optimal maximin program. Suppose the maximin criterion is adopted as a welfare measure. It is upper semicontinuous in the product topology. Therefore, Weierstrass's Theorem implies it achieves its maximum value over any product continuous budget constraint. Hence, $U^* = \inf_t \{c_t : \mathbf{c} \in \mathbf{B}(k_0)\}$ has an optimal solution $\mathbf{c}^*$. Many other objectives can be shown to yield optimal programs in $\mathbf{B}(k_0)$. ◀

This particular existence result is a special case of those found in the next section. It illustrates how the various ingredients are combined to demonstrate optimal programs exist.

Basic Existence Theorem. *Suppose the basic assumptions are satisfied, $u(c) \le a + bc^\gamma/\gamma$, and $f(k) \le \alpha + \beta k$ with $\beta \ge 1$ and $b, \alpha \ge 0$. If $\beta^\gamma \delta < 1$ and either $a = 0$ or $\delta < 1$, then an optimal path exists.*

Proof. Let $\theta > \beta \ge 1$ with $\theta^\gamma \delta < 1$. Now $c_t \le f^t(k_0)$ and $f^t(k_0) \le \alpha + \alpha\theta + \cdots + \alpha\theta^{t-1} + \theta^t k_0 = \alpha(\theta^t - 1)/(\theta - 1) + \theta^t k_0$ by induction. Since $\theta > 1$, $c_t \le [k_0 + \alpha/(\theta - 1)]\theta^t$. Let $A = b[k_0 + \alpha/(\theta - 1)]^\gamma/\gamma$ and let $g_t(c_t) = u(c_t) - a - A\theta^{\gamma t} \le 0$ for feasible $\mathbf{c}$. On the feasible set, the partial sums $S_T(\mathbf{c}) = \sum_{t=1}^T \delta^{t-1} g_t(c_t)$ form a decreasing sequence of upper semicontinuous functions. Proposition 2.1 implies their limit is upper semicontinuous. Now $\sum_{t=1}^\infty \delta^{t-1} g_t(c_t) = U(\mathbf{c}) - a/(1 - \delta) - A/(1 - \theta^\gamma \delta)$. Thus $U(\mathbf{c})$ is upper semicontinuous on the compact set $\mathbf{B}(k_0)$. By the Weierstrass Theorem, an optimal path exists. $\square$

Note how this theorem fits in with the example in Section 4.2.1. Take $a = \alpha = 0$, $b = 1$, $\gamma = 1$, and $\beta = 2$. When $2\delta < 1$, the theorem applies, while there are problems when $2\delta > 1$. The relation between β, δ, and γ is sharp. If it is violated, the conclusion can fail.

▶ Example 2: Upcounting. One interesting feature of the analysis is that we may not need discounting when $u \le 0$. For example, if $u(c) = -1/\sqrt{c}$, $f(k) = 2k$ and $\delta = 1.2$, we have $\alpha = 2$ and $\gamma = -1/2$. The conditions of the theorem are satisfied as $1.2/\sqrt{2} < 1$. The only danger is that all paths may have $U(\mathbf{c}) = -\infty$; this does not happen in this example. The sequences $k_t = k_0(3/2)^t$ and $c_t = k_0(3/2)^{t-1}/2$ are feasible and yield $U(\mathbf{c}) > -\infty$.

This sort of upcounted case may easily occur in a social welfare context. Suppose the population growth factor is 1.2, and that each individual's consumption at each time is given equal weight in a social welfare function—then $\delta = 1.2$ is the implicit discount factor. Some forms of felicity, such as $u(c) = c$, are ruled out by the requirement that a welfare maximum exist. Other forms $(u(c) = -1/\sqrt{c})$ do have maxima, and pass Koopmans's screening test. ◄

The Basic Existence Theorem must be used with care. It is possible $U(\mathbf{c}) = -\infty$ for all feasible consumption profiles. This is not a problem when $\delta < 1$ and $f'(0+) > 1$ (as when f satisfies an Inada condition at the origin). For small k, $f(k) = f(0) + \int_0^k f'(x)\,dx > f(0) + k$. Given initial stocks $k_0 > 0$, choose an expansible stock $k' \le k_0$ with $f(k') > k'$. The consumption path $c_1 = f(k_0) - k'$, $c_t = f(k') - k'$ is feasible and $U(\mathbf{c}) > -\infty$. One example where $U(\mathbf{c}) = -\infty$ for all feasible consumption paths is Gale's (1967) cake-eating model (see Examples 1.5 and 3.4).

► Example 3: Nonclassical models. The hypotheses of the Basic Existence Theorem do not posit the concavity of the production function. Special forms of nonconvex production functions arise in applications, particularly in the economics of the fishery. Clark (1971) and Skiba (1978) introduced a class of nonconvex models defined by a convex-concave production function. These functions allow for increasing returns to scale for small values of the capital stock and decreasing returns to scale for large values. Suppose f satisfies the basic assumptions with $f(0) = 0$ and there is a maximum sustainable stock $k^M = f(k^M) > 0$. The crucial convex-concave property of the production function is captured by the following condition:

Nonclassical Technology. There exists an inflection point, $0 < k_I < k^M$, such that $f''(k) > 0$ for $k < k_I$ and $f''(k) < 0$ for $k > k_I$.

Thus, f is *convex* on the interval $[0, k_I]$ but concave on $[k_I, \infty)$. The *average product function* $a(k) = f(k)/k$ has the traditional upside-down U shape. The average product is maximized at k_A. The marginal product is greater (less) than the average product if the capital stock input is less (greater) than k_A. Therefore, the region of increasing returns to scale is $[0, k_A]$ while $[k_A, \infty)$ is the decreasing returns to scale region. Moreover, it can be shown that $k_I < k_A \le k^M$. The compactness of $\mathbf{B}(k_0)$ and $\mathbf{F}(k_0)$ follow from Tychonoff's Theorem just as in the case of a convex model. Existence of an optimum for any upper semicontinuous objective functional on the budget set follows.

The nonconvex production function structure implies the model is not convex: we therefore follow the literature by calling this production function *nonclassical* in contrast to the *classical* case arising in a convex model. ◄

The uniqueness of the solution may be demonstrated if u and f are also assumed to be strictly concave functions.

Basic Uniqueness Theorem. *Suppose, in addition to the basic assumptions, that u is strictly concave and f is concave. Then there is a unique optimal program.*

The proof is quite standard, and omitted. It consists of showing if there are two solutions, then their strict convex combination (which is a feasible program owing to the concavity of f) must offer a higher utility (because u is strictly concave) than the utility achieved at the given optimal allocations. However, this contradicts the optimality of the given programs. Thus, there is a unique program.

4.2.4 Extended Utilitarianism

Undiscounted models are used to illustrate the basic techniques and elaborate on the importance of uniqueness results in the basic theory in this subsection. After demonstrating the basic results, we conclude this section with a brief discussion of an alternative welfare criterion defined on ℓ^∞—the long-run average criterion.[5]

A wider range of undiscounted models can be considered using a modified optimality criterion. We say $\mathbf{c}'$ *overtakes* $\mathbf{c}$ if

$$\liminf_{T\to\infty} \sum_{t=1}^{T} [u(c_t') - u(c_t)] > 0.$$

An easy calculation shows that $\mathbf{c}'$ is eventually better than $\mathbf{c}$ by some strictly positive amount. A feasible path $\mathbf{c}$ is *weakly maximal* if it is not overtaken by any feasible path. Thus, $\mathbf{c}$ is weakly maximal if

$$\liminf_{T\to\infty} \sum_{t=1}^{T} [u(c_t') - u(c_t)] \le 0$$

for all feasible $\mathbf{c}'$.[6]

▶ Example 4: Weak maximality and the cake-eating problem. The borderline case where $\beta^\gamma \delta = 1$ may not even have weakly maximal programs, as demonstrated by the cake-eating example with $\delta = 1$ and $u(c) = \sqrt{c}$ (any strictly concave subutility function will do). Here, $\beta = 1$ and $\gamma = 1/2$, so $\beta^\gamma \delta = 1$. Suppose a path $\mathbf{c}$ has $c_t \neq c_{t+1}$ for some t. By the strict concavity of u, the path with consumption $(c_t + c_{t+1})/2$ at times t and $t+1$ overtakes $\mathbf{c}$. Since this program is feasible if $\mathbf{c}$ is feasible, $\mathbf{c}$ cannot be

---

[5] The long-run average is not the only such alternative utilitarian criterion. There is a considerable literature on the subject. Two recent examples are Blackorby, Bossert, and Donaldson (1995a; 1995b).

[6] Hieber (1981) catalogs the variety of possible optimality criteria related to the weakly maximal welfare measure.

weakly maximal. Thus, weakly maximal paths must have equal consumption in all time periods. The only feasible path with equal consumption at all times is $c_t = 0$ for all t, which is clearly not weakly maximal. In fact, it is overtaken by every other feasible path! This model has the further interesting property that $J(k_0) = +\infty$, which can be seen by considering paths of the form $c_t = k_0/n$ for $t \leq n$ and $c_t = 0$ otherwise. The weak maximality criterion flunks Koopmans's test and may be rejected for this model on the grounds it cannot deliver a "best" action. Finally, we note that introducing discounting ($\delta < 1$) allows optimal programs to exist for utility functions such as $U(\mathbf{c}) = \sum_{t=1}^{\infty} \delta^{t-1} \sqrt{c_t}$. ◀

Consider the undiscounted Ramsey model introduced in Example 3.3 using the renormalized utility function as a welfare measure. Weakly maximal programs exist in this case. Before proving the existence of a weakly maximal path we establish the class of good programs is nonempty. We say a capital stock k is *expansible* if $f(k) > k$. Expansible stocks offer the planner the option of accumulating capital. The set of expansible stocks in the classical Ramsey model is the interval $(0, k^M)$ where k^M is the maximum sustainable stock.

Lemma 1. *There is a good program from any expansible stock.*

Proof. There are two cases: (i) $k_0 \geq k_g$ and (ii) $0 < k_0 < k_g$. In the first case, the golden-rule stock can be reached in one step by following the program $k_0 = k$, $c_1 = f(k) - k_g$, and $c_{t+1} = c_g$, $k_{t+1} = k_g$ for all $t \geq 1$.

In the second case, define $h(k) = f(k) - k$. Clearly h is increasing for k smaller than k_g. Hence, for $k_0 \leq k \leq k_g$ it follows that $0 < h(k_0) \leq h(k) \leq h(k_g)$. Choose a natural number N such that $0 < (k_g - k_0)/N \leq h(k_0)/2$. Define $(\mathbf{c}, \mathbf{x})$ as follows: $x_0 = k_0$, $x_{t+1} = x_t + (k_g - k_0)/N$ for $t = 0, 1, 2, \ldots, N - 1$; $x_t = k_g$ for $t \geq N$ with $c_{t+1} = f(x_t) - x_{t+1}$ for all $t \geq 0$. Note that for $t = 0, 1, \ldots, N - 1$ we have $c_{t+1} = (f(x_t) - x_t) + (x_t - x_{t+1}) \geq h(x_t) - (k_g - k_0)/N > 0$, by the choice of N. Also, $x_N = k_g$ implies $c_{t+1} = c_g$ for $t \geq N$. Thus, the program $(\mathbf{c}, \mathbf{x})$ eventually reaches the golden rule and offers positive consumption at each time. Therefore, this is a good program.[7] □

If $u(0) = 0$, then the path of pure accumulation may be used to define a good program. Follow the path of pure accumulation until the golden-rule stock is achieved and maintain that capital stock thereafter while enjoying the golden-rule consumption flow. Since the path of pure accumulation reaches the golden rule in a finite number of periods, this is a good program. The lemma is required to handle the cases arising when $u(0) = -\infty$ and the path of pure accumulation leads to a bad program.

---

[7] This proof is due to Majumdar and Mitra (1982) and is adapted from a nonconvex model.

We notice that if the initial stocks happen to equal the golden-rule stocks, then maintaining consumption at the golden-rule level is weakly maximal. The golden-rule pair (c_g, k_g) is referred to as the *stationary optimal program*. The next theorem generalizes this special case of existence of a weakly maximal program to an arbitrary expansible stock.

Undiscounted Existence Theorem. *Suppose u and f satisfy the basic assumptions and are strictly concave. Then for any expansible initial capital stock, a weakly maximal program exists for the undiscounted model.*

Proof. The objective U_R is upper semicontinuous on $\mathbf{B}(k_0)$ with respect to the topology of pointwise convergence. For each N define the partial sum $U_R^N(\mathbf{c}) = \sum_{t=1}^{N}[u(c_t) - u(c_g)]$ where c_g is the golden-rule consumption flow. Clearly $U_R(\mathbf{c}) = \inf_N U_R^N(\mathbf{c})$ since the value loss terms are non-negative. Each U_R^N is a σ-continuous (sub)utility function on $\mathbf{B}(k_0)$; U_R is the pointwise infimum of continuous functions and must then be upper semicontinuous.

Let $U^* = \sup\{U_R(\mathbf{c}) : \mathbf{c} \in \mathbf{B}(k_0)\}$; note $U^* > -\infty$ since a good program exists for any expansible k_0. Choose a maximizing sequence $\mathbf{c}_\nu \in \mathbf{B}(k_0)$ so that $U_R(\mathbf{c}_\nu) \to U^*$. Since $\mathbf{B}(k_0)$ is compact, there is a subsequence, also denoted $\mathbf{c}_\nu$, which converges to some $\mathbf{c}^* \in \mathbf{B}(k_0)$. Now $U_R(\mathbf{c}^*) \geq \limsup_{\nu \to \infty} U_R(\mathbf{c}_\nu) = U^*$. As $U_R(\mathbf{c}^*) > -\infty$, $\mathbf{c}^*$ is a good path. Therefore, $U_R(\mathbf{c}^*) \geq U_R(\mathbf{c}')$ for all feasible $\mathbf{c}'$.

If $\mathbf{c}$ overtakes $\mathbf{c}^*$, $\mathbf{c}$ is good and $\sum_{t=1}^{T}[u(c_t) - u(c_g)] = \sum_{t=1}^{T}[u(c_t) - u(c_t^*)] + \sum_{t=1}^{T}[u(c_t^*) - u(c_g)]$. Letting $T \to \infty$ shows that $U_R(\mathbf{c}) > U_R(\mathbf{c}^*)$. Thus $\mathbf{c}$ cannot be feasible. It follows that $\mathbf{c}^*$ cannot be overtaken by any feasible program, so $\mathbf{c}^*$ is weakly maximal. $\square$

A more general existence proof in the same spirit is found in Brock (1970b). Strict concavity of the felicity and production functions is important in showing good programs converge to the golden rule. Consider $f(k) = \min\{1 + k, 2k, 3\}$ and $u(c) = c$. This model has multiple golden-rule stocks. All k in $[1, 2]$ are golden-rule stocks. Any sequence with $1 \leq k_t \leq 2$ for t large is good as the corresponding value loss $L(k_{t-1}, k_t)$ is 0. The simultaneous flat spots in the utility and production functions make this possible. Such behavior is more common in multisector models. The set of points with value loss zero is referred to there as a *von Neumann facet*.[8]

Under the conditions of the Undiscounted Existence Theorem, there is a unique weakly maximal program. Moreover, that path converges asymptotically to the golden rule. Given the Basic Uniqueness Theorem, we observe many TAS (extended) utilitarian criteria generate a unique

---

[8] McKenzie (1986) shows how to accommodate von Neumann facets in general reduced-form models with TAS payoff functions.

optimal program. However, there are criteria exhibiting multiple optima.

▶ Example 5: Long-run average optimal paths. Suppose the economy is specified by a one-sector technology having a maximum sustainable stock $k^M > 0$ and the felicity and production functions satisfy the basic assumptions and are strictly concave. A program $\mathbf{c} \in \mathbf{B}(k_0)$ is *long-run average optimal* if, for any other attainable program $\mathbf{c}' \in \mathbf{B}(k_0)$,

$$\limsup_{T \to \infty} \frac{1}{T} \sum_{t=1}^{T} [u(c_t') - u(c_t)] \leq 0.$$

The weakly maximal path found for the renormalized utility function is one of many long-run average optimal programs. Indeed, *any* good program is a long-run average optimal program. Just observe for any two good paths

$$\lim_{T \to \infty} \frac{1}{T} \sum_{t=1}^{T} [u(c_t') - u(c_t)] = 0,$$

because $c_t, c_t' \to c_g$.

The long-run average optimality criterion is an example of a welfare function where the class of optima is so large as to be of little interest to a planner. The multiplicity of optima does not call for a specific plan to be chosen in order to achieve a "best" allocation of resources. A *metacriterion* would need to be invoked in order to determine a course of action. The only real recommendation from this objective is to not choose a bad path. In contrast, the uniqueness property of the optimum for the overtaking criterion tells the planner to choose one particular program. There is no ambiguity about the overtaking optimal course of action. ◀

4.3 Multisector Capital Accumulation Models

In this section, we examine production in multisector models. The technology will be described by a set Y of net output vectors contained in a Riesz subspace $\mathbf{E}$ of s^m. Positive components of $\mathbf{y} \in Y$ represent outputs, negative components are inputs. The economy starts with an endowment $\omega \in \mathbf{E}_+$. The feasible output sequences are those for which the endowment can supply the inputs. That is, feasible sequences are those in $\mathbf{Y}(\omega) = \{\mathbf{y} \in Y : \mathbf{y} \geq -\omega\}$. When combined with the endowment, these yield consumption sequences in the positive orthant of $\mathbf{E}$. The following conditions (or subsets thereof) will be imposed on the technology set Y.

Technology Assumptions. Suppose $(\mathbf{E}, \mathbf{E}')$ is a symmetric Riesz dual pair with $Y \subset \mathbf{E} \subset s^m$.

(T1) Y is a $\sigma(\mathbf{E}, \mathbf{E}')$-closed set (closure).

(T2) Y is a convex set (convexity).

(T3) $\mathbf{0} \in Y$ (inaction).

(T4) $Y \cap \mathbf{E}_+ = \{\mathbf{0}\}$ (no free lunch).

(T5) $\mathbf{E}_- \subset Y$ (free disposal).

(T6) For each $\bar{\mathbf{y}} \in \mathbf{E}$ the set $\{\mathbf{y} \in Y : \mathbf{y} \geq \bar{\mathbf{y}}\}$ is order bounded (boundedness).

(T7) Whenever $\mathbf{y} \in Y$, $\mathbf{y} \geq \mathbf{x}$ with $\mathbf{x} \leq \mathbf{0}$, and $N > 0$, there is an $M > N$ and $\mathbf{z} \in Y$ with $\mathbf{z} \geq \mathbf{x}$ and $\mathbf{z}$ obeys $z_t = y_t$ for $t = 1, \ldots, N$ and $z_t \leq 0$ for $t > M$ (shutdown).

We will generally use the dual pairing (s^m, c_{00}) or $(\ell^\infty(\beta), \ell^1(1/\beta))$. Assumptions (T1)–(T5), closure, convexity, inaction, no free lunch, and free disposal, are fairly standard. When convexity and inaction are taken together, they imply that commodities are infinitely divisible. Assumption (T4) says that if anything is produced, some components of the production vector must be negative—something must be used as input.

Assumption (T6) says that if inputs are bounded, outputs must be bounded too. Assumptions (T1) and (T6) establish compactness of the feasible set because $\sigma(\mathbf{E}, \mathbf{E}')$-closed and bounded subsets of $\mathbf{E}$ are $\sigma(\mathbf{E}, \mathbf{E}')$-compact. Given an endowment ω, the feasible set $\mathbf{Y}(\omega)$ is compact.

In finite dimensional spaces, assumption (T6) is redundant. It is implied by (T1)–(T4). This is not true in when $\mathbf{E}$ is infinite dimensional, hence the additional assumption. Interestingly, if Y is a cone, (T6) implies (T4)! If there were a $\mathbf{y} \in Y$ with $\mathbf{y} > \mathbf{0}$, then $\lambda \mathbf{y} \in Y$ for all $\lambda > 0$. This would mean $\mathbf{Y}(\mathbf{0})$ is not bounded, and (T4) also holds.

Other assumptions could be substituted for assumption (T6). For example, the assumption below, that a minimal amount of input is needed to produce output, implies assumption (T6) when $(\mathbf{E}, \mathbf{E}') = (s^m, c_{00})$.

Input Requirement Assumption. For every $\mathbf{y} \in Y$, and each t and $\delta \geq 1$, there is an $\epsilon > 0$ such that $|y_\tau^-| > \epsilon$ for some $\tau < t$ whenever $|y_t^+| > \delta$.

Lemma 2. Let $(\mathbf{E}, \mathbf{E}') = (s^m, c_{00})$. If Y satisfies (T2), (T3), and the input requirement assumption, then assumption (T6) is satisfied.

Proof. Suppose (T6) is not satisfied. Then we can find a sequence $\mathbf{y}^\nu \in \{\mathbf{y} \in Y : \mathbf{y} \geq \bar{\mathbf{y}}\}$ which is unbounded. Let t be the first time at which y_t^ν is unbounded. By passing to a subsequence, if necessary, we may assume y_{it}^ν is positive and monotonically increases to ∞ for some i. Let $\alpha_t = \max\{1, \max_i\{y_{it}\}\} > 0$. Note $\mathbf{y}/\alpha_t \in Y$ by combining convexity and $\mathbf{0} \in Y$. Apply the input requirement assumption with $\delta < y_t^\nu/\alpha_t$. There is an $\epsilon > 0$ with $|(y_\tau^\nu)^-/\alpha_t| > \epsilon$ for some $\tau < t$ when $\nu \geq N$. As there are finitely many $\tau < t$, and finitely many goods, some sequence $y_{j\tau}^\nu$ has to converge to $-\infty$. This is impossible since $\mathbf{y}^\nu \geq \bar{\mathbf{y}}$. $\square$

Assumption (T7) allows eventual termination of any production process. It is related to Bewley's (1972) exclusion assumption. Exclusion sets forth a fixed sequence of termination times. It must be possible to terminate the process at these times. Prescott and Lucas (1972) require immediate termination be possible. Unlike these conditions, the shutdown condition does not require that it be possible to terminate the process at a given time. It may take some time to bring the process to an end, and the time taken may depend on the production process being used.

Both assumptions (T6) and (T7) are satisfied by standard capital accumulation models, where the production set is the sum of periodwise production sets $\bar{Y}_t$. They also hold in "neo-Austrian" capital accumulation models (e.g., Hicks, 1973; Atsumi, 1991) even when production cannot be truncated at an arbitrary point in time.[9]

4.3.1 The von Neumann and Malinvaud Models

The *von Neumann model* (1937) starts by defining a collection of fundamental production processes (*activities*). There are n activities producing m goods. The n-vector z_t denotes the intensity of each activity at time t. The m-vectors a_t and b_t respectively denote the inputs and output at time t. The technology is described by two $m \times n$ matrices, the input matrix A and the output matrix B. Given intensity z_t, the inputs required are $a_t = Az_t$ and the outputs produced are $b_{t+1} = Bz_t$. Thus a_{ij} is the input of good i required by activity j when j is run at unit intensity. Similarly, b_{ij} is the output of good i by activity j when j is run at unit intensity. The columns of A and B denote the activities. The rows of A represent inputs, while the rows of B represent outputs. One activity may produce many goods (joint production), and many activities may produce the same good (production processes are substitutes).

The set of feasible input–output combinations is $T_N = \{(a, b) : a \geq Az,\ 0 \leq b \leq Bz$ for some $z \geq 0\}$. Note that we allow free disposal of both inputs and outputs. Typically, we require that the following *KMT conditions* (Kemeny, Morgenstern, and Thompson, 1956) be satisfied. The matrices A and B have non-negative entries, each column of A has a strictly positive entry, and each row of B has a strictly positive entry. Since each column (activity) in A has a positive entry, all activities require the input of something. Since each row (output) of B has a positive entry, all outputs can be produced by some activity.

---

[9] Atsumi (1991) notes there is a subtle problem in transforming a neo-Austrian model into the von Neumann model in its classical form. The output matrix of the von Neumann model is assumed to have only nonnegative entries. In Atsumi's neo-Austrian case some products may appear in the output matrix as negative entries. Loś (1976) extended the von Neumann model to allow negative entries in the output matrix. McKenzie (1991) also elaborates on this issue.

Under the KMT conditions, T_N is a closed, convex cone. There is free disposal of inputs and outputs since if $(a, b) \in T_N$ and if $a' \geq a$ and $0 \leq b' \leq b$, then $(a', b') \in T_N$. You cannot produce something from nothing, $(0, b) \in T_N$ implies $b = 0$. The economy can produce all goods in the sense that for all i, there is $(a, b) \in T_N$ with $b_i > 0$. Since T_N is convex, it follows there is an $(a, b) \in T_N$ with $y \gg 0$.[10] We can regard **b** − **a** as a net output vector for this technology. Positive entries denote outputs, negative entries denote inputs.

A sequence $(a_t, b_t) \in \mathbb{R}_+^{2m}$ is *feasible* from b_1 if there are activity levels z_t with $b_t \geq a_t \geq A z_t$ and $b_{t+1} \leq B z_t$ (equivalently $(a_t, b_{t+1}) \in T_N$ and $a_t \leq b_t$) for all $t = 1, 2, \ldots$. Here a_t is the capital stock drawn from the goods available at time t, which is used as an input to production of output b_{t+1} at time $t + 1$. A feasible sequence uses the outputs in one period as the inputs in the next period. The economy starts with an endowment b_1 of goods available for use as either inputs or consumption in the first period.

The *Malinvaud model* generalizes the von Neumann model by starting with a sequence of technology sets $T_t \subset \mathbb{R}_+^{2m}$ for $t = 1, \ldots$. We say the model is *stationary* if $T_t = T$ for all t. We always require T_t satisfy the following conditions in the Malinvaud model:

Malinvaud Technology Assumptions. A set $T \subset \mathbb{R}_+^{2m}$ is a Malinvaud technology set if:

(M1) T is a closed set (closure).

(M2) T is a convex set (convexity).

(M3) $(0, 0) \in T$ (inaction).

(M4) $(0, b) \in T$ implies $b = 0$ (no free lunch).

(M5) If $(a, b) \in T$ and $a' \geq a$, $0 \leq b' \leq b$, then $(a', b') \in T$ (free disposal).

(M6) There is $(a, b) \in T$ with $b \gg 0$ (productivity).

Of course, $T_t = T_N$ is a Malinvaud technology whenever the KMT conditions are satisfied. Note that we do not require constant returns here, unlike Malinvaud (1953). Indeed, we include technologies limited by primary factors in the Malinvaud technology category.

▶ Example 6: The von Neumann model with fixed labor supply. We start with the standard von Neumann model represented by the matrices (A, B) satisfying the KMT conditions. We assume there is one unit of labor available to the economy in each period. Labor is a primary factor of production. Each process requires one unit of labor input when run at unit intensity. Let $e = (1, \ldots, 1)$ be the m-dimensional row vector with a 1 in each component. Define the set $T_N^* = \{(a, b) : a \geq A z, 0 \leq b \leq B z$ for

---

[10] The notation $x \gg y$ means $x_i > y_i$ for every i.

some $z \geq 0$ and $ez \leq 1$}. Then T_N^* is a Malinvaud technology. Moreover, this technology set is compact. ◀

We can derive a technology set from a Malinvaud technology. Let $Y = \{\mathbf{y} = \mathbf{b} - \mathbf{a} : (a_t, b_{t+1}) \in T_t$ and $b_1 = 0\}$. This is clearly convex (T2) and contains $\mathbf{0}$ (T3). The no free lunch condition (T4) holds: if $\mathbf{y} = \mathbf{b} - \mathbf{a} > \mathbf{0}$, then $b_t \geq a_t$ for every t. But then $a_1 = 0$, which implies $b_2 = 0$, and so $a_2 = 0$, etc. Thus $\mathbf{y} = \mathbf{0}$ is the only non-negative element of Y. Free disposal in T implies free disposal (T5) in Y. Moreover, since $(0, 0) \in T_t$, we can halt production at any time, satisfying assumption (T7). We will usually utilize the production set Y, which enables us to work in terms of consumption sequences. An alternative that is often used in conjunction with the Malinvaud technology is the *reduced-form model*, where utility is specified in terms of capital inputs and outputs, instead of consumption. On the surface, the reduced-form model seems more general as we can write consumption in terms of capital inputs and outputs. However, this generality is an illusion. In the cases where consumers actually do get utility from the stocks of capital goods, they can be incorporated separately in the list of commodities.

▶ Example 7: The neoclassical multisector model. There are $m + 1$ "final goods" consisting of one pure consumption good and m pure capital goods. Labor is the only primary factor. We begin by defining the properties of neoclassical production functions. Cobb-Douglas and CES production functions are standard examples of neoclassical production functions.

Neoclassical Production Function. A function $F \colon \mathbb{R}_+^{m+1} \to \mathbb{R}_+$ is neoclassical if:

(1) $F \in \mathcal{C}^2(\mathbb{R}_{++}^{m+1}, \mathbb{R}_{++})$;
(2) $F(\lambda x) = \lambda F(x)$, for all $k \in \mathbb{R}_+^{m+1}$ and $\lambda \geq 0$;
(3) F is concave;
(4) $DF(x) \gg 0.$[11]

Suppose production possibilities are described by $m + 1$ neoclassical production functions F^j for $j = 0, 1, \ldots, m$. There is no joint production. Each production process produces only one output. Sector 0 is the consumption goods sector; capital goods are produced in sectors $j = 1, 2, \ldots, m$. Let $F^j(\ell^j, a^{1j}, \ldots, a^{mj})$ denote the production function of sector j using labor input ℓ^j and capital inputs $(a^{1j}, a^{2j}, \ldots, a^{mj})$ for $j = 0, 1, \ldots, m$. Here a^{ij} is the input of capital good i in sector j and ℓ^j is the input of labor into sector j.

We will represent the technology set using a transformation function. The economy is assumed to have one unit of labor available at each time.

---

[11] $DF(x)$ is the gradient of F.

The *transformation function* is

$$\mathcal{T}(a, b) = \sup \; F^0(\ell^0, a^{10}, \ldots, a^{m0})$$

$$\text{s.t. } F^j(\ell^j, a^{1j}, \ldots, a^{mj}) \geq b_j \text{ for } j = 1, 2, \ldots, m$$

$$\sum_{j=0}^{m} a^{ij} \leq a_i \text{ for } i = 1, 2, \ldots, m$$

$$\sum_{j=0}^{m} \ell^j \leq 1 \text{ and } \ell^j, x_j^i \geq 0 \text{ for all } i, j.$$

In other words, $\mathcal{T}(a, b)$ is the maximal consumption that can be obtained by combining a unit of labor with capital stock a, while leaving a vector of capital goods b available for the future.

The transformation function $\mathcal{T}$ is concave in both arguments, non-decreasing in the capital goods input components a, and non-increasing in the capital goods output b. It is differentiable if each F^j is strictly quasi-concave and if all inputs are necessary (Benhabib and Nishimura, 1979). Moreover, $\mathcal{T}(0, 0) = 0$ since the underlying production functions are neoclassical. A Malinvaud technology set is derived from this neoclassical model by defining it to be the input–output combinations (a, b) lying in the domain of $\mathcal{T}$.

If u is the felicity function over consumption, then we write $v(a, b) = u(\mathcal{T}(a, b))$ to be the transformed felicity function defined over beginning and end-of-period capital stocks. The function $v(a, b)$ is also an example of a reduced-form felicity function. Similar considerations apply with recursive utility, yielding a reduced-form aggregator $V(a, b, y) = W(\mathcal{T}(a, b), y)$. ◄

We need the following lemma to show that Y is product closed (T2) and that product boundedness (T6) is satisfied in the general Malinvaud model.

Lemma 3. *Let T satisfy (M1)–(M4). For all $\alpha > 0$ there is a $\beta > 0$ such that whenever $(a, b) \in T$ with $|a| \leq \alpha$, then $|b| \leq \beta$.*

Proof. Suppose not. Then there are pairs $(a^n, b^n) \in T_t$ with $|b^n| > n$ and $|a^n| \leq \alpha$. By convexity, $\frac{1}{|b^n|}(a^n, b^n) \in T_t$. Now there is a subsequence such that $b^{n_j}/|b^{n_j}| \to b^* \neq 0$. Note that $a^{n_j}/|b^{n_j}| < \alpha/n_j \to 0$. By closure, $(0, b^*) \in T_t$. But this violates the no free lunch condition. This contradiction establishes the result. □

Corollary 1. *Let each T_t satisfy (M1)–(M4). The derived production set Y then obeys assumption (T6) for (s^m, c_{00}).*

Proof. Suppose $\mathbf{y} \in Y$ and $\mathbf{y} \geq \bar{\mathbf{y}}$. Write $\mathbf{y} = \mathbf{b} - \mathbf{a}$. We know $b_1 = 0$, so $0 \leq a_1 \leq -\bar{y}_1$. By the lemma, b_2 is bounded by some constant vector

$\beta_2 \in \mathbb{R}^m_+$. But then $\beta_2 - a_2 \geq b_2 - a_2 \geq \bar{y}_2$, so a_2 is bounded by $\beta_2 - \bar{y}_2$. Again applying the lemma shows b_3 is bounded. By induction, $\mathbf{Y}(-\bar{\mathbf{y}})$ is bounded. $\square$

Corollary 2. *Let each T_t satisfy (M1)–(M4). The derived production set Y is product closed.*

Proof. Let $\mathbf{y}^\nu \to \mathbf{y}$ with $\mathbf{y}^\nu \in Y$. We can write $\mathbf{y}^\nu = \mathbf{b}^\nu - \mathbf{a}^\nu$.

Our first objective is to show that $\{\mathbf{a}^\nu\}$ and $\{\mathbf{b}^\nu\}$ are bounded. We proceed by induction. Suppose $\{a^\nu_t\}$ is bounded. By the lemma, $\{b^\nu_{t+1}\}$ is bounded. Now $a^\nu_{t+1} = b^\nu_{t+1} - y^\nu_{t+1}$. Boundedness of $\{a^\nu_{t+1}\}$ follows from boundedness of $\{b^\nu_{t+1}\}$ and $\{y^\nu_{t+1}\}$. Moreover, $b^\nu_1 = 0$, so $a^\nu_1 = y^\nu_1$. Now $\{a^\nu_1\}$ is bounded since it converges (to y_1). This starts the induction, and we conclude $\{\mathbf{a}^\nu\}$ and $\{\mathbf{b}^\nu\}$ are bounded.

In s^m_+, bounded sequences have convergent subsequences. Take a subsequence where $\mathbf{a}^{\nu_j}$ and $\mathbf{b}^{\nu_j}$ converge to $\mathbf{a}$ and $\mathbf{b}$. Now $\mathbf{y}^{\nu_j} = \mathbf{b}^{\nu_j} - \mathbf{a}^{\nu_j} \to \mathbf{b} - \mathbf{a}$. But $\mathbf{y}^{\nu_j} \to \mathbf{y}$, which means that $\mathbf{y} = \mathbf{b} - \mathbf{a} \in Y$. Therefore Y is closed. $\square$

In short, we have now shown the following.

Corollary 3. *Suppose each T_t satisfies (M1)–(M5). The derived production set Y satisfies (T1)–(T7) for (s^m, c_{00}).*

The productivity condition (M6) is not required for the derivation of (T1)–(T7). This allows us to consider models containing both primary and produced goods.

4.3.2 The Feasible Correspondence

A *correspondence* from a set A to a set B is a mapping that associates a non-empty subset of B with every element of A. We write $\psi \colon A \twoheadrightarrow B$ to denote that ψ is a correspondence from A to B. An example is the feasible correspondence $\mathbf{Y}(\omega)$. It is a correspondence from s^m_+ to s^m. Non-emptiness follows from the fact that $\{\mathbf{0}\} \subset \mathbf{Y}(\omega)$. We say $\psi \colon A \twoheadrightarrow B$ is *lower semicontinuous at* x if for every open V that intersects $\psi(x)$, there is a neighborhood N of x such that $\psi(x')$ intersects V for every $x' \in N$. A correspondence is *upper semicontinuous at* x if for every open V with $\psi(x) \subset V$, there is a neighborhood N of x with $\psi(x') \subset V$ for every $x' \in N$. A correspondence is *upper (lower) semicontinuous* if it is upper (lower) semicontinuous at every x. A correspondence is *continuous* if it is both lower and upper semicontinuous. Finally, a correspondence f is *closed* if for every x and y, whenever $x^\nu \to x$ and $y^\nu \to y$ with $y^\nu \in \psi(x^\nu)$, we have $y \in \psi(x)$.[12] There is a close relation between closed and upper semicontinuous correspondences. A closed-valued upper semi-

---

[12] Klein and Thompson (1984) is a good reference on correspondences.

continuous correspondence is closed, and a closed correspondence whose range is contained in a compact set is upper semicontinuous.[13]

When the technology assumptions hold under the product topology, the feasible correspondence $\mathbf{Y}(\omega)$ is well behaved. Not only is it a compact-valued and closed correspondence, but it is also a lower semicontinuous correspondence from s_+^m to s^m.

Proposition 2. *Suppose convexity, inaction, and the shutdown condition hold for $Y \subset s^m$ under the product topology. Then $\mathbf{Y}(\omega)$ is a product lower semicontinuous correspondence.*

Proof. Note $\mathbf{0} \in \mathbf{Y}(\omega)$. Let V be open with $V \cap \mathbf{Y}(\omega) \neq \emptyset$. Recall that the sets $G(\mathbf{x}, \epsilon, N) = \{\mathbf{x} \in s^m : |x_t - z_t| < \epsilon \text{ for } t = 1, \dots, N\}$ form a basis for the product topology. Take $\mathbf{y} \in V \cap \mathbf{Y}(\omega)$ and $\epsilon, N > 0$ with $G(\mathbf{y}, \epsilon, N) \subset V$. If $y_{it} = 0$ for all $t = 1, \dots, N$, $\mathbf{0} \in V$ which immediately implies lower semicontinuity as $\mathbf{0} \in \mathbf{Y}(\omega')$ for all ω'. We now consider the case where $y_{it} \neq 0$ for some $t \leq N$. By the eventual shutdown condition, we can take M large enough that $\mathbf{z}$ given by the shutdown condition is in Y. Further, $\mathbf{y} \geq -\omega$, $\mathbf{z} \geq -\omega$. Clearly $\mathbf{z} \in \mathbf{Y}(\omega)$, and $G(\mathbf{z}, \epsilon, M) \subset G(\mathbf{z}, \epsilon, N) = G(\mathbf{y}, \epsilon, N) \subset V$.

Let $\alpha < \min_{t \leq M}\{\epsilon/|z_{it}|\} < \infty$, and consider $(1-\alpha)\mathbf{z} = (1-\alpha)\mathbf{z} + \alpha\mathbf{0} \in Y$. Because $|(1-\alpha)z_{it} - z_{it}| = \alpha|z_{it}| < \epsilon$ for $t = 1, \dots, M$, we have $(1-\alpha)\mathbf{z} \in G(\mathbf{z}, \epsilon, M)$. Let $\delta = \min_{t \leq M}\{\alpha\omega_{it} : \omega_{it} \neq 0\}$.

We now show that $(1-\alpha)\mathbf{z} \in \mathbf{Y}(\omega')$ whenever $\omega' \in G(\omega, \delta, M)$. Let $\omega' \in G(\omega, \delta, M)$. Then $(1-\alpha)z_{it} \geq -(1-\alpha)\omega_{it} = -\omega_{it} + \alpha\omega_{it} \geq -\omega_{it} + \delta \geq -\omega_{it}'$ whenever $t = 1, \dots, M$. Moreover, since $z_{it} = 0$ for $t > M$, $(1-\alpha)\mathbf{z} \geq -\omega'$, and so $(1-\alpha)\mathbf{z} \in \mathbf{Y}(\omega')$. This establishes lower semicontinuity. $\square$

4.4 The Existence and Sensitivity of Optimal Paths

The Basic Existence and Uniqueness Theorems are extended to the broader class of recursive utility functions in this section. Existence is quite straightforward. The existence of optimal paths is just one of the useful facts that follow from continuity of the utility function and compactness of the feasible set. When the aggregator defines a continuous utility function, a modern version of Weierstrass's Theorem, the Maximum Theorem, can be used to show continuity of optimal paths.[14] For example, when the feasible set (and hence the optimal path) depends continuously on a parameter vector ω, the maximizer correspondence $\mu(\omega)$ will be continuous.

---

[13] These are standard results, see Klein and Thompson (1984, Theorems 7.1.15 and 7.1.16).

[14] Magill and Nishimura (1984) also use the Maximum Theorem to obtain continuous policy functions with recursive utility.

4.4.1 The Maximum Theorem

We start with a form of the Maximum Theorem that is well adapted to our purposes.[15]

Maximum Theorem. *Suppose ψ is a compact-valued correspondence from X to Z.*

(1) *If U is upper semicontinuous on Z, there exists a $z^* \in \psi(x)$ such that $U(z^*) = \sup\{U(z) : z \in \psi(x)\}$.*

(2) *If Z is compact, U is continuous, and ψ is lower semicontinuous and closed, then the value function $J(x) = \sup U(\psi(x))$ is continuous and the maximizer correspondence $\mu(x) = \arg\max\{U(z) : z \in \psi(x)\}$ is closed.*

(3) *If in addition, U is strictly concave, then $\mu(x)$ is a continuous function of x.*

Proof. Part (1) is just the Weierstrass Theorem. An upper semicontinuous function must attain its maximum over any compact set.

We next show J is lower semicontinuous. Let α be arbitrary and take x_0 with $J(x_0) > \alpha$. Let $z_0 \in \mu(x_0)$. Let $\epsilon > 0$ so that $J(x_0) - \epsilon > \alpha$ and choose an open set U with $z_0 \in U$ and $|U(z) - U(z_0)| < \epsilon$ for $z \in U$. Now $\psi(x_0) \cap U \neq \emptyset$, so by lower semicontinuity of the correspondence ψ, there is a neighborhood N of x_0 with $\psi(x) \cap U \neq \emptyset$ for $x \in N$. Then if $x \in N$, there is a $z_1 \in \psi(x) \cap V$ with $U(z_1) > U(z_0) - \epsilon > \alpha$. It follows that $J(x) > J(x_0) - \epsilon > \alpha$ for all $x \in N$. Thus $J^{-1}(\alpha, \infty)$ is open.

Now we show μ is closed. Let $x^n \to x$ and $z^n \in \mu(x^n)$ with $z^n \to z$. Since ψ is a closed correspondence, $z \in \psi(x)$. Then $\lim J(x^n) = \lim U(z^n) = U(z)$ by continuity of U. But $\lim J(x^n) \geq J(x)$ because J is lower semicontinuous. Thus $J(x) = U(z)$ and so $z \in \mu(x)$.

We need only show upper semicontinuity of J to show J is continuous. Recall that closed correspondences mapping into compact sets are upper semicontinuous. Now let α be arbitrary with $J(x_0) < \alpha$. Choose ϵ with $J(x_0) + \epsilon < \alpha$. Set $W = \{z : U(z) < J(x_0) + \epsilon\}$ and $F = \{z : z \in \psi(x_0)\}$. Of course $F \subset W$, F is compact, and W is open. For each $z \in F$, take an open set U_z with $z \in U_z \subset W$. The collection $\{U_z\}$ covers F, so it has a finite subcover $\{U_i\}_{i=1}^{I}$. Let $U = \cap_{i=1}^{I} U_i$. Then U is open with $F = \psi(x_0) \subset U \subset W$. By upper semicontinuity of ψ, we may choose a neighborhood N of x_0 with $\psi(x) \subset U$ for $x \in N$. For $x \in N$ and $z \in \psi(x)$, $U(z) < J(x_0) + \epsilon$ because $\psi(x) \subset U \subset W$. Thus $J(x) \leq J(x_0) + \epsilon$ for $x \in N$ and $x \in J^{-1}(-\infty, \alpha)$. Thus J is upper semicontinuous. That completes part (2).

Finally, part (3) is immediate since if U is strictly concave there is a unique maximizer. Thus μ is actually a function: either closedness or

---

[15] For other forms, see Berge (1963) or Klein and Thompson (1984).

upper semicontinuity as a correspondence implies continuity as a function. $\square$

This form of the Maximum Theorem will demonstrate continuity of the optimal paths and value function. The next order of business is to put all of the pieces together.

4.4.2 Optimal Paths

We start by showing how to employ the β-topologies. The first step is to show that the feasible set is actually compact. This turns out to be fairly easy, since the β-topology often coincides with the product topology, which is quite easy to work with. The following lemma shows that the β-topology and product topology coincide on any α-bounded set whenever $\alpha < \beta$.[16]

Lemma 4. *The product topology and the β-topology coincide on any α-bounded set for $1 \leq \alpha < \beta$.*

Proof. Since both topologies are metric, it suffices to work with sequences. Let A be the α-bounded set, and $\mathbf{x}, \mathbf{x}^\nu \in A$.

If $\mathbf{x}^\nu \to \mathbf{x}$ in the β-topology, $|x_t^\nu - x_t| \to 0$, which implies product convergence.

Now suppose $\mathbf{x}^\nu \overset{p}{\to} \mathbf{x}$ and let $\epsilon > 0$. Let M be an α-bound for A, and choose T with $M(\alpha/\beta)^T/2 < \epsilon$. Now consider $G(\epsilon, T, \mathbf{x})$. There is an N with $\mathbf{x}^\nu \in G(\epsilon, T, \mathbf{x})$ for $\nu \geq N$. Thus $|x_t^\nu - x_t|/\beta^t \leq |x_t^\nu - x_t| < \epsilon$ for $\nu \geq N$ and $t \leq T$. For $t > T$, $|x_t^\nu - x_t|/\beta^t \leq 2M\alpha^t/\beta^t < 2M(\alpha/\beta)^T < \epsilon$. Thus $\mathbf{x}^\nu \to \mathbf{x}$ in the β-topology. $\square$

It is crucial that $\beta > \alpha$. Majumdar (1975) gives an example illustrating why norm-bounded feasible sets are not compact in the norm topology. The same sort of problem would occur here if $\beta = \alpha$. In fact, $\beta = \alpha = 1$ is precisely Majumdar's case. This also occurs in Example 2.4. With Lemma 4 in hand, we can now state the main existence theorem.

Existence Theorem. *Suppose that $\mathbf{Y}(\boldsymbol{\omega})$ is α-bounded when $\boldsymbol{\omega} \in \ell_+^\infty(\alpha)$ with $1 \leq \alpha < \beta$.*

(1) *If U is β-upper semicontinuous, and Y satisfies (T1) and (T6), an optimal path exists. That is, there is a $\mathbf{c}^*$ with $U(\mathbf{c}^*) \geq U(\mathbf{c})$ for all $\mathbf{c} \in \mathbf{Y}(\boldsymbol{\omega})$.*

(2) *If U is β-continuous, and Y satisfies assumptions (T1)–(T3), (T5), and (T6), the value function $J(\boldsymbol{\omega}) = \sup U(\mathbf{Y}(\boldsymbol{\omega}))$ is α-continuous, and the maximizer correspondence, mapping $\ell_+^\infty(\alpha)$ into $\ell_\beta^\infty(\alpha)$ is closed.*

(3) *If in addition, U is strictly concave, then $\mu(\boldsymbol{\omega})$ is a continuous function of $\boldsymbol{\omega}$.*

---

[16] A subset of s^1 which is bounded in the α-norm is called α-*bounded*.

Proof. The product and β-topologies coincide on α-bounded sets. Assumptions (T1) and (T6) imply $\mathbf{Y}(\omega)$ is compact-valued. Lower semicontinuity of $\mathbf{Y}$ is a local property, so we confine our attention to an α-neighborhood V of ω. This is bounded below by some $\chi \in \ell^\infty(\alpha)$, so $\mathbf{Y}(V) \subset \mathbf{Y}(\chi)$, which is compact. Lemma 4 and Proposition 2 tell us that $\mathbf{Y}(\omega)$ is an α to β-lower semicontinuous correspondence. The Maximum Theorem then yields the result. $\square$

▶ Example 8: The Ramsey model. One application is to a one-sector model of optimal capital accumulation (*Ramsey model*). In the classical Ramsey model previously introduced, the technology is described by a (gross) *production function*. The production function f is a continuous, nondecreasing function $f: \mathbb{R}_+ \to \mathbb{R}_+$. Note that $f(0) \geq 0$. In the time-varying Ramsey model, the technology is given given by a sequence, $\{f_t\}_{t=1}^\infty$, of such production functions. Production is *stationary* if $f_t = f$ and the corresponding model is then said to be stationary.

We can write the Ramsey model in Malinvaud form by setting $T_t = \{(a, b) : 0 \leq b \leq f_t(a)\}$. We map the initial capital stock k into $\omega(k) = (f(k), 0, 0, \ldots)$. The term $f(k)$ appears in the endowment because the Ramsey model is defined in terms of an initial capital stock at time 0, yielding output $f(k)$ as endowment at time 1. By abuse of notation, we refer to $\mathbf{Y}(\omega(k))$ by the shorthand $\mathbf{Y}(k)$. This satisfies (T1), (T3), (T5), and (T6). If f is concave, it satisfies (T2), and $f(0) = 0$ implies (T4).

Define f^t inductively by $f^1 = f_1$ and $f^t = f_t \circ f^{t-1}$. The *path of pure accumulation* is $\{f^t(k)\}_{t=1}^\infty$. When $\lim[f^t(k)/\alpha^t] < \infty$, $\mathbf{Y}(k)$ is an α-bounded subset of $\ell_+^\infty(\beta)$. More generally, we call the technology α-*bounded* if $\mathbf{Y}(k)$ is α-bounded. This happens in the case of exogenous technical progress where $f_t(x) = e^{nt}x^\rho$. The path of pure accumulation from k is $f^t(k) = \exp(n(t + \rho(t-1) + \cdots + \rho^{t-1}))k^{\rho^t}$. This grows at asymptotic rate $\exp\{n/(1-\rho)\}$, so the technology is α-bounded for $\alpha > \exp\{n/(1-\rho)\}$. As any concave production function obeys $f(x) \leq f(a) + \xi(x-a)$ whenever ξ is a supergradient at a (e.g., $\xi = f'(a)$), it is α-bounded for any $\alpha > \xi$. Thus, any stationary, concave, production technology is α-bounded for all $\alpha > f'(\infty)$.

Suppose the technology is α-bounded and U is upper semicontinuous on $\ell_+^\infty(\beta)$ with $\beta > \alpha$. The Existence Theorem establishes the existence of at least one optimal path.[17]

Let's now confine our attention to the classical case where f is concave,

---

[17] In fact, we could use the weaker condition that U be continuous on $\ell_+^\infty(\Theta)$ with Θ the path of pure accumulation, i.e., $\theta_t = f^t(k)$. Continuity of U can be obtained for a general class of aggregators and production functions by using upper and lower approximations like those used by Streufert (1990). Alternatively, a brute force calculation will also often show $W(c_1, W(c_2, \ldots))$ converges uniformly to a continuous utility function in this case.

so that (T2) is satisfied. Because $k \mapsto \omega(k)$ is α-continuous, $\mathbf{Y}(k)$ is a β-lower semicontinuous correspondence. The Existence Theorem then yields a β-closed maximizer correspondence $\mu(k)$.

Now suppose U is strictly concave. There is then a unique optimal capital-consumption path $\{k_t(k), c_t(k)\}_{t=1}^{\infty}$. Of course, $0 \leq k_{t+1}(k) + c_{t+1}(k) \leq f_t(k_t(k))$. Define the *consumption policy function* $g(k) = c_1(k)$. The policy function gives the optimal consumption level as a function of the previous period's capital stock. By the Existence Theorem, g exists and is continuous. There is an associated *capital policy function* $h(k) = f(k) - g(k)$. The optimal paths are then $c_t(k) = g(k_{t-1}(k))$ with $c_1 = g(k)$ and $k_t(k) = h(k_{t-1}(k)) = f(k_{t-1}(k)) - g(k_{t-1}(k))$.

One consequence is that $c_t(k)$ is continuous in k for each t. In general, $\mathbf{c}(k)$ is only β-continuous for $\beta > \alpha$, but not α-continuous. However, in this case we can also show a turnpike result: optimal paths converge monotonically to a unique steady state. This implies α-continuity. Details of the turnpike property for this model are in Section 5.2.3. ◄

▶ Example 9: Nonconvex Ramsey model. In fact, we obtain a closed maximizer correspondence in the Ramsey model even if f_t is not concave. We exploit the special features of the one-sector model. Recall the one-sector feasible set defined by $\mathbf{Y}(k_0) = \{(\mathbf{c}, \mathbf{k}) : (\mathbf{c}, \mathbf{k})$ is feasible from $k\}$, and the sets of feasible capital and consumption programs $\mathbf{F}(k) = \{\mathbf{k} : (\mathbf{c}, \mathbf{k}) \in \mathbf{Y}(k)$ for some $\mathbf{c}\}$ and $\mathbf{B}(k) = \{\mathbf{c} : (\mathbf{c}, \mathbf{k}) \in \mathbf{Y}(k)$ for some $\mathbf{k}\}$, respectively. We will show $\mathbf{F}(k)$ is a continuous correspondence. It easily follows that $\mathbf{B}(k)$ is also continuous. The maximizer correspondence is then upper semicontinuous by the Maximum Theorem.

For k' near k, $\mathbf{F}(k') \subset \mathbf{F}(k+1)$. Locally, everything takes place in a closed α-bounded set, and we may use the product topology. First we note that $\mathbf{F}$ is upper semicontinuous. Since closed α-bounded sets are product compact, it is enough to show $\mathbf{F}$ is a closed correspondence. Suppose $k^\nu \to k$ and $\mathbf{k}^\nu \to \mathbf{k}$ with $\mathbf{k}^\nu \in \mathbf{F}(k^\nu)$. Since f is continuous, the feasibility constraints hold in the limit, and $\mathbf{k} \in \mathbf{F}(k)$.

For lower semicontinuity, it is enough to show lower semicontinuity for the basic open sets $G(\mathbf{y}, \epsilon, N) = \{\mathbf{x} \in s_+^1 : |x_t - y_t| < \epsilon$ for all $t < N\}$. Let $\epsilon, N > 0$ be given. Take $\mathbf{y} \in \mathbf{F}(k)$. By continuity of the f_t, we can choose δ with $|f^t(k') - f^t(k)| < \epsilon$ for all $t \leq N$ when $|k - k'| < \delta$. For any such k', take the path $x_t = \min\{y_t, f^t(k')\}$. Note that $f^t(k') + \epsilon > f^t(k) \geq y_t$ for $t \leq N$, so $y_t \geq x_t > y_t - \epsilon$ for all $t \leq N$. Hence $\mathbf{x} \in G(\mathbf{y}, \epsilon, N)$. Further, $f_{t+1}(x_t) = \min\{f_{t+1}(y_t), f^{t+1}(k')\} \geq x_{t+1}$ and $x_1 \leq f_1(k')$, so $\mathbf{x} \in \mathbf{F}(k')$. It follows $\mathbf{F}(k') \cap G(\mathbf{y}, \epsilon, N) \neq \emptyset$ whenever $|k - k'| < \delta$, establishing lower semicontinuity.

In the nonconcave case, we do not necessarily get unique optimal paths. Amir, Mirman, and Perkins (1991) and Dechert and Nishimura (1983), using a nonconvex stationary technology, find that optimal paths converge to zero if the initial capital stock is below some critical value. Optimal paths starting above the critical value converge to a steady state that lies above the critical value. If utility is sufficiently concave, it may be optimal to remain at the critical value if you start there. In such cases, the optimal paths will be unique, so our theorem implies they are β-continuous for $\beta > \alpha$. They assume a maximum sustainable stock, so $\alpha = 1$ will do here. In this case, $\mathbf{c}(k)$ is not α-continuous because of the long-run jump as you cross the critical capital stock value. ◄

Two endogenous growth models were introduced in Chapter 1. The Existence Theorem applies to these models for suitable choices of recursive objectives.

► Example 10: A convex endogenous growth model. The first endogenous growth model we consider is Gale and Sutherland's (1968) model. They call a convex production function f *strongly productive* if $f(x + h) \geq f(x) + \gamma h$ for some $\gamma > 1$ whenever $h > 0$. When f is differentiable, this implies $f'(x) \geq \gamma$ for all x. Suppose f is differentiable and let $\bar{\gamma} = \lim_{x \to \infty} f'(x)$. Let $\beta > \bar{\gamma}$ and choose α, $\beta > \alpha > \bar{\gamma}$ and $\bar{x}$ with $f'(\bar{x}) < \alpha$. By concavity $f(x) \leq f(\bar{x}) + f'(\bar{x})(x - \bar{x}) \leq f(\bar{x}) + \alpha x$. The budget set is α-bounded. Since $\beta > \alpha$, any β-myopic utility function realizes a maximum over the budget set by the Existence Theorem. In fact, any β-myopic utility function for $\beta > \bar{\gamma}$ will have optimal paths.

Jones and Manuelli (1988) consider examples of the form $f(x) = \gamma x + x^\rho$ for $\gamma > 1$ and $0 < \rho < 1$. Here $\bar{\gamma} = \gamma$. It follows that any β-myopic utility function achieves a maximum on the budget set provided $\beta > \gamma$. Thus, an optimal (endogenous) growth path exists provided the planner exhibits a sufficient degree of impatience relative to the asymptotic growth rate γ. Put differently, an optimal action exists provided myopia overcomes the prospects for increasing levels of consumption in the (distant) future. ◄

► Example 11: A human capital model. The second example of an endogenous growth model described in Chapter 1 is Lucas's (1988) human capital model (Example 1.7). Recall there are two types of capital stocks, one physical (denoted x) and the other human (denoted h). Production of goods requires both types of capital inputs. Let h_{1t} be the human capital devoted to producing current output goods; h_{2t} is the amount of human capital engaged in knowledge accumulation. The planner controls the proportion of human capital allocated to each use at each time. Let $\eta_t \in [0, 1]$ be the share of human capital in current output production at time t; similarly, $1 - \eta_t$ is the proportion of human capital in the knowledge sector at time t. The equations governing the evolution of the state variables x and h are $h_{t+1} = \mu(1 - \eta_t)h_t$ and $c_t + x_t = x_{t-1}^\alpha (\eta_t h_t)^{1-\alpha-\beta}$ where $\mu, \alpha, \beta > 0$, $1 - \alpha - \beta > 0$, and $0 < \alpha, \beta < 1$. The labor input has been normalized at one unit in these expressions. We may choose the units of human capital so that $h_0 = 1$ represents the initial endowment of human capital. Consumption in Lucas's model can never exceed the path of pure accumulation constructed by letting human capital grow at the maximum possible rate μ. Of course, this bound is weak in the sense that it cannot be actually attained by any consumption profile. However, it serves as a comparison program which constrains the growth of consumption and which is suitable for establishing the existence of an optimal program. Let $h_t = \mu^t$ (as $h_0 = 1$) denote the maximum potential level of human capital at time t. Let $\bar{x}_t = \mu^t \bar{x}_{t-1}^\alpha$ denote the path of pure accumulation (starting from k_0) when the maximum possible human capital is allocated to goods production. Then consumption in the planner's budget set must satisfy the inequality $c_t \leq \bar{x}_t$. It follows that consumption cannot grow faster than would be the case if the economy enjoyed exogenous technical progress with growth factor $\mu > 1$. The path of pure accumulation grows at the asymptotic rate $(\mu - 1)/(1 - \alpha)$. As in Example 8 and the preceding discussion it is possible to show optimal programs exist for upper semicontinuous utility functions defined on a suitable space $\ell_+^\infty(\beta)$. ◄

► Example 12: Von Neumann models. Of course, the Existence Theorem also applies to full multisector models. The only trick to handling them is to derive an appropriate growth rate. This is easily done in the von Neumann model by the following lemma.

Lemma 5. *Let T_N be a von Neumann technology satisfying the KMT conditions. There is an $\alpha > 0$ with $\|b\| \leq \alpha\|a\|$ whenever $(a, b) \in T_N$.*

Proof. This is trivially true if $b = 0$. We examine the case $b \neq 0$. Note $a \neq 0$ also by the no free lunch condition. Let z be an associated activity vector, so $0 \leq b \leq Bz$ and $0 \leq Az \leq a$. There is some i with $b_i > 0$. Since $b_i \leq \sum_j b_{ij} z_j$, there is a j with $z_j > 0$. Now the KMT conditions yield a k with $a_{kj} > 0$. It follows that $Az \neq 0$. Now $\|b\| \leq \|Bz\|$ and $\|Az\| \leq \|a\|$, so $\|b\|/\|a\| \leq \|Bz\|/\|Az\|$. It is enough to show that $\|Bz\|/\|Az\|$ is bounded.

By homogeneity of degree zero, and the fact that $z \neq 0$, we can restrict z to the simplex $\Delta = \{z \in \mathbb{R}_+^n : \sum_i z_i = 1\}$. But on the simplex, $\|Az\| \neq 0$, so $\|Bz\|/\|Az\|$ is continuous. It therefore has a maximum α. □

The von Neumann model uses an initial endowment $b \in \mathbb{R}_+^m$. We again translate to the technology set using the mapping $\omega(b) = (b, 0, 0, \ldots)$. For $\mathbf{y} \in \mathbf{Y}(b)$ (again abusing notation), $\mathbf{y} = \mathbf{b} - \mathbf{a}$ with $a_t \leq b_t$ for $t \geq 1$ and $b_1 = 0$, $a_1 \leq b$. Inducting with the lemma, we find $\|a_t\| \leq \|b_t\| \leq \alpha^{t-1}\|b\|$. Thus $\mathbf{Y}(b)$ is α-bounded, and the Existence Theorem applies. If the utility function is strictly concave and β-continuous for $\beta > \alpha \geq 1$, we even obtain a unique optimal path that is β-continuous. ◄

Variations on these techniques are possible. Although we have focused on capital stocks, the Maximum Theorem also yields continuity in technological parameters whenever the feasible correspondence is continuous in those parameters. Stronger forms of the Maximum Theorem allow the utility function to depend on some parameters α. If the bounds of the Continuous Existence Theorem (Chapter 3) hold uniformly in α, the optimal paths will be continuous in α.[18] A simple example is an optimal growth model with additively separable utility $W(c,y) = u(c) + \delta y$. Take $(k, \delta) = \omega \in \Omega = \mathbb{R}_+ \times [0, \bar{\delta}]$ with a strictly concave, bounded u and $\bar{\delta} < 1$. With a stationary concave production function f, a unique optimal path $\{c_t(k, \delta)\}$ exists. Further, $\{c_t(k, \delta)\}$ is β-continuous, hence $c_t(k, \delta)$ is a continuous function of (k, δ) for all $(k, \delta) \in \Omega$. A non-separable example in a similar vein is the EH form $W(c,y) = [-1+y]e^{\delta - u(c)}$. When $\delta < u(0)$, this yields a β-continuous utility function for any $\beta > \alpha$.

4.5 Recursive Dynamic Programming

We begin our discussion of dynamic programming with recursive utility by examining the one-sector TAS case. This serves as a detailed example allowing us to explore the structures needed for a recursive utility generalization.

4.5.1 Dynamic Programming with TAS Utility

We again consider the Ramsey problem, the problem of maximizing the sum $\sum_{t=1}^{\infty} \delta^{t-1} u(c_t)$ given an initial capital stock k and production function f. This time, instead of the direct method, we approach the optimal growth problem via dynamic programming, using the *value function* $J(k) = \sup\{U(\mathbf{c}) : \mathbf{c} \in \mathbf{B}(k)\}$. The value function always exists, although it may be either $+\infty$ or $-\infty$. If it is a continuous function, we will be able to use it to find optimal paths. We establish Bellman's equation using the Principle of Optimality. The classic statement of the Principle of Optimality is:[19]

The Principle of Optimality. An optimal policy has the property that whatever the initial state and initial decision are, the remaining decisions must constitute an optimal policy with regard to the state resulting from the first decision.

The Optimality Principle says once on the optimal path, it is optimal to stay there. Optimal choices are time consistent. This idea underlies the following proof, although it is a bit obscured due to the use of the supremum rather than a maximum. If the maximum does exist, the epsilons can be dispensed with, making clear how the Principle of Optimality

---

[18] Details may be found in Boyd (1990a).
[19] Bellman (1957, p. 83).

is employed. *Bellman's equation* is the analytical implementation of the Principle of Optimality. The basic methodology of dynamic programming is to solve the optimization problem by finding the solution to Bellman's equation. The value function stores all the relevant information necessary to solve the original problem.[20]

Bellman's Equation. *Under the basic assumptions,*

$$J(k) = \sup \{u(c) + \delta J(f(k) - c) : 0 \leq c \leq f(k)\}.$$

Proof. Let $\epsilon > 0$, and take a feasible path $\mathbf{c}$ with $U(\mathbf{c}) > J(k) - \epsilon$. The path $\mathbf{c}' = \{c_{t+1}\}_{t=1}^{\infty}$ is feasible from $f(k) - c_1$, and so $U(\mathbf{c}') \leq J(f(k) - c_1)$. Thus $J(k) - \epsilon < U(\mathbf{c}) = u(c_1) + \delta \sum_{t=1}^{\infty} \delta^{t-1} u(c_{t+1}) = u(c_1) + \delta U(\mathbf{c}') \leq u(c_1) + \delta J(f(k) - c_1)$. It follows that $J(k) - \epsilon \leq \sup \{u(c) + \delta J(f(k) - c)\}$. Because ϵ was arbitrary, $J(k) \leq \sup\{u(c) + \delta J(f(k) - c)\}$.

For step two, fix $\epsilon > 0$. Take any $c \in [0, f(k)]$ and choose $\mathbf{c}$ feasible from $f(k) - c$ with $U(\mathbf{c}) \geq J(f(k) - c) - \epsilon/\delta$. Letting $\mathbf{c}^* = (c, \mathbf{c})$, we obtain $U(\mathbf{c}^*) = u(c) + \delta U(\mathbf{c}) \geq u(c) + \delta J(f(k) - c) - \epsilon$. As $\mathbf{c}^*$ is feasible from initial stocks k, $\epsilon + J(k) \geq \sup\{u(c) + \delta J(f(k) - c)\}$. Since ϵ was also arbitrary, $J(k) \geq \sup\{u(c) + \delta J(f(k) - c)\}$. Combining this with the previous paragraph yields Bellman's equation. $\square$

Our next problem is to solve Bellman's equation. If we also show that Bellman's equation has a unique solution, we will know we have found the value function. Define the *Bellman operator* T by the formula:

$$(T\xi)(k) = \sup\{u(c) + \delta\xi(f(k) - c) : 0 \leq c \leq f(k)\}. \tag{1}$$

This operator returns a candidate value function for each trial value function ξ input (defined over the domain of initial capital stocks). When u is continuous on $[0, \infty)$, the Maximum Theorem shows that the Bellman operator maps continuous functions into continuous functions. Further, the supremum is actually attained. A function solves the Bellman equation if and only if it is a fixed point of the Bellman operator. A weighted contraction mapping argument will show that the Bellman operator has a unique fixed point, which must be the value function.

Suppose u is non-decreasing and continuous on $\mathbb{R}_+$. For convenience, we normalize $u(0) = 0$. Let $\varphi > 0$ be increasing and continuous with $u(f(k))/\varphi(k)$ bounded. The Bellman operator is clearly monotone. Further,

$$(T0)(k) = \sup\{u(c) : 0 \leq c \leq f(k)\} = u(f(k)),$$

---

[20] There are many treatments of dynamic programming. We recommend Stokey and Lucas (1989) for an exhaustive treatment of dynamic programming in deterministic and stochastic models. Streufert's (1997) chapter surveys deterministic and stochastic dynamic programming using his biconvergence technique.

which is φ-bounded. Finally,

$$T(\xi + A\varphi)(k) = \sup\{u(c) + \delta\xi(f(k) - c) + \delta A\varphi(f(k) - c)\}$$
$$\leq (T\xi)(k) + A\delta\varphi(f(k))$$

since φ is increasing. Provided that $\delta \sup_x \varphi(f(x))/\varphi(x) < 1$, the conditions of the Weighted Contraction Mapping Theorem (see Chapter 2) hold. In sum, we have the following proposition:

Proposition 3. *Suppose the basic assumptions hold, u is continuous on $\mathbb{R}_+$ with $u(0) = 0$, and there is an increasing continuous function $\varphi > 0$ with $\theta = \sup_x[\varphi(f(x))/\varphi(x)] < 1$ and $u(f(x))/\varphi(x)$ bounded. Then the Bellman's equation has a unique continuous solution.*

The fact that T is a contraction actually gives more information. Consider $\xi_n(k) = T^n(0)(k)$. Then $\|\xi_n - TJ\|_\varphi \leq \theta\|\xi_{n-1} - J\|_\varphi$, where $\|\cdot\|_\varphi$ denotes the φ-norm introduced in Chapter 2. By induction, we obtain $\|\xi_n - J\|_\varphi \leq \theta^n\|\xi_0 - J\|_\varphi = \theta^n\|J\|_\varphi$ since $\xi_0 = 0$. Thus $\xi_n \to J$ in the space of φ-bounded continuous functions. This fact allows us to numerically approximate the value function to any desired degree of accuracy.

Define the *consumption policy correspondence*

$$\mathbf{g}(k) = \{c : u(c) + \delta J(f(k) - c) = J(k)\}.$$

The policy correspondence gives the optimal consumption level as a function of the previous period's capital stock. The Maximum Theorem guarantees that $\mathbf{g}$ is non-empty and upper semicontinuous. There is an associated *capital policy correspondence*

$$\mathbf{h}(k) = f(k) - \mathbf{g}(k).$$

For simplicity, assume the policy correspondence is single-valued.[21] Denote the consumption and capital policy functions by $g(k)$ and $h(k)$ respectively, where $h(k) = f(k) - g(k)$. Define $c_t = g(k_{t-1})$ with $c_1 = g(k)$ and $k_t = h(k_{t-1}) = f(k_{t-1}) - g(k_{t-1})$. Clearly $\mathbf{c}$ and $\mathbf{k}$ are feasible from k. Further, $|J(k) - \sum_{t=1}^T \delta^{t-1}u(c_t)| = \delta^T|J(h^T(k))|$ where h^T is the Tth iterate of h. As $0 \leq h(k) \leq f(k)$,

$$\delta^T|J(h^T(k))| \leq \delta^T \max\{|J(0)|, |J(f^T(k))|\}$$
$$\leq \delta^T \max\{|J(0)|, \|J\|_\varphi\varphi(f^T(k))\}.$$

---

[21] If not, take a selection from $\mathbf{g}$. For example, if $\mathbf{g}$ is compact and convex-valued one could take the barycentric selection, $b(\mathbf{g}(k)) = \left(\int_{g(k)} g\, d\mu\right)/|\mathbf{g}(k)|$, where $g \in \mathbf{g}(k)$, $|\mathbf{g}(k)|$ is the Lebesgue measure of the set $\mathbf{g}(k)$ (which is the length of an interval since the correspondence is a compact convex subset of $\mathbb{R}_+$), and the integral is taken in the sense of Lebesgue.

This last term is dominated by the maximum of

$$\delta^T |J(0)| \text{ and } \|J\|_\varphi \delta^T \left[\sup_x \frac{\varphi(f(x))}{\varphi(x)}\right]^T \varphi(k).$$

These converge to zero provided $\delta \sup_x \varphi(f(x))/\varphi(x) < 1$. Hence $U(\mathbf{c}) = J(k)$, and $\mathbf{c}$ is an optimal path.

A class of models covered by Proposition 3 are those where $f(x) \leq \alpha + \beta x$ with $\beta > 1$ and $u(c) = c^\gamma$ for $0 < \gamma \leq 1$. Set $\varphi(x) = \lambda + x^\gamma$ where λ obeys $1 + \alpha^\gamma/\lambda \leq \beta^\gamma$. Then $\varphi(f(x)) \leq \lambda + (\alpha + \beta x)^\gamma \leq \lambda + \alpha^\gamma + \beta^\gamma x^\gamma \leq \beta^\gamma(\lambda + x^\gamma) = \beta^\gamma \varphi(x)$. The Bellman equation has a unique solution provided $\beta^\gamma \delta < 1$.

One example is the case where $u(c) = c^\gamma$ and $f(k) = \beta k$ with $0 < \gamma \leq 1$ and $\beta^\gamma \delta < 1$. This satisfies the hypothesis of Proposition 3. The value function has the form $J(k) = Ak^\gamma$; the constant A can be determined by substituting this functional form in the Bellman equation, and solving for A. The fact that Ak^γ solves the Bellman equation verifies that it is the value function since Proposition 3 implies solutions to the Bellman equation are unique.

The proposition does not cover cases such as $u(c) = \log c$ since this felicity is not continuous over $\mathbb{R}_+$. Nevertheless, when $f(k) = k^\rho$, the value function has the form $J(k) = A + \rho(1 - \delta\rho)^{-1} \log k$.[22] Again, the constant A can be determined by using Bellman's equation. However, unlike the previous case, the fact that this function solves the Bellman equation does *not* imply it is the value function. Since we do not have a strict contraction, the Bellman equation may have several solutions, only one of which is the true value function. Other techniques must be employed to demonstrate that this is really the value function, and even to show that optimal paths exist.[23] Care *must be exercised* when the contraction argument fails. The possibility of multiple solutions to the Bellman equation or that $J(k) = -\infty$ cannot always be ruled out in such circumstances.

4.5.2 Recursive Utility and Multisector Models

The weak separability property (limited independence) that recursive utility possesses is sufficient to do dynamic programming. Not surprisingly, the Weighted Contraction Theorem is also useful here. The usual Principle of Optimality applies, yielding *Bellman's equation*

$$J(k) = \sup\{W(c, J(f(k) - c)) : 0 \leq c \leq f(k)\}.$$

---

[22] We will prove this in Section 5.1.
[23] Boyd's (1990b) symmetry technique handles this problem as explained in the next chapter.

Indeed, the same argument used to establish the Bellman equation in the TAS case applies to the aggregator model.

Define the *Bellman operator* by

$$(T\xi)(k) = \sup\{W(c, \xi(f(k) - c)) : 0 \le c \le f(k)\}.$$

When W is continuous on $\mathbb{R}_+ \times \mathbb{R}_+$, the Maximum Theorem shows that the Bellman operator maps continuous functions into continuous functions. Further, the supremum is actually attained for each continuous function ξ. A function solves the Bellman equation if and only if it is a fixed point of the Bellman operator. A contraction mapping argument analogous to the TAS case will now show that the Bellman operator has a unique fixed point, which must be the value function.

Suppose $W(\cdot, y)$ is continuous on $\mathbb{R}_+$, again normalize so $W(0,0) = 0$, and let $\varphi > 0$ be increasing and continuous with $W(f(k),0)/\varphi(k)$ bounded. Again, the Bellman operator is clearly monotone. Further,

$$(T0)(k) = \sup\{W(c,0) : 0 \le c \le f(k)\} = W(f(k), 0) \le \varphi(k).$$

Finally,

$$T(\xi + A\varphi)(k) = \sup\{W(c, \xi(f(k) - c)) + A\varphi(f(k) - c)\}$$
$$\le (T\xi)(k) + A\delta\varphi(f(k))$$

since φ is increasing. Provided that $\delta \sup_x \varphi(f(x))/\varphi(x) < 1$, the conditions of the Weighted Contraction Mapping Theorem hold. In sum, we have the following proposition:

Proposition 4. *Suppose $W(\cdot, 0)$ is continuous on $\mathbb{R}_+$ with $W(0,0) = 0$, and there is an increasing continuous $\varphi > 0$ with*

$$\theta = \delta \sup_x [\varphi(f(x))/\varphi(x)] < 1$$

and $W(f(x),0)/\varphi(x)$ bounded. Then the Bellman equation has a unique continuous solution.

The value function can be numerically approximated by the same iterative procedure used in the TAS case to calculate J. Proposition 3 is clearly a special case of Proposition 4. Hence, all the TAS cases incorporated under Proposition 3 remain valid applications of Proposition 4.

▶ **Example 13: EH utility with constant returns to scale.** Consider the Epstein-Hynes aggregator $W(c,y) = (-1 + y)e^{-v(c)}$ with $v(0) > 0$ coupled with the linear production function, $f(x) = \beta x$ for $\beta > 1$. We first transform the aggregator so that $W(0,0) = 0$. Let $U_0 = U(0) = (1 - e^{v(0)})^{-1} < 0$. The equivalent normalized aggregator is $V(c,y) = U_0 + (-1 + y + U_0)e^{-v(c)}$. Thus $V(f(x),0) = -U_0 + (-1 + U_0)e^{-v(\beta x)}$. Because $U_0 < 0$, $V(f(x),0) \le -U_0$. This constant bound means we may take $\varphi = 1$, and the hypotheses of the theorem are trivially satisfied. ◀

▶ **Example 14: KDW utility with constant returns to scale.** Consider the KDW aggregator $W(c, y) = (\delta/d) \log(1 + ax^b + dy)$ where $a, b, d, \delta > 0$, $b, \delta < 1$. This is clearly concave, continuous, and increasing. Moreover, $W_2 = \delta/(1 + ax^b + dy) \leq \delta$. Again consider $f(x) = \beta x$ for $\beta > 1$. No transformation is necessary here as $W(0, 0) = 0$. Now $W(f(x), 0) = \log(1 + a\beta^b x^b)$. Let $\varphi(x) = N + \log(1 + a\beta^b x^b)$ with N chosen so that $(1 + (b/N) \log \beta) < \delta^{-1}$. Then

$$\delta \frac{\varphi(f(x))}{\varphi(x)} = \delta \frac{N + \log(1 + a\beta^{2b} x^b)}{N + \log(1 + a\beta^b x^b)}$$

$$\leq \delta \frac{N + b \log \beta + \log(1 + a\beta^b x^b)}{N + \log(1 + a\beta^b x^b)}$$

$$\leq \delta \left[1 + \frac{b}{N} \log \beta \right] < 1.$$

Again, the hypotheses of the theorem are satisfied. ◀

The KDW example highlights the power of the aggregator method, just as in Example 3.9. Unlike the TAS and UEH cases, we are unable to write down the utility function for the KDW aggregator. Nonetheless, such utilities have quite intuitive representations in terms of Fisherian diagrams. It is easy to build aggregators incorporating reasonable economic hypotheses, that do not have closed-form representations. That's exactly how the KDW aggregator arose. Fortunately, the lack of closed-form solutions is not a major barrier to numerically computing the value function or optimal paths. The iterative techniques introduced earlier in this section work equally well in the KDW case.

Streufert (1990) provides an alternative to contraction mapping methods. He considers the case where there are best and worst paths. These yield upper and lower partial sums. He considers the case where they both converge to the recursive utility function (biconvergence). He shows that the value function is the unique admissible solution to the Bellman equation, where admissibility rules out certain obviously absurd functions.[24]

Dynamic programming is not limited to the one-sector case. The Principle of Optimality applies in many multisector models. Sorger (1992a) extends the dynamic programming result of Proposition 4 to the case of aggregators defined in the reduced form over beginning and end-of-period capital stocks (as discussed in Chapter 3).

One such case is a stationary Malinvaud model where the endowment is concentrated at time 0. Let T be the Malinvaud technology set and $b \in \mathbb{R}_+^m$ the initial endowment. The feasible set is $\mathbf{Y}((b, 0, 0, \dots))$. The

---

[24] Streufert has continued this line of work in more abstract settings—see his (1992) paper and (1997) survey article.

by now usual Principle of Optimality argument yields the *Bellman equation* $J(b) = \sup\{W(u(b - a), J(b')) : (a, b') \in T, a \leq b\}$. Note that we write the value function in terms of the initial endowment rather than an initial capital stock. We can again define a Bellman operator $(T\xi)(b) = \sup\{W(u(b - a), \xi(b')) : (a, b') \in T, a \leq b\}$. Repeating the contraction argument establishes the following proposition.

Proposition 5. *Suppose $W(u(\cdot), 0)$ is continuous on $\mathbb{R}_+^m$ with $W(u(0), 0) = 0$, and there is a non-decreasing continuous $\varphi > 0$ with*

$$\theta = \delta \sup\{[\varphi(b)/\varphi(a)] : (a, b) \in T\} < 1$$

and $\sup\{W(u(b), 0)/\varphi(b)\} < \infty$. Then the Bellman equation has a unique continuous solution.

4.5.3 Dynamic Programming and Extended Utilitarianism

Bellman's equation may be defined for the renormalized utility function $U_R(\mathbf{c})$ arising in the extended utilitarian case of the classical Ramsey model. The value function for the program $J(k) = \sup\{U_R(\mathbf{c}) : \mathbf{c} \in B(k)\}$ for $k_0 \equiv k$ will satisfy this equation. We notice the existence of a good program implies $J(k) > -\infty$. Unfortunately, contraction techniques cannot be used to demonstrate this is the only possible solution to the Bellman equation.[25] However, contraction arguments are not the only game in town. The special structure of the undiscounted optimization problem can be used to show J is the unique solution of the Bellman equation within a suitable class of functions. The key to proving this result is the observation that $J(k_g) = 0$ since the golden-rule profile is weakly maximal in the class of programs available to the planner starting with initial stocks k_g. The particular value taken by J at the golden-rule stock is the consequence of the renormalization of the zero point of the utility function U_R: note $U_R(c_g, c_g, \dots) = 0$. This uniqueness theorem is due to Dana and Le Van (1990b) in the case of a general n-capital good model cast in a reduced form (the so-called "stationary model" in McKenzie, 1986). A somewhat simpler treatment is possible for the classical one-sector Ramsey model studied below. We maintain all the assumptions that u and f are increasing, strictly concave, $f(0) = 0$, $f'(0+) = \infty$, and that there is a maximum sustainable stock k^M. We restrict our attention to initial stocks which are expansible. Hence, we consider the domain of J to be the interval $(0, k^M)$. These maintained assumptions imply J is strictly concave, increasing, and continuous on $(0, k^M)$. The last fact follows from concavity since any concave function is continuous on the

---

[25] Streufert's biconvergence techniques also fail in this case—a bad program is not lower convergent.

interior of its domain. The normalization $J(k_g) = 0$ implies $J(k) < \infty$ also holds for all $k \in (0, k^M)$.

Bellman's equation is

$$J(k) = \sup\{u(c) + J(f(k) - c) : 0 \leq c \leq f(k)\} - u_g,$$

where $u_g \equiv u(c_g)$ denotes the golden-rule felicity. Dana and Le Van's uniqueness result is as follows.

Proposition 6. J is the unique continuous solution to the Bellman equation that satisfies $J(k_g) = 0$ and is continuous on $(0, k^M)$.

The main steps in their proof are summarized by the following three lemmas which together prove the proposition.

Lemma 6. If I is any other solution to the Bellman equation that is upper semicontinuous and satisfies $I(k_g) = 0$, then $I(k) \leq J(k)$ for all $k \in (0, k^M)$.

Proof. Let I be any other upper semicontinuous function on $(0, k^M)$ satisfying $I(k_g) = 0$. Let k be such that $I(k) > -\infty$. Then for some program $(\mathbf{c}, \mathbf{k}) \in \mathbf{Y}(k)$,

$$I(k) = \sum_{t=1}^{T}[u(c_t) - u_g] + I(k_T).$$

Since I is upper semicontinuous, I is bounded from above. Thus for some M,

$$I(k) - M \leq \sum_{t=1}^{T}[u(c_t) - u_g],$$

for every T. Therefore $(\mathbf{c}, \mathbf{k})$ is a good program and converges to the golden rule: $(c_t, k_t) \to (c_g, k_g)$ as $t \to \infty$. Hence

$$I(k) \leq J(k) + \limsup_{T \to \infty} I(k_T).$$

The upper semicontinuity of I, combined with $k_T \to k_g$, and $I(k_g) = 0$, implies $\limsup_{T \to \infty} I(k_T) \leq I(k_g) = 0$. Thus $I(k) \leq J(k)$. $\square$

Lemma 7. If I is any other solution to the Bellman equation that is upper semicontinuous and satisfies $I(k_g) = 0$, then I is continuous at k_g.

Proof. Suppose $\mathbf{k}$ is a sequence in $(0, k^M)$, such that $k_t \to k$ for $k \in (0, k^M)$. Since k_g is expansible, for all t large enough we have $\bar{c}_t = f(k_t) - k_g > 0$. As I solves the Bellman equation, we have the inequality $I(k_t) \geq u(\bar{c}_t) - u_g + I(k_g)$ for t large enough. Thus $\liminf_{t \to \infty} I(k_t) \geq 0 \geq \limsup_{t \to \infty} I(k_t)$, implying $\lim_{t \to \infty} I(k_t) = 0$. Hence I is continuous at k_g. $\square$

Lemma 8. *If I is any other solution to the Bellman equation that is upper semicontinuous and satisfies $I(k_g) = 0$, then $I(k) = J(k)$ for all $k \in (0, k^M)$.*

Proof. Let I be any other upper semicontinuous solution to the Bellman equation satisfying $I(k_g) = 0$. Suppose $k \in (0, k^M)$ and let $(\mathbf{c}, \mathbf{k})$ be the weakly maximal program starting from those initial stocks. Then

$$I(k) \geq \sum_{t=1}^{T} [u(c_t) - u_g] + I(k_T).$$

As $(\mathbf{c}, \mathbf{k})$ is a good path, $k_t \to k_g$ as $t \to \infty$ and I continuous at k_g imply

$$I(k) \geq \lim_{T \to \infty} \sum_{t=1}^{T} [u(c_t) - u_g] = J(k).$$

Lemma 6 implies $I(k) \leq J(k)$. Hence $I(k) = J(k)$ for all $k \in (0, k^M)$ and J is the unique continuous solution to the Bellman equation satisfying the normalization condition. $\square$

The proof of Proposition 6 actually shows a little more: J is the unique solution of the Bellman equation in the class of upper semicontinuous functions satisfying the normalization property.

4.6 Characterization of Optimal Paths

At this point we have existence of optimal paths under control. Moreover, we know some rudimentary properties of the optimal paths and value function. We are ready to characterize the optimal paths. We begin with an intuitive treatment of the optimality conditions focused on the interpretation of the transversality condition. This is followed by a rigorous derivation of conditions completely characterizing an optimal program in Malinvaud models.

4.6.1 No-Arbitrage Conditions

We present a heuristic derivation of the Euler equations and transversality condition below. Our presentation emphasizes the necessary conditions for an optimum are the implications of the absence of arbitrage profits along an optimal program. We assume preferences are expressed by a β-myopic utility function and there is a one-sector technology defined by an increasing strictly concave differentiable function f satisfying $f(0) = 0$ and $f'(0+) = \infty$. The latter condition is called the *Inada condition* at the origin. We also assume $f(k^M) = k^M > 0$ for some k^M defines the maximum sustainable stock. Let $(\mathbf{c}, \mathbf{k})$ denote an optimal consumption and capital sequence.

The Kuhn-Tucker conditions for an optimal path are known as the *Euler* or *no-arbitrage equations* and are necessary conditions for optimality. These conditions are given in (1) when the utility function is assumed to be differentiable in each period's consumption separately and satisfies the Inada condition $U_t(c_1, c_2, \ldots, c_{t-1}, 0+, c_{t+1}, c_{t+2}, \ldots) = \infty$. Formally, if $(\mathbf{c}, \mathbf{k})$ is optimal, then for each t:

$$U_{t+1}(\mathbf{c})f'(k_t) \le U_t(c_t), \tag{2}$$

with equality if $k_t > 0$. If U fails to satisfy the Inada condition, then inequality (2) can also hold in the opposite sense if $k_t = f(k_{t-1})$. The Inada condition rules this out since it would not allow $c_t = 0$ in an optimal plan.[26] In the one-sector model, we call an optimal path $(\mathbf{c}, \mathbf{k})$ *regular* if $c_t > 0$, $k_t > 0$ for all t. For simplicity, this section focuses on regular optimal paths. If the optimal path is regular, then (2) becomes an equality.

The interpretation of the Euler condition is that a one-period reversed arbitrage, an arbitrage that immediately returns to the original path, is not profitable on an optimal path. This means that the cost calculated at $t = 1$ from acquiring an extra unit of capital at time t, $U_t(\mathbf{c})$, is at least as great as the benefit realized at time $t + 1$, discounted back to $t = 1$, from selling that additional unit of capital at $t + 1$ for consumption. The extra unit of capital yields $f'(k_t)$ units of consumption good at time $t + 1$; each unit of that good is worth $U_{t+1}(\mathbf{c})$ utils in period 1. For the discounted Ramsey model with TAS utility discount factor δ, the Euler equation for regular optima takes the form

$$\delta f'(k_t)u(c_{t+1}) = u'(c_t).$$

The necessary condition for a stationary optimal path in the TAS case becomes $c = f(k) - k$ and $\delta f'(k) = 1$; the unique solution to the Euler equation is called the *discounted golden rule*, denoted (c^δ, k^δ). The golden-rule case arises when $\delta = 1$.

The *transversality condition* holds along a path $(\mathbf{c}, \mathbf{k})$ if

$$\lim_{t \to \infty} k_t U_t(\mathbf{c}) = 0.$$

The necessity of the transversality condition can be interpreted as a type of no-arbitrage condition for *unreversed arbitrages*, arbitrages which never return to the original path. This interpretation of the transversality condition was originally suggested by Gray and Salant (1983) and applied

---

[26] We show this in Lemma 5.1.

to the Ramsey problem by Becker and Majumdar (1989).[27] We develop the intuition behind the transversality condition for the recursive utility model by showing how it follows from arguing no unreversed arbitrage should be profitable along an optimal path.

Assume $(\mathbf{c}, \mathbf{k})$ is optimal. Suppose the planner decides to increase the first period's consumption; this is possible if the planner foregoes one unit of capital (to be used for next period's production). The marginal gain to the planner is $U_1(\mathbf{c})$ in units of utility at time 1. Let T be a natural number. A *T-period reversed arbitrage* occurs if at time $T+1$ the planner reacquires the unit of capital foregone at time 1. After time $T+1$, the arbitrage no longer affects the path.

There are two costs incurred by the acquisition at time $T+1$. First, there is the *direct cost* or *repurchase cost* of foregone consumption which arises from converting a unit of consumption at time $T+1$ to a unit of capital to be saved for the next period's production. This direct cost equals $U_{T+1}(\mathbf{c})$ in utils of time period 1. The *indirect cost* arises because the *net* marginal product of that unit of capital is lost to the planner in every period between $t = 2$ and $t = T+1$; this is a foregone shadow interest loss. The indirect cost at time t in utils of time 1 is

$$U_t(\mathbf{c})[f'(k_{t-1}) - 1].$$

Adding those lost utils yields the present value (focal date 1) of the indirect costs of the arbitrage as the figure

$$\sum_{t=2}^{T+1} U_t(\mathbf{c})[f'(k_{t-1}) - 1].$$

Therefore, the total cost of this arbitrage equals the sum of the direct and indirect costs:

$$\sum_{t=2}^{T+1} U_t(\mathbf{c})[f'(k_{t-1}) - 1] + U_{T+1}(\mathbf{c}).$$

A necessary condition for the optimality of the program $(\mathbf{c}, \mathbf{k})$ is that for any T the marginal benefit of a T-period reversed arbitrage is equal to its marginal (discounted) cost. Thus

$$U_1(\mathbf{c}) = \sum_{t=2}^{T+1} U_t(\mathbf{c})[f'(k_{t-1}) - 1] + U_{T+1}(\mathbf{c}). \tag{3}$$

---

[27] Several papers have been devoted to general characterization results for additive objectives with special emphasis on proving the necessity of the transversality condition. We mention Ekeland and Scheinkman (1986), Peleg (1970; 1974), Peleg and Zilcha (1977), Ponstein (1984), Shinotsuka (1990), and Weitzman (1973).

For $T = 1$, the equation above reduces to the Euler equation.

Equation (3) contains no further information. We can rewrite (3) as

$$0 = \sum_{t=1}^{T} (U_{t+1}(\mathbf{c})f'(k_{t-1}) - U_t(\mathbf{c})). \tag{4}$$

From (4), it is clear that the unprofitability of one-period reversed arbitrages, expressed via the Euler equations, implies the unprofitability of any T-period reversed arbitrage. However, this is not the end of the story.

The infinite horizon means the planner should also contemplate the profitability of an *unreversed arbitrage* in which the unit of capital is permanently sacrificed at $t = 1$. There are no repurchase costs associated with an unreversed arbitrage, hence the zero marginal profit condition for an unreversed arbitrage must be

$$U_1(\mathbf{c}) = \sum_{t=2}^{\infty} U_t(\mathbf{c})[f'(k_{t-1}) - 1]. \tag{5}$$

But (3) and (5) can hold as $T \to \infty$ only if

$$\lim_{T \to \infty} U_T(\mathbf{c}) = 0,$$

which implies the transversality condition since the capital stocks are bounded. Thus, the transversality condition expresses the zero marginal profit condition for the open-ended arbitrages which are only admissible in the infinite horizon context.

The Euler equations and the transversality condition are necessary for optimality. For concave optimal growth models—the case where utility and production functions are concave—the Euler equations and transversality conditions are also sufficient to identify an optimal program. We will formally prove this result, the *Complete Characterization Theorem*, in the next subsection.

▶ Example 15: An asset pricing example. Consols are perpetuities promising to pay r dollars per year. If the market interest rate is ρ, then the price of the consol is r/ρ—the present discounted value of the future cash streams. This price is found by summing the geometric series whose terms are $r/(1+\rho)^t$, where $\rho > 0$. This pricing formula can be justified on arbitrage grounds. Suppose there are zero coupon bonds paying \$1 on date t and nothing otherwise for $t = 1, 2, \ldots$. These bonds are the Arrow securities for this dated commodity model—they pay on one date only. The price of a zero coupon bond paying off at time t is $1/(1+\rho)^t$. Clearly, the consol is equivalent to buying an infinite number of zero coupon bonds with r units of bonds maturing at each time t. Arbitrage considerations imply the security offering r dollars at each date is equivalent to purchasing this infinite sequence of zero coupon bonds and therefore trades for the same price. Moreover, the consol's price must be the sum of the values of the zero coupon bonds.[28]

We reexamine this simple asset pricing story within the following simple model. Our purpose is to show how the Euler equations are not always sufficient for optimality, even in convex models. This example also illustrates the type of equilibrium concept we will explore in later chapters. The transversality condition plays an important role in rounding up the "right" candidate solution. This example is a discrete time version of a problem introduced by Benveniste and Scheinkman (1982).

At time t, a household holds x_t units of an asset. In time $t + 1$ this returns r units of a consumption good and the asset can be sold for price p_{t+1}. Income can be consumed. The budget constraint is $c_t + p_t x_t = r x_{t-1} + p_t x_{t-1}$. The initial endowment is $x = 1$. The representative infinitely lived investor-consumer maximizes $\sum_{t=1}^{\infty} \delta^{t-1} u(c_t)$ by choice of a budget feasible program. We write $\delta^{-1} = (1 + \varrho)$. We look for equilibrium price sequences: these have $x_t = x = 1$ and $c_t = c = rx = r$ for all t.

The Euler equations along an equilibrium profile reduce to $p_t = \delta(r + p_{t+1})$. This can be rewritten as $p_{t+1} = (1 + \varrho)p_t - r$. This is a first-order difference equation. The solution is $p_t = (1+\varrho)^{t-1} p_1 - (\frac{r}{\varrho})[(1+\varrho)^{t-1} - 1] = (1 + \varrho)^{t-1}[p_1 - \frac{r}{\varrho}] + \frac{r}{\varrho}$. There are an infinite number of price systems satisfying the Euler equation characterizing equilibrium—one solution for each initial price.

Efficient markets would imply the absence of arbitrage opportunities and therefore require $p_1 = r/\varrho$. Prices with $p_1 > r/\varrho$ create a *bubble*. Prices continue to rise simply because people expect them to rise—the market tries to live off its dreams. Prices with $p_1 < r/\varrho$ yield a strange type of negative bubble as prices become negative in finite time. It costs real resources to dispose of the asset. This negative bubble can be ruled out by appealing to free disposal—a budget constraint of the form $c_t + p_t x_t \leq r x_{t-1} + p_t x_{t-1}$. The Euler equations themselves do not provide any further information. Trying any other *finite* reversed arbitrage places no additional restrictions on the selection of an equilibrium price. These arbitrages also yield the Euler equations. Put differently, no T-period reversed arbitrage restricts the initial choice of p_1.

The other possibility is to consider the implication of the fact that no unreversed arbitrage shows a profit. Decrease consumption at time 1 by ϵ, and then eat the extra interest income in all subsequent time periods. As our asset holding is permanently decreased by ϵ/p_1, we receive extra

---

[28] This type of arbitrage argument has been widely applied to more complex valuation problems. See Ross (1976; 1978) for further details.

interest income of $\epsilon r/p_1$ in all subsequent time periods. Thus period 1 consumption falls by the amount $\Delta c_1 = -\epsilon$ while $\Delta c_t = \epsilon r/p_1$ measures the increment in consumption available for all $t > 1$. The opposite unreversed arbitrage, where consumption is increased in the first period, is also feasible. Following the logic used earlier in this section, we see an unreversed arbitrage cannot be profitable and must therefore satisfy the condition:

$$-\epsilon u'(c) + \sum_{t=2}^{\infty} \delta^{t-1} u'(c)\frac{\epsilon r}{p_1} = -\epsilon u'(c)\left[1 - \frac{\delta r}{p_1(1-\delta)}\right]$$

$$= \epsilon u'(c)\left[-1 + \frac{r}{p_1 \varrho}\right] = 0.$$

Thus, $p_1 = r/\varrho$ must hold for an equilibrium price system. The individual's optimizing behavior rules out all bubbles, both positive and negative. The market cannot live on its dreams. Prices reflect market fundamentals—the price is the discounted value of future income streams. Pricing consistent with efficient markets emerges in equilibrium. The optimizing behavior of the investor imposes a transversality condition on the equilibrium price path.[29]

This example shows that the Euler equations, corresponding to reversed arbitrages, do not fully characterize an optimum. At least one additional condition is required—the transversality condition. ◄

▶ Example 16: Extended utilitarianism and arbitrages. The optimal program for the undiscounted Ramsey model converges to the golden rule. Thus $c_t \to c_g, k_t \to k_g$ implies $u'(c_t)k_t \to u'(c_g)k_g$ since u' is continuous. However, this violates the transversality condition as $u'(c_g)k_g > 0$. This observation has led many earlier writers on optimal growth to conclude the transversality condition is not, in general, a necessary condition for a dynamic optimization problem. However, this conclusion is premature. The logic of unreversed arbitrages can be used to resolve the puzzle regarding the necessity of the transversality condition. The key observation is any good program must converge to the golden rule. *Any* unreversed arbitrage must necessarily give rise to a *bad program*. Therefore, any unreversed arbitrage cannot offer a profit. Thus, all unreversed arbitrages being bad programs is a necessary condition for optimality in the undiscounted model. The economically meaningful transversality condition is precisely this point—no unreversed arbitrage can produce a profit. The undiscounted model satisfies this condition. The heuristic argument used to derive the transversality condition earlier in this section breaks down in

---

[29] Transversality conditions can even play a similar role in models with incomplete markets, as in Magill and Quinzii (1994).

the undiscounted case because there are infinite losses from pursuing an unreversed arbitrage. We conclude the undiscounted model does *not* generate a real counterexample to the necessity of the transversality condition. The fact that $u'(c_t)k_t \to 0$ fails here simply reminds us this convergence property is merely the implication of unprofitable unreversed arbitrages which do not offer infinite losses. ◄

4.6.2 Complete Characterization of Optimal Paths

Optimal paths for the Malinvaud model are characterized in this section. We confine our attention to the Malinvaud model because it uses a recursive production structure that interacts with recursive preferences in a simple way. More general theorems could be proved, but they would provide much less guidance in concrete practical situations than the theorems below.

A useful envelope theorem and the Euler equations are developed first. We then proceed to the main result that the Euler equations, together with the transversality condition, completely characterize optimal paths for a large class of aggregators.

The following assumptions will be maintained throughout this section. The utility function U obeys $U(\mathbf{0}) = 0$ and is concave and φ-bounded on $\ell_+^\infty(\beta)$ for some φ with $\|\varphi \circ S\|_\varphi < 1/\delta$. In addition, the feasible set $\mathbf{Y}(b) \equiv \mathbf{Y}((b, 0, \dots))$ is α-bounded for each initial stock $b \in \mathbb{R}_+^m$. The production set Y is generated by a Malinvaud technology sequence T_t. Under these conditions, the value function $J(b)$ is defined and continuous in initial endowment b. When U is differentiable with respect to consumption at time t, denote $\partial U/\partial c_t \in \mathbb{R}^m$ by U_t or $D_t U$ and $\partial U/\partial c_{it}$ by U_{it} or $D_{it}U$. Except as noted, assume U is differentiable at each time. Finally, an optimal path $\mathbf{c}^* = \mathbf{y}^*$ is *regular* if there are associated input and output sequences $\mathbf{a}^*$ and $\mathbf{b}^*$ with $(a_t^*, b_{t+1}^*) \in \text{int } T_t$ and $b_t^* \gg a_t^*$ for every t.[30]

Envelope Theorem. *The value function J is non-decreasing and concave. If U is differentiable with respect to consumption in period 1, and optimal paths are regular, then J is differentiable and obeys $D_b J(b) = U_1(\mathbf{c})$ where $\mathbf{c}$ is any optimal path from b.*

Proof. The value function is increasing because the feasible set grows when the initial stock increases. The free disposal property of Malinvaud models ensures this. Concavity follows since U is concave and $\alpha \mathbf{Y}(k) + (1 - \alpha)\mathbf{Y}(k') \subset \mathbf{Y}(\alpha k + (1 - \alpha)k')$ for $0 \le \alpha \le 1$.

Differentiability is established as follows.[31] Let $h > 0$, $\mathbf{h} = (he^i, 0, \dots)$ where e^i is the ith basis vector, and let $\mathbf{c}$ be an optimal path with initial

---

[30] Analogous results for non-regular paths in the one-sector Ramsey model may be found in Boyd (1990a).

[31] This method is adapted from Mirman and Zilcha (1975).

endowment b so that $J(b) = U(\mathbf{c})$. Clearly, $J(b+h e^i) \geq U(\mathbf{c}+\mathbf{h})$ and thus $J(b + h e^i) - J(b) \geq U(\mathbf{c} + \mathbf{h}) - U(\mathbf{c})$. Dividing by h and taking the limit shows that the right-hand derivative $D_i^+ J(b)$ satisfies $D_i^+ J(b) \geq U_{i1}(\mathbf{c})$.[32] Since $\mathbf{c}$ is regular, $c_1 = b - a_1$ is non-zero. We may then repeat this with $-c_1 < h < 0$, to show $D_i^- J(b) \leq U_{i1}(\mathbf{c}) \leq D_i^+ J(b)$. As J is concave, $D_i^+ J(b) \leq D_i^- J(b)$, thus $D_b J(b) = U_1(\mathbf{c})$. $\square$

Corollary 4. *Suppose U is recursive, the aggregator is differentiable, and optimal paths are regular. Then $D_b J(b) = W_1(c_1, U(S\mathbf{c}))$ where $\mathbf{c}$ is any optimal path from y.*

Henceforth, assume that U is differentiable at each time t. Define $p_t = U_t(\mathbf{c}^*)$. Let $(a, b) \in T_s$. Consider the path $c_t(\epsilon) = c_t^*$ for $t \neq s, s+1$, $c_s(\epsilon) = b_s^* - [(1-\epsilon) a_s^* + \epsilon a] = c_s^* + \epsilon(a_s^* - a)$ and $c_{s+1}(\epsilon) = [(1-\epsilon) b_{s+1}^* + \epsilon b] - a_{s+1}^* = c_{s+1}^* - \epsilon(b_{s+1}^* - b)$. This is feasible for $0 < \epsilon < 1$ by convexity of Y. Let $g(\epsilon) = U(\mathbf{c}(\epsilon))$. Now g achieves a maximum at 0. Thus $0 \geq g'(0+) = p_s(a_s^* - a) - p_{s+1}(b_{s+1}^* - b)$. In this case, we may rearrange to obtain:

$$p_{s+1} b_{s+1}^* - p_s a_s^* \geq p_{s+1} b_{s+1} - p_s a_s \text{ for all } (a_s, b_{s+1}) \in T_s,$$

where $p_s = U_s(\mathbf{c}^*)$ and s is arbitrary. We refer to these equations as the *Euler equations*.[33] More generally, when U is concave but not necessarily differentiable, we obtain prices p_s that simultaneously support T and the utility function U.

▶ **Example 17: Stationary differentiable one-sector model.** In the stationary one-sector model, $(a, b) \in T$ means $0 \leq b \leq f(a)$. The Euler inequalities translate to $p_{s+1}(f(a_s^*) - f(a)) \geq p_s(a_s^* - a)$. Regularity implies $f(a_{s-1}^*) > a_s^* > 0$, so $a_s^* - a$ can be either positive or negative for feasible a near a_s^*. When f is differentiable, dividing by $(a_s^* - a)$ and letting $a \to a_s^*$ shows $p_{s+1} f'(a_s^*) = p_s$. Recalling that $p_s = U_s$, we obtain the usual Euler equations $U_{s+1} f'(a_s^*) = U_s$.

Since $U_s(\mathbf{c})/U_{s+1}(\mathbf{c}) = 1 + R_{s,s+1}(\mathbf{c})$, we can rewrite the Euler equations as:

$$f'_{s+1}(a_s^*) = 1 + R_{s,s+1}(\mathbf{c}^*) = 1 + R(S^{s-1}\mathbf{c}^*).$$

That is, the net marginal product of capital is equal to the marginal rate of impatience. In the additively separable case $1 + R_{s,s+1}(\mathbf{c}) = u'(c_s)/\delta u'(c_{s+1})$, so these reduce to the usual Euler equations. ◀

▶ **Example 18: Reduced-form models.** Here we may write utility as a function $V(\mathbf{k})$ of the capital stock sequence. When the path is regular, we may perturb it as above, yielding the Euler equations $V_t(\mathbf{k}^*) = 0$. In

---

[32] We use D_i^+ and D_i^- to denote the right- and left-hand derivatives in the ith direction.
[33] As we will presently show, it can be used to derive the usual Euler equations.

the TAS case, $V(\mathbf{k}) = \sum_{t=1}^{\infty} \delta^{t-1} v(k_{t-1}, k_t)$, so $V_t = \delta^{t-1} D_2 v(k_{t-1}, k_t) +$ $\delta^t D_1 v(k_t, k_{t+1})$ with D_i denoting the gradient vector with respect to the first or second set of coordinates, as $i = 1, 2$. The Euler equations become $D_2 v(k_{t-1}, k_t) + \delta D_1 v(k_t, k_{t+1}) = 0$. ◄

▶ Example 19: Neoclassical two-sector model. We can apply the reduced-form Euler equations to the neoclassical model of Example 7. For simplicity, consider the two-sector case.[34] The two production sectors are described by neoclassical production functions F^0 and F^1. Sector zero produces a consumption good, and sector one produces capital. Capital input a is allocated to the two sectors so $a^0 + a^1 \leq a$. There is one unit of labor available in each time period which is also allocated to the two sectors, so $\ell^0 + \ell^1 \leq 1$. The transformation function

$$T(a, b) = \sup F^0(\ell^0, a^0)$$
$$\text{s.t. } F^1(\ell^1, a^1) \geq b$$
$$a^0 + a^1 \leq a, \ell^0 + \ell^1 \leq 1$$

expresses the maximum consumption that can be obtained from input stock a while leaving output stock b. Given a consumption-based felicity function u, reduced-form felicity becomes $v(a, b) = u(T(a, b))$.

We can write the Lagrangian as $\mathcal{L} = F^0(\ell^0, a^0) + \lambda[F^1(\ell^1, a^1) - b] +$ $\mu[a - a^0 - a^1] + \nu[1 - \ell^0 - \ell^1]$. Assuming an interior solution, the first-order conditions are $\partial F^0/\partial a^0 = \mu$, $\partial F^0/\partial \ell^0 = \nu$, $\lambda \partial F^1/\partial a^1 = \mu$, and $\lambda \partial F^1/\partial \ell^1 = \nu$.[35] Solving for λ, we find

$$\lambda = \frac{\partial F^0/\partial \ell^0}{\partial F^1/\partial \ell^1} = \frac{\partial F^0/\partial a^0}{\partial F^1/\partial a^1}.$$

This also implies that the marginal rate of technical substitution between capital and labor must be the same in both sectors. The Envelope Theorem tells us that $\partial T/\partial a = \mu = \partial F^0/\partial a^0$, which is the marginal product of capital in the consumption sector. It also tells us that

$$\partial T/\partial b = -\lambda = -\frac{\partial F^0/\partial a^0}{\partial F^1/\partial a^1},$$

which is the marginal rate of transformation of capital into consumption.[36]

---

[34] Note that the capital input is produced at time $t-1$ while the labor input is supplied at time t. Thus production at time t is $F^j(\ell_t^j, k_{t-1}^j)$. A fuller discussion of the two-sector model appears in Section 6.3.2.

[35] Notice that even in CES cases other than Cobb-Douglas, we might not have interior solutions. In that case T might not be smooth even though each of the F^i is smooth.

[36] A more explicit application of duality methods to transformation function occurs in Benhabib and Nishimura (1979).

We now apply Example 18's Euler equations along a path $\mathbf{k}$ to the reduced form v. The Euler equations are

$$u'(c_t)D_2\mathcal{T}(k_{t-1},k_t) + \delta u'(c_{t+1})D_1\mathcal{T}(k_t,k_{t+1}) = 0,$$

where $c_t = \mathcal{T}(k_{t-1},k_t)$. Substituting in our expressions for $D_i\mathcal{T}$ and rearranging, this becomes

$$\frac{u'(c_t)}{\delta u'(c_{t+1})} = \frac{\partial F^0(\ell_{t+1}^0,k_t^0)}{\partial k_t^0} \times \frac{\partial F^1(\ell_t^0,k_{t-1}^0)/\partial k_{t-1}^1}{\partial F^0(\ell_t^0,k_{t-1}^0)/\partial k_{t-1}^0},$$

which says that the marginal rate of substitution between consumption in adjacent time periods must equal the marginal rate of transformation of consumption into capital times the marginal (consumption) product of capital. Alternatively, we can view this in arbitrage terms as saying that, at the margin, we are indifferent between consuming a unit today or devoting the resources used to produce that unit of consumption to capital production (MRT), and then turning that extra capital into extra consumption tomorrow (MP). ◄

The Euler equations are instrumental in proving the Transversality Theorem.

Transversality Theorem. *Suppose U is recursive, non-decreasing, and differentiable at each time. A regular path $\mathbf{c}^*$ is optimal if and only if the Euler equations hold and $p_t a_t^* \to 0$ as $t \to \infty$ (the transversality condition).*

Proof. Suppose $\mathbf{c}^*$ is optimal. As above, the optimal path must satisfy the Euler equations. Note that $a_t^* > 0$ for all t by regularity and the no free lunch condition. Let J_t denote the value function at time t. Note $c_t^* > 0$. Since $J_t(0) = 0$, and J_t is concave, $J_t(b) \geq D_t J(b) \cdot b \geq 0$ for all $b \geq 0$. Setting $b = b_t^*$ yields $J_t(b_t^*) \geq D_t J(b_t^*) \cdot b_t^*$. Now $J_t(b_t^*) = U(S^{t-1}\mathbf{c}^*)$. Multiplying through by δ^{t-1}, and using the facts that $\delta \geq W_2$ and $J_t(b_t^*) = W_1(c_t^*, J(S^t\mathbf{c}^*))$ we find

$$0 \leq U_t(\mathbf{c}^*) \cdot b_t^* \leq \delta^{t-1}U(S^{t-1}\mathbf{c}^*).$$

Now consider the right-hand side. We have:

$$\delta^{t-1}U(S^{t-1}\mathbf{c}^*) \leq \delta^{t-1}\|U\|_\varphi \varphi(S^{t-1}\mathbf{c}^*)$$

$$\leq \delta^{t-1}\|U\|_\varphi \left[\frac{\varphi(S^{t-1}\mathbf{c}^*)}{\varphi(S^{t-2}\mathbf{c}^*)}\right] \cdots \left[\frac{\varphi(S\mathbf{c}^*)}{\varphi(\mathbf{c}^*)}\right]$$

$$\leq [\delta\|\varphi \circ U\|_\varphi]^{t-1}\|U\|_\varphi.$$

We see that the last term converges to 0 as $t \to \infty$ due to the fact that $\delta\|\varphi \circ S\|_\varphi < 1$. Thus $U_t(\mathbf{c}^*) \cdot b_t^* = p_t \cdot b_t^* \to 0$. The Euler equations with

$(a, b) = (0, 0)$ show $p_t b_t^* \geq p_{t-1} a_{t-1}^*$, so the transversality condition holds. The sufficiency of the transversality condition is implied by the following lemma since U is continuous. □

Lemma 9. *Suppose U is product lower semicontinuous on the feasible set. Then a path $\mathbf{c}^* = \mathbf{b}^* - \mathbf{a}^*$ is optimal if it satisfies the Euler equations and the transversality condition is satisfied.*

Proof. Consider an arbitrary feasible path $\mathbf{c} = \mathbf{b} - \mathbf{a}$. Define an approximate utility function $\hat{U}_N$ by

$$\hat{U}_N(\mathbf{c}) = U(c_1, \ldots, c_N, c_{N+1}^*, c_{N+2}^*, \ldots).$$

Since U is concave, we have

$$\hat{U}_N(\mathbf{c}) - U(\mathbf{c}^*) \leq \sum_{t=1}^{N} p_t[b_t - b_t^* - a_t + a_t^*].$$

Rearranging, we find

$$\hat{U}_N(\mathbf{c}) - U(\mathbf{c}) \leq p_1[b_1 - b_1^*] + \sum_{t=1}^{N-1} p_{t+1}[b_{t+1} - b_{t+1}^*]$$

$$+ \sum_{t=1}^{N-1} p_t[a_t^* - a_t] + p_N[a_N^* - a_N]$$

$$\leq p_1[b_1 - b_1^*] + p_N[a_N^* - a_N]$$

$$+ \sum_{t=1}^{N-1} \{p_{t+1}[b_{t+1} - b_{t+1}^*] + p_t[a_t^* - a_t]\}.$$

The summation is non-positive by the Euler equations. Since b_1^* is the endowment and $\mathbf{c}$ is feasible, the first term is also non-positive. The right-hand side gets bigger if we throw them away. Thus $\hat{U}_N(\mathbf{c}) - U(\mathbf{c}^*) \leq p_N(a_N^* - a_N) \leq p_N a_N^*$. Letting $N \to \infty$ and using the transversality condition shows $\limsup \hat{U}_N(\mathbf{c}) \leq U(\mathbf{c}^*)$. By lower semicontinuity of U, $U(\mathbf{c}) \leq \limsup \hat{U}_N(\mathbf{c}) \leq U(\mathbf{c}^*)$ for all feasible $\mathbf{c}$. Therefore $\mathbf{c}^*$ is optimal. □

Note that we did not require regularity in the lemma. There are a number of related results in the literature. Ekeland and Scheinkman (1986) use functional bounds to show necessity of the transversality condition in a number of cases where utility is not bounded below. In particular, they are able to handle the logarithmic case. Their results even apply to some models with nonconvex technologies, such as Skiba (1978).

Shinotsuka (1990) takes a different approach. His technique applies most easily to multisectoral models where the feasible set is uniformly bounded and U is upper semicontinuous. He uses perturbation methods, defining a function $\varphi(\mathbf{h}) = \sup_{\mathcal{F}} U(\mathbf{c} + \mathbf{h})$ where $\mathcal{F}$ is the feasible set. Provided there is a path in the ℓ^∞-interior of $\mathcal{F}$ with finite utility, he shows $\varphi \colon c_0 \to \mathbb{R}$ is continuous on a neighborhood of zero. Note $\varphi(\mathbf{0})$ is the value function. As φ is also concave, it has a derivative at zero. The derivative is in $(c_0)^* = \ell^1$, and is given by $\varphi' = (U_t(\mathbf{c}^*))$. As a_t^* is bounded, the transversality condition follows.

It is easy to show that a similar result holds when U is not differentiable, with supergradients replacing derivatives. The steps are very similar to those taken above.

4.7 Conclusion

Logical necessity forces us to grapple with existential questions. However, when all is said and done, the existence of an optimum remains neither more nor less than saying membership in the set of optimal programs is non-empty. L. C. Young (1969, p. 122) argued that existence of an optimum was a "first step, a mere formality, something like the acquisition of a passport." Indeed, he suggests that foreign travel would be less exciting if it consisted mainly of the struggle to get a passport rather than taking a grand tour of exotic places. Our approach to the existence of an optimum emphasizing the machinery needed to solve the problem is, as Young notes, also a matter of finding proper definitions.

We go part way towards taking our grand tour when we fully characterize optimal programs whose existence we have already established for a variety of models. The Euler equations (or inequalities) and the transversality condition become in our travel analogy the equivalent of glossy brochures and travel books giving hints of what to expect when we arrive at our destination. The necessary and sufficient conditions are a means of conjecturing solutions—of imagining what we might find—and they are a means of answering our travel questions. The implications of optimizing behavior remain our goal. The existence and characterization theories are merely the stepping stones preparing our trip. We have arranged our passport, packed our bags, and mapped out the territory to explore. The ship is waiting.

CHAPTER 5

Statics and Dynamics of Optimal Paths

5.1 Introduction

In Chapter 4, we characterized optimal paths. It's now time to find out what they look like. We start by returning to the simple explicit TAS model of Example 1.1. Once we understand its properties, we will be ready to proceed to more general models. Let utility be $U(\mathbf{c}) = \sum_{t=1}^{\infty} \delta^{t-1} \log c_t$ and describe production by the production function $f(k) = k^{\rho}$ where $0 < \rho < 1$. The Euler equations tell us $1/c_t = \delta\rho(k_t)^{\rho-1}/c_{t+1}$ along the optimal path. Moreover, the transversality condition $\lim_{t\to\infty} \delta^t \rho(k_t)^{\rho-1}/c_t = 0$ must hold. These equations completely characterize the solution.

To understand the properties of the optimal path a little better, we approach by an indirect route. The first thing to note is that there is a special initial capital stock which exactly reproduces itself on the optimal path. We denote this stock by k^{δ} or $k(\delta)$, and refer to it as the *modified* or *discounted golden rule*. Consumption is then constant and given by $c^{\delta} = (k^{\delta})^{\rho} - k^{\delta}$. The Euler equations reduce to $\delta\rho(k^{\delta})^{\rho-1} = 1$. Thus $k^{\delta} = (\delta\rho)^{1/(1-\rho)}$ and $c^{\delta} = (1 - \delta\rho)(\delta\rho)^{\rho/(1-\rho)} > 0$. Since the Euler equations and transversality condition are sufficient for optimality, this path is optimal from initial stock k^{δ}. In fact, it is the unique optimal path from k^{δ} by strict concavity.

What about other initial stocks? One easy way to determine the general optimal paths is to use the special properties of this utility function. Its indifference map possesses several *symmetries*. What is a symmetry? One particularly elegant definition of symmetry is due to Hermann Weyl. Richard Feynman paraphrases it by saying that "a thing is symmetrical if there is something that you can do to it so that after you have finished doing it it looks the same as it did before."[1] One familiar type of symmetry is homotheticity. When we multiply two consumption bundles by a common positive constant factor, our preference between them remains

---

[1] See Feynman (1965, p. 84) and Feynman et al. (1963, p. 52-1). Weyl's (1952) lectures contain his thoughts on various notions of symmetry, and their manifestations in art, nature, and mathematics.

the same. The indifference map is unchanged. The utility function above, $U(\mathbf{c}) = \sum_{t=1}^{\infty} \delta^{t-1} \log c_t$, is clearly homothetic.

More generally, we say that an invertible transformation T of the consumption set is a *symmetry* of a preference relation $\succsim$ if $\mathbf{c} \succsim \mathbf{c}'$ if and only if $T\mathbf{c} \succsim T\mathbf{c}'$. Preferences are homothetic if $T\mathbf{c} = \lambda \mathbf{c}$ is a symmetry for every $\lambda > 0$. Note that if T is a symmetry for $\succsim$, and if $\mathbf{c} \in \mathbf{F}$ is a best point in $\mathbf{F}$, then $T\mathbf{c}$ is a best point in $T\mathbf{F}$, and vice versa. Symmetries transform optima into optima.

Our utility function above enjoys another symmetry property that is closely related to production. Define the *dilation* T_λ by $(T_\lambda \mathbf{c})_t = \lambda^{\rho^t} c_t$. Now

$$
\begin{aligned}
U(T_\lambda \mathbf{c}) &= \sum_{t=1}^{\infty} \delta^{t-1} \log \lambda^{\rho^t} c_t \\
&= \sum_{t=1}^{\infty} \delta^{t-1} \log c_t + \sum_{t=1}^{\infty} \delta^{t-1} \log \lambda^{\rho^t} \\
&= U(\mathbf{c}) + \frac{\rho}{1 - \delta\rho} \log \lambda.
\end{aligned}
$$

This transformation preserves the preference order because it merely adds a common constant to the utility function.

Production is also well behaved under this symmetry. Let $S_\lambda(\mathbf{c}, \mathbf{k}) = (T_\lambda \mathbf{c}, T_\lambda \mathbf{k})$. Then $S_\lambda \mathbf{Y}(k_0) = \mathbf{Y}(\lambda k_0)$, as is easily seen by manipulating the equation $c_t + k_t = (k_{t-1})^\rho$. Multiplying by λ^{ρ^t}, we find $(T_\lambda \mathbf{c})_t + (T_\lambda \mathbf{k})_t = ((T_\lambda \mathbf{k})_{t-1})^\rho$. Thus multiplying the initial stock by λ applies T_λ to the feasible consumption set, and so maps optima to optima. Now set $\lambda = (k_0/k^\delta)$. The optimal path $k_t = k^\delta$ for initial stock k^δ is mapped to the optimal path $k_t = (k_0/k^\delta)^{\rho^t} k^\delta = k_0^{\rho^t}(\delta\rho)^{(1-\rho^t)/(1-\rho)}$ for initial stock k_0. Because $\lim_{t\to\infty} \rho^t = 0$, $\lim_{t\to\infty} k_t = k^\delta$. The optimal path converges to the golden-rule stock. Moreover, the convergence is monotonic: $k_t \uparrow k^\delta$ if $k_0 < k^\delta$, and $k_t \downarrow k^\delta$ if $k_0 > k^\delta$.

We know that $J(k^\delta) = U(\mathbf{c}^\delta) = (1 - \delta\rho)^{-1} \log c^\delta$ where $\mathbf{c}^\delta$ is the constant sequence $(c^\delta, c^\delta, \dots)$. Applying the transformation T_λ with $\lambda = k_0/k^\delta$, we find that $J(k_0) = U(T_\lambda \mathbf{c}_g) = J(k^\delta) + \rho(1 - \delta\rho)^{-1} \log(k_0/k^\delta)$. We can now substitute in Bellman's equation and differentiate to find the consumption policy function $g(k) = (1 - \delta\rho)k^\rho$ and the capital policy function $h(k) = \delta\rho k^\rho$. The steady state is easily found using the capital policy function. It is the point where the policy function intersects the 45 degree line, $k^\delta = h(k^\delta)$.[2]

---

[2] For more on the use of symmetries in optimal growth and dynamic equilibrium, see Boyd (1990b).

This example illustrates the most important facts about the standard one-sector model. Optimal paths are monotonic, even with a nonconvex technology. Optimal paths converge to a steady state.[3] In this chapter we investigate conditions leading to convergence or divergence of optimal paths. We start by examining one-sector models, and then move on to the multisector case. For a broad class of models, we can establish that a steady state exists. Another class of models exhibits sustained monotonic growth. However, neither monotonicity nor convergence is characteristic of optimal growth in general. In two-sector models, cycles, and even chaotic behavior, are possible. Cycles can also occur in more complex one-sector models, such as those involving adjustment costs or joint production.

5.2 One-Sector Models

This section focuses on differentiable one-sector models with concave production functions and strictly concave recursive utility U. The aggregator W is assumed to obey either (W1) or (W1'), and also (W2) with Lipschitz bound $\delta < 1$. We require $U_t(\mathbf{c}) > 0$ exist whenever $U(\mathbf{c}) > -\infty$, and that $f' > 0$ on $\mathbb{R}_{++}$. Further, assume that the feasible set $\mathbf{F}(k)$ is α-bounded, and that U is β-upper semicontinuous for some $\beta > \alpha$. If U is time additive separable, this implies $0 < \delta < 1$ and that $u' > 0$ on $\mathbb{R}_{++}$; we also require $u'' < 0$ on $\mathbb{R}_{++}$. These conditions ensure that the existence theory of Chapter 4 applies, and optimal paths exist. Moreover, the optimal path is unique because utility is strictly concave and the production function is concave. Many of the results below can be obtained under weaker conditions, but at the cost of considerably complicating the exposition.

5.2.1 The Inada Conditions

The Euler equations are one of our main tools for investigating the properties of optimal paths. We would like to use them to characterize optimal paths. However, we have only derived the standard Euler equations as necessary conditions when optimal paths are regular. There are two ways to work around this. One is to allow for boundary points by using a Kuhn-Tucker inequality when $k_t = 0$ or $c_t = 0$. Modified Euler equations of this sort are presented in Boyd (1990a). The other, and simpler, method is to guarantee interiority by imposing the Inada conditions. The *Inada conditions* come in two parts: the Inada utility condition is $U_t^+(\mathbf{c}) = +\infty$

---

[3] For $k_0 < k^\delta$, the optimal accumulation and consumption increase over time. The theory of capital accumulation that takes the one-sector model as prototype is what Bliss (1975) calls the *orthodox vision*.

when $c_t = 0$; the Inada production conditions are $f'(0+) = +\infty$ and $f'(\infty) \sup W_2 < 1$. When U is time additive separable, the Inada utility condition becomes $u'(0+) = +\infty$, and the production condition is $\delta f'(\infty) < 1$. We have:

Lemma 1. *Suppose the Inada condition for utility is satisfied and $f(0) = 0$ and $f'(k) > 0$ for $k \geq 0$. Whenever $k > 0$ and $J(k) > -\infty$, any optimal path is regular, it obeys $c_t, k_t > 0$ for all t.*

Proof. Let **c** be optimal and suppose $c_s = 0$. If $c_{s+1} > 0$, then $f(k_s) - k_{s+1} = c_{s+1} > 0$, so $f(k_s) > k_{s+1}$ and hence $k_s > 0$. Take $\Delta > 0$ small enough that $k_s > \Delta$ and $f(k_s - \Delta) > k_{s+1}$. We try an arbitrage between times s and $s + 1$ that accelerates consumption. Increase consumption by Δ at time s by taking the path **c'** defined by $c'_t = c_t$ for $t \neq s, s + 1$, $c'_s = c_s + \Delta$, and $c'_{s+1} = f(k_s - \Delta) - k_{s+1} = c_{s+1} + f(k_s - \Delta) - f(k_s)$, which is feasible. Now $0 \geq U(\mathbf{c'}) - U(\mathbf{c})$. Dividing by Δ, and letting $\Delta \to 0^+$, we find $0 \geq U_s(\mathbf{c}) - U_{s+1}(\mathbf{c})f'(k_s)$. But the right-hand side is $+\infty$. This contradiction shows that $c_{s+1} = 0$ also. Once consumption reaches 0, it must stay there.

Now let s be the earliest time with $c_s = 0$. If $s = 1$, $c_t = 0$ for all t. Thus $J(k) = U(\mathbf{0})$. Of course, this is impossible if $U(\mathbf{0}) = -\infty$, so we may assume $U(\mathbf{0})$ is finite. But then, the path $\mathbf{c}^* = (f(k), 0, 0, \dots)$ is feasible, and yields utility $W(k, U(\mathbf{0})) > W(0, U(\mathbf{0})) = U(\mathbf{0})$. This is also impossible as **c** is optimal. Thus $s > 1$.

Note that all of the capital must be used up at s. No more consumption will take place, and we would be made better off by consuming any leftover capital. Try an arbitrage between s and $s - 1$ that delays consumption. Let $\Delta > 0$ and define **c'** by $c'_t = c_t$ for $t \neq s - 1, s$, $c'_{s-1} = c_{s-1} - \Delta$, and $c'_s = f(\Delta)$. This is feasible for small Δ. Again, $0 \geq U(\mathbf{c'}) - U(\mathbf{c})$. We again divide by Δ, and let $\Delta \to 0^+$. This yields $0 \geq -U_{s-1}(\mathbf{c}) + U_s(\mathbf{c})f'(0)$. The right-hand side is $+\infty$ by the Inada condition on U. This contradiction shows that there is no s with $c_s = 0$. $\square$

▶ **Example 1: Is $f(0) = 0$ important?** The Inada conditions on u are not enough to guarantee interiority by themselves. It is important that $f(0) = 0$. Examine the following TAS example. Let $u(c) = \sqrt{c}$, $f(k) = 1 + 2k$ and $\delta < 1$. Consider the stationary path $k = 0$, $c = 1$. Since $u'(1) = 1/2 > \delta/2 = \delta f'(0)u'(0)$, it does not pay to try to accumulate capital. This path is optimal, but not interior. This type of situation arises in models with incomplete markets and borrowing constraints.[4] ◀

▶ **Example 2: Positive marginal products and regularity.** If we had imposed the Inada condition on production, we would not need the separate hypothesis that $J(k) > -\infty$ for $k > 0$. However, $f'(k) > 0$ is not sufficient to

---

[4] See Becker (1980), Becker and Foias (1987; 1994), Becker, Boyd and Foias (1991) and Sorger (1994a; 1995).

guarantee this. Consider the production function $f(k) = k/2$, with TAS felicity $u(c) = -1/c$ and discount factor $1/2 < \delta < 1$. The path of pure accumulation is $k_t = k/2^{t-1}$, so $u(c_t) \leq -2^{t-1}/k$ on any feasible path. But then $U(\mathbf{c}) \leq \sum_{t=1}^{\infty}(2\delta)^{t-1}/k = -\infty$, so $J(k) = -\infty$ for all k. ◀

By imposing the Inada conditions, we make certain that all optimal paths are regular. This means that the Euler *equations* are *necessary* for optimality.

5.2.2 Stationary States in One-Sector Models

As in the example of Section 5.1, the first order of business is to discover whether there are any optimal programs from k that are stationary: that is, are there optimal paths where $k_t = k$ and $c_t = c = f(k) - k$ for all t? Such a program is referred to as a *stationary optimal program*. The associated capital stock k is called a *stationary optimal stock* or *steady state*. When $f(0) = 0$, there is an obvious trivial steady state at $k = 0$. The more interesting question is whether there is a non-trivial steady state.

Recall that the *marginal rate of impatience*, R, is defined by

$$1 + R(S^{t-1}\mathbf{c}) = \frac{U_1(S^{t-1}\mathbf{c})}{U_2(S^t\mathbf{c})} = \frac{W_1(c_t, U(S^t\mathbf{c}))}{W_2(c_t, U(S^t\mathbf{c}))W_1(c_{t+1}, U(S^{t+1}\mathbf{c}))}.$$

Under the Inada conditions, optimal paths are regular, and must obey the Euler equations. We can rewrite the Euler equations using the marginal rate of impatience as $1 + R(S^{t-1}\mathbf{c}) = f'(k_t)$.

Define the *steady-state rate of impatience* $\varrho(c)$ by $\varrho(c) = R(c, c, \dots)$. This is the marginal rate of impatience, evaluated along the constant consumption path $\mathbf{c} = (c, c, \dots)$. Of course, $\varrho(c) > 0$. The upper and lower norms of marginal impatience impose bounds on $\varrho(c)$, with $\delta^{-1} - 1 \leq \underline{\varrho} \leq \varrho(c) \leq \bar{\varrho}$ where δ is the Lipschitz bound on W from assumption (W2). The upper norm $\bar{\varrho}$ may be infinite, depending on both the aggregator and the program space. If k is a steady state capital stock, $c = f(k) - k$ is the corresponding consumption level. Any steady state will have to satisfy the stationary Euler equation, $1 + \varrho(f(k) - k) = f'(k)$. At a minimum, this requires $\underline{\varrho} \leq f'(k) - 1 \leq \bar{\varrho}$. In fact, the range of $\varrho(f(k) - k)$ may be even smaller than the range of ϱ because not all consumption levels may be attainable as stationary programs. Steady states cannot lie above the stock that yields the maximum sustainable consumption, where $f'(k) = 1$.

To aid in calculations, define the utility of constant consumption c by $\Phi(c) = U(c, c, \dots)$. Utility corresponding to a constant capital stock k is $\Psi(k) = \Phi(f(k) - k)$. The steady-state rate of impatience can be written in terms of the aggregator and Ψ as $1 + \varrho(c) = 1/W_2(c, \Phi(c))$. With additively separable preferences, $\varrho(c)$ reduces to the constant rate of impatience $\varrho = \delta^{-1} - 1$, so $\delta = 1/(1 + \varrho)$.

Proposition 1. *Suppose f is concave and k satisfies $f'(k) = 1 + \varrho(f(k)-k)$ and $f(k) > k$. Then k is a steady state.*

Proof. Because $f(k) - k > 0$, the path $(k, k, \dots)$ is interior. The Euler equations and transversality condition hold on this path, and so k is a steady state. □

Non-trivial steady states are now completely characterized. This reduces the problem of finding a steady state to finding a k with $f(k) > k$ and $f'(k) = 1 + \varrho(f(k) - k)$. We can think of $f'(k) - 1$ as the long-run demand for capital, and $\varrho(f(k) - k)$ as the long-run supply of capital. To have a steady state, supply and demand must intersect.

Corollary 1. *Suppose f is concave, that $f'(0+) > 1 + \varrho(0)$, and that $f'(k) < 1 + \varrho(f(k) - k)$ for some k. Then a non-trivial steady state exists.*

Proof. The function $g(k) = f'(k) - 1 - \varrho(f(k) - k)$ is continuous on $\mathbb{R}_{++}$ with $g(0) < 0$ and $g(k) > 0$ for some k, so there is at least one k with $g(k) = 0$ by the Intermediate Value Theorem. Moreover, these k form a compact set. Take the first such k, and call it k^*. Since $f'(k) > 1 + \varrho(f(k) - k) > 1$ for $0 < k < k^*$, $f(k^*) > k^*$. Thus $c^* = f(k^*) - k^* > 0$; we have an interior path, and hence a steady state by Proposition 1. □

Similar arguments show:

Corollary 2. *Suppose f is concave with $f'(0) > 1 + \bar{\varrho}$ and $f'(k) < 1 + \underline{\varrho}$. Then a non-trivial steady state exists.*

Corollary 3. *Suppose $\varrho(c) > 0$ is finite for all c, f is concave, and the Inada production conditions are satisfied. Then a non-trivial steady state exists.*

The conditions for existence of a steady state in these concave models are even less stringent when the technology is bounded. Then $f'(\infty) < 1$. In fact, if there is a maximum sustainable stock k^M, $f'(k) < 1 + \varrho(f(k) - k)$ is satisfied for $k \geq k^M$. In that case, we need only worry about the first condition, $f'(0) > 1 + \varrho(0)$.

If $f'' < 0$, there will be at most one steady state in the TAS, UEH, and KDW cases as $1 + \varrho$ is non-decreasing while f' is decreasing.[5] The long-run capital supply and demand curves can intersect at most once. In the TAS model, we denote a unique steady state by k^δ or $k(\delta)$ to indicate its dependence on the discount factor.

When the range of f' is too small, there may not be a steady state. This is especially true in the TAS case where the range of $\varrho = \delta^{-1} - 1$ is a single point. In the TAS case with $f(k) = \beta k$, steady states exist if and only if $\beta = \delta^{-1}$. When ϱ is decreasing, there may be multiple steady states.

---

[5] This only holds up to the maximum sustainable consumption. That is all we need as larger stocks cannot be steady states anyway because $f' < 1$ there.

▶ Example 3: Uzawa-Epstein-Hynes utility. The UEH aggregator given by $W(c, y) = u(c) + ye^{-v(c)}$ has $\Phi(c) = u(c)/(1 - e^{-v(c)})$ and $\varrho(c) = e^{v(c)} -$ 1. Now $\varrho' = v'e^v$. Because $v' > 0$, the marginal rate of impatience is increasing in steady-state consumption. Also, $1 + \varrho(0) = e^{v(0)} > 1$. A steady state exists provided $f'(0+) > e^{v(0)}$. Here $\varrho(f(k) - k)$ is increasing in k below the maximum sustainable stock, so there is only one possible intersection of supply and demand—one possible steady state. ◀

▶ Example 4: KDW utility. In the KDW case, $W(c, y) = (\delta/d) \log(1 + ac^b + dy)$ where $a, b, d, \delta > 0$, $b, \delta < 1$. Then $1 + \varrho(c) = (1 + ac^b + d\Phi(c))/\delta = e^{d\Phi(c)/\delta}$. This is also increasing in steady-state consumption c because steady-state utility Φ is increasing in c. Again, there is at most one steady state. ◀

▶ Example 5: Decreasing rate of impatience. Take $a, b > 0$ with $b < 4a$ and a function $\varphi: \mathbb{R}_+ \to \mathbb{R}_+$ obeying $\varphi' > 0$, $\varphi'' < 0$, $0 \le \varphi \le b$ and $\varphi(0) = 0$. Define $W(c, y) = \sqrt{\varphi(c)(a + y)}$. Set $\mathcal{Y} = \mathbb{R}_+$. Then W is strictly concave on $\mathbb{R}_+ \times \mathcal{Y}$, and

$$W_2 = \frac{1}{2}\sqrt{\frac{\varphi(c)}{a + y}} \le \frac{1}{2}\sqrt{\frac{b}{a + y}} \le \sqrt{\frac{b}{4a}} < 1.$$

It follows that this aggregator defines a strictly concave recursive utility function on all of s_+^1. Now

$$1 + \varrho(c) = \frac{1}{W_2(c, \Phi(c))} = 2\sqrt{\frac{a + \Phi(c)}{\varphi(c)}}.$$

The function Φ solves $\Phi = \sqrt{\varphi(c)(a + \Phi)}$, or $\Phi^2 = \varphi(c)(a + \Phi)$. Substituting in, $1 + \varrho(c) = 2\Phi(c)/\varphi(c)$. Applying the quadratic formula, we find

$$\Phi(c) = \frac{\varphi(c) \pm \sqrt{\varphi^2(c) + 4a\varphi(c)}}{2}.$$

As $\Phi \in \mathcal{Y}$, only the positive root works. Thus

$$1 + \varrho(c) = 1 + \sqrt{1 + \frac{4a}{\varphi(c)}}$$

and so

$$\varrho(c) = \sqrt{1 + \frac{4a}{\varphi(c)}}.$$

Because φ is increasing, ϱ is decreasing in c, takes the value $+\infty$ at 0, and is bounded below by $\sqrt{1 + 4a/b} > \sqrt{2}$. In this case, some production functions may yield multiple steady states. ◀

When f (or even u) is not concave, the Euler equations are still necessary for optimality, and solutions to $f'(k) = 1 + \varrho(f(k) - k)$ are candidates for a steady state, but they may or may not be optimal, depending on the form of U and f.

5.2.3 Monotonicity and Turnpikes in TAS Models

Although steady states can be optimal programs, many optimal paths are not stationary. What do these non-stationary optimal paths look like? In this section we concentrate on TAS models and temporarily relax our maintained assumptions to admit both *concave* and *nonconcave* production functions. We shall establish that: optimal paths cannot cross one another. Optimal paths are monotonic. The turnpike property holds— optimal paths converge either to steady states or to infinity.

Non-Crossing Lemma. *Let $(\mathbf{c}, \mathbf{k})$ and $(\mathbf{c}', \mathbf{k}')$ be optimal from k_0 and k_0', respectively. Suppose $J(k_0) > -\infty$. If $k_0 < k_0'$, then $k_1 \leq k_1'$.*

Proof. Note that $J(k_0') > J(k_0) > -\infty$. Suppose, by way of contradiction, that $k_1 > k_1'$. Define c^* and c^{**} by $c^* = f(k_0) - k_1'$ and $c^{**} = f(k_0') - k_1$. Then $c_1' = f(k_0') - k_1' > c^* > f(k_0) - k_1 = c_1$ and similarly $c_1' > c^{**} > c_1$. We now use the Bellman equation to compare $\mathbf{k}$ with $(k_0, k_1', k_2', \ldots)$ and $\mathbf{k}'$ with $(k_0', k_1, k_2, \ldots)$. This yields $J(k_0) = u(c_1) + \delta J(k_1) \geq u(c^*) + \delta J(k_1')$ and $J(k_0') = u(c_1') + \delta J(k_1') \geq u(c^{**}) + \delta J(k_1)$.

Adding these, and subtracting $\delta[J(k_0') + J(k_0)]$, shows $u(c_1) + u(c_1') \geq u(c^{**}) + u(c)$. Further, $c_1 + c_1' = c^* + c^{**}$. There is a θ, $0 < \theta < 1$, with $c^* = \theta c_1' + (1 - \theta)c_1$ and $c^{**} = (1 - \theta)c_1' + \theta c_1$. Strict concavity of u now implies $u(c^*) + u(c^{**}) > u(c_1) + u(c_1')$. This is impossible. Thus $k_1 \leq k_1'$. $\square$

This does not rule out the possibility of crossing in two steps, first catching up to the higher path, and then surpassing it in a later period. With a little more detailed knowledge about the optimal path (that the Euler equations are necessary), we can show $k_1 < k_1'$. That will rule out the possibility of even catching a higher path.

One application of the Inada conditions is to show optimal paths are strictly monotonic. In fact, any interior optimal paths are monotonic. Suppose $\mathbf{k}$ and $\mathbf{k}'$ are optimal from k and k' with $k < k'$ and $k_1' = k_1$. The path $(k', k_1, k_2, \ldots)$ is then optimal from k' by the Principle of Optimality. Applying the Euler equations to this path and to $\mathbf{k}$ shows $u'(c_1) = \delta f'(k_1) u'(c_2)$ and $u'(c_1') = \delta f'(k_1) u'(c_2)$. Thus $u'(c_1) = u'(c_1')$. Since u is strictly concave and $c_1 \neq c_1'$, this is impossible. If $k' > k$, then $k_1' > k_1$. Comparison of the paths starting at k and k_1 shows that if $k_1 > k$, then $k_2 > k_1$. Induction establishes $k_t > k_{t-1}$ for all t. The case $k_1 < k$ is similar. In sum,

Monotonicity Theorem. *If an optimal path is an interior path, it is either a steady state or its capital stocks are strictly monotonic.*

Corollary 4. *If the Inada felicity condition holds, $f(0) = 0$, and $f' > 0$ for $k \geq 0$, then any non-stationary optimal path has strictly monotonic capital stocks.*

The Monotonicity Theorem also tells us about the long-run behavior of optimal capital paths. The sequence k_t is either strictly increasing or strictly decreasing. It converges either to a finite limit k^* (possibly zero), or to $+\infty$. Moreover, if $k_t \to k^*$, $c_t = f(k_{t-1}) - k_t \to f(k^*) - k^* = c^*$, so consumption converges too. It is clear that c^* can only be zero if k^* is zero, otherwise it would be better to consume the extra capital k^*. Now consider the Euler equations $u'(c_t) = \delta f'(k_t) u'(c_{t+1})$. Letting $t \to \infty$, we find $u'(c^*) = \delta f'(k^*) u'(c^*)$. Unless $c^* = k^* = 0$, $1 = \delta f'(k^*)$. If $f'' < 0$, k_t converges either to zero, or to the (unique) steady state k^δ, or to $+\infty$. More generally, we have:

TAS Turnpike Theorem. *If an optimal path $\mathbf{k}$ is interior, then k_t converges either to zero, or to a k^δ with $\delta f'(k^\delta) = 1$, or to infinity.*

Corollary 5. *Suppose the Inada utility condition holds, and that $f'(\infty) < 1$ and $f'' < 0$. Then any optimal path converges to k^δ.*

Proof. The concavity of f yields a unique steady state k^δ. Since $f' < 1$ for large k, optimal paths must be bounded, which rules out convergence to ∞. Finally, if $k_t \to 0$, $\delta f'(k_t) > 1$ for t large. But then $u'(c_t) = \delta f'(k_t) u'(c_{t+1}) > u'(c_{t+1})$, so $c_{t+1} > c_t$ for t large. But $c_t \to 0$ since $k_t \to 0$. This contradiction rules out convergence to 0, so all optimal paths must converge to k^δ. □

Differential Approach

Life is much easier when the value function is twice continuously differentiable.[6] Suppose that $f'', u'' < 0$ and $f'(0+) = u'(0+) = +\infty$. It immediately follows that J is concave, so $J'' \leq 0$. The Bellman equation tells us to maximize $u(c) + \delta J(f(k) - c)$. The first-order necessary conditions are $u'(c^*) = \delta J'(f(k) - c^*)$. The consumption function g exists and obeys $u'(g(k)) = \delta J'(f(k) - g(k))$. The Implicit Function Theorem guarantees g is differentiable. By the chain rule, $u'' g' = \delta J'' [f' - g']$. Thus $f' > g' = \delta J'' f' / (u'' + \delta J'') > 0$. Current consumption g is increasing in the capital stock, but does not increase as fast as output increases. Thus, (gross) savings, which are given by the capital policy function $h(k) = f(k) - g(k)$, are also increasing. We have $h' = u'' / (u'' + \delta J'') > 0$.

---

[6] Araujo (1991) and Santos (1991) establish conditions for twice differentiability of J in the one-sector model and multisector models, respectively. Santos (1992) gives conditions for smoothness in parameters of the model, such as the discount factor. See also Boldrin and Montrucchio (1989).

It follows that if $k_1 > k_0$, $k_2 = h(k_1) > h(k_0) = k_1$. Optimal (capital) paths are monotonic. Further, since $g' > 0$, consumption is monotonic too.

A similar technique can be used to examine the effects of a change in the discount factor. Consider consumption as a function of both the capital stock and the discount factor. Then $g(k, \delta)$ obeys $u'(g(k, \delta)) = \delta J_k(f(k) - g(k, \delta), \delta)$, where $J_k = \partial J/\partial k$. Again, g is differentiable in (k, δ) by the Implicit Function Theorem. Differentiating the first-order condition yields $u'' g_\delta = J_k + \delta J_{k\delta} - \delta J_{kk} g_\delta$, so $g_\delta = (J_k + \delta J_{k\delta})/(u'' + \delta J_{kk}) < 0$. In this case we must sign $J_{k\delta}$ before proceeding. Becker (1985b) uses an induction argument to establish $J_{k\delta} \geq 0$.[7] Thus an increase in the discount factor (increase in patience) results in a decrease in current consumption. Since $h(k, \delta) = f(k) - g(k, \delta)$, savings will increase. These matters are discussed further in Chapter 7.

Nonclassical Models

In all these cases, the felicity function u is concave, so optimal paths are monotonic. However, there is still the problem of characterizing the limiting capital stock. The function $G(k) = f(k) - \delta^{-1}k$ will prove useful in characterizing the long-run behavior of optimal paths. Notice that $G' = 0$ at steady states.

Lemma 2. *Suppose* $(\mathbf{c}, \mathbf{k})$ *is optimal from* k. *Then* $(1 - \delta) \sum_{t=1}^{\infty} \delta^{t-1} c_t \geq f(k) - k$.

Proof. Let $c = (1 - \delta) \sum_{t=1}^{\infty} \delta^{t-1} c_t$. Then $u(c) \geq (1 - \delta) \sum_{t=1}^{\infty} \delta^{t-1} u(c_t)$ by Jensen's inequality.[8] As $(1 - \delta)^{-1} = \sum_{t=1}^{\infty} \delta^{t-1}$, $\sum_{t=1}^{\infty} \delta^{t-1} u(c) \geq \sum_{t=1}^{\infty} \delta^{t-1} u(c_t)$. If $f(k) - k > c$, $c_1' = f(k) - k > c$ is feasible. This yields higher utility than $\mathbf{c}$. Since $\mathbf{c}$ is optimal, this is impossible, thus $f(k) - k \leq c$. $\square$

Non-Optimality Lemma. *Suppose a path* $\mathbf{k}$ *with initial stock* k *obeys* $G(k_t) \leq G(k)$ *with strict inequality for some* t. *Then* $\mathbf{k}$ *is not optimal.*

Proof. Suppose $G(k_t) \leq G(k)$ with strict inequality for some t. We have

$$c_t = f(k_{t-1}) - k_t$$
$$= f(k_{t-1}) - \delta^{-1} k_{t-1} + \delta^{-1} k_{t-1} - k_t$$
$$= G(k_t) + \delta^{-1} k_{t-1} - k_t.$$

---

[7] Note however that his earlier argument (Becker, 1983b) is incomplete as it ignores the dependence of the value function on the discount factor. We discuss this dependence further in Chapter 7, on comparative dynamics.

[8] *Jensen's inequality* says that if u is concave and $\sum_{t=1}^{\infty} \alpha_t = 1$ for $\alpha_t \geq 0$, then $u(\sum_{t=1}^{\infty} \alpha_t c_t) \geq \sum_{t=1}^{\infty} \alpha_t u(c_t)$. It is a standard consequence of concavity. For example, see Aliprantis and Border (1994, pp. 325–326).

Multiplying by δ^{t-1} and summing over t yields

$$\sum_{t=1}^{\infty} \delta^{t-1} c_t = \sum_{t=1}^{\infty} \delta^{t-1} G(k_t) + \sum_{t=1}^{\infty} [\delta^{t-2} k_{t-1} - \delta^{t-1} k_t]$$
$$< (1-\delta)^{-1} G(k) + \delta^{-1} k = (1-\delta)^{-1} [f(k) - k].$$

Lemma 2 now shows that this path cannot be optimal. $\square$

It follows that if G has a global maximum, it is a steady state. The Non-Optimality Lemma allows us to strengthen the corollary to the TAS Turnpike Theorem.

Corollary 6. *Suppose the Inada production and utility conditions hold, and that $f'' < 0$. Then any optimal path converges to k^δ.*

Proof. Suppose $\mathbf{k}$ is optimal with $k_t \to \infty$. Take t large enough that $\delta f'(k_t) < 1$. Because $G' < 0$ for $k > k_t$, the Non-Optimality Lemma implies the path $(k_t, k_{t+1}, \dots)$ is not optimal from k_t. Thus all optimal paths are bounded. The arguments from Corollary 5 now apply. $\square$

▶ **Example 6: Linear technology.** Suppose $f(k) = \alpha + \beta k$, so $G(k) = \alpha + \beta k - \delta^{-1} k$ and $G'(k) = \beta - \delta^{-1}$. Unless $\beta = \delta^{-1}$, this model does not have a steady state. If $\beta = \delta^{-1}$, all initial stocks are steady states. If $\beta \neq \delta^{-1}$, the TAS Turnpike Theorem gives us two alternatives: either $k_t \downarrow 0$ or $k_t \uparrow +\infty$. If $\beta < \delta^{-1}$, a path with $k_t \uparrow \infty$ has $G(k_t) < G(k)$, and cannot be optimal by the Non-Optimality Lemma. All optimal paths must converge to 0. On the other hand, if $\beta > \delta^{-1}$, any path with $k_t \downarrow 0$ cannot be optimal, and all optimal paths grow without bound. ◀

Dechert and Nishimura (1983) gave a comprehensive analysis of the renewable resource (fishery) model of Clark (1971). Much of their analysis used the function G. They examined the case where f has increasing returns for low levels of k, followed by a region of diminishing returns once k is large enough. Related work on more general nonconvex models can be found in the papers by Skiba (1978), Majumdar and Mitra (1982), and Majumdar and Nermuth (1982). We follow Dechert and Nishimura and assume:

Dechert-Nishimura Conditions.

(DN1) Felicity u is $\mathcal{C}^2$ on $(0, \infty)$. If u is bounded from below, it is continuous on $[0, \infty)$. The discount factor $\delta < 1$;

(DN2) Felicity obeys $u' > 0$, $u'' < 0$ and $u'(0+) = \infty$;

(DN3) The production function f is $\mathcal{C}^2$ on $[0, \infty)$ with $f' > 0$ and $f(0) = 0$;

(DN4) There is an inflection point $k_I > 0$ with $f'' > 0$ for $k < k_I$ and $f'' < 0$ for $k > k_I$;

(DN5) There is a $k_b > k_I$ with $f(k_b) = k_b$ and $f(k) < k$ for $k > k_b$.

Since production is bounded and the discount factor is less than unity, optimal paths exist, although $J(k) = -\infty$ is possible. The Inada condition $u'(0+) = \infty$, together with $f(0) = 0$ and $f' > 0$, ensures that $c_t, k_t > 0$ for all t. Thus optimal paths are monotonic whenever $J(k) > -\infty$.[9] As all feasible paths are bounded, convergence to $+\infty$ is impossible. The TAS Turnpike Theorem then shows that all optimal paths converge to a steady state, or to 0.

Under (DN3)–(DN5), there are at most two points with $\delta f'(k) = 1$. Denote these by k_* and k^*. If there is only one, denote it by k^*. If δ is small, such a point may not exist. Note that $k_* < k_I \leq k^*$. There are three cases to distinguish:

Discounting Conditions.

  (1) Mild discounting: $G'(0) \geq 0$.
  (2) Intermediate discounting: $G'(0) < 0$ and there is a k with $G(k) > 0$.
  (3) Strong discounting: $G(k) < 0$ for all k.

Under mild discounting either $k_* = 0$ $[\delta f'(0) = 1]$ or k_* does not exist. In this case, G is hump-shaped with a maximum at k^*.

Proposition 2. *Under mild discounting, all optimal paths starting from $k > 0$ converge to k^*.*

Proof. The point k^* is a steady state since it is a global maximum for G. Thus if $k_t \neq k^*$, $G(k_t) < G(k^*)$. By the Non-Optimality Lemma, such a path is not optimal from k^*. As paths are bounded, the only option for paths starting above k^* is to converge to k^*. If $k < k^*$, $k_t \downarrow 0$ would imply $G(k_t) < G(k)$. These are again ruled out, so all optimal paths must converge to k^*. $\square$

Under intermediate discounting, $G(0) = 0$. As $G'(0) < 0$, G first declines to a minimum at $k_* > 0$, then increases to a global maximum at k^*, and finally decreases thereafter. Optimal paths have three possible modes of convergence by the TAS Turnpike Theorem. They can converge to 0, k_*, or k^*. Notice that $k_* < k_I < k^*$. Let z^* be the unique $z^* > 0$ with $G(z^*) = 0$ and $z^* \leq k^*$. We first examine the paths starting at or above z^*.

Lemma 3. *Suppose $k \geq z^*$. Under intermediate discounting, all optimal paths from k converge to k^*.*

Proof. First note that k^* is optimal since any other path from k^* has $G(k_t) < G(k^*)$. By the Non-Crossing Lemma, any path with $k > k^*$ cannot cross k^* and thus decreases to k^*.

---

[9] Dechert and Nishimura implicitly assume $J(k) > -\infty$.

Now suppose $z^* \leq k < k^*$ and k_t does not converge to k^*. By the TAS Turnpike Theorem, k_t decreases to k_* or 0. In either case, $G(k_t) \leq G(k)$ with strict inequality for some t. As this is impossible for an optimal path, $k_t \uparrow k^*$. $\square$

The next issue is the status of k_*. It is possible that k_* is a steady state. If it is a steady state, it must be unstable. This holds under any discounting condition.

Lemma 4. *No optimal path with $k \neq k_*$ converges to k_*.*

Proof. Suppose by way of contradiction that a path $\mathbf{k}$ is optimal from $k \neq k_*$, and converges to k_*. By the Monotonicity Theorem, $k_t \to k_*$ monotonically. There are two possibilities: either $k_* \leq k_t < k$ (when $k > k_*$), or $k < k_t \leq k_*$ (when $k < k_*$). In either case $G(k_t) < G(k)$ for all t. By the Non-Optimality Lemma, such a path cannot be optimal. $\square$

There are now two possibilities. In the first, remaining at k_* is optimal, and optimal paths with $k < k_*$ converge to 0 while optimal paths with $k > k_*$ converge to k^*. Dechert and Nishimura's Lemma 4 describes a case where remaining at k_* is not optimal. If $(\delta^{-1} - 1)u''(c_*) + \delta u'(c_*)f''(k_*) > 0$, k_* is not a steady state. When k_* is not a steady state, they use the Euler equations to show that optimal paths starting at sufficiently low stocks must converge to 0. By the Non-Crossing Lemma, it follows that there is a critical level k_c, with $k_c \leq z^*$ such that optimal paths starting below k_c converge to 0 while those starting above k_c converge to k^*. Further, if $k_c \neq k_*$, the fact that $\mathbf{k}(k)$ is a closed correspondence implies there are optimal paths from k_c converging to 0 and to k^*, respectively.

The analysis of the strong discounting case is similar. Here, if δ is sufficiently small, neither k^* nor k_* exist. In the extreme case when even k^* is not optimal, all optimal paths converge to the origin.

One further point to note is that we can sometimes obtain monotonicity results for consumption. By the Euler equations, $u'(c_t) = \delta f'(k_t)u'(c_{t+1})$. Since marginal utility is decreasing, $c_t < c_{t+1}$ when $\delta f'(k_t) > 1$ and $c_t > c_{t+1}$ when $\delta f'(k_t) < 1$. Under mild discounting, this immediately shows that all optimal consumption paths are monotonic because $\delta f'(k_t) > 1$ for $k < k^*$ and $\delta f'(k_t) < 1$ for $k > k^*$. Under intermediate discounting, if $k_* = k_c$, all optimal consumption paths are monotonic. If $k_* \neq k_c$, consumption along paths starting near k_c will either decrease and then increase, or the reverse, even though capital is monotonic. Which happens depends on whether $k_c < k_*$ or $k_c > k_*$.

5.2.4 Monotonicity and Turnpikes in Recursive Models

Similar monotonicity results hold when preferences are recursive, but not necessarily additive. Monotonicity and turnpike results were established by Beals and Koopmans (1969), and under slightly weaker conditions by

Magill and Nishimura (1984).[10] Something does have to be given up to obtain the extra generality. In this section, we confine our attention to concave production functions and strictly concave utility, unlike Section 5.2.3. The basic strategy is the same. We prove optimal paths are monotonic and that they cannot cross. Convergence to a steady state (or infinity) then follows.

Monotonicity Theorem. *Suppose* $\partial R/\partial c_1 < 0$. *For any initial stock* k, $k_t(k)$ *is a strictly increasing function of* k *and the optimal path* $\mathbf{k}(k)$ *is strictly monotonic.*

Proof. The strict concavity means $\mathbf{k}(k)$ is single-valued, hence continuous. Let $k < k'$, and let $\mathbf{k} = \mathbf{k}(k)$, $\mathbf{k}' = \mathbf{k}(k')$ be optimal. Suppose $k_1 = k_1'$. By the Principle of Optimality, $k_t = k_t'$ for $t = 2, 3, \dots$. Further, $c_1 = f(k) - k_1 < f(k') - k_1' = c_1'$ and $c_2 = f(k_1) - k_2 = c_2'$. Thus $c_t' = c_t$ for $t = 2, 3, \dots$. The Euler equations yield $R(c_1, c_2, \dots) = f'(k_1) = f'(k_1') = 1 + R(c_1', c_2', \dots)$. Since $c_t' = c_t$ for $t = 2, 3, \dots$, $R(c_1, c_2, \dots) = R(c_1', c_2, \dots)$. But this is impossible since R is decreasing in c_1 and $c_1 < c_1'$. Thus $k_1 \neq k_1'$.

Now suppose $k_1 > k_1'$. Since $k_1(0) = 0 < k_1' < k_1(k)$, and $k_1(k)$ is continuous, there is a k'' with $0 < k'' < k$ and $k_1(k'') = k_1'$. This is impossible by the preceding argument. Therefore k_1 is strictly increasing. Since $k_t(k)$ is the tth iterate of k_1, it too is strictly increasing. Further, $\mathbf{k}(k)$ is strictly monotonic by the usual argument. $\square$

A close look at the proof shows that we really only require that $\partial R/\partial c_1$ never be zero, not that it be negative. However, the requirement that $\partial R/\partial c_1 < 0$ is quite natural. Remember, R is the marginal rate of substitution between consumption today and consumption tomorrow. As we increase today's consumption, we expect the rate of substitution to fall. In the additive case, it must fall as $\partial R/\partial c_1 = u''(c_1)/\delta u'(c_2)$. In the more general recursive case it is equivalent to requiring

$$\partial[W_1(c_1, u)/W_2(c_1, u)]/\partial c_1 < 0.$$

It says that the indifference curves in (c_1, u)-space are convex to the origin.[11]

As before, monotonicity immediately implies that optimal paths converge either to 0, or to a steady state, or to $+\infty$.

Initial stocks can be divided into three disjoint sets. Let $\mathcal{I}^0 = \{k : k = 0$ or $f'(k) = 1 + \varrho(f(k) - k)\}$, $\mathcal{I}^+ = \{k : f'(k) > 1 + \varrho(f(k) - k)\}$, and

---

[10] Boyer (1975) and Iwai (1972) examined recursive utility models with one sector. They utilized dynamic programming ideas and conjectured the presence of multiple steady states in some cases.

[11] This condition also appears in our treatment of comparative dynamics in Chapter 7.

$\mathcal{I}^- = \{k : f'(k) < 1 + \varrho(f(k) - k)\}$. For $k \in \mathcal{I}^0$, the Euler equations and transversality condition are clearly satisfied by the stationary path $k_t = k$. Thus every element of $\mathcal{I}^0$ is a steady state. The Euler equations also show that all steady states are in $\mathcal{I}^0$. Accumulation is definitely possible in $\mathcal{I}^+$ since $f'(k) > 1 + \varrho(f(k) - k) > 1$.

Recursive Non-Optimality Lemma. *Suppose $k \in \mathcal{I}^+$ ($k \in \mathcal{I}^-$) and $k_t \le k$ ($k_t \ge k$) for $t < n$ with $k_t = k$ for $t \ge n$. Then $U(\mathbf{c}) \le \Psi(k)$, and $\mathbf{k}$ is not optimal.*

Proof. First suppose $k \in \mathcal{I}^+$. That $U(\mathbf{c}) \le \Psi(k)$ is trivial for $n = 1$. We proceed by induction. Suppose $U(\mathbf{c}) \le \Psi(k)$ when $n = m \ge 1$ and consider a path $\mathbf{k}$ with $k_t \le k$ and $k_t = k$ for $t \ge m + 1$. If $k_m = k$, $U(\mathbf{c}) \le \Psi(k)$ by the induction hypothesis, so we may suppose $k_m < k$.

First consider the path $\mathbf{k}'$ defined by $k'_t = k$ for $t \ne m$ and $k'_m = k + \Delta$. Obviously $f'(k) > 1$, so this path will be feasible from k for $\Delta > 0$ small enough. Taking a Taylor expansion shows

$$\begin{aligned} U(\mathbf{c}') - U(\mathbf{c}) &= -U_m(\mathbf{c})\Delta + U_{m+1}(\mathbf{c})\Delta f' + o(\Delta)\Delta \\ &= (W_2)^{m-1}[-W_1 + W_2 W_1 f']\Delta + o(\Delta)\Delta \\ &= W_1(W_2)^{m-1}[W_2 f' - 1]\Delta + o(\Delta)\Delta \end{aligned}$$

where all derivatives are evaluated at k. Now

$$1 + \varrho(f(k) - k) = 1/W_2(k, \Psi(k)) < f'(k)$$

as $k \in \mathcal{I}^+$. So $W_2 f' > 1$ and Δ may be chosen small enough that $U(\mathbf{c}') > \Psi(k)$. Note that remaining at k cannot be optimal.

Now take λ, $0 < \lambda < 1$ with $\lambda(k + \Delta) + (1 - \lambda)k_m = k$. (Here $\lambda = (k - k_m)/(k - k_m + \Delta)$.) Then $\mathbf{k}'' = \lambda \mathbf{k}' + (1 - \lambda)\mathbf{k}$ satisfies the hypotheses of the lemma for $n = m$, so $U(\mathbf{c}'') \le \Psi(k)$ by the induction hypothesis. Now $\Psi(k) \ge U(\mathbf{c}'') \ge \lambda U(\mathbf{c}') + (1 - \lambda)U(\mathbf{c}) > \lambda \Psi(k) + (1 - \lambda)U(\mathbf{c})$. Thus $\Psi(k) > U(\mathbf{c})$. The inequality holds for all n by induction. Further, since the stationary path $k_t = k$ is feasible and not optimal, $\mathbf{k}$ cannot be optimal.

The case of $k \in \mathcal{I}^-$ is similar. $\square$

This result is very similar to the Non-Optimality Lemma of Section 5.2.3. Let's again consider the additively separable case. Then $\mathcal{I}^+$ and $\mathcal{I}^-$ are the regions where $G'(k) > 0$, and $G'(k) < 0$, respectively, while $\mathcal{I}^0 = \{0\} \cup \{k : G'(k) = 0\}$. Moreover, since $f'' < 0$, there is a unique steady state k^δ. Then $\mathcal{I}^+ = (0, k(\delta))$, $\mathcal{I}^- = (k(\delta), \infty)$ and $\mathcal{I}^0 = \{0, k(\delta)\}$.

Using the Recursive Non-Optimality Lemma, we can prove a turnpike result. Since both $\mathcal{I}^+$ and $\mathcal{I}^-$ are open, they are the countable union of open intervals. The endpoints of these intervals must be in $\mathcal{I}^0$.[12] Now

---

[12] Note that $\mathcal{I}^0$ may contain points other than these endpoints.

label the endpoints $\bar{k}_i$ such that $\bar{k}_i < \bar{k}_{i+1}$. We allow $+\infty$ as the largest $\bar{k}_i$. If $k \notin (\bar{k}_i, \bar{k}_{i+1})$, the optimal path cannot cross the steady states at the endpoints, so $k_t \in (\bar{k}_i, \bar{k}_{i+1})$. Further, since k_t is monotonic, it must converge to some $\bar{k}$. Taking the limit in the Euler equations shows $f'(\bar{k}) = 1 + \varrho(f(\bar{k}) - \bar{k})$. The optimal path converges to one of the endpoints. Similarly, if k is greater than all of the steady states it converges either to the largest steady state, or to ∞. The next theorem shows that $k_t \to \bar{k}_{i+1}$ when $k \in (\bar{k}_i, \bar{k}_{i+1}) \subset \mathcal{I}^+$ and $k_t \to \bar{k}_i$ when $k \in (\bar{k}_i, \bar{k}_{i+1}) \subset \mathcal{I}^-$.

Recursive Turnpike Theorem. *Suppose* $\partial R/\partial c_1 < 0$. *If* $k \in (\bar{k}_i, \bar{k}_{i+1}) \subset \mathcal{I}^+$, *the optimal path obeys* $k_t \uparrow \bar{k}_{i+1}$; *if* $k \in (\bar{k}_i, \bar{k}_{i+1}) \subset \mathcal{I}^-$, *it obeys* $k_t \downarrow \bar{k}_{i+1}$; *and if* $k \in \mathcal{I}^0$, $k_t = k$ *is the optimal path.*

Proof. When $k \in \mathcal{I}^0$, the path $k_t = k$ satisfies the Euler equations and transversality condition. Thus it is optimal.

Consider the case where $k \in \mathcal{I}^+$. We know that k_t is strictly monotonic. Suppose k_t is decreasing. Take a sequence of feasible paths $\mathbf{k}^\nu$ such that $\mathbf{k}^\nu \to \mathbf{k}$ in the product topology with $k_t^\nu \leq k$ for all t and $k_t^\nu = k$ for large t. (This is possible since $f' > 1$ and $f(k) > k$ on $[k_t^\nu, k]$.) Then $U(\mathbf{k}^\nu) \leq \Psi(k)$ by the Recursive Non-Optimality Lemma. Since U is product continuous on the feasible set, $U(\mathbf{k}) \leq \Psi(k)$, contradicting the fact that $\mathbf{k}$ is optimal. Thus k_t is increasing. By the Non-Crossing Lemma, $k_t < \bar{k}_{i+1}$. Taking the limit in the Euler equations shows the limit point is in $\mathcal{I}^0$. It must be $\bar{k}_{i+1}$.

The case $k \in \mathcal{I}^-$ is similar, except that the optimal path may simply be truncated to obtain the desired $\mathbf{k}^\nu$. $\square$

Uzawa-Epstein-Hynes preferences have an upward sloping long-run supply curve. When the technology is sufficiently productive, there is a unique steady state. The Recursive Turnpike Theorem implies that the steady state is stable. Initial stocks above the steady state lead to optimal paths that converge downward to the steady state, while initial stocks below the steady state lead to upward convergence.

The preferences from Example 5 are somewhat different. In that case, the long-run supply curve is *downward* sloping. If the technology is sufficiently productive, sustained growth results. When the technology is somewhat less productive, there will be steady states, and there may even be multiple steady states. If so, their stability depends on whether the long-run supply curve cuts upward (stable) or downward (unstable) through the long-run demand curve as capital increases.

5.2.5 Growing Economies

So far, we have focused on models with steady states. Not all economies have steady states. Even so, we still know that optimal paths are monotonic, and that they must grow in $\mathcal{I}^+$ and shrink in $\mathcal{I}^-$. We focus on the growing case. When preferences are TAS, this is the case where $G' > 0$ for all k (equivalently $f' > \delta^{-1} = 1 + \varrho$). In such economies, all optimal paths must grow without bound.

▶ Example 7: Homogeneous TAS felicity. One of the simplest cases occurs under constant returns and homothetic preferences. The only constant returns production functions have the form $f(k) = \beta k$. In the additive case, the economy grows if the growth overcomes discounting, that is $\beta\delta > 1$. We use a symmetry argument to find the solution. Consider the effect of an expansion of the initial capital stock by a factor λ. Clearly, $\mathbf{F}(\lambda k) = \lambda\mathbf{F}(k)$. Opportunities expand by the factor λ. When preferences are homothetic, multiplication by λ is a symmetry. Thus $\lambda\mathbf{c}^*$ is optimal from λk whenever $\mathbf{c}$ is optimal from k. We need only find the optimal path from a single point to find all optimal paths. Take the optimal capital path $\mathbf{k}$ and define $\lambda^* = k_1/k$. Now $\lambda^*\mathbf{k}$ is optimal from $k_1 = \lambda^*k$. Thus $k_2 = \lambda^*k_1$, $k_3 = \lambda^*k_2$, etc. The optimal path grows at a constant factor λ^*.

The standard case is to take homogeneous felicity $u(c) = c^\gamma/\gamma$ for $\gamma < 1$, $\gamma \neq 0$. We assume $\beta\delta > 1$ and $\beta^\gamma\delta < 1$. The Basic Existence Theorem ensures an optimal path exists. For λ^* to be the optimal growth factor, it must satisfy the Euler equations. Thus $u'(c)/\delta u'(\lambda^*c) = \beta$. Now $u'(c) = c^{\gamma-1}$, so $1/\delta(\lambda^*)^{\gamma-1} = \beta$. Rearranging, we find $\lambda^* = (\beta\delta)^{1/(1-\gamma)}$ is the optimal growth factor. Notice that $\lambda^* > 1$ because $\beta\delta > 1$ and $\gamma < 1$. The economy grows. ◀

▶ Example 8: Dolmas model. Dolmas (1996a) considered the aggregator $W(c, y) = c^\gamma[1 + \delta y/c^\gamma]^\rho/\rho$ for $0 < \delta$, $\rho < 1$, and $0 < \gamma < 1$. The corresponding utility function is then homogeneous of degree γ. Because of homotheticity, $\mathrm{MRS}_{t,t+1}$ along $\alpha\mathbf{c}$ is the same as along $\mathbf{c}$. Thus $\varrho(c)$ is independent of the level of c. It is constant, as in the TAS case. Homotheticity also implies that $\mathrm{MRS}_{t,t+1}$ along a path that grows at a constant rate is independent of the level of c or time t. The marginal rate of impatience on such a path depends only on its growth rate.

Consider the production function $f(k) = \beta k$, as in Example 7. The Existence Theorem yields an optimum whenever $\beta^\gamma\delta < 1$. The symmetry argument from Example 7 now applies and shows that the optimal path grows at a constant rate. We need only determine the rate. For this, we again employ the Euler equations. Note that $W(\lambda c, \lambda^\gamma y) = \lambda^\gamma W(c, y)$. It follows that $W_1(\lambda c, \lambda^\gamma y) = \lambda^{\gamma-1}W_1(c, y)$. Suppose $\mathbf{c} = (c, \lambda c, \lambda^2 c, \dots)$ grows by the factor λ, then

$$\beta = 1 + R(\mathbf{c}) = \frac{W_1(c, U(\lambda\mathbf{c}))}{W_2(c, U(\lambda\mathbf{c}))W_1(\lambda c, U(\lambda^2\mathbf{c}))} = \frac{1}{\lambda^{\gamma-1}W_2(c, U(\lambda\mathbf{c}))}.$$

Computing, we obtain

$$W_2(c, U(\lambda \mathbf{c})) = \delta[1 + \delta U(\lambda \mathbf{c})/c^\gamma]^{\rho-1} = \delta[1 + \delta z(\lambda)]^{\rho-1},$$

where $z(\lambda) = U(\lambda, \lambda^2, \ldots)$. Now $z(\lambda) = \lambda^\gamma[1 + \delta z(\lambda)]^\rho/\rho$. This has a unique solution, and $z(\lambda)$ is increasing with $z(\lambda) \to \infty$ as $\lambda \to \infty$. Moreover, z is continuous with $z(0) = 0$.

The optimal growth factor λ obeys the balanced growth Euler equation

$$\delta\beta = \lambda^{1-\gamma}[1 + \delta z(\lambda)]^{1-\rho}. \tag{1}$$

The right-hand side is continuous and increasing in λ. It takes the value 0 when $\lambda = 0$, and is $+\infty$ for $\lambda = +\infty$. There is then a unique λ^* that solves the Euler equation. Optimal paths grow at that λ^*. However, unlike the preceding TAS case, λ^* may be less than one. The economy may shrink instead of growing.

This can happen when $\rho = 1/2$. A short computation shows $z(1) = 2\delta + 2\sqrt{1 + \delta^2}$. Substituting this in (1) for $\lambda = 1$, we find the right-hand side becomes $\delta + \sqrt{1 + \delta^2}$. If $1 < \beta < 1 + \sqrt{1 + \delta^{-2}}$, the right-hand side of (1) is already larger than the left hand side at $\lambda = 1$ and the solution to (1) occurs in $(0, 1)$. The economy must shrink. If β is large enough, with $\beta > 1 + \sqrt{1 + \delta^{-2}}$, sustained growth occurs. ◄

Nonlinear technologies can also lead to sustained growth. This occurs whenever f' remains above $1 + \bar{\varrho}$ for all capital stocks. In that case, the Recursive Turnpike Theorem implies that capital must continue to accumulate. By Proposition 3.4, we can never have $c_{t+1} \le c_t$ in such circumstances, so $c_{t+1} > c_t$ for all t. Both capital and consumption grow over time.

▶ Example 9: Convex endogenous growth. Jones and Manuelli (1988) introduce the production function $f(k) = \gamma k + x^\rho$ where $\gamma > 1$ and $0 < \rho < 1$. Here $f'(0) = +\infty$ and $f'(\infty) = \gamma$. With TAS utility, this model will have a unique steady state if $\delta\gamma < 1$, but $\delta\gamma \ge 1$ implies $G' > 0$ and optimal paths must grow forever. The Basic Existence Theorem yields an optimal path if felicity is logarithmic and $\delta < 1$ or if felicity is homogeneous, $u(c) = c^{1-\sigma}/(1 - \sigma)$ for $\sigma \ge 0$, and if $\delta\gamma^{1-\sigma} < 1$. In either case, there are utility functions leading to sustained growth. Dolmas's utility functions yield very similar results for this technology. ◄

The growth that we see in Examples 7–9 depends on the properties of both the technology and of preferences. If we consider a model with utility generated from the EH aggregator $W(c, y) = -1 + e^{-v(c)}y$, neither the linear technology nor the Jones-Manuelli technology can generate sustained growth. Individuals with Epstein-Hynes utility become more and more impatient as they become wealthier. Eventually, they become impatient enough to stabilize the economy at a steady state.

There is not a clear consensus on whether people become more or less patient as steady-state income rises. Irving Fisher (1930, p. 72) argued that impatience decreases as steady-state consumption rises. According to him, "Poverty bears down heavily on all portions of a man's expected life. But it increases the want for immediate income *even more* than it increases the want for future income." However, even if this is true for small consumption levels, it might not hold when comparing wealthy and wealthier. Hayek (1941, p. 228) considered the possibility that impatience would increase at high wealth levels, resulting in convergence to a steady state. Curiously, the other possibility he considers is not that consumers would become less patient, but that returns to investment would decrease, again yielding a steady state. He apparently thought the possibility of sustained growth too implausible to consider.

5.3 Steady States in Multisectoral Models

In one-sector models, the existence of steady states follows from the Intermediate Value Theorem. Discounted multisector models are somewhat more complex, requiring the Kakutani Fixed Point Theorem. Below, we show existence of steady states in both discounted and undiscounted TAS models, and in discounted recursive models.

5.3.1 Stationary Optimal Programs for Additive Utility

We focus first on the time additive separable case, and start by characterizing steady states in the consumption-based model. We then switch over to the more convenient reduced-form model. A pair (a^*, b^*) is a *discounted golden rule* if $u(b^* - a^*) \geq u(\delta b + (1 - \delta)b^* - a)$ for all $(a, b) \in T$ with $\delta b + (1 - \delta)b^* - a \geq 0$. Of course, this admits 0 as a possible discounted golden rule, albeit an uninteresting one. The discounted golden rule is *non-trivial* if $u(b^* - a^*) > u(0)$. In the multisector context, a pair (a^*, b^*) is a *stationary optimal program* if setting $c_t^* = b^* - a^*$ for every t maximizes utility $\sum_{t=1}^{\infty} \delta^{t-1} u(c_t)$ among all programs $\mathbf{c}$ that are feasible from b^*: that obey $c_t = b_t - a_t$ with $(a_t, b_{t+1}) \in T$ for $t = 1, 2, \ldots$ with $b_1 = b^*$.

Proposition 3. *Suppose u is differentiable. A pair (a^*, b^*) is a discounted golden rule if and only if it is a stationary optimal program.*

Proof (only if). Suppose (a^*, b^*) is a discounted golden rule. Let $(\mathbf{a}, \mathbf{b})$ be feasible from b^*. To simplify notation, we set $b^1 = b^*$. Let

$$\bar{a} = (1 - \delta) \sum_{t=1}^{\infty} \delta^{t-1} a_t$$

and

$$\bar{b} = \delta^{-1}(1 - \delta) \sum_{t=2}^{\infty} \delta^{t-1} b_t.$$

Note $\bar{b} = (1 - \delta) \sum_{t=1}^{\infty} \delta^{t-1} b_{t+1}$. Now $(\bar{a}, \bar{b}) \in T$ because T is closed and convex and $(a_t, b_{t+1}) \in T$ for all t. Let $\bar{c} = (1 - \delta)b^* + \delta\bar{b} - \bar{a} = (1 - \delta) \sum_{t=1}^{\infty} \delta^{t-1}(b_t - a_t) \geq 0$. Since (a^*, b^*) is a discounted golden rule, $u(b^* - a^*) \geq u(\bar{c})$. Also, by concavity of u, $u(\bar{c}) \geq (1-\delta) \sum_{t=1}^{\infty} u(c_t)$. Combining, and multiplying by $(1 - \delta)^{-1} = \sum_{t=1}^{\infty} \delta^{t-1}$, we find $\sum_{t=1}^{\infty} \delta^{t-1} u(b^* - a^*) \geq \sum_{t=1}^{\infty} \delta^{t-1} u(c_t)$. Therefore (a^*, b^*) is a stationary optimal program.

Proof (if). Now suppose (a^*, b^*) is a stationary optimal program. If $(a, b) \in T$ with $c = \delta b + (1 - \delta)b^* - a \geq 0$, then $c - c^* = \delta(b - b^*) + (a^* - a)$ where $c^* = b^* - a^*$. By concavity, $u(c^*) + p[\delta(b - b^*) + a^* - a] \geq u(c)$ where $p = Du(c^*)$. Now employ the Euler equations at (a^*, b^*). Here $p_t = \delta^{t-1}p$, so $\delta p b^* - p a^* \geq \delta p b - p a$. This implies $u(c^*) \geq u(c)$, which means (a^*, b^*) is a discounted golden rule. $\square$

The fact that u is differentiable was only used in the "if" part, and only to derive supporting prices. Not surprisingly, a similar argument using supporting prices (or supergradients) works if u is merely concave. We now recast the definition of a discounted golden rule in a reduced-form model. Let $v : T \subset \mathbb{R}_+^{2m} \to \mathbb{R} \cup \{-\infty\}$ denote the reduced-form felicity function. There are a number of conditions we will impose on our reduced-form models. The first set is:

TAS Reduced Form. A TAS reduced-form model is a triple (T, v, δ) where $T \subset \mathbb{R}_+^{2m}$ is a Malinvaud technology set, $0 < \delta \leq 1$, and $v : T \to \mathbb{R} \cup \{-\infty\}$ obeys (R1)–(R2). If (R3) holds, we say the model is *bounded*. If (R4) holds, we call the model δ-*normal*.

(R1) v is concave, finite on int T, upper semicontinuous on T, and lower semicontinuous at all points where $v(a, b) > -\infty$.

(R2) If $(a, b) \in T$, and $a' \geq a$, $0 \leq b' \leq b$, then $v(a', b') \geq v(a, b)$ (monotonicity).

(R3) There is a $\beta > 0$ such that $\|b\| < \|a\|$ whenever $(a, b) \in T$ with $\|a\| > \beta$.

(R4) There is $(\bar{a}, \bar{b}) \in T$ such that $\bar{a} \leq \delta\bar{b}$ and $v(\bar{a}, \bar{b}) > v(0, 0)$.

The assumption of lower semicontinuity at points where $v(a, b) > -\infty$ only bites on the boundary of T. Concavity and the fact that v is finite on the interior of T implies v is continuous there. We include the undiscounted case ($\delta = 1$) as a possibility in our definitions.

Boundedness does *not* mean that T is necessarily a bounded set. It *does* imply that all feasible paths are bounded. It also implies that if $(k, k, \dots)$ is feasible, $\|k\| \leq \beta$. Any steady state k must have $\|k\| \leq \beta$. It is an easy induction using the following lemma to show feasible paths are bounded by the maximum of β and the norm of the initial stock when the technology is bounded.

Lemma 5. *Suppose a bounded Malinvaud technology set T obeys the boundedness postulate (R3). Then $\|b\| \leq \max\{\beta, \|a\|\}$ for all $(a, b) \in T$.*

Proof. When $\|a\| > \beta$, this follows immediately from the definition, so we may suppose $\|a\| \leq \beta$. If $\|b\| > \beta$, take $a' \geq a$ with $\beta < \|a'\| < \|b\|$. Then $(a', b) \in T$ by free disposal. But then $\|b\| < \|a'\| < \|b\|$ by boundedness, so $\|b\| > \beta$ is impossible. $\square$

We say an input stock $\bar{a}$ is *expansible* if there is $\bar{b}$ with $(\bar{a}, \bar{b}) \in T$ such that $\bar{a} \ll \bar{b}$ and $v(\bar{a}, \bar{b}) > v(0, 0)$.[13] Note that any expansible stock is δ-normal for $\delta \geq \max\{\bar{a}_i/\bar{b}_i\} < 1$, while the $\bar{a}$ given by δ-normality is expansible if $\bar{a} \gg 0$. There is one other useful concept related to the notion of an expansible stock. If the model is δ-normal for $\delta = 1$, we refer to the associated input $\bar{a}$ as a *weakly expansible stock*.

A stock k is a *golden-rule stock* if $(k, k) \in T$ and $v(k, k) \geq v(a, b)$ for all $(a, b) \in T$ with $a \leq (1 - \delta)k + \delta b$. When $\delta < 1$, we will sometimes refer to a golden-rule stock as a *discounted golden-rule stock*. A golden rule is *non-trivial* if $v(k, k) > v(0, 0)$. As in the consumption case, remaining at a non-trivial golden rule is optimal.

We will only show the existence of non-trivial golden rules when the technology is both bounded and δ-normal. The one-sector model provides some insight into the existence result. The TAS Turnpike Theorem tells us that only two things can go wrong in one-sector models, at either zero or infinity. The δ-normality condition rules out cases where all optimal paths converge to zero, and is a generalization of the requirement that $\delta f'(0+) > 1$ in the one-sector model. Boundedness is crucial, it rules out convergence to infinity. As Section 5.2.5 shows, discounted golden rules may not exist if the technology is not bounded, even in the one-sector case. Dolmas (1996b) shows that the combination of constant returns and δ-normality leads to sustained growth in multisector TAS models.[14]

The undiscounted case is easier, and we do it first.[15]

Theorem 1. *Suppose the TAS reduced-form model $(T, v, 1)$ satisfies (R1)– (R3) with weakly expansible stock $\bar{a}$. Then this undiscounted model has a non-trivial golden-rule stock.*

Proof. Since T is bounded, $\|b\| < \|a\|$ whenever $\|a\| > \beta$. Thus all

---

[13] The notation $x \ll y$ means $x_i < y_i$ for all i.

[14] In fact, Dolmas's argument only needs constant returns for the δ-normal stock.

[15] Mitra (1992) has identified conditions on the technology which, together with differentiability of the value function, imply the existence of a non-trivial golden-rule stock even when nonconvexities are present. See Majumdar and Peleg (1992) for related results.

$(a, b) \in T$ with $a \leq b$ obey $\|a\| \leq \beta$. It follows that $\{(a, b) \in T : a \leq b\}$ is compact. By the Weierstrass Theorem, $v(a, b)$ has a maximum over $\{(a, b) \in T : a \leq b\}$ at some $(a^*, b^*) \in T$ with $a^* \leq b^*$. By monotonicity, $v(a^*, a^*) \geq v(a^*, b^*)$, so a^* is a golden-rule stock. Finally, $(\bar{a}, \bar{b}) \in T$ and $\bar{b} \geq \bar{a}$, so $v(a^*, a^*) \geq v(\bar{a}, \bar{b}) > v(0, 0)$. This means a^* is a non-trivial golden rule. $\square$

When v is strictly concave, this golden rule is unique. In that case, we denote the undiscounted golden rule by k_g. It is considerably harder to show that discounted golden rules exist. We state the result here as Theorem 2, but it is actually a corollary to the Recursive Golden Rule Existence Theorem below.

Theorem 2. *Suppose the TAS reduced-form model (T, v, δ) satisfies (R1)–(R4). Then a non-trivial discounted golden-rule stock exists.*

5.3.2 Stationary Optimal Programs for Recursive Utility

This section proves the existence of a non-trivial stationary optimal program in a reduced-form multisectoral capital accumulation model with recursive preferences. A variety of techniques have been used to show existence of steady states in TAS models. For example, Sutherland (1970), Hansen and Koopmans (1972), Peleg and Ryder (1974), Cass and Shell (1976), Flynn (1980), and McKenzie (1982) utilize duality and the Kakutani Fixed Point Theorem to show that steady states exists. Khan and Mitra's (1986) existence result proceeds via a purely primal method, again using Kakutani's Fixed Point Theorem. Becker and Foias (1986) used Ky Fan's inequality and an indirect route to establish their existence result. Boyd (1996) established the existence of a stationary optimal program when utility is recursive.

The key to Boyd's proof is a new form of δ-normality that is appropriate for use with recursive preferences. Under some mild conditions on the aggregator, non-trivial steady states exist when the technology is bounded and δ-normal. The actual proof is akin to those in McKenzie (1986) or Khan and Mitra (1986).

We start by recasting the reduced-form model for recursive utility. Let $\mathcal{Y} \subset [-\infty, +\infty)$ be a closed interval.

Recursive Reduced Form. A recursive reduced-form model is a pair (T, W) where $T \subset \mathbb{R}_+^{2m}$ is a Malinvaud technology set, and $W : T \to \mathcal{Y}$ obeys (RR1)–(RR5).

(RR1) $W(a, b, y)$ is finite whenever $(a, b) \in \operatorname{int} T$ and $y \in \mathcal{Y}$ is finite. If $-\infty \in \mathcal{Y}$, then $W(a, b, -\infty) = -\infty$ for all $(a, b) \in T$. W is both upper semicontinuous and lower semicontinuous on $T \times \mathcal{Y}$.[16]

---

[16] This means W is continuous as an extended real-valued function.

(RR2) The derivative $W_3 \equiv \partial W / \partial y$ exists and is continuous in (a, b, y) whenever $W(a, b, y) > -\infty$. Moreover, $0 < \delta^- \leq W_3 \leq \delta^+ < 1$ for some δ^- and δ^+.

(RR3) Let $y \in \mathcal{Y}$. Each W_y^n defined inductively by $W_y^0(\mathbf{k}) = y$ and $W_y^n(\mathbf{k}) = W(k_0, k_1, W_y^{n-1}(S\mathbf{k}))$ is concave in $\mathbf{k}$.

(RR4) If $a' \geq a$, $0 \leq b' \leq b$ and $y' \geq y$ then $W(a', b', y') \geq W(a, b, y)$ (monotonicity).

(RR5) For all $(a, b), (a', b') \in T$ and $y, y' \in \mathcal{Y}$ with $y, y' > -\infty$, W obeys $W(a, b, y) > W(a', b', y)$ if and only if $W(a, b, y') > W(a', b', y')$ (limited independence).

Assumption (RR1) is meant to include commonly used cases, such as the additively separable aggregator $W(a, b, y) = \log(f(a) - b) + \delta y$ with $\delta < 1$. This example also illustrates that continuity of W with respect to (a, b) does not follow from (RR2). The concavity assumption (RR3) implies concavity of the derived utility function. Notice that (RR1)–(RR3) correspond to (W1)–(W3) for consumption-based aggregators. Monotonicity (RR4) is standard in reduced-form models. Finally, (RR5) is Koopmans's limited independence axiom transposed to the reduced-form case.

Although the existence theorems of Chapter 4 do not apply directly to this model, the fact that $\mathcal{Y}$ is bounded above makes it easy to adapt the "partial summation" method from Section 3.5.4 to show that utility exists and is upper semicontinuous. Temporarily set $y = \sup \mathcal{Y}$. Of course, $W(a, b, y) \leq y$ for all $(a, b) \in T$. Define W_y^n as above. An easy induction shows that $W_y^n(\mathbf{k}) \leq W_y^{n-1}(\mathbf{k})$ for all n, so it has an infimum. Define $U(\mathbf{k}) = \inf_n W_y^n(\mathbf{k})$. The Lipschitz condition implicit in (RR2) implies that $|W_v^n(\mathbf{k}) - W_w^n(\mathbf{k})| \leq (\delta^+)^n |v - w|$ for any finite $v, w \in \mathcal{Y}$. As a result, the infimum of W_v^n does not depend on v. The function U is now recursive as $U(\mathbf{k}) = \inf W_y^n(\mathbf{k}) = \inf W(k_0, k_1, W_y^{n-1}(S\mathbf{k})) = W(k_0, k_1, \inf W_y^{n-1}(S\mathbf{k})) = W(k_0, k_1, U(S\mathbf{k}))$. The infimum is upper semicontinuous in the product topology. Condition (RR3) guarantees that U is concave.

When $(k, k) \in T$, define $\Phi(k) = U(k, k, \ldots)$. If $(k, k) \in T$ and $W(k, k, y) > -\infty$ for some finite $y \in \mathcal{Y}$, then the Lipschitz condition from (RR2) implies there is a finite $v \in \mathcal{Y}$, with $W(k, k, v) \geq v$. Then $W_v^n(k, k, \ldots) \geq v$ for all n, so $\Phi(k) \geq v > -\infty$. Of course Φ inherits upper semicontinuity from U.

As is well known, discounted golden rules may not exist if the technology is not bounded, even in one-sector models. This occurs in models that generate balanced growth, as in Examples 7–9 above. However, boundedness is not enough to guarantee the existence of steady states. If the technology is not sufficiently productive, all optimal paths may converge to 0. We need a joint assumption on W and T to ensure that productivity can compensate for discounting. Define $\delta_k = W_3(k, k, \Phi(k))$. Let $\delta = \inf \delta_k \geq \delta^- > 0$. We use a generalization of the δ-normality assumption from the additive case.

δ-**Normality Assumption.** The reduced-form model (T, W) is δ-normal if there is a pair $(\bar{a}, \bar{b}) \in T$ such that $0 \ll \bar{a} \leq \delta \bar{b}$ and $W(\bar{a}, \bar{b}, y) > \Phi(0)$ for some $y \in \mathcal{Y}$.

We will only show the existence of non-trivial golden rules when the technology is both bounded and δ-normal. The δ-normality condition rules out cases where all optimal paths converge to 0, and is a generalization of the requirement that $\delta f'(0+) > 1$ in the one-sector model.

▶ Example 10: δ-normality in the one-sector TAS model. Suppose the felicity function u and production function f are both concave, increasing and differentiable. The reduced-form aggregator is $W(a, b, y) = u(f(a) - b) + \delta y$. The δ-normality condition then requires $(\bar{a}, \bar{b})$ with $f(\bar{a}) \geq \bar{b}$ and $\delta \bar{b} \geq \bar{a} > 0$ and that $u(f(\bar{a}) - \bar{b}) > u(f(0))$. Since u is increasing, this last condition can be written $f(\bar{a}) - \bar{b} > f(0)$. Thus $f(\bar{a}) - \delta^{-1}\bar{a} > f(0)$. Applying the Mean Value Theorem, we find an a, $0 \leq a \leq \bar{a}$ with $f(\bar{a}) = f(0) + f'(a)\bar{a}$. Substituting and simplifying, $(f'(a) - \delta^{-1})\bar{a} > 0$, so $f'(a) > \delta^{-1}$ for some a. The δ-normality condition simply asserts that the marginal product is greater than δ^{-1} for some capital stocks. This can be combined with boundedness to yield a steady state. If the technology is also bounded, $f'(a) < 1$ for a sufficiently large, and there is some $a > 0$ with $\delta f'(a) = 1$. ◀

Notice that (RR2) implies there is a finite $\bar{y} \in \mathcal{Y}$ with $W(\bar{a}, \bar{b}, \bar{y}) \geq \bar{y}$. To find one, take any $y > -\infty$. If $W(\bar{a}, \bar{b}, y) < y$, the fact that the slope of $W(\bar{a}, \bar{b}, \cdot)$ lies strictly between 0 and 1 means that there is a $\bar{y} < y$ with $W(\bar{a}, \bar{b}, \bar{y}) \geq \bar{y}$. Once we have $\bar{y}$, $W(\bar{b}, \bar{b}, \bar{y}) \geq \bar{y}$ by (RR4). This implies $W_{\bar{y}}^n(\bar{b}, \bar{b}, \dots)$ is non-decreasing, and so $\Phi(\bar{b}) \geq \bar{y}$.

Now define $K = \{k \in \mathbb{R}_+^m : (k, k) \in T \text{ and } \Phi(k) \geq \bar{y}\}$. We will find a steady state in K. Of course, $\|k\| \leq \beta$ whenever $k \in K$. Note that K is compact and convex. It is non-empty because it contains $\bar{b}$.

Both Φ and δ_k are defined on K. However, we will have to work with the entire set of potential initial stocks, $T_1 = \{a : \|a\| \leq \beta \text{ and } (a, b) \in T \text{ for some } b\}$. Let $k \in T_1$. Because K is compact and convex, there is a unique nearest point to k in K. Denote it by $g(k)$. The function g is continuous by the Maximum Theorem. We use g to extend Φ and δ_k to all of T_1 by composing them with g. Denote the extension of Φ by Ψ, so $\Psi(k) = \Phi(g(k))$. By abuse of notation, we denote the extension of δ_k by δ_k.

For $k \in T_1$, define $\phi(k) = \{(a, b) \in T : a \leq (1 - \delta_k)k + \delta_k b\}$. This correspondence is illustrated in Figure 1. For $k \in T_1$, $(\bar{a}, \bar{b}) \in \phi(k)$, so $\phi(k)$

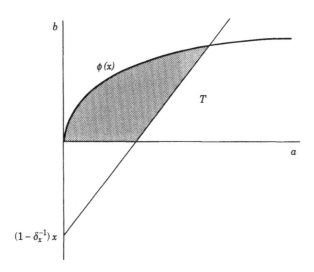

Figure 1:   The correspondence $\phi(x)$.

is non-empty and $\phi\colon T_1 \twoheadrightarrow T$ is a correspondence. The boundedness of the model implies $\phi(k)$ is bounded. Suppose $(a,b) \in \phi(k)$ with $\|a\| > \beta$. Then using (R3), we find $\|a\| \leq (1 - \delta_k)\|k\| + \delta_k\|b\| \leq (1 - \delta_k)\|k\| + \delta_k\|a\|$. But then, $\|a\| \leq \|k\| \leq \beta$. It follows that $\|a\| \leq \beta$ for all $(a,b) \in \phi(k)$. In that case, $\|b\| \leq \beta$ too, as we could otherwise take $a' \geq a$ with $\|b\| > \|a'\| > \beta$ and $(a',b) \in T$. This would violate (R3). The boundedness implies $\phi(k)$ is compact. It is also clearly convex.

Recursive Golden Rule. A stock $k \in K$ is a recursive golden rule if $(k,k) \in T$ and $W(k,k,\Phi(k)) \geq W(a,b,\Phi(k))$ for all $(a,b) \in \phi(k)$.

When W is additively separable, with $W(a,b,y) = v(a,b) + \delta y$, this definition reduces to the usual definition of a discounted golden rule. A recursive golden rule is *non-trivial* if $\Phi(k) > \Phi(0)$. Our first result is that a recursive golden rule is a stationary optimal program.

Recursive Golden Rule Optimality Theorem. *Suppose axioms (RR1)–(RR4) hold, the technology is bounded, and (T,W) is δ-normal. If k is a recursive golden rule, the stationary path $(k,k,\dots)$ is optimal from k.*

Proof. By δ-normality, $\phi(k)$ has an interior. The mapping $(a,b) \mapsto W(a,b,\Phi(k))$ is concave on $\phi(k)$, and has a maximum at (k,k). Thus there is a vector (p,q) which supports both W and $\phi(k)$. In other words, $W(a,b,\Phi(k)) \leq W(k,k,\Phi(k)) + p(a - k) + q(b - k)$ for all $(a,b) \in T$, and $(p,q) = \lambda(p',q') + \sum_{i=1}^{m} \lambda_i(e_i, -\delta_k e_i)$ for some $\lambda, \lambda_i \geq 0$ where (p',q')

supports T.[17] That is, $p'a + q'b \leq pk + qk$ for all $(a, b) \in T$.

Let $\mathbf{x}$ be feasible from k and $\mathbf{k} = (k, k, \dots)$. Then $W^n_{\Phi(k)}(\mathbf{k}) = U(\mathbf{k}) = \Phi(k)$. Because $W^n_{\Phi(k)}$ is concave, and W is continuously differentiable and non-decreasing in the third argument, we have

$$W^n_{\Phi(k)}(\mathbf{x}) - W^n_{\Phi(k)}(\mathbf{k}) \leq p(x_0 - k) + \sum_{t=1}^{n-1}(\delta_k p + q)\delta_k^{t-1}(x_t - k) + \delta_k^n q(x_n - k).$$

Recalling that $x_0 = k$, taking the limit as $n \to \infty$ yields

$$U(\mathbf{x}) \leq U(\mathbf{k}) + \sum_{t=1}^{\infty}(\delta_k p + q)\delta_k^{t-1}(x_t - k).$$

Now $\delta_k p + q = \lambda \delta_k p' + \lambda q' + \sum_{i=1}^{m} \lambda_i(\delta_k e_i - \delta_k e_i) = \lambda \delta_k p' + \lambda \delta_k q'$. Consider the convex combination $(1 - \delta_k)^{-1} \sum_{t=1}^{\infty} \delta_k^{t-1}(x_{t-1}, x_t) \in T$.[18] By the support property of (p', q'),

$$\sum_{t=1}^{\infty} \delta_k^{t-1}(p'x_{t-1} + q'x_t) \leq \sum_{t=1}^{\infty} \delta_k^{t-1}(p'k + q'k). \tag{2}$$

Since $\mathbf{x}$ is feasible from $x_0 = k_0$, we can rewrite Equation 2 to obtain $\sum_{t=1}^{\infty} \delta_k^{t-1}(\delta_k p' + q)(x_t - k) \leq 0$. But $\delta_k p + q = \delta_k p' + q'$, so $U(\mathbf{x}) \leq U(\mathbf{k})$. Thus $\mathbf{k}$ is optimal from k. $\square$

Although it is obscured a bit because we must handle corner solutions and non-differentiable cases, the basic idea is that the first-order conditions for a recursive golden rule imply the Euler equations along the corresponding stationary path.[19]

▶ Example 11: Golden rules in two-sector neoclassical models. Consider the two-sector neoclassical model of Examples 4.7 and 4.19. Using the transformation function T, we find $W(a, b, y) = u(T(a, b)) + \delta y$ and $\Phi(k) = (1 - \delta)^{-1} u(T(k, k))$. Thus recursive golden rules must maximize $W(a, b, \Phi(k)) = u(T(a, b)) + \delta(1 - \delta)^{-1}u(T(k, k))$ over $\phi(k)$. This is equivalent to maximizing $T(a, b)$ over $\phi(k)$. Assuming T is smooth and the solution is interior, we form the Lagrangian $\mathcal{L} = T(a, b) + \lambda[(1 - \delta)k + \delta b - a]$. The first-order conditions must be satisfied at (k, k). They are $D_1 T(k, k) = \lambda$ and $D_2 T(k, k) = -\delta\lambda$. Letting $c = T(k, k)$, we find

---

[17] Here e_i denotes the ith standard basis vector of $\mathbb{R}^m$.

[18] This construction has been used in a primal context by Dechert and Nishimura (1983) and Khan and Mitra (1986).

[19] Remember that even in neoclassical models with CES technologies other than Cobb-Douglas, the transformation function T, and hence the reduced-form felicity, might not be smooth.

$u'(c)D_2\mathcal{T}(k,k) + \delta u'(c)D_1\mathcal{T}(k,k) = u'(c)[-\lambda\delta + \delta\lambda] = 0$. Thus the Euler equations are satisfied along the path $(k,k,\ldots)$. The transversality condition is also obviously satisfied, and so $(k,k,\ldots)$ is optimal from k.

We can also interpret the first-order conditions $D_1\mathcal{T}(k,k) = \lambda$ and $D_2\mathcal{T}(k,k) = -\delta\lambda$ using Example 4.19. We know $D_1\mathcal{T} = \partial F^0/\partial a^0$ and $D_2\mathcal{T} = -(\partial F^0/\partial a^0)/(\partial F^1/\partial a^1)$. Substituting and rearranging we see that $1 = \delta(\partial F^1/\partial a^1)$. The marginal product of capital used in the production of future capital must equal the inverse of the discount factor, just as in the one-sector model. Since we are at a steady state, the marginal rate of transformation between capital and consumption is the same in all periods. This implies that the marginal rate of transformation from current consumption to next period's consumption is also the inverse of the discount factor.[20] ◄

Since recursive golden rules are steady states by the Recursive Golden Rule Optimality Theorem, we have reduced the problem to showing that recursive golden rules exist. Given a stock $k \in T_1$, the *implicit programming problem* is to solve

$$V(k) = \sup\{W(a,b,\Psi(k)) : (a,b) \in \phi(k)\}.$$

The function $V(k)$ is called the *marginal function*.

This problem can be solved because $\phi(k)$ is compact and $W(a,b,\Psi(k))$ is upper semicontinuous in (a,b). Because (T,W) is δ-normal, not only is $(\bar{a},\bar{b}) \in \phi(k)$ for all $k \in K$, but $V(k) \geq W(\bar{a},\bar{b},\Psi(k))$. Since $\Psi(k) \geq \bar{y}$, it follows that $V(k) \geq W(\bar{a},\bar{b},\bar{y}) \geq \bar{y} > -\infty$. We may examine the set of solutions $\mu(k)$. More formally, the *marginal correspondence* $\mu(k)$ is given by

$$\mu(k) = \{(a,b) \in \phi(k) : W(a,b,\Psi(k)) = V(k)\}.$$

Note that $\mu(k)$ is also non-empty, compact, and convex for each $k \in K$. Thus a stock $k \in K$ is a recursive golden rule if and only if $(k,k) \in \mu(k)$.

We now recast this characterization of recursive golden rules. Project μ onto the input space T_1.[21] This defines a new correspondence ψ on T_1. It is illustrated in Figure 2. A $k \in K$ is a recursive golden rule if and only if $k \in \psi(k)$. Naturally, we will use the Kakutani Fixed Point Theorem to prove recursive golden rules exist. Before proceeding, we state the Kakutani Fixed Point Theorem.[22]

Kakutani Fixed Point Theorem. *Let* $X \subset \mathbb{R}^m$ *be non-empty, compact, and convex and* $\xi\colon X \twoheadrightarrow X$ *be convex-valued and either a closed or an*

---

[20] At the steady state, the rate of interest is $\delta^{-1} - 1$, whether measured in consumption terms or in capital terms. This need not hold on other paths. For more discussion see Section 6.3, and especially subsections 6.3.2 and 6.3.3.

[21] Notice that we cannot guarantee that the projection projects $\mu(k)$ into K itself.

[22] See Klein and Thompson (1984, pp. 101–102) for a proof.

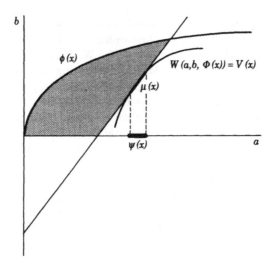

Figure 2:   The correspondence $\psi(x)$.

upper semicontinuous correspondence. Then there is an $x \in X$ with $x \in \xi(x)$.

The proof of existence of stationary optimal programs now proceeds through a series of lemmas. We start with a preliminary lemma that shows Φ and δ_k are continuous on T_1. Next we prove that ϕ has a lower semicontinuity property in Lemma 7. We then use that fact to establish $\mu(k)$ is a closed correspondence in Lemma 8. Clearly, ψ is then a compact and convex-valued, closed correspondence on T_1. The Kakutani Fixed Point Theorem yields a fixed point of ψ. Such a fixed point must be in K, and is hence a recursive golden rule. Finally, an appeal to the Recursive Golden Rule Optimality Theorem shows that the path $(k, k, \ldots)$ is optimal from k, and is thus a stationary optimal program.

Lemma 6. *The function Ψ and the mapping $k \mapsto \delta_k$ are continuous on T_1.*

Proof. Because g is continuous, it is enough to show δ_k and $\Phi(k)$ are continuous on K. Let $\epsilon > 0$ and $k \in K$.

We first show that for $k' \in K$,

$$|W_{\Phi(k)}^n(\mathbf{k}') - \Phi(k)| \leq (1 - \delta^+)^{-1}|W(k', k', \Phi(k)) - W(k, k, \Phi(k))|.$$

This is established by induction. When $n = 1$, it follows because $(1 - \delta^+)^{-1} \geq 1$ and $W(k', k', \Phi(k)) = W^1(\mathbf{k}')$. Now suppose it holds for n.

Then

$$|W_{\Phi(k)}^{n+1}(\mathbf{k}') - \Phi(k)| = |W(k', k', W_{\Phi(k)}^n(\mathbf{k}')) - \Phi(k)|$$
$$\leq |W(k', k', W_{\Phi(k)}^n(\mathbf{k}')) - W(k', k', \Phi(k))| + |W(k', k', \Phi(k)) - \Phi(k)|$$
$$\leq \delta^+ |W_{\Phi(k)}^n(\mathbf{k}') - \Phi(k)| + |W(k', k', \Phi(k)) - \Phi(k)|$$
$$\leq \frac{\delta^+}{1 - \delta^+} |W(k', k', \Phi(k)) - \Phi(k)| + |W(k', k', \Phi(k)) - \Phi(k)|$$
$$\leq (1 - \delta^+)^{-1} |W(k', k', \Phi(k)) - W(k, k, \Phi(k))|.$$

The claim now follows by induction.

Because $W(k, k, \Phi(k)) > -\infty$, (RR1) implies we may pick $\eta > 0$ with $|W_{\Phi(k)}^n(\mathbf{k}') - \Phi(k)| < \epsilon/2$ for $\|k' - k\| < \eta$. Letting $n \to \infty$ shows $|\Phi(k') - \Phi(k)| < \epsilon$ for $\|k' - k\| < \eta$.

Now $\delta_k = W_3(k, k, \Phi(k))$. By (RR2) and the continuity of Φ, δ_k is also continuous. $\square$

Lemma 7. *Suppose $(x, v) \in \phi(k)$ with $(x, v) \neq (\bar{a}, \bar{b})$. If $\epsilon > 0$, there is α with $0 < \alpha < \min\{1, \epsilon/(\|(x, v) - (\bar{a}, \bar{b})\|)\}$ and $\eta > 0$ such that $((1 - \alpha)x + \alpha\bar{a}, (1 - \alpha)v + \alpha\bar{b}) \in \phi(k')$ whenever $\|k' - k\| < \eta$.*

Proof. Let $z = (1 - \alpha)x + \alpha\bar{a}$ and $w = (1 - \alpha)v + \alpha\bar{b}$. By convexity of T, $(z, w) \in T$. Then define

$$q(k') = (1 - \alpha)(\delta_{k'} - \delta_k)v + [(1 - \delta_{k'})k' - (1 - \alpha)(1 - \delta_k)k] + \alpha(\delta_{k'} - \delta)\bar{b}.$$

Note that q is continuous in k' and that $q(k) = \alpha(1 - \delta_k)k + \alpha(\delta_k - \delta)\bar{b} \geq 0$. There are now two cases to consider. First, if $\delta_k > \delta$, $q(k) \gg 0$. It follows that $q(k') \gg 0$ for k' near k. Second, if $\delta_k = \delta$, the first and third terms of $q(k')$ are always non-negative, and the middle term is non-negative when k' is sufficiently near k. Either way, we may choose $\eta > 0$ with $q(k') \geq 0$ for $\|k' - k\| < \eta$.

Using α to form a convex combination of $x \leq (1 - \delta_k)k + \delta_k v$ and $\bar{a} \leq \delta\bar{b}$, we find

$$z \leq (1 - \delta_{k'})k' + \delta_{k'}w - q(k') \leq (1 - \delta_{k'})k' + \delta_{k'}w$$

for $\|k' - k\| < \eta$. It follows that $(z, w) \in \phi(k')$ for $\|k' - k\| < \eta$. $\square$

Lemma 8. *The correspondence $\mu: T_1 \twoheadrightarrow T$ is a closed correspondence.*

Proof. As in Lemma 6, we may restrict our attention to K. Suppose $(a^n, b^n) \in \mu(k^n)$ with $(a^n, b^n) \to (a, b)$ and $k^n \to k$. Then $(a, b) \in T$ by closure and $a \leq (1 - \delta_k)k + \delta_k b$, so $(a, b) \in \phi(k)$. Since W and Φ are upper semicontinuous and W is non-decreasing in y, $V(k) \geq W(a, b, \Phi(k)) = \limsup W(a_n, b_n, \Phi(k_n)) = \limsup V(k^n)$. To complete the proof we need only show $W(a, b, \Phi(k)) = \limsup W(a^n, b^n, \Phi(k^n)) \geq V(k)$.

Note that $W(a, b, \Phi(k)) \geq \limsup V(k^n) \geq W(\bar{a}, \bar{b}, \Phi(k))$. Suppose $V(k) > W(a, b, \Phi(k))$. Then $V(k) > W(\bar{a}, \bar{b}, \Phi(k))$. Take $(x, v) \in \phi(k)$ with $W(x, v, \Phi(k)) = V(k)$. By Lemma 7, we can construct a subsequence of the k^n (also labeled k^n) and $\alpha^n < 1/n$ with $(x^n, v^n) \in \phi(k^n)$ where $x^n = (1 - \alpha^n)x + \alpha^n\bar{a}$ and $v^n = (1 - \alpha^n)v + \alpha^n\bar{b}$.

Now $W(x^n, v^n, \Phi(k^n)) \leq V(k^n)$ because $(x^n, v^n) \in \phi(k^n)$. Furthermore,

$$W(x^n, v^n, \Phi(k^n)) \geq (1 - \alpha^n)W(x, v, \Phi(k^n)) + \alpha^n W(\bar{a}, \bar{b}, \Phi(k^n))$$

by concavity. Rearranging and using $V(k^n) \geq W(x^n, v^n, \Phi(k^n))$, we obtain

$$\alpha^n[W(x, v, \Phi(k^n)) - W(\bar{a}, \bar{b}, \Phi(k^n))] \geq W(x, v, \Phi(k^n)) - V(k^n).$$

Let $\epsilon > 0$. We know

$$[W(x, v, \Phi(k^n)) - W(\bar{a}, \bar{b}, \Phi(k^n))] \to [V(k) - W(\bar{a}, \bar{b}, \Phi(k))] > 0$$

by Lemma 6 and the continuity of W in y. For n large, we then have $\epsilon > [W(x, v, \Phi(k^n)) - V(k^n)]$. But $W(x, v, \Phi(k^n)) \to V(k)$, so $\epsilon/2 + V(k^n) > V(k)$ for n large. It follows that $V(k) \geq \limsup V(k^n) \geq \liminf V(k^n) \geq V(k)$, and so $W(a, b, \Phi(k)) = V(k)$. This shows μ is closed. $\square$

We are now ready to show that recursive golden rules exist.

Recursive Golden Rule Existence Theorem. *Suppose (RR1)–(RR5) are satisfied, the technology is bounded, and the pair (T, W) is δ-normal. Then a non-trivial recursive golden rule exists.*

Proof. Define a correspondence $\psi \colon T_1 \twoheadrightarrow T_1$ by $\psi(k) = \{a \in T_1 : (a, b) \in \mu(k) \text{ for some } b\}$. We know that ψ maps into T_1 because ϕ and μ are bounded by β. It is clear that ψ has convex, compact non-empty values. It is also closed. Let $k^n \to k$ and $a^n \to a$ with $a^n \in \psi(k^n)$. Take b^n with $(a^n, b^n) \in \mu(k^n)$. Because T is bounded, and $\|a^n\| \leq \beta$, $\|b^n\| \leq \beta$. By passing to a subsequence, we may assume $b^n \to b$. But then $(a, b) \in \mu(k)$ because μ is closed. Hence ψ is closed.

Now apply the Kakutani Fixed Point Theorem to obtain k with $k \in \psi(k)$. There is a b with $(k, b) \in \mu(k)$. Then $k \leq (1 - \delta_k)k + \delta_k b$, which implies $k \leq b$. By free disposal $(k, k) \in T$, and by monotonicity $W(k, k, \Psi(k)) \geq W(k, b, \Psi(k)) = V(k)$. Now $V(k) = W(k, k, \Psi(k)) \geq W(\bar{a}, \bar{b}, \Psi(k))$. Then use limited independence to find

$$W(k, k, \bar{y}) \geq W(\bar{a}, \bar{b}, \bar{y}) \geq \bar{y}.$$

Induction then shows $W_{\bar{y}}^n(\mathbf{k}) \geq \bar{y}$ where $\mathbf{k} = (k, k, \dots)$. Taking the limit as $n \to \infty$ yields $\Phi(k) \geq \bar{y}$, so $k \in K$. Therefore k is a recursive golden rule.

For non-triviality, we use (RR5) to see that

$$\Phi(k) = W(k, k, \Phi(k)) \geq W(\bar{a}, \bar{b}, \Phi(k)) > W(0, 0, \Phi(k)).$$

It follows that $W^n_{\Phi(k)}(\mathbf{0})$ is non-increasing. Taking the limit shows $\Phi(k) > \Phi(0)$. $\square$

Although (RR5) is a natural extension of Koopmans's limited independence axiom to the reduced-form context, we can also consider models where it does not hold. Such models might arise naturally if capital stocks are valued independently of consumption, as can happen in natural resource models.[23] Steady states will still exist in a broad range of such models.

Corollary 7. *Suppose (RR1)–(RR4) hold, the technology is bounded, the pair (T, W) is δ-normal, there is a finite $\bar{y}$ with $\Phi(-a) \geq \bar{y}$, and $W(\bar{a}, \bar{b}, y) > W(0, 0, y)$ for all $y \in \mathcal{Y}$ with $y \geq \bar{y}$. Then a non-trivial recursive golden rule exists.*

Proof. Define K using $\bar{y}$ in the hypotheses of the theorem. Condition (RR5) is used twice above, both times in the proof of the Recursive Golden Rule Existence Theorem. The first use is now superfluous as $\Phi(k) \geq \bar{y}$ because $(k, k) \in T$.

The second use is in demonstrating non-triviality. By the Recursive Golden Rule Optimality Theorem, the stationary path $(k, k, \ldots)$ is optimal from k, thus

$$\Phi(k) = W(k, k, \Phi(k)) \geq U(k, 0, \ldots) = W(k, 0, \Phi(0)).$$

By monotonicity, $W(k, k, \Phi(k)) \geq W(k, k, \Phi(0))$, so $\Phi(k) \geq \Phi(0)$. Then

$$W(k, k, \Phi(k)) \geq W(\bar{a}, \bar{b}, \Phi(k)) > W(0, 0, \Phi(k)) \geq W(0, 0, \Phi(0)) = \Phi(0)$$

establishes non-triviality. $\square$

In fact, we did not use two of the Malinvaud technology conditions. Neither inaction (M3) nor no free lunch (M4) was required.[24] As we have seen, stationary optimal programs will exist in a wide variety of multisector models with recursive utility. This provides a firm foundation for the local analysis of steady states in Section 5.4.

One important difference between recursive models and additively separable models is that the discount factor can adjust in recursive models. As a result, it is common for one-sector recursive models to have steady states even when the economy can grow at a high rate. In contrast, Dolmas

---

[23] Majumdar and Mitra (1994a) discuss TAS models where capital is valued independently from consumption.

[24] This is explicit in Boyd (1996).

(1996b) shows that with TAS utility, δ-normal technologies that exhibit constant returns to scale yield sustained growth. The general question of existence of steady states when the technology is unbounded remains open for more general recursive utility functions.

5.4 Stability of Multisectoral Models

The next order of business is to examine the stability of optimal paths in multisectoral models. We focus on the time additive separable case, where a more complete theory is available. The path to the turnpike result, that optimal paths converge to a steady state, is longer and more complex than in the one-sector model.

As in the one-sector model, we start by establishing the existence of a stationary optimal path. This was accomplished in Section 5.3. Next, we look at the undiscounted models. Under strict concavity these have a unique golden rule. As in Chapter 4, we can show that optimal paths exist, and must converge to the golden rule. Moreover, any optimal path in the discounted model must visit a neighborhood of the golden rule, provided the discounting is mild. This means that stationary optimal paths must be near the golden rule. When felicity is smooth, we can use the Implicit Function Theorem to obtain a unique steady state when near the golden rule. Some additional conditions allow us to extend the uniqueness result.

Once we have a unique steady state, the problem is to show optimal paths converge there. Following Scheinkman (1976), we focus on smooth models and linearize the Euler equations. We find that the linearized system is saddlepoint stable—that for each initial capital stock there is a unique solution that converges to the steady state. The Stable Manifold Theorem shows when this approximation is valid. We can then show that optimal paths starting within a neighborhood of the steady state must converge there. Finally, all optimal paths must converge to the steady state because they visit the neighborhood where our approximation holds, and thereafter converge.

5.4.1 The Undiscounted Model

We now examine the undiscounted model. If k_g is a steady state, (k_g, k_g) maximizes $v(a, b)$ over $\{(a, b) \in T : a \leq b\}$. The analysis becomes more complex if (k_g, k_g) happens to be on the boundary of T. This possibility does not arise in the one-sector model since such a point would yield zero consumption. Various conditions can likewise rule out the boundary case in the multisector model. We will simply postulate that $(k_g, k_g) \in \text{int}\, T$ with $v(k_g, k_g) > v(0, 0)$, which we describe by saying k_g is *interior*. Note that this implies the existence of an expansible stock because for n large enough, $(k_g, k_g + e/n) \in T$ and $v(k_g, k_g + e/n) > v(0,0)$. When k_g is interior, we can find a price vector that supports v at (k_g, k_g).

Lemma 9. *Suppose (R1), (R2) hold. When k_g is interior, there is a* $p^* \in \mathbb{R}_+^m$ *with* $v(a,b) + p^*(b-a) \le v(k_g, k_g)$.

Proof. Because k_g is interior, $G = \{(a,b) \in T : a \le b\}$ has an interior. Now v is concave, and has a maximum at (k_g, k_g). Thus there is a vector (p,q) which supports both v and G at (k_g, k_g). In other words, $v(a,b) \le v(k_g, k_g) + p(a - k_g) + q(b - k_g)$ for all $(a,b) \in T$, where $(p,q) = \lambda(p', q') + \sum_{i=1}^m \lambda_i(e_i, -e_i)$ for some $\lambda, \lambda_i \ge 0$ with (p', q') supporting T. Because $(k_g, k_g) \in \text{int } T$, $\lambda = 0$, so $p = -q = (\lambda_1, \ldots, \lambda_m) \ge 0$. Now set $p^* = p$ to obtain the result. $\square$

If v is strictly concave, there will be a unique golden-rule stock, and the inequality above will be strict for $(a,b) \ne (k_g, k_g)$. If v is merely concave, there may be many points with $v(a,b) + p^*(b-a) = v(k_g, k_g)$. The collection of all such points is referred to as the *von Neumann facet*. The von Neumann facet is not merely of technical interest. It can arise whenever there is a flat in the technology (e.g., under constant returns) and felicity is not strictly concave. Since the list of capital may well contain goods that are not consumed, this can easily happen. Nonetheless, in the interest of simplicity, we confine our attention to the strictly concave case. However, a similar analysis can be carried out in the general case.[25] We next demonstrate that all good paths converge to the golden rule. The key step is the Radner-Atsumi Lemma.[26] Roughly speaking, the Radner-Atsumi Lemma says that the value loss $L(a,b) = p^*(a-b) - v(a,b) + v(k_g, k_g)$ is bounded below by some constant ρ for all (a,b) outside some "neighborhood" of (k_g, k_g).

Radner-Atsumi Lemma. *Suppose (R1)–(R3) hold, v is strictly concave, and k_g is interior. Let $\epsilon, M > 0$. Then there is a $\rho > 0$ with $v(a,b) + p^*(b-a) < v(k_g, k_g) - \rho$ whenever $(a,b) \in T$ with $\|a\| \le M$ and $|v(a,b) - v(k_g, k_g)| + \|a - k_g\| + \|b - k_g\| > \epsilon$.*

Proof. Suppose not. Then there is a sequence $(a^n, b^n) \in T$ with $\|a^n\| \le M$ obeying

$$|v(a^n, b^n) - v(k_g, k_g)| + \|a^n - k_g\| + \|b^n - k_g\| > \epsilon \qquad (3)$$

and

$$\lim_n [v(a^n, b^n) + p^*(b^n - a^n)] \ge v(k_g, k_g). \qquad (4)$$

---

[25] These issues are beyond the scope of this work. For details on the von Neumann facet, see McKenzie (1983; 1986).

[26] See Radner (1961) and Atsumi (1965).

The sequence $\{b^n\}$ is bounded because the technology is bounded and inputs $\{a^n\}$ are bounded (by M). Thus we may find convergent subsequences, which we also denote by $\{a^n\}$, $\{b^n\}$, with limits a and b, respectively. By closure, $(a, b) \in T$. By upper semicontinuity of v, $v(a, b) + p^*(b - a) \geq v(k_g, k_g)$, so $v(a, b) + p^*(b - a) = v(k_g, k_g)$ by the support property. But then $(a, b) = (k_g, k_g)$ by strict concavity. Now (4) implies $v(k_g, k_g) = v(a, b) \geq \lim_n v(a^n, b^n) \geq v(k_g, k_g)$, so $\lim_n v(a^n, b^n) = v(k_g, k_g)$. But then $|v(a^n, b^n) - v(k_g, k_g)| + \|a^n - k_g\| + \|b^n - k_g\| \to 0$, contradicting (3). This contradiction establishes the result. □

We can now show that optimal paths converge to the golden rule. The Radner-Atsumi Lemma will imply that any program that does not converge to the golden rule is a bad program—a program that accumulates an infinite value loss.

Undiscounted Turnpike Theorem. *Suppose* $\mathbf{k}$ *is good from initial stock* k_0, *(R1)–(R3) hold,* k_g *is interior, and* v *is strictly concave. Then* $k_t \to k_g$.

Proof. Let $\epsilon > 0$ and suppose $\|k_t - k_g\| > \epsilon$ infinitely often. Note that path $\mathbf{k}$ is bounded as are all feasible paths. Let $\rho > 0$ be given by the Radner-Atsumi Lemma. Now $v(k_{t-1}, k_t) - v(k_g, k_g) < p^*(k_{t-1} - k_t) - \rho$ when $\|k_t - k_g\| > \epsilon$, and $v(k_{t-1}, k_t) - v(k_g, k_g) \leq p^*(k_{t-1} - k_t)$ otherwise. Let $N(T)$ be the number of $t \leq T$ with $\|k_t - k_g\| > \epsilon$.

Consider the partial sums

$$\sum_{t=1}^{T}[v(k_{t-1}, k_t) - v(k_g, k_g)] \leq -N(T)\rho + \sum_{t=1}^{T} p^*(k_t - k_{t-1})$$

$$\leq -N(T)\rho + p^* k_T - p^* k_0.$$

Now $p^* k_T$ is bounded and $N(T) \to \infty$, so the right-hand side converges to $-\infty$. This contradicts the fact that $\mathbf{k}$ is good. Therefore $\|k_t - k_g\| > \epsilon$ for only finitely many t. As $\epsilon > 0$ was arbitrary, $k_t \to k_g$. □

Thus all good paths converge to the steady state. We can try to proceed as in Section 4.2.4, construct a renormalized utility function, and establish the existence of weakly maximal paths. There is a potential stumbling block. All feasible programs might be infinitely bad. This possibility can be ruled out if it is possible to accumulate capital until you reach the steady state, while keeping utility above $-\infty$. In the concave one-sector model, it is enough that $f(k_g) > k_g$ and $u(c) > -\infty$ for $c > 0$. In the multisector model, the following Reachability Theorem shows it is possible to accumulate enough to reach the steady state.

Reachability Theorem. *Suppose (R1)–(R3) hold, that* $\bar{a}$ *is expansible to* $\bar{b}$, *and that* k_g *is interior. Given* $k \geq \bar{a}$, *there is an integer* N *and* $k_0, \ldots, k_N$ *with* $k_0 = k$, $k_N = k_g$ *and* $(k_{n-1}, k_n) \in T$ *for* $n = 1, \ldots, N$.

Proof. Take $\hat{k} \gg k_g$ with $(\hat{k}, \hat{k}) \in T$, which is possible since (k_g, k_g) is interior. Then take α, $0 < \alpha < 1$ with $\hat{a} = (1 - \alpha)\bar{a} + \alpha\hat{k} \geq k_g$. This is possible because $\hat{k} \gg 0$. Letting $\hat{b} = (1 - \alpha)\bar{b} + \alpha\hat{k}$, we find $(\hat{a}, \hat{b}) \in T$. Let $\beta = \min_i\{\hat{b}_i/\hat{a}_i\} > 1$. Thus $\hat{a}$ can be expanded by a factor of β.

Now $(k_0, \bar{b}) \in T$ by free disposal as $k_0 = k \geq \bar{a}$. Take $\lambda > 0$ such that $\lambda\beta\hat{a} \leq \bar{b}$. Such a λ exists because $\bar{b} \gg 0$. Let N be the least integer with $\beta^N\lambda \geq 1$ and define $k_0 = k$, $k_n = \lambda\beta^n\hat{a}$ for $\lambda\beta^n < 1$ and $k_N = k_g$. Note that $(\lambda\beta^n\hat{a}, \lambda\beta^{n+1}\hat{a}) \in T$ for $n = 2, \ldots, N - 1$ by concavity of T. Thus $(k_{n-1}, k_n) \in T$ for $n = 2, \ldots, N - 1$. Recalling that $k_0 = k \geq \bar{a}$ and $k_1 = \lambda\beta\hat{a} \leq \bar{b}$, we see $(k_0, k_1) \in T$ by free disposal. Finally, since $\lambda\beta^N\hat{a} \geq \hat{a} \geq k_g = k_N$, $(k_{N-1}, k_N) \in T$ by free disposal. $\square$

The restriction that the initial stock be greater than some expansible stock is actually quite mild. Under the other conditions of the theorem, any strictly positive stock will qualify. This is implied by the following lemma.

Lemma 10. *Suppose (R1), (R2) hold, that $\bar{a}$ is expansible to $\bar{b}$, and that k_g is interior. Then there is a stock a' expansible to b' with $(a', b') \in \text{int } T$ and $\lambda a'$ expansible to $\lambda b'$ for $0 < \lambda \leq 1$.*

Proof. Take U open with $(k_g, k_g) \in \text{int } T$. Consider $(a', b') = \frac{1}{2}(\bar{a}, \bar{b}) + \frac{1}{2}(k_g, k_g) \in \frac{1}{2}(\bar{a}, \bar{b}) + \frac{1}{2}U \subset T$. Then $(a', b') \in \text{int } T$ with $a' \ll b'$. As $v(a', b') \geq \frac{1}{2}v(\bar{a}, \bar{b}) + \frac{1}{2}v(k_g, k_g) > v(0, 0)$, (a', b') is expansible.

Set $V = \frac{1}{2}(\bar{a}, \bar{b}) + \frac{1}{2}U$. Because $(0, 0) \in T$, $\lambda V \subset T$ for $0 < \lambda < 1$. It follows that $(\lambda a', \lambda b') \in \text{int } T$. If $v(0, 0) = -\infty$, $v(\lambda a', \lambda b') > v(0, 0)$ since $(\lambda a', \lambda b') \in \text{int } T$. If $v(0, 0) > -\infty$, $v(\lambda a', \lambda b') \geq \lambda v(a', b') + (1 - \lambda)v(0, 0) > v(0, 0)$, which completes the lemma. $\square$

Corollary 8. *Under the above hypotheses, there is an expansible $\bar{a} \leq k$ whenever $k \gg 0$.*

We now proceed as in the one-sector undiscounted case. Define the *value loss* $L(k_{t-1}, k_t) = p^*(k_{t-1} - k_t) - v(k_{t-1}, k_t) + v(k_g, k_g) \geq 0$ and let the *renormalized utility function* be given by

$$U_R(\mathbf{k}) = p^*(k_0 - k_g) - \sum_{t=1}^{\infty} L(k_{t-1}, k_t).$$

It then follows that $U_R(\mathbf{k}) = \lim_{T \to \infty} \sum_{t=1}^{T}[v(k_{t-1}, k_t) - v(k_g, k_g)] > -\infty$ whenever $\mathbf{k}$ is good. Conversely, if $U_R(\mathbf{k})$ is finite, $L(k_{t-1}, k_t) \to 0$. By the Radner-Atsumi Lemma, $k_t \to k_g$, and the finiteness of $U_R(\mathbf{k})$ then implies $\mathbf{k}$ is good. It is then easy to see that if $U_R(\mathbf{k}^*)$ is finite and $U_R(\mathbf{k}^*) \geq U_R(\mathbf{k})$ for all feasible $\mathbf{k}$, then $\mathbf{k}^*$ is weakly maximal.

Existence Theorem for Undiscounted Models. *Suppose (R1)–(R3) are satisfied, that k_g is interior, and there is an expansible $\bar{a}$ with $k \geq \bar{a}$. Then a weakly maximal path exists from k.*

Proof. The function U_R is upper semicontinuous, and the feasible set is compact, so U_R can be maximized over the feasible set at some path $\mathbf{k}^*$. Apply the preceding lemma to obtain an expansible a'. Consider paths starting from $\bar{b}$. Set $k_0 = k$ and $k_1 = \bar{b}$, so $(k_0, k_1) \in T$ by free disposal, and $v(k_0, k_1) \geq v(\bar{a}, \bar{b}) > -\infty$. The Reachability Theorem, applied to $\bar{b}$, using the expansible stock a', yields a path from $k_2 = \bar{b}$ to $k_N = k_g$ for some N. Moreover, $v(k_{t-1}, k_t) > -\infty$ since $v(\lambda a', \lambda b') > -\infty$ for $0 < \lambda \leq 1$. The path $\mathbf{k}$ is then good with $U_R(\mathbf{k}) > -\infty$. As a result, $U_R(\mathbf{k}^*) > -\infty$, and hence is weakly maximal. $\square$

5.4.2 The Visit Lemma

The steady state for the undiscounted case turns out to be close to steady states for the discounted case, provided the discount factor is near 1. Let $\{k_t^\delta\}_{t=1}^\infty$ denote the optimal path from k_0 when the discount factor is δ. The next result, Scheinkman's (1976) Visit Lemma, says that any neighborhood of k_g is entered by optimal paths provided δ is sufficiently large, where the meaning of "sufficiently large" depends on the neighborhood in question. The Visit Lemma is reminiscent of the original turnpike theorems, which said, roughly speaking, that the optimal path of a finite horizon model would be near the "turnpike" (here represented by the steady state) most of the time. As Dorfman, Samuelson, and Solow (1958, p. 331) put it: "[I]f origin and destination are far enough apart, it will always pay to get on to the turnpike and cover distance at the best rate of travel, even if this means adding a little mileage at either end."

Visit Lemma. *Suppose (R1)–(R3) hold with v strictly concave and k_g interior. Let $\bar{a}$ be expansible. Given M and $\epsilon > 0$, there is a $\delta(\epsilon) < 1$ such that whenever $\delta(\epsilon) \leq \delta \leq 1$, and $k_0 \geq \bar{a}$ with $M \geq \|k_0\|$, any optimal path $\{k_t^\delta\}$ from k_0 has $\|k_t^\delta - k_g\| \leq \epsilon$ for some t.*

Proof. Suppose, by way of contradiction, that $\|k_t^\delta - k_g\| > \epsilon$ for all t. By the Radner-Atsumi Lemma, there is a $\rho > 0$ with $v_t^\delta + p^*(k_t^\delta - k_{t-1}^\delta) < v^* - \rho$ where $v_t^\delta = v(k_{t-1}^\delta, k_t^\delta)$ and $v^* = v(k_g, k_g)$. Multiplying by δ^{t-1}, and summing, we obtain

$$\sum_{t=1}^\infty \delta^{t-1} v_t^\delta + \sum_{t=1}^\infty \delta^{t-1} p^*(k_t^\delta - k_{t-1}^\delta) < \sum_{t=1}^\infty \delta^{t-1} v^* - \frac{\rho}{1-\delta}.$$

Telescoping the second term on the left, we find

$$\sum_{t=1}^\infty \delta^{t-1} v_t^\delta + \sum_{t=1}^\infty (\delta^{t-1} - \delta^t) p^* k_t^\delta - p^* k_0 < \sum_{t=1}^\infty \delta^{t-1} v^* - \frac{\rho}{1-\delta}.$$

Since $\delta^{t-1} - \delta^t > 0$, this yields

$$\sum_{t=1}^{\infty} \delta^{t-1} v_t^\delta - p^* k_0 < \sum_{t=1}^{\infty} \delta^{t-1} v^* - \frac{\rho}{1-\delta}. \tag{5}$$

Now apply the Reachability Theorem to obtain a feasible path $\mathbf{k}'$ from k_0 that reaches k_g at some time T. Denote $v(k'_{t-1}, k'_t)$ by v'_t. As $\mathbf{k}^\delta$ is optimal, $\sum_{t=1}^{\infty} \delta^{t-1} v_t^\delta \geq \sum_{t=1}^{\infty} \delta^{t-1} v'_t = \sum_{t=1}^{T} \delta^{t-1} v'_t + \sum_{t=T+1}^{\infty} \delta^{t-1} v^*$. Since $\sum_{t=1}^{T} \delta^{t-1} v'_t$ is continuous in δ, it has a lower bound $V > -\infty$ for all δ, $0 \leq \delta \leq 1$. Substituting in (5), we find

$$V - p^* k_0 < \sum_{t=1}^{T} \delta^{t-1} v^* - \frac{\rho}{1-\delta} \leq T v^* - \frac{\rho}{1-\delta}.$$

This condition is violated for δ bigger than some $\delta(\epsilon) < 1$, and hence there is a t with $\|k_t^\delta - k_g\| \leq \epsilon$ for $\delta \geq \delta(\epsilon)$. □

The Visit Lemma lets us show that steady states are close to k_g. Let $K(\delta)$ denote the collection of non-trivial discounted golden rules for (T, v, δ). Although $K(1)$ is a singleton, we cannot yet conclude $K(\delta)$ is a singleton for $\delta < 1$. However, we can show that all the steady states for (T, v, δ) must be close to k_g when δ is close to 1. We first impose an additional interiority condition:

Interiority of Steady States.

(R5) There is a $\delta^* < 1$ with $\{(k, k) : k \in K(\delta)\} \subset \text{int } T$ for $\delta > \delta^*$.

Corollary 9. *Under the conditions of the Visit Lemma and (R5), let $\bar{a}$ be expansible and suppose $k^\delta \geq \bar{a}$ whenever $k^\delta \in K(\delta)$ for $\delta > \delta^*$. For any $\epsilon > 0$, there is a $\delta(\epsilon) > \delta^*$ such that $\|k^\delta - k_g\| < \epsilon$ for any $k^\delta \in K(\delta)$ whenever $\delta \geq \delta(\epsilon)$.*

Proof. Note $K(\delta) \subset T_1$ and take M bounding the set K. Apply the Visit Lemma to the optimal path $(k^\delta, k^\delta, \ldots)$. □

5.4.3 Uniqueness of Steady States

The next step is to examine the structure of $K(\delta)$ in a neighborhood of k_g. Under appropriate conditions, we will show that $K(\delta)$ is a singleton, $\{k(\delta)\}$, for δ sufficiently near 1. In addition, $k(\delta)$ will be a smooth function. To show this, we need a differentiability assumption.

Smoothness Assumption.

(R6) The reduced-form felicity function $v(a, b)$ is strictly concave on T and is ℓ times continuously differentiable on int T with $\ell \geq 3$; $D^2 v$ is negative definite on int T.

The restriction on ℓ will be important in Section 5.4.5. For the present we only need $\ell \geq 2$. We will use the Euler equations to show that steady states are unique for δ close to 1. The reduced-form Euler equations (Example 4.18) for the optimal path are

$$\delta \frac{\partial v}{\partial a^j}(k_t, k_{t+1}) + \frac{\partial v}{\partial b^j}(k_{t-1}, k_t) = 0$$

for $t = 1, 2, \ldots$ and $j = 1, \ldots, m$, where $\partial v/\partial a$ and $\partial v/\partial b$ denote derivatives with respect to inputs a and outputs b. We will sometimes write the Euler equations as $\delta v_1(k_t, k_{t+1}) + v_2(k_{t-1}, k_t) = 0$ with $v_1 = [\partial v/\partial a_j]$ and $v_2 = [\partial v/\partial b_j]$. We denote the left-hand side of the Euler equations by $E(k_{t-1}, k_t, k_{t+1}, \delta)$. Since E involves the derivatives of v, it is in $C^{\ell-1}$. At a steady state k, we have

$$\delta \frac{\partial v}{\partial a^i}(k, k) + \frac{\partial v}{\partial b^i}(k, k) = 0. \tag{6}$$

Denote the matrices of partial derivatives by $A = [\partial^2 v/\partial a^i \partial a^j] = v_{11}$, $B = [\partial^2 v/\partial a^i \partial b^j] = v_{21}$, and $C = [\partial^2 v/\partial b^i \partial b^j] = v_{22}$, all evaluated at $k_1 = k_2 = k$.[27] Thus

$$D^2 v = \begin{bmatrix} v_{11} & v_{21} \\ v_{12} & v_{22} \end{bmatrix} = \begin{bmatrix} A & B \\ B' & C \end{bmatrix}.$$

We know that (6) is satisfied at all $k \in K(\delta)$. Our plan is to use the Implicit Function Theorem on (6) to obtain a unique solution. This requires that the derivative of $E(k, k, k, \delta)$ with respect to k is non-singular. This derivative is $\delta A + \delta B' + B + C$. We start by examining the unique golden rule k_g at $\delta = 1$.

Lemma 11. *Suppose (R1)–(R6) hold. Then the matrix $A + B + B' + C$ is non-singular at the golden rule k_g.*

   Proof. Suppose $A + B + B' + C$ is singular at k_g. Then there is a non-zero vector x with $(A + B + B' + C)x = 0$. Let x' denote the transpose of x. We now have

$$0 = x'[A + B + B' + C]x = [x', x'] \begin{bmatrix} A & B \\ B' & C \end{bmatrix} \begin{bmatrix} x \\ x \end{bmatrix} = [x', x']D^2 v \begin{bmatrix} x \\ x \end{bmatrix}.$$

But the last term is negative since $D^2 v$ is negative definite and $x \neq 0$. This contradiction shows $A + B + B' + C$ is non-singular. $\square$

   The fact that $D^2 v$ is continuous yields the following corollary.

---

[27] Hence A, B, and C are functions of k.

Corollary 10. *Under (R1)–(R6), there is a neighborhood $\mathcal{U}_0 \times \mathcal{V}_0$ of $(k_g, 1)$ where $\delta A + \delta B' + B + C$ is non-singular.*

We will need the Implicit Function Theorem, which we state without proof.[28]

Implicit Function Theorem. *Let $\Phi: \mathbb{R}^n \to \mathbb{R}^m$ be C^q on an open connected set D containing a point x_0 where $\Phi(x_0) = 0$, and suppose $q \geq 1$ and $1 \leq m < n$. Write $x \in \mathbb{R}^n$ as (y, z) with $y \in \mathbb{R}^{n-m}$, $z \in \mathbb{R}^m$. Suppose $D_z\Phi(x_0)$ is invertible. Then there exists a neighborhood $\mathcal{U}$ containing x_0, an open set $\mathcal{V}$ containing y_0 and a C^q function $\phi : \mathcal{V} \to \mathbb{R}^m$ such that $D_z\Phi$ is invertible on $\mathcal{U}$ and $\{x \in \mathcal{U} : \Phi(x) = 0\} = \{x \in \mathcal{U} : y \in \mathcal{V}, z = \phi(y)\}$.*

The Implicit Function Theorem yields a unique stationary solution to the Euler equations on a neighborhood $\mathcal{U} \times \mathcal{V} \subset \mathcal{U}_0 \times \mathcal{V}_0$ since $A + B' + B + C$ is non-singular. The Visit Lemma tells us that optimal paths eventually enter the neighborhood $\mathcal{U}$, provided δ is large enough, so there is actually a unique discounted golden rule for δ large. As Brock (1973) has shown, this argument can be adapted to the case where $\delta B' + \delta A + C + B$ is non-singular at all steady states for $\delta > \delta^*$.

Uniqueness and Smoothness of Steady States. *Suppose (R1)–(R6) hold and $\delta A + \delta B' + B + C$ is non-singular at all steady states with $\delta > \delta^*$. Then there is a unique steady state for each $\delta > \delta^*$. In addition, the function $k(\delta)$ is $C^{\ell-1}$ for $\delta > \delta^*$.*

Proof. Suppose there is some $\delta > \delta^*$ where the steady state is not unique. Let $\bar{\delta} = \sup\{\delta > \delta^* : K(\delta) \text{ is not a singleton}\}$. Now consider a steady state $\bar{k}$ for $\bar{\delta}$. Because $\bar{\delta}A + \bar{\delta}B' + B + C$ is non-singular, the Implicit Function Theorem yields an open neighborhood $\mathcal{U} \times \mathcal{V}$ of $(\bar{k}, \bar{\delta})$, where the steady-state Euler equations have a unique solution $\bar{k}(\delta)$.

Take a sequence $\delta^n \uparrow \bar{\delta}$ where $K(\delta^n)$ has at least two elements. For n large enough, there is at least one element of $K(\delta^n)$ outside of $\mathcal{U}$. Call it k^n. Since the k^n all lie in K, they have a convergent subsequence. Call the limit k^*. Note $k^* \notin \mathcal{U}$. Since the Euler equations are continuous, we may take the limit of $E(k^n, k^n, k^n, \delta^n) = 0$ to find $E(k^*, k^*, k^*, \bar{\delta}) = 0$. But then $k^* \neq \bar{k}$ is a steady state for $\bar{\delta}$.

We may again apply the Implicit Function Theorem: there is a neighborhood $\mathcal{U}' \times \mathcal{V}'$ of $(k^*, \bar{\delta})$ with a unique stationary solution $k^*(\delta)$ to the Euler equations. Now consider $\delta^n \in \mathcal{V} \cap \mathcal{V}'$ with $\delta^n \downarrow \bar{\delta}$ and $\delta^n > \bar{\delta}$. Then $\bar{k}(\delta^n) \to \bar{k}$ and $k^*(\delta^n) \to k^*$. For some δ^n, we must have $\bar{k}(\delta^n) \neq k^*(\delta^n)$, contradicting the definition of $\bar{\delta}$. This contradiction establishes uniqueness for all $\delta > \delta^*$.

Given a unique $k(\delta)$ solving the steady-state Euler equations, the Implicit Function Theorem implies $k \in C^{\ell-1}$ because $E \in C^{\ell-1}$. □

---

[28] The proof is well known, e.g., Section 4–6 of Fleming (1965).

5.4.4 Local Analysis of Steady States

Since Poincaré, mathematicians have known that the eigenvalues associated with Hamiltonian dynamical systems come in reciprocal pairs. In many economic problems, this reciprocity implies that steady states are saddlepoints—there are equal numbers of stable and unstable roots. There are as many eigenvalues with modulus greater than one as have modulus less than one.

The saddlepoint property plays an important role in capital theory. Saddlepoint instability is characteristic of optimal growth problems (Kurz, 1968a). By Becker's (1981) Equivalence Principle, saddlepoint instability is also characteristic of perfect foresight equilibria.[29] Further, it is instrumental in Scheinkman's (1976) construction of the stable manifold. The Stable Manifold Theorem then describes the behavior of optimal paths near a steady state. In particular, it implies that optimal paths converge to the steady state.

The saddlepoint property is intimately related to various other stability and regularity properties of optimal paths. Under a symmetry condition, DasGupta and McKenzie (1984; 1985; 1990) show that the saddlepoint property implies local strong dynamic regularity, and is equivalent to both local asymptotic stability and the dominant diagonal block condition used by Araujo and Scheinkman (1977). Combining this with Araujo and Scheinkman's arguments shows the saddlepoint property is equivalent to global asymptotic stability—all optimal paths converge to the steady state.

This section investigates the saddlepoint property. We have found that paths must visit the undiscounted golden rule when the discount rate is low (the Visit Lemma). This allowed us to show the corresponding steady states are near k_g. In the differentiable case, we can employ the Implicit Function Theorem to show steady states are unique. We can now rewrite the Euler equations as a first-order dynamical system, and linearize. This system enjoys the saddlepoint property. In the next section, the saddlepoint property will be used to derive properties of the stable manifold, and prove a turnpike theorem.

Let k^δ denote the unique steady state. When confusion is possible, we use A_δ, B_δ, and C_δ to denote the matrices A, B, and C evaluated at k^δ. We are now ready to start analyzing the behavior of the optimal path near k^δ. We focus on the generic case where B_δ is non-singular.

Non-Singularity Assumption.

(R7) The matrix B_δ is non-singular.

---

[29] The Equivalence Principle is taken up in Chapter 6.

Consider the Euler equations $E(k_{t-1}, k_t, k_{t+1}, \delta) = 0$ again in a neighborhood of k^δ. Then $\partial E / \partial k_{t+1} = \delta B'_\delta$ at k^δ. Under (R7), the Implicit Function Theorem yields a $C^{\ell-1}$ capital policy function $k_{t+1} = G(k_{t-1}, k_t, \delta)$ valid on a neighborhood of $(k^\delta, k^\delta, \delta)$. Its derivatives with respect to k_{t-1} and k_t are $G_1 = -(\delta B')^{-1} E_1 = -(\delta B')^{-1} B$ and $G_2 = -(\delta B')^{-1}(\delta A + C)$. Using G, we can rewrite the Euler equations as a first-order system on $\mathbb{R}_+^{2m}$. Let $y_t = k_{t+1}$, $z_t = (k_t, y_t)'$ and define $F \colon \mathbb{R}_+^{2m} \to \mathbb{R}_+^{2m}$ by

$$F(z_t) = \begin{bmatrix} y_t \\ G(k_t, y_t, \delta) \end{bmatrix},$$

so $z_{t+1} = F(z_t)$. Notice that we need to specify both k_0 and k_1 to find k_2 using the policy function. There are many solutions to the Euler equations, parametrized by k_1. However, only one choice of k_1 will produce the unique optimal path. This is not surprising as the Euler equations are not sufficient for optimality—the transversality condition is also required.

The matrix

$$D_z F = \begin{bmatrix} 0 & I \\ -(\delta B'_\delta)^{-1} B_\delta & -(\delta B'_\delta)^{-1}(\delta A_\delta + C_\delta) \end{bmatrix}$$

is non-singular since B_δ is non-singular. The equations $z_{t+1} = (D_z F) z_t$ are referred to as the *linearized Euler equations*. We will be interested in the eigenvalues of $D_z F$, which are the roots of the characteristic polynomial $\det[\lambda^2 I + \lambda(\delta B'_\delta)^{-1}(\delta A_\delta + C_\delta) + (\delta B'_\delta)^{-1} B_\delta]$. When B_δ is non-singular, these are the roots of $p_\delta(\lambda) = \det[\delta B'_\delta \lambda^2 + (\delta A_\delta + C_\delta)\lambda + B_\delta] = 0$. The linearization approximately describes the behavior of optimal paths near k^δ.

We must show that the roots have the proper modulus. We say the *saddlepoint property* holds provided there are no unit roots, and that roots come in pairs, with one member of each pair having modulus less than one, while the other has modulus greater than one.[30] In that case, the linearized Euler equations exhibit saddlepoint instability. Most solutions to the linearized Euler equations are explosive. There is only one choice of first-period stocks that yield a path that converges to the steady state.

Before analyzing the eigenvalues, we need the following well-known result concerning the factorization of polynomials. This allows us to establish that roots come in reciprocal pairs. This proposition is an easy and basic consequence of the Fundamental Theorem of Algebra and the fact that such a factorization must be unique (see Hoffman and Kunze,

---

[30] This definition is standard in growth theory, and is stronger than the usual usage in dynamical systems.

1971, pp. 136–138). The importance of this factorization is that it takes multiplicity of roots into account.[31]

Proposition 4. *Let $p(\lambda)$ be a polynomial of degree m over the reals. It has a unique factorization of the form*

$$p(\lambda) = \alpha \prod_{i=1}^{j} (\lambda - \lambda_i)^{m_i}$$

where α is a constant, the λ_i are the distinct roots of p, the m_i are their multiplicities, and $\sum_{i=1}^{j} m_i = m$. The roots may be complex, but they occur in conjugate pairs.

The above factorization will be used in the following lemma on paired roots.

Lemma 12. *Suppose $p(\lambda)$ is a polynomial of degree m that satisfies $p(\lambda) = \gamma \lambda^m p(1/\delta \lambda)$ for some constant γ with $p(0) \neq 0$. Then both λ_i and $1/\delta \lambda_i$ are roots of the same multiplicity m_i.*

Proof. Use the proposition to factor $p(\lambda)$.

$$p(\lambda) = \gamma \lambda^m p(1/\delta \lambda) = \gamma \lambda^m \alpha \prod_{i=1}^{j} [(\delta \lambda)^{-1} - \lambda_i]^{m_i}$$

$$= \gamma \alpha \prod_{i=1}^{j} [\delta^{-1} - \lambda_i \lambda]^{m_i} = \alpha' \prod_{i=1}^{j} [\lambda - (\delta \lambda_i)^{-1}]^{m_i}.$$

Unique factorization guarantees that both λ_i and $1/\delta \lambda_i$ are roots of multiplicity m_i. $\square$

The characteristic polynomial $p_\delta(\lambda) = \det[\delta B'_\delta \lambda^2 + (\delta A_\delta + C_\delta)\lambda + B_\delta]$ then obeys

$$p_\delta(\lambda) = \lambda^{2m} \delta^m \det[B'_\delta + (\delta A_\delta + C_\delta)(\delta \lambda)^{-1} + \delta B_\delta (\delta \lambda)^{-2}]$$

$$= \lambda^{2m} \delta^m \det[\delta B_\delta (\delta \lambda)^{-2} + (\delta A_\delta + C_\delta)(\delta \lambda)^{-1} + B'_\delta]$$

$$= \lambda^{2m} \delta^m \det[\delta B'_\delta (\delta \lambda)^{-2} + (\delta A_\delta + C_\delta)(\delta \lambda)^{-1} + B_\delta]$$

since A and C are again symmetric. We have shown that p_δ obeys $p_\delta(\lambda) = \lambda^{2m} \delta^m p_\delta(1/\delta \lambda)$. Lemma 12 now implies that both λ_i and $1/\delta \lambda_i$ are roots of the same multiplicity. This establishes the following theorem.

---

[31] Many authors have assumed, either explicitly or implicitly, that the roots are unique. We allow for multiple roots by following the approach in Boyd (1989b).

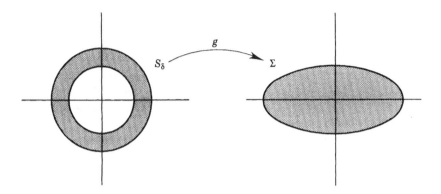

Figure 3:   The mapping g.

Paired Root Theorem. *Suppose roots are counted according to multiplicity. Under (R7), the characteristic roots of the reduced-form optimization problem occur in pairs* $\{\lambda_i, 1/\delta\lambda_i\}$.

The paired root property is the major step in establishing the saddle-point property. Only one step remains: showing the roots have the proper modulus. This can be accomplished when δ is near 1. Let S_δ be the annulus in the complex plane $\{z \in \mathbb{C} : 1 \leq |z| \leq 1/\delta\}$ illustrated in the left side of Figure 3.[32] By the Paired Root Theorem, the saddlepoint property is equivalent to having no roots in S_δ. We can derive the saddlepoint property for δ near 1 by using the fact that there are no unit roots when $\delta = 1$.

▶ Example 12: Symmetric cross terms. The analysis can be simplified when the matrix of cross partial derivatives B is symmetric, as occurs with a single capital good. We need only look at an $m \times m$ matrix rather than a $2m \times 2m$ matrix. For a matrix M let $\sigma(M) = \{\lambda : \det[\lambda I - M] = 0\}$ denote the *spectrum* (the set of roots) of M. Define $\Sigma = \{z : (\operatorname{Re} z)^2/(1 + \delta)^2 + (\operatorname{Im} z)^2/(1 - \delta)^2 \leq 1\}$. We claim that the saddlepoint property is equivalent to $\Sigma \cap \sigma(B^{-1}(\delta A + C)) = \emptyset$.

Proof of Claim. We must show $\sigma(D_z F) \cap S = \emptyset$. The set of roots is $\sigma(D_z F) = \{\lambda : \det[\delta B'\lambda^2 + (\delta A + C)\lambda + B] = 0\}$. With B symmetric, $\sigma(D_z F) = \{\lambda : \det[B^{-1}(\delta A + C) - g(\lambda)] = 0\}$, where $g(\lambda) = -(\delta\lambda^2 + 1)/\lambda$. Since g is at most 2 to 1, and $g(1/\delta\lambda) = f(\lambda)$ for $\lambda \neq 0$, we find $\sigma(D_z F) = \{\lambda : g(\lambda) \in \sigma(B^{-1}(\delta A + C))\}$. Now g maps S onto the elliptical region

---

[32] $\mathbb{C}$ denotes the complex numbers. When $z = x + iy \in \mathbb{C}$, we denote its real part x by $\operatorname{Re} z$ and its imaginary part y by $\operatorname{Im} z$.

$\Sigma = g(S) = \{z : (\text{Re}\, z)^2/(1+\delta)^2 + (\text{Im}\, z)^2/(1-\delta)^2 \le 1\}$ as shown in Figure 3. It immediately follows that the saddlepoint property is equivalent to $\Sigma \cap \sigma(B^{-1}(\delta A + C)) = \emptyset.$ □

We know A and C are negative definite since $D^2 v$ is negative definite. Thus $-(\delta A + C)$ is positive definite and so has a square root D. Now $\sigma(B^{-1}(\delta A + C)) = -\sigma(B^{-1}D^2) = -\sigma(DB^{-1}D)$. Moreover, $-\sigma(DB^{-1}D) \subset \mathbb{R}$ because the spectrum of a symmetric matrix is real. Since $\Sigma \cap \mathbb{R} = [-(1+\delta),(1+\delta)]$, the saddlepoint property is then equivalent to $\sigma(B^{-1}(\delta A + C)) \cap [-(1+\delta),(1+\delta)] = \emptyset$, which is the same condition derived by DasGupta and McKenzie (1984). ◀

We can derive the saddlepoint property in a different way when δ is near 1. This method relies on the continuity of the characteristic polynomial, combined with the fact that the undiscounted model has no unit roots. It does not require a symmetry condition.

Lemma 13. *Under (R7), if $\lambda \ne 0$ solves $p_1(\lambda) = 0$, then $|\lambda| \ne 1$.*

Proof. Suppose $p_1(\lambda) = \det[\lambda^2 B' + (A + C)\lambda + B] = 0$ with $|\lambda| = 1$. Since $\lambda \ne 0$, we can multiply by $(\bar{\lambda})^m$ to obtain $\det[\lambda B' + (A+C) + \bar{\lambda}B] = 0$. Take $x \ne 0$ in the null space of $\lambda B' + (A + C) + \bar{\lambda}B$. Letting x^* denote the Hermitian conjugate of x,[33] form

$$x^*[\lambda B' + A + C + \bar{\lambda}B]x = [\bar{\lambda}x^*, x^*] \begin{bmatrix} A & B \\ B' & C \end{bmatrix} \begin{bmatrix} \lambda x \\ x \end{bmatrix} < 0$$

as $D^2 v$ is negative definite. However, the expression is zero since x is in the null space of $\lambda B' + A + C + \bar{\lambda}B$. This contradiction shows that $|\lambda| \ne 1$. □

Lemma 14. *Under (R1)–(R7), there is a $\delta_1 \ge \delta^*$ so that the saddlepoint property holds at all steady states for $\delta > \delta_1$.*

Proof. We know $p_1(\lambda) \ne 0$ for $|\lambda| = 1$. Because p_1 is continuous in λ there will be a δ_0 with $p_1(\lambda) \ne 0$ for $\lambda \in S_{\delta_0}$. Let $\epsilon = \min\{|p_1(\lambda)| : \lambda \in S_{\delta_0}\} > 0$. Now $p_\delta(\lambda)$ is continuous in δ because $k(\delta)$ is continuous and $v \in C^2$. Choose $\delta_1 \ge \delta_0$ so that $|p_\delta(\lambda)| \ge \epsilon/2$ on S_{δ_0} for $\delta \ge \delta_1$. It follows that p_δ has no roots in $S_\delta \subset S_{\delta_0}$ for $\delta \ge \delta_1$, so the saddlepoint property holds for $\delta \ge \delta_1$. □

5.4.5 Local and Global Stability

When the saddlepoint property holds, the Stable Manifold Theorem applies, and describes the asymptotic behavior of the system near the steady state.[34]

---

[33] Recall that the *Hermitian conjugate* is the complex conjugate of the transpose.

[34] Scheinkman (1976) showed how the Stable Manifold Theorem could be used to prove the turnpike property.

Let $S\colon \mathbb{R}^m \to \mathbb{R}^m$ be an invertible linear transformation. We say S is *hyperbolic* if it has no roots of unit modulus. In that case, we can decompose $\mathbb{R}^m$ and S into direct sums $\mathbb{R}^m = E_1 \oplus E_2$ and $S = S_1 \oplus S_2$ with $S(E_i) \subset E_i$. Moreover, E_i can be chosen so that the eigenvalues of S_1 all have modulus less than one, and the eigenvalues of S_2 all have modulus greater than one. We can then choose norms on E_i so that S_1 and S_2^{-1} are strict contractions.[35] Define the *skewness* by $\rho = \max\{\|S_1\|, \|S_2^{-1}\|\}$. Our choice of norm ensures $\rho < 1$. Let $E(r)$ denote the ball in E of radius r about 0, and similarly for $E_i(r)$.

Given a set $X \subset \mathbb{R}^m$, denote the set of k-times continuously differentiable functions on X by $C^k(X)$. We topologize $C^k(X)$ by defining an ϵ-ball about f to be all $g \in C^k$ where $\|D^l f - D^l g\|_\infty < \epsilon$ for $l = 1, \ldots, k$. Thus convergence in C^k means uniform convergence of the function and its first k derivatives. For $f\colon X \to \mathbb{R}^m$, define the *Lipschitz norm* by $\mathrm{Lip}_X(f) = \inf\{\epsilon : \|f(x) - f(y)\| \leq \epsilon \|x - y\| \text{ for all } x, y \in X\}$. Note that when X is convex, $\mathrm{Lip}_X(f) = \|Df\|_\infty$ if the latter exists. Given a transformation S, let $N_\delta^k(S) = \{f \in C^k(E(r)) : \|f(0)\| \leq \delta \text{ and } \mathrm{Lip}_{E(r)}(f - S) < \delta\}$. Define $W^r = \{x \in E(r) : f^n(x) \in E(r), n = 1, \ldots\}$. This is the portion of the *stable manifold* in $E(r)$. It consists of all points whose trajectory $f^t(x)$ remains within $E(r)$. The stable manifold is characterized by the Stable Manifold Theorem for a Point.[36]

Stable Manifold Theorem for a Point. *Given $0 < \rho < 1$ and $r > 0$, there exists a constant ϵ (independent of r) and a constant η, $\epsilon > \eta > 0$, such that if S is a hyperbolic linear isomorphism of $\mathbb{R}^m$ with skewness ρ, and $f\colon E(r) \to \mathbb{R}^m$ satisfies $\|f(0)\| \leq \eta$ and $\mathrm{Lip}_{E(r)}(f - S) < \epsilon$, then there is a unique map $g_f\colon E_1(r) \to E_2(r)$ such that the graph of g_f is W^r. Moreover, g_f has the following properties:*

(1) *$\mathrm{Lip}_{E_1(r)}(g_f) \leq 1$;*
(2) *g_f is as differentiable as f;*
(3) *$f \mapsto g_f$ is a continuous map from $N_\eta^k(S)$ to $C^k(E_1(r), E_2(r))$;*
(4) *$f \restriction W^r$ is a strict contraction on W^r.*

Because $f \restriction W^r$ is a strict contraction, $f^n(x) \to 0$ whenever $x \in W^r$. Thus W^r is the portion of the stable manifold within distance r of 0.

We now have all the pieces required for the Multisector Turnpike Theorem. If the saddlepoint property holds at $D_z F$, then $D_z F$ is hyperbolic and both E_1 and E_2 have dimension m. Let $z^\delta = (k^\delta, k^\delta)'$ and define $f(z) = F(z + z^\delta) - z^\delta$. Note that $f^n(z) = F^n(z + z^\delta) - z^\delta$. The stable manifold for f is a translate of the stable manifold of F. This transformation just changes coordinates so the steady state is at the origin, for

---

[35] See Nitecki (1971, Chapter 2).
[36] See Hirsch and Pugh (1970) or Nitecki (1971) for a proof.

our convenience.

Now consider $f(z) - S \cdot z$ where $S = D_z f|_0$. By Taylor's Theorem, $f(w) - S \cdot w = f(z) - S \cdot z + o(w - z)$, where $o(x)$ denotes a function with $\lim_{z \to 0} \|o(x)\| / \|x\| = 0$. By taking $r < 1$ small enough, $\text{Lip}_{E(r)}(f - S) < \epsilon$. By (R6) $D^2 f$ is continuous in δ, so we can choose an r that works simultaneously for all $\delta > \delta_1$. Of course $\|f(0)\| = 0 < \eta$. The Stable Manifold Theorem gives us a unique function g on $E_1(r)$. This function depends on δ in a continuous way. We now want to use g to define a function that takes an initial stock near 0 (the translate of k^δ), and yields a corresponding stock for the next period that puts us on the stable manifold. The optimal path from our initial stock will then be found by repeated application of the contraction f to this point of W. By the Stable Manifold Theorem, it will converge to the steady state at 0.

Basically, we want to project W down onto a neighborhood of 0 in an invertible fashion. The map we want is then the inverse. Intuitively, this will work if the stable manifold W has dimension m, and no components are vertical at the steady state. This is accomplished by showing that Q_1 defined below is invertible.

Take an invertible matrix Q such that $Q^{-1} S Q = \Lambda$ where $\Lambda = \Lambda_1 \oplus \Lambda_2$ is in Jordan form, with all eigenvalues with modulus less than one in Λ_1, and all eigenvalues with modulus greater than one in Λ_2.[37] Write Q as

$$Q = \begin{bmatrix} Q_1 & Q_2 \\ Q_3 & Q_4 \end{bmatrix}.$$

Before continuing, we must show that Q_1 is invertible.

Lemma 15. *Under (R1)–(R7), Q_1 is invertible if the saddlepoint property holds at k^δ.*

Proof. Using $SQ = Q\Lambda$, the formula for S, and the fact that each submatrix is $m \times m$, we find $Q_3 = Q_1 \Lambda_1$ and $Q_4 = Q_2 \Lambda_2$. Now suppose Q_1 is not invertible. Take $z \neq 0$ with $Q_1 z = 0$, and define $k_t = Q_1 \Lambda_1^t z$ for $t = 0, 1, \ldots$. Notice that at least $k_1 = Q_3 z \neq 0$ as Q is invertible. Also, $k_0 = 0$. Because the eigenvalues of Λ_1 have modulus less than one, $k_t \to 0$.

Rather than considering the original optimization problem, we now turn to a related quadratic optimization problem.[38] Define

$$w(k_{t-1}, k_t) = [k'_{t-1}, k'_t] D^2 v|_{z^\delta} \begin{bmatrix} k_{t-1} \\ k_t \end{bmatrix}.$$

Since $D^2 v$ is negative definite, w is strictly concave with maximum at zero. Let I be the product of compact intervals in $\mathbb{R}^m$ with $0 \in \text{int}\, I$

---

[37] See Hoffman and Kunze (1971) for information on the Jordan form.

[38] We adapt this trick from Scheinkman (1976).

and $\{k_t\} \subset \text{int } I$ and take $I \times I$ as the technology set. Then maximize $\sum_{t=1}^{\infty} \delta^{t-1} w(k_{t-1}, k_t)$. Although this technology does not quite fit our framework, it is easy to see that the Euler equations and transversality condition are necessary and sufficient for an optimum. The Euler equations can be written as $\delta B'_\delta k_{t+1} + (\delta A_\delta + C_\delta) k_t + B_\delta k_{t-1} = 0$. We solve for $k_{t+1} = -(\delta B'_\delta)^{-1}[(\delta A_\delta + C_\delta) k_t + B_\delta k_{t-1}]$ and rewrite as a first-order system, obtaining $z_{t+1} = S z_t$. Thus the actual Euler equations for w are the same as the linearized Euler equations for v. Note that the unique steady state is at 0.[39]

Now

$$
S \begin{bmatrix} k_t \\ k_{t+1} \end{bmatrix} = SQ \begin{bmatrix} \Lambda_1^t z \\ 0 \end{bmatrix} = Q\Lambda \begin{bmatrix} \Lambda_1^t z \\ 0 \end{bmatrix} = Q \begin{bmatrix} \Lambda_1^{t+1} z \\ 0 \end{bmatrix} = \begin{bmatrix} k_{t+1} \\ k_{t+2} \end{bmatrix},
$$

so k_t satisfies the Euler equations. Moreover,

$$
\lim_{t\to\infty} \delta^t w_1(k_t, k_{t+1}) k_t = \lim_{t\to\infty} 2\delta^t z'[AQ_1\Lambda_1^t + B'Q_1\Lambda_1^{t+1}]'Q_1\Lambda_1^t z = 0
$$

since all the roots of Λ_1 have modulus less than one.[40] It follows that k_t is optimal. But this is impossible as zero is the only optimal path from $k_0 = 0$. This contradiction shows Q_1 is invertible. □

Now that we have Q_1 invertible, we can construct our desired projection. Let $y \in W^r = \text{gr } g$, where $\text{gr } g$ denotes the graph of g. Because $y \in \text{gr } g$, we can write $y = w + g(w)$ for some $w \in E_1(r)$.[41] Now E_1 is composed of linear combinations of the columns of $[Q'_1, (Q_1\Lambda)']'$. Thus any element of E_1 has the form $w = [(Q_1 x)', (Q_1\Lambda x)']'$ for some $x \in \mathbb{R}^m$. By a slight abuse of notation, we write this as $(w_1, w_2) = (Q_1 x, Q_1\Lambda x)$. Moreover, this x is unique because Q_1 is invertible. In fact, $x = Q_1^{-1} w_1$. Substituting, we have $y_1 = Q_1 x + g_1(Q_1 x, Q_1\Lambda x)$ for some $x \in \mathbb{R}^m$.

Consider the map $\phi(x) = Q_1 x + g_1(Q_1 x, Q_1\Lambda x)$, taking as domain D all points with $\|(Q_1 x, Q_1\Lambda x)\| < r$. Note that 0 is in the interior of D. The map ϕ is $C^{\ell-1}$ since f is. It also maps D onto the projection of W^r on its first m components by construction. Moreover, the Lipschitz condition on g implies that ϕ is one-to-one on D. It follows that ϕ is invertible on D. Let y_1 denote the first m components of y and y_2 the last m components. Now define $h(y_1) = Q_1\Lambda\phi^{-1}(y_1) + g_2(Q_1\phi^{-1}(y_1), Q_1\Lambda\phi^{-1}(y_1))$. Then h is a continuous map, and $(y_1, h(y_1)) \in W^r$ for all y_1 sufficiently small.

This h map gives us a stock for the first period that puts us on the stable manifold. Applying f and translating over to k^δ shows that the

---

[39] A modified version of this argument applies when $\delta = 1$. See Scheinkman (1976).

[40] Notice how this argument requires the roots have modulus less than $\delta^{-1/2}$. It fails on all of the unstable roots, which have modulus greater than δ^{-1}.

[41] Keep in mind that we are regarding $\text{gr } g$, E_1, and E_2 as embedded in $\mathbb{R}^{2m}$.

Euler equations are satisfied. By the Stable Manifold Theorem, f is a contraction on W^r, so $f^t(k) \to 0$, and the translates converge to k^δ. But then the translates must obey the transversality condition, and so be the unique optimal path from k. Thus h is actually the capital policy function.

Moreover, if we start at any initial stock, the Visit Lemma implies we will eventually approach within r of k^δ. Henceforth, the path must converge to k^δ. Thus all optimal paths from initial stocks that are greater than some expansible stock must converge to the unique steady state k^δ. We sum up these results in a theorem.

Multisector Turnpike Theorem. *Suppose (R1)–(R7) hold. If $1 > \delta > \delta_1$, the optimal path converges to the unique steady state k^δ.*

Notice that the map g defining the stable manifold depends smoothly on δ. In contrast, the policy function h is only known to be continuous. There are two obstacles to declaring it smooth. The first concerns ϕ^{-1} above. If we knew $D\phi$ was invertible, the Inverse Function Theorem would imply ϕ^{-1} is as smooth as ϕ. Unfortunately, it is not easy to get information about $D\phi$. Second, there may be problems constructing Q in a smooth way, especially if eigenvalues are repeated. Scheinkman (1976) uses a slightly different method that finesses the second problem. However, the first problem remains.

Under somewhat stronger conditions, it is possible to show the policy function is smooth: see Santos (1991; 1992) and Boldrin and Montrucchio (1989). The relation between smoothness, the saddlepoint property, and the turnpike property are discussed further in Araujo and Scheinkman (1977) and DasGupta and McKenzie (1984; 1985; 1990).

5.5 Cycles and Chaos in Optimal Growth

All these stability results may leave you with the wrong impression that optimal paths *always* converge to a steady state. This is not so. In fact, there are even one-sector examples where any optimal path starting off the stationary state *never* converges.

▶ Example 13: Sutherland's optimal cycles. The earliest example of optimal cycles was due to Sutherland (1970). His example is a reduced-form, one-sector model. The technology set is $T = [0,1]^2$, while felicity is $v(x, y) = -(9x^2 + 11xy + 4y^2) + 43x$. The discount factor is $\delta = 1/3$. The Euler equation, $v_2(k_{t-1}, k_t) + \delta v_1(k_t, k_{t+1}) = 0$, becomes $-11k_{t-1} - 8k_t + [-18k_t - 11k_{t+1} + 43]/3 = 0$. This can be rewritten as $43 - 33k_{t-1} - 42k_t - 11k_{t+1} = 0$. The stationary solution is $k_t = 1/2$ for all t.

This equation has roots $(-21 \pm \sqrt{78})/11$, which are approximately -1.11 and -2.71. The general solution is $k_t = 1/2 + \alpha r_1^t + \beta r_2^t$ where

$r_1 = (-21 + \sqrt{78})/11$ and $r_2 = (-21 - \sqrt{78})/11$. Since both roots are negative, the solution will oscillate. As both roots have modulus greater than one, the system is unstable. Further, k_t passes 0 or 1 in finite time. At this point, optimal paths are no longer interior, and the above Euler equation breaks down. Taking the constraints into account, we see that oscillation between 0 and 1 is optimal. (If $k_t = k_{t+2} = 1$ and $k_{t+1} = 0$, $v_2 + \delta v_1 = -1/3 < 0$, which is okay since the constraint $k_{t+1} \geq 0$ binds. The case with $k_t = k_{t+2} = 0$ and $k_{t+1} = 1$ is similar.) ◄

Although interesting, Sutherland's example has been viewed by many as unconvincing. It cannot be derived from a production function and felicity function depending only on consumption. Samuelson (1973) recounts that he suspected that either the joint production or the bang-bang nature of the solution was responsible for the oscillations in Sutherland's example. He did not feel oscillations could happen in a well-behaved model—one that is derived from primitives and has a reasonable felicity function. Weitzman (see Samuelson, 1973) showed that cycles are possible in a simple example using Cobb-Douglas felicity and a linear technology.

► Example 14: Weitzman's interior cycles. Weitzman's example contains three goods: bread, grape juice, and wine. The technology is linear. One unit of labor is available at each time. It can be used in the production of either bread or grape juice. One unit of labor can produce one unit of bread, or one unit of grape juice. Wine is produced by letting grape juice ferment for one period. Only bread and wine are consumed. Denote the amounts of bread, grape juice, and wine available in period t by $c_{1t}, c_{2t},$ and c_{3t}. The constraints are $c_{2t} = 1 - c_{1t}$, $c_{3t} = c_{2,t-1}$, and $c_{1t}, c_{2t}, c_{3t} \geq 0$. Felicity is Cobb-Douglas, $u(c_{1t}, c_{3t}) = (c_{1t} c_{3t})^{1/2}$. Denote c_{1t} by c_t. Thus $c_{2t} = 1 - c_t$ and $c_{3t} = 1 - c_{t-1}$. The initial endowment of grape juice is $c_{20} = c_0 = c$.

Reduced-form utility is $v(c_{t-1}, c_t) = \sqrt{c_t(1 - c_{t-1})}$ and the technology set is $T = [0,1] \times [0,1]$. The Euler equation is $\delta^t[(1 - c_{t-1})/c_t]^{1/2} = \delta^{t+1}[c_{t+1}/(1 - c_t)]^{1/2}$, thus $\delta^2 c_{t+1} c_t = (1 - c_{t-1})(1 - c_t)$. The steady state is at $c = 1/(1 + \delta)$ so $\delta c = 1 - c$. However, there are also cycles. Take $\delta = 1/2$, $c = 1/6$. Then $c_t = 1/6$ for t even and $c_t = 20/21$ for t odd is optimal. ◄

5.5.1 The Existence of Cycles

What causes these cycles? Are there conditions that guarantee the existence of cycles? As usual, we turn to the Euler equations for help. The plan is to iterate the Euler equations, and then show that the second iterate has fixed points besides the steady states. These will be the desired cycles.

We will examine a reduced-form model with one capital good and a bounded technology. In addition to (R1)–(R7), we assume that:

Sign Change Assumption.

(R8) A steady state k^δ exists for all δ, $\delta_0 < \delta < 1$, and there are δ^+ and δ^-, $\delta_0 \le \delta^- < \delta^+ \le 1$ with $v_{22} + \delta^- v_{11} > (1 + \delta^-)v_{12}$ at k^{δ^-} and $v_{22} + \delta^+ v_{11} < (1 + \delta^+)v_{12}$ at k^{δ^+}.

In our discussion of the saddlepoint property, we set $A = v_{11}$, $B = v_{12} = v_{21}$, $C = v_{22}$. When $B = v_{12} < 0$, $0 < B^{-1}(\delta^- A + C) < 1 + \delta^-$ at k^{δ^-} and $B^{-1}(\delta^+ A + C) > 1 + \delta^+$ at k^{δ^+}. It follows that the saddlepoint property holds at δ^+ and fails at δ^-. Further, since k^δ solves $v_2(k, k) + \delta v_1(k, k) = 0$, the Implicit Function Theorem shows that $\delta \to k^\delta$ is continuously differentiable. Benhabib and Nishimura (1985) exploit these facts to obtain the existence of cycles.

Let $P^+ = \{\delta : v_{22} + \delta v_{11} < (1+\delta)v_{12} \text{ at } k^\delta\}$, $P^0 = \{\delta : v_{22} + \delta v_{11} = (1+\delta)v_{12} \text{ at } k^\delta\}$, and $P^- = \{\delta : v_{22} + \delta v_{11} > (1+\delta)v_{12} \text{ at } k^\delta\}$. When $v_{12} < 0$, the saddlepoint property holds on P^+ and fails on P^-. By assumption, $\delta^+ \in P^+$ and $\delta^- \in P^-$, so both P^+ and P^- are non-empty. The roots of linearized Euler equations solve $\delta v_{12}\lambda^2 + (v_{22} + \delta v_{11})\lambda + v_{12} = 0$, so $\delta\lambda^2 + (v_{22} + \delta v_{11})\lambda/v_{12} + 1 = 0$. Descartes's Rule of Signs implies that there are no positive roots.[42] Further, as both roots are real (the discriminant $[(v_{22} + \delta v_{11})/v_{12}]^2 - 4\delta$ is positive since $D^2 v$ is negative definite), both are negative. Label them with $\lambda_1 \le \lambda_2$. A simple calculation shows that $\lambda_1, \lambda_2 < -1$ when $\delta \in P^-$, $\lambda_1 = -1/\delta$ and $\lambda_2 = -1$ when $\delta \in P^0$, and $\lambda_1 < -1 < \lambda_2 < 0$ when $\delta \in P^+$.

As before, define the policy function $G(k_{t-1}, k_t, \delta)$ implicitly via the Euler equation $v_2(k_{t-1}, k_t) + \delta v_1(k_t, G) = 0$. A short calculation shows $G_1 = -\delta^{-1}$ and $G_2 = -(v_{22} + \delta v_{11})/\delta v_{12}$. Again, set $y_t = k_{t+1}$, $z_t = (k_t, y_t)'$ and define $F_\delta : \mathbb{R}_+^{2m} \to \mathbb{R}_+^{2m}$ by

$$F_\delta(z_t) = \begin{bmatrix} y_t \\ G(k_t, y_t, \delta) \end{bmatrix}.$$

We first prove a preliminary technical lemma. Denote the unit m sphere by $S^m = \{x \in \mathbb{R}^{m+1} : \|x\| = 1\}$. The unit sphere is a smooth manifold both in its own right, and as the boundary of the unit ball.[43] We use ∂A to denote the boundary of the set A.

Lemma 16. *Suppose $A, B \subset \mathbb{R}^m$ are non-empty sets with $A \subset \text{int } B$, A compact, and B convex. Then there is $\mathcal{M}$, a manifold with boundary,*

---

[42] See Uspensky (1948, p. 121).

[43] Manifolds (with and without boundary) and diffeomorphisms are studied in differential topology. Standard mathematical references are Milnor (1965) and Guillemin and Pollack (1974). Mas-Colell (1985) gives an exhaustive development of the techniques of differential topology as applied to Walrasian competitive analysis.

such that $\mathcal{M} \subset \text{int } B$ *and* $A \subset \text{int } \mathcal{M}$. *Moreover,* $\mathcal{M}$ *can be chosen so its boundary* $\partial \mathcal{M}$ *is diffeomorphic to* S^{m-1}.

Proof. If B is not bounded, we intersect it with a ball containing A in its interior. Thus we assume B is bounded without loss of generality. Choose ϵ with $0 < \epsilon < \text{dist}(A, \partial B)$. Define $C = \{x \in B : \text{dist}(x, \partial B) \geq \epsilon/2\}$.

We claim the set C is convex. Let $x, y \in C$. Clearly $z = \alpha x + (1 - \alpha)y \in B$ for all α with $0 < \alpha < 1$. We must show $z \in C$. If not, $\text{dist}(z, \partial B) < \epsilon/2$. Take $w \in \partial B$ with $\|w - z\| = \text{dist}(z, \partial B) < \epsilon/2$ and choose $\delta > 0$, $\|w - z\| + \delta < \epsilon/2$. Now consider $x + w - z + u$ where $\|u\| < \delta$. As $\|w - z + u\| < \epsilon/2 < \text{dist}(x, \partial B)$, $x + w - z + u \in B$. Similarly, $y + w - z + u \in B$. By convexity, $w + u = \alpha x + (1 - \alpha)y + w - z + u \in B$. Since u was arbitrary with $\|u\| < \delta$, $w \in \text{int } B$, which contradicts $w \in \partial B$. Thus $z \in C$ and C is convex.

By the construction of C, it is clear that C is compact with $C \subset \text{int } B$, $A \subset \text{int } C$. Moreover, $\text{dist}(\partial C, \partial B) = \epsilon/2 \leq \text{dist}(\partial C, \partial A)$.

Now fix $x_0 \in \text{int } C$. For $u \in S^{m-1}$, let $\phi(u) = \sup\{\alpha > 0 : x_0 + \alpha u \in C\}$. The function ϕ exists by compactness of C and the fact that $x_0 \in \text{int } C$. Moreover, the convexity of C implies ϕ is continuous. Thus it may be approximated by a smooth ψ with $|\psi(u) - \phi(u)| < \epsilon/4$ for $u \in S^{m-1}$.[44] Define $\mathcal{M} = \{x_0 + \alpha u : u \in S^{m-1}$ and $0 \leq \alpha \leq \psi(u)\}$. Note that $\mathcal{M} \subset \text{int } B$ and $A \subset \text{int } \mathcal{M}$. Finally, to show $\mathcal{M}$ is a manifold with boundary, it is enough to see that the boundary is smooth. Let B^m denote the unit m-ball. Notice that the mapping $\varphi(u) = x_0 + \psi(u/\|u\|)u$ is smooth from $B^m \setminus \{0\}$ to $\mathcal{M} \setminus \{x_0\}$ with smooth inverse given by $\varphi^{-1}(x) = (x - x_0)/\psi(\frac{x - x_0}{\|x - x_0\|})$. Clearly $\partial \mathcal{M}$ is diffeomorphic to S^{m-1}. $\square$

To prove that there are fixed points of the second iterate of the Euler equations that are not steady states, we will count the fixed points using the degree. Suppose $\mathcal{M}$ and $\mathcal{N}$ are manifolds without boundary with $\mathcal{M}$ compact, $\mathcal{N}$ connected, and $f : \mathcal{M} \to \mathcal{N}$ smooth. We say that $y \in \mathcal{N}$ is a *regular point* of f if Df_x is invertible for all $x \in f^{-1}(y)$. If y is a regular point, we can define the *degree* of f at y by $\deg f = \sum_{x \in f^{-1}(y)} \text{sgn det } Df_x$. The degree does not depend on the choice of y and is a homotopy invariant; it is the same for all homotopic maps.[45]

Existence of Two-Cycles. *Under assumptions (R1)–(R8), there is at least one* $\delta \in [\delta^-, \delta^+]$ *such that two-cycles exist.*

Proof. Consider fixed points of the second iterate of F_δ. These are points with $z = F_\delta(F_\delta(z))$. Define $M_\delta(z) = z - F_\delta(F_\delta(z))$. Zeros of M_δ are then 2-cycles (which may also be steady states). When evaluated at

---

[44] The Stone-Weierstrass Theorem implies we could even require ψ to be a polynomial.
[45] A *(differentiable) homotopy* between functions f and g mapping X to $\mathbb{R}$ is a differentiable function $H : X \times [0, 1] \to \mathbb{R}$ with $H(x, 0) = f(x)$ and $H(x, 1) = g(x)$. See Milnor (1965) or Guillemin and Pollack (1974) for more on degrees and homotopies.

the steady state k^δ, the chain rule implies $DM_\delta = I - J^2$, where J denotes the steady state value of DF_δ. As J has roots λ_1 and λ_2, DM has roots $1 - \lambda_i^2$. (If $S^{-1}JS = \Lambda$, $S^{-1}(I - J^2)S = I - \Lambda^2$ is the diagonalization of DM_δ.) Thus $\det DM_\delta = [1 - \lambda_1^2(\delta)][1 - \lambda_2^2(\delta)]$. It follows that $\det DM_\delta$ is negative on P^+ and positive on P^-.

Define $Z(\delta) = \{z : M_\delta(z) = 0\}$. Since $Z(\delta)$ consists of steady states and 2-cycles, and technology is bounded by (R3), $Z(\delta)$ is contained in the ball of radius β. As $Z(\delta) = M_\delta^{-1}(\{0\})$, $Z(\delta)$ is closed, and hence compact. Finally, for $\delta \in P_+ \cup P_-$, DM_δ is invertible. This implies the points of $Z(\delta)$ are isolated, and hence $Z(\delta)$ is finite for $\delta \in P^+ \cup P^-$.

Define $z(\delta) = (k^\delta, k^\delta)$. Because $\delta \mapsto k^\delta$ is continuous, $z([\delta^-, \delta^+])$ is compact. As $z(\delta)$ is always in the interior of T, $z([\delta^-, \delta^+])$ is bounded away from the boundary of T. If $Z(\delta)$ is not uniformly bounded away from ∂T for all $\delta \in [\delta^-, \delta^+]$, there is a δ where $Z(\delta)$ contains at least one point other than the steady state k^δ. This is the desired cycle of period 2, and we are done.

Otherwise, $Z(\delta)$ is uniformly bounded away from ∂T for $\delta \in [\delta^-, \delta^+]$. Apply Lemma 16 to find a manifold $\mathcal{M}$ with $\mathcal{M} \subset \mathrm{int}\, T$ and $Z(\delta) \subset \mathrm{int}\, \mathcal{M}$. Moreover, the boundary $\partial \mathcal{M}$ is diffeomorphic to the sphere S^{2m-1}, which orients $\partial \mathcal{M}$. As $\partial \mathcal{M} \cap Z(\delta) = \emptyset$, M_δ is never 0 on $\partial \mathcal{M}$ for $\delta \in [\delta^-, \delta^+]$. It follows that $\hat{M}_\delta = M_\delta / \|M_\delta\|$ is smooth on $\partial \mathcal{M}$. We will compute the degree of $\hat{M}_\delta$.

Both $\partial \mathcal{M}$ and S^{2m-1} are manifolds without boundary, with $\partial \mathcal{M}$ compact and S^{2m-1} connected. Set $\delta(t) = \delta^- + t(\delta^+ - \delta^-)$ to define a homotopy $\hat{M}_{\delta(t)}(z)$ between $\hat{M}_{\delta^-}(z)$ and $\hat{M}_{\delta^+}(z)$. Because the degree is a homotopy invariant, $\deg_{\partial \mathcal{M}} \hat{M}_{\delta^-} = \deg_{\partial \mathcal{M}} \hat{M}_{\delta^+}$. In fact, we have shown the degree is constant as δ varies over $[\delta^-, \delta^+]$.

We now calculate the degree. Temporarily fix $\delta \in P^+ \cup P^-$. Then $Z(\delta) = \{z_i\}$ is finite, and we may take finitely many disjoint balls B_i centered at z_i with $Z(\delta) \subset \cup_i B_i$ and $B_i \subset \mathrm{int}\, \mathcal{M}$. Let $\mathcal{N} = \mathcal{M} \setminus (\cup_i B_i)$. Orient $\partial \mathcal{M}$ as above and ∂B_i negatively. Because M_δ is never 0 on $\mathcal{N}$, $\hat{M}_\delta$ is smooth on $\mathcal{N} = \mathcal{M} \setminus (\cup_i B_i)$. It follows that its degree is zero on $\partial \mathcal{N}$. Thus $\deg_{\partial \mathcal{M}} \hat{M}_\delta = \sum_i \deg_{\partial B_i} \hat{M}_\delta$ where each B_i has the usual orientation. Now $\deg_{\partial B_i} \hat{M}_\delta = \mathrm{sgn}\det DM_\delta|_{z_i}$.[46] Putting this together, we find $\deg_{\partial \mathcal{M}} \hat{M}_\delta = \sum_{z \in Z(\delta)} \mathrm{sgn}\det DM_\delta|_z$ for $\delta \in P^+ \cup P^-$. This formula holds for any $\delta \in P^+ \cup P^-$.

If there were no two-cycles, $Z(\delta)$ would consist entirely of steady states. In that case, DM_δ would be positive on P^- and negative on P^+. The degree would count the number of steady states on P^- and the negative

---

[46] The degree of $\hat{M}_\delta$ is called the *index* of M_δ. Its computation is standard. See Milnor (1965).

of the number of steady states on P^+. Because the sum must be the same in both cases, and since there *are* steady states, there must be values of δ where $Z(\delta)$ contains elements that are not steady states. Transversality is automatically satisfied, and these are the required cycles of period 2. $\square$

Remark. The proof actually shows that there are cycles either for all $\delta \in P^+$ or for all $\delta \in P^-$, depending on the sign of the degree.

Benhabib and Nishimura have further results along these lines, and the Sutherland example fits their criteria. Their method cannot be used to establish the existence of odd-period cycles since the determinant of the Jacobian of odd iterates is always positive at steady states. It also fails for 2^n-cycles when $n > 1$ since we only show that $Z(\delta)$ contains elements which are not steady states. An explicit counting of $Z(\delta)$, as we do later for the tent map, would be required to show more.

The sign of v_{12} determines the behavior of optimal paths. The case $v_{12} \geq 0$ also determines comparative dynamics properties as shown in Chapter 7.

Lemma 17. *Suppose $(k, h(k)) \in \text{int} T$ where h is the policy function. Then h is increasing at k if $v_{12}(k, h(k)) > 0$ and decreasing at k if $v_{12}(k, h(k)) < 0$.*

Proof. We know h is single-valued by the strict concavity of v. By the Maximum Theorem h is continuous. There is then a neighborhood N of k with $(k, h(x)), (x, h(k)) \in T$ for all $x \in N$. Let $\mathbf{k}$ and $\mathbf{x}$ be optimal from k and x respectively, so $k_1 = h(k)$ and $x_1 = h(x)$. The paths $(k, x_1, x_2, \ldots)$ and $(x, k_1, k_2, \ldots)$ are then feasible. It follows that $J(k) = v(k, k_1) + \delta J(k_1) \geq v(k, x_1) + \delta J(x_1)$, and $J(x) = v(x, x_1) + \delta J(x_1) \geq v(x, k_1) + \delta J(k_1)$. Thus $v(k, k_1) + v(x, x_1) - v(x, k_1) - v(k, x_1) \geq 0$. By the Fundamental Theorem of Calculus, we have $\int_{k_1}^{x_1} \int_k^x v_{12}(s, t) \, ds \, dt \geq 0$. If $v_{12} < 0$, $x_1 - k_1$ and $x - k$ have opposite signs, and if $v_{12} > 0$, $x_1 - k_1$ and $x - k$ have the same sign. $\square$

There are two corollaries. The first is immediate, the second provides another turnpike result.

Corollary 11. *If $v_{12} > 0$ on $\text{int} T$, interior optimal paths are monotonic. If $v_{12} < 0$ on $\text{int} T$, interior optimal paths oscillate.*

Corollary 12. *If $v_{12} > 0$ on $\text{int} T$, interior optimal paths converge monotonically to a steady state. If $v_{12} < 0$ on $\text{int} T$, interior optimal paths converge to a steady state or a cycle of period 2.*

Proof. The first part follows from monotonicity and boundedness, as before. Now suppose $v_{12} < 0$ so the policy function h is decreasing. If $k_1 < k_3$, $k_2 = h(k_1) > h(k_3) = k_4$. Thus $k_3 = h(k_2) < h(k_4) = k_5$. It follows that $k_1 < k_3 < k_5 < \cdots$, and $k_2 > k_4 > k_6 > \cdots$. As both the even order terms and odd order terms are monotonic, they converge to

k_{even} and k_{odd}. If $k_{even} = k_{odd}$, the Euler equations yield a steady state, and if $k_{even} \neq k_{odd}$, the Euler equations imply we have a cycle of period 2. Similar arguments apply if $k_1 > k_3$. □

Interestingly, a similar argument works with recursive preferences in the one-sector case, as shown by Benhabib, Majumdar, and Nishimura (1987).[47] However, instead of depending on whether $v_1(k, k')$ is increasing or decreasing in k', the recursive case depends on whether $W_1(k, k', J(k'))$ is increasing or decreasing in k'. Generally speaking, this condition is somewhat unsatisfying as it depends on the value function J.

▶ Example 15: Two-sector neoclassical model. We can get some insight into the nature of these cycles by examining the case of a neoclassical technology with one capital good. Consumption given input a and output b is $\mathcal{T}(a, b)$, where $\mathcal{T}$ is the transformation function. Then $v(a, b) = u(\mathcal{T}(a, b))$ where u is felicity. We have $v_{12} = u'\mathcal{T}_{12} + u''\mathcal{T}_1\mathcal{T}_2$. Consider the case $u(c) = c$. Then $v_{12} = \mathcal{T}_{12}$. We can regard $\{(b, c) : c = \mathcal{T}(a, b)\}$ as the production possibilities frontier given input a. The condition $\mathcal{T}_{12} < 0$ says that the slope of the production frontier, $\mathcal{T}_2$, becomes steeper (more negative) as the amount of capital input a rises. This would happen if production of the consumption good were more capital intensive than production of the capital good.[48] ◀

In another paper, Benhabib and Nishimura (1979) use the Hopf Bifurcation Theorem to find cycles in a continuous time model. Benhabib and Rustichini (1990) construct an eight-parameter family of examples using a three-sector model with Cobb-Douglas production to show that cycles can occur at discount factors arbitrarily close to one. Moreover, the cycles are robust under small perturbations of the parameters. Cartigny and Venditti (1995) show that cycles can emerge in symmetric multisector models.[49] These analyses suggest that cycles are relatively easy to obtain in multisector models.[50]

5.5.2 Chaotic Dynamics

Benhabib and Nishimura were able to exhibit cycles by using the policy function and the Euler equations. The properties of the policy function can also be examined by using dynamic programming. The capital policy function $h(x)$ solves Bellman's equation, $\max\{v(x, y) + \delta J(y)\}$. The optimal path is then written as $k_{t+1} = h(k_t)$. When $\delta = 0$, Boldrin and

---

[47] See also Benhabib and Nishimura (1988).

[48] A fuller discussion may be found in Benhabib and Nishimura (1985).

[49] Here "symmetric" means that the matrix of mixed second partial derivatives, v_{12}, is symmetric.

[50] See Nishimura and Sorger (1996) for a recent survey of the literature on cycles and chaos.

Montrucchio (1986) show that *any* continuous function can be an optimal policy function. Define v by $v(x, y) = -\|y\|^2/2 + \langle y, h(x) \rangle - L\|x\|^2/2$. By the Cauchy-Schwartz inequality, $\langle y, h(x) \rangle \leq \|y\|^2/2 + \|h(x)\|^2/2$, thus $v(x, y) \leq \|h(x)\|^2/2 - L\|x\|^2/2 = v(x, h(x))$, and v attains its maximum at $h(x)$. For appropriate choice of L, v will be concave. They then use a continuity argument to show that *any* proposed policy function may be approximated arbitrarily well by the optimal policy function of a discounted problem (with δ small). They go on to show that any C^2 function on T may be a policy function for δ sufficiently small.[51]

The fact that any continuous function can be a policy function has strong implications. Even very simple continuous policy functions can yield very complex dynamics.

▶ **Example 16: The tent map.** Define $f(x) = 2x$ for $0 \leq x \leq 1/2$ and $f(x) = 2(1 - x)$ for $1/2 \leq x \leq 1$. This is the *tent map*.[52] You can think of this map as stretching the interval out to double its length, and then folding it back upon itself, like pulling taffy. It illustrates how complex optimal paths can be. Both the set of rational numbers and the set of irrational numbers are invariant under the map f. Notice that f has two fixed points, 0 and 2/3, as shown in the left panel of Figure 4. Now consider the second iterate $f^2(x) = f(f(x))$. This has four fixed points, shown in the right panel of Figure 4. They occur at 0, 2/5, 2/3 and 4/5. Two are fixed points of f, the other two constitute a cycle of period 2 (2-cycles). In general, the nth iterate has 2^n fixed points. Two of these are fixed points of f. If m divides n, others will be fixed points of f^m (cycles of period m). As $2 + \cdots + 2^{n/2} < 2^n$, there will be fixed points of f^n that are not fixed points of any f^m for $m \leq n$. Thus there will be cycles of period n that do not contain cycles of any lesser period. For example, f^3 has $2^3 = 8$ fixed points, 2 of which have period 1. Thus f has $6/3 = 2$ distinct 3-cycles. They are $2/7, 4/7, 6/7$ and $2/9, 4/9, 8/9$. Similarly, f^4 has $2^4 = 16$ fixed points. Four are fixed points of f^2 (this includes the fixed points of f). This leaves 12 fixed points, which constitute $12/4 = 3$ distinct 4-cycles of f.

Consider a rational number written in lowest terms $r = p/2^n q$ with $0 \leq r \leq 1$ and q not divisible by 2. After n applications of f, we obtain a number of the form p'/q. Now consider $r = p/q$ with q not divisible by 2. Regardless of whether $f(r) = 2p/q$ or $f(r) = 2(q - p)/q$, the number is still in lowest terms. Since there are at most $q - 1$ rational numbers of this form, p/q ends up in a cycle with period at most $q - 1$. It follows that all rational numbers are eventually mapped to either a fixed point, or a

---

[51] Neumann et al. (1988) show a similar result for a broader class of policy functions in the one-dimensional case.

[52] A smooth map with similar properties on $[0, 1]$ is the logistic map $f(x) = 4x(1 - x)$.

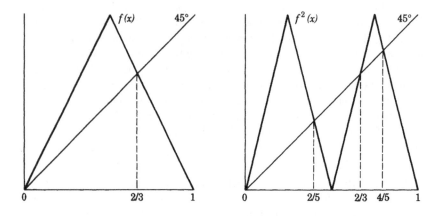

Figure 4:   The fixed points of the tent map f are at 0 and 2/3 (left panel), while the fixed points of f^2 are at 0, 2/5, 2/3, and 4/5 (right panel).

cycle.

The behavior of the tent map on the irrational numbers is completely different. If x is irrational, so is $f(x)$. Further, $f^n(x) = a_n + b_n x$ for some rational numbers a_n and b_n. It follows that x cannot be a fixed point of any iterate of f since any fixed point of f^n obeys $x = f^n(x) = a_n + b_n x$ and so $x = a_n/(1 - b_n)$ is rational. Irrational numbers wander around seemingly at random (chaotically) under repeated application of f.[53] The tent map is a prototypical chaotic map, and shows that chaotic capital accumulation may be optimal.[54] ◄

The peculiar behavior of the tent map exemplifies one of the problems that can arise when simulating a chaotic model. Computer simulation of this dynamical system involves the use of rational numbers. Such simulations *always* result in convergence to a cycle, regardless of the precision of the simulation. Nevertheless, convergence to a cycle is a zero probability

---

[53] For most initial values the iterates of this particular tent map look like they were generated from an IID process. The iterates of other tent maps, with peaks located at other points in the interval, have the autocorrelation coefficients of an AR(1) process for almost all initial values. See Sakai and Tokumaru (1980). Brock and Dechert (1988) use this fact to show that linear techniques cannot distinguish between data generated from tent maps and data generated by a stochastic process.

[54] There are several concepts of chaos available. For us, a map is *chaotic* if cycles of every positive period exist, and there is an uncountable set S, containing no periodic points, with $\limsup_{n \to \infty} |f^n(x) - f^n(y)| > 0$ and $\liminf_{n \to \infty} |f^n(x) - f^n(y)| = 0$ for all $x, y \in S$ with $x \neq y$, and $\limsup_{n \to \infty} |f^n(x) - f^n(y)| > 0$ whenever $x \in S$ and y is a periodic point. This is sometimes referred to as "Li-Yorke" chaos.

event. For almost all initial values, paths do not converge to a cycle, but rather wander chaotically. In contrast, a theoretical analysis allows us to detect the chaos. There are general criteria available that can be used to test for chaos.

In the one-sector case, the presence of 3-cycles implies chaos (Li and Yorke, 1975). Boldrin and Montrucchio (1986) showed that the policy function could have 3-cycles, for discount factors sufficiently near 0. The question of whether small discount factors were necessary was left unanswered by Boldrin and Montrucchio. Sorger (1992a; 1992b) shows that the logistic map could not be a policy function for discount factors larger than $1/2$.[55] Montrucchio (1994) and Sorger (1994b) have further refined these bounds, and extended them to all policy functions. Finally, Mitra (1995) has shown that 3-cycles cannot occur if the discount factor is larger than $(3 - \sqrt{5})/2$ (about 0.38), and that for any discount factor smaller than $(3 - \sqrt{5})/2$, there are reduced-form models that exhibit cycles of period 3.[56]

Relatively little is known about chaos in the general multisector case. However, it is known that two-sector models are a rich source of examples of both cyclic and chaotic trajectories. Indeed, the recent example of Nishimura and Yano (1995) indicates how to construct a two-sector model exhibiting ergodically chaotic optimal accumulation for a discount factor arbitrarily close to one.[57] Since some discounted multisector models exhibit chaotic solutions it is reasonable to believe this behavior will be robust with a more general recursive utility specification.

5.6 Conclusion

Bliss (1975) describes the *orthodox vision* of capital accumulation as the view that capital accumulation is "accompanied by a continuous increase in consumption per capita, by a continuous decline in the rate of interest and by a continuous increase in the real wage rate."[58] The standard one-sector Ramsey model is the archetypical dynamic model that embodies

---

[55] Sorger's methods can also be applied to some multisectoral models.

[56] Brock and Dechert (1991) contains more information on chaos in optimal growth models.

[57] Intuitively, a policy function h exhibits *ergodic chaos* if the "scrambled set" of initial values for which "chaotic dynamics" occurs has positive Lebesgue measure and the sequence of iterates $\{h^t\}$ obtained for each initial value in the scrambled set approximates an ergodic and absolutely continuous distribution which is invariant under h and which characterizes the limiting statistical properties (e.g., mean and variance) of the deterministic chaotic trajectories. For precise definitions see Majumdar and Mitra (1994b) and the presentation by Boldrin and Woodford (1990).

[58] Bliss (1975, p. 279).

the orthodox vision provided the Equivalence Principle (discussed in the next chapter) is used to justify the statements about factor prices. He goes on to argue that the orthodox vision is invalid in multisector models. The culprit, in Bliss's view, is that the rate of interest has no interpretation in that setup.

We have shown that the orthodox vision stands up in a class of one-sector recursive utility models. However, the fundamental underlying premise of the orthodox theory—the continuous accumulation of capital—is suspect in a variety of other single capital good models. The emergence of cycles and chaotic trajectories for optimal accumulation programs (and their dual competitive equilibria via the Equivalence Principle) casts doubt on the very core of the orthodox vision. What idea, if any, can take the place of the orthodox vision is unknown. The inherent nonlinearities of our optimal accumulation models suggest a pessimistic resolution of this problem. A sweeping replacement of the orthodox vision would appear to be an unattainable goal. The current emphasis on numerical simulations in macroeconomic models serves to underscore this point.

CHAPTER **6**

Equivalence Principles
and Dynamic Equilibria

6.1 Introduction

In the theory of dynamic models of competitive equilibrium one focus of attention is the instability of the price system known as the "saddlepoint instability" problem. Hahn (1966) first noted this problem in the context of a multisector model with the simple savings assumption that workers do not save and capitalists do not consume. He argued that if there is short-run perfect foresight with perfect capital markets, then for any given initial endowment of capital goods, not all initial price vectors lead to balanced growth. Shell and Stiglitz (1967) gave an example of a model where there is a unique set of initial prices that lead to balanced growth; for all other initial prices, at some finite time in the future, the perfect foresight assumption would be violated.

Following a suggestion of Meade, Hahn (1966) conjectured that if the government were to enforce an accumulation plan that was "efficient," then shadow prices associated with that plan would satisfy the short-run perfect foresight (Euler) equations of the model. If this notion is correct, then a planned economy is led to select the correct initial prices required to realize a stable path of accumulation. To verify this conjecture requires the "efficiency" problem used to calculate the appropriate "efficiency" prices has the desired stability property and that in fact the solution to the "efficiency" problem satisfies the perfect foresight equations of the given descriptive model. One may suppose the "efficiency" problem to take the strong form of an optimal growth problem. The saddlepoint property often holds for optimal growth paths. As a result, there is a unique initial price (or next period's capital stock) which supports convergence to the optimal path. Hahn's (1966) question can then be reinterpreted to ask whether there are competitive mechanisms that choose the correct initial price. As we saw in the asset pricing model of Section 4.6.1, short-run maximization, satisfying the Euler equations only, is not enough. A transversality condition is required. Any equilibrium model must find a way to deal with this *Hahn problem*.

In this chapter we examine the Hahn problem for one-sector and multisector models. The one-sector case with TAS utility is explored in some detail in the next section. We show the solutions to a perfect foresight equilibrium model also solve an optimal growth model and vice versa. This result is a form of the fundamental theorems of welfare economics adapted to a dynamic framework. Thus we establish an *Equivalence Principle* connecting optimal growth theory and equilibrium analysis. Perfect markets and perfect planning form a dual pair of resource allocation problems: a market equilibrium is a social optimum and a social optimum is a market equilibrium. The notion of an equivalence between a centralized planning model's optimal solutions and decentralized equilibrium solutions is implicit in much of the growth literature. The formal structure of this equivalence and the class of descriptive models for which this method is applicable were discussed by Becker (1981; 1982a; 1983a; 1985a) and are summarized in this chapter.[1] One interesting feature of the equivalence is that it holds for models with borrowing constraints. These constraints appear as non-negativity restrictions on individual capital holdings at each time. Although borrowing constraints are usually regarded as market imperfections, they actually serve to make the equilibrium optimal in our model.

In general, the analysis of dynamic market equilibrium problems is difficult owing to the non-stationary nature of the agents' optimization problems. The prices used to define a household's budget constraint may fluctuate over time. The validity of the Equivalence Principle for a class of optimal-growth/market-equilibrium models greatly simplifies the analysis of the market equilibrium problem; the properties enjoyed by an equilibrium may be read off from those of the optimal growth model. In particular, the existence, uniqueness, stability, and comparative dynamics properties of a market equilibrium solution follow from the analogous properties of the dual optimal growth model.[2]

A more significant role for the Equivalence Principle is that it provides

---

[1] Brock (1974) sketches the idea for a Equivalence Principle in one-sector models. A related idea in a partial equilibrium adjustment cost model of an industry may be found in Lucas and Prescott (1971) and Scheinkman (1977). In Lucas and Prescott (1971), consumers' demands had no intertemporal feature. Scheinkman (1977) formulated a model with intertemporal maximization problems for a representative consumer and producer, but did not include capital accumulation.

[2] For example, Brock (1974) discusses the relation between rational expectations equilibrium and both deterministic and stochastic one-sector optimal growth models. The steady state behavior of the two systems differs. Brock points out that the modified golden-rule condition for the TAS Ramsey model, $\delta f'(k^\delta) = 1$, is really a form of the Dynamic Nonsubstitution Theorem, and can be connected to the labor theory of value (see Burmeister and Dobell, 1970, and Bliss, 1975, for textbook treatments). In this case the exogenous rate of impatience and the properties of the technology determine the steady state level of capital independently of the specific form of the felicity function. Brock observes that in the related stochastic model, the stationary state depends

a *mechanism* by which a decentralized economy can achieve a social optimum. This aspect of the Equivalence Principle (as well as its proof) is closely tied to the necessity of the transversality condition in the market equilibrium model. The central idea will be to match the Euler equations and transversality conditions for the decentralized equilibrium problem to the analogous equations for the optimal growth model. Hence, the economically important feature of this process is the demonstration that the competitive economy's equilibrium path obeys an appropriate transversality condition.

As we saw in Chapter 4, the transversality condition is a type of no-arbitrage condition across *infinitely* many dates; the passage from an Euler necessary condition representing the no-arbitrage property for any finite number of dates to a condition stretching over the indefinite future has always been bothersome to capital theorists. Consequently, the interpretation of the necessity of the transversality condition has been an important issue in the debates over both the meaning and the possibility of decentralization in infinite horizon capital accumulation models. This is particularly so in discussions of the Hahn problem. We will return to the interpretation of the transversality condition in our commentary at the conclusion of this chapter.

The fact that an equilibrium solves an optimization problem and vice versa also has some surprising applications to economies with various types of distortions. We will illustrate this twist off the Equivalence Principle in the next section using a model of capital income taxation.

We also present another decentralized resource allocation mechanism called a *recursive competitive equilibrium*. This concept exploits the dynamic programming possibilities that are present when private agents' utility functions are recursive. The representative household's solution to a particular stationary dynamic programming problem will be seen to be equivalent to solving the dynamic programming problem characterizing the solution to the corresponding optimal growth model. Hence, the perfect foresight solution will also be the same as the recursive competitive equilibrium in economies with a representative agent.[3]

---

on the felicity function as well as the fixed rate of impatience and the given production function. Hence, the labor theory of value implied for the one-sector deterministic case does not carry over to the stochastic case. For more on the stochastic Equivalence Principle see Brock (1982). Brock and Mirman (1972) and Mirman and Zilcha (1975) explore the one-sector stochastic modified golden rule and the properties of optimal programs with technological uncertainty.

[3] This equivalence only applies in deterministic settings.

6.2 Equivalence Principles for One-Sector Models

The simplest examples of Equivalence Principles occur in one-sector models. The basic market equilibrium model is based on the postulate of a representative household with perfect foresight about the time paths of output and factor prices. The representative household axiom is a proxy for the assumption of a large number of identical households. In equilibrium, no household will have an incentive to deviate from the behavior of the average or representative agent.[4]

There are two alternative ways to define the household's intertemporal budget constraint. The first form is sequential; current prices are used to value goods in any period and a one-period rental-interest rate for capital goods is the price which links adjacent periods. This approach is symmetric to the recursive structure of the constraints in the optimal growth model. The alternative model is formulated with present value prices; agents are allowed to borrow and lend subject to the repayment of all debts as time stretches to infinity. In this view of the budget constraint, anticipated labor income may be fully capitalized to the present.

The sequential economy is essentially Hicks's "spot economy" (1946, Chapter 10). Trading takes place in a sequence of spot markets for current goods. Households save some of their goods, which they sell to firms in the succeeding period. There is no intertemporal trade, only storage. Because capital goods depreciate completely in the next period, this spot economy is equivalent to an economy where the firms lease capital goods from the households, establishing a one-period rental-interest rate.[5]

This latter formulation of the sequential economy also recalls Arrow's (1953) security model. However, there is an important difference between the securities in this model and Arrow's securities. Our securities are all issued by the firms. Households cannot issue securities. This precludes consumption loans, whereas Arrow's model involves pure exchange, and *all* loans are consumption loans. Markets are complete in Arrow's model, and incomplete in the sequential economy.

The present value model is a form of Hicks's "futures economy" (1946, Chapter 10). There is a complete set of forward markets. All consumption and production decisions are made in the initial period using present value prices. Households can consume any of their income in any period they desire. Markets are complete.

On the face of it, these two models seem quite different. The futures

---

[4] The limitations of representative agent models are the subject of Kirman (1992).

[5] Alternatively, the firms could issue bonds, using the proceeds to purchase capital goods in the current period. They pay off the bonds out of their earnings in the next period.

economy has complete markets. Not surprisingly, the usual welfare theorems hold there (see Chapter 8). The spot economy has incomplete markets. As a result, we cannot adapt Arrow's (1953) arguments to conclude that the complete futures economy and incomplete spot economy have the same equilibria. However, in the representative household world, these two views of the budget constraint are essentially the same. When one (representative) agent wishes to borrow for consumption purposes, all other agents wish the same. There are no lenders to be found. The borrowing constraint will not bind in equilibrium. Because of this, it makes no difference whether we model the budget constraint in present value form or in sequential form as demonstrated in Sections 6.2.1 and 6.2.2.[6]

We will begin the development of the Equivalence Principles by assuming TAS utility. Throughout this section, we will assume felicity obeys $u \geq 0$, $u(0) = 0$, $u' > 0$, $u'' < 0$, and $u'(0+) = \infty$, and that the production function obeys $f \geq 0$, $f(0) = 0$, $f' > 0$, $f'' < 0$, $f'(0+) = \infty$, and $f'(\infty) < 1$. The second Inada condition on production ensures the existence of a maximum sustainable stock k^M. The more general recursive utility case is examined in Section 6.2.3 below.

6.2.1 The Perfect Foresight Equivalence Theorem

The *Perfect Foresight Equivalence Principle* applies to a model where a representative household's budget constraint is written so that there is one expenditure equals income constraint for each period. It turns out that we can extend this Equivalence Principle to a one-parameter family of closely related problems that allow a particular tax distortion to be present in the market economy. The Equivalence Principle matching the social optimum and the market equilibrium occurs for the distortion free economies. For the distorted economies, we find that a Ramsey optimal growth model with slightly altered objective characterizes the solution to the perfect foresight equilibrium model with a tax distortion.

Perfect Foresight Competitive Equilibrium
We consider a representative consumer perfect foresight model with capital taxation. The household perfectly anticipates future returns to capital and labor. Capital income is taxed at a constant rate.[7] Labor is supplied inelastically. This simplifies the analysis and isolates the effects of the capital tax. The tax revenue is returned to consumers in a lump sum paid during each period. In this way, the analysis is conducted for a compensated tax.

---

[6] The form of the budget constraint does make a difference if there is no representative agent. We discuss this further in Section 6.4.

[7] Strictly speaking, the tax is placed on capital income and wealth.

The household maximizes lifetime utility determined by a TAS utility representation. The utility discount factor is a given constant. The household accumulates capital and provides for consumption at each time from disposable income derived by the rental of capital, supply of labor, and government transfer payments. Since the current price of capital is always one, there are no capital gains to include in current income.

The household's capital is required to be non-negative. This amounts to a borrowing constraint. Households cannot borrow against future wage income. Rather than being a market imperfection, some constraint of this nature is required. Without such a constraint, the household's problem would have no solution. It would possible for individuals to live on their dreams, to engage in a Ponzi scheme–an unreversed arbitrage where current consumption is financed by borrowing, and the debt is perpetually rolled over. The constraint rules out these schemes, and, in equilibrium, does not otherwise bind our representative agents.

A perfect foresight equilibrium rules when the representative household's planned accumulation program agrees with static profit maximization in the production sector. The production sector's decision is myopic and uses the pre-tax return to capital to calculate desired capital demand at each time. As there are no capital gains in this one-sector model, capital income coincides with total rental income. The capital income tax places a wedge between the unit gross and net returns to capital. This model is a discrete time variant of Chamley's (1981) perfect foresight capital taxation model.

θ-Perfect Foresight Competitive Equilibrium. Given θ with $0 \leq \theta < 1$, a θ-perfect foresight competitive equilibrium (θ-PFCE) is a sequence of 6-tuples $\{r_t, R_t, g_t, w_t, c_t, k_t\}_{t=1}^{\infty}$ obeying:

(1) $r_t = (1 - \theta)R_t$;
(2) $R_t = f'(k_{t-1})$;
(3) $w_t = f(k_{t-1}) - R_t k_{t-1}$;
(4) $g_t = \theta R_t k_{t-1}$;
(5) $\{c_t, k_t\}$ maximizes $\sum_{t=1}^{\infty} \delta^{t-1} u(c_t)$ such that $c_t + k_t = w_t + g_t + r_t k_{t-1}$ with $k_0 = k$.

The first condition gives the net return to capital r_t in terms of the gross return R_t and tax rate θ. The second condition is that firms maximize profits at each time t. The third defines wages w_t. Implicitly, we assume that the household inelastically supplies one unit of labor and the production function f is derived from a constant returns to scale production function F by $f(k) = F(k, 1)$. The fourth condition defines government revenues. These are transferred back to the consumer in lump-sum fashion. The final condition is that the representative consumer maximizes utility given his budget constraint.

A 0-PFCE corresponds to the no-distortion case and is abbreviated as PFCE. Thus, the θ-PFCE concept defines a one-parameter class of equilibria defined for $\theta \in [0, 1)$, with the extreme case $\theta = 0$ corresponding to an undistorted market equilibrium.

In a θ-PFCE the sequence $\{r_t, R_t, g_t, w_t\}$ is self-justifying: the representative household's optimal program $\{c_t, k_t\}$ and the profit condition (2) can be combined with the wage distribution equation (3), the government's balanced budget condition (4), and the household's budget constraint in condition (5) to obtain for each time t,

$$c_t + k_t = f(k_{t-1}).$$

Thus, planned supply of capital equals planned demand for capital and consumption plus capital for next period's production equals total output at each time. The definition of θ-PFCE anticipates the interiority of equilibrium programs (e.g., condition (2) since the Inada conditions apply to u and f) and reflects the underlying constant returns to scale technology.

The PFCE Equivalence Principle

The analysis of a perfect foresight competitive equilibrium is greatly facilitated by noting that any θ-PFCE outcome corresponds formally to the solution that would result from a central planner optimizing a particular welfare function. The central planning problem takes the form of a one-sector Ramsey optimal growth model where the planner's preferences are represented by a TAS utility function with discount factor $\delta(1 - \theta)$ and felicity u. Hence, the planner and household discount future utilities by different factors but share a common felicity function. This implies that the planner's pure rate of time preference exceeds the household's pure rate of time preference by a factor reflecting the tax rate. In the case where there is no tax distortion, the discount factors of the planner and household agree.

The Equivalence Principle will tell us that for an undistorted economy, the market equilibrium outcome is the same as the central planner's solution and is a Pareto optimum. In the case of a positive tax distortion, the equilibrium profile is not a Pareto optimum when the household's utility function is used as the welfare criterion. Hence, there is a welfare loss when capital is taxed. We emphasize that solving the planner's optimization problem in the case of a capital tax is an auxiliary problem whose solution enables us to solve the equilibrium problem by reducing it to a single optimization problem of the familiar Ramsey variety.[8]

---

[8] See Kehoe, Levine, and Romer (1992) for a broader exploration of dynamic models with distortions. They show how many such models can be studied using a suitably designed optimization problem with side conditions. Stokey and Lucas (1989, Chapter

Equivalence Theorem (θ-PFCE). *The sequence $\{r_t, R_t, g_t, w_t, c_t, k_t\}_{t=1}^{\infty}$ is a θ-PFCE if and only if $\{c_t, k_t\}$ maximizes $\sum_{t=1}^{\infty}[\delta(1-\theta)]^{t-1}u(c_t)$ (the θ-social welfare function) such that $c_t + k_t = f(k_{t-1})$ and $c_1 + k_1 = f(k)$.*

Proof. Since $w_t + g_t + r_t k_{t-1} = f(k_{t-1})$ by (1)–(4), it is enough to compare the Euler and transversality conditions. The Euler equations for the household's problem are $u'(c_t) = \delta r_t u'(c_{t+1})$. Using conditions (1) and (2), we see that this is equivalent to $u'(c_t) = \delta(1-\theta)f'(k_t)u'(c_{t+1})$ which are the Euler equations for the θ-social welfare function.

The transversality condition for the household is $\delta^t u'(c_t)k_t \to 0$.[9] As $\delta \geq \delta(1-\theta)$, this implies $[\delta(1-\theta)]^t u'(c_t)k_t \to 0$ which is the transversality condition for θ-social welfare maximization. Conversely, if c_t and k_t maximize θ-social welfare, c_t and k_t converge to non-zero steady-state values. This establishes the transversality condition for the household.   □

This equivalence immediately yields information about the equilibrium. We know optimal paths for the θ-social welfare function exist, are unique, and are monotonic. By the Equivalence Theorem, equilibrium paths exist, are unique, and are monotonic. If $\theta = 0$, then a market equilibrium is a Pareto optimum and vice versa. If $\theta > 0$, there is a welfare loss since the wrong social welfare function is being maximized. (The Euler equations for $\theta = 0$ are clearly violated.) In the long run, there is complete shifting of the tax burden as $\delta r = 1$ in the steady state. The long-run net return to capital is unaffected by taxation.

We can use this Equivalence Principle to further analyze the effect of unanticipated changes in the tax rate. Let $k(\theta)$ denote the steady-state level of capital, given tax rate θ. Thus $\delta(1-\theta)f'(k(\theta)) = 1$, so $dk/d\theta = f'/[(1-\theta)f''] < 0$ and $dR/d\theta = f''(k(\theta))(dk/d\theta) > 0$. The effect of increases in θ on steady-state government revenues is uncertain. We will see in the next chapter how easily we can analyze the effect of changes in θ on the dynamic equilibrium path by using the comparative dynamic analysis developed there.

6.2.2 The Fisher Equivalence Theorem

The microeconomic foundation for the present value investment criterion is the *Fisher Separation Principle*. This principle derives from Fisher's "second approximation," which portrays the intertemporal consumption–investment decision of agents as a two-stage process.[10] In the first stage,

---

18) and Coleman (1991) discuss fixed point or *direct* techniques for analyzing distorted economies in cases where the *indirect* method adopted by us fails.

[9] We will show this condition holds for perfect foresight equilibria more generally for the broader class of recursive utility functions in Section 6.2.3 below.

[10] See Fisher (1907; 1930) for the original development of this idea and Hirshleifer (1970) for a more contemporary viewpoint.

investment opportunities are exploited to realize a maximum value of initial wealth. The solution to the first stage problem is found by maximizing the net present value over all feasible projects. Given competitive prices (and implicit discount rates), all agents whose intertemporal preference relations satisfy a mild nonsatiation requirement will be led to choose the same wealth maximizing investment projects. In the second stage, those agents take their maximized wealth and access perfect capital markets to borrow and lend in order to obtain the most preferred lifetime consumption pattern.

The Fisher competitive equilibrium is the infinite horizon analogue of the Fisher Separation Principle. There is a single lifetime household budget constraint; the savings–investment decision is separated from the consumption decision. Consumers maximize utility given their maximized wealth obtained as residual claimants to the discounted profit streams of firms. Those firms in turn maximize the discounted sum of their profits. Letting $R = \{r_t\}$ be the sequence of interest rates and $q_t = \prod_{\tau=1}^{t}(1+r_\tau)^{-1}$ be the discounted price of time t consumption, define the profit function by $\pi(k, R) = \max\{\sum_{t=1}^{\infty} q_t[f(k_{t-1}) - (1 + r_t)k_{t-1}] : k_0 = k\}$.[11]

Fisher Competitive Equilibrium. A sequence $\{r_t, c_t, k_t\}_{t=1}^{\infty}$ forms a Fisher competitive equilibrium (FCE) if:

(1) $\pi(k, R) = \sum_{t=1}^{\infty} q_t[f(k_{t-1}) - (1 + r_t)k_{t-1}]$ where $k_0 = k$;
(2) Consumers maximize $\sum_{t=1}^{\infty} \delta^{t-1}u(c_t)$ subject to the budget constraint $\sum_{t=1}^{\infty} q_t c_t = \pi(k, R) + k$;
(3) The market clearing condition $c_t = f(k_{t-1}) - k_t$ holds.

Equivalence Theorem (FCE). *The sequence $\{r_t, c_t, k_t\}_{t=1}^{\infty}$ is an FCE if and only if $\{c_t, k_t\}$ maximizes $\sum_{t=1}^{\infty} \delta^{t-1}u(c_t)$ such that $c_t + k_t = f(k_{t-1})$ with $k_0 = k$.*

Proof. The consumer's Euler equation is $u'(c_t) = (\delta q_t/q_{t+1})u'(c_{t+1}) = \delta(1 + r_{t+1})u'(c_{t+1})$. Using the firm's first-order condition, this becomes $u'(c_t) = \delta f'(k_t)u'(c_{t+1})$, which is the Euler equation for maximizing welfare.

As before, it now suffices to consider the transversality condition. Consider a Fisher competitive equilibrium. For all T, it obeys

$$\sum_{t=1}^{T} q_t c_t = \sum_{t=1}^{T} q_t[f(k_{t-1}) - k_t]$$

$$= k - q_T k_T + \sum_{t=1}^{T} q_t[f(k_{t-1}) - (1 + r_t)k_{t-1}].$$

[11] In the Fisher model we are using r_t to be an interest rate although we used the same symbol to stand for the interest factor in the last subsection.

Letting $T \to \infty$ and using (1) and the constraint from the consumer's problem shows $q_t k_t \to 0$. Now $q_{t+1}/q_t = \delta u'(c_{t+1})/u'(c_t)$. Taking the product from $t = 1$ to T gives $q_{T+1}/q_1 = \delta^T u'(c_{T+1})/u'(c_1)$. Multiplying by k_{T+1} and letting $T \to \infty$ yields the transversality condition for the social welfare problem. Thus any Fisher competitive equilibrium maximizes social welfare.

Conversely, the transversality condition for the social welfare problem shows $q_t k_t = q_1 \delta^t u'(c_t) k_t / u'(c_1) \to 0$. For any alternative path $\mathbf{x}$ such that $\sum_{t=1}^{\infty} q_t x_t = \pi(k, R) + k$, $\delta^{t-1}[u(c_t) - u(x_t)] \geq \delta^{t-1} u'(c_t)(c_t - x_t)$. Again using the fact that $\delta^t u'(c_t) = q_t[u'(c_1)/q_1]$ shows $\delta^{t-1}[u(c_t) - u(x_t)] \geq [u'(c_1)/\delta q_1] q_t (c_t - x_t)$. Summing over t from 1 to T and letting $T \to \infty$, we get, using $c_t = f(k_{t-1}) - k_t$ as above, $\sum_{t=1}^{\infty} \delta^{t-1}[u(c_t) - u(x_t)] \geq -\lim_{t \to \infty} (q_t k_t)(u'(c_1)/\delta q_1) = 0$. Thus c_t solves the consumer's problem. $\square$

Combining the θ-PFCE Equivalence Theorem for $\theta = 0$ and the FCE Equivalence Theorem yields the following observation.

Corollary 1. *The sequence* $\{r_t, c_t, k_t\}_{t=1}^{\infty}$ *is an FCE if and only if the sequence* $\{r_t^*, R_t^*, g_t^*, w_t^*, c_t, k_t\}_{t=1}^{\infty}$ *is a PFCE where* $R_t^* = r_t^*$, $r_t^* = r_t + 1$, $g_t^* = 0$, *and* $w_t^* = f(k_{t-1}) - (1 + r_t)k_{t-1}$ *for all* t.

6.2.3 The Equivalence Theorem and Transversality

The Equivalence Theorems demonstrated in the previous two sections easily generalize to include a class of recursive utility functions. The appropriate collection of recursive utility functions will be the ones that satisfy the condition

$$\lim_{t \to \infty} \delta^{t-1} U(S^t \mathbf{c}) = 0$$

for all consumption programs satisfying the representative household's budget constraints. This condition is nothing more than the *transversality condition* from Section 4.6. In this section we will establish that this transversality condition holds for the PFCE paths of one-sector models obeying all of the technology conditions applicable to the previous Equivalence Theorems.[12]

The following assumptions will be maintained throughout this section. The recursive utility function U obeys $U(\mathbf{0}) = 0$ and is concave and φ-bounded on $\ell_+^\infty(\beta)$ for some φ with $\|\varphi \circ S\|_\varphi < 1/\delta$. Under these conditions, the household's transversality condition holds for any $\mathbf{c} \in \ell_+^\infty(\beta)$. Here we choose the weight β to contain all feasible programs for the opti-

---

[12] Of course the Inada condition for recursive utility must be used now as stated in Section 4.6.1.

mal growth model

$$\max U(\mathbf{c})$$
$$\text{s.t. } c_t + x_t \leq f(x_{t-1}),$$
$$c_t \geq 0, \ x_t \geq 0, \text{ and } x_0 \leq k,$$

where k is the starting capital stock and f is the one-sector production function. The maximum sustainable stock is k^M and it is assumed to be positive. We suppose that there is no capital tax and notice that any equilibrium program for the PFCE problem must be a feasible path in the corresponding optimal growth model. Hence, we can restrict our attention to equilibrium consumption sequences lying in $\ell_+^\infty(\beta)$. In particular, we note that the equilibrium sequence of wages must be in that set and therefore

$$\lim_{t \to \infty} \delta^{t-1} U(S^t \mathbf{w}) = 0,$$

implying

$$\lim_{t \to \infty} \delta^{t-1}[U(S^t \mathbf{c}) - U(S^t \mathbf{w})] = 0 \tag{1}$$

for any PFCE consumption stream.

Given the equilibrium sequences of rental and wage rates r_t and w_t, respectively, define a sequence of optimal return functions $J_t : [0, k^M] \to \mathbb{R}_+$ by setting

$$J_t(y_t') = \sup W(c_t', U(S^t \mathbf{c}'))$$

by choice of non-negative sequences $\mathbf{c}'$ and $\mathbf{x}'$ subject to

$$c_t' + x_t' = y_t'$$
$$c_s' + x_s' = w_s' + (1 + r_s)x_{s-1}', \text{ for } s \geq t,$$

where W is the aggregator corresponding to U. Note that at time t the wage and rental as well as the previous period's capital are fixed, so y_t' is determined from those data. The last period's capital stock may differ from that period's stock realized in the given PFCE. Clearly $J_t(0) \geq 0$ and J_t is non-decreasing in y_t'; thus $J_t \geq 0$. By mimicking the arguments in Chapter 4, we claim without further proof that J_t is a concave function on $[0, k^M]$, has a finite value at y_t corresponding to the PFCE output level at time t, and is C^1 on $(0, k^M)$. The derivative of J_t at the PFCE y_t has the envelope property

$$J_t'(y_t) = W_1(c_t, U(S^t \mathbf{c})).$$

Since J_t is concave, we have the inequality

$$
\begin{aligned}
J_t(y_t) - J_t(0) &\geq J_t'(y_t)y_t \\
&\geq W_1(c_t, U(S^t\mathbf{c}))f(x_{t-1}) \qquad (2) \\
&\geq W_1(c_t, U(S^t\mathbf{c}))x_t
\end{aligned}
$$

by $y_t = f(x_{t-1}) \geq x_t$ in a PFCE. But

$$
U_t(\mathbf{c}) = W_2(c_1, U(S\mathbf{c})) \cdots W_2(c_{t-1}, U(S^{t-1}\mathbf{c}))W_1(c_t, U(S^t\mathbf{c})).
$$

Let $\delta = \max\{W_2(c_i, U(S^i\mathbf{c})) : 1 \leq i \leq t - 1\}$; the properties of W imply that $0 < \delta < 1$. Thus $U_t(\mathbf{c}) \leq \delta^{t-1}W_1(c_t, U(S^t\mathbf{c}))$. Multiplying (2) through by δ^{t-1}, using the fact that $x_t \geq 0$, and simplifying implies

$$
\delta^{t-1}[J_t(y_t) - J_t(0)] \geq U_t(\mathbf{c})x_t \geq 0.
$$

But $J_t(y_t) = U(S^t\mathbf{c})$ and $J_t(0) \geq U(S^t\mathbf{w})$, hence

$$
\delta^{t-1}[U(S^t\mathbf{c}) - U(S^t\mathbf{w})] \geq U_t(\mathbf{c})x_t \geq 0. \qquad (3)
$$

Letting $t \to \infty$, (1) and (3) imply that $U_t(\mathbf{c})x_t \to 0$, which is the household's transversality condition.

Notice the crucial role played by the non-negativity constraint. Without it, we could not use the above squeezing argument. The borrowing constraint is the key to showing transversality. It enters the argument twice, first in showing the maximization problem is well-posed, and second in the squeezing argument. Although borrowing constraints are usually thought of as market imperfections, this borrowing constraint actually *perfects* the market structure of the PFCE.

The Inada condition implies the household will never desire zero consumption, hence the Euler conditions will be equalities in both the household and central planner's problems. The proof of the Equivalence Principle proceeds by matching the Euler or no-arbitrage and transversality conditions of the optimality and equilibrium models as before. In the equilibrium model the transversality condition need only be a valid necessary condition in a perfect foresight equilibrium. Put differently, the household sector's transversality condition may not be valid for an *arbitrary* profile of wages and rentals. The matching of the first-order conditions in the two frameworks proves the Equivalence Principle because those conditions are *complete characterizations* of the agents' problems in the respective frameworks. The necessity of the transversality condition in the PFCE setting is also an extreme form of the efficient markets' hypothesis since it may be interpreted as saying that the present discounted price of a unit of capital is equal to the discounted sum of the stream of future rental rates—just transpose the heuristic reasoning for the transversality condition given in Chapter 4 into the PFCE setup.

The same basic reasoning can also be used to link the Fisher competitive equilibrium and the PFCE solution. Hence, both the Fisher and PFCE Equivalence Principles carry over to the recursive utility case.

Equivalence Theorem. *The sequence* $\{r_t, w_t, c_t, k_t\}_{t=1}^{\infty}$ *is a PFCE (FCE with* $w_t = f(k_{t-1}) - (1 + r_t)k_{t-1}$*) if and only if* $\{c_t, k_t\}$ *maximizes* $U(\mathbf{c})$ *such that* $c_t + k_t = f(k_{t-1})$ *with* $k_0 = k$, $c_t \geq 0$, *and* $k_t \geq 0$.

The conditions of the theorem are only *sufficient* for the Equivalence Principle to obtain. The case of TAS utility with log felicity and Cobb-Douglas production can be shown to lead to an Equivalence Theorem by using the symmetry technique found in Section 5.1.

The properties of a PFCE may now be inferred from the analogous properties exhibited by the corresponding Ramsey optimum. If the optimal capital sequence is monotone, then the equilibrium capital stock is too.[13] If capital is increasing along the optimum, then the rental rate is falling and the wage is rising. The orthodox vision of capital accumulation obtains. Capital income is increasing along the optimum-equilibrium path whenever the neoclassical production function F underlying f has an elasticity of substitution greater than or equal to unity. In particular, capital income increases as capital increases if production is Cobb-Douglas. Through the Equivalence Principle, the Ramsey optimization model leads to a general theory of the *functional distribution of income*.

6.2.4 Recursive Competitive Equilibrium and Equivalence

Real business cycle research has increasingly focused on decentralized dynamic programming solutions to the planner's problem. Prescott and Mehra (1980) introduced a decentralized mechanism that highlights the recursive structure of production and utility. This concept, *stationary recursive competitive equilibrium (RCE)*, is yet another way to implement an optimal solution in the one-sector model. Prescott and Mehra used a stochastic one-sector model with an expected discounted utility objective. We illustrate their idea in the deterministic one-sector framework, but adapt it to accommodate a recursive utility objective.[14]

The representative producers and households continue to be decision makers just as in the PFCE setup. However, the representative household's decision problem is recast as a *dynamic programming problem*. This formulation of the equilibrium model emphasizes the capacity of agents

---

[13] A sufficient condition for the optimal capital sequence to be monotone is found in Chapter 5's Monotonicity Theorem.

[14] The deterministic TAS case can be found in Cooley and Prescott (1995). We follow their schema in our formulation of the RCE model.

to make decisions at each time instead of once and for all time at the beginning of the horizon. The recursive structure of the representative household's utility function combined with a stationary technological environment will imply that the RCE solution is time consistent: the representative household's decision rule is independent of calendar time and will always be the same decision given its state variables. This household distinguishes between its capital stock, k, which it controls, and the economy-wide or aggregate capital stock, K, which it takes as given. Of course one of the equilibrium conditions is $k = K$. We use the convention that lower-case letters denote variables under the control of individual decision making units while upper-case letters are reserved for the corresponding aggregate variables.

The representative household solves a stationary dynamic programming problem of the type discussed in Chapter 4 at each stage. The state variables are (k, K). Let $j(k, K)$ be the household's value function. The household also assumes that firms will maximize myopic profits, so it assumes that

$$1 + r(K) = f'(K)$$
$$w(K) = f(K) - f'(K)K$$

will be the market rental factor and wage rate, respectively. This household also takes as given a function $X(K)$ which tells it how the economy's capital stock evolves. We assume capital does not depreciate in this section, so the evolution of the aggregate capital stock follows

$$K' = K + X(K),$$

and the household's capital stock evolves according to the transition rule

$$k' = k + x,$$

where x is the household's investment in capital goods and primes denote next-period values of the state variables. The household's decision variables are its consumption, c, and investment, x. The Bellman equation for its dynamic programming problem is

$$j(k, K) = \sup_{c, x \geq 0} \{W(c, j(k', K'))\}$$
$$\text{s.t. } c + x \leq r(K)k + w(K),$$
$$k' = k + x,$$
$$K' = K + X(K),$$

where W is the household's aggregator function.

Let $d(k, K)$ be the policy function that solves the household's dynamic programming problem. Since all the households in this economy are assumed to be alike, it must be the case that $d(k, K) = D(K)$, where $D(K)$ is the per capita policy function for the planner's dynamic programming problem.

Recursive Competitive Equilibrium. A recursive competitive equilibrium is a value function, $j\colon \mathbb{R}^2_+ \to \mathbb{R}$, and a policy function, $d\colon \mathbb{R}^2_+ \to \mathbb{R}_+$, which gives decisions $c(k, K)$, $x(k, K)$ for the representative household; an aggregate per capita policy function for the planner's problem, $D\colon \mathbb{R}_+ \to \mathbb{R}_+$, which gives aggregate decisions $C(K)$ and $X(K)$; and factor price functions $1 + r(K)$ and $w(K)$ such that:

(1) The functions $c(k, K)$ and $x(k, K)$ solve the household's dynamic programming problem given the value function $j(k, K)$, the aggregate investment function $X(K)$, and the factor price functions $1 + r(K)$ and $w(K)$;

(2) The factor price functions $1 + r(K)$ and $w(K)$ satisfy the profit maximization conditions for an interior solution;

(3) Individual and aggregate decisions are consistent: $d(k, K) = D(K)$ for all K;

(4) The aggregate resource constraint holds: $C(K) + X(K) = f(K)$.

If (j, d, D, r, w) is a recursive competitive equilibrium, then it is clear that $j(k, K)$ coincides with the planner's value function $J(K)$ and $D(K)$ is that problem's policy function. Therefore, every RCE solves the planner's problem and vice versa (provided the transversality condition holds in the RCE). Moreover, the PFCE, FCE, and RCE solutions agree.

RCE Equivalence Principle. *The functions (j, d, D, r, w) constitute a recursive competitive equilibrium if and only if the sequence $\{c_t, k_t\}_{t=1}^{\infty}$ defined by $c_t = f(k_{t-1}) - k_t$ and $k_t - k_{t-1} = d(k_{t-1}, K_{t-1})$, $K_t \equiv k_t$ for all t with $K_0 = k_0 = k$, maximizes $W(c_1, U(Sc))$ subject to $c_t + k_t \le f(k_{t-1})$, $c_t, k_t \ge 0$, and $k_0 = k$.*

The main interest in the RCE solution arises in its capacity to link a decentralized equilibrium to the solution of a dynamic programming problem in stochastic decentralized economies. Moreover, the RCE formulation appears to offer some advantages in treating stochastic dynamic economies with money and tax distortions.[15]

---

[15] Hansen and Prescott (1995) and Danthine and Donaldson (1995) address these points. The stochastic analogue of a θ-PFCE is presented in the latter paper along with other models with distortions that can be addressed using the RCE solution concept.

6.3 Multisector Equivalence Principles

The Equivalence Principle for one-sector models has a natural extension to the multisector case. We focus here on the two-sector extension since it embodies the central differences with the one-sector model. The basic strategy will remain the same: we will match the no-arbitrage conditions and the transversality conditions for equilibrium and central planning problems.

6.3.1 The Portfolio Equilibrium Condition

The major difference between one-sector and multisector perfect foresight equilibrium models lies in the form taken by the no-arbitrage condition. This is easily illustrated for a two-sector model. Suppose there are two sectors consisting of a consumption goods sector and a capital goods sector. The capital and consumption goods are distinct commodities. Suppose that i_{t+1} is the one-period interest rate measured in units of a numéraire commodity, r_{t+1} is the rental rate on a unit of capital measured in the numéraire's units, and q_{t+1} is the unit purchase price for a unit of capital measured in the numéraire's units. We suppose that the purchase of a unit of capital at time t entitles its owner to receive the rental flows from the next period on as long as the unit remains in service. Suppose further for simplicity that capital does not depreciate. One requirement for a perfect foresight equilibrium is that there are no one-period reversed arbitrage opportunities. Suppose the model follows an equilibrium path with those prices and at time t the household decision maker acquires another unit of capital. This costs this household q_t units of the numéraire. The opportunity cost of this action in units of the numéraire is $i_{t+1}q_t$, the interest charge that could have been otherwise earned. To reverse this capital acquisition at time $t+1$ the household will sell that unit of capital for q_{t+1} units of the numéraire. This gives a capital gain (loss) equal to $q_{t+1} - q_t$. The household also gets to keep the one-period rental, r_{t+1}. This one-period reversed arbitrage is unprofitable if the marginal revenue equals the marginal cost reckoned in units of the numéraire. That is

$$i_{t+1}q_t = r_{t+1} + q_{t+1} - q_t. \tag{4}$$

Equation (4) reflects the absence of arbitrage opportunities in a perfect foresight competitive equilibrium. It is also called the *portfolio equilibrium condition* because it expresses the absence of arbitrage opportunities in the manner in which the agent's wealth is held.[16] We can rearrange this

---

[16] Some capital theorists refer to (4) as the *perfect foresight equation*.

equation to get

$$i_{t+1} = \frac{r_{t+1}}{q_t} + \frac{q_{t+1} - q_t}{q_t},\tag{5}$$

which says that the one-period interest rate, i_{t+1}, equals the capital good's *own rate of return*, r_{t+1}/q_t, plus the *capital gain yield*, $(q_{t+1} - q_t)/q_t$.

Notice for the one-sector model that $q_t = 1$. This is the price of the consumption good in units of the numéraire commodity (chosen to be current consumption) since the capital and consumption goods are identical. Hence, there is no capital gain yield in that case and we get

$$i_{t+1} = r_{t+1}.$$

The interest rate equals the rental rate for capital goods. Thus, even if there is a single capital good, the portfolio equilibrium condition differs when the one-sector model is compared to the two-sector model.

In models with several distinct capital goods the portfolio equilibrium condition (5) applies to each capital good separately. If there are m types of distinct capital goods, then portfolio equilibrium is expressed by the equation:

$$i_{t+1} = \frac{r_{t+1}^i}{q_t^i} + \frac{q_{t+1}^i - q_t^i}{q_t^i}, \text{ for } i = 1, \ldots, m,\tag{6}$$

where the superscript labels the rental and prices for capital good of type i. Equation (6) tells us that at each time, a capital asset's rate of return (own rate of return plus capital gain yield) must equal the economy's one-period interest rate. With many capital goods households have a variety of options for holding their wealth. The rates of return on any portfolio of capital assets must be equalized or there will be a one-period reversed arbitrage opportunity.[17] Hence, equation (6) is the condition expressing the absence of such arbitrage opportunities.

The major pricing differences between one-sector models and multisector models concern the form of the portfolio equilibrium condition.[18] Since the major difference already shows up in the two-sector case, we focus our presentation of the multisector Equivalence Principle on that simpler model.

6.3.2 The Two-Sector Equivalence Theorem

The two-sector perfect foresight equilibrium model with an infinitely lived representative agent is specified by a *household sector*, a *consumption*

---

[17] This equilibrium condition plays an important role in Walras's (1954, pp. 268–269) theory of capital formation and credit.

[18] The dimension of the state space is also important. However, this is less of an issue in the context of the Hahn problem since the basic difficulty he raised occurs in a two-sector model with an aggregate capital stock.

goods sector, and a *capital goods sector*. The latter two sectors constitute the *production sector*.

The Household Sector

In the PFCE, the representative household maximizes a recursive utility function $U(\mathbf{c}) = W(c_1, U(S\mathbf{c}))$ subject to a sequences of budget constraints, one for each period:

$$c_t + q_t[k_t - (1 - \mu)k_{t-1}] = r_t k_{t-1} + w_t, \text{ for } t = 1, 2, \ldots,$$

where q_t is the current price of capital in units of consumption at time t, r_t is the one-period rental price of capital at time t in terms of current consumption, w_t is the current wage rate, and μ, $0 \leq \mu \leq 1$, is the depreciation rate.[19] Further, the household's choices of capital and consumption must be non-negative at each time and $k_0 = k$ must hold, where k is the household's endowment of the capital good. Once again, the non-negativity restriction on the household's capital stock is interpreted as a borrowing constraint.

The household's maximization problem has the first-order condition

$$\frac{U_t}{U_{t+1}} = \frac{1}{q_t}[r_{t+1} + q_{t+1}(1 - \mu)]$$

for an interior solution. The ratio U_t/U_{t+1} defines an *implicit interest factor* for the one-period consumption goods loaned at time t and repaid at time $t+1$. By identifying $1 + i_{t+1} = U_t/U_{t+1}$, the household's first-order condition is readily seen to be the portfolio equilibrium condition.

The Fisher competitive equilibrium problem corresponding to this perfect foresight setup recasts the budget constraint in the form

$$\sum_{t=1}^{\infty} \left(\prod_{s=1}^{t} \frac{1}{(1 + i_s)} \right) c_t \leq W,$$

where i_s is the one-period interest rate as before, and W is the household's wealth, consisting of its initial capital stock and the present value of future labor income. In this framework, the present value price of a unit of consumption delivered at t is $\prod_{s=1}^{t}(1 + i_s)^{-1}$. Hence, the present value of a unit of capital at t is $\left(\prod_{s=1}^{t}(1 + i_s)^{-1}\right)q_t$ and $\left(\prod_{s=1}^{t}(1 + i_s)^{-1}\right)w_t$ is the discounted wage paid at t. In the sequel, we focus on the perfect foresight model and leave the development of the analogous Fisher model to the reader.

---

[19] Capital goods are allowed to depreciate at an exponential rate.

The Production Sector

The production sector is composed of the consumption goods industry and the capital goods industry. The output of each sector utilizes capital and labor inputs according to neoclassical production functions. Producers are assumed to maximize profits at each time t given output and factor prices. We assume that the consumption at time t is the numéraire (we use a current value price system) and q_t is the purchase price of capital at time t. The current rental and wage rates are given by r_t and w_t respectively. As with the one-sector model, capital produces output with a one-period lag.

The consumption goods sector's production function is given by $y_t^0 = F^0(k_{t-1}^0, \ell_t^0)$, where k_{t-1}^0 is the capital input at time $t - 1$ that is used to produce consumption goods at time t, ℓ_t^0 is the labor input utilized during period t by this sector, and y_t^0 is the output of consumption goods at time t.[20] This sector's profit maximizing problem is specified for each time t as the following program:

$$\max \; y_t^0 - r_t k_{t-1}^0 - w_t \ell_t^0$$
$$\text{s.t. } y_t^0 \leq F^0(k_{t-1}^0, \ell_t^0),$$
$$k_{t-1}^0, \ell_t^0 \geq 0.$$

The household sector is the residual claimant on this sector's profit. However, under the constant returns to scale assumption that will govern production in this sector, profits will always be zero.

The capital goods sector's production function is $y_t^1 = F^1(k_{t-1}^1, \ell_t^1)$, where k_{t-1}^1 is the capital input at time $t - 1$ that is used to produce capital goods at time t, ℓ_t^1 is the labor input utilized during period t by this sector, and y_t^1 is the output of capital goods at time t. This sector's profit maximizing problem is specified for each time t as the following program:

$$\max \; q_t y_t^1 - r_t k_{t-1}^1 - w_t \ell_t^1$$
$$\text{s.t. } y_t^1 \leq F^1(k_{t-1}^1, \ell_t^1),$$
$$k_{t-1}^1, \ell_t^1 \geq 0.$$

The household sector is also the residual claimant on this sector's profit. As before, the constant returns to scale assumption means that profits will always be zero.

All intertemporal decisions are undertaken in the household sector. This implies production decisions need only maximize one-period profits

---

[20] The use of (k, y) rather than (a, b), as in previous chapters, is intended to emphasize that there is only one capital good.

at each time. For example, let π_t^0 denote the consumption goods sector profits at time t (measured using current consumption as the numéraire). Suppose the one-period interest rate is i_t and let $\prod_{s=1}^{t}(1+i_s)^{-1}$ denote the present value of a unit of consumption at time t. This sector's present value objective is $\sum_{t=1}^{\infty} \left(\prod_{s=1}^{t}(1+i_s)^{-1} \right) \pi_t^0$ where $\pi_t^0 = F^0(k_{t-1}^0, \ell_t^0) - r_t k_{t-1}^0 - w_t \ell_t^0$. We observe that π_t^0 depends only on k_{t-1}^0 and ℓ_t^0. Hence, profits attained at time t depend only on the decisions taken at time t and on nothing else. Therefore, maximization of discounted profits is equivalent to static or periodwise optimization at each time.

We assume that each production function is neoclassical, as defined in Example 4.7. Moreover, we assume that capital is *essential* for production of either sector's goods, that is $F^i(0, \ell_t^i) = 0$. We also assume there is a maximum sustainable stock in the capital goods sector when that sector absorbs the entire labor supply. This means there is a $k^M > 0$ such that $F^1(k, 1) < \mu k$ for all $k > k^M$ and $F^1(k, 1) > \mu k$ for all $k < k^M$. It also means we are taking $\mu > 0$ in the sequel. Moreover, this condition implies that the path of pure accumulation is bounded and therefore any feasible program starting from the given initial capital stocks must be bounded too.

The Transformation Function

We can also recast the production sector's problem in terms of the reduced-form model covered in Chapter 4. To this end we recall that the *transformation function* $\mathcal{T}(k, y)$ is given by:

$$\mathcal{T}(k, y) = \max F^0(k^0, \ell^0)$$
$$\text{s.t. } F^1(k^1, \ell^1) \geq y$$
$$k^0 + k^1 \leq k, \quad \ell^0 + \ell^1 \leq 1,$$

where all choice variables are to be non-negative. The transformation function records the maximum output of the consumption goods sector for a given level of capital (that can be allocated across the two sectors) and for a given output target assigned to the capital goods producing sector.

The transformation function can be shown to inherit many of the properties of the underlying sectoral production functions. It is concave in (k, y), increasing in k for each y, and decreasing in y for each k. We let $D \subseteq \mathbb{R}_+ \times \mathbb{R}_+$ be the domain of $\mathcal{T}$. It is a closed convex set with $(0, 0)$ as one element. Under suitable conditions, it can also be shown that $\mathcal{T}$ is C^2 on the interior of its domain.

The transformation function may be used to replace the pair of profit maximizing problems faced by the consumption and capital goods sectors by a single profit maximization problem. All static allocations of capital and labor between sectors are subsumed in the maximizing behavior stored in the transformation function. All intertemporal decisions are taken by the household in this model. Therefore, given perfect input and output markets, the production sector need only solve a *static* optimization problem at each date. The specific problem is to choose the capital input level and output of new capital goods that maximize one-period profit, given the current price for investment goods, q_t, and the current rental rate for capital goods, r_t. The specific optimization problem at time t can be stated as:

$$\max \mathcal{T}(k_{t-1}, y_t) + q_t y_t - r_t k_{t-1},$$

where y_t is the output of new investment goods and k_{t-1} is the total capital available at the end of period $t-1$ for producing output at time t. In equilibrium, the balance condition $y_t = k_t - (1 - \mu)k_{t-1}$ must hold. Assuming this static profit maximization problem has an interior solution, we find that

$$r_t = \mathcal{T}_1(k_{t-1}, y_t)$$
$$q_t = -\mathcal{T}_2(k_{t-2}, y_t),$$

where $\mathcal{T}_1(k, y) = \partial \mathcal{T}(k, y)/\partial k$ and $\mathcal{T}_2(k, y) = \partial \mathcal{T}(k, y)/\partial y$. These form the first-order conditions. The concavity of the transformation function implies these conditions are also sufficient to solve this myopic optimization problem.

Perfect Foresight Equilibrium

The definition of a perfect foresight competitive equilibrium for the two-sector model is entirely analogous to the one-sector case. We require the representative household to forecast sequences of prices and calculate optimal consumption and capital paths subject to a sequence of budget constraints, one for each period. The production sectors choose their input combinations and outputs to maximize each period's profits given the factor prices and output prices at that time. There is a market clearing condition too: the household's demand for consumption at each time equals the output of the consumption goods sector, the household's demand for investment goods (new capital less last period's capital plus replacement capital) equals the output of the capital goods sector, and the input demands for each sector balance with the available supply at each time. Thus, the prices forecast by the household sector and the production sectors are self-justifying in an equilibrium configuration.

Perfect Foresight Competitive Equilibrium. In the two-sector model, a sequence $\{w_t, r_t, q_t, c_t, k_t, k_t^0, k_t^1, \ell_t^0, \ell_t^1\}_{t=1}^{\infty}$ is a perfect foresight competitive equilibrium (PFCE) if:

   (1) $k_t^0, k_t^1, \ell_t^0, \ell_t^1$ maximize profit in each sector at each time t;

(2) The output market clears, at each t, $c_t = F^0(k_t^0, \ell_t^0)$ and $k_t - (1 - \mu)k_{t-1} = F^1(k_t^1, \ell_t^1)$;

(3) The input market clears, at each t, $k_t^0 + k_t^1 = k_t$ and $\ell_t^0 + \ell_t^1 = 1$;

(4) $\{c_t, k_t\}$ maximizes $U(\mathbf{c})$ subject to $c_t + q_t[k_t - (1 - \mu)k_{t-1}] = w_t + r_t k_{t-1}$ and $c_t, k_t \geq 0$ for each t with $k_0 = k$.

Notice that zero profits are achieved in both sectors when a PFCE program is followed. This means that the model has a Walrasian flavor on the production side where the dissolution and formation of firms can be represented in terms of the flow of entrepreneurial factors between sectors which may use them in different proportions. In this context, we interpret labor as the entrepreneurial factor.[21] The interest rate for one-period consumption loans is implicitly determined using the household's first-order condition by setting $1 + i_{t+1} = U_t/U_{t+1}$.

The definition of a PFCE can be simplified using the transformation function.

Perfect Foresight Competitive Equilibrium. Given a transformation function $\mathcal{T}$, a sequence $\{w_t, r_t, q_t, c_t, k_t, y_t\}_{t=1}^{\infty}$ constitutes a perfect foresight competitive equilibrium (PFCE) if:

(1) (k_{t-1}, y_t) maximizes $\mathcal{T}(k, y) + q_t y - r_t k$ over all (k, y) in the domain of $\mathcal{T}$ at each time t;

(2) $w_t = \mathcal{T}(k_{t-1}, y_t) + q_t y_t - r_t k_{t-1}$;

(3) At each t, $c_t = \mathcal{T}(k_{t-1}, y_t)$ and $k_t - (1 - \mu)k_{t-1} = y_t$ (market clearing);

(4) $\{c_t, k_t\}$ maximizes $U(\mathbf{c})$ subject to $c_t + q_t[k_t - (1 - \mu)k_{t-1}] = w_t + r_t k_{t-1}$ and $c_t, k_t \geq 0$ for each t with $k_0 = k$.

The wage rate is the residual payment to the fixed labor (equivalently, entrepreneurial) factor in this version of the two-sector PFCE problem.

The Optimal Growth Problem

We can define the optimal growth problem solved by an omniscient central planner following the intertemporal preference of the household in a straightforward manner. This problem is:

$$\sup U(\mathbf{c})$$
$$\text{s.t. } c_t = F^0(k_t^0, \ell_t^0)$$
$$k_t - (1 - \mu)k_{t-1} = F^1(k_t^1, \ell_t^1)$$
$$k_t^0 + k_t^1 \leq k_t, \ \ell_t^0 + \ell_t^1 \leq 1, \text{ for each } t,$$
$$\text{and } k_0 \leq k \text{ given.}$$

---

[21] See also McKenzie (1994).

The transformation function can be used to state the reduced form of the two-sector optimal growth problem in the following format:

$$\sup A\left(k_0, k_1, V(\mathbf{k})\right)$$
$$\text{s.t. } (k_{t-1}, k_t) \in D \text{ for } t = 1, 2, \ldots,$$
$$k_0 \leq k \text{ given.}$$

The reduced-form recursive utility function has aggregator $A(a, b, V) = W(\mathcal{T}(a, b - (1 - \mu)a), V)$, expressed in terms of capital input a and output b. Then utility is

$$V(\mathbf{k}) = W(\mathcal{T}(k_0, k_1 - (1 - \mu)k_0), W(\mathcal{T}(k_1, k_2 - (1 - \mu)k_1), W(\cdots)))$$
$$= U(\mathcal{T}(k_0, k_1 - (1 - \mu)k_0), \mathcal{T}(k_1, k_2 - (1 - \mu)k_1), \ldots).$$

We will use the reduced form of the optimum growth problem to derive the Equivalence Principle. The technology conditions (supplemented by Inada conditions as needed) give us a unique interior optimal program. The corresponding Euler conditions can readily be seen to be expressed by the following equation:

$$\frac{U_t}{U_{t+1}} = \frac{-\mathcal{T}_1(t, t+1) + \mathcal{T}_2(t, t+1)(1 - \mu)}{\mathcal{T}_2(t-1, t)}, \tag{7}$$

where we let $\mathcal{T}_2(t - 1, t) = \mathcal{T}_2(k_{t-1}, k_t - (1 - \mu)k_{t-1})$, $\mathcal{T}_1(t, t+1) = \mathcal{T}_1(k_t, k_{t+1} - (1 - \mu)k_t)$, and U_t is the partial derivative of U with respect to consumption at time t. The corresponding transversality condition is:

$$\lim_{t \to \infty} U_t k_t = 0. \tag{8}$$

This condition is automatically satisfied because the optimal capital sequence is interior and bounded (by the technology conditions).

The Equivalence Theorem
Suppose that the household solves its optimization problem given profiles of capital goods prices, rentals, and wages. Provided the resulting solution is interior in the sense that consumption and capital are always positive, we can write down the no-arbitrage condition for a PFCE as the equation:

$$\frac{U_t}{U_{t+1}} = \frac{r_{t+1} + q_{t+1}(1 - \mu)}{q_t}. \tag{9}$$

The corresponding transversality condition is (8). The balance condition $y_t = k_t - (1 - \mu)k_{t-1}$ obtains in an equilibrium. Define $w_t = \mathcal{T}(k_{t-1}, y_t) + q_t y_t - r_t k_{t-1}$, $r_t = \mathcal{T}_1(k_{t-1}, y_t)$, and $q_t = -\mathcal{T}_2(k_{t-2}, y_t)$, and let the implicit interest rate connecting the two periods, i_{t+1}, be the marginal rate of impatience calculated at the optimal consumption sequence, that is

$$i_{t+1} = \frac{U_t}{U_{t+1}} - 1.$$

With this substitution the no-arbitrage condition (9) matches (7)—the no-arbitrage condition for an optimum. Hence, the first-order conditions for a PFCE solution agree with the first-order conditions for our optimal growth problem and the corresponding transversality conditions also match. Hence, every solution to the optimal growth problem is a PFCE and vice versa. This is the *Equivalence Principle for Two-Sector Models*:

Two-Sector Equivalence Theorem. *The sequence* $\{q_t, w_t, r_t, c_t, k_t\}_{t=1}^{\infty}$ *is a PFCE if and only if* $\{c_t, k_t\}$ *maximizes* $U(\mathbf{c})$ *such that* $c_t = \mathcal{T}(k_{t-1}, k_t - (1 - \mu)k_{t-1})$ *with* $k_0 = k$.

This version of the Equivalence Principle can be extended to a many capital goods model by using the reduced-form representations introduced in the last chapter. Hence, we can conclude that in a variety of circumstances, the solution to an optimal growth model is a perfect foresight competitive equilibrium and vice versa. Moreover, there is a natural extension of this Equivalence Principle to encompass the two-sector RCE model. Hence, the RCE solution is yet another avenue for implementing the two-sector optimal growth solution in a decentralized economy.

6.3.3 Dynamics and the Two-Sector Equivalence Theorem

We can read off the properties of an equilibrium program by translating the properties of the optimum growth solution into the equilibrium framework. One immediate implication of this equivalence is that there is a unique equilibrium program from a given starting stock whenever the dual optimal growth model has a unique solution. The Equivalence Principle applied to the one- and two-sector models allows us to draw on the analysis of optimal paths found in Chapter 5. The perfect foresight equilibrium model will exhibit a monotonic capital sequence or oscillatory capital sequence whenever the dual optimal growth model does. In particular, there can be cyclic solutions or even chaos in a two-sector perfect foresight equilibrium regime because there are two-sector optimal growth models with those properties. Boldrin (1989) presents conditions for an abstract two-sector model with discounted TAS utility to exhibit cyclic and chaotic capital and consumption trajectories. Those cases only occur when there are factor intensity reversals along the optimal program dual to the PFCE path. Boldrin and Deneckere (1990) give an explicit example of such a two-sector model. A low discount rate is needed to produce the chaotic solutions since otherwise the perfectly foreseeing household would try to arbitrage anticipated fluctuations in the rate of return to capital. Their example also relies on a Leontief fixed coefficient production function in the investment goods sector and a Cobb-Douglas production function in the consumption goods sector.

The potential for oscillatory programs to arise in two-sector models implies that the competitive equilibrium path need not converge to a modified golden-rule program. However, the uniqueness of the optimum implies the price sequences placing the economy on the perfect foresight path are uniquely determined given the initial data.

Notice that although the equilibrium program is uniquely determined given the initial data, the path need not be stable in the sense that it need not converge to a modified golden rule. Thus, the Hahn question is really not about determining whether or not the economy can select the right initial prices or next period's capital stock to lead to a long-run steady-state solution. The presence of heterogeneous capital goods is also not the problem since Hahn's question can be raised in a two-sector model having an aggregate capital variable. The crucial issue is whether or not the competitive economy imposes on itself a transversality condition. When it does, then the resulting competitive equilibrium has the same properties as the corresponding optimum. The famous unseen hand produces a social optimum. For economies with infinitely lived representative agents, the absence of arbitrage applied to reversed and unreversed arbitrage opportunities leads to conditions which determine the prices consistent with an equilibrium configuration.

The orthodox vision of capital accumulation fails to hold on several fronts when a two-sector model is examined instead of a one-sector economy. First, the equilibrium accumulation path need not be monotonic. Second, in the case of a monotonic capital path, there is no price that serves as *the* rate of interest, even though the wage rate increases as capital increases.[22] There is a sequence of (implicit) one-period interest rates, i_{t+1}, which vary from period to period. There is also a sequence of own rates of return to capital, which generally differ from the implicit interest rate. Both rates have a claim to being rates of interest. There is *no single rate of interest* that can decline as capital accumulation progresses.

6.4 Transversality and the Hahn problem

The Equivalence Principle provides a solution to the Hahn problem. The question raised by Hahn was formulated in a multisector model, but the basic issue arises in one- and two-sector models. Put briefly, the Hahn

---

[22] This is Bliss's (1975, pp. 292–297) critique of the orthodox vision.

question is what determines the "correct choice" of the initial price of capital (in present value terms) or equivalently, what determines the initial consumption or the next period's capital stock in a *decentralized* market economy?

Originally, Hahn's problem was bound up with whether or not the equilibrium path was stable. His contention was that the saddlepoint character of the long-run, steady-state equilibrium opened the possibility (and probability) that a decentralized economy would choose the "wrong" initial prices (or equivalent consumption or next period's capital stocks) and fail to converge to the long-run equilibrium. This potential instability was supposed to be a fundamental flaw in dynamic market economies. There was no obvious choice of a mechanism to place the economy on the stable manifold belonging to the steady state. However, stability is *not* the real economic issue. There are cyclic or even chaotic equilibria in two-sector models because there are corresponding equivalent two-sector optimal growth models according to the Equivalence Principle. The stability issue is intertwined with the choice of the initial price (consumption or next period's capital stock) consistent with the perfect foresight solution in the one-sector case because of the monotonicity property and, in the case of discounted TAS utility and some recursive utility specifications, the turnpike property.

Therefore, the Equivalence Principle tells us that whenever there is a *unique* socially optimal path, then there is a unique initial present value price (or consumption or next period's capital stocks) which places the economy on the perfect foresight path. The decentralized perfect foresight market economy imposes a transversality condition on itself in equilibrium which gives an efficient market's connection between the initial price and the anticipated rental stream. The market cannot live on its dreams and no price bubble can persist.

The Equivalence Principle gives a rigorous answer to Hahn's conjecture that shadow prices associated with an optimum could be used to place the economy on the perfect foresight path. This *theoretical* solution to the Hahn problem shows the central issue is not the economy's stability, but rather the capacity of competitive agents to choose the correct starting prices that result in perfect foresight and market clearing at all future time. Of course, it would seem that one has to accept the infinitely lived agent and long-run perfect foresight assumptions for this to be an acceptable solution. Hahn (1985, pp. 5–6) states that he does not and makes his view of the matter quite clear:

> I took my result to show that warranted paths of the economy as defined by Harrod did not in general seek the steady state. It never occurred to me that anyone would wish to posit perfect foresight

over the infinite future. But I was wrong. Such a postulate is now commonplace. It still strikes me as dotty.

Stiglitz (1990, pp. 13–15) argues that infinitely lived representative agent models of the type described here ignored the basic question posed by Hahn. His point is that "individuals are not infinitely lived, and the market institutions which would ensure that the transversality condition be satisfied do not exist."[23] There are not enough futures markets in place now to allow speculators to arbitrage a bubble that they believe will burst in the distant future. The PFCE Equivalence Principles developed in this chapter are about the relationship between perfect markets and perfect planning. It is no surprise that the imperfect market equilibrium as described by Hahn and Stiglitz is found wanting in comparison to its perfect market counterpart. The PFCE solution compares a perfect planner's solution and a perfect market equilibrium. It is an idealized theoretical answer to the Hahn problem in representative agent economies.[24]

Hahn's question can also be posed in heterogeneous agent economies. The futures economy (FCE) is the subject of Chapter 8. The usual welfare theorems apply. The spot economy (PFCE) is a bit trickier. A PFCE does exist (Becker, Boyd, and Foias, 1991), but may not be Pareto optimal. Becker (1980) first examined the one-sector case with heterogeneous discount factors. In the steady state, the borrowing constraint binds on most agents. Such an equilibrium is *not* Pareto optimal and cannot solve a planner's problem. Becker and Foias (1987) showed that equilibria converge to the steady state in a large class of these models.[25] These equilibria are also not Pareto optimal.

It might seem that this ends any hope of a general Equivalence Principle for heterogeneous agent spot economies. However, Magill and Quinzii (1994) obtain an equivalence result for infinite horizon exchange economies with incomplete financial markets. They introduce two types of borrowing constraints. The *implicit debt constraint* requires that debts be uniformly bounded. The *explicit debt constraint* puts an upper bound on the amount of debt allowed. In their terminology, a PFCE has an explicit debt constraint of zero. Magill and Quinzii find that the futures (FCE) version

---

[23] Stiglitz (1990, p. 15).

[24] See Burgstaller (1995) for another attack on the interpretation of the PFCE Equivalence Principle. He objects that there is no stock (equity) market in the equilibrium model. However, the representative consumer is the residual claimant in the PFCE models when labor is the entrepreneurial factor. This immortal agent's foresight coupled with market clearing at each time and the non-negativity of capital holding is responsible for the transversality condition obtaining along an equilibrium.

[25] Cycles and chaotic equilibria may also exist. See Becker and Foias (1994) and Sorger (1994a; 1995). A turnpike theorem for the case of identical discount factors was established by Hernández (1991).

of their model, which they call an *equilibrium with transversality condition*, has the same equilibrium allocations as the model with implicit debt constraint. Moreover, if the explicit debt constraint is set larger than the implicit bound for a particular equilibrium, the explicit debt model also yields that equilibrium. The equilibrium is optimal when the explicit debt constraint is strong enough to rule out Ponzi schemes, but weak enough that it does not bind in any particular period.

The importance of debt constraints in spot economies cannot be overemphasized. Borrowing constraints are not necessarily a market imperfection. Rather, they frequently serve to perfect the market. They rule out Ponzi-type unreversed arbitrages and ensure that the transversality condition must hold, thus providing a solution to the Hahn problem.

The Equivalence Principle adapted to stochastic models has been the cornerstone of the "real business cycle theory" of Lucas, Prescott, Kydland, and others. According to a critique by Hahn and Solow (1995) these models have two fundamental premises. First, the macroeconomy should be an exact aggregation of the underlying microeconomic structure. Second, the only appropriate micro model is one based on intertemporal utility maximization, subject only to budget and technological constraints. When combined with the immortal representative household assumption the resulting macro model is firmly rooted in perfect foresight behavior, infinite time optimization, and universal perfect competition. Hahn and Solow (1995, p. 2) object:

> What Ramsey took to be a normative model, useful for working out what an omniscient planner should do, has been transformed into a model for interpreting last year's and next year's national accounts.
>
> Of course, that is the economics of Dr. Pangloss, and it bears little relation to the world.

Hahn and Solow (1995, p. 2) go on to say that "no account has been given of how and why a decentralized economy *could* (italics added) behave as if guided by a Ramsey maximizer." They argue that the Equivalence Principle is irrelevant once missing markets or other imperfections are admitted to the story.

Our coverage of the Equivalence Principle emphasizes its idealism. But it also shows how certain imperfections such as missing markets (due to debt constraints) are not the problem either, since they help eliminate open-ended arbitrage opportunities. The rigorous treatment of the Euler and transversality conditions within perfect foresight optimizing behavior in a perfectly competitive world tells us when a decentralized economy behaves as if guided by a Ramsey maximizer. It also serves the purpose of highlighting the key assumptions underlying such a conclusion. For Hahn and Solow (1995, p. 140) the real problem lies in the assumption of an immortal representative agent, correctly predicting economic variables out to infinity. They simply do not believe *macroeconomic* insights are possible "with so extravagant an expectational hypothesis" (p. 140). Thus, while the theory is about idealized settings, there is the real problem of whether or not it is applicable. Consequently, the significance of these models remains controversial.

6.5 Transversality and Decentralization

Questions about the meaning of the transversality condition have been raised since its importance was first recognized by Malinvaud (1953). Koopmans (1957) posed the problem of how an optimum over an infinite horizon can be decentralized via a price mechanism when there are an infinite number of agents, each operating over one period of time.[26] He wondered how the task of meeting the transversality condition could be pinned down on any particular decision maker. As we have seen, the transversality condition asserts that the absence of unreversed arbitrage profits is a necessary condition for equilibrium or optimality. For Ramsey's infinitely lived all-seeing and all-knowing central planner, the verification of the transversality condition is no more difficult than doing any other computation. Hence, the perfect central planner has no problem verifying *all* the conditions for optimality. The problem lies with the equilibrium side of the story. If we maintain the hypothesis that there is an infinitely lived representative agent, then there is no reason why that immortal individual should be unable to look sufficiently far into the future and verify the transversality condition for any candidate equilibrium program. Koopmans's concern applies in the case where individual agents are finitely lived, but that is a different modeling assumption than the one we have pursued throughout this volume.[27]

The real critique of the Equivalence Principle is whether or not the infinitely lived agent assumption is a useful *modeling fiction*. We contend that it is for many problems. One way to support that claim is to show how this modeling framework leads to interesting "laws of change" showing how an economy's equilibrium or optimal program responds to changes in the model's underlying parameters. This is our next task.

---

[26] See Koopmans (1957, pp. 111–112).

[27] See Becker and Majumdar (1989) for a survey of decentralization results for one-sector models. Agents in that framework can verify in some case the first-order conditions and another condition based on a finite number of periods' prices and achieve an optimal accumulation program. The symposium volume edited by Majumdar (1992) contains several papers devoted to characterizing the decentralization of competitive programs when consumers and producers are able to see a limited number of future prices.

CHAPTER 7

Comparative Dynamics

7.1 Introduction

Up to now we have answered many questions about the optimization problems underlying our approach to dynamic economics. We have shown how those problems yield solutions and described conditions when the optimum is uniquely determined by the underlying data. We have also described how those models can be interpreted as intertemporal competitive equilibria. As Samuelson (1947) and Hicks (1946) have shown, we are ultimately interested in the implications of optimizing behavior whether it be that of a central planner or a household (or producer) in a market oriented economy. The characterization conditions of an optimum (or equilibrium) are to be subjected to further analysis in order to deduce the properties exhibited by an optimal (or equilibrium) path of capital accumulation and consumption. In a decentralized economy, we seek knowledge about the time paths of the various prices for goods and factors as well as the evolution and distribution of income and wealth. Finally, we are interested in the laws of change which describe the response of the optimum to shifts in the various economically important parameters or the initial data (the initial capital stock). This is called the problem of *comparative dynamics*. The optimization structure of the choice problem as well as its stability properties are combined to deduce the ways in which a parameter shift (e.g., the rate of time preference in a TAS utility model) induces a change in the dynamics of the model. In practice, these different analytical levels are often interconnected rather than taken up in sequence.

In Chapter 5 we saw how various infinite horizon optimal capital accumulation programs might evolve. We examined stability of the long-run steady state (turnpike theory) and explored the possibility of nonconvergence and cyclic or even chaotic solutions. In those problems we held constant the underlying primitives of the model—preferences and technology. We varied the initial conditions—the starting capital stock value. Turnpike theorems can then be viewed as one type of comparative dynamics result whereby all optimal programs converge to a particular program independently of the magnitude of the initial capital stock. In this chapter we will be concerned with comparative dynamics results based on changing a preference parameter.[1] The results we will demonstrate are closely linked to the stability properties of the underlying model. We will also use the previous chapter's Equivalence Principle to draw inferences about the comparative dynamics properties of market models. In particular, we will use the θ-PFCE Equivalence Theorem to explore the implications of a tax reform in that model.

A good way to introduce the questions addressed in this chapter is to examine an example. We return to the TAS Example 1.1 that was further explored in Section 5.1. Recall that utility is $U(\mathbf{c}) = \sum_{t=1}^{\infty} \delta^{t-1} \log c_t$ and production is described by the production function $f(k) = k^\rho$ where $0 < \rho < 1$. We showed using a symmetry argument that the value function (here written to include the parameters δ and ρ as arguments) is $J(k_0, \delta, \rho) = J(k_g, \delta, \rho) + \frac{\rho}{1-\delta\rho} \log(k_0/k_g)$, where k_0 is the starting stock and k_g is the steady-state stock (which also depends on δ and ρ). We also showed the consumption policy function is $g(k, \delta, \rho) = (1 - \delta\rho)k^\rho$ and the capital policy function is $h(k, \delta, \rho) = \delta\rho k^\rho$. Given the parameter values (δ, ρ), the steady state is a fixed point of the capital policy function, $k_g(\delta, \rho) = h(k_g(\delta, \rho), \delta, \rho)$. We can use these functions to determine the sensitivity of the optimal path to changes in the underlying taste and technology parameters (δ, ρ).

Suppose that δ undergoes an exogenous increase. The planner has become more patient because his discount factor rose. What happens to the new optimal program as compared to the old? We begin by observing that the new steady-state capital stock increases. The steady-state capital stock must satisfy the Euler equation, which takes the form $\delta\rho(k_g(\delta, \rho))^{\rho-1} = 1$. Differentiate this with respect to δ and solve to show that

$$\frac{\partial k_g(\delta, \rho)}{\partial \delta} = \frac{k_g(\delta, \rho)}{\delta(1 - \rho)} > 0.$$

Therefore, an increase in the discount factor increases steady-state capital. This is the steady-state *capital deepening* response to a change in the discount factor. A routine calculation also shows that steady-state consumption increases with δ. This is called *nonparadoxical consumption behavior* in the capital theory literature.[2] These results are interesting,

---

[1] Comparative dynamics results can also be obtained for parametric changes in technology. For example, the exponent of the Cobb-Douglas production function could be varied, or the production function could be multiplied by a constant. Faugère (1993) considers comparative dynamics for two classes of parametric changes that increase marginal productivity and permit both Hicks neutral and Hicks labor saving changes.

[2] See Burmeister and Turnovsky (1972) for a general discussion of capital deepening. Burmeister (1980) surveys the steady-state theory for multisector models, capital deepening, nonparadoxical consumption, and their connections to the so-called Cambridge controversies.

but they do not tell us the whole story. When the planner's discount factor increases, the planner recomputes the entire optimal program, not just the steady state. The planner undertakes a new optimal accumulation program that is based on examining *all* of the feasible programs starting from the stocks on hand prior to the parameter change.

We can use the policy functions to show the change in the trajectory the planner will follow from a given starting stock when the discount factor increases. The first period's capital stock was $k_1(\delta, \rho) = h(k_0, \delta, \rho) = \delta \rho k_0^\rho$. Differentiate this with respect to δ to get

$$\frac{\partial k_1(\delta, \rho)}{\partial \delta} = \rho k_0^\rho > 0.$$

Hence, the first period's capital stock increases. This is the *impact effect* of the parameter change because it represents the initial response of the planner to the new parameter value. Observe for periods $t = 2, 3, \ldots$ that $k_t(\delta, \rho) = \delta \rho [k_{t-1}(\delta, \rho)]^\rho$; by successive substitutions we find

$$k_t(\delta, \rho) = (\delta \rho)^{1 + \rho + \cdots + \rho^{t-1}} k_0^{\rho^t}.$$

Differentiation with respect to δ implies

$$\frac{\partial k_t(\delta, \rho)}{\partial \delta} = (1 + \rho + \cdots + \rho^t) \rho (\delta \rho)^{\rho + \rho^2 + \cdots + \rho^{t-1}} k_0^{\rho^t} > 0.$$

Therefore, the capital stock also rises in every other period compared to the original optimal program's capital stock. Thus, we may conclude that for each $t \geq 1$, the optimal capital stock is increasing in the discount factor:

$$k_t(\delta', \rho) > k_t(\delta, \rho) \text{ whenever } \delta' > \delta.$$

Hence, we can say that there is a *generalized capital deepening response* to an increase in the discount factor because the economy's capital stock increased at each time.

It is also interesting to point out that the impact effect on consumption is in the opposite direction from the impact on the first period's capital stock. The first period's consumption must fall because that consumption and the new first period's capital stock must still add up to the economy's initial endowment of output, k_0^ρ, which is unchanged by the shift in the discount factor.

How far can we extend the generalized capital deepening response to a parameter change? In this chapter we will investigate the following hypothesis:

Generalized Capital Deepening Hypothesis. *Aggregate capital stocks increase at each time in response to an increase in the discount factor.*

We will explore this hypothesis first in a time additive utility model in the reduced form. We will then see to what extent we can demonstrate the generalized capital deepening response holds when we look at recursive utility.

The comparative dynamics results derived below are based on two related techniques. The first is a backward induction dynamic programming argument which will be valid for sufficiently smooth value functions. We will then observe that this approach is a smooth version of some lattice programming techniques introduced by Topkis (1978). Those methods will be applied to the recursive case in a one-sector model.

Comparative dynamics properties in the general m-sector optimal accumulation model with discounted additive utility were developed by Araujo and Scheinkman (1977; 1979) and McKenzie (1986). They showed that the present value of the stream of increments in the capital stock (vector) is positive at the initial support prices. In this situation the optimal path is termed *dynamically regular*.[3] Their result is an application of the Implicit Function Theorem in the Banach space of bounded sequences of real m-vectors. This sensitivity result is obtained by inverting the infinite Jacobian matrix derived from the discrete Euler conditions for an optimal path. They showed that the existence of this inverse follows from basic assumptions on the curvature properties of the felicity function. The invertibility of the Jacobian implies that the stationary optimal state satisfies the strong turnpike property, i.e., it is globally asymptotically stable and a regular saddlepoint. The latter property means that the $2m$ eigenvalues associated with the linearized Euler equations at the steady state exhibit m roots with modulus smaller than one and m roots with modulus larger than one.[4] This links the comparative dynamics and stability properties of the model in the fashion of Samuelson's Correspondence Principle. Brock (1986) and Burmeister and Long (1977) have proposed a Revised Correspondence Principle for capital theoretic models. It says that a steady state is nonparadoxical if and only if it is a regular saddlepoint. We will see below for the reduced-form aggregate capital model with cyclic optimal programs that the Revised Correspondence Principle need not hold.[5]

---

[3] A generalized capital deepening response in an aggregative model is dynamically regular. The initial present support price sequence is $\{p_t\}$. The capital deepening response implies that at each time t, $p_t k_t(\delta', \rho) > p_t k_t(\delta, \rho)$. Summing over all t shows the increments in the capital stock exhibit the dynamic regularity property.

[4] The local analysis of steady states was reviewed in Sections 5.4.4 and 5.4.5.

[5] This does not contradict their single capital good results since they work in a continuous time setup and the cyclic case does not occur when there is one good.

Comparative dynamics results were also developed by DasGupta and McKenzie (1985) under a symmetry condition applicable to the aggregate model.[6] They focus on changes in the discount factor when the initial capital stock is a locally asymptotically stable steady state. They prove a strong regularity property: the increments in the capital stock have a positive value at the initial support prices at each time following the initial period. In the aggregate model, given positive prices, this implies that the capital stocks increase at each time. We will show this for the case of monotonic optimal capital sequences by an alternative method and extend their result to an arbitrary initial state. We will also show that their result does not extend to cyclic optimal solutions.[7]

The arguments used throughout this chapter are based on *dynamic programming techniques*. We will initially employ a twice continuously differentiable value function to obtain our results. Araujo and Scheinkman (1979) first conjectured that this condition could be used to derive comparative dynamics conclusions. Santos's (1992) results on the smoothness of the value function in its initial capital stock and parameter arguments provide a set of sufficient conditions for meeting that smoothness requirement. The advantage of making such a strong smoothness assumption is that the results are made intuitive and elementary methods may be used in the proofs. Moreover, this method can be extended to some recursive utility models. Furthermore, attention is clearly put on the dynamically feasible (efficient) alternatives open to the planner when a parameter shifts. The direct comparison of steady states is thereby avoided, since it generally is not possible or optimal, if feasible, for the planner to jump to the new steady state in one step.[8]

7.2 The Reduced-Form TAS Model

We consider an aggregate capital TAS reduced-form model (T, v, δ) where $T \subset \mathbb{R}_+^2$ is a Malinvaud technology set, $0 < \delta < 1$, and $v: T \to \mathbb{R}_+$. We have defined here a special case of the general TAS reduced-form model as set out in Chapter 5. The main difference aside from the number of capital goods is the requirement that the one-period return function $v(a, b)$ be bounded below (by zero). Otherwise, we impose (R1)–(R7).

---

[6] They require the matrix of second-order cross partials of the utility function to be a symmetric matrix. See Example 5.12 for the local stability analysis with this symmetry assumption. DasGupta and McKenzie (1990) derive dynamic regularity with weaker conditions in a reduced-form model.

[7] This will not contradict their result, since their local stability hypothesis is not met in our example.

[8] Burmeister (1980) raised this issue in his critique of the Cambridge controversies.

Recall from Section 4.3.1 that the definition of a Malinvaud technology set includes the conditions that T be a closed convex set containing $(0,0)$. We also assume (in conjunction with (R5)) that v is a strictly concave function and twice continuously differentiable on the interior of T with $v(0,0) = 0$. We let $J(k,\delta)$ denote the optimal value function obtained by solving the optimal growth problem:

$$J(k,\delta) = \sup \sum_{t=1}^{\infty} \delta^{t-1} v(k_{t-1}, k_t)$$

$$\text{s.t. } (k_{t-1}, k_t) \in T \text{ for } t = 1, 2, \ldots$$

$$\text{and } k_0 = k \text{ given.}$$

We let $k(\delta)$ denote the stationary optimal program given δ (it is assumed to be unique in the following discussion).

7.2.1 Comparative Dynamics for Monotonic Programs

We recall from Section 5.5.1 that the sign of v_{12} determines whether or not the optimal capital sequence from starting stock k is monotonic or oscillatory. Our first comparative dynamics result applies in the case where $v_{12} \geq 0$ for all $(a,b) \in T$. The main result is that an increase in δ provides a larger capital stock at each time $t \geq 1$ along the new optimal program as compared with the old. As capital rises at $t = 1$, single-period utility initially decreases below the original current level but eventually increases over the original steady-state level.[9]

The results in this section are valid for δ near 1. In this case we know that the stationary optimal program is a regular saddlepoint and locally asymptotically stable as shown in Section 5.4. Furthermore, this steady state is globally asymptotically stable by the Turnpike Theorem.

We will assume throughout that the discount factor lies in the interval $\Delta = [\underline{\delta}, \bar{\delta}]$, for $0 < \underline{\delta} < \bar{\delta} < 1$ where $\underline{\delta}$ and $\bar{\delta}$ are given parameters. These discount factors are used to create a closed interval to which we may apply contraction mapping techniques to demonstrate our comparative dynamics results. We also assume that the economy's initial capital stock is smaller than the maximum sustainable stock, k^M. The optimal capital sequence, $\{k_t(k,\delta)\}_{t=1}^{\infty}$, depends on the starting stock and the value of the discount parameter $\delta \in \Delta$. We assume that $k_0 > 0$ and $\{k_t(k,\delta)\}_{t=1}^{\infty}$ is an interior optimum in the sense that $0 < k_t(k,\delta) < k^M$ holds for all

---

[9] The presentation here follows Becker (1985b) for the reduced-form model and Becker (1983b) for the one-sector case. Dutta (1985; 1987) derives analogous results for the one-sector model using an approach that relaxes the strong smoothness conditions assumed in our analysis. Dutta (1993) surveys comparative dynamics results for aggregate models of capital accumulation as well as other closely related sensitivity issues.

t. The value function J is a concave function which is increasing in k for each δ. We also assume that J is a twice continuously differentiable assumption of k and δ. Santos (1992) gives sufficient conditions on the underlying technology and felicity function for J to be twice continuously differentiable.[10]

The stationarity of the model and dynamic programming considerations yield the Bellman optimality equation: for each $\delta \in \Delta$ and $k \in [0, k^M]$,

$$J(k, \delta) = \sup_b \{v(k, b) + \delta J(b, \delta) : (k, b) \in T\}. \tag{1}$$

The first-order condition for an interior solution to (1) is given by

$$v_2(k, b) + \delta J_1(b, \delta) = 0.$$

The assumed concavity and smoothness properties of v and J (with $v_{11} < 0$ and $J_{11} \leq 0$) yield

$$D \equiv D(k, b, \delta) = v_{22}(k, b) + \delta J_{11}(b, \delta) < 0.$$

The Implicit Function Theorem applies to yield a once continuously differentiable optimal policy function, ψ, defined on a neighborhood of (k, δ) so that $\psi(k, \delta) = b$. The partial derivatives of ψ at (k, δ) are

$$\psi_1(k, \delta) = -\frac{v_{21}(k, b)}{D}; \tag{2}$$

$$\psi_2(k, \delta) = -\frac{\delta J_{12}(b, \delta) + J_1(b, \delta)}{D}. \tag{3}$$

Since $v_{21} > 0$, $\psi_1 > 0$. If $J_{12} \geq 0$, then $\psi_2 > 0$ as $J_1 > 0$. We will show below in Lemma 1 that if $v_{21} = v_{12} > 0$, then $J_{12} \geq 0$.[11]

Equations (2) and (3) are the *impact effects* of a change in k and δ, respectively. The term ψ_1 is the analogue of the marginal propensity to save. The term ψ_2 gives the change in the end-of-current-period stocks (saving) due to a change in the discount factor. That $\psi_2 > 0$ when $J_{12} \geq 0$ is not surprising given the usual interpretation of J_1 as the current demand price for capital. This says that if δ is marginally increased, an additional

---

[10] He adds a curvature condition to the maintained assumptions on the one-period return function in addition to our smoothness assumptions and assumes that the optimal program is an interior one.

[11] The proof is similar to the one in the third appendix of Danthine and Donaldson (1981). Their proof applies to an uncertainty model. Here, the assumption that J is sufficiently smooth is needed to assure that the limits taken yield a sufficiently smooth J. The lattice programming methods discussed in Section 7.3 ameliorate the necessity of assuming J is twice continuously differentiable.

unit of capital is worth more than its original shadow price, so that there is a gain to increasing stocks. In effect, the current price of additional "consumption" has increased with δ, and there is a benefit to increasing the stocks available for next period's production—hence $\psi_2 > 0$.

Lemma 1. *If J is twice continuously differentiable and $v_{12} > 0$, then $J_{12} \geq 0$.*

Proof. Put $F^0(k, b, \delta) = v(k, 0)$. Then define $F^1(k, b, \delta) = v(k, b) + \delta v(b, 0)$; let

$$M^1(k, \delta) = \sup_b \{F^1(k, b, \delta) : (k, b) \in T\}. \tag{4}$$

Problem (4) has an interior solution for $(k, \delta) \in (0, k^M) \times (\underline{\delta}, \bar{\delta})$; the first-order necessary condition is

$$F_2^1 = v_2 + \delta v_1 = 0. \tag{5}$$

The second-order sufficient condition $F_{22}^1 < 0$ obtains as

$$F_{22}^1 = v_{22} + \delta v_{11} \equiv D^1 < 0. \tag{6}$$

The Implicit Function Theorem yields the policy function ψ^1 with $b = \psi^1(k, \delta)$ and partial derivatives at (k, δ):

$$\psi_1^1 = -\frac{v_{12}}{D^1} > 0 \text{ if } v_{21} > 0; \tag{7}$$

$$\psi_2^1 = -\frac{v_1}{D^1} > 0 \text{ if } v_1 > 0. \tag{8}$$

We can compute the first and second derivatives of M^1 and M^2. The necessary condition (5) implies the envelope relations $M_1^1 = F_1^1$, $M_2^1 = F_3^1 = v(b, 0) \geq 0$.

The second derivatives of M^1 are found from the relation

$$M_1^1(k, \delta) = v_1(k, \psi^1(k, \delta)) = F_1^1(k, \psi^1(k, \delta), \delta).$$

From (6) and (7), after simplification,

$$M_{11}^1 = \frac{\det D^2 v + \delta(v_{11})^2}{D^1} < 0,$$

since $D^1 < 0$, $\det D^2 v \equiv v_{11}v_{22} - (v_{12})^2 > 0$ and $v_{11} < 0$. Also $M_{12}^1 = v_{12}\psi_2^1 > 0$ by $v_{12} > 0$ and (8). Moreover, $M_2^1 = v(\psi^1(k, \delta), 0)$ implies that $M_{22}^1 = v_1\psi_2^1 > 0$ by (7).

For $n \geq 2$ define

$$F^n(k, b, \delta) = v(k, b) + \delta M^{n-1}(b, \delta);$$
$$M^n(k, \delta) = \sup_b \{F^n(k, b, \delta) : (k, b) \in T\}.$$

Notice M^n, $F^n \geq 0$ because $v \geq 0$. The induction hypothesis is

$$M_1^{n-1} = F_1^{n-1} > 0, \ M_2^{n-1} \geq 0,$$
$$M_{11}^{n-1} < 0, \ M_{22}^{n-1} > 0, \ \text{and} \ M_{12}^{n-1} > 0. \tag{9}$$

The procedure applied to F^1 and M^1 can be used on F^n and M^n to yield a policy function ψ^n with $\psi^n(k, \delta) = b$. Specifically,

$$F_2^n = 0 \ \text{and} \ F_{22}^n = v_{22} + \delta M_{11}^{n-1} \equiv D^n < 0,$$

by the induction assumption. Furthermore,

$$\psi_1^n = -\frac{v_{12}}{D^n} > 0 \ \text{since} \ v_{21} > 0;$$

$$\psi_2^n = -\frac{\delta M_{12}^{n-1} + M_1^{n-1}}{D^n} > 0 \ \text{by (9)}. \tag{10}$$

The envelope relations $M_1^n = F_1^n = v_1 > 0$, $M_2^n = F_3^n = M^{n-1} + \delta M_2^{n-1} \geq 0$ hold and yield as above the relation,

$$M_{11}^n = \frac{\det D^2 v + \delta v_{11} M_{11}^{n-1}}{D^n} < 0$$

by $\det D^2 v > 0$, $v_{11} < 0$, and $M_{11}^{n-1} < 0$ from the induction hypothesis (9). Also

$$M_{12}^n = v_{12}\psi_2^n > 0 \ \text{by} \ v_{12} > 0 \ \text{and (10)};$$
$$M_{22}^n = (M_1^{n-1} + \delta M_{21}^{n-1})\psi_2^n + 2M_2^{n-1} + \delta M_{22}^{n-1}.$$

The induction hypothesis (9) yields $M_{22}^n > 0$, since $M_{22}^{n-1} > 0$. This completes the induction.

We are now ready to show $J_{12} \geq 0$. Modify our discounted dynamic programming technique by letting the state space be $S = [0, k^M] \times [\underline{\delta}, \bar{\delta}]$ and the action space be $\{b \in [0, k^M] : (x, b) \in T \ \text{for some} \ x\}$. Define a continuous and compact-valued feasibility correspondence γ, by $\gamma(k, \delta) = \{b \in [0, k^M] : (k, b) \in T\}$. Define a transition operator $\tau \colon S \times \Delta \times [0, k^M] \to S \times \Delta$ by $\tau(k, \delta, b) = (b, \delta)$. Let the one-period reward function be $v(k, b)$, and observe that it is bounded and continuous on the state space. The Bellman operator can be shown to be a contraction, so there is a unique bounded continuous function $M \colon S \to \mathbb{R}$ such that M satisfies

$$M(k, \delta) = \sup_{b \in \gamma(k, \delta)} \{v(k, b) + \delta M(\tau(k, \delta, b), \delta)\}.$$

The function M can be computed by successive approximations. In our case, $\{M^n\}$ converges to M and thereby computes this function. *By assumption*, the optimal return function is the twice continuously differentiable function J and we may conclude that $M \equiv J$.[12]

The function J so found inherits the properties of the functions M^n in the approximating sequence; in particular, $J_{12} \geq 0$. To see this, let (k_0, δ_0) be arbitrary, $k > k_0$, $\delta > \delta_0$ and observe that

$$0 \leq \int_{k_0}^{k} \int_{\delta_0}^{\delta} M_{12}^n(s, t) \, ds \, dt$$
$$= M^n(k, \delta) - M^n(k_0, \delta) - M^n(k, \delta_0) + M^n(k_0, \delta_0).$$

Let $n \to \infty$ (so $M^n \to J$ pointwise, J twice continuously differentiable), and rearrange to get

$$J(k, \delta_0) - J(k_0, \delta_0) \leq J(k, \delta) - J(k_0, \delta).$$

Divide by $k - k_0$; letting $k \to k_0$ gives

$$J_1(k_0, \delta) - J_1(k_0, \delta_0) \geq 0.$$

Divide by $\delta - \delta_0$; letting $\delta \to \delta_0$ gives $J_{12}(k_0, \delta_0) \geq 0$. $\square$

Define $\{k_t(k, \delta)\}$ recursively by setting $k_0(k, \delta) = k$ and $k_t(k, \delta) = \psi(k_{t-1}(k, \delta), \delta)$ for $t \geq 1$. The path $\{k_t(k, \delta)\}$ satisfies the Euler equations and is optimal for the corresponding optimal growth problem. Let $k_{1t} = \partial k_t / \partial k$ and $k_{2t} = \partial k_t / \partial \delta$. Then equation (2) implies $k_{11} = \psi_1(k_0, \delta) > 0$ and equation (3) implies $k_{21} = \psi_2(k_0, \delta) > 0$. Make the induction assumption that $k_{2,t-1} \geq 0$, where $t \geq 2$. Then the chain rule yields from (2) and (3)

$$k_{2t} = \psi_1 k_{2,t-1} + \psi_2 > 0. \tag{11}$$

Therefore, $k_{2t} \geq 0$ for all $t \geq 1$. As $\psi_2 > 0$, $k_{2t} > 0$ for all t follows. This is summarized below.

Capital Deepening Theorem. *If $v_{12} > 0$, J is twice continuously differentiable, and $k(\delta)$ is the unique stationary optimal state for each δ, $\underline{\delta} < \delta < \bar{\delta}$, then $\partial k_t / \partial \delta > 0$ for $t = 1, 2, \ldots$.*

The induction argument yielding the Capital Deepening Theorem leads to a decomposition of the change in stocks due to an increase in δ into two effects: a *time preference effect* and a *capital stock effect*. The time preference effect is given by the second term in (11), which is positive by (3). This term has the same interpretation as the impact effect (3) because capital is held fixed with stocks k_t. The first term in (11) picks up the effect of an increased capital input available at the beginning of

---

[12] This is where the certainty case differs from the uncertainty case studied by Danthine and Donaldson (1981).

the period as a result of the increment in the previous period's terminal stocks. The term $\psi_1(k_{t-1}, \delta)$ gives the increase in terminal stocks at the end of period $t-1$ (to produce goods in period t) per unit increase in beginning period stocks. The term $k_{2,t-1}$ gives the increment in stocks available at the beginning of the period. Thus, the product of those two terms is the increment in the end-of-period stocks as a result of increases in previous periods' capital induced by a marginal increase in the discount factor. The two effects work in the same direction for $t \geq 1$, so capital increases at each stage along the new optimal program as compared with the old. The induction is begun by observing that initial stocks k are fixed at time 0, and the discount factor effect leads to an increase in the stocks available at time 1.

The Capital Deepening Theorem is illustrated in Figure 1 for the case $k = k(\delta)$. The case $k \neq k(\delta)$ is similar and left to the reader. The new discount factor is δ^* with $\delta < \delta^*$. The stable manifold corresponding to the new steady-state stock $k(\delta^*)$ is $S^* s^*$. Since the steady state is nonparadoxical $k(\delta^*) > k(\delta)$.[13] Felicity contours are also drawn in Figure 1 for reference in the following paragraph. The indifference curves are easily shown to have the indicated shape. Increasing values of v lie in the southeast direction. In the case $k = k(\delta)$, continuity considerations imply that $k(\delta^*)$ is sufficiently near $k(\delta)$ so that $k(\delta)$ lies in a neighborhood of $k(\delta^*)$ for which the local stable manifold $S^* s^*$ for δ^* represents the optimal path with initial condition $k(\delta)$.

The initial increment in stocks k_1 at $t = 0$ necessarily results in a decrease in utility achieved within the period starting at $t = 0$. This utility loss represents the cost of foregone "consumption" in order to realize a greater terminal stock to produce next period's goods. The convergence property of the new optimal program and $k_{2t} > 0$ imply that for $\delta < \delta^*$, there is a $T(\delta^*)$ such that if $t \geq T(\delta^*)$, then

$$v(k_t(k, \delta^*), k_{t+1}(k, \delta^*)) > v(k_t(k, \delta), k_{t+1}(k, \delta)); \qquad (12)$$

i.e., utility eventually increases over the previously obtained level (see Figure 1). Further, (12) holds when $k_t(k, \delta)$ and $k_{t+1}(k, \delta)$ are replaced by $k(\delta)$, provided that t is large enough. The optimality of the program for δ^* when the δ-optimal program is still available (as k is fixed) implies that this utility tradeoff results in a positive benefit less cost condition, where the δ^* factor discounts benefits and costs. The transition path from one steady state to another in this case is shown in Figure 1. The steady-

---

[13] The steady state satisfies the Euler equation, $v_2(k(\delta), k(\delta)) + \delta v_1(k(\delta), k(\delta)) = 0$. Under appropriate Inada conditions, the uniqueness of the steady state implies the left-hand side is decreasing in k. Differentiation then yields $k'(\delta) > 0$; the steady state is nonparadoxical.

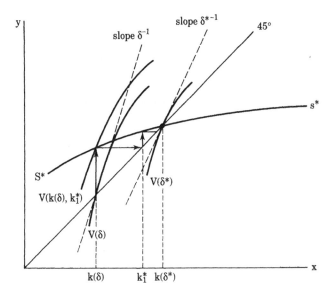

Figure 1:   The Capital Deepening Theorem.

state levels of utility are $v(\delta)$ and $v(\delta^*)$. The general result is summarized as:

Utility Transition Theorem. *If* $v_{12} > 0$, J *is twice continuously differentiable, and* $k(\delta)$ *is the unique stationary optimal state for each* δ, $\underline{\delta} < \delta < \bar{\delta}$, *then utility within each period eventually increases along the new path as compared to the old in response to an increase in the discount factor.*

▶ **Example 1: The one-sector model.** The one-sector model with production function $f(x)$ and felicity function $u(c)$ leads to a reduced-form model satisfying the condition $v_{12} > 0$. Notice that $v(a, b) = u(f(a) - b)$ is the reduced-form felicity and under our standard concavity and differentiability assumptions $v_{12} = -f'u'' > 0$. Assuming the value function is sufficiently smooth, we conclude from Lemma 1 that $J_{12} \geq 0$ holds in this model.[14] Hence, there is a capital deepening response when the planner's discount factor increases. Moreover, as in our opening example, the consumption level initially falls to pay for the additions to the capital stock at the initial impact of this parameter change. Eventually, consumption

---

[14] Becker (1983a) has a gap in the argument that is repaired with our analysis.

along the new path surpasses the old steady-state consumption level.

The Equivalence Principle also allows us to derive comparative dynamics results for perfect foresight equilibria. The increase in capital implies factor returns also change in response to the shift in the discount factor. Consider the case where the initial capital stock is smaller than the economy's steady-state stock (given the discount factor). Capital and consumption will be monotonically increasing with limits equal to the steady-state capital and consumption levels. In terms of factor prices, we can express this monotonicity property in terms of the *factor-price frontier*, $H(1+r)$, defined by

$$w = H(1+r) \equiv f(G(1+r)) - (1+r)G(1+r),$$

where $f'(G(1+r)) = 1+r$ implicitly defines G and where $1+r$ is the total return to capital in a PFCE. The factor-price frontier represents the trade-off between the wage rate and the return to capital; clearly $H'(1+r) < 0$ holds too.

If capital is increasing along the optimal path, then $\{1+r_t\}$ is decreasing (because $f'' < 0$) and $\{w_t\}$ is increasing because the factor-price frontier is decreasing. When the economy responds to an increased discount factor by providing a larger capital stock, then the return to capital falls at each time in comparison to the old equilibrium path while simultaneously raising the economy's wage bill at each time. ◄

▶ Example 2: The two-sector model. The two-sector model with a linear felicity and transformation function with $\mathcal{T}_{12} \geq 0$ has a capital deepening response. Benhabib and Nishimura (1985) show that $\mathcal{T}_{12} \geq 0$ holds when the capital goods sector is always more capital intensive than the consumption goods sector.[15] The condition $\mathcal{T}_{12} \geq 0$ means there are no factor intensity reversals along the optimal path. Hence, the capital deepening hypothesis applies to this class of two-sector models. ◄

7.2.2 Comparative Dynamics for Oscillating Programs

The purpose of this section is to examine the difficulties in extending the previous comparative dynamics results to the case $v_{12} < 0$. As noted in Chapter 5, this situation leads to oscillating solutions. The discussion in this section is heuristic, since certain technical details are omitted.

We showed in Chapter 5 that cycles of period 2 were possible when $v_{12} < 0$ held. The possibility of non-trivial periodic cycles leads to a counterexample to the Capital Deepening Theorem when $v_{12} < 0$. A 2-cycle, $\{(k^*, k_1^*), (k_1^*, k^*), (k^*, k_1^*), \dots\}$, is shown in Figure 2. There is a

---

[15] See Nishimura and Sorger (1996) for a survey of conditions on two-sector models that give rise to monotonic programs and cycles.

unique unstable steady state, $k(\delta)$. The discount factor is the largest one for which a non-trivial periodic solution exists (clearly $\delta < 1$). The crucial observation is that for δ' near enough to 1 we know the corresponding steady state will be globally asymptotically stable by the Turnpike Theorem. Therefore, for $\delta^* = \delta + d\delta$ with $d\delta > 0$ very small, $k(\delta) < k(\delta^*)$, since both steady states are nonparadoxical. For $k = k^*$, the optimal path for δ^* converges asymptotically to $k(\delta^*)$. This is shown in Figure 2 using the negatively sloped stable manifold S^*s^*. It is the damped oscillatory program starting at k^*. By the continuity of the steady state in the discount factor the choice of $d\delta$ can be made small enough so that $k(\delta^*) < k_1^*$ with $k^* < k_1^*$. The δ^*-optimal path initiated at k^* oscillates, and the convergence to $k(\delta^*)$ implies that eventually $k_t(k^*,\delta) < k_1^*$. But this means that there are an infinite number of periods in which capital along the new optimal path is smaller than along the old path (which is the cycle for δ).

The backward induction calculation used in the previous section appears to break down when $v_{12} < 0$, $k(\delta)$ is globally asymptotically stable, and is a regular saddlepoint. If $v_{12} < 0$, then (2) implies that $\psi_1 < 0$. The sign of ψ_2 requires an order of magnitude estimate of v_{12}; the proof of Lemma 1 shows that the sign of J_{12} is not determined if $v_{12} < 0$, unless other information is available. Consequently, our induction argument may fail.

This counterexample shows that for one capital good models in discrete time, the Strong Correspondence Principle conjectured by Burmeister and Long (1977) is false. Specifically, $k(\delta)$ in Figure 2 is nonparadoxical; yet it is not a regular saddlepoint. That is, regularity (Burmeister and Turnovsky's sense) does not imply stability, a result due to DasGupta (1985).[16] Burmeister and Long (1977) established the equivalence between efficient paradoxical steady states and a non-regular saddlepoint structure for one capital good models in continuous time. The locally unstable $k(\delta)$ with $v_{12} < 0$ in the discrete time linear approximation system has both of its characteristic roots with modulus greater than one. Hence, their result does not obtain in discrete time. Suppose the oscillating solution is stable and a regular saddlepoint is present. Let this solution be the "steady state" compared to $k(\delta^*)$. In this case, the conjectured correspondence principle also fails, since the δ-optimal oscillating solution is greater (less) than $k(\delta^*)$ infinitely often.

▶ Example 3: Two-sector models and joint production. Two-sector models

---

[16] DasGupta (1985) provides a quadratic counterexample for a discrete capital good, discrete time model. Previously, Levhari, Liviatan, and Luski (1974) showed the Strong Correspondence Principle fails if there are at least two capital goods in a discrete time framework (also see Benhabib and Nishimura, 1981, for a multisector example of an unstable steady state where regularity holds).

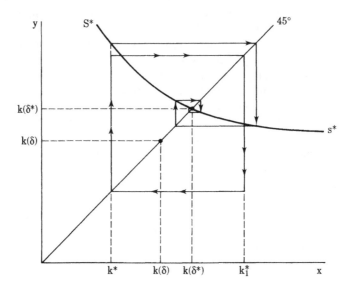

Figure 2:   Cycles and the Capital Deepening Counterexample.

are known to generate cycles or even chaos when there are factor intensity reversals. Benhabib and Nishimura (1985) have also shown that if the capital goods sector is less capital intensive than the consumption goods sector, then $\mathcal{T}_{12} < 0$ occurs where $\mathcal{T}$ is the transformation function.[17] These models are the ones for which we expect the capital deepening hypothesis to fail.

Liviatan and Samuelson (1969) introduced a one capital good joint production model. The transformation function $\mathcal{T}^*(a, y)$ gives the maximum output of the consumption good for a given capital input, a, and target output of investment goods, y. We can relate the following period's capital stock, b, to y according to the formula $y = b - (1 - \eta)a$, where $\eta \in [0, 1]$ is the depreciation rate. Hence, we can rewrite the transformation function as $\mathcal{T}(a, b) = \mathcal{T}^*(a, b - (1 - \eta)a)$. They observed that there could be multiple steady states in the corresponding reduced-form TAS model if $\mathcal{T}_{12} < 0$. They interpreted this condition to mean that capital is an inferior input in the production process. In this case, we expect cycles to exist for a sufficiently small discount factor based on the results in Chapter 5.

---

[17] See Nishimura and Sorger (1996) for a summary of recent work showing cycles can exist when each sector has a Cobb-Douglas production function.

Hence, we do not expect this joint production model to display a capital deepening response in this case. ◄

7.2.3 Comparative Dynamics and Capital Income Tax Reform

The Capital Deepening and Utility Transition Theorems may be combined with the θ-PFCE Equivalence Theorem (Chapter 6) for one-sector models to analyze the comparative dynamics impact of an unanticipated capital tax reform.[18] The θ-PFCE Equivalence Theorem implies that a change in the discount factor in the artificially constructed planner's problem is equivalent to an unanticipated change in the capital tax rate. Hence, we can read off the comparative dynamics properties of such a tax reform by examining the corresponding changes in the planner's "optimal" solution. The decomposition of the change in capital at each time due to the tax reform can be interpreted here as a *stock effect* and a *pure incentive effect*. The capital stock effect shows how a tax change increases savings as capital is larger in every period (other than time 0). The pure incentive effect shows how the change in the terms of trade between the present and the future serves to increase saving. Other properties are also deduced using these methods. For example, the transition between steady states that arises from a partial reduction in the tax rate at time 0 is completely characterized. This reform of the tax policy leads to an increased capital stock at each time, initially lower consumption and eventually larger consumption, a larger after-tax rate of return to capital at each time, a smaller before-tax return to capital at each time, a larger wage rate at each time, and a welfare gain. The change in government revenue at each time is ambiguous. Each variable converges to the long-run steady state appropriate for the new tax rate. These results represent the power of our optimization framework and the equivalence idea for simplifying the analysis of tax distortions in a dynamic economy.

The optimization problem solved by the planner in the θ-PFCE Equivalence Theorem is represented by the reduced-form model

$$J(k, 1 - \theta) = \sup \sum_{t=1}^{\infty} (\delta(1 - \theta))^{t-1} u(f(k_{t-1}) - k_t)$$

$$\text{s.t. } (k_{t-1}, k_t) \in T \text{ for } t = 1, 2, \ldots$$

$$\text{and } k_0 = k \text{ given.}$$

Here T is the domain of $v(a, b) = u(f(a) - b)$. Notice how the capital tax rate modifies the planner's discount factor. If we let $H(R)$ denote the factor price frontier with R the total pre-tax return to capital, and let r

---

[18] This section summarizes the results of Becker (1985a).

denote the after-tax total return to capital, then we can say something about how the distorted economy's factor prices change with tax reforms. As with the no-tax case, if $\{k_t\}$ is increasing, then the total return to capital declines and the wage rate rises just as in the undistorted case. But the steady state must satisfy $\delta\bar{r} = 1$, where $\bar{r}$ is the steady-state net rate of return to capital (we use overbars to denote steady-state values throughout this section). Thus, profit maximization conditions for PFCE imply

$$\delta(1 - \theta)f'(\bar{k}) = 1.$$

Therefore, the steady-state rate of return to capital is independent of the tax rate. This implies that the capital income tax is shifted to the labor income component in the long run. The shifting of the tax does *not* mean that long-run total income is the same with and without the tax—the long-run stock of capital is smaller given the tax. In general, the properties of $\{g_t\}$, the equilibrium sequence of government revenue, are indeterminate other than $g_t \to \bar{g} = \theta\bar{R}\bar{k}$, where $\bar{R}$ is the steady-state gross return to capital. Since, R_t and k_{t-1} move in opposite directions as t increases, $\{g_t\}$ can be increasing, decreasing, or oscillating. However, if capital income $R_t k_{t-1}$ is increasing in the total capital stock, then we can say that the government's revenue also converges monotonically to the steady-state level $\bar{g}$. This occurs if production is Cobb-Douglas, or more generally the neoclassical production function has an elasticity of substitution greater than or equal to one.

The main responses of the θ-PFCE to a partial tax reform are summarized in the next theorem.

Tax Reform Theorem. *Given a θ-PFCE, a small unanticipated reduction in the tax rate from θ to θ^* at time 0 induces an increase in the capital stock in the θ^*-PFCE as compared to the θ-PFCE for each $t \geq 1$. Consumption in the θ^*-PFCE eventually exceeds consumption in the θ-PFCE. Moreover, the partial tax reform reduces the gross capital return at each time and increases the wage at each time. If the θ-PFCE is a steady state, then the net return to capital increases at each time as well and welfare also increases.*

We will not give a detailed proof of this result, but rather focus on how it is connected to the Capital Deepening Theorem. The idea is to exploit the θ-PFCE Equivalence Principle to reduce the tax reform problem to an analysis of the following Bellman equation:

$$J(k, \Theta) = \max_{0 \leq b \leq f(k)} \{u(f(k) - b) + \delta\Theta J(b, \Theta)\},$$

where we make the change of variable $\Theta = 1 - \theta$ and notice that an increase in Θ is equivalent to a tax cut. Let $\psi(k, \Theta)$ denote the optimal policy function. Transpose the proof of the Capital Deepening Theorem to this setting to show that $J_{12} \geq 0$ and conclude that $\psi_1 > 0$ and $\psi_2 > 0$. In the same manner, we can show that $k_{2t} = \psi_1 k_{2,t-1} + \psi_2$. The pure incentive effect of a tax reform is measured by the term ψ_2 while the capital stock effect is $\psi_1 k_{2,t-1}$.

The gross return to capital is $R_t(k, \Theta) = f'(k_{t-1}(k, \Theta))$. Differentiation with respect to Θ shows us that $\partial R_t / \partial \Theta = f''(k_{t-1}(k, \Theta))k_{2,t-1} < 0$ since $f'' < 0$. The negative slope of the factor price frontier implies the wage rises. This agrees with intuition since the tax reform increases the capital stock at each time.

In general, the change in the after-tax total return is ambiguous. Differentiating $r_t(k_{t-1}(k, \Theta)) = \Theta R_t(k, \Theta)$ with respect to Θ shows that the sign of $\partial r_t / \partial \Theta$ is indeterminate:

$$\frac{\partial r_t}{\partial \Theta} = \Theta \frac{\partial R_t}{\partial \Theta} + R_t.$$

The first term in this expression is negative and the second is positive, so their sum could be either sign. However, in specific examples, exact knowledge of the R_t function would be available and the sign of $\partial r_t / \partial \Theta$ could be calculated given numerical values for the parameters of the model.

Since $r_t(k, \Theta)$ and $r_t(k, \Theta^*)$, for $\Theta^* > \Theta$ sufficiently close to Θ, have the same limit δ^{-1}, it follows that the sequences $\{r_t(k, \Theta)\}$ and $\{r_t(k, \Theta^*)\}$ are asymptotically equal. If the economy is initially in long-run equilibrium with the tax rate θ, then $r_t(\bar{k}, \Theta) = \delta^{-1}$ for all t. Since $r_t(\bar{k}, \Theta^*) \downarrow \delta^{-1}$ (because $f(\bar{k})$ is unchanged by assumption and the Θ^*-PFCE capital sequence is increasing), it follows that $r_t(\bar{k}, \Theta^*) > \delta^{-1}$ for all t. Thus, the response to the tax reform from an initial steady state is for the after-tax return to capital to *increase* over the previous after-tax return and then monotonically decline as capital accumulates to realize the pre-tax reform long-run return, δ^{-1}. Notice that the pre-tax return falls and is always smaller after the reform than before. The increase in the post-tax return is the incentive signal to the household to increase capital stocks as the after-tax rate of return exceeds its long-run value. In effect, the wedge between net and gross returns becomes smaller as the tax rate is reduced. Thus, in the important case of a transition between steady states, the properties of the after-tax return to capital may be deduced. The result is driven by the fixed long-run rate of return defined by the household's constant pure rate of time preference.

The change in the government revenue on a period-by-period basis is ambiguous when the tax rate is reduced since $g_t = (1 - \Theta)R_t k_{t-1}$ implies

$$\frac{\partial g_t}{\partial \Theta} = -R_t k_{t-1} + (1 - \Theta)\left(k_{t-1}\frac{\partial R_t}{\partial \Theta} + R_t\frac{\partial k_{t-1}}{\partial \Theta}\right).$$

The sign of the expression in the parentheses cannot be determined by the previous analysis: therefore, the overall sign in the above expression is ambiguous. One cannot conclude that a reduction in the tax rate increases or decreases government revenue at any given t. This ambiguity arises because the gross return to capital falls at the same time capital is increasing.

The change in the tax rate induces a change in welfare. In general, there is insufficient information to conclude that the tax cut raises welfare. However, if the initial situation corresponds to a steady-state equilibrium, then it is possible to show that welfare rises with a capital tax reform.[19]

7.3 A Primer of Lattice Programming

The dynamic programming argument showing $v_{12} \geq 0$ implied $J_{12} \geq 0$ in Lemma 1 used the assumed twice continuous differentiability of the value function in an essential fashion. The critical problem was to show that the pointwise limit of the successive approximations, $\{M_n\}$, inherited the property $M_{12}^n \geq 0$ that had been established by induction for each term n. The lattice programming approach initiated by Topkis (1978) is a technique that allows us to obtain our comparative dynamics conclusion without making the artificial smoothness assumption characteristic of the dynamic programming approach of the previous section.[20] This freedom from smoothness conditions yields a bonus: we can extend our dynamic programming methods to some problems with multiple solutions (as might arise in concave rather than strictly concave optimization problems). Moreover, the comparative dynamics properties of TAS utility with nonclassical production and recursive utility models with a classical technology can be successfully analyzed by these methods.[21]

There is a second reason for exploring lattice programming methods in a comparative dynamics context. Milgrom and Shannon (1994) have argued that traditional comparative statics results obtained either by Implicit Function Theorem methods or revealed preference arguments have

---

[19] See Becker (1985b) for details.

[20] Granot and Veinott (1985) is another important contribution to lattice programming theory.

[21] Mendelssohn and Sobel (1980) presented the earliest application of Topkis's methods in the economics literature. They applied lattice programming methods to a stochastic dynamic programming model with a fishery application. Amir, Mirman, and Perkins (1991) showed how to use lattice programming with a TAS utility function and nonclassical technology. Amir (1996) links lattice programming to reduced-form TAS models. We'll summarize his results in Section 7.4. Hertzendorf (1995) examines comparative dynamics in the neoclassical one-sector recursive utility model. We will discuss his results in Section 7.5.

relied on superfluous smoothness hypotheses or unnecessary convex structures. Lattice programming methods focus on the underlying ordinal structures in the model that are responsible for *monotone comparative statics* results—theorems showing that a decision variable in an optimization problem increases with increases in an underlying parameter's value.[22] The lattice programming approach to comparative dynamics has a similar motivation, namely to expose the economically important conditions that support the capital deepening hypothesis.

7.3.1 More about Lattices

We met the concept of a lattice in Chapter 2 where it was used to discuss Riesz spaces. Here we examine lattices in more detail for the express purpose of setting up our presentation of lattice programming theory in Sections 7.3.2 and 7.3.3.[23]

Partial Order. Let X be a set. A partial order on X is a binary relation $\geq_X$ on X such that, for $x, y, z \in X$,

(1) $x \geq_X x$ for any $x \in X$ (reflexivity);
(2) $x \geq_X y$ and $y \geq_X x$ imply $x = y$ (anti-symmetry);
(3) $x \geq_X y$ and $y \geq_X z$ imply $x \geq_X z$ (transitivity).

We use $\geq$ in place of the more cumbersome $\geq_X$ when there is no ambiguity.

Poset. A set X equipped with a partial order $\geq$ is called a partially ordered set, or a poset.

We will write $\{X, \geq\}$ for a poset when it is necessary to specify the order. Suppose that X is a poset where x and y are two of its elements. Let $x \vee y = \sup\{x, y\}$ denote the *least upper bound*, or *join*, of x and y in X, if it exists, and let $x \wedge y = \inf\{x, y\}$ denote the *greatest lower bound*, or *meet*, of x and y in X, if it exists. Two elements x and y of a poset are *unordered* if neither $x \geq y$ nor $y \geq x$ holds. A poset is a *chain* if it does not contain an unordered pair of elements. We note that $\mathbb{R}$ is a chain, whereas $\mathbb{R}^2$ is not a chain (with the usual componentwise order).

Lattice. A poset X is a lattice if for every pair of elements x and y in X,

---

[22] Other recent papers developing lattice programming methods and monotone comparative statics are Marx (1993), Milgrom (1994), Milgrom and Roberts (1994a; 1995), Shannon (1995), and Topkis (1995). Game theorists have also exploited lattice programming methods. See Topkis (1979), Milgrom and Roberts (1990), and Vives (1990) for supermodular games emphasizing strategic complementarities. See Milgrom and Roberts (1994b) for a "textbook" exposition with examples drawn from standard microeconomic theory.

[23] There is an intentional overlap with Chapter 2 to make this chapter self-contained.

the join $x \vee y$ and the meet $x \wedge y$ exist in X. Thus, X is a lattice if it is closed with respect to the operations join and meet.

The set $X = \mathbb{R}^n$ is a lattice with the usual componentwise order. The vector spaces such as s^m and ℓ_∞ introduced in Chapter 2 are lattices with their standard componentwise orders. In our exposition of lattice programming we will only work with finite dimensional spaces. We will also need subsets of $\mathbb{R}^n$ that are lattices in their own right. These sets are called sublattices and they are closed with respect to the operations of join and meet.

Sublattice. A subset S of a poset X is a sublattice if for every pair of elements x and y in S, the join $x \vee y$ and the meet $x \wedge y$ exist in S.

By a *closed order interval* we mean either the entire lattice X or a set of one of the three types: (i) all $x \geq a$, (ii) all $x \leq b$, or (iii) all x such that $a \leq x \leq b$. A closed order interval is a sublattice of X. The positive orthant of $\mathbb{R}^n$, $\mathbb{R}^n_+$, is a sublattice of $\mathbb{R}^n$.[24] However, the elements of a hyperplane contained in $\mathbb{R}^n$ generally do not form a sublattice. For example, $\{(x_1, x_2) \in \mathbb{R}^2 : x_1 + x_2 = 1\}$ is not a sublattice of $\mathbb{R}^2$ with the componentwise order. If X is a lattice, then we use $L(X)$ to denote the set of all sublattices of X. The set $L(X)$ is a poset under the ordering $\geq_L$ defined by $A \geq_L B$ if and only if $a \vee b \in A$ and $a \wedge b \in B$ whenever $a \in A$ and $b \in B$.[25]

A sublattice S of X is *complete* if for every non-empty subset S' of S, $\inf(S')$ and $\sup(S')$ both exist and are elements of S. Complete sublattices have a topological characterization. The *order interval topology* of a lattice X is that which results by taking the closed order intervals of the lattice as a subbasis for the closed sets of the space.[26] For example, the order interval topology on $\mathbb{R}$ with its usual order is the topology for which the sets $\mathbb{R}$, $[x, \infty)$, and $(-\infty, x]$ form a subbasis for the closed sets. Hence, the order interval topology corresponds to the usual topology in this case. The Frink-Birkhoff Theorem characterizes complete sublattices.[27]

Frink-Birkhoff Theorem. *Let X be a lattice and S a sublattice. Then S is complete if and only it is compact in the order interval topology.*

Corollary 1. *A sublattice of $\mathbb{R}^m$ is complete if and only if it is compact in the usual topology.*

Given two or more lattices, we can define new lattices by taking direct products and equipping the product lattice with the coordinatewise order.

[24] When $\mathbb{R}^n$ or its subsets are considered as posets, the usual componentwise order is always assumed unless indicated otherwise.
[25] A useful characterization of the sublattices of the product of N lattices may be found in Topkis (1976).
[26] See Section 2.2.2 on closed subbases.
[27] See Birkhoff (1967, p. 250) and Frink (1942).

This product order is understood to be the order relation on every product lattice encountered in this chapter. If S is a sublattice of $X \times T$ where X and T are lattices, then each *section* $S_t = \{x : (x,t) \in S\}$ corresponding to a fixed $t \in T$ is a sublattice of X. Let $\Pi_T S$ denoting the *projection* of S on T be defined as the set $\{t : S_t \neq \emptyset\}$. It is a sublattice of T.

In our model the underlying lattice X is the direct product of lattices X_α, where $\alpha \in A$ indexes the product's factors. The interval topology turns out to be equivalent to the product topology on X if each X_α is a lattice with a greatest and least element. Generally though, the product topology is also finer than the interval topology (the converse is not true—consider $\mathbb{R}^2 = \mathbb{R} \times \mathbb{R}$ with the usual order and observe that $\{(x,y) : y \geq 0\}$ is closed in the product topology but not in the interval topology).[28]

If X and Y are posets, then a function $f \colon X \to Y$ is *non-decreasing* if $x_1 \geq_X x_2$ in X implies $f(x_1) \geq_Y f(x_2)$ in Y. Let X be a lattice. A map F from a poset P to $L(X)$ is *ascending* if $p_1 \geq_P p_2$ in P implies $F(p_1) \geq_L F(p_2)$, i.e., if $x_1 \in F(p_1)$ and $x_2 \in F(p_2)$ imply: (i) $x_1 \vee x_2 \in F(p_1)$ and (ii) $x_1 \wedge x_2 \in F(p_2)$. The map F is *expanding* if $F(p_1) \supset F(p_2)$.

▶ Example 4: Malinvaud technologies. Let $T \subset \mathbb{R}_+^{2m}$ be a Malinvaud technology set satisfying conditions (M1)–(M6). Generally speaking, the section $T_a = \{b \in \mathbb{R}_+^m : (a,b) \in T\}$ will not be a sublattice of $\mathbb{R}_+^m$ for $m > 1$ as it will not usually contain the coordinatewise maximum of the bs.

For a one capital good model, the section T_a is not only a lattice, but a closed order interval. The projection $\{a \in \mathbb{R}_+^m : T_a \neq \emptyset\} = \mathbb{R}_+^m$, so the projection is a sublattice of itself.

In the single capital good case, it is also easy to show that a map from $\mathbb{R}_+$ to $L(\mathbb{R}_+)$ defined by $a \mapsto T_a$ is expanding by free disposal. The map is also ascending in a. Take $a_1 \geq a_2$, $(a_1,b_1) \in T$, and $(a_2,b_2) \vee T$. Then $(a_1,b_2) \in T$ by free disposal. Now $b_1 \vee b_2$ is either b_1 or b_2, which are both in T_{a_1}. Also, $b_1 \wedge b_2$ is either b_1 or b_2. The former is in T_{a_2} by construction, and if $b_1 \wedge b_2 = b_1$, $b_1 \in T_{a_2}$ by free disposal. ◀

▶ Example 5: Nonclassical technology. Suppose that f is the one-sector nonclassical production function presented in Example 4.3. It has an inflection point k_I and a maximum sustainable stock, k^M. Its graph appears in Figure 3. Let $T = \{(x,y) \in \mathbb{R}_+^2 : f(x) - y \geq 0\}$ be the corresponding production set. Its section $T_x = \{y \in \mathbb{R}_+ : f(x) - y \geq 0\}$ is non-empty for each $x \geq 0$ and is a closed interval. Hence, it is a sublattice of $\mathbb{R}_+$. Two sections are shown in Figure 3. The projection $\{x \in \mathbb{R}_+ : T_x \neq \emptyset\} = \mathbb{R}_+$, so it is a sublattice too. As with the previous example, the section T_x is ascending and expanding in x. Just repeat the the argument above with the points shown in Figure 3. ◀

---

[28] These observations are due to Birkhoff and Frink. See Topkis (1978, p. 313) for further elaboration.

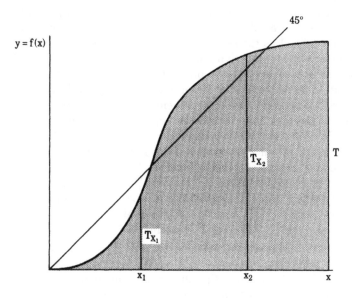

Figure 3:   Nonclassical production sections. T_{x_1} and T_{x_2} are sections of T with $x_1 < x_2$.

7.3.2 An Introduction to Monotone Comparative Statics

The basic problem analyzed using lattice programming is concerned with determining when the solution to an optimization problem is an increasing function of an underlying parameter.[29] We introduce here the basic sufficient condition for this to happen by developing an example.[30]

A function $f: X \times A \to \mathbb{R}$, where A is a poset and X is a lattice, has *increasing differences* in its two arguments x and α if for all $x \geq x'$, the difference

$$f(x, \alpha) - f(x', \alpha)$$

is non-decreasing in α.[31] If $X = \mathbb{R}$ and $A = \mathbb{R}_+$ and f is a twice continuously differentiable function, then we can give a simple differential criterion for f to have increasing differences in its two arguments.[32]

---

[29] The lattice programming technique also can be applied when there are multiple solutions to the optimization problem.

[30] This example was motivated by Ross (1983).

[31] Some lattice programmers use the term *isotone differences* to describe this property.

[32] This is a special case of Topkis's (1978) characterization of supermodularity. We

Lemma 2. *If $X = \mathbb{R}$, $A = \mathbb{R}_+$, and f is a twice continuously differentiable function, then f has increasing differences in x and α if and only if $f_{\alpha x} \geq 0$.*[33]

Proof. If $f_{\alpha x} \geq 0$, then for $x_1 > x_2$ and $\alpha_1 > \alpha_2$,

$$\int_{x_2}^{x_1} \int_{\alpha_2}^{\alpha_1} f_{\alpha x}(x, \alpha) \, d\alpha \, dx \geq 0, \text{ so}$$

$$\int_{x_2}^{x_1} \frac{\partial}{\partial x}[f(x, \alpha_1) - f(x, \alpha_2)] \, dx \geq 0.$$

Therefore

$$f(x_1, \alpha_1) - f(x_2, \alpha_1) - (f(x_1, \alpha_2) - f(x_2, \alpha_2)) \geq 0.$$

Hence, f has increasing differences.

To prove the converse we suppose that $f(x', \alpha) - f(x, \alpha)$ is non-decreasing in α and that f is twice continuously differentiable. If $\alpha_1 > \alpha_2$ and $x_1 > x$, then the increasing differences property implies

$$f(x_1, \alpha_1) - f(x, \alpha_1) \geq f(x_1, \alpha_2) - f(x, \alpha_2).$$

Since $x_1 - x > 0$, we have

$$\frac{f(x_1, \alpha_1) - f(x, \alpha_1)}{x_1 - x} \geq \frac{f(x_1, \alpha_2) - f(x, \alpha_2)}{x_1 - x}.$$

Let $x_1 \to x$ to obtain

$$f_x(x, \alpha_1) \equiv \frac{\partial}{\partial x} f(x, \alpha_1) \geq \frac{\partial}{\partial x} f(x, \alpha_2) \equiv f_x(x, \alpha_2)$$

when $\alpha_1 \geq \alpha_2$. Hence $f_x(x, \alpha_1) - f_x(x, \alpha_2) \geq 0$, and for $\alpha_1 > \alpha_2$,

$$\frac{f_x(x, \alpha_1) - f_x(x, \alpha_2)}{\alpha_1 - \alpha_2} \geq 0.$$

Therefore, as $\alpha_1 \downarrow \alpha_2$, we have

$$f_{\alpha x}(x, \alpha) \geq 0,$$

because f is twice continuously differentiable. $\square$

We can see how the smooth version of the increasing differences condition can lead to a monotone comparative statics result. Let $x(\alpha) =$

---

discuss this further in Section 7.3.3.

[33] Here $f_{\alpha x} = \partial^2 f / \partial \alpha \partial x$ is the second-order cross partial derivative of f.

argmax$_x$ $f(x, \alpha)$ where f is twice continuously differentiable. Here x is the decision variable, α is the parameter, and $f_x(x(\alpha), \alpha) = 0$ is the first-order condition. We assume here that the second-order sufficient condition for a maximum is satisfied—$f_{xx}(x(\alpha), \alpha) < 0$. By using the standard Implicit Function Theorem argument we can assert that $x(\alpha)$ is a continuously differentiable function and $x'(\alpha) = -f_{\alpha x}/f_{xx}$, where in the neighborhood of $x(\alpha)$, $f_{xx} < 0$ by the second-order sufficient condition for a maximum. Therefore, if f has increasing differences in its two arguments, then we can conclude that $f_{\alpha x} \geq 0$ and $x'(\alpha) \geq 0$, with a strict inequality whenever $f_{\alpha x} > 0$. The increasing differences condition determines the sign of $f_{\alpha x}$ and this is enough to show that the decision variable is a non-decreasing function of the parameter.

Now let's examine the nonsmooth counterpart of this elementary optimization problem. Let $M(\alpha) = \sup_{x \in X} f(x, \alpha)$ and $m(\alpha) = \{x \in X : f(x, \alpha) = M(\alpha)\}$. We suppose that the conditions of the Weierstrass Theorem are met (X is a compact subset of $\mathbb{R}$ and f is upper semicontinuous in f for each α). We note that since $m(\alpha)$ is a non-empty subset of the closed bounded interval X, we can conclude that $m(\alpha)$ contains its maximal and minimal elements. Let $h(\alpha)$ be the selection from $m(\alpha)$ that yields the maximal optimizer in $m(\alpha)$ for each $\alpha \in A$. Notice that we must assume that A is a poset if we are to impose the increasing differences property on f. We want to show that $h(\alpha_1) \geq h(\alpha_2)$ whenever $\alpha_1 > \alpha_2$. Consider $x \in X$ with $x \leq h(\alpha_2)$. Then $f(h(\alpha_2), \alpha_2) \geq f(x, \alpha_2)$, or

$$f(h(\alpha_2), \alpha_2) - f(x, \alpha_2) \geq 0. \tag{13}$$

Applying increasing differences to (13) yields $f(h(\alpha_2), \alpha_1) - f(x, \alpha_1) \geq 0$. No element smaller than $h(\alpha_2)$ can be $h(\alpha_1)$. Because X is a chain, $h(\alpha_1) \geq h(\alpha_2)$—this optimal policy selection is a non-decreasing function of the parameter. This argument does not assume the uniqueness of an optimizer given the parameter value. However, if $m(\alpha)$ is a singleton for each α, then we may conclude that the optimal solution is a non-decreasing function of the parameter value.

7.3.3 Topkis's Theorems

We have just seen how the increasing differences property might be used to produce a monotone comparative statics result. Topkis's theorems and their generalizations by Milgrom, Roberts, and Shannon are built on a generalization of increasing differences called supermodularity.[34]

---

[34] Strictly speaking, the recent papers by Milgrom et al. utilize the weaker concept of quasi-supermodularity. However, we will not need their industrial strength versions of Topkis's results and hence limit our discussion to the case of supermodular functions.

Supermodular Function. A function $f \colon X \to \mathbb{R}$ defined on the lattice X is said to be supermodular if $f(x_1 \wedge x_2) + f(x_1 \vee x_2) \geq f(x_1) + f(x_2)$ for all $x_1, x_2 \in X$. If the inequality is strict, then f is strictly supermodular.

Every real-valued function defined on $\mathbb{R}$ is supermodular since $\mathbb{R}$ is a chain. If $X = \mathbb{R}^2$, then f is supermodular if and only if f has increasing differences in its two arguments. Hence, if f is also twice continuously differentiable, then f has non-negative mixed partial derivatives. Topkis (1978) showed that f defined on $\mathbb{R}^n$ is supermodular if and only if $f(x + \epsilon e^i) - f(x)$ is non-decreasing in x_j for all $i \neq j$, $\epsilon > 0$, and x, where e^i is the ith unit vector in $\mathbb{R}^n$. For example, on $\mathbb{R}^3$, one of the conditions would be

$$f(x + \epsilon, y_1, z_1) - f(x, y_1, z_1) \geq f(x + \epsilon, y_2, z_2) - f(x, y_2, z_2)$$

when $(y_1, z_1) \geq (y_2, z_2)$. There are two other related conditions for supermodularity to hold on $\mathbb{R}^3$. If f is differentiable on $\mathbb{R}^n$, then f is supermodular if and only if $\partial f / \partial x_i$ is non-decreasing in x_j for all $i \neq j$ and x. If f is twice continuously differentiable on $\mathbb{R}^n$, then f is supermodular if and only if $\partial^2 f / \partial x_i \partial x_j \geq 0$ for all $i \neq j$ and all x.

Supermodular functions have been known by other names in different settings. For example, when f is a neoclassical production function defined on $\mathbb{R}_+^m$, then the supermodularity of f is equivalent to assuming all factors are *normal*—an increase in one factor raises the marginal product of all other factors.[35] Hence, supermodularity is a generalized form of Edgeworth complementarity.

Rewrite the inequality defining a supermodular function f as

$$f(x \vee y) - f(x) \geq f(x \wedge y) - f(y).$$

This says that on the four-point sublattice $\{x, y, x \wedge y, x \vee y\}$ the change in f's value in response to an increase in some of its arguments is a non-decreasing function of the levels of the other variables. The arguments of the function are complementary since increasing some of them increases the payoffs to increasing the others. The requirement that the domain of f be a lattice can be interpreted as a technical form of complementarity. The lattice property implies that an increase in the value of some variables is always compatible with increasing the others as well. Similarly, decreasing some variables always allows decreases in the other variables.[36]

---

[35] See Rader (1968) for a more detailed study of normal inputs in the neoclassical theory of the firm and general equilibrium theory. Consult Samuelson (1974) for a general review of complementarity in consumer and producer theory.

[36] For a more detailed discussion of the connections between supermodularity and complementarity consult Milgrom and Roberts (1994b; 1995).

Supermodularity is preserved under a variety of operations. The following results are drawn from Topkis (1978). The first two items follow easily from the definition of a supermodular function.

Supermodularity Lemma.

(1) If f and g are supermodular, and $\alpha, \beta \geq 0$, then $\alpha f + \beta g$ is supermodular.

(2) If $\{f_n\}$ is a sequence of supermodular functions with pointwise limit f^*, then f^* is supermodular.

(3) If f is supermodular and increasing and $g \colon \mathbb{R} \to \mathbb{R}$ is increasing and convex, then $g \circ f$ is supermodular.

The preceding lemma tells us that the composition of an increasing supermodular function with an increasing convex function is supermodular. Unfortunately, this result is not valid for increasing concave functions. Figure 4 shows the problem. Let f be any supermodular function defined on $\mathbb{R}^2$ and let $f^{ij} = f(x_i, y_j)$ for $i, j = 1, 2$. We can express the increasing differences condition (which is equivalent to supermodularity here) as the inequality $f^{11} - f^{21} \geq f^{12} - f^{22}$. Figure 4 shows the points f^{ij} plotted on the horizontal axis against their values $g(f^{ij})$ where g is an increasing concave function. The graph has been drawn so that $g(f^{11}) - g(f^{21}) < g(f^{21}) - g(f^{22})$ holds. Thus, the composition of f with an increasing concave function may reverse the ordering of differences. An increasing convex function g composed with this f would preserve those differences, and hence $h \colon \mathbb{R}^2 \to \mathbb{R}$ defined by $(x, y) \mapsto h(x, y) = g(f(x, y))$ is a supermodular function.

The standard lattice programming problem is concerned with the maximization of a supermodular function over a lattice. The first result is the lattice programming analogue of the Weierstrass Theorem.[37]

Lattice Optimization Theorem. *If f is a supermodular function on a lattice X, then the set $m(f, X) = \mathrm{argmax}\{f(x) : x \in X\}$ is a sublattice of X. If X is a non-empty lattice that is compact in a topology finer than the interval topology and f is supermodular and upper semicontinuous on X, then the $m(f, X)$ is a non-empty, compact, and complete sublattice of X and hence has a greatest and least element.*

Proof. Choose any x and y in $m(f, X)$. As f is supermodular on X

---

[37] The existence of maximal and minimal optimizers can be demonstrated directly using the order structure. A real-valued function f defined on the lattice X is **order upper semicontinuous** at $x \in X$ if for any net $\{x^\lambda\}$ in X with $x^\lambda \overset{o}{\to} x$, $\limsup_\lambda f(x^\lambda) \leq f(x)$. Milgrom and Roberts (1990) proved that if f is an order semicontinuous supermodular function on a complete lattice X taking values in $\mathbb{R} \cup \{-\infty\}$, then f has a maximum on X. Moreover, the set of maximizers of f is a complete sublattice of X, and has both largest and smallest elements.

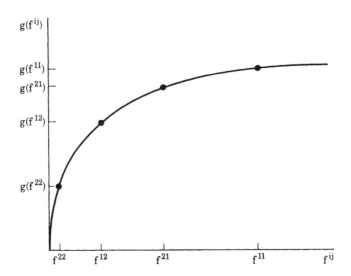

Figure 4:   Increasing differences are not preserved when a concave function is composed with a supermodular function. Here $f^{11} - f^{21} > f^{12} - f^{22}$, but $g(f^{11}) - g(f^{21}) < g(f^{12}) - g(f^{22})$.

and $x, y \in m(f, X) \subset X$, it follows that

$$0 \geq f(x \vee y) - f(x) \geq f(y) - f(x \wedge y) \geq 0.$$

Hence $m(f, X)$ is a sublattice. Since f is upper semicontinuous and X is compact, $m(f, X)$ is non-empty and compact in a topology finer than the interval topology. Therefore, the Frink-Birkhoff Theorem implies $m(f, X)$ is complete. $\square$

   This result tells us that there are always two selections that can be drawn from $m(f, X)$, one taking the greatest element of $m(f, X)$, the other taking the least element. If these coincide, then $m(f, X)$ is a singleton.

   We are now ready to state Topkis's Theorems.[38]

Topkis's Value Function Theorem. *Suppose X and T are lattices, S is a sublattice of $X \times T$, f is supermodular on S, S_t is the section of S at*

---

[38] These are reformulated versions of Theorems 4.3 and 6.1–6.3 in Topkis (1978). We have transposed his results for minimization problems into the corresponding maximization cases.

$t \in T$, and $g(t) = \sup_{x \in S_t} f(x, t)$ is finite on the projection $\Pi_T S$. Then g is supermodular on $\Pi_T S$.

Proof. Choose any $t, u \in \Pi_T S$, $x \in S_t$, and $y \in S_u$. Since S is a sublattice, $(x \lor y, t \lor u) = (x, t) \lor (y, u) \in S$ and $(x \land y, t \land u) = (x, t) \land (y, u) \in S$. Thus

$$g(t \lor u) + g(t \land u) \geq f(x \lor y, t \lor u)$$
$$+ f(x \land y, t \land u) \geq f(x, t) + f(y, u), \quad (14)$$

where the latter inequality follows from the assumed supermodularity of f. Now take the supremum of the right-hand side of (14) over $x \in S_t$ and $y \in S_u$ to conclude that g is supermodular. $\square$

Topkis's Value Function Theorem tells us that the maximization operation preserves supermodularity. The value function of a lattice programming problem with supermodular objective is itself supermodular.

The next result establishes a set of sufficient conditions for the optimal solutions of a lattice programming function to be monotone increasing in their parameters. Let

$$m(f, S_t) = \operatorname{argmax}_{x \in S_t} f(x, t).$$

We first state a verification lemma that sets out a sufficient condition for $m(f, S_t)$ to be ascending in $t \in T$.

Lemma 3. *Suppose S is a lattice, T is a poset, $S_t \subset S$ is ascending in t on T, and*

$$f(x \land y, t) + f(x \lor y, u) \geq f(x, t) + f(y, u) \quad (15)$$

for all t and u in T with $u \geq t$, $x \in S_t$, and $y \in S_u$. Then $m(f, S_t)$ is ascending in t on $T^* = \{t \in T : m(f, S_t) \neq \emptyset\}$.

Proof. The Lattice Programming Theorem and (15) imply that each $m(f, S_t)$ is a sublattice of S. Pick t and u in T^* with $t \leq u$. Then pick $x \in m(f, S_t)$ and $y \in m(f, S_u)$. Because S_t is ascending in t, we have $x \land y \in S_t$ and $x \lor y \in S_u$. Then by (15) and the optimality of $x \in S_t$ and $y \in S_u$,

$$0 \leq f(x, t) - f(x \land y, t) \leq f(x \lor y, u) - f(y, u) \leq 0. \quad (16)$$

Therefore equality holds in (16) and we may conclude that $x \land y \in m(f, S_t)$ and $x \lor y \in m(f, S_u)$. Hence $m(f, S_t)$ is ascending in t on T^*. $\square$

Topkis's Monotonicity Theorem. *Suppose S is a lattice, T is a poset, S_t is ascending in t on T, $f(x, t)$ is supermodular in $x \in S$ for each $t \in T$, $f(x, t)$ has increasing differences in $(x, t) \in S \times T$, each S_t is compact in a topology finer than the interval topology, and $f(x, t)$ is* upper semicontinuous in $x \in S$ for each $t \in T$. Then $m(f, S_t)$ is ascending and thus has a least element, $\underline{s}_t$, and greatest element, $\bar{s}_t$, both of which are non-decreasing in $t \in T$.

Proof. We verify inequality (15) to show that $m(f, S_t)$ is ascending. Since S_t is ascending in t, we have $x \vee y \in S_u$. Since $y \leq x \vee y$, the increasing differences hypothesis implies

$$f(x \vee y, u) - f(y, u) \geq f(x \vee y, t) - f(y, t). \tag{17}$$

The supermodularity of $f(x, t)$ in x for each t implies

$$f(x \vee y, t) - f(y, t) \geq f(x, t) - f(x \wedge y, t). \tag{18}$$

Combine inequalities (17) and (18) to yield (15):

$$f(x \vee y, u) - f(y, u) \geq f(x \vee y, t) - f(y, t) \geq f(x, t) - f(x \wedge y, t).$$

The Lattice Programming Theorem implies that $m(f, S_t)$ is non-empty and its least and greatest elements exist. It remains to show that they are non-decreasing in t. Note that $m(f, S_t)$ is a complete sublattice. Since $m(f, S_t)$ is ascending, we have for any $x \in m(f, S_t)$ and $y \in m(f, S_u)$ that $x \wedge y \in m(f, S_t)$ and $x \vee y \in m(f, S_u)$ when $u \geq t$. Therefore, $\inf m(f, S_t) \leq x \wedge y \leq y$ and $x \leq x \vee y \leq \sup m(f, S_u)$, and hence $\underline{s}_t = \inf m(f, S_t) \leq \inf m(f, S_u) = \underline{s}_u$ and $\bar{s}_t = \sup m(f, S_t) \leq \sup m(f, S_u) = \bar{s}_u$. □

7.4 Lattice Programming and the TAS Model

Amir (1996) has shown how to apply Topkis's theorems to TAS reduced-form models. He allows the technology to reside in $\mathbb{R}_+^{2m}$, so there are m capital goods. He does not assume either the technology is convex or the reduced-form felicity is concave in keeping with the spirit of lattice programming methods. He shows how the closely allied concepts of supermodularity and increasing differences can be combined to prove that the optimal capital sequence is non-decreasing and there is a capital deepening response for increases in the discount factor. We will illustrate his results using the aggregative reduced-form TAS model with discounting. The technology set $T \subset \mathbb{R}_+^2$ satisfies (M1), (M3)–(M6).[39] T is a Malinvaud technology when (M2), convexity, is also satisfied. However, this is not required in our application of the lattice programming technique. Define the section $T_k = \{b \geq 0 : (k, b) \in T\}$. It is a non-empty set

---

[39] The Malinvaud conditions (M1)–(M6) were introduced in Section 4.3.1.

for each $k \geq 0$. Moreover, T_k will be a sublattice of $\mathbb{R}_+$, and the map $k \mapsto T_k$ is ascending and expanding, as in Examples 4 and 5. Further, the correspondence $k \mapsto T_k$ is assumed to be compact-valued, and upper semicontinuous. These conditions are met if $T = \{(k, b) \in \mathbb{R}_+^2 : k \leq f(b)\}$ when f is an increasing continuous function with $f(0) = 0$.[40] Hence, we allow classical and nonclassical production functions to generate the technology set.

The reduced-form felicity function, $v(k, b)$, satisfies the following:

Reduced-Form Felicity Conditions. $v\colon T \to \mathbb{R}_+$ satisfies the following conditions:

- (V1) $v(a, b)$ is non-decreasing in a for each b.
- (V2) v is supermodular in $(a, b) \in T$.
- (V3) There is a $K > 0$ such that $|v(a, b)| \leq K$ for all $(a, b) \in T$ (boundedness).
- (V4) v is upper semicontinuous in each $(a, b) \in T$.
- (V5) If $(a, b) \in T$, and $a' \geq a$, $0 \leq b' \leq b$, then $v(a', b') \geq v(a, b)$ (monotonicity).

The boundedness assumption is for technical purposes and can be relaxed to some extent.[41]

7.4.1 Monotonicity of Optimal Capital Policy Functions

We show first how to obtain monotonic optimal capital sequences by showing the optimal capital policy correspondence is ascending. As in Section 7.2.1, we consider the recursion:

$$J_n(k) = \sup_{b \in T_k} \{v(k, b) + \delta J_{n-1}(b)\}, \text{ for } n = 1, 2, \ldots, \quad (19)$$

where $J_0(k) \equiv 0$. Here J_n is the value function when there are n periods of consumption remaining and J is the value function of the corresponding infinite horizon Bellman equation:[42]

$$J(k) = \sup_{b \in T_k} \{v(k, b) + \delta J(b)\}. \quad (20)$$

We let

$$G_n(k) = \operatorname{argmax}\{v(k, b) + \delta J_{n-1}(b) : b \in T_k\}$$

and

$$G(k) = \operatorname{argmax}\{v(k, b) + \delta J(b) : b \in T_k\}.$$

---

[40] See Example 4.8.

[41] See Amir (1996) for the details.

[42] In Section 7.2.1, we found it convenient to start one period later. In that case we assumed $v_2 > 0$, so $J_1(k) = v(k, 0)$.

These sets give the current optimal capital decisions when the starting stock is k and there are n (or infinitely many) periods remaining. We note that our technology and felicity conditions yield upper semicontinuous J_n and J, allowing us to replace the sup operator with the max operator in (19) and (20).

It is straightforward to show that J_n and J are non-decreasing in k. We have $J_1(k) = \max_{b \in T_k} v(k, b)$ since $J_0(k) \equiv 0$. Since $v(a, \cdot)$ is supermodular (because it is defined on a chain) we can apply Topkis's Value Function Theorem to conclude that J_1 is supermodular. We continue this by applying an induction argument. Assume that J_{n-1} is supermodular. Then the objective in (19) is supermodular as the sum of two supermodular functions (by the Supermodularity Lemma). Applying Topkis's Value Function Theorem once again, we conclude that J_n is supermodular. But supermodularity is preserved by taking the pointwise limit of the sequence $\{J_n\}$ (by the Supermodularity Lemma). Standard dynamic programming theory tells us that $J = \lim_n J_n$, hence J is supermodular.

We can apply Topkis's Monotonicity Theorem to the problems (19) and (20) because $v(k, b) + \delta J_{n-1}(b)$ and $v(k, b) + \delta J(b)$ also have increasing differences (they are supermodular functions on $\mathbb{R}^2$). Let $\underline{g}_n(k) = \inf G_n(k)$, $\bar{g}_n(k) = \sup G_n(k)$ and let $\underline{g}(k) = \inf G(k)$, $\bar{g}(k) = \sup G(k)$. Topkis's Monotonicity Theorem implies G_n and G are ascending, $\underline{g}_n$, $\bar{g}_n$, $\underline{g}$, and $\bar{g}$ are non-decreasing. If G_n and G are singleton sets for each k, then we conclude the optimal capital policy function is non-decreasing. We summarize this discussion in the following theorem due to Amir (1996).

Amir's Capital Stock Monotonicity Theorem. *Consider the reduced-form TAS model with one capital good and discount factor δ. Suppose that the technology conditions (M1), (M3)–(M6) are met, $k \mapsto T_k$ is a compact-valued and upper semicontinuous correspondence, and the felicity conditions hold. Then*

(1) *J_n and J are non-decreasing in k;*
(2) *J_n and J are supermodular on $\mathbb{R}_+$;*
(3) *$\underline{g}_n$, $\bar{g}_n$, $\underline{g}$, and $\bar{g}$ are non-decreasing in k.*

This result tells us that a sufficient condition for a discounted TAS infinite horizon one capital good model to yield a non-decreasing optimal capital policy selection is that the one-period return function be supermodular and the related lattice theoretic technology properties obtain. By iterating the optimal policy function for the infinite horizon we can conclude that the optimal capital sequence is monotonic too, provided it is uniquely determined by the initial capital stock. We reiterate that this result applies to nonclassical as well as classical technologies.

▶ Example 6: Capital accumulation and wealth effects. Kurz (1968b) introduced the following discounted TAS model of optimal capital accumulation. The wealth effect or capital stock effect can arise in fishery models where the biomass (the capital stock) enters the one-period reward function.[43] The planner solves the problem

$$J(k) = \sup \sum_{t=1}^{\infty} \delta^{t-1} u(c_t, k_{t-1})$$

$$\text{s.t. } c_t + k_t \leq f(k_{t-1}), \text{ for } t = 1, 2, \ldots,$$

$$c_t \geq 0, k_t \geq 0 \text{ and } k_0 \leq k.$$

The production function in Kurz's model is a strictly concave neoclassical one and the reduced-form felicity is $v(k_{t-1}, k_t) = u(f(k_{t-1}) - k_t, k_{t-1})$ where u is strictly concave. This function will be supermodular if u is twice continuously differentiable and $v_{12} \geq 0$. The latter condition is met if $v_{12} = -u_{11}f' - u_{21} \geq 0$. In particular, if $u(c, k) = \varphi(c) + \xi(k)$, then $u_{12} = 0$ and $v_{12} \geq 0$. In this case, there is a unique optimal capital stock for each initial stock and the optimal capital sequence will be nondecreasing (in fact, this can be strengthened to "increasing" given the concavity hypotheses). By way of contrast, Majumdar and Mitra (1994a) show in concave wealth effects problems that if $v_{12} < 0$, then the optimal capital sequence can be cyclic or even chaotic.

We notice that the lattice programming technique allows us to couple a nonclassical production function with a wealth effect in the utility function to produce monotonic optimal capital sequences. The supermodularity condition $v_{12} \geq 0$ can be met without assuming either a neoclassical technology set or a concave objective. This is important since many renewable resource models posit a nonclassical technology. Hence, the lattice programming approach to obtaining qualitative information on the structure of optimal solutions can be pushed to give new results in nonconcave problems of economic interest. ◄

7.4.2 The Capital Deepening Theorem

We used the smooth form of supermodularity to demonstrate the capital deepening property for concave aggregative reduced-form models in Section 7.2. The induction argument told us that we had a sequence of supermodular value functions (where the nth term in the sequence gave the optimal value for the n-stage problem). By applying the Supermodularity Lemma, we can now conclude that the limit value function is also

---

[43] See Majumdar and Mitra (1994a) for an extensive defense of this model and a more complete discussion of the rationale for assuming capital can be an argument of the utility function in renewable resource management problems. They also defend this assumption in the context of optimal growth models.

supermodular without appealing to an auxiliary smoothness hypothesis.[44] However, we can weaken the smoothness and concavity requirements by applying lattice programming methods throughout. The basic argument will be similar—induction on the number of stages. We apply Topkis's theorems to obtain the capital deepening conclusion. The advantage of applying the purely lattice theoretic methodology is that we can unify the neoclassical and nonclassical models. The original result along these lines was obtained by Amir, Mirman, and Perkins (1991). We continue to follow Amir's (1996) reduced-form presentation, but restrict our focus to the one good reduced-form model.

We can address the capital deepening hypothesis for this aggregative model by reconsidering the recursion (19) and Bellman equation (20) with explicit recognition that the value functions depend on the discount factor as well as the current capital stock. These equations are written out as

$$J_n(k, \delta) = \sup_{b \in T_k} \{v(k, b) + \delta J_{n-1}(b, \delta)\}, \text{ for } n = 1, 2, \ldots; \tag{21}$$

$$J(k, \delta) = \sup_{b \in T_k} \{v(k, b) + \delta J(b, \delta)\}. \tag{22}$$

We let $J_0(k, \delta) \equiv 0$ in the n-stage recursion (21). The optimal policy correspondences are denoted by $G_n(k, \delta)$ for the n-stage problem and $G(k, \delta)$ for the infinite horizon problem. Analogous notation is used for their least and largest selections. The same type of induction argument used to demonstrate monotonicity can be used to establish the capital deepening hypothesis. We let $\Delta = [\underline{\delta}, \bar{\delta}]$ where $0 < \underline{\delta} < \bar{\delta} < 1$ are fixed (as in Section 7.2.1).[45]

Amir's Capital Deepening Theorem. *Consider the reduced-form TAS model with one capital good and discount factor $\delta \in \Delta$. Suppose that the technology conditions (M1), (M3)–(M6) are met, $k \mapsto T_k$ is a compact-valued and upper semicontinuous correspondence, and the felicity conditions hold. Then*

(1) *J_n and J are supermodular on $\mathbb{R}_+ \times \Delta$;*
(2) *For $\delta_1 \geq \delta_2$ in Δ, $\underline{g}_n(\cdot, \delta_1) \geq \underline{g}_n(\cdot, \delta_2)$, $\bar{g}_n(\cdot, \delta_1) \geq \bar{g}_n(\cdot, \delta_2)$, $\underline{g}(\cdot, \delta_1)$ $\geq \underline{g}(\cdot, \delta_2)$, and $\bar{g}(\cdot, \delta_1) \geq \bar{g}(\cdot, \delta_2)$.*

Proof. The first step is to demonstrate that J_n is supermodular in $(k, \delta) \in \mathbb{R}_+ \times \Delta$ using an induction argument. For $n = 1$, J_1 is independent

---

[44] The contortions surrounding the smoothness of J arose in Section 7.2 because we could not be sure that the sequence J_n and its first two derivatives converged uniformly to J and its first two derivatives. We needed the second derivatives to deduce a comparative dynamics result. Dynamic programming theory only got us the convergence of J_n to J pointwise.

[45] This condition ensures that $J_n \to J$ via a routine dynamic programming argument.

of δ, and supermodular on $\mathbb{R}_+$ by the second part of Amir's Monotonicity Theorem. Hence, J_1 is supermodular in (k, δ) on $\mathbb{R}_+ \times \Delta$. The induction hypothesis is J_{n-1} is supermodular in (x, δ) on $\mathbb{R}_+ \times \Delta$. We claim that J_n has the desired supermodularity property because the maximand on the right-hand side of (21) is supermodular in (k, b, δ) on $T \times \Delta$. Since v is supermodular in (k, b) by assumption, we need only prove that $\delta J_{n-1}(b, \delta)$ is supermodular on $T_k \times \Delta$. The Supermodularity Lemma then tells us the sum $v(k, b) + \delta J_{n-1}(b, \delta)$ is supermodular on $T \times \Delta$. To see that $\delta J_{n-1}(b, \delta)$ is supermodular on $T_k \times \Delta$ we note that the induction hypothesis implies that for $\delta_1 \geq \delta_2$ and $b_1, b_2 \in T_k$,

$$J_{n-1}(b_1 \vee b_2, \delta_1) - J_{n-1}(b_1, \delta_1)$$
$$\geq J_{n-1}(b_2, \delta_2) - J_{n-1}(b_1 \wedge b_2, \delta_2) \geq 0. \quad (23)$$

Multiplication of the left-hand side of (23) by δ_1 and the remainder of (23) by δ_2 does not change the sense of the inequality. Thus

$$\delta_1 J_{n-1}(b_1 \vee b_2, \delta_1) - \delta_1 J_{n-1}(b_1, \delta_1) \geq \delta_2 J_{n-1}(b_2, \delta_2) - \delta_2 J_{n-1}(b_1 \wedge b_2, \delta_2).$$

Therefore, $\delta J_{n-1}(b, \delta)$ is supermodular on $T_k \times \Delta$. Topkis's Value Function Theorem now implies that $J_n(k, \delta)$ is supermodular. By induction, we conclude that this is true for all n. Since $J_n(k, \delta) \to J(k, \delta)$ pointwise, we infer from the Supermodularity Lemma that J is supermodular too.

We apply Topkis's Monotonicity Theorem to (21) and (22) to conclude that for $\delta_1 \geq \delta_2$ in Δ, $\underline{g}_n(\cdot, \delta_1) \geq \underline{g}_n(\cdot, \delta_2)$, $\bar{g}_n(\cdot, \delta_1) \geq \bar{g}_n(\cdot, \delta_2)$, $\underline{g}(\cdot, \delta_1) \geq \underline{g}(\cdot, \delta_2)$, and $\bar{g}(\cdot, \delta_1) \geq \bar{g}(\cdot, \delta_2)$. $\square$

We conclude this discussion of lattice programming with a TAS objective with the following observations about our capital income tax model.

▶ Example 7: Capital income tax reform and capital deepening. The Θ-PFCE Equivalence Theorem can be combined with lattice programming theory. Let

$$J(k, \Theta) = \max \sum_{t=1}^{\infty} (\delta\Theta)^{t-1} u(f(k_{t-1}) - k_t)$$
$$\text{s.t. } (k_{t-1}, k_t) \in T = \{(a, b) \in \mathbb{R}_+^2 : f(a) - b \geq 0\}$$

represent the reduced-form model solved by the artificial planner (recall $\Theta \equiv 1 - \theta$, where θ is the tax rate). J can be shown to be supermodular in Θ by mimicking our previous arguments. This result shows that the smoothness conditions used to analyze the capital income tax problem can be significantly relaxed while preserving the main economic conclusion: an unanticipated capital income tax reform yields a capital deepening response. ◀

7.5 Recursive Utility Models

Topkis's theorems can be applied when utility is recursive. The additive structure is not crucial for obtaining monotonicity theorems or capital deepening responses.

7.5.1 Recursive Utility, Monotonicity, and Lattice Programming

Consider the one-sector Ramsey model with recursive utility expressed by the aggregator $W(c, y)$. If $W_{12} \geq 0$, then W is supermodular and the conditions of Topkis's theorems are met. The optimal capital sequence is monotonic. Unfortunately, some interesting aggregators are not supermodular. For instance, the Epstein-Hynes and KDW aggregators have the opposite property—$W_{12} < 0$. However, there is an alternative criterion for programs to be monotonic in the Ramsey model. We proved in Section 5.2.4 that one-sector Ramsey models with recursive utility had monotonic optimal capital sequences if the marginal rate of impatience is a decreasing function of the first period's consumption, i.e., $\partial R/\partial c_1 < 0$. This was seen to be equivalent to the requirement that $\partial \left[W_1(c_1, y)/W_2(c_1, y) \right]/\partial c_1 < 0$, which means that the indifference curves in (c_1, y)-space are convex to the origin. This hypothesis also means that y enters W like a *normal good* in demand theory.[46] If the aggregator is supermodular and concave, then it satisfies this normality condition for monotonicity as $\partial \left[W_1(c_1, y)/W_2(c_1, y) \right]/\partial c_1 = W_{11} W_2^{-1} - W_1 W_2^{-2} W_{21}$.[47] However, the converse is false because the Epstein-Hynes and KDW aggregators satisfy this normality condition, but neither are supermodular. For example, in the KDW case, $W_1/W_2 = abc^{b-1}/d$, where $a, b, d > 0$ and $b < 1$. Hence, $\partial[W_1/W_2]/\partial c_1 = ab(b-1)c_1^{b-2} < 0$ and this aggregator is normal.

7.5.2 Increasing Impatience and Recursive Utility

The investigation of the capital deepening hypothesis for TAS models was greatly facilitated by the fact that there was a natural parameter, the discount factor, that could be used to describe how the planner could become more patient. In the broader family of recursive utility functions the discount parameter varies over time or across steady states. Hence, we must find a way to define a decrease in impatience if we hope to analyze the sensitivity of an optimal program with respect to a change in impatience.

---

[46] Milgrom and Shannon (1994) observe that this condition alone is sufficient for monotonicity of the optimal capital sequence—no convexity hypotheses are necessary.

[47] Joshi (1995) considers recursive utility under uncertainty. He shows how to link supermodularity of the aggregator to stochastic monotonicity in optimal growth models.

One way to describe a change in impatience is to find a one-parameter family of recursive utility functions that has the property that an increase in that parameter's value corresponds to our intuitive idea that the planner's rate of impatience has decreased or the planner has become more patient. Hertzendorf (1995) proposed a one-parameter family of aggregators that is suitable for a sensitivity analysis.[48] He assumes that all aggregators are non-negative and we make this auxiliary assumption here too. The key observation is that if $W(c, y)$ is an aggregator, then W_2 is the marginal value of an additional util received in the next period. Hence, W_2 is the discount factor at the point (c, y). In the additive case, $W_2 = \delta$ is the discount factor and an increase in δ increases W_2 everywhere. This motivates us to think of a more general situation: an aggregator W^* discounts the future less heavily than an aggregator W, if for all admissible (c, y) we have $W_2^*(c, y) > W_2(c, y)$. Hertzendorf notes that there is more than one possible way to parameterize an increase consistent with saying one aggregator discounts the future less heavily than another. He goes on to suggest a one-parameter family of functions that will do this. The TAS aggregator is $W(c, y) = v(c) + \delta y$; recursive substitution leads to the TAS utility function. An increase in δ increases W_2 by adding a constant amount to it. We can also do this for more general aggregators.

Reduction in the Rate of Impatience. Let $W^\delta(c, y) = W(c, y) + \delta y$. When δ increases, then we say there has been a reduction in the rate of impatience.

Since $W_2^\delta = W_2 + \delta$, an increase in δ uniformly increases the discount factor.[49] Given a "primitive" aggregator W, the one-parameter family of aggregators $\{W^\delta\}$ gives us a parametric partial ordering of aggregators: $W^{\delta_1} \geq W^{\delta_2}$ if and only if $\delta_1 \geq \delta_2$. We will use this continuum of aggregators to study the impact of a change in δ on the optimal capital sequence. Hence, the capital deepening hypothesis for recursive utility models is interpreted as saying the optimal capital stock increases at each time when δ increases.

▶ **Example 8: TAS utility.** Let $W(c, y) = v(c) + \beta y$, where $v \geq 0$ and $0 < \beta < 1$. The perturbed family of aggregators takes the form $W^\delta(c, y) = v(c) + (\beta + \delta)y$. Recursive substitution yields the utility function $U^\delta(\mathbf{c}) = \sum_{t=1}^\infty (\beta + \delta)^{t-1} v(c_t)$. The marginal rate of impatience between any two adjacent periods is $v'(c_t)/(\beta + \delta)v'(c_{t+1})$, which reduces to $1/(\beta + \delta)$ in a steady state. Thus, the planner's rate of impatience in a steady state has decreased for each $\delta > 0$ compared to the original rate of impatience $\beta^{-1} - 1$. Hence, the perturbation in the discount factor introduced above

---

[48] Our summary of capital deepening results for recursive utility is based on his paper.
[49] This increase in the discount factor decreases impatience whether measured by marginal rate of impatience or by continuity. If $W_{22} \geq 0$, it also decreases the steady state rate of impatience.

is equivalent to an increase in the discount factor and therefore a reduction in the rate of impatience. ◄

▶ **Example 9: Epstein-Hynes utility.** Let $V(c, y) = (-1 + y) \exp(-v(c))$, where $y \leq 0$, $v(c) > 0$, $v' > 0$, and $v'' < 0$. Since $V \leq 0$, we renormalize it to give the adjusted aggregator $W(c, y) = [y + \nu/(1 - \nu)] \exp(-v(c)) - 1/(1 - \nu)$ where $\nu = \exp(v(0))$.[50] The perturbed family of aggregators is given by $W^\delta(c, y) = [y + \nu/(1 - \nu)] \exp(-v(c)) - 1/(1 - \nu) + \delta y$. Its steady-state marginal rate of impatience is $1 + \varrho^\delta(c) = 1/(\exp(-v(c)) + \delta)$ and it decreases as δ increases. Hence, an increase in δ reduces the steady-state rate of impatience. Thus, our definition of a decrease in impatience is consistent with a reduction in the steady-state rate of impatience. ◄

7.5.3 Capital Deepening and Recursive Utility

Lattice programming theory can yield a capital deepening theorem for recursive utility when we add the auxiliary assumption $W_{22} \geq 0$ to the supermodularity condition $W_{12} \geq 0$. The aggregator need not be concave in this situation, so we may lose uniqueness of the optimal program given the underlying parameters. However, this is not a problem since Topkis's methods work as easily with optimal policy correspondences as with policy functions. Of course, the key step is to prove the value function is supermodular and this is where the supplementary condition $W_{22} \geq 0$ is critical as we will show in the one-sector model by following Hertzendorf's (1995) argument.

The hypothesis $W_{22} \geq 0$ may appear odd since we have generally focused on aggregators satisfying the opposite inequality. The TAS and EH aggregators satisfy $W_{22} = 0$, so they are consistent with this convexity condition. However, the TAS aggregator is supermodular ($W_{12} = 0$) whereas the EH aggregator is not since $W_{12} < 0$. Hence, we need an example of a non-TAS supermodular aggregator with $W_{22} \geq 0$ in order to show how our lattice theoretic methods can accommodate some recursive utility functions beyond those already covered by Amir's theorems.

▶ **Example 10: The UEH aggregator.** Recall that the Uzawa-Epstein-Hynes aggregator is given by $W(c, y) = u(c) + e^{-v(c)}y$. We require $u \geq 0$, $u' > 0$, $v' < 0$, $u'' < 0$, $(v')^2 < v''$, $v(0) > 0$, and $y \geq 0$. This ensures that utility exists (by the Continuous Existence Theorem, or by examining the utility sums), and is non-negative, increasing and concave. A routine computation shows $W_1 = u'(c) - v'(c)e^{-v(c)}y > 0$, $W_2 = e^{-v(c)} > 0$, $W_{11} = u''(c) + [(v'(c))^2 - v''(c)]e^{-v(c)}y < 0$, $W_{12} = W_{21} = -v'e^{-v(c)} > 0$ and $W_{22} = 0$. This aggregator is supermodular and obeys $W_{22} \geq 0$. If $W^\delta(c, y) = u(c) + (e^{-v(c)} + \delta)y$, then an increase in δ will correspond

---

[50] This adjustment of the EH utility scale was discussed in Section 3.5.1.

to a decrease in the steady-state rate of impatience which is given by $1 + \varrho^\delta(c) = (W_2^\delta)^{-1} = 1/(e^{-v(c)} + \delta)$. ◀

Consider the one-sector optimal growth problem

$$J(x, \delta) = \sup W^\delta(x - k_0, W^\delta(f(k_0) - k_1, W^\delta(f(k_1) - k_2, \dots)) \cdots)$$
$$\text{s.t. } k_t \le f(k_{t-1}), \text{ for } t = 1, 2, \dots, \text{ and } 0 \le k_0 \le x,$$

where x is given, $\delta \in \Delta = [0, \bar{\delta}]$ for $0 < \bar{\delta} < 1$, and $W^\delta(x - k, y) = W(x - k, y) + \delta y$.[51] This model has a slightly different dating scheme than our earlier ones—the initial x is the given amount of output that can be consumed or saved at time $t = 0$. The decision, k_0, determines current consumption $c_0 = x - k_0$ and next period's output $f(k_0) = x_1$ and so on. We assume:

Hertzendorf Conditions.

(1) The aggregator $W: \mathcal{D} \subset \mathbb{R}_+^2 \to \mathbb{R}_+$ is continuous and strictly increasing in both arguments. Moreover, $W(c, y)$ is strictly concave in c for each y and $\bar{\beta} \equiv \sup_y W_2$ obeys $\bar{\beta} + \bar{\delta} < 1$;

(2) The production function $f: \mathbb{R}_+ \to \mathbb{R}_+$ is continuous, non-decreasing, and there is a maximum sustainable stock $k^M > 0$.

The Bellman equation for this problem is

$$J(x, \delta) = \sup_{0 \le k \le x} \{W(x - k, J(f(k), \delta)) + \delta J(f(k), \delta)\}.$$

Let $\psi(x, \delta) = \text{argmax}_{0 \le k \le x}\{W(x - k, J(f(k), \delta)) + \delta J(f(k), \delta)\}$ be the *optimal policy correspondence*.

Consider the one-sector optimal growth problem with $n+1$-period horizon defined by

$$J_{n+1}(x, \delta) =$$
$$\sup W^\delta(x - k_0, W^\delta(f(k_0) - k_1, W^\delta(f(k_1) - k_2, \dots)), W^\delta(f(k_n), 0))$$
$$\text{s.t. } k_t \le f(k_{t-1}), \text{ for } t = 1, 2, \dots, n+1, \text{ and } 0 \le k_0 \le x.$$

The objective for the $n + 1$-stage problem is found by recursively substituting the aggregator back into its second argument n times. The final period's consumption is $f(k_n)$, which implies $k_{n+1} = 0$. Let $J_0(k, \delta) = 0$ and define the Bellman equation and associated functions F_n for this $n+1$-stage problem for $n \ge 0$ by

$$J_{n+1}(x, \delta) = \sup_{0 \le k \le x} F_n(x, k, \delta);$$
$$F_n(x, k, \delta) = W(x - k, J_n(f(k), \delta)) + \delta J_n(f(k), \delta).$$

---

[51] The restriction $\bar{\delta} < 1$ is used to show that the Bellman operator is a strict contraction.

Hertzendorf's Capital Deepening Theorem. *Let W and f satisfy the Hertzendorf conditions. If in addition, $W_{12} \geq 0$ and $W_{22} \geq 0$, then*

(1) $J_n(k, \delta)$ *is supermodular on* $\mathbb{R}_+ \times \Delta$ *for all* $n = 1, 2, \ldots$;

(2) $J_n(k, \delta) \to J(k, \delta)$ *for each* $(k, \delta) \in \mathbb{R}_+ \times \Delta$ *satisfying* $\sup_y W_2 + \delta < 1$;

(3) *The optimal policy correspondence* $\psi(k, \delta)$ *is ascending in* δ.

We prove this theorem using an induction argument analogous to the ones used to prove capital deepening theorems with TAS utility. This step shows that J_n is supermodular in (x, δ) for each n. Once this is done, we have the second part of the theorem by combining a dynamic programming argument with the Supermodularity Lemma.

Define the sublattice $A = \{(x, \delta, k) \in \mathbb{R}_+ \times \Delta \times \mathbb{R}_+ : k \in [0, x]\} \subset \mathbb{R}_+ \times \Delta \times \mathbb{R}_+$. The section of A at x is $A_x = \{(k, \delta) : (x, \delta, k) \in A\} = \{(k, \delta) : 0 \leq k \leq x, \text{ and } 0 \leq \delta \leq \bar{\delta}\}$. The projection of A on $\mathbb{R}_+ \times \Delta$ is $\Pi_{\mathbb{R}_+ \times \Delta} A = \{(x, \delta) : A_x \neq \emptyset\}$. The key step verifying that F_n is supermodular is given in Lemma 4. This uses the induction hypothesis and the supermodularity of J_{n+1} will follow from Topkis's Value Function Theorem. By induction we conclude that J_n is supermodular for all n.

The Bellman operator T that takes bounded continuous functions on $\mathbb{R}_+$ into bounded continuous functions on $\mathbb{R}_+$ is defined by the equation

$$(T\xi)(x, \delta) = \sup_{0 \leq k \leq x} \{W(x - k, \xi(f(k))) + \delta\xi(f(k))\}.$$

The Bellman operator is clearly monotone and a strict contraction since $\tilde{\beta} + \delta \leq \bar{\beta} + \bar{\delta} < 1$. Therefore $J_n \to J$ pointwise and the Supermodularity Lemma implies that J inherits the supermodular property from the sequence of supermodular functions $\{J_n\}$. Topkis's Monotonicity Theorem implies that the optimal capital policy correspondence $\psi(x, \delta)$ is ascending.

The induction argument designed to show J_n is supermodular in (x, δ) begins by showing J_1 is supermodular. Since $J_0 \equiv 0$ and W is supermodular we have $J_1(x, \delta) = W(x, 0) = \sup_{0 \leq k \leq x} W(x - k, 0)$ is supermodular by Topkis's Value Function Theorem. The verification that F_n is supermodular is given by the following result. It is the recursive utility analogue of Lemma 1.

Lemma 4. *If W and f satisfy the Hertzendorf conditions and J_n is supermodular on $\mathbb{R}_+ \times \Delta$, then F_n is supermodular on $A \subset \mathbb{R}_+ \times \Delta \times \mathbb{R}_+$.*

Proof. Since F_n is a function of three variables we must show that it has increasing differences in (x, δ), (x, k), and (k, δ). Beginning with (x, δ), F_n will have increasing differences in (x, δ) if for all $(x_1, k, \delta_1) \geq (x_2, k, \delta_2)$:

$$W(x_1 - k, J_n(f(k), \delta_1)) - W(x_2 - k, J_n(f(k), \delta_1))$$
$$\geq W(x_1 - k, J_n(f(k), \delta_2)) - W(x_2 - k, J_n(f(k), \delta_2)).$$

Rewrite this inequality as the following integral:

$$\int_{x_2}^{x_1} W_1(x - k, J_n(f(k), \delta_1)) \, dx \geq \int_{x_2}^{x_1} W_1(x - k, J_n(f(k), \delta_2)) \, dx.$$

Since $J_n(f(k), \delta_1) \geq J_n(f(k), \delta_2)$ and $W_{12} \geq 0$, the integrand on the left is greater. This implies F_n has increasing differences in (x, δ).

We now claim F_n has increasing differences in (x, k). This will be the case if for $(x_1, \delta, k_1) \geq (x_2, \delta, k_2)$ we obtain:

$$W(x_1 - k_1, J_n(f(k_1), \delta)) - W(x_2 - k_1, J_n(f(k_1), \delta))$$
$$\geq W(x_1 - k_2, J_n(f(k_2), \delta)) - W(x_2 - k_2, J_n(f(k_2), \delta)).$$

Once again we can replace differences by integrals:

$$\int_{x_2}^{x_1} W_1(x - k_1, J_n(f(k_1), \delta)) \, dx \geq \int_{x_2}^{x_1} W_1(x - k_2, J_n(f(k_2), \delta)) \, dx.$$

The facts that $(x - k_1) \leq (x - k_2)$, $J_n(f(k_1), \delta) \geq J_n(f(k_2), \delta)$, and that $W_{11} \leq 0$ and $W_{12} \geq 0$ imply that the left-hand integrand is larger than the right-hand integrand. Therefore, F_n has increasing differences in (x, k).

The final step is to show that F_n has increasing differences in (k, δ). Let $(k_1, \delta_1) \geq (k_2, \delta_2)$ and set $J^{ij} = J_n(f(k_i), \delta_j)$. The induction hypothesis implies that J_n has increasing differences in (k, δ) since f is increasing. The Supermodularity Lemma tells us that the composition of an increasing supermodular function and an increasing convex function is supermodular. Therefore, for each fixed $a \geq 0$, $W(a, J_n(f(k), \delta))$ is supermodular in (k, δ). The reason is that $W(a, \cdot)$ is an increasing convex function, so its composition with J_n is supermodular too. Let $a = y - k_2$, then

$$W(x - k_2, J^{11}) - W(x - k_2, J^{12}) \geq W(x - k_2, J^{21}) - W(x - k_2, J^{22}). \quad (24)$$

Because $W_{12} \geq 0$, $k_1 \geq k_2$, and $J^{11} \geq J^{12}$ we can assert

$$\int_{k_2}^{k_1} \int_{J^{12}}^{J^{11}} W_{12}(x - k, J) \, dJ \, dk \geq 0, \text{ or that}$$

$$\int_{k_2}^{k_1} W_1(x - k, J^{11}) \, dk \geq \int_{k_2}^{k_1} W_1(x - k, J^{12}) \, dk.$$

Hence,

$$W(x - k_1, J^{11}) - W(x - k_2, J^{11}) \geq W(x - k_1, J^{12}) - W(x - k_2, J^{12}).$$

By rearranging terms we find that

$$W(x - k_1, J^{11}) - W(x - k_1, J^{12}) \geq W(x - k_2, J^{11}) - W(x - k_2, J^{12}). \quad (25)$$

Combining (24) and (25) yields

$$W(x - k_1, J^{11}) - W(x - k_1, J^{12}) \geq W(x - k_2, J^{21}) - W(x - k_2, J^{22}).$$

Since $J_n(f(k), \delta)$ is supermodular in (k, δ), it also has increasing differences in those variables, so

$$J^{11} - J^{21} \geq J^{12} - J^{22}. \quad (26)$$

Multiplying the left-hand side of (26) by δ_1 and the right-hand side by δ_2 does not change the sense of the inequality since $\delta_1 \geq \delta_2$. Therefore, carrying out the multiplications and rearranging yields

$$\delta_1 J^{11} - \delta_2 J^{12} \geq \delta_1 J^{21} - \delta_2 J^{22}. \quad (27)$$

Inequalities (26) and (27) prove that F_n has increasing differences in (k, δ).□

Hertzendorf's Theorem implies that there are least and greatest elements of the optimal policy correspondence which are non-decreasing sequences in δ. Thus for all $t \geq 0$, $\bar{k}_t(x, \delta_1) = \sup \psi_t(x, \delta_1) \geq \bar{k}_t(x, \delta_2) = \sup \psi_t(x, \delta_2)$, where $\psi_t(x, \delta)$ is defined recursively by $\psi_0(x, \delta) = k_0$ and $\psi_t(x, \delta) = \psi(\psi_{t-1}(x, \delta), \delta)$ for $t \geq 1$. Similar conclusions can be drawn for the least element of the optimal policy correspondence.

A close look at the proof of Lemma 4 reveals how the convexity condition $W_{22} \geq 0$ enters the analysis in proving F_n has increasing differences in (k, δ). That part of the proof is similar to the demonstration of Amir's Capital Stock Monotonicity Theorem for TAS utility functions. A TAS aggregator composed with J_n would be supermodular. Moreover, nonclassical and neoclassical (concave) production functions are accommodated by this result. In this sense, Hertzendorf's Theorem generalizes Amir's Theorem.

One interesting problem is to explore the prospects of obtaining a positive capital deepening result when the aggregator is concave. Hertzendorf obtained a partial answer to this by returning to the Implicit Function Theorem approach presented in Section 7.2. He postulates a twice continuously differentiable value function and shows that if the initial capital stock is a steady state, the aggregator is concave and obeys a curvature restriction, and the production function is strictly concave, then there is a capital deepening response to a decrease in impatience. The specific curvature condition needed is $(1 + W_{22}J_2) > 0$ at the given initial steady-state output x (and with $\delta = 0$). This condition has the following interpretation. The marginal value of a future util delivered in one period viewed from today is $W_2(x, J(x, \delta)) + \delta$. Differentiate this with respect to δ to get $W_{22}J_2 + 1$. By requiring this expression to be positive, Hertzendorf ensures that an increase in δ (starting from $\delta = 0$) does indeed increase the marginal value of future utility along the new optimal solution. This complementarity between the marginal value of future utility and δ leads to a monotone comparative dynamics result: the capital stock along the new path is larger than the initial steady-state stock in each period.

7.6 Conclusion

Comparative dynamics tells us how a capital accumulation model's optimal or equilibrium solution varies with changes in underlying parameters. We have seen that interesting qualitative results are obtainable in the one-sector model provided certain ordinal properties of the planner or representative household's objective function are satisfied. These conditions are designed to start from a qualitative statement such as "the planner has become more patient" and produce a conclusion such as "the optimal capital stock increases at each time." We have returned to the theme announced in Chapter 1 about exploiting the order structure of our optimization problems to obtain qualitative results. We used the order structure of the commodity and parameter spaces as well as the order imposed by the passage of time (via the induction arguments) to deduce monotone comparative dynamics theorems. The passage from differential methods based on the Implicit Function Theorem to lattice programming theory was a process of abstraction that sought to extract the essential properties of our optimization models responsible for monotone comparative dynamics results. The benefit obtained from this exercise in structural excavation is the extension of our basic capital deepening result to nonclassical models and some recursive utility models.

CHAPTER **8**

Dynamic Competitive Equilibrium

8.1 Introduction

In previous chapters we have analyzed the properties of optimal paths in a single-agent framework. It is now time to consider equilibrium models, where there are many interacting agents. The key questions addressed in this chapter are the existence of equilibrium and its welfare properties. The welfare properties considered include not only the First and Second Welfare Theorems, but also core equivalence.

Many theorems have been proved concerning the existence of competitive equilibrium in infinite dimensional spaces, dating back to Peleg and Yaari (1970) and Bewley (1972).[1] Unfortunately, most of these theorems rely on consumption sets that are precisely equal to the positive orthant. Magill (1981), Aliprantis and Brown (1983), Jones (1984), Mas-Colell (1986), Yannelis and Zame, (1986) and Zame (1987) are other examples.[2] Although such consumption sets simplify the existence and core equivalence problems, they also suffer from two major inadequacies. First, they do not allow trade in personal services, even when production is absent; nor do they allow differentiated labor inputs in production. Second, they do not allow for substitution between goods on the subsistence boundary of the consumption possibility set.

Major exceptions to this include Stigum (1973), Back (1988), Boyd and McKenzie (1993), and Chichilnisky and Heal (1993). Stigum's results involve complex restrictions on the location of the trading set, and require that the tail of any vector in the trading set be replaceable by a suitable tail of another vector in the trading set. Chichilnisky and Heal use preferences defined on the entire space, which will usually not be possible in our framework. Back's results require that the trading set have a finite lower bound, and that vectors in the trading set be approximated by suitable vectors that also lie in the trading set. We will adopt the method of Boyd and McKenzie, which has the advantage of also proving core equivalence.

Boyd and McKenzie build on the work of Peleg and Yaari (1970) and

---

[1] Bewley (1991) is another classic addressing the existence question in ℓ^∞—it first appeared as a working paper in 1973.

[2] Mas-Colell and Zame (1991) provide a survey of this literature.

Aliprantis, Brown, and Burkinshaw (1987a; 1987b).[3] The method of proof is indirect. It is based on Edgeworth's (1881) conjecture: the core of the economy shrinks to the competitive equilibrium as the economy grows large. We adopt the same line of argument, and show that any allocation that is in the equal treatment core of every replica economy is a competitive equilibrium. An appeal to Scarf's Theorem on non-emptiness of the core then yields the existence of equilibrium.[4]

Before proceeding to the proofs of existence of equilibrium, and of core equivalence, we must clarify some basics concerning the *correct topology* to use, and the *nature of the competitive equilibrium*. This is done in Section 8.2. At this point we are also able to establish the existence of individually rational Pareto optima. In Section 8.3, we show the existence of the core, and of the equal treatment core in replica economies. Section 8.4 contains the basic core equivalence result. As usual, nearly all of the effort is expended in showing that core allocations are also equilibrium allocations. With these results in hand, we also establish the basic welfare theorems, and relate equilibria to social welfare maxima. Section 8.5 extends the results of Section 8.4 to the case where discounting is extremely heterogeneous, which applies to recursive utility. Concluding remarks are in Section 8.6.

8.2 Dynamic Economies

There are some points that need clarification before we may lay out the assumptions. One of the first problems that we encounter concerns the trading sets. Not only does each consumer have his own trading set, but these sets may lie in different commodity spaces. We have seen that different aggregators lead naturally to different commodity spaces. It may seem natural to take the largest commodity space (or the supremum), as this will encompass all of the consumption sets. Unfortunately, that causes difficulties. The trading sets will no longer be closed in the new commodity space. We cannot simply take the closure as that may include vectors where preferences cannot be defined. It may include vectors that the consumer cannot even conceive of.

We are forced to work with the intersection of the commodity spaces so that all trading sets are closed. Under appropriate conditions, this will not be a severe limitation. Even once we have everything in a common commodity space, there is an issue of which topology to use. If we require

---

[3] Similar methods have been used by Araujo and Monteiro (1994). Also, see McKenzie (1992).

[4] That Scarf's Theorem yields a non-empty core for multiagent capital accumulation games was also shown by Becker (1982b; 1992).

that the trading sets be closed and preferences be continuous in the wrong topology, we may be unable to find an equilibrium. Indeed, as Araujo (1985) points out using the following example, there may not be any individually rational Pareto optima.

▶ Example 1: Nonexistence of individually rational Pareto optima in ℓ^∞. We specialize Araujo's (1985) example to the following exchange economy. Use ℓ^∞ as the commodity space and let $\tau = \sigma(\ell^\infty, ba)$. Then there is a τ-continuous linear functional $\mathbf{p} > \mathbf{0}$ that is purely finitely additive; a Banach limit will do. Let $\omega_1 = \omega_2$ be uniformly bounded above zero with $\omega_{11} = 1$. By taking a scalar multiple, we may assume $\mathbf{p}\omega_2 > 1$. Set $U_1(\mathbf{x}_1) = x_{11} + \mathbf{p} \cdot \mathbf{x}_1$ and $U_2(x_2) = \mathbf{q} \cdot \mathbf{x}_2 + \mathbf{p} \cdot \mathbf{x}_2$ where $\mathbf{q} \in \ell^1_+$, $q_t > 0$ for $t > 1$. Notice that agent 1 does not value any specific goods from period 2 onwards. He only cares about them asymptotically because $\mathbf{p}$ is purely finitely additive. Let $(\bar{\mathbf{x}}_1, \bar{\mathbf{x}}_2)$ be a Pareto optimal allocation. Consumption at any specific time $t > 1$ can be costlessly transferred to agent 2, who benefits from it. Thus $\bar{x}_{1t} = 0$ for $t > 1$. As there are 2 units of consumption available at time 1, $U_1(\bar{\mathbf{x}}_1) \leq 2$. But $U_1(\omega_1) = \omega_{11} + \mathbf{p} \cdot \omega_1 > 2$, so any Pareto optimum is not individually rational, and hence there cannot be an equilibrium. ◀

The real problem in Araujo's example is that there is not a common topology where preferences are continuous and the feasible set is compact. Such difficulties can even arise in $\mathbb{R}^n$. Boyd (1989a) illustrates this in $\mathbb{R}^2$ in a very similar fashion.

▶ Example 2: Nonexistence of individually rational Pareto optima in $\mathbb{R}^2$. Define utility functions on $\mathbb{R}^2_+$ by $U_1(x, y) = y$ if $x > 0$ and $U_1(x, y) = 0$ if $x = 0$, and $U_2(x, y) = x + y$. Note that U_1 is concave since if $x > 0$ or $x' > 0$, $U(\alpha x + (1 - \alpha)x', \alpha y + (1 - \alpha)y') = \alpha y + (1 - \alpha)y' \geq \alpha U(x, y) + (1 - \alpha)U(x', y')$, while if $x = x' = 0$, $U(\alpha x + (1 - \alpha)x', \alpha y + (1 - \alpha)y') = 0 = U(x, y) + (1 - \alpha)U(x', y')$. Give $\mathbb{R}^2$ the discrete topology. Both utility functions are continuous, and both are weakly monotonic. Let the endowments be $\omega_1 = \omega_2 = (1, 1)$. (Any strictly positive endowments will do.) Like the Araujo example, this exchange economy has no individually rational Pareto optimal allocations. If the allocation $((x_1, y_1), (x_2, y_2))$ is individually rational, then $U_1(x_1, y_1) \geq 1$. Thus $x_1 > 0$. Now consider the allocation $((x_1/2, y_1), (x_2 + x_1/2, y_2))$. This is a Pareto improvement over the original allocation. Of course, this economy cannot have an equilibrium. ◀

Once we have found a topology where preferences are continuous and the feasible set is compact, another issue appears. Should we require that prices be represented by continuous linear functionals? If we require continuity, we may rule out some economically reasonable prices. Consider the following example from Zame (1987).

▶ **Example 3: Nonexistence of dual equilibrium prices.** The consumption set is ℓ_+^1. To avoid excessive sub- and superscripting, we denote x_t by $x(t)$. There is one consumer with utility function $U(\mathbf{x}) = \sum_{t=1}^{\infty} x(t)$ and endowment $\boldsymbol{\omega} = (2^{-2t})$. The production set is the cone generated by the negative orthant and vectors of the form $-\mathbf{e}_k + 2\mathbf{e}_{k+1}$ where k is not a power of 2. As a result, no goods may be carried over to period $2^s + 1$ from period 2^s. As Zame notes, any equilibrium price system $\mathbf{p}$ must obey $p(t) \geq 2p(t+1)$ for t not a power of 2 and $p(2^s) = p(2^{s+1})$. But the only way $\mathbf{p}$ can satisfy these relations and remain in $(\ell^1)' = \ell^\infty$ is if $\mathbf{p} = \mathbf{0}$. Thus there is no equilibrium dual price vector.

Although Zame is correct in noting that this economy has no equilibrium with prices in the dual, it would be a mistake to think that there are no economically reasonable equilibria. Boyd (1989a) constructs such an equilibrium. Let $0 < k \leq 2^{s-1}$ and consider $t = k + 2^{s-1}$. Then $c(t) \leq \sum_{j=1}^{k} 2^{k-j} \omega(j + 2^{s-1}) = \sum_{j=1}^{k} 2^{(k-3j-2^s)} = \frac{1}{7} 2^{(k-2^s)} [1 - 2^{-3k}]$. It follows that $c(t)$ grows no faster than $z(t) = 2^{(k-2^s)}$. The feasible set is contained in the Riesz ideal $\mathbf{Z}$ generated by $\mathbf{z}$. The space $\mathbf{Z}$ is the Riesz ideal recommended by Aliprantis, Brown, and Burkinshaw (1987a; 1987b). Set $p(k + 2^{s-1}) = 2^{(2^{s-1}-k)}$ for $0 < k \leq 2^{s-1}$ (note $p(2^s) = 1$). Thus $p(t)z(t) \leq 2^{-2^{s-1}}$ when $2^{s-1} < t \leq 2^s$. As this is summable, $\mathbf{p}$ is a linear functional on $\mathbf{Z}$, even though it is not continuous on all of ℓ^1. The price vector $\mathbf{p}$ can also be extended to ℓ_+^1 by setting $\mathbf{p}(\mathbf{x}) = \lim_{T \to \infty} \sum_{t=1}^{T} p(t)x(t)$. This converges either to a finite number or to $+\infty$. Some vectors in ℓ_+^1 may have a positively infinite value, but that is not a barrier to economic interpretation. It just means that they are not in the budget set. ◀

How do we decide which prices are economically reasonable? Edgeworth's (1881) conjecture provides one answer. We allow the consumers to trade until all potential gains from trade are achieved, attaining a core allocation. If the economy is very large, the absence of further trading opportunities pins down the exchange rate between any pair of commodities. These exchange rates are the economically natural prices. As we saw in Example 3, and will see again in Section 8.4, the equilibrium prices need not lie in the dual of the commodity space.

8.2.1 Infinite Horizon Economies

With these examples in mind, we start by considering the case where there is a common Riesz ideal $\ell^\infty(\beta)$ with $\beta \geq 1$ that contains all trading sets and the technology set.[5] Let $\sigma = \sigma(\ell^\infty(\beta), \ell^1(1/\beta))$ denote the weak* topology on $\ell^\infty(\beta)$. Consumer h is characterized by a set of feasible net

---

[5] This assumption will be relaxed in Section 8.5.

trades, X^h, and a utility function U^h defined on X^h. The corresponding preference relation is denoted $\succ_h$. Each net trade specifies how much a consumer receives from the economy, and how much that consumer supplies to the economy. We use the general equilibrium convention that for consumers, positive components denote demands and negative components denote supplies. The *trading set* contains all the net trades the consumer can evaluate that are consistent with consumer survival, and with any other physical constraints that limit the consumer's trading possibilities.

The case where consumers may consume any bundle in the positive orthant, and are able to sell a fixed endowment ω, corresponds to the trading set $\ell_+^\infty(\beta) - \omega$. In fact, any trading set that contains its greatest lower bound can be thought of in terms of endowments which are fully alienable. However, confining our attention to such endowments would be an economically unnatural restriction.

One obvious case is where labor services are traded. If a consumer can supply two different types of labor, differing in disutility, they must necessarily be treated as two different goods. It does not make sense to think of this consumer as having an alienable endowment of both kinds of labor. The consumer should be able to supply up to 24 hours of each in a day, but this would lead to the absurd result that he can supply 48 hours of labor services in a day. Trying to incorporate the physical constraint that there are only 24 hours in a day means that we must exclude the greatest lower bound of consumption—labor services cannot be fully alienable. When trading sets do not contain their greatest lower bounds, this type of restriction is easily accommodated.

Another case where the endowment picture is on the wrong track concerns survival constraints. Although a consumer needs food to survive and provide labor services, there are many different combinations of food that suffice. Corn can be substituted for wheat along the survival boundary. In the intertemporal context, even more possibilities are open. Survival prospects may depend not only on consumption today, but on consumption in neighboring periods. The amount of food needed for survival now depends on what we had for lunch earlier today, and for dinner yesterday. By allowing a lower bound on the trading set to lie outside it, we permit intertemporal dependence in the survival constraint.

Consumer Assumptions. The trading sets X^h and utility functions U^h obey:

(C1) Each X^h is σ-closed.
(C2) Each X^h is convex.
(C3) There is a $\omega \in \ell_+^\infty$ with $-\omega$ a lower bound for each X^h.
(C4) Each U^h is concave and upper semicontinuous on X^h.

(C5) Whenever $\mathbf{x} \in X^h$ and $\mathbf{z} \geq \mathbf{x}$ with $z_t \gg x_t$ for some t, then $U^h(\mathbf{z}) > U^h(\mathbf{x})$. (periodwise monotonicity)

Except for the unusual form of monotonicity (C5), these assumptions are fairly standard. The notation $-\omega$ is used for the lower bound because the negative of the aggregate endowment serves as a lower bound in endowment economies. Because $\omega \in \ell^\infty$, there is uniform upper bound on the amount of non-produced goods a consumer may supply to the economy at any time.[6] Notice that (C5) is a natural form of monotonicity in infinite horizon models. In fact, when utility is recursive, it is implied by the more usual form that $\mathbf{x} \gg \mathbf{z}$ implies $\mathbf{x} \succ \mathbf{z}$. Let $X = \sum_{h=1}^{H} X^h$ be the aggregate trading set and let $R^h(\mathbf{x}^h) = \{\mathbf{z} \in X^h : \mathbf{z} \succsim_h \mathbf{x}^h\}$ denote h's weakly preferred set for $\mathbf{x}^h$.

Our technology assumptions are based on the technology assumptions (T1)–(T6) from Section 4.3 using the dual pair $(\ell^\infty(\beta), \ell^1(1/\beta))$. Elements of the technology set Y are net outputs. Negative components denote inputs to production; positive components denote outputs.

Technology Assumptions.

(S1) Y is a σ-closed set.

(S2) Y is a convex cone.

(S3) $\mathbf{0} \in Y$.

(S4) $Y \cap \ell_+^\infty(\beta) = \{\mathbf{0}\}$.

(S5) $\ell_-^\infty(\beta) \subset Y$.

(S6) For each $\bar{\mathbf{y}} \in \ell^\infty$ the set $\{\mathbf{y} \in Y : \mathbf{y} \geq \bar{\mathbf{y}}\}$ is β-bounded.

(S7) Y contains no straight lines.

Assumptions (S1) and (S3)–(S5) are (T1) and (T3)–(T5). Assumption (S2) strengthens (T2), requiring that Y is a cone; (S6) weakens (T6), requiring that uniformly bounded inputs lead to bounded outputs. Production is also irreversible (S7). We only concern ourselves with the case of uniformly bounded inputs because consumers may not provide anything larger. As usual, models with a finite number of firms subject to diminishing returns to scale can be put in this framework by adding entrepreneurial factors (McKenzie, 1959; 1994). Example 5 considers a finite number of firms in each period using stationary Malinvaud technologies. These can be handled by using a entrepreneurial factor in each period. Problems can arise if these diminishing returns firms earn infinite discounted profits in equilibrium. Sun and Kusumoto (1996) have adapted the Peleg-Yaari argument to that context.

We will be examining models with a finite number, H, of consumers. Thus inputs from the consumer sector will be bounded by $-H\omega \in \ell_+^\infty$.

---

[6] We relax this restriction in the remark at the end of Section 8.4.1.

Inputs of produced goods may grow over time, but those will net out in the net output vector.

An *infinite horizon economy* is a collection $\mathcal{E} = \{X^h, U^h, Y\}_{h=1}^H$ of trading sets, utility functions, and a common technology set. We will also require some joint assumptions on consumers and technology.

We say a bundle $\mathbf{x}^h$ is *individually rational* if $\mathbf{x}^h \succsim_h \mathbf{z}^h$ for all $\mathbf{z}^h \in X^h \cap Y$. This means that $\mathbf{x}^h$ is at least as good as any bundle of goods that h may obtain by using his resources in conjunction with the common technology Y. The bundle $\mathbf{x}^h$ is *strongly individually rational* if it is *better* than anything h can achieve on his own, if $\mathbf{x}^h \succ_h \mathbf{z}^h$ for all $\mathbf{z}^h \in X^h \cap Y$. For $I \subset \{1, \ldots, H\}$, define $\mathbf{x}^I = \sum_{h \in I} \mathbf{x}^h$.

The economy is *irreducible* if whenever I_1, I_2 is a non-trivial partition of $\{1, \ldots, H\}$, and $\mathbf{x}^{I_1} + \mathbf{x}^{I_2} \in Y$ with $\mathbf{x}^h \in X^h$, there are $\mathbf{z}^{I_1} + \mathbf{z}^{I_2} \in Y$ with $\mathbf{z}^h \succ_h \mathbf{x}^h$ for all $h \in I_1$ and for each $h \in I_2$, $\mathbf{z}^h \in \alpha_h X^h$ for some $\alpha_h > 0$.[7] Irreducibility requires that for any allocation, no matter how we partition the consumers, one group is able to supply a bundle of goods that, when used with the common technology, can make the other group strictly better off. Each subgroup, and indeed, each individual, always has bundles available for supply that are valued by others in the economy, at least in some proportion.

We now strengthen the concept of irreducibility. Recall that $\mathbf{x}$ is an *extreme point* of a convex set C if there do not exist distinct $\mathbf{x}', \mathbf{x}'' \in C$ and α, $0 < \alpha < 1$, with $\mathbf{x} = \alpha \mathbf{x}' + (1 - \alpha) \mathbf{x}''$. The economy is *strongly irreducible* if whenever I_1, I_2 is a non-trivial partition of $\{1, \ldots, H\}$, and $\mathbf{x}^{I_1} + \mathbf{x}^{I_2} \in Y$ with $\mathbf{x}^h \in X^h$, there are $\mathbf{z}^{I_1} + \mathbf{z}^{I_2} \in Y$ with $U^h(\mathbf{z}^h) > U^h(\mathbf{x}^h)$ for $h \in I_1$ and for $h \in I_2$, $\mathbf{z}^h \in X^h$ with $U^h(\mathbf{z}^h) > -\infty$ when $\mathbf{x}^h$ is strongly individually rational and not an extreme point of X^h and $\mathbf{z}^h \in \alpha_h X^h$ for some $\alpha_h > 0$ otherwise. This differs from irreducibility in that the consumers must actually be able to make the improving trades— unless they are at an extreme point of their survival boundary, or unless they have not previously benefited from trade. It is needed to show that replicas of a consumer receive indifferent net trades in the core of replica economies. Notice that strict monotonicity implies strong irreducibility when the trading sets are translates of the positive orthant and consumers have non-negative and non-zero endowments.

We use the notation $(\mathbf{x}\|_t\mathbf{y})$ to denote $(x_1, \ldots, x_t, y_{t+1}, \ldots)$, where the tail of $\mathbf{y}$ replaces the tail of $\mathbf{x}$ after time t. The vector $\mathbf{e}_s$ is defined by $e_{it} = 1$ if $t = s$ and $e_{it} = 0$ otherwise.

---

[7] Irreducibility was introduced by McKenzie (1959). This version is based on McKenzie (1981), which incorporated ideas of Moore (1975) into the definition. See Khan (1993) for a discussion of the role of irreducibility in equilibrium existence, and Hammond (1993) for a general discussion of irreducibility and related concepts.

Joint Assumptions.

(J1) There exist $\bar{\mathbf{x}}^h \leq \mathbf{0}$ with $\bar{\mathbf{x}}^h \in X^h - Y$ and $\bar{\mathbf{x}} = \sum_h \bar{\mathbf{x}}^h \ll \mathbf{0}$ with $\bar{\mathbf{x}}$ constant over time.

(J2) The economy is strongly irreducible.

(J3) For any $\mathbf{x} \in X^h$, $\mathbf{y} \in Y$ and $\delta > 0$ there is a τ_0 such that for each $\tau > \tau_0$ there is an $\alpha > 0$ with $\delta(\mathbf{e}_1 + \cdots + \mathbf{e}_{\tau+1}) + (\mathbf{x} - \mathbf{y}\|_\tau \alpha \bar{\mathbf{x}}^h) \in R^h(\mathbf{x}) - Y$.

Combining $\bar{\mathbf{x}}^h \in X^h - Y$ with $\bar{\mathbf{x}}^h \leq \mathbf{0}$ and free disposal (S5), we find $\mathbf{0} \in X^h - Y$. Thus each consumer can survive using only his or her own resources together with the production technology. The assumption that $\bar{\mathbf{x}} \ll \mathbf{0}$ is a strong form of viability.

Assumption (J3) says that if we give a consumer a small amount of all goods in early periods, he or she is able to use the technology to produce enough to attain a given utility level and eventually supply some fraction of $\bar{\mathbf{x}}^h$ to the economy. The basic idea is to accumulate enough capital. This will be automatically satisfied in many standard capital accumulation models (see Examples 4 and 5). The growth rate of $\bar{\mathbf{x}}$, currently set to zero, will ultimately determine how fast equilibrium prices converge to zero. Notice also that because $\bar{\mathbf{x}}^h \ll \mathbf{0}$, any smaller α will also work. In particular, α may be set to zero. Assumption (J3) plays a key role in normalizing prices.

▶ Example 4: One-sector models with diminishing returns. Consider the one-sector representative agent case with recursive utility function U and production function f. Suppose U is concave and φ-bounded on $\ell_+^\infty(\beta)$ for some φ with $\|\varphi \circ S\|_\varphi < 1/\delta$. We require the production function be strictly concave and obey $f \geq 0$, $f' > 0$, $f(0) = 0$, and the Inada condition $f'(0) = +\infty$. Further, suppose the technology is α-bounded for some $\alpha, \beta > \alpha \geq 1$. Consider the weak* topology on $\ell^\infty(\beta)$, $\sigma = \sigma(\ell^\infty(\beta), \ell^1(1/\beta))$.

At first glance, this model does not appear to fit our framework because the technology does not exhibit constant returns to scale. However, such production functions are commonly regarded as deriving from a neoclassical production function with one capital good. The corresponding neoclassical production function is $F(a^0, a^1) = a^0 f(a^1/a^0)$ for $a^0, a^1 > 0$ and $F(a^0, a^1) = 0$ otherwise. As in the neoclassical model of Example 4.7, good 0 is labor while good 1 is the produced good. The corresponding Malinvaud technology set is $T = \{(a^0, a^1, b^0, b^1) : 0 \leq b^1 \leq F(a^0, a^1), b^0 = 0\}$. Notice that it obeys the Malinvaud axioms (M1)–(M5). It fails (M6) because labor is a primary good and cannot be produced. Construct the technology set Y as in Section 4.3.1, but relative to $\ell^\infty(\beta)$. The feasible set is not affected by the relativization. Then $Y = \{\mathbf{y} \in \ell^\infty(\beta) : \mathbf{y} = \mathbf{b} - \mathbf{a}$ with $(a_t, b_{t+1}) \in T_t$ and $b_1 = 0\}$. By Corollary 4.3, the technology conditions (S1)–(S6) are satisfied. The fact that inputs must precede outputs implies Y contains no straight lines. If both $\mathbf{y}, -\mathbf{y} \in Y$, then $y_1 = 0$. But since there is no input in period 1, no output can be produced in period 2, implying $y_2 = 0$. Proceeding by induction, we find $\mathbf{y} = \mathbf{0}$.

The representative consumer has initial endowment $k \geq 0$. The consumer can supply up to one unit of labor in each period. Utility is translated into this framework by letting it depend solely on consumption. It is not influenced by the amount of labor supplied. The trading set has a product structure with $X = \prod_{t=1}^{\infty} X_t$. Define the trading set at time 1 by $X_1 = \{(x^0, x^1) : x^0 \geq -1 \text{ and } x^1 \geq -k\}$ and the time t trading set by $X_t = \{(x^0, x^1) : x^0 \geq -1 \text{ and } x^1 \geq 0\}$ for $t = 2, \ldots$. The consumer is endowed with k units of capital at time 1, and also has one unit of labor available at each time. The consumption sequence corresponding to a net trade $\mathbf{x}$ is $\mathbf{c} = ((x_1^0 + 1, x_1^1 + k), (x_1^0 + 1, x_1^1), \ldots)$. The consumer supplies labor inelastically, and has utility $U(\mathbf{c}) = U(x_1^1 + k, x_1^1, x_2^1, \ldots)$. Conditions (C1)–(C5) are satisfied.

We now consider the joint assumptions. By the Inada conditions, there is a stock $\bar{k}$ and constant $\gamma > 1$ with $0 < \bar{k} < k$ and $f(\bar{k}) > \gamma\bar{k}$. Set $\bar{b}^1 = \min\{f(\bar{k})/\gamma, k\}$. Let $\bar{a}_t^0 = 1/\gamma$ and $\bar{a}_t^1 = \bar{k}/\gamma$. For $t > 1$ set $\bar{b}_t^1 = \bar{b}^1$, so $\bar{k} < \bar{b}_t^1 \leq F(a_t^0, a_t^1) = F(1, \bar{k})/\gamma = f(\bar{k})/\gamma$. Of course we set $\bar{b}_1^1 = 0$. The vector $\bar{\mathbf{x}} = ((-1, \bar{b}^1), (-1, 0), \ldots) - \bar{\mathbf{b}} + \bar{\mathbf{a}}$ lies in $X - Y$ and has the constant value $((1 - \gamma)/\gamma, (\bar{k} - \gamma\bar{b}^1)/\gamma) \ll 0$. Thus (J1) is satisfied. Monotonicity combined with the fact that the positive orthant is contained in each trading set implies (J2).

For (J3), suppose $\mathbf{x} \in X$, $\mathbf{y} \in Y$ and $\delta > 0$ are given. Choose α with $\delta \geq \alpha\bar{b}^1$. Now

$$(-1, 0) + (-\delta, -\delta) + \alpha(1/\gamma, \bar{k}/\gamma) = (-1 - \delta + \alpha/\gamma, -\delta + \bar{k}/\gamma)$$
$$\leq \alpha((\gamma - 1)/\gamma, (\gamma\bar{b}^1 - \bar{k}/\gamma)).$$

Thus using $(-\delta, -\delta)$ at time $\tau + 1$, we can produce sufficient output to supply $\alpha\bar{x}$. The vector $\delta\mathbf{e}_{\tau+1} + (\mathbf{0}\|_\tau \alpha\bar{\mathbf{x}})$ is then in $X - Y$. Now pick τ_0 so that $\delta(\mathbf{e}_1 + \cdots + \mathbf{e}_\tau) + (\mathbf{x}\|_\tau ((-1, 0), \ldots)) \in R(\mathbf{x})$ for $\tau > \tau_0$. This is possible by continuity of preferences and the product nature of X. Then $\delta(\mathbf{e}_1 + \cdots + \mathbf{e}_{\tau+1}) + (\mathbf{x} - \mathbf{y}\|_\tau \alpha\bar{\mathbf{x}}) \in R(\mathbf{x}) - Y$ for all $\tau > \tau_0$, establishing (J3). ◄

▶ Example 5: Multisector models with diminishing returns. A multisectoral model with diminishing returns to scale can also be put into the constant returns framework of this chapter. Suppose production is described by a Malinvaud technology set $T \subset \mathbb{R}_+^m \times \mathbb{R}_+^m$ that does not exhibit constant returns to scale. Following McKenzie (1959; 1994), we convert this to a constant returns technology by introducing an artificial "entrepreneurial" factor, which we label good zero. Let $D \subset \mathbb{R}_+^{m+1} \times \mathbb{R}_+^{m+1}$ be defined by

$$D = \mathrm{cl}\{(\lambda, a, 0, b) : \lambda > 0 \text{ and } (a, b) \in \lambda T\}.$$

As the closure of a convex set, D is both closed (M1) and convex (M2). It is clear that D inherits the free disposal property (M5) from T. The inaction postulate (M3) holds because $(1/n, 0, 0, 0) \in D$ for all n and D is closed.

We must show (M4) holds. Suppose $(0, 0, \mu, b) \in D$ with $(\mu, b) > 0$. Clearly $\mu = 0$ by construction. Moreover, this point can only be in D as a limit, so there are $\lambda^n > 0$ and $(a^n, b^n) \in \lambda^n T$ with $\lambda^n \to 0$, $a^n \to 0$, and $b^n \to b$. For n large, $\lambda^n / \|b^n\| < 1$. Combining inaction and convexity for T, we find $(\lambda^n / \|b^n\|)(a^n / \lambda^n, b^n / \lambda^n) \in T$ for n large. That is, $(a^n / \|b^n\|, b^n / \|b^n\|) \in T$ for n large. Since $\{b^n / \|b^n\|\}$ is a bounded sequence, we may extract a convergent subsequence. Denoting its limit by b^*, and letting $n \to \infty$ along that subsequence, we find $(0, b^*) \in T$ with $\|b^*\| = 1$. But this is impossible by (M4) for T, contradicting $(\mu, b) > 0$. Thus (M4) holds for D as well. As in Example 4, D does not satisfy the productivity condition (M6) because good 0 cannot be produced. Construct Y relative to $\ell^\infty(\beta)$ from D. Conditions (S1)–(S6) are now satisfied by Corollary 4.3.

Suppose further that the technology is α-bounded and $\beta > \alpha \geq 1$. Let U be U recursive, concave and φ-bounded on $\ell_+^\infty(\beta)$ for some φ with $\|\varphi \circ S\|_\varphi < 1/\delta$. Suppose $X = \prod_{t=1}^\infty X_t$. Extend trading sets and preferences to include the entrepreneurial factor, leaving the consumer indifferent to it, as in Example 4. Endow the consumer with one unit of the entrepreneurial factor in each period and a capital stock $k \gg 0$ in the first period. The consumer conditions (C1)–(C5) are satisfied as in Example 4.

If there is a $\gamma > 1$ and $(a, b) \in T$ with $b > \gamma a \gg 0$, a stock that is expansible by a factor $\gamma > 1$, we can mimic the remaining arguments of Example 4 to show the joint assumptions are satisfied. ◄

This example shows why some sort of joint condition on consumption and production is needed. The production sector alone cannot necessarily produce positive outputs of all goods after the first period. Inputs of labor or other non-produced goods may be required. A joint condition on consumption and production is then needed to obtain positive output of all goods.

Competitive Equilibrium. A competitive equilibrium for an infinite horizon economy $\mathcal{E} = \{X^h, U^h, Y\}_{h=1}^H$ is a collection $\{\mathbf{x}^h, \mathbf{y}, \mathbf{p}\}_{h=1}^H$ with $\mathbf{p} \in s^m$ such that:

(1) $\mathbf{y} \in Y$, $\limsup_{\tau \to \infty} \sum_{t=1}^\tau p_t y_t = 0$ and $\limsup_{\tau \to \infty} \sum_{t=1}^\tau p_t z_t \leq 0$ whenever $\mathbf{z} \in Y$;

(2) $\mathbf{x}^h \in X^h$ with $\limsup_{\tau\to\infty} \sum_{t=1}^{\tau} p_t x_t^h \leq 0$ and $U^h(\mathbf{z}^h) \leq U^h(\mathbf{x}^h)$
for all $\mathbf{z}^h \in X^h$ with $\liminf_{\tau\to\infty} \sum_{t=1}^{\tau} p_t z_t^h \leq 0$;

(3) $\sum_{h=1}^{H} \mathbf{x}^h = \mathbf{y}$.

The first condition is a form of profit maximization. The limit supremum handles cases where profits may not converge. We then require that even under the most optimistic interpretation, total profits will not be positive.[8] This deserves elaboration. Remember that all paths are infinite paths. If a path can be "terminated," this means that it has a zero tail. Condition (1) implies a "terminated" path cannot show a profit.

Profit conditions in neoclassical models (such as those covered by the Equivalence Principle) place the profit condition on each single period's production process. In effect, producers are taken to have a one-period horizon and foresight is concentrated in the household sector. However, there is no clear rationale for traders being prevented from exercising their foresight to combine processes into infinite paths which may have positive value. Condition (1) rules out such possible profit, effectively excluding this arbitrage activity. It embodies the requirement that there are no unreversed arbitrage opportunities in an equilibrium.

The second condition is utility maximization. The consumer chooses a best net trade in his budget set, where the consumer uses the most optimistic interpretation of which vectors are in the budget set. If the sequence of values of a net trade over the first T periods has several limit points, the consumer uses the one that yields the lowest cost for the net trade.

Our results will show that $\mathbf{p}$ is summable. The ℓ^∞ lower bound on the trading sets then implies $\sum_{t=1}^{\tau} p_t z_t^h$ converges either to a finite value or to $+\infty$ for all $\mathbf{z}^h \in X^h$. Thus $\mathbf{p}\mathbf{z}^h = \sum_{t=1}^{\infty} p_t z_t^h$ is well defined on X^h.[9] In this trading set formulation, both income and spending are included in $\mathbf{p}\mathbf{z}^h$. We can rewrite $\mathbf{p}\mathbf{z}^h = \mathbf{p}\mathbf{z}_+^h - \mathbf{p}\mathbf{z}_-^h$ by using the positive and negative parts of $\mathbf{z}^h$. The budget constraint is then $\mathbf{p}\mathbf{z}_+^h \leq \mathbf{p}\mathbf{z}_-^h$. Since the positive components represent purchases, the left-hand side is spending. Similarly, the right-hand side is income. The income received from the sale of goods must be at least as large as spending. Notice that income is not given exogenously by some endowment. Rather, it arises endogenously as part of the consumer's optimal choice, and varies with the net trade.

Condition (3) is the usual market clearing condition. We let $CE(\mathcal{E})$ denote the set of competitive equilibrium allocations for $\mathcal{E}$. This formulation of equilibrium avoids the problems of Example 3.

Remark: Fisher competitive equilibrium. The Fisher competitive equilib-

---

[8] A similar condition was used by Stigum (1973).

[9] Thus it really makes no difference whether the budget set is formulated using the limit, limsup, or liminf.

rium now appears as a special case. This is easy to see in the one-sector case of Example 4. The budget constraint for the model of Example 4 can be rewritten to say that the discounted value of consumption must be no more than the discounted sum of wage income plus the value of the initial capital stock. The neoclassical multisector case may be handled similarly.

▶ Example 6: An economy of firms. Consider an economy with f explicit firms. Each firm is subject to diminishing returns to scale. Firm j's production possibilities are described by a Malinvaud technology set T_j. Besides their endowments of goods, consumers are entitled to a share, possibly null, of each firm's profits. Consumer h's share of firm j's profits is denoted θ_{hj}. We require $\theta_{hj} \geq 0$ and $\sum_{h=1}^{H} \theta_{hj} = 1$ for each firm j. All of the firm's profits are allocated to the households. We slightly modify the approach of Example 5 to recast this firms economy into our framework.

Let $D_j = \text{cl}\{(a, \lambda_j e_j, b, 0) : \lambda_j > 0 \text{ and } (a, b) \in \lambda_j T_j\}$. The arguments of Example 5 apply to show each D_j obeys (M1)–(M5). Now let $D = \sum_{j=1}^{f} D_j \subset \mathbb{R}_+^{m+f} \times \mathbb{R}_+^{m+f}$. The aggregate technology set D inherits properties (M2)–(M5) from the D_j. A little extra effort is required to show D is closed. We could simply apply Choquet's Theorem (Section 8.4) since $D_j \subset \mathbb{R}_+^{m+f} \times \mathbb{R}_+^{m+f}$ for each j. However, an elementary argument is available. Let $z^n \in D$, so $z^n = \sum_{j=1}^{f} z_j^n$ for some $z_j^n \in D_j$, and suppose $z^n \to z$. For n larger than some N, $z^n \leq z + e$. The non-negativity of z_j^n implies that for each j, $0 \leq z_j^n \leq z + e$ for $n \geq N$. Each sequence $\{z_j^n\}_{n=1}^{\infty}$ is then bounded, and so has a convergent subsequence. Denote its limit by z_j. Passing to the subsequence, we find $z^n \to \sum z_j$. But $z^n \to z$, so $z = \sum z_j$. Because each D_j is closed, $z \in D$. Thus D is also closed. The corresponding technology set obeys (S1)–(S6) by Corollary 4.3, and (S7) because inputs precede outputs, as in Example 4.

Replace consumer h's trading set X^h by $Z^h = \{(\mathbf{x}, \mathbf{w}) : \mathbf{x} \in X^h \text{ and } \mathbf{w} \in s^f \text{ with } \mathbf{w} \geq -\sum_{j=1}^{f} \theta_{hj} e_j\}$ and define a new utility function V^h on Z^h by $V^h(\mathbf{x}, \mathbf{w}) = U^h(\mathbf{x})$. The new trading sets and utility functions will inherit (C1)–(C5) from X^h and U^h.

Deriving conditions for the T_j that insure (J1)–(J3) hold in the constant returns setting is more complex, and we will simply impose (J1)–(J3) in this example. The case of one diminishing returns firm is simpler. See Example 4 for the one-sector case.

Now consider an equilibrium in the constant returns setup. We will write the price at time t as (p_t, π_t). Because the technology is derived from Malinvaud technologies, profit maximization is equivalent to maximizing each $p_{t+1} b_{t+1}^j - p_t a_t^j - \pi_{j,t} \alpha_j$ by choice of $(a_t^j, b_{t+1}^j) \in \alpha_j T_j$. As consumers do not derive utility from consumption of the entrepreneurial factors, each consumer will supply all of the entrepreneurial factors he can. The total supply will be one unit for each firm in each period. Market clearing implies that $\alpha_j = 1$. The firm will earn zero profit due to constant returns to scale, so $\pi_{j,t} = p_{t+1}b_{t+1}^j - p_t a_t^j$. The price of the entrepreneurial factor is exactly the maximum possible discounted profit from time t for the diminishing returns firm. The income that consumer h receives from sale of the entrepreneurial factor is then $\theta_{hj}\pi_{j,t}$, which is h's share of profits of firm j in the diminishing returns setup. Consumer h chooses a best point $(\mathbf{x}^h, \mathbf{w}^h) \in Z^h$ with $\limsup_{\tau \to \infty} \sum_{t=1}^{\tau}(p_t x_t^h + \pi_t w_t^h) \leq 0$ by setting $\mathbf{w}^h = -\sum_{j=1}^{f} \theta_{hj}\mathbf{e}_j$ and choosing a best $\mathbf{x}^h \in X^h$ with $\limsup_{\tau \to \infty} \sum_{t=1}^{\tau}(p_t x_t^h - \sum_{j=1}^{f} \theta_{hj}\pi_{j,t}) \leq 0$. In other words, the consumer chooses the best point he can afford based on his share of the profits.[10] ◀

8.2.2 Existence of Pareto Optima

The first potential stumbling block was the possible nonexistence of individually rational Pareto optima as illustrated in Example 1. Our assumptions remove that obstacle. Infinite horizon economies obeying the consumer, technology, and joint assumptions have such Pareto optima. In fact, the existence of individually rational Pareto optima follows from a subset of these assumptions.

An *allocation* $\mathbf{X}$ is a collection $(\mathbf{x}^1, \ldots, \mathbf{x}^H)$ with $\mathbf{x}^h \in X^h$ for each h. An allocation $\mathbf{X}$ is *feasible* if $\sum_{h=1}^{H} \mathbf{x}^h \in Y$. Denote the set of feasible allocations by $\mathcal{F}$. Of course, the set of feasible allocations is non-empty, compact, and convex. A feasible allocation $\mathbf{X}$ is *Pareto optimal* if there is no other feasible allocation $\mathbf{Y}$ with $\mathbf{y}^h \succsim_h \mathbf{x}^h$ for all h and $\mathbf{y}^i \succ_h \mathbf{x}^i$ for some i.

Lemma 1. *Under (C1)–(C3), (S1), (S2), (S5), (S6), and (J1), the set of feasible allocations is non-empty, σ-compact, and convex.*

Proof. Convexity and σ-closure of $\mathcal{F}$ follow from the convexity and σ-closedness of Y and each X^h. By assumption (J1), there is an $\bar{\mathbf{x}} \in X - Y$ with $\bar{\mathbf{x}} \ll \mathbf{0}$. By free disposal, $\mathbf{0} \in X - Y$, which means $\mathcal{F}$ is non-empty. By Tychonoff's Theorem, we need only show $\mathcal{F}$ is compact in each factor, and by Alaoglu's Theorem, it is enough to show each factor is β-bounded to complete the proof.

First note that $X \cap Y$ is β-bounded by assumption (S6) and the fact that X is bounded below by $-H\omega$. Let $\hat{y}$ be an upper bound for $X \cap Y$ and let $\mathbf{X} \in \mathcal{F}$. Then $-\omega \leq \mathbf{x}^h \leq \hat{y} - \sum_{i \neq h} \mathbf{x}^i \leq \hat{y} + (H-1)\omega$. □

---

[10] Our equilibrium existence theorem will imply discounted profits are summable. Sun and Kusumoto's (1996) existence theorem applies to some cases where the discounted profits are not summable. They are consequently able to relax (J3) insofar as it pertains to the entrepreneurial factors.

Theorem 1. *Suppose assumptions (C1)–(C5), (S1), (S2), (S5), (S6), and (J1) hold. An individually rational Pareto optimum exists.*

Proof. For $\mathbf{X} \in \mathcal{F}$, define $R(\mathbf{X}) = \{\mathbf{Y} \in \mathcal{F} : \mathbf{y}^h \succsim_h \mathbf{x}^h \text{ for all } h\}$. Order $\{R(\mathbf{X})\}$ by $R(\mathbf{X}) \geq R(\mathbf{Y})$ if and only if $R(\mathbf{X}) \subset R(\mathbf{Y})$. This corresponds to Pareto ordering of $\mathbf{X}$ and $\mathbf{Y}$. Let $\mathcal{S}$ be the collection of all $R(\mathbf{Y})$ for feasible allocations $\mathbf{Y}$ that are individually rational for all agents. Note that $\mathcal{S}$ is non-empty by monotonicity and (J1). Let $\mathcal{R}$ be a chain in $\mathcal{S}$.[11] If $\mathcal{U} = \{R(\mathbf{X}_i)\}_{i=1}^m$ is a finite subset of $\mathcal{R}$, $\cap_{i=1}^m R(\mathbf{X}_i) = R(\max_i \mathbf{X}_i)$ is non-empty by transitivity, where $\max_i \mathbf{X}_i$ is defined using the Pareto ranking $\mathbf{X} \succsim \mathbf{Y}$ if and only if $\mathbf{x}^h \succsim_h \mathbf{y}^h$ for all h. Since each element of $\mathcal{R}$ is σ-compact, and the intersection of any finite subset is non-empty, $\cap_{R \in \mathcal{R}} R$ is non-empty. For any $\mathbf{X} \in \cap_{R \in \mathcal{R}} R$, $R(\mathbf{X})$ is an upper bound for $\mathcal{R}$. By Zorn's Lemma, there is a maximal element R^* of $\mathcal{S}$.[12] Any element of R^* is now an individually rational Pareto optimum. $\square$

8.3 The Core and Edgeworth Equilibria

With the preliminaries out of the way, we are ready to consider the core. A *coalition* is a non-empty subset of $\{1, \ldots, H\}$. An allocation $\mathbf{X}$ is *feasible for a coalition* S if $\sum_{h \in S} \mathbf{x}^h \in Y$. A coalition S can *improve* on the allocation $\mathbf{X}$ if there is an allocation $\mathbf{Z}$ that is feasible for S with $U^h(\mathbf{z}^h) > U^h(\mathbf{x}^h)$ for every $h \in S$. Thus an improving coalition makes all of its members better off. The *core*, denoted $C(\mathcal{E})$, is the set of all allocations that do not admit any improvements by any coalition. Define $U : \mathcal{F} \to \mathbb{R}^H$ by $U(\mathbf{X}) = (U^1(\mathbf{x}^i), \ldots, U^H(\mathbf{x}^H))$. Then $U(\mathcal{F})$ is bounded above because all the U^h are upper semicontinuous and $\mathcal{F}$ is compact. For any coalition S define $V(S) = \{x \in \mathbb{R}^H : x^h \leq U^h(\mathbf{x}^h) \text{ for } \mathbf{X} \text{ that is feasible for } S\}$. Note that $V(S)$ is closed, non-empty and *comprehensive* ($x \in V(S)$ and $z \leq x$ implies $z \in V(S)$). Because $U(\mathcal{F})$ is bounded above, the projection of $V(S)$ into $\mathbb{R}^S$ is also bounded above.

8.3.1 Existence of Core Allocations

Let $\mathcal{B}$ be a non-empty family of subsets of $\{1, \ldots, H\}$. Define $\mathcal{B}_h = \{S \in \mathcal{B} : h \in S\}$. A family $\mathcal{B}$ is *balanced* if there exists non-negative weights λ_S with $\sum_{S \in \mathcal{B}_h} \lambda_S = 1$ for all h. A *V-allocation* or *utility allocation* is

---

[11] Recall that a chain is a totally ordered set.

[12] *Zorn's Lemma* states that if every chain in a partially ordered set $\mathcal{S}$ has an upper bound, then $\mathcal{S}$ contains a maximal element. See Aliprantis and Border (1994, p. 13). In the finite dimensional case it is straightforward to show the existence of individually rational Pareto optima using Zorn's Lemma. The case of infinite dimensional exchange economies is more delicate, e.g., Aliprantis, Brown and Burkinshaw (1989, p. 153).

an element of $V(1, \ldots, H)$. A coalition can improve on a V-allocation x if there is a $z \in V(S)$ with $z_h > x_h$ for all $h \in S$. The *core* of V is the set of V-allocations that cannot be improved on by any coalition. Note that x is in the core of V if and only if the corresponding $\mathbf{X}$ is in the core of $\mathcal{E}$.

Theorem (Scarf). *Suppose* $\cap_{S \in \mathcal{B}} V(S) \subset V(1, \ldots, H)$ *whenever* $\mathcal{B}$ *is a balanced family. Then V has a non-empty core.*

Proof. See Scarf (1967). □

Theorem 2. *Under assumptions (C1)–(C4), (S1)–(S6), and (J1), the infinite horizon economy $\mathcal{E}$ has a non-empty core.*

Proof. Let $\mathcal{B}$ be a balanced family of sets with balancing weights λ_S and let $(x^1, \ldots, x^H) \in \cap_{S \in \mathcal{B}} V(S)$. For each coalition $S \in \mathcal{B}$, there are $\mathbf{x}_S^h \in X^h$ for $h \in S$ with $\sum_{h \in S} \mathbf{x}_S^h = \mathbf{y}_S \in Y$ and $U^h(\mathbf{x}_S^h) \geq x^h$. Now consider $\mathbf{x}^h = \sum_{S \in \mathcal{B}_h} \lambda_S \mathbf{x}_S^h$. Because $\mathbf{x}^h$ is a convex combination of the $\mathbf{x}_S^h$ and U^h is concave, we have $U^h(\mathbf{x}^h) \geq x^h$. Also,

$$\sum_{h=1}^{H} \mathbf{x}^h = \sum_{h=1}^{H} \left(\sum_{S \in \mathcal{B}_h} \lambda_S \mathbf{x}_S^h \right) = \sum_{S \in \mathcal{B}} \left(\sum_{h \in S} \lambda_S \mathbf{x}_S^h \right) = \sum_{S \in \mathcal{B}} \lambda_S \mathbf{y}_S \in Y.$$

Thus $\mathbf{X}$ is feasible for the entire economy. It follows that $(x_1, \ldots, x_H) \in V(1, \ldots, H)$. Scarf's Theorem shows the core of V is non-empty, and therefore the core of $\mathcal{E}$ is non-empty. □

8.3.2 Replicas and Edgeworth Equilibria

The *r-fold replica* of the economy $\mathcal{E}$ is the economy defined by $\mathcal{E}_r = \{U^{hi}, X^{hi}, Y\}_{h,i=1}^{H,r}$ with $X^{hi} = X^h$ and $U^{hi} = U^h$. Each agent h is replaced by r clones, whom we refer to as agents of type h. The *equal treatment core* of $\mathcal{E}_r$, denoted $K(\mathcal{E}_r)$, is the set of core allocations that give identical net trades to each agent of the same type. Note that $K(\mathcal{E}_r) \subset \mathcal{F}$. Define the set of *Edgeworth equilibria* $EE(\mathcal{E})$ by $EE(\mathcal{E}) = \cap_{r=1}^{\infty} K(\mathcal{E}_r)$. In this context, the Edgeworth conjecture states that the set of Edgeworth equilibria coincides with the set of competitive equilibria. In this section, we will show that Edgeworth equilibria exist. We start with a preliminary lemma that shows all agents of the same type receive the same utility in the core. Using this lemma, we can show that the equal treatment core is non-empty.

Lemma 2. *Suppose (C2), (C4), (S1), and (J2) hold. If $\{\mathbf{x}^{hj}\} \in C(\mathcal{E}_r)$, then $U^h(\mathbf{x}^{hi}) = U^h(\mathbf{x}^{hj})$ for all $h = 1, \ldots, H$ and $i, j = 1, \ldots, r$.*

Proof. Take $\mathbf{X} = (\mathbf{x}^{hj})$ in the core of $\mathcal{E}_r$ and suppose there is some i, k, l with $U^i(\mathbf{x}^{ik}) \neq U^i(\mathbf{x}^{il})$. For each $h = 1, \ldots, H$, choose $j(h)$ so that $U^h(\mathbf{x}^{hj(h)}) \leq U^h(\mathbf{x}^{hj})$ for all $j = 1, \ldots, r$. Thus $hj(h)$ is a worst-off agent of type h. Now form the coalition of these worst-off agents of each type, $S = \{hj(h)\}_{h=1}^{H}$, and give $hj(h)$ the net trade $\mathbf{x}^{h} = (1/r)\sum_{j=1}^{r}\mathbf{x}^{hj}$.

For each h, it follows by concavity that $U^{h}(\mathbf{x}^{h}) \geq U^{h}(\mathbf{x}^{hj(h)})$. Moreover, $U^{i}(\mathbf{x}^{i}) > U^{i}(\mathbf{x}^{ij(i)})$. Now $\sum_{\{hj\}\in S}\mathbf{x}^{hj} = (1/r)\sum_{h=1}^{H}\sum_{j=1}^{r}\mathbf{x}^{hj} \in Y$ since $\mathbf{X}$ is a feasible allocation and Y is a cone.

We now use strong irreducibility to spread the gains received by $ij(i)$ to the entire coalition S. Let $I_1 = \{h : h \neq i\}$ and $I_2 = \{i\}$. By construction, $\mathbf{x}^i$ is not an extreme point of X^i as it is the convex combination of at least two distinct elements of X^i. Strong irreducibility now yields a feasible allocation $(\mathbf{z}^1, \ldots, \mathbf{z}^H)$ with $U^h(\mathbf{z}^h) > U^h(\mathbf{x}^h)$ for $h \in I_1$. Now take the convex combination $\lambda \mathbf{x}^h + (1 - \lambda)\mathbf{z}^h$. For $\lambda < 1$, this is preferred to $\mathbf{x}^h$ by all members of I_1. By concavity of U^i, we can choose λ near enough to 1 that $\lambda \mathbf{x}^i + (1 - \lambda)\mathbf{z}^i$ is preferred by i to $\mathbf{x}^i$. With such a λ, $(\lambda \mathbf{x}^h + (1 - \lambda)\mathbf{z}^h)$ improves on $\mathbf{x}^h$, and hence improves on the original allocation for all members of S. This contradicts the fact that $\mathbf{X}$ is in the core. $\square$

Lemma 3. *Suppose (C2), (C4), (S1), and (J2) hold. The equal treatment core of $\mathcal{E}_r$ is non-empty if the core of $\mathcal{E}_r$ is non-empty.*

Proof. We know that all agents of the same type receive indifferent net trades in the core. Give each agent of type h the average net trade received by agents of type h. This weakly increases utility, and is feasible, so it is in the core. As all agents of the same type get the same net trade, it is in the equal treatment core. $\square$

Since the core of each $\mathcal{E}_r$ is non-empty by Theorem 2, we have:

Corollary 1. *Under (C1)–(C4), (S1)–(S6), and (J1)–(J2), $K(\mathcal{E}_r) \neq \emptyset$ for any $r \geq 1$.*

Existence of Edgeworth Equilibrium. *Under (C1)–(C4), (S1)–(S6), and (J1)–(J2), $EE(\mathcal{E})$ is non-empty.*

Proof. Fix r. We first show $K(\mathcal{E}_r)$ is closed. As $K(\mathcal{E}_r) \subset \mathcal{F}$, this will imply $K(\mathcal{E}_r)$ is compact. Let $\{\mathbf{X}_\nu\} = \{(\mathbf{x}_\nu^h)\}$ be a convergent net of allocations in $K(\mathcal{E}_r)$ with $\lim \mathbf{x}_\nu^h = \mathbf{x}^h$. Take the r-fold replicas $\mathbf{X}_\nu^r = (\mathbf{x}_\nu^{hj})$ of $\mathbf{X}_\nu$. Clearly equal treatment holds in the limit, so if $\mathbf{X}$ is not in $K(\mathcal{E}_r)$, there must be a coalition S in the replica economy that can improve on $\mathbf{X}^r$. There is then a feasible allocation $\mathbf{Z} = (\mathbf{z}^{hj})$ with $U^h(\mathbf{z}^{hj}) > U^h(\mathbf{x}^{hj})$ for all $\{hj\} \in S$. Because U^h is upper semicontinuous, $U^h(\mathbf{x}^{hj}) \geq \limsup U^h(\mathbf{x}_\nu^{hj})$. But then $U^h(\mathbf{z}^{hj}) > U(\mathbf{x}_\nu^{hj})$ for all $\{hj\} \in S$ when ν is sufficiently large. This contradicts the fact that $\mathbf{X}_\nu$ is in $K(\mathcal{E}_r)$. We conclude that $\mathbf{X}_\nu \in K(\mathcal{E}_r)$.

The $K(\mathcal{E}_r)$ now form a nested sequence of non-empty compact sets. Because they are nested, they have the finite intersection property. The intersection $\cap K(\mathcal{E}_r) = EE(\mathcal{E})$ is therefore non-empty. $\square$

8.4 The Core and Competitive Equilibrium

Edgeworth's (1881) conjecture says that in large economies, the core allocations will coincide with the competitive equilibrium. The price system then arises naturally. The relative price of two goods is the common rate of exchange for those goods between any pair of traders. By taking this approach, we do not place prior restrictions on the types of prices—the types of trades—that are permissible. Rather than being required *a priori* to be in ℓ^1, our endogenous price system turns out to be in ℓ^1 because preferences and technology interact in a particular fashion. This interaction is summed up in the joint assumptions, especially (J1) and (J3). Because the ℓ^1 prices are not dual prices, we avoid the problems pointed out in Zame's example (Example 3).

We will prove the form of the Edgeworth conjecture shown by Debreu and Scarf (1963) for finite horizon exchange economies, and extended to some infinite production economies by Peleg and Yaari (1970), and Aliprantis, Brown, and Burkinshaw (1987b). In this form, the Edgeworth conjecture says that the set of Edgeworth equilibria coincides with the set of competitive equilibria. Our proof is most similar to that of Boyd and McKenzie (1993).

Once core equivalence is established, we will also examine the First and Second Welfare Theorems, and the equivalence of equilibria and social welfare maxima.

8.4.1 Core Equivalence

We start by showing that any Edgeworth equilibrium is a competitive equilibrium. Take $\mathbf{X} \in EE(\mathcal{E})$. Let G be the convex hull of $\cup_{h=1}^{H} R_h(\mathbf{x}^h)$. If $\mathbf{z} \in G$, there are $\alpha_h \geq 0$, $\sum_h \alpha_h = 1$ and $\mathbf{z}^h \in R_h(\mathbf{x}^h)$ with $\mathbf{z} = \sum_h \alpha_h \mathbf{z}^h$. When the α_h are rational, we can take r large enough that $r\alpha^h$ is an integer for each h. Then $\mathbf{z}$ can be interpreted as an aggregate net trade for a coalition with $r\alpha_h$ members of type h. Such net trades will be feasible if they lie in Y, if $\mathbf{0} \in rG - Y$. Using the fact that Y is a cone ($rY = Y$) we can rewrite this last condition as $\mathbf{0} \in G - Y$. By Lemma 4, G is closed. Normalizing net trades in $\mathcal{E}_r$ by the replication factor r, we can interpret G as the closure of the set of normalized net trades that are possible for some coalition in some replica.

Now examine $G - Y$, which is closed by Lemma 5. If there were a negative element of $G - Y$, it would mean that we could increase our aggregate net trade while maintaining feasibility. Although it is intuitively clear that this is not possible because $\mathbf{X}$ is in the core, it does require proof because we have taken the closure of the net trades. This is accomplished in Lemma 6. This brings us to the heart of the proof, weakly separating

$G - Y$ from zero. The vector that performs this separation will be our equilibrium price vector.

We construct a vector which will be used to normalize prices. The fact that $G - Y$ does not intersect the negative orthant allows us to approximately separate $(G - Y) \cap \ell^\infty$ from $\mathbf{0}$ with parameter ϵ, where the parameter is based on our normalization (Lemma 7). The resulting sets of ϵ-price vectors form a nested collection of non-empty compact sets, and so have an intersection (Lemma 8). Any element of the intersection can be used for the separation. We take an element of that intersection. The vector may be in ba, so we remove its finitely additive part using the Yosida-Hewitt Theorem.[13] The normalization ensures the ℓ^1 part is non-zero. Lemma 9 shows that the ℓ^1 part of this separating vector also separates. We finish the proof by using irreducibility to show that it is is equilibrium price vector.

It is important that the equilibrium price system lies in ℓ^1 rather than ba. If the equilibrium price turned out to be a purely finitely additive measure (such as a Banach limit), then a sufficiently foresighted trader would have an arbitrage opportunity. If this price system in ba gave to a stream of goods a value different from the value arrived at by trading on each date separately, then a sure profit of arbitrary magnitude could be obtained through trading both ways. Put differently, a price in ba which is a pure charge must represent a "bubble." Capital goods would not be priced according to their fundamental value, the value of the discounted sum of one-period rentals.[14] This arbitrage opportunity eliminates the arbitrageur's budget constraint and excludes the possibility of competitive equilibrium when the arbitrageur's preferences have no satiation point. Hence, if trading sets lie in $\ell^\infty(\beta)$, price systems in ba cannot be realized in a competitive equilibrium. This forces us to focus on conditions that yield a price system in ℓ^1, or perhaps even $\ell^1(1/\beta)$. Assumption (J3) plays a key role in this.

Armed with the above intuition, we proceed to the details of the proof.

Lemma 4. *Under (C1)-(C4), (S1)-(S6), and (J1)-(J2), G is σ-closed.*

Proof. We know that each X^h is bounded below by $-\omega$, and therefore G is bounded below by $-\omega$. Suppose $\mathbf{z}_\nu \in G$ with $\mathbf{z}_\nu \to \mathbf{z}$. We can then write $\mathbf{z}_\nu = \sum_{h=1}^H \alpha_h^\nu \mathbf{w}_\nu^h$ where $\alpha_h^\nu \geq 0$, $\sum_{h=1}^H \alpha_h^\nu = 1$, and $\mathbf{w}_\nu^h \in R_h(\mathbf{x}^h) \subset X^h$. Let $\mathbf{z}_\nu^h = \alpha_h^\nu \mathbf{w}_\nu^h$.

The sequence $\{\alpha_h^\nu\}$ is bounded, so by passing to a subsequence, we can assume it converges. If any of the sequences $\{\mathbf{z}_\nu^h\}$ were unbounded, the fact that each $\{\mathbf{z}_\nu^h\}$ is bounded below would imply that $\{\mathbf{z}_\nu\}$ is also

---

[13] See Section 2.3.5 for the Yosida-Hewitt Theorem.
[14] Gilles (1989) and Gilles and LeRoy (1992) interpreted pure charges as bubbles, our discussion follows McKenzie (1993).

unbounded. Therefore each $\{z_\nu^h\}$ is bounded, and by Alaoglu's Theorem, we can extract a convergent subsequence. It follows that we can assume $z_\nu^h \to z^h$.

Let $I = \{h : \alpha_h > 0\}$. For $h \in I$, $w_\nu^h = z_\nu^h/\alpha_h^\nu \to z^h/\alpha_h$. Call the limit w^h. Because X^h is closed, $w^h \in X^h$ for $h \in I$. For $h \notin I$, $-\alpha_h^\nu \omega \le z_\nu^h$. Letting $\nu \to \infty$ shows $z^h \ge 0$. By monotonicity, $z^h/\alpha_h + \sum_{i \notin I} z^i \in R^h(x^h)$ for $h \in I$. Moreover, $\sum_{h \in I} \alpha_h(z^h/\alpha_h + \sum_{i \notin I} z^i) = \sum_{i=1}^H z^i = z$. Therefore $z \in G$. $\square$

We now know that both G and Y are closed, and want to conclude that $G - Y$ is closed. Unfortunately, the sum of two closed convex sets need not be closed, even in $\mathbb{R}^m$, and even if the sets are cones.

▶ Example 7: The sum of closed convex cones need not be closed. In $\mathbb{R}^3$, let $A = \{(0,0,z) : z \le 0\}$ and $B = \{(x,y,z) \ge 0 : (x-z)^2 + y^2 \le z^2\}$. Clearly both are closed convex cones. As such, their sum is their convex hull. Now consider the point $(0,1,0)$. It is not in $A + B$ since any point in $A+B$ with a non-zero y coordinate must also have a non-zero x coordinate. However, for any $\epsilon > 0$, the point $(\epsilon, 1, 0)$ is in $A + B$ since it is the sum of $(0, 0, -(1+\epsilon^2)/2\epsilon) \in A$ and $(\epsilon, 1, (1+\epsilon^2)/2\epsilon) \in B$. Thus $(0,1,0)$ is in the closure of $A + B$, and $A + B$ is not closed. ◀

The sum $A + B$ in Example 7 has a special property. It contains a straight line (the z-axis). This is the main thing that can go wrong. In $\mathbb{R}^m$, it is fairly easy to show that the sum is closed if it contains no straight lines. Choquet (1962) has shown a similar result for more general topological vector spaces using the weak topology.[15]

Choquet's Theorem. *If Z is convex, weakly complete, and contains no straight lines, then for any weakly closed sets $X, Y \subset Z$, $X + Y$ is also weakly closed.*

Because $\ell^\infty(\beta)$ is a complete space, we can specialize and obtain:

Corollary 2. *If $Z \subset \ell^\infty(\beta)$ is convex, σ-closed, and contains no straight lines, then for any σ-closed sets $X, Y \subset Z$, $X + Y$ is σ-closed.*

We are now ready to conclude $G - Y$ is closed.

Lemma 5. *Suppose (C1)–(C4), (S1)–(S7), and (J1)–(J2) hold. Then $G - Y$ is σ-closed.*

Proof. Recall that $G - Y \subset -\omega + \ell_+^\infty(\beta) - Y$. Both $G + \omega$ and $-Y$ are closed and contained in $-Y$ (note $\ell_+^\infty(\beta) \subset -Y$ by free disposal). By assumption, Y contains no straight lines. We now apply Corollary 2 to obtain the result. $\square$

---

[15] Further results of this type may be found in Dieudonné (1966), Fan (1965), Jameson (1972), and Khan and Vohra (1987).

Debreu and Scarf's (1963) argument can now be adapted to show that $G - Y$ does not intersect the negative orthant.

Lemma 6. *Under (C1)–(C5), (S1)–(S6), and (J1)–(J2), there are no* $z \in G$ *and* $y \in Y$ *with* $z \leq y$ *and* $z_t \ll y_t$ *for some* t.

Proof. By periodwise monotonicity, such a pair z', y' would imply the existence of another pair, z, y with $z = \sum_{h=1}^{H} \alpha_h z^h$ for some $z^h \succ_h x^h$, weights $\alpha_h \geq 0$ with $\sum_{h=1}^{H} \alpha_h = 1$, and $y \in Y$. Let $I = \{h : \alpha_h > 0\}$.

For every $h \in I$ and positive integer k, let a_h^k be the smallest integer greater than or equal to $k\alpha_h$. By assumptions (J1) and (S5), there is $y^h \in X^h \cap Y$. Let $w_k^h = (k\alpha_h/a_h^k)(z^h - y^h) + y^h$. As w_k^h is a convex combination of z^h and y^h, it lies in X^h. Letting $k \to \infty$, we find $w_k^h \to z^h$ because $a_h^k \to 1$. By the concavity of U^h, $U^h(w_k^h) \to U^h(z^h)$, so $U^h(w_k^h) > U^h(x^h)$ for large k. We now fix k large.

Also,

$$\sum_{h \in I} a_h^k w_k^h = \sum_{h \in I} (k\alpha_h z^h - k\alpha_h y^h + a_h^k y^h) = ky + \sum_{h \in I} (a_h^k - k\alpha_h) y^h.$$

As $0 \leq a_h^k - k\alpha_h \leq 1$, $\sum_{i \in I} a_h^k w_k^h \in Y$. Thus the coalition formed of a_h^k consumers of type h for each $h \in I$ can improve on $\mathbf{X}$. This improving coalition can be formed when the economy is replicated $\max_{h \in I}\{a_h^k\}$ times. But then $\mathbf{X} \notin EE(\mathcal{E})$, which contradicts our original construction of G. We conclude that it is impossible to choose the pair z', y' above. This contradiction establishes the lemma. $\square$

The next step is to construct the vector used to normalize prices. Choose α and τ such that

$$v^h = e_1 + \cdots + e_{\tau+1} + (x^h\|_\tau \alpha \bar{x}^h) \in R^h(x^h) - Y$$

for all h. This is possible by assumption (J3) and monotonicity. Let $\chi^h = v^h + 2e_1$. By the definition of v^h and monotonicity, $\chi^h \in \ell^\infty \cap (G - Y)$, as is $\theta^h = \chi^h - \alpha \bar{x}^h \geq \chi^h$. Note that $\theta_t^h = 0$ for $t = \tau + 2, \ldots$. Define θ and χ by

$$\chi \equiv \frac{1}{H} \sum_{h=1}^{H} \chi^h;$$

$$\theta \equiv \frac{1}{H} \sum_{h=1}^{H} \theta^h = -\frac{\alpha\bar{x}}{H} + \chi.$$

(1)

For $0 < \epsilon < 1$, we define the ϵ-price set $P(\epsilon)$ by

$$P(\epsilon) = \{\mathbf{p} \in ba : \mathbf{p}\theta = 1 \text{ and } \mathbf{p}z \geq -\epsilon \text{ for all } z \in (G - Y) \cap \ell^\infty\}.$$

Lemma 7. *Suppose (C1)–(C5), (S1)–(S7), and (J1)–(J3) hold. For any ϵ, $0 < \epsilon < 1$, there is $\mathbf{q} \in P(\epsilon)$ such that $\mathbf{q} \geq 0$ and $|q_1| > 0$. Moreover, whenever $\mathbf{p} \in P(\epsilon)$, $\mathbf{pz} \leq 0$ for all $\mathbf{z} \in Y \cap \ell^\infty$.*

Proof. Let $\epsilon > 0$. By Lemma 6, $-\epsilon \mathbf{e}_1 \notin G - Y$. We know $G - Y$ is σ-closed and $\{-\epsilon \mathbf{e}_1\}$ is trivially compact, so there is a non-zero vector $\mathbf{p} \in \ell^1(1/\beta)$ and $\delta > 0$ with $\mathbf{pz} \geq -\epsilon \mathbf{pe}_1 + \delta$ for any $\mathbf{z} \in G - Y$. Periodwise monotonicity and the separation condition imply $\mathbf{p} \geq 0$, so $\mathbf{p} \cdot \mathbf{e}_1 = p_1 \cdot e_1 = |p_1|$, where $|\cdot|$ is the ℓ^1-norm on $\mathbb{R}^m$. Thus

$$\mathbf{pz} > -\epsilon |p_1| \text{ for all } \mathbf{z} \in G - Y. \tag{2}$$

Since $\mathbf{0} \in G - Y$, $|p_1| > 0$.

Now $v^h \in G - Y$, so $\mathbf{p}v^h > -\epsilon |p_1|$ and $\mathbf{p}\theta^h = 2|p_1| + \mathbf{p}v^h - \mathbf{p}\bar{\mathbf{x}}^h \geq (2 - \epsilon)|p_1|$. As $0 < \epsilon < 1$, $\mathbf{p}\theta^h > |p_1|$, and so $\mathbf{p}\theta > |p_1|$. Define $\mathbf{q} = \mathbf{p}/\mathbf{p}\theta$ and consider $\mathbf{z} \in G - Y$. If $\mathbf{qz} \geq 0$, then $\mathbf{qz} \geq -\epsilon$. If $\mathbf{qz} < 0$, $\mathbf{qz} > \mathbf{pz}/|p_1| \geq -\epsilon$ by equation (2). Thus $\mathbf{q} \in P(\epsilon)$.

Now let $\mathbf{p} \in P(\epsilon)$. Since $Y = Y + Y$ and $\mathbf{0} \in G - Y$, it follows that $-Y \cap \ell^\infty \subset (G - Y) \cap \ell^\infty$. Therefore, $\mathbf{pz} \leq \epsilon$ for all $\mathbf{z} \in Y \cap \ell^\infty$. As Y is a cone, this implies $\mathbf{pz} \leq 0$ for all $\mathbf{z} \in Y \cap \ell^\infty$. □

We now take the intersection of the ϵ-price sets. Let

$$P = \cap_{0 < \epsilon < 1} P(\epsilon).$$

The set P will be our price set. The next order of business is to show P is non-empty, and that elements of P separate $G - Y$ and $\mathbf{z}$

Lemma 8. *Suppose (C1)–(C5), (S1)–(S7), and (J1)–(J3) hold. Then $P = \cap_{0 < \epsilon < 1} P(\epsilon)$ is non-empty. Moreover, $\mathbf{p} \in P$ implies $\mathbf{pz} \geq 0$ for all $\mathbf{z} \in (G - Y) \cap \ell^\infty$.*

Proof. The previous lemma shows each $P(\epsilon)$ is non-empty. Now regard $P(\epsilon)$ as a subset of ba. As such, it is $\sigma(ba, \ell^\infty)$-closed since the inner product is $\sigma(ba, \ell^\infty)$-continuous.

Let $\mathbf{p} \in P(\epsilon)$ be arbitrary. Consider $\chi = \theta + \alpha \bar{\mathbf{x}}/H$, which is in $(G - Y) \cap \ell^\infty$ by construction. Thus $\mathbf{p}\theta + \alpha \mathbf{p}\bar{\mathbf{x}}/H = \mathbf{p}\chi \geq -\epsilon$. Using the normalization $\mathbf{p}\theta = 1$, we obtain $-\mathbf{p}\bar{\mathbf{x}} \leq H(1 + \epsilon)/\alpha$. As in the proof of Lemma 7, $\mathbf{p} \geq 0$. We now use the fact that $\bar{\mathbf{x}}$ is constant and strictly negative to find $\delta > 0$ with $\bar{\mathbf{x}} \leq -\delta \mathbf{e}$. Then $\delta \|\mathbf{p}\|_1 = \delta \mathbf{pe} \leq \mathbf{p}\bar{\mathbf{x}} \leq H(1 + \epsilon)/\alpha$. The set $P(\epsilon)$ is bounded in ba. By Alaoglu's Theorem, $P(\epsilon)$ is $\sigma(ba, \ell^\infty)$-compact.

As the $P(\epsilon)$ are a nested family of non-empty compact sets, their intersection is non-empty by the finite intersection property.

Finally, the property that $\mathbf{pz} \geq 0$ for all $\mathbf{z} \in (G - Y) \cap \ell^\infty$ follows because $\mathbf{pz} \geq -\epsilon$ for all ϵ, $0 < \epsilon < 1$. □

Take any $\mathbf{p} \in P$. The Yosida-Hewitt Theorem allows us to decompose $\mathbf{p} = \mathbf{p}^* + \mathbf{p}_f$ where $\mathbf{p}^* \in \ell^1$ and $\mathbf{p}_f$ is a pure charge. Since θ is finitely non-zero, $\mathbf{p}_f \theta = 0$. The normalization $\mathbf{p}\theta = 1$ then implies $\mathbf{p}^*\theta = 1$. This ensures $\mathbf{p}^*$ is non-trivial. The next step is to show $\mathbf{p}^*$ separates $\mathbf{0}$ from $G - Y$, not merely from $(G - Y) \cap \ell^\infty$.

Lemma 9. *Suppose (C1)–(C5), (S1)–(S7), and (J1)–(J3) hold. The sequence $\mathbf{p}^*$ satisfies:*

(1) $\lim_{\tau \to \infty} \sum_{t=1}^{\tau} p_t^* x_t \geq 0$ *for all* $\mathbf{x} \in G$;

(2) $\limsup_{\tau \to \infty} \sum_{t=1}^{\tau} p_t^* y_t \leq 0$ *for all* $\mathbf{y} \in Y$.

Proof. Let $\mathbf{z} = \mathbf{w} - \mathbf{y}$ with $\mathbf{w} \in G$ and $\mathbf{y} \in Y$. Define $\mathbf{w}^- = \mathbf{w} \wedge \mathbf{0}$. For $\mathbf{w} \in X^h$, $-\omega \leq \mathbf{w}^-$, so $\mathbf{w}^- \in \ell^\infty$. Now $\mathbf{p}^*\mathbf{w} = \mathbf{p}^*(\mathbf{w} - \mathbf{w}^-) + \mathbf{p}^*\mathbf{w}^-$. The first term is either finite or $+\infty$ and the second term is finite. Thus $\mathbf{p}^*\mathbf{w}$ is either finite or $+\infty$.

Now consider $\mathbf{z} \in G - Y$. We can write $\mathbf{z}$ as a convex combination, $\mathbf{z} = \sum_{h=1}^{H} \alpha_h \mathbf{z}^h$, with $\mathbf{z}^h \in R^h(\mathbf{x}^h) - Y$. For τ large and $\epsilon > 0$,

$$\epsilon(\mathbf{e}_1 + \cdots \mathbf{e}_{\tau+1}) + (\mathbf{z}^h \|_\tau \mathbf{0}) \in R^h(\mathbf{x}^h) - Y$$

by assumption (J3) and monotonicity. Thus

$$\epsilon(\mathbf{e}_1 + \cdots \mathbf{e}_{\tau+1}) + \sum_{h=1}^{H} \alpha_h (\mathbf{z}^h \|_\tau \mathbf{0})$$
$$= \epsilon(\mathbf{e}_1 + \cdots \mathbf{e}_{\tau+1}) + (\mathbf{z} \|_\tau \mathbf{0}) \in (G - Y) \cap \ell^\infty.$$

Apply $\mathbf{p}$ to see

$$\epsilon \|p^*\|_1 + \liminf_{\tau \to \infty} \sum_{t=1}^{\tau} p_t^* z_t \geq 0.$$

Since $\epsilon > 0$ was arbitrary, this implies $\liminf_{\tau \to \infty} \sum_{t=1}^{\tau} p_t^* z_t \geq 0$. Finally, the facts that $G \subset G - Y$ and $-Y \subset G - Y$ imply the conclusion. $\square$

At this point we have found the equilibrium prices, and proved the key separation property. However, the separation property only yields a quasi-equilibrium. As usual, if there is a cheaper point than $\mathbf{x}^h$ in the consumption set, consumer h will actually be maximizing utility. Let $P^h(\mathbf{x}) = \{\mathbf{z} \in X^h : U^h(\mathbf{z}) > U^h(\mathbf{x})\}$ denote the strictly preferred set.

Proposition 1. *Suppose U^h is concave. If there is a $\mathbf{w} \in X^h$ with $\mathbf{pw} < 0$ and if $\mathbf{pz} \geq 0$ whenever $\mathbf{z} \in P^h(\mathbf{x})$, then $\mathbf{pz} > 0$ for all $\mathbf{z} \in P^h(\mathbf{x})$.*

Proof. Suppose $\mathbf{z} \in P^h(\mathbf{x})$ and $\mathbf{pz} = 0$. Consider $\mathbf{z}_\alpha = \alpha\mathbf{w} + (1 - \alpha)\mathbf{z}$ for $0 < \alpha < 1$. Now $U^h(\mathbf{z}_\alpha) \geq \alpha U^h(\mathbf{w}) + (1 - \alpha)U^h(\mathbf{z})$. For α small, $U^h(\mathbf{z}_\alpha) > U^h(\mathbf{x})$, so $\mathbf{pz}_\alpha \geq 0$. But $\mathbf{pz}_\alpha < 0$. This contradiction shows that $\mathbf{pz} > 0$. $\square$

A point $\mathbf{w} \in X^h$ with $\mathbf{pw} < 0$ will be referred to as a *cheap point*.

Theorem 3. *Under the consumer, technology, and joint assumptions, any Edgeworth equilibrium is a competitive equilibrium with prices in ℓ^1.*

Proof. Let $\mathbf{X}$ be an Edgeworth equilibrium and set $\mathbf{y}^* = \sum_h \mathbf{x}^h$. Thus market clearing is immediate. Construct $G - Y$ as above, and take ℓ^1-prices $\mathbf{p}^*$ that support $G - Y$. By Lemma 9, $\limsup_{\tau \to \infty} \sum_{t=1}^{\tau} p_t^* y_t \le 0$ for all $\mathbf{y} \in Y$. In particular, this holds for $\mathbf{y}^*$. Because $\mathbf{y}^* = \sum_h \mathbf{x}^h$ is bounded below by $-H\omega \in \ell^\infty$, $\sum_t p_t^* y_t^*$ converges. Moreover, Lemma 9 also implies $\mathbf{p}^* \mathbf{y}^* = \mathbf{p}^*(\sum_h \mathbf{x}^h) \ge 0$, so $\sum_{t=1}^{\infty} p_t^* y_t^* = 0$. Profits are maximized at $\mathbf{y}^*$.

By Lemma 9 and Proposition 1, it is enough to show that every consumer has a cheap point. First notice that (J1), combined with the fact that $\mathbf{p}^* \ge 0$, implies there is at least one consumer with a cheap point since $\mathbf{p}^* \bar{\mathbf{x}} < 0$.

Let I_1 be the set of consumers with cheap points, and I_2 the rest of the consumers. We know I_1 is non-empty.

Suppose both I_1 and I_2 are non-empty. By strong irreducibility, there are $\alpha_h > 0$ and $\mathbf{z}^h \in \alpha_h X^h$ for $h \in I_2$ and $\mathbf{z}^h \in P^h(\mathbf{x}^h)$ for $h \in I_1$ such that $\mathbf{y} = \mathbf{z}_{I_1} + \mathbf{z}_{I_2} \in Y$. Now $0 = \mathbf{p}^* \mathbf{y} = \mathbf{p}^* \mathbf{z}_{I_1} + \mathbf{p}^* \mathbf{z}_{I_2}$. Since each consumer in I_1 has a cheap point, $\mathbf{p}^* \mathbf{z}_{I_1} > 0$ by Proposition 1. Then $\mathbf{p}^* \mathbf{z}_{I_2} < 0$, which implies some member of I_2 has a cheap point. But I_2 consists of the consumers without cheap points. This contradiction shows I_2 is empty.

Thus all consumers have cheap points. Proposition 1 combined with Lemma 9 shows that consumer h maximizes utility at $\mathbf{x}^h$, so we have an equilibrium. $\square$

Core Equivalence Theorem. *Under the consumer, technology, and joint assumptions, an allocation is an Edgeworth equilibrium if and only if it is a competitive equilibrium with price vector in ℓ^1.*

Proof. We have already proven the "only if" part, and the "if" part follows by standard arguments. $\square$

As a bonus, we also get existence of equilibrium because Edgeworth equilibria exist.

Competitive Equilibrium Existence Theorem. *Whenever the consumer, technology, and joint assumptions hold, a competitive equilibrium exists with price vector in ℓ^1.*

Remark: Riesz Ideals and Competitive Equilibrium. A similar result holds if $\ell^\infty(\beta)$ is replaced by a principal Riesz ideal $\ell^\infty(\gamma)$ with $\gamma \gg 0$. Let γ^{-1} be defined by $\gamma_{it}^{-1} = 1/\gamma_{it}$ and let $\sigma = \sigma(\ell^\infty(\gamma), \ell^1(\gamma^{-1}))$. Suppose also that $\bar{\mathbf{x}}$ is a strictly negative vector with $\ell^\infty(\bar{\mathbf{x}}) \subset \ell^\infty(\gamma)$, and $\omega \in \ell^\infty(\bar{\mathbf{x}})$, and modify the consumer, technology, and joint assumptions accordingly, replacing $\ell^\infty(\beta)$ by $\ell^\infty(\gamma)$ and ℓ^∞ by $\ell^\infty(\bar{\mathbf{x}})$. Then core equivalence still holds, but equilibrium prices are in $\ell^1(\bar{\mathbf{x}}^{-1})$ instead of ℓ^1 as the proof of Lemma 7 then shows that each $P(\epsilon)$ is bounded in $\ell^\infty(\bar{\mathbf{x}})$.

The case where the Riesz ideal is all of s^m is covered in Boyd and McKenzie (1993).

8.4.2 The Welfare Theorems

Core equivalence is a strong result in comparison to the welfare theorems. Typically, similar techniques can be used to prove the welfare theorems, and that is also the case here. We consider both theorems.[16]

The proof of the First Welfare Theorem is fairly standard.

First Welfare Theorem. *Suppose (C2), (C4), and (C5) hold. Suppose further that $\{\mathbf{x}^h, \mathbf{y}, \mathbf{p}\}$ is a competitive equilibrium with $p \in \ell^1$. Then the allocation $\mathbf{X} = (\mathbf{x}^h)$ is Pareto optimal.*

Proof. As usual, this result only requires local nonsatiation, which follows from monotonicity and convexity. Suppose $\mathbf{Z} \succsim \mathbf{X}$. For each h, $\mathbf{e}_1 + \mathbf{z}^h \succ_h \mathbf{z}^h$. It follows that the convex combination $\epsilon(\mathbf{e}_1 + \mathbf{z}^h) + (1 - \epsilon)\mathbf{z}^h = \epsilon\mathbf{e}_1 + \mathbf{z}^h \succ_h \mathbf{x}^h$ for all $0 < \epsilon < 1$. Thus $\epsilon|p_1| + \mathbf{p}\mathbf{z}^h > 0$. Letting $\epsilon \to 0$, we find $\mathbf{p}\mathbf{z}^h \geq 0$. Now suppose $\mathbf{Z}$ is a Pareto improvement over $\mathbf{X}$. Then for some i, $\mathbf{z}^i \succ_i \mathbf{x}^i$, and cannot be in i's budget set, so $\mathbf{p}\mathbf{z}^i > 0$. Summing the $\mathbf{p}\mathbf{z}^h$, we find $\sum_h \mathbf{p}\mathbf{z}^h > 0$. But this implies $\mathbf{Z}$ cannot be feasible because if $\sum_h \mathbf{z}^h$ were in Y, it would have a non-positive value. No Pareto improvements are feasible, and so $\mathbf{X}$ is Pareto optimal. $\square$

Before moving to the Second Welfare Theorem, we must define an equilibrium with transfer payments.

Equilibrium with Transfer Payments. An equilibrium with transfer payments for the infinite horizon economy $\mathcal{E} = \{X^h, U^h, Y\}_{h=1}^H$ is a collection $\{\mathbf{x}^h, T^h, \mathbf{y}, \mathbf{p}\}_{h=1}^H$ with $\mathbf{p} \in s^m$ such that:

(1) $\mathbf{x}^h \in X^h$ with $\liminf_{\tau \to \infty} \sum_{t=1}^\tau p_t x_t^h \leq T^h$. Whenever $U^h(\mathbf{z}) > U^h(\mathbf{x}^h)$, we have $\liminf_{\tau \to \infty} \sum_{t=1}^\tau p_t z_t > T^h$;

(2) $\sum_h T^h \leq 0$;;

(3) $\mathbf{y} \in Y$, $\limsup_{\tau \to \infty} \sum_{t=1}^\tau p_t y_t = 0$ and $\limsup_{\tau \to \infty} \sum_{t=1}^\tau p_t z_t \leq 0$ whenever $\mathbf{z} \in Y$;

(4) $\sum_{h=1}^H \mathbf{x}^h = \mathbf{y}$.

If T^h is positive, it represents a lump-sum subsidy; if it is negative, it is a lump-sum tax. Since the sum of the transfers is non-positive, tax receipts are sufficient to cover the subsidies.

---

[16] See Becker (1991b) for a survey of the available welfare theorems in infinite dimensional spaces.

Second Welfare Theorem. *Suppose the consumer, technology, and joint assumptions hold. Let $\{\mathbf{x}^h\}_{h=1}^H$ be a Pareto optimum. Set $\mathbf{y} = \sum_{h=1}^H \mathbf{x}^h$. There is a $\mathbf{p}^* \in \ell^1$ and, for each h, $T^h \in \mathbb{R}$ such that $\{\mathbf{x}^h, T^h, \mathbf{y}, \mathbf{p}^*\}_{h=1}^H$ is a competitive equilibrium with transfer payments.*

Proof. Let $B = \sum_{h=1}^H R^h(\mathbf{x}^h)$. We follow the basic core equivalence argument of Section 8.4.1. By Corollary 2, B is closed, as is $B - Y$ (corresponding to Lemmas 4 and 5). Lemma 6 holds for B and Y as $\mathbf{z} \in B$ and $\mathbf{y} \in Y$ with $\mathbf{z} \le \mathbf{y}$ and $z_t \ll y_t$ would violate Pareto optimality of the allocation $\mathbf{X}$. Lemmas 6 and 7 apply in the new setting, so we obtain the equilibrium price vector $\mathbf{p}^*$ as before. Lemma 9 holds, needing only minor modifications to the proof. Now define the transfers by $T^h = \mathbf{p}^* \cdot \mathbf{x}^h$. Irreducibility implies that every consumer has a cheap point. Finally, Proposition 1, adjusted for the transfers, shows we have an equilibrium with transfers. $\square$

8.4.3 Representation of Equilibrium as Welfare Maximum

The welfare theorems link competitive equilibria and Pareto optima. As usual, we can represent any Pareto optimum as the solution to a maximization problem by using a social welfare function. Alternatively, we can rewrite the definition of Pareto optimality as a collection of H maximization problems. Both formulations allow us to further characterize equilibria.

We start with the social welfare approach. Using the notation of Section 8.3, define $\mathcal{U} = U(\mathcal{F})$ and $\mathcal{V} = V(1,\ldots,H)$. Then $\mathcal{U}$ is the set of feasible utility allocations, and $\mathcal{V}$ is its comprehensive hull. Note that $\mathcal{V} = \{v \in \mathbb{R}^H : \text{there is } u \in \mathcal{U} \text{ with } v \le u\}$ is convex. If $u^* \in \mathbb{R}^H$ is a Pareto optimal utility allocation, then $\mathcal{V}$ and $\{u \in \mathbb{R}^H : u > u^*\}$ are disjoint non-empty convex sets. We may separate them with a vector $\lambda \in \mathbb{R}_+^H$ so that $\lambda \cdot v \le \lambda \cdot u^* \le \lambda \cdot u$ for all $v \in \mathcal{V}$ and $u > u^*$. But then u^* solves a maximization problem. Specifically, it maximizes $\lambda \cdot u$ over the set $\mathcal{V}$. Clearly $u^* \in \mathcal{U} \subset \mathcal{V}$, so it also maximizes $\lambda \cdot u$ over $\mathcal{U}$. Finally, $\mathcal{U} = U(\mathcal{F})$, so the given Pareto optimum solves:

$$\max \sum_{h=1}^H \lambda_h U^h(\mathbf{x}^h)$$
$$\text{s.t. } \mathbf{x}^h \in X^h, \quad \sum_{h=1}^H \mathbf{x}^h \in Y.$$

The alternative approach is to maximize each agent's utility under the constraint that every other agent's utility is not reduced. We solve

$$\max U^h(\mathbf{x}^h)$$
$$\text{s.t. } \mathbf{x}^h \in X^h, \quad \sum_{h=1}^{H} \mathbf{x}^h \in Y$$
$$U^i(\mathbf{x}^i) \geq U^{*i} \text{ for } i \neq h$$

for every h.

In the case where preferences are TAS, with all agents having the same discount factor δ, much of our machinery for the single-agent case may be brought to bear on this problem. In that case, $\sum_{h=1}^{H} \lambda_h U^h(\mathbf{x}^h) = \sum_h \lambda_h (\sum_t \delta^t u^h(x_t^h)) = \sum_t \delta^t (\sum_h \lambda_h u^h(x_t^h))$. Thus the Pareto optimum solves a single agent's TAS utility maximization problem with mH goods and felicity function given by $\sum_h \lambda_h u^h(x_t^h)$. The Euler equations for this single-agent problem characterize the equilibrium. Some additional information regarding the welfare weights λ_h might even allow us to conclude that the equilibrium converges to a steady state.[17] There is a complication when analyzing changes in the initial capital stock. The initial capital stock affects the weights λ_h. The weights must also be altered when the distribution of initial capital changes. Dana and Le Van (1990a) analyze the properties of the mapping between capital stocks and weights.

When there are heterogeneous discount factors, the problem is not so simple. It is impossible to aggregate the felicity functions due to the change in discount factor. Let δ_h be the discount factor for agent h. If the weights on utilities are λ_h, the weight on h's felicity at time t is $\delta_h^{t-1}\lambda_h$. The relative weights change over time, and in the long run only the most patient consumers matter.[18] One way to handle this problem in a recursive way is to rewrite the maximization problem using next period's utility as a state variable. Either of the formulations of the maximization problem can be rewritten in this fashion.

Lucas and Stokey (1984) used the weighted utility formulation. Let's specialize to the case of recursive utility functions defined over consumption sequences with aggregator W^h, Malinvaud technology T, and each consumer endowed with an initial capital stock k^h. Let $U(k)$ denote the utility possibility set from endowment $k = \sum_h k^h$. The weighted utility

---

[17] Although he works in a dual context, some of the arguments in Bewley (1982) can be interpreted as getting control over the welfare weights. This is also true of Yano (1984a; 1984b; 1985).

[18] One effect of this is that impatient consumers will consume nothing in the long run. The dynamics of this model have been studied by Coles (1985). A related model with borrowing constraints was introduced in Becker (1980).

maximization problem can be rewritten as:

$$\max \sum_{h=1}^{H} \lambda_h W^h(c^h, u^h)$$
$$\text{s.t. } (\textstyle\sum_h (k^h - c^h), k') \in T, \quad (u^1, \ldots, u^h) \in U(k').$$

Thus we maximize social welfare by choosing current consumption and next period's utility levels under the constraints that future utilities be feasible from next period's capital stock, and that next period's capital stock be feasible given current consumption and the capital endowment. Notice that next period's utility is Pareto optimal from the capital k'. Under additional conditions as detailed in Lucas and Stokey (1984) and Dana and Le Van (1990a; 1991a), we can map the Pareto optimum in the next period into a new set of utility weights that support it. In the additive case, the new weights would be proportional to $\lambda_h \delta_h$. This allows the social welfare problem to be reformulated as a dynamic programming problem involving both capital stocks and utility weights. Dana and Le Van (1990a) use this to derive Euler equations for a given Pareto optimum, and were able to modify Scheinkman's (1976) argument to show a turnpike result under some regularity conditions.[19]

An alternative approach, taken by Benhabib, Jafarey, and Nishimura (1988) that is also examined by Dana and Le Van (1990a; 1991b) is to maximize each agent's utility under the constraint that all other agents receive a reference level of utility.[20]

8.5 Models with Very Heterogeneous Discounting

So far, the model does not allow much heterogeneity in discounting. All the action takes place within the same commodity space. However, from Section 3.5, we know that different aggregators naturally lead to different associated commodity spaces. When consumers discount the future sufficiently differently, we should not expect them to all use the same commodity space. In this section we modify our assumptions to handle these possibilities, piggy-backing on the results of Section 8.4.

The restriction that all consumers have consumption sets that are closed in the same $\ell^\infty(\beta)$ is rather severe. The only restrictions on con-

---

[19] See Chapter 5 for a presentation of Scheinkman's argument. Scheinkman's original argument also implied that a regularity condition hold for cases near the undiscounted case, whereas Dana and Le Van assume the appropriate regularity condition.

[20] This method was previously used by Epstein (1987a; 1987c) to derive similar results in continuous time models.

sumers are supposed to come through their budget and survival (trading) sets. We cannot arbitrarily cut the survival set down to lie within $\ell^\infty(\beta)$.

If we think back to the construction of recursive utility from the aggregator, we find that there were limitations imposed on the spaces where we could construct a recursive utility function. Here the agent's imagination, his ability to evaluate consumption profiles, places a limitation on the trading set. Paths that grow too fast cannot be evaluated. The actual limiting space may vary across consumers. Typically, we would expect to obtain a utility function on some $\ell^\infty(\beta_h)$ for consumer h, with different β_hs for different consumers.

We can now prove a more general core equivalence theorem, that does not require the technology set and all the trading sets to lie in a common Riesz ideal.

Suppose $X^h \subset \ell^\infty(\beta_h)$ with $\beta_h \geq 1$ and that the consumer assumptions are satisfied for h using the $\sigma_h = \sigma(\ell^\infty(\beta_h), \ell^1(1/\beta_h))$ topology. Let $\beta = \min_h \beta_h$. Further, assume that the technology set is a cone, obeys (T1)–(T5) from Section 4.3 for $(\mathbf{E}, \mathbf{E}')$ with $\ell^\infty(\beta) \subset \mathbf{E}$ and σ stronger than the relative $\sigma(\mathbf{E}, \mathbf{E}')$ topology on $\ell^\infty(\beta)$, and obeys (S6)–(S7) above. Let $\mathcal{E} = \{X^h, U^h, Y\}$ and consider the associated infinite horizon economy $\mathcal{E}' = \{X^h \cap \ell^\infty(\beta), U^h, Y \cap \ell^\infty(\beta)\}$. Suppose further that $\mathcal{E}'$ obeys (J1), (J2), and (J3*) below. We refer to these as the *generalized consumer, technology, and joint assumptions*.

Assumption.

(J3*) For any $\mathbf{x} \in X^h$, $\mathbf{y} \in Y$, and $\delta > 0$ there is a τ_0 such that for each $\tau > \tau_0$, there is $\alpha > 0$ with $\delta(\mathbf{e}_1 + \cdots + \mathbf{e}_{\tau+1}) + (\mathbf{x} - \mathbf{y}\|_\tau \alpha \bar{\mathbf{x}}^h) \in [R^h(\mathbf{x}) \cap \ell^\infty(\beta) - Y \cap \ell^\infty(\beta)]$.

This assumption strengthens (J3) slightly. There is the extra restriction to $\ell^\infty(\beta)$ at the end. Of course, if $X^h, Y \subset \ell^\infty(\beta)$, this restriction is moot. Notice that in the presence of the consumer and technology assumptions, $R^h(\mathbf{x}) \cap \ell^\infty(\beta) - Y \cap \ell^\infty(\beta) = (R^h(\mathbf{x}) - Y) \cap \ell^\infty(\beta)$ because if $\mathbf{z} = \mathbf{w} - \mathbf{y} \in (R^h(\mathbf{x}) - Y) \cap \ell^\infty(\beta)$ with $\mathbf{w} \in R^h(\mathbf{x})$ and $\mathbf{y} \in Y$, we can write $\mathbf{y} = \mathbf{w} - \mathbf{z}$. Since $R^h(\mathbf{x})$ is bounded below in $\ell^\infty(\beta)$, $\mathbf{y}$ is bounded below. But this implies $\mathbf{y} \in \ell^\infty(\beta)$ by the technology assumptions. Thus $\mathbf{w} = \mathbf{z} + \mathbf{y}$ is also in $\ell^\infty(\beta)$, demonstrating $\mathbf{z} \in R^h(\mathbf{x}) \cap \ell^\infty(\beta) - Y \cap \ell^\infty(\beta)$.

Lemma 10. *If the generalized consumer, technology, and joint assumptions hold for an infinite horizon economy $\mathcal{E}$, then the associated economy $\mathcal{E}'$ obeys the consumer, technology, and joint assumptions.*

Proof. The key point is that on $\ell^\infty(\beta)$, the σ-topology is stronger than the σ_h- and $\sigma(\mathbf{E}, \mathbf{E}')$-topologies. Thus the $X^h \cap \ell^\infty(\beta)$ and $Y \cap \ell^\infty(\beta)$ are σ-closed. $\square$

This immediately implies $EE(\mathcal{E}') = CE(\mathcal{E}') \neq \emptyset$. Notice that feasible allocations for the economy $\mathcal{E}$ are always in $\ell^\infty(\beta)^H$. This follows because inputs are uniformly bounded, and by (S6), outputs lie in $\ell^\infty(\beta)$. The larger trading sets enhance the possibility of forming an improving coalition, so the set of Edgeworth equilibria must shrink. The larger trading sets also enhance the possibility of purchasing a better net trade, so the set of equilibria must also shrink. Clearly $CE(\mathcal{E}) \subset EE(\mathcal{E})$. We now have $CE(\mathcal{E}) \subset EE(\mathcal{E}) \subset EE(\mathcal{E}') = CE(\mathcal{E}')$, so if we show that $CE(\mathcal{E}') \subset CE(\mathcal{E})$, then both economies have the same competitive equilibria and the same Edgeworth equilibria.

Theorem 4. *Suppose the generalized consumer, technology, and joint assumptions hold for an infinite horizon economy $\mathcal{E}$. Then $CE(\mathcal{E}) = CE(\mathcal{E}')$ where $\mathcal{E}'$ is the associated economy in $\ell^\infty(\beta)$.*

Proof. By the above remarks, we need only show $CE(\mathcal{E}') \subset CE(\mathcal{E})$. Suppose we have a competitive equilibrium $\{\mathbf{x}^h, \mathbf{y}^*, \mathbf{p}^*\}$ for $\mathcal{E}'$. We must first show that the price sequence $\mathbf{p}^*$ is in ℓ^1. Consider the vector θ that was used to normalize prices. Because $\theta \in c_{00}$, $\mathbf{p}^*\theta < -\infty$. Moreover, from equation (1), $\mathbf{p}^*\theta \geq \mathbf{p}^*\chi > 0$ by periodwise monotonicity and the equilibrium conditions. Let $\mathbf{q} = \mathbf{p}^*/(\mathbf{p}^*\theta)$. It is easy to see $\mathbf{q} \in P$. As before, we use the Yosida-Hewitt Theorem to decompose $\mathbf{q}$ into ℓ^1 and pfa parts. However, the fact that $\mathbf{p}^*$ is a sequence means the pfa part is zero. Thus $\mathbf{p}^* \in \ell^1$. It is also easy to see that $\mathbf{p}^*$ satisfies the separation condition in Lemma 8, restricted to $\ell^\infty(\beta)$.

We next show that profits are always non-positive. Let $\mathbf{y} \in Y$. Consider $\mathbf{x}^h - \mathbf{y} \in R^h(\mathbf{x}^h) - Y$ and let $\delta > 0$. By (J3*), there is $\alpha > 0$ so that

$$\delta(\mathbf{e}_1 + \cdots + \mathbf{e}_{\tau+1}) + (\mathbf{x}^h - \mathbf{y}\|_\tau \alpha \bar{\mathbf{x}}^h) \in R^h(\mathbf{x}^h) \cap \ell^\infty(\beta) - Y \cap \ell^\infty(\beta)$$

for τ sufficiently large. Thus

$$\delta(\mathbf{e}_1 + \cdots + \mathbf{e}_{\tau+1}) + \frac{1}{H}\left(\sum_h \mathbf{x}^h - H\mathbf{y}\Big\|_\tau \sum_h \alpha \bar{\mathbf{x}}^h\right) \in G \cap \ell^\infty(\beta) - Y \cap \ell^\infty(\beta)$$

for τ large. By the separation condition, we have

$$\delta\|p^*\|_1 - \sum_{t=1}^\tau p_t^* y_t + \frac{1}{H}\sum_h \sum_{t=1}^\tau p_t^* x_t^h + \frac{1}{H}\sum_{t=\tau+1}^\infty \sum_h \alpha p_t^* \bar{x}_t^h \geq 0.$$

Letting $\delta \to 0$ we obtain

$$\frac{1}{H}\sum_h \sum_{t=1}^\tau p_t^* x_t^h + \frac{1}{H}\sum_{t=\tau+1}^\infty \sum_h \alpha p_t^* \bar{x}_t^h \geq \sum_{t=1}^\tau p_t^* y_t.$$

Then letting $\tau \to \infty$, and using the facts that $\mathbf{p}^*(\sum_h \mathbf{x}^h) = 0$ (because we started with an equilibrium) and that $\bar{\mathbf{x}}^h$ is bounded and $\mathbf{p}^*$ summable, we find $\limsup_{\tau \to \infty} \sum_{t=1}^{\tau} p_t^* y_t \leq 0$ for any $\mathbf{y} \in Y$. Thus the profit condition is satisfied.

Now we handle the larger budget sets. Let $\mathbf{z} \in R^h(\mathbf{x}^h)$ and $\delta > 0$. By $(J3^*)$ there are $\alpha > 0$ and τ_0 with

$$\delta(\mathbf{e}_1 + \cdots + \mathbf{e}_{\tau+1}) + (\mathbf{z}\|_\tau \alpha \bar{\mathbf{x}}^h) \in R^h(\mathbf{x}^h) \cap \ell^\infty(\beta) - Y \cap \ell^\infty(\beta)$$

whenever $\tau > \tau_0$. Again the separation condition yields

$$\delta\|p^*\|_1 + \sum_{t=1}^{\tau} p_t^* z_t + \alpha \sum_{t=\tau+1}^{\infty} p_t^* \bar{x}_t^h \geq 0.$$

Letting $\delta \to 0$ and then $\tau \to \infty$ we find $\mathbf{p}^* \mathbf{z} \geq 0$. Thus we have a quasi-equilibrium. The proof of Theorem 3 yields a cheap point for h for $\mathcal{E}'$, and hence for $\mathcal{E}$. By Proposition 1, the quasi-equilibrium is actually an equilibrium. $\square$

Remark: The Welfare Theorems. The welfare theorems also apply in this setting.

As Examples 4–6 indicate, the framework developed above encompasses many capital accumulation models. When preferences are recursive, we can employ the machinery developed in the previous chapters.

▶ **Example 8: Equilibrium with recursive utility.** We temporarily work in terms of consumption goods rather than net trades. Consider an aggregator for consumer h that obeys conditions (W1)–(W3) of Section 3.5, and generates a continuous utility function on $\ell_+^\infty(\beta_h)$ for some $\beta_h \geq 1$ via the Continuous Existence Theorem. We take this as the consumption set for consumer h and set $\mathcal{X} = \mathbb{R}_+^m$. We also suppose consumer h has an endowment $\boldsymbol{\omega}^h \in \ell_+^\infty(\beta_h)$, yielding $X^h = -\boldsymbol{\omega}^h + C^h$ as the trading set. For purposes of this example, we take $\boldsymbol{\omega}^h \in \ell^\infty$, and also require $\boldsymbol{\omega}_1$ be strictly positive. This is the case of bounded resources and potential labor supply. A similar example could be constructed when resources and potential labor supply grow over time.

Let $\sigma_h = \sigma(\ell^\infty(\beta_h), \ell^1(\beta_h^{-1}))$. Assumption (W3) ensures that the resulting utility function is concave. We also assume that if $x \gg w$, $W(x,y) > W(w,y)$ for all $x, w \in \mathcal{X}$. This implies periodwise monotonicity. Thus (C1)–(C5) are satisfied for the σ_h-topology.

Let technology be given by a constant returns Malinvaud technology set as in Example 5. As in that example, we will assume there is some strictly positive stock that is expansible by a factor $\gamma > 1$. By Lemma 4.3, there is an upper bound β^* on the growth rate of the economy, given uniformly bounded inputs. We require that $\beta^* \leq \beta \equiv \min_h \beta_h$. Letting $\sigma = \sigma(\ell^\infty(\beta), \ell^1(\beta^{-1}))$, we find find that (S1)–(S7) hold for $Y \cap \ell^\infty(\beta)$, as in Example 5.

Now consider the associated economy $\mathcal{E}'$. The generalized consumer and technology assumptions hold. The only conditions left to check for this capital accumulation economy are the joint conditions.

For (J1), it is enough that ω provide sufficient inputs to produce a constant stream of output of all goods. This follows from γ-expansibility because ω_1 is strictly positive.[21]

If the aggregator is strictly monotonic, strong irreducibility (J2) follows. Finally, the arguments of Examples 4 and 5 establish (J3*). ◄

8.6 Conclusion

All of the basic equilibrium questions, existence, the welfare theorems, core equivalence, can be addressed in intertemporal models. For a broad range of models, equilibria exist, the welfare theorems and core equivalence hold, and equilibria can be represented as solutions to a social welfare problem. To show and properly exploit these facts requires *all* of the preceding chapters. The order and temporal structures emphasized in Chapter 2 play an important role in existence and core equivalence. The aggregator representation from Chapter 3 yields exactly the properties we need here. The same compactness and continuity issues that arose in showing the existence of optimal paths in Chapter 4 arise here in the context of Pareto optimality and social welfare maximization. The Equivalence Principle from Chapter 6 foreshadows the interplay between optimality and equilibrium in this chapter. Finally, the turnpike and comparative dynamics results of Chapters 5 and 7 apply to the social welfare representation of equilibria.

---

[21] If the technology is not γ-expansible, (J1) may fail. This happens in the cake-eating example, and may also occur in models with an essential exhaustible resource.

References

C. D. Aliprantis and Kim C. Border (1994), *Infinite Dimensional Analysis: A Hitchhiker's Guide*, Springer-Verlag, New York.

C. D. Aliprantis and D. J. Brown (1983), Equilibria in markets with a Riesz space of commodities, *J. Math. Econ.* **11**, 189–207.

C. D. Aliprantis and O. Burkinshaw (1978), *Locally Solid Riesz Spaces*, Academic Press, New York.

C. D. Aliprantis and O. Burkinshaw (1985), *Positive Operators*, Academic Press, New York.

C. D. Aliprantis, D. J. Brown, and O. Burkinshaw (1987a), Edgeworth equilibria, *Econometrica* **55**, 1109–1137.

C. D. Aliprantis, D. J. Brown, and O. Burkinshaw (1987b), Edgeworth equilibria in production economies, *J. Econ. Theory* **43**, 252–291.

C. D. Aliprantis, D. J. Brown, and O. Burkinshaw (1989), *Existence and Optimality of Competitive Equilibria*, Springer-Verlag, New York.

Rabah Amir (1996), Sensitivity analysis of multi-sector optimal economic dynamics, *J. Math. Econ.* **25**, 123–141.

Rabah Amir, Leonard J. Mirman, and William R. Perkins, (1991), One-sector nonclassical optimal growth: optimality conditions and comparative dynamics, *Internat. Econ. Rev.* **32**, 625–644.

Alosio P. de Araujo (1985), Lack of equilibria in economies with infinitely many commodities: the need for impatience, *Econometrica* **53**, 455–462.

Alosio P. de Araujo (1991), The once but not twice differentiability of the policy function, *Econometrica* **59**, 1383–1393.

Alosio P. de Araujo and P. K. Monteiro (1994), The general existence of extended price equilibria with infinitely many commodities, *J. Econ. Theory* **63**, 408–416.

Alosio P. de Araujo and Jose A. Scheinkman (1977), Smoothness, comparative dynamics, and the turnpike property, *Econometrica* **45**, 601–620.

Alosio P. de Araujo and Jose A. Scheinkman (1979), Notes on comparative dynamics, in *General Equilibrium, Growth, and Trade: Essays in Honor of Lionel W. McKenzie* (Jerry R. Green and Jose A. Scheinkman, eds.), Academic Press, New York.

Kenneth J. Arrow (1953), Le rôle des valeurs boursièrs pour la répartition la meilleure des risques, *Économétric* **11**, 41–47; (1964), The role of securities in the optimal allocation of risk-bearing, (translation), *Rev. Econ. Studies* **31**, 91–96.

Hiroshi Atsumi (1965), Neoclassical growth and the efficient program of capital accumulation, *Rev. Econ. Studies* **32**, 127–136.

Hiroshi Atsumi (1991), On the rate of interest in a 'neo-Austrian' theory of capital, in *Value and Capital: Fifty Years Later* (Lionel W. McKenzie and Stefano Zamagni, eds.), Macmillan Press, London.

Robert J. Aumann and Lloyd S. Shapley (1994), Long-term competition: a game theoretic analysis, in *Essays in Game Theory in Honor of Michael Maschler* (Nimrod Megiddo, ed.), Springer-Verlag, New York.

Kerry Back (1988), Structure of consumption sets and existence of equilibria in infinite dimensional commodity spaces, *J. Math. Econ.* **17**, 88–99.

Robert J. Barro and Xavier Sala-i-Martin (1992), Convergence, *J. Polit. Econ.* **100**, 223–251.

Robert J. Barro and Xavier Sala-i-Martin (1995), *Economic Growth*, McGraw-Hill, New York.

Richard Beals and Tjalling C. Koopmans (1969), Maximizing stationary utility in a constant technology, *SIAM J. Appl. Math.* **17**, 1001–1015.

Robert A. Becker (1980), On the long-run steady state in a simple dynamic model of equilibrium with heterogeneous households, *Quart. J. Econ.* **95**, 375–382.

Robert A. Becker (1981), The duality of a dynamic model of equilibrium and an optimal growth model: the heterogeneous capital goods case, *Quart. J. Econ.* **48**, 271–300.

Robert A. Becker (1982a), The equivalence of a Fisher competitive equilibrium and a perfect foresight competitive equilibrium in a multi-sectoral model of capital accumulation, *Internat. Econ. Rev.* **23**, 19–34.

Robert A. Becker (1982b), The existence of core allocations in a one sector model of capital accumulation, *Econ. Letters* **9**, 201–207.

Robert A. Becker (1983a), A simple dynamic model of equilibrium with adjustment costs, *J. Econ. Dyn. Control* **6**, 79–98.

Robert A. Becker (1983b), Comparative dynamics in the one-sector optimal growth model, *J. Econ. Dyn. Control* **6**, 99–107.

Robert A. Becker (1985a), Capital income taxation and perfect foresight, *J. Pub. Econ.* **26**, 147–167.

Robert A. Becker (1985b), Comparative dynamics in aggregate models of optimal capital accumulation, *Quart. J. Econ.* **100**, 1235–1256.

Robert A. Becker (1991a), An example of the Peleg and Yaari economy, *Econ. Theory* **1**, 200–204.

Robert A. Becker (1991b), The fundamental theorems of welfare economics in infinite commodity spaces, in *Equilibrium Theory with Infinitely Many Commodities* (M. Ali Khan and Nicholas Yannelis, eds.), Springer-Verlag, New York.

Robert A. Becker (1992), Cooperative capital accumulation games and the core, in *Economic Theory and International Trade: Essays in Memoriam J. Trout Rader* (Wilhelm Neuefeind and Raymond G. Riezman, eds.), Springer-Verlag, New York.

Robert A. Becker and John H. Boyd III (1990), Teoriá de la utilidad recursiva: tiempo discreto, *Cuadernos Economicos de ICE* **46**, 103–160.

Robert A. Becker and John H. Boyd III (1993), Recursive utility: discrete time theory, *Hitotsubashi J. Econ.* **34** (Special Issue), 49–98.

Robert A. Becker, John H. Boyd III, and Ciprian Foias (1991), The existence of Ramsey equilibrium, *Econometrica* **59**, 441–460.

Robert A. Becker and Ciprian Foias (1986), A minimax approach to the implicit programming problem, *Econ. Letters* **20**, 171–175.

Robert A. Becker and Ciprian Foias (1987), A characterization of Ramsey equilibrium, *J. Econ. Theory* **41**, 173–184.

Robert A. Becker and Ciprian Foias (1994), The local bifurcation of Ramsey equilibrium, *Econ. Theory* **4**, 719–744.

Robert A. Becker and Mukul Majumdar (1989), Optimality and decentralization in infinite horizon economies, *in Joan Robinson and Modern Economics Theory* (G. Feiwel, ed.), Macmillan Press, London.

Richard Bellman (1957), *Dynamic Programming*, Princeton University Press, Princeton, NJ.

Jess Benhabib, Saqib Jafarey, and Kazuo Nishimura (1988), The dynamics of efficient intertemporal allocations with many agents, recursive preferences and production, *J. Econ. Theory* **44**, 301–320.

Jess Benhabib, Mukul Majumdar, and Kazuo Nishimura (1987), Global equilibrium dynamics with stationary recursive preferences, *J. Econ. Behav. Org.* **8**, 429–452.

Jess Benhabib and Kazuo Nishimura (1979), The Hopf bifurcation and the existence and stability of closed orbits in multisector models of optimal economic growth, *J. Econ. Theory* **21**, 421–444.

Jess Benhabib and Kazuo Nishimura (1981), Stability of equilibrium in dynamic models of capital theory, *Internat. Econ. Rev.* **22**, 275–293.

Jess Benhabib and Kazuo Nishimura (1985), Competitive equilibrium cycles, *J. Econ. Theory* **35**, 284–306.

Jess Benhabib and Kazuo Nishimura (1988), On endogenous cycles in discrete time optimal growth models, *in Optimal Control Theory and Economic Analysis, 3* (G. Feichtinger, ed.), North-Holland, Amsterdam.

Jess Benhabib and Aldo Rustichini (1990), Equilibrium cycling with small discounting, *J. Econ. Theory* **52**, 423–432.

L. M. Benveniste and Jose A. Scheinkman (1982), Duality theory for dynamic optimization models of economics: the continuous time case, *J. Econ. Theory* **27**, 1–19.

C. Berge (1963), *Topological Spaces*, Macmillan Co., New York.

Truman Bewley (1972), Existence of equilibria in economies with infinitely many commodities, *J. Econ. Theory* **27**, 514–540.

Truman Bewley (1982), An integration of equilibrium theory and turnpike theory, *J. Math. Econ.* **10**, 233–267.

Truman Bewley (1991), A theorem on the existence of competitive equilibria in a market with a finite number of agents and whose commodity space is L_∞, *in Equilibrium Theory with Infinitely Many Commodities* (M. Ali Khan and Nicholas Yannelis, eds.), Springer-Verlag, New York.

K. P. S. Bhaskara Rao and M. Bhaskara Rao (1983), *Theory of Charges*, Academic Press, New York.

Garrett Birkhoff (1967), *Lattice Theory*, American Mathematical Society, Providence, RI.

Charles Blackorby, Walter Bossert, and David Donaldson (1995a), Intertemporally consistent population ethics: classical utilitarian principles, *in Social
Choice Re-Examined* (Kenneth J. Arrow, Amartya Sen and K. Suzumura,
eds.), Macmillan Press, London.

Charles Blackorby, Walter Bossert, and David Donaldson (1995b), Intertemporal population ethics: critical-level utilitarian principles, *Econometrica* **63**,
1303–1320.

Charles Blackorby, Daniel Primont, and R. Robert Russell (1978), *Duality, Separability and Functional Structure*, North-Holland, Amsterdam.

David Blackwell (1965), Discounted dynamic programming, *Annals Math. Stats.*
36, 226–235.

Christopher J. Bliss (1975), *Capital Theory and the Distribution of Income*,
North-Holland, Amsterdam.

Eugen von Böhm-Bawerk (1912), *Kapital und Kapitalzins*, Verlag von Gustav
Fischer, Stuttgart; English translation (1959), *Capital and Interest*, Liber-
tarian Press, South Holland, Illinois.

Michele Boldrin (1989), Paths of optimal growth in two-sector models, *in Eco-
nomic Complexity: Chaos, Sunspots, Bubbles, and Nonlinearity* (William A.
Barnett, John Geweke, and Karl Shell, eds.), Cambridge University Press,
Cambridge, UK.

Michele Boldrin and Raymond J. Deneckere (1990), Sources of complex dynamics in two-sector growth models, *J. Econ. Dyn. Control* **14**, 627–653.

Michele Boldrin and Luigi Montrucchio (1986), On the indeterminacy of capital
accumulation paths, *J. Econ. Theory* **40**, 26–39.

Michele Boldrin and Luigi Montrucchio (1989), On the differentiability of the
policy function, Working Paper, UCLA.

Michele Boldrin and Michael Woodford (1990), Equilibrium in models displaying
fluctuations and chaos: a survey, *J. Mon. Econ.* **25**, 189–222.

John H. Boyd III (1986), *Preferences, Technology and Dynamic Equilibria*,
Ph.D. Dissertation, Indiana University.

John H. Boyd III (1989a), The existence of equilibrium in infinite-dimensional
spaces: some examples, Working Paper, University of Rochester.

John H. Boyd III (1989b), Reciprocal roots, paired roots and the saddlepoint
property, Working Paper, University of Rochester.

John H. Boyd III (1990a), Recursive utility and the Ramsey problem, *J. Econ.
Theory* **50**, 326–345.

John H. Boyd III (1990b), Symmetries, dynamic equilibria and the value function, *in Conservation Laws and Symmetry: Applications to Economics and
Finance* (R. Sato and R. Ramachandran, eds.), Kluwer Academic Publishers, Boston.

John H. Boyd III (1996), The existence of steady states in multisector capital
accumulation models, *J. Econ. Theory* **71**, 289–297.

John H. Boyd III and Lionel W. McKenzie (1993), The existence of competitive
equilibrium over an infinite horizon with production and general consumption sets, *Internat. Econ. Rev.* **34**, 1–20.

Marcel Boyer (1975), An optimal growth model with stationary non-additive
utilities, *Can. J. Econ.* **8**, 216–237.

William A. Brock (1970a), An axiomatic basis for the Ramsey-Weizsäcker overtaking criterion, *Econometrica* **38**, 927–929.

William A. Brock (1970b), On existence of weakly maximal programmes in a multi-sector economy, *Rev. Econ. Studies* **37**, 275–280.

William A. Brock (1973), Some results on the uniqueness of steady states in multisector models of optimum growth when future utilities are discounted, *Internat. Econ. Rev.* **14**, 535–559.

William A. Brock (1974), Comments on Radner's "Market equilibrium under uncertainty", *in Frontiers of Quantitative Economics, vol. II* (Michael D. Intrilligator and David A. Kendrick, eds.), North-Holland, Amsterdam.

William A. Brock (1982), Asset prices in a production economy, *in The Economics of Information and Uncertainty* (John J. McCall, ed.), University of Chicago Press, Chicago.

William A. Brock (1986), A revised version of Samuelson's correspondence principle: applications of recent results on the asymptotic stability of optimal control to the problem of comparing long-run equilibrium, *in Models of Economic Dynamics* (Hugo F. Sonnenschein, ed.), Springer-Verlag, New York.

William A. Brock and W. Davis Dechert (1988), Theorems on distinguishing deterministic from random systems, *in Dynamic Econometric Modeling, Proceedings of the Third International Symposium in Economic Theory and Econometrics* (William A. Barnett, E. R. Berndt, and Halbert White, eds.), Cambridge University Press, Cambridge, UK.

William A. Brock and W. Davis Dechert (1991), Non-linear dynamical systems: instability and chaos in economics, *in Handbook of Mathematical Economics, vol. IV* (Werner Hildenbrand and Hugo Sonnenschein, eds.), North-Holland, Amsterdam.

William A. Brock and David Gale (1969), Optimal growth under factor augmenting progress, *J. Econ. Theory* **1**, 229–243.

William A. Brock and Leonard J. Mirman (1972), Optimal economic growth and uncertainty: the discounted case, *J. Econ. Theory* **4**, 479–513.

Donald J. Brown and Lucinda M. Lewis (1981), Myopic economic agents, *Econometrica* **49**, 359–368.

P. Buckholtz and J. Hartwick (1989), Zero time preference with discounting, *Econ. Letters* **29**, 1–6.

André Burgstaller (1995), *Property and Prices: Toward a Unified Theory of Value*, Cambridge University Press, Cambridge, UK.

Edwin Burmeister (1980), *Capital Theory and Dynamics*, Cambridge University Press, Cambridge, UK.

Edwin Burmeister and A. Rodney Dobell (1970), *Mathematical Theories of Economic Growth*, Macmillan Press, London.

Edwin Burmeister and Ngo Van Long (1977), On some unresolved questions in capital theory: an application of Samuelson's correspondence principle, *Quart. J. Econ.* **91**, 289–314.

Edwin Burmeister and Stephen J. Turnovsky (1972), Capital deepening response in an economy with heterogeneous capital goods, *Amer. Econ. Rev.* **62**, 842–853.

Donald Campbell (1985), Impossibility theorems and infinite horizon planning, *Social Choice and Welfare* **2**, 283–293.

P. Cartigny and A. Venditti (1995), Endogenous cycles in discrete symmetric multisector growth models, *J. Opt. Theory Appl.* **86**, 17–36.

David Cass and Karl Shell (1976), The structure and stability of competitive dynamical systems, *J. Econ. Theory* **12**, 31–70.

Christophe Chamley (1981), The welfare cost of capital income taxation in a growing economy, *J. Polit. Econ.* **89**, 468–496.

Graciela Chichilnisky (1993), The cone condition, properness, and extremely desirable commodities, *Econ. Theory* **3**, 177–182.

Graciela Chichilnisky and Geoffrey M. Heal (1993), Competitive equilibrium in Sobolev spaces without bounds on short sales, *J. Econ. Theory* **59**, 364–384.

Graciela Chichilnisky and Peter J. Kalman (1980), Application of functional analysis to models of efficient allocation of economic resources, *J. Opt. Theory Appl.* **30**, 19–32.

G. Choquet (1962), Ensembles et cônes convexes faiblement complets, *Comptes Rendus de l'Academie des Sciences, Paris* **254**, 1908–1910.

C. W. Clark (1971), Economically optimal policies for the utilization of biologically renewable resources, *Math. Biosci.* **17**, 245–268.

S. Clemhout and H. Wan, Jr. (1986), Common-property exploitations under risks of resource extinctions, *in Dynamic Games and Application in Economics* (T. Başar, ed.), Springer-Verlag, New York.

Wilbur John Coleman, II (1991), Equilibrium in a productive economy with an income tax, *Econometrica* **59**, 1091–1104.

Jeffrey L. Coles (1985), Equilibrium turnpike theory with constant returns to scale and possibly heterogeneous discount factors, *Internat. Econ. Rev.* **26**, 671–679.

John B. Conway (1967), The strict topology and compactness in the space of measures: II, *Trans. Amer. Math. Soc.* **126**, 474–486.

Thomas F. Cooley (ed.) (1995), *Frontiers of Business Cycle Research*, Princeton University Press, Princeton, NJ.

Thomas F. Cooley and Edward C. Prescott (1995), Economic growth and business cycles, *in Frontiers of Business Cycle Research* (Thomas F. Cooley, ed.), Princeton University Press, Princeton, NJ.

Rose-Anne Dana and Le Van Cuong (1990a), On the structure of Pareto-optima in an infinite horizon economy where agents have recursive preferences, *J. Opt. Theory Appl.* **64**, 269–292.

Rose-Anne Dana and Le Van Cuong (1990b), On the Bellman equation of the overtaking criterion, *J. Opt. Theory Appl.* **67**, 587–600.

Rose-Anne Dana and Le Van Cuong (1991a), Equilibria of a stationary economy with recursive preferences, *J. Opt. Theory Appl.* **71**, 289–313.

Rose-Anne Dana and Le Van Cuong (1991b), Optimal growth and Pareto optimality, *J. Math. Econ.* **20**, 155–180.

Jean-Pierre Danthine and John B. Donaldson (1981), Stochastic properties of fast vs. slow growing economies, *Econometrica* **49**, 1007–1033.

Jean-Pierre Danthine and John B. Donaldson (1995), Computing equilibria of nonoptimal economies, in *Frontiers of Business Cycle Research* (Thomas F. Cooley, ed.), Princeton University Press, Princeton, NJ.

Swapan DasGupta (1985), A local analysis of stability and regularity of stationary states in discrete symmetric optimal capital accumulation models, *J. Econ. Theory* **36**, 302–318.

Swapan DasGupta and Lionel W. McKenzie (1984), The comparative statics and dynamics of stationary states, Working Paper, University of Rochester.

Swapan DasGupta and Lionel W. McKenzie (1985), A note on comparative statics and dynamics of stationary states, *Econ. Letters* **18**, 333–338.

Swapan DasGupta and Lionel W. McKenzie (1990), The comparative statics and dynamics of stationary states, in *Preferences, Uncertainty and Optimality: Essays in Honor of Leonid Hurwicz* (John S. Chipman, Daniel McFadden, and Marcel K. Richter, eds.), Westview Press, Boulder, CO.

Gerard Debreu (1954a), Valuation equilibrium and Pareto optimum, *Proc. Nat. Acad. Sci.* **40**, 588–592.

Gerard Debreu (1954b), Representation of a preference ordering by a numerical function, in *Decision Processes* (R. M. Thrall, C. H. Coombs and R. L. Davis, eds.), Wiley, New York.

Gerard Debreu (1959), *Theory of Value: An Axiomatic Analysis of Economic Equilibrium*, Yale University Press, New Haven.

Gerard Debreu (1960), Topological methods in cardinal utility theory, in *Mathematical Methods in the Social Sciences, 1959* (Kenneth J. Arrow, Samuel Karlin, and Patrick Suppes, eds.), Stanford University Press, Stanford.

Gerard Debreu and Herbert Scarf (1963), A limit theorem on the core of an economy, *Internat. Econ. Rev.* **4**, 235–246.

W. Davis Dechert and Kazuo Nishimura (1980), Existence of optimal paths and the turnpike property: the non-convex case with unbounded stocks, Working Paper, SUNY-Buffalo.

W. Davis Dechert and Kazuo Nishimura (1983), A complete characterization of optimal growth paths in an aggregated model with a non-concave production function, *J. Econ. Theory* **31**, 332–354.

Peter A. Diamond (1965), The evaluation of infinite utility streams, *Econometrica* **33**, 170–177.

J. Dieudonné (1966), Sur la séparation des ensembles convexes, *Math. Ann.* **163**, 1–3.

James F. Dolmas (1995), Time-additive representations of preferences when consumption grows without bound, *Econ. Letters* **47**, 317–326.

James F. Dolmas (1996a), Balanced-growth-consistent recursive utility, *J. Econ. Dyn. Control* **20**, 657–680.

James F. Dolmas (1996b), Endogenous growth in multisector Ramsey models, *Internat. Econ. Rev.* **37**, 403–421.

Robert Dorfman, Paul A. Samuelson, and Robert M. Solow (1958), *Linear Programming and Economic Analysis*, McGraw-Hill, New York.

Nelson Dunford and Jacob T. Schwartz (1957), *The Theory of Linear Operators, Part I: General Theory*, Wiley-Interscience, New York.

Prajit K. Dutta (1985), *Social and Private Time-Preference: Does the Choice of a Discount Factor Matter?*, Ph.D. Dissertation, Cornell University.

Prajit K. Dutta (1987), Capital deepening and impatience equivalence in stochastic aggregative growth models, *J. Econ. Dyn. Control* **11**, 519–530.

Prajit K. Dutta (1991), What do discounted optima converge to? A theory of discount rate asymptotics in economic models, *J. Econ. Theory* **55**, 64–94.

Prajit K. Dutta (1993), On specifying the parameters of a development plan, *in Capital, Investment and Development: Essays in Memory of Sukhamoy Charkravarty* (Kaushik Basu, Mukul Majumdar, and Tapan Mitra, eds.), Basil Blackwell, Cambridge, MA.

Frances Y. Edgeworth (1881), *Mathematical Psychics*, C. Kegan Paul & Co., London.

Ivar Ekeland and Jose A. Scheinkman (1986), Transversality conditions for some infinite horizon discrete time optimization problems, *Math. Oper. Res.* **11**, 216–229.

Larry G. Epstein (1983), Stationary cardinal utility and optimal growth under uncertainty, *J. Econ. Theory* **31**, 133–152.

Larry G. Epstein (1986), Implicitly additive utility and the nature of optimal economic growth, *J. Math. Econ.* **15**, 111–128.

Larry G. Epstein (1987a), The global stability of efficient intertemporal allocations, *Econometrica* **55**, 329–355.

Larry G. Epstein (1987b), Impatience, *in The New Palgrave: A Dictionary of Economics* (John Eatwell, Murray Milgate, and Peter Newman, eds.), Macmillan Press, New York.

Larry G. Epstein (1987c), A simple dynamic general equilibrium model, *J. Econ. Theory* **41**, 68–95.

Larry G. Epstein and J. Allan Hynes (1983), The rate of time preference and dynamic economic analysis, *J. Polit. Econ.* **91**, 611–635.

Larry G. Epstein and Stanley E. Zin (1989), Substitution, risk aversion, and the temporal behavior of consumption and asset returns: a theoretical framework, *Econometrica* **57**, 937–969.

M. C. Escher and J. L. Locher (1984), *The Infinite World of M. C. Escher*, Abrandale Press/Harry Abrams, New York.

Ky Fan (1965), A generalization of the Alaoglu-Bourbaki theorem and its applications, *Math. Zeitschr.* **88**, 48–60.

Christophe Faugère (1993), *Essays on the Dynamics of Technical Progress*, Ph.D. Dissertation, University of Rochester.

Richard Feynman (1965), *The Character of Physical Law*, The MIT Press, Cambridge, MA.

Richard Feynman, Robert B. Leighton and Matthew Sands (1963), *The Feynman Lectures on Physics, vol. I*, Addison-Wesley, Reading, MA.

Peter C. Fishburn (1970), *Utility Theory for Decision Making*, Wiley, New York.

Irving Fisher (1907), *The Rate of Interest*, Macmillan Co., New York.

Irving Fisher (1930), *The Theory of Interest*, Macmillan Co., New York.

Wendell H. Fleming (1965), *Functions of Several Variables*, Addison-Wesley, Reading, MA.

James Flynn (1980), The existence of optimal invariant stocks in a multi-sector economy, *Rev. Econ. Studies* **47**, 809–811.

Orrin Frink (1942), Topology in lattices, *Trans. Amer. Math. Soc.* **51**, 569–582.

David Gale (1967), On optimal development in a multi-sector economy, *Rev. Econ. Studies* **34**, 1–18.

David Gale and W. R. S. Sutherland (1968), Analysis of a one good model of economic development, *in Mathematics of the Decision Sciences: Part II* (G. B. Dantzig and A. F. Veinott, eds.), American Mathematical Society, Providence, RI.

Christian Gilles (1989), Charges as equilibrium prices and asset bubbles, *J. Math. Econ.* **18**, 155–167.

Christian Gilles and Stephen F. LeRoy (1992), Bubbles and charges, *Internat. Econ. Rev.* **33**, 323–339.

James Gleick (1987), *Chaos: Making of a New Science*, Viking, New York.

W. M. Gorman (1968a), Conditions for additive separability, *Econometrica* **36**, 605–609.

W. M. Gorman (1968b), The structure of utility functions, *Rev. Econ. Studies* **35**, 367–390.

Frieda Granot and Arthur F. Veinott (1985), Substitutes, complements and ripples in network flows, *Math. Oper. Res.* **10**, 471–497.

Jo Anna Gray and Stephen W. Salant (1983), Transversality conditions in infinite-horizon models, Working Paper, Washington State University.

Victor Guillemin and Alan Pollack (1974), *Differential Topology*, Prentice-Hall, Englewood Cliffs.

Frank Hahn (1966), Equilibrium dynamics with heterogeneous capital goods, *Quart. J. Econ.* **80**, 633–646.

Frank Hahn (1985), *Money, Growth and Stability*, The MIT Press, Cambridge, MA.

Frank Hahn and Robert M. Solow (1995), *A Critical Essay on Modern Macroeconomic Theory*, The MIT Press, Cambridge, MA.

Peter J. Hammond (1993), Irreducibility, resource relatedness, and survival in equilibrium with individual nonconvexities, *in General Equilibrium, Growth and Trade II: The Legacy of Lionel W. McKenzie* (Robert A. Becker, Michele Boldrin, Ronald Jones, and William Thomson, eds.), Academic Press, New York.

Gary D. Hansen and Edward C. Prescott (1995), Recursive methods for computing equilibria of real business cycles, *in Frontiers of Business Cycle Research* (Thomas F. Cooley, ed.), Princeton University Press, Princeton, NJ.

Terje Hansen and Tjalling C. Koopmans (1972), On the definition and computation of a capital stock invariant under optimization, *J. Econ. Theory* **5**, 487–523.

Friedrich A. Hayek (1941), *The Pure Theory of Capital*, University of Chicago Press, Chicago.

Alejandro Hernández D. (1991), The dynamics of equilibrium allocations with borrowing constraints, *J. Econ. Theory* **55**, 180–191.

Mark N. Hertzendorf (1995), Recursive utility and the rate of impatience, *Econ. Theory* **5**, 51–65.

John R. Hicks (1946), *Value and Capital*, Oxford University Press, Oxford.

John R. Hicks (1965), *Capital and Growth*, Oxford University Press, Oxford.

John R. Hicks (1973), *Capital and Time: A Neo-Austrian Theory*, Oxford University Press, Oxford.

Gerhard Hieber (1981), *On Optimal Growth Paths with Variable Technology*, Oelgeschlager, Gunn & Hain, Cambridge, MA.

M. W. Hirsch and C. Pugh (1970), Stable manifolds and hyperbolic sets, *Proc. Symp. Pure. Math.* **14**, 133–163.

Jack Hirshleifer (1970), *Investment, Interest and Capital*, Prentice-Hall, Englewood Cliffs, NJ.

Kenneth Hoffman and Ray Kunze (1971), *Linear Algebra*, Second Edition, Prentice-Hall, Englewood Cliffs, NJ.

Katsuhito Iwai (1972), Optimal economic growth and stationary ordinal utility —a Fisherian approach, *J. Econ. Theory* **5**, 121–151.

Saqib Jafarey (1988), Recursive utilities and the stability of intertemporal allocations, Working Paper, SUNY-Buffalo.

G. J. O. Jameson (1972), The duality of pairs of wedges, *Proc. London Math. Soc.* **24** (Series 3), 531–547.

Larry E. Jones (1984), A competitive model of commodity differentiation, *Econometrica* **52**, 507–530.

Larry E. Jones and Rodolfo E. Manuelli (1988), A model of optimal equilibrium growth, Working Paper, Northwestern University.

Larry E. Jones and Rodolfo E. Manuelli (1990), A convex model of equilibrium growth: theory and policy implications, *J. Polit. Econ.* **82**, 1008–1038.

Sumit Joshi (1995), Recursive utility and optimal growth under uncertainty, *J. Math. Econ.* **24**, 601–617.

Nicholas Kaldor (1961), Capital accumulation and economic growth, *in The Theory of Capital* (F. A. Lutz and D. C. Hague, eds.), St. Martin's Press, New York.

Y. Kannai (1970), Continuity properties of the core of a market, *Econometrica* **38**, 791–815.

Timothy J. Kehoe, David K. Levine, and Paul M. Romer (1992), On characterizing equilibria of economies with externalities and taxes as solutions to optimization problems, *Econ. Theory* **2**, 43–68.

John L. Kelley (1955), *General Topology*, Springer-Verlag, New York.

J. G. Kemeny, Oskar Morgenstern, and G. L. Thompson (1956), A generalization of the von Neumann model of an expanding economy, *Econometrica* **24**, 115–135.

M. Ali Khan (1993), Lionel W. McKenzie on the existence of competitive equilibrium, *in General Equilibrium, Growth and Trade II: The Legacy of Lionel W. McKenzie* (Robert A. Becker, Michele Boldrin, Ronald Jones, and William Thomson, eds.), Academic Press, New York.

M. Ali Khan and Tapan Mitra (1986), On the existence of a stationary optimal stock for a multi-sector economy: a primal approach, *J. Econ. Theory* **40**, 319–328.

M. Ali Khan and Rajiv Vohra (1987), On sufficient conditions for the sum of two weak* closed sets to be weak* closed, *Archiv der Mathematik* **48**, 328–330.

Alan P. Kirman (1992), Whom or what does the representative individual represent?, *J. Econ. Perspectives* **6**, 117–136.

E. Klein and A. C. Thompson (1984), *Theory of Correspondences*, Wiley, New York.

Tjalling C. Koopmans (1957), *Three Essays on the State of Economic Science*, McGraw-Hill, New York.

Tjalling C. Koopmans (1960), Stationary ordinal utility and impatience, *Econometrica* **28**, 287–309.

Tjalling C. Koopmans (1967), Objectives, constraints and outcomes in optimal growth models, *Econometrica* **35**, 1–15.

Tjalling C. Koopmans (1972a), Representation of preference orderings over time, *in Decision and Organization* (C. B. McGuire and Roy Radner, eds.), North-Holland, Amsterdam.

Tjalling C. Koopmans (1972b), Representation of preference orderings with independent components of consumption, *in Decision and Organization* (C. B. McGuire and Roy Radner, eds.), North-Holland, Amsterdam.

Tjalling C. Koopmans (1985), *The Scientific Papers of Tjalling C. Koopmans, vol. II*, The MIT Press, Cambridge, MA.

Tjalling C. Koopmans, Peter A. Diamond, and Richard E. Williamson (1964), Stationary utility and time perspective, *Econometrica* **82**, 82–100.

David M. Kreps (1977), Decision problems with expected utility criteria, I: upper and lower convergent utility, *Math. Oper. Res.* **2**, 45–53.

Mordecai Kurz (1968a), The general instability of a class of competitive growth processes, *Rev. Econ. Studies* **35**, 155–174.

Mordecai Kurz (1968b), Optimal economic growth and wealth effects, *Internat. Econ. Rev.* **9**, 348–357.

D. Levhari, N. Liviatan, and I. Luski (1974), The social discount rate, consumption, and capital, *Quart. J. Econ.* **88**, 117–126.

T.-Y. Li and J. A. Yorke (1975), Period three implies chaos, *Amer. Math. Monthly* **82**, 985–992.

N. Liviatan and P.A. Samuelson (1969), Notes on turnpikes: stable and unstable, *J. Econ. Theory* **1**, 454–475.

J. Łoś (1976), Extended von Neumann models and game theory, *in Computing Equilibria How and Why* (J. Łoś and M. W. Łoś, eds.), North-Holland, Amsterdam.

Robert E. Lucas, Jr. (1988), On the mechanics of economic development, *J. Mon. Econ.* **22**, 3–43.

Robert E. Lucas, Jr. and Edward C. Prescott (1971), Investment under uncertainty, *Econometrica* **39**, 659–682.

Robert E. Lucas, Jr. and Nancy L. Stokey (1984), Optimal growth with many consumers, *J. Econ. Theory* **32**, 139–171.

Angus Maddison (1982), *Phases of Capitalist Development*, Oxford University Press, Oxford.

Michael J. P. Magill (1981), An equilibrium existence theorem, *J. Math. Anal. Appl.* **84**, 162–169.

Michael J. P. Magill and Kazuo Nishimura (1984), Impatience and accumulation, *J. Math. Anal. Appl.* **98**, 270–281.

Michael J. P. Magill and Martine Quinzii (1994), Infinite Horizon Incomplete Markets, *Econometrica* **62**, 853–880.

Mukul Majumdar (1975), Some remarks on optimal growth with intertemporally dependent preferences in the neoclassical model, *Rev. Econ. Studies* **42**, 147–153.

Mukul Majumdar (ed.) (1992), *Decentralization in Infinite Horizon Economies*, Westview Press, Boulder.

Mukul Majumdar and Tapan Mitra (1982), Intertemporal allocations with a non-convex technology: the aggregate framework, *J. Econ. Theory* **27**, 101–136.

Mukul Majumdar and Tapan Mitra (1994a), Periodic and chaotic programs of optimal intertemporal allocation in an aggregative model with wealth effects, *Econ. Theory* **4**, 649–676.

Mukul Majumdar and Tapan Mitra (1994b), Robust ergodic chaos in discounted dynamic optimization models, *Econ. Theory* **4**, 677–688.

Mukul Majumdar and Manfred Nermuth (1982), Dynamic optimization in non-convex models with irreversible investment: monotonicity and turnpike results, *Zeitschrift für Nationalokonomie*, 339–362.

Mukul Majumdar and Bezalel Peleg (1992), A note on optimal development in a multi-sector nonconvex economy, *in Equilibrium and Dynamics: Essays in Honor of David Gale* (Mukul Majumdar, ed.), St. Martin's Press, New York.

Edmond Malinvaud (1953), Capital accumulation and efficient allocation of resources, *Econometrica* **21**, 233–268; Efficient capital accumulation: a corrigendum, *Econometrica* **30**, 570–573.

Leslie M. Marx (1993), Monotonicity of solution sets for parameterized optimization problems, The Center for Mathematical Studies in Economics and Management Science, Northwestern University.

Andreu Mas-Colell (1985), *The Theory of General Economic Equilibrium*, Cambridge University Press, Cambridge, UK.

Andreu Mas-Colell (1986), The price equilibrium existence problem in topological vector lattices, *Econometrica* **54**, 1039–1053.

Andreu Mas-Colell and W. R. Zame (1991), Equilibrium theory in infinite dimensional spaces, *in Handbook of Mathematical Economics, vol. IV* (Werner Hildenbrand and Hugo Sonnenschein, eds.), North-Holland, Amsterdam.

Lionel W. McKenzie (1959), On the existence of general equilibrium for a competitive market, *Econometrica* **22**, 147–161.

Lionel W. McKenzie (1981), The classical theorem on the existence of general equilibrium, *Econometrica* **49**, 819–841.

Lionel W. McKenzie (1982), A primal route to the turnpike and Liapounov stability, *J. Econ. Theory* **26**, 194–209.

Lionel W. McKenzie (1983), Turnpike theory, discounted utility and the von Neumann facet, *J. Econ. Theory* **30**, 330–352.

Lionel W. McKenzie (1986), Optimal economic growth, turnpike theorems and comparative dynamics, *in Handbook of Mathematical Economics, vol. III* (Kenneth J. Arrow and Michael D. Intriligator, eds.), North-Holland, Amsterdam.

Lionel W. McKenzie (1991), Comment on Atsumi's rate of interest in a 'Neo-Austrian' theory of capital, in *Value and Capital: Fifty Years Later* (Lionel W. McKenzie and Stefano Zamagni, eds.), Macmillan Press, London.

Lionel W. McKenzie (1992), Existence of competitive equilibrium in a growing economy, in *Economic Theory and International Trade: Essays in Memoriam J. Trout Rader* (Wilhelm Neuefeind and Raymond G. Riezman, eds.), Springer-Verlag, New York.

Lionel W. McKenzie (1993), Achieving a general consumption set in an infinite model of competitive equilibrium, *Hitotsubashi J. Econ.* **34** (Special Issue), 5–21.

Lionel W. McKenzie (1994), Equilibrium, trade and capital accumulation, RCER Working Paper, No. 395, University of Rochester.

Thomas McKeown (1976), *The Modern Rise of Population*, Academic Press, New York.

Roy Mendelssohn and Matthew J. Sobel (1980), Capital accumulation and the optimization of renewable resource models, *J. Econ. Theory* **23**, 243–260.

Paul Milgrom (1994), Comparing optima: do simplifying assumptions affect conclusions?, *J. Polit. Econ.* **102**, 607–615.

Paul Milgrom and John Roberts (1990), Rationalizability, learning, and equilibrium in games with strategic complementarities, *Econometrica* **58**, 1255–1277.

Paul Milgrom and John Roberts (1994a), Comparing equilibria, *Amer. Econ. Rev.* **84**, 441–459.

Paul Milgrom and John Roberts (1994b), Monotone methods for comparative statics analysis: a note for graduate students, Version 1.5, Working Paper.

Paul Milgrom and John Roberts (1995), Complementarities and fit: strategy, structure, and organizational change in manufacturing, *J. Account. and Econ.* **19**, 179–208.

Paul Milgrom and Chris Shannon (1994), Monotone comparative statics, *Econometrica* **62**, 157–180.

John W. Milnor (1965), *Topology from the Differentiable Viewpoint*, University of Virginia Press, Charlottesville, VA.

Leonard J. Mirman and Itzhak Zilcha (1975), On optimal growth under uncertainty, *J. Econ. Theory* **11**, 329–339.

Tapan Mitra (1992), On the existence of a stationary optimal stock for a multisector economy with nonconvex technology, in *Equilibrium and Dynamics: Essays in Honor of David Gale* (Mukul Majumdar, ed.), St. Martin's Press, New York.

Tapan Mitra (1995), A exact discount factor restriction for period three cycles in dynamic optimization models, *J. Econ. Theory* **69**, 281–305.

Luigi Montrucchio (1994), Dynamic complexity of optimal paths and discount factors for strongly concave problems, *J. Opt. Theory Appl.* **80**, 385–406.

James Moore (1975), The existence of compensated equilibrium and the structure of the Pareto efficiency frontier, *Internat. Econ. Rev.* **16**, 267–300.

Dean Neumann, Thomas O'Brien, John Hoad, and Kyoo Kim (1988), Policy functions for capital accumulation paths, *J. Econ. Theory* **46**, 205–214.

Kazuo Nishimura and Gerhard Sorger (1996), Optimal cycles and chaos: a survey, *Studies in Nonlinear Dynamics and Econometrics* **1**.

Kazuo Nishimura and Makoto Yano (1995), Nonlinear dynamics and chaos in optimal growth: an example, *Econometrica* **63**, 981–1001.

Zbigniew Nitecki (1971), *Differentiable Dynamics*, The MIT Press, Cambridge, MA.

Maurice Obstfeld (1990), Intertemporal dependence, impatience, and dynamics, *J. Mon. Econ.* **26**, 45–75.

Maurice Obstfeld and Kenneth Rogoff (1996), *Foundations of International Macroeconomics*, The MIT Press, Cambridge, MA.

Bezalel Peleg (1970), Efficiency prices for optimal consumption plans, III, *J. Math. Anal. Appl.* **32**, 630–638.

Bezalel Peleg (1974), On competitive prices for optimal consumption plans, *SIAM J. Appl. Math.* **26**, 239–253.

Bezalel Peleg and Harl E. Ryder, Jr. (1974), The modified golden rule of a multi-sector economy, *J. Math. Econ.* **1**, 193–198.

Bezalel Peleg and Menahem E. Yaari (1970), Markets with countably many commodities, *Internat. Econ. Rev.* **11**, 369–377.

Bezalel Peleg and Itzhak Zilcha (1977), On competitive prices for optimal consumption plans, II, *SIAM J. Appl. Math.* **32**, 627–630.

J. Ponstein (1984), Dualizing optimization problems in mathematical economics, *J. Math. Econ.* **13**, 255–272.

Edward C. Prescott and Robert E. Lucas, Jr. (1972), A note on price systems in infinite dimensional spaces, *Internat. Econ. Rev.* **13**, 416–422.

Edward C. Prescott and Rajnish Mehra (1980), Recursive competitive equilibrium: the case of homogeneous households, *Econometrica* **48**, 1365–1380.

Trout Rader (1968), Normally factor inputs are never gross substitutes, *J. Polit. Econ.* **76**, 38–43.

Trout Rader (1981), Utility over time: the homothetic case, *J. Econ. Theory* **25**, 219–236.

Roy Radner (1961), Paths of economic growth that are optimal with regard only to final states, *Rev. Econ. Studies* **28**, 98–104.

John Rae (1834), *Statement of Some New Principles on the Subject of Political Economy*, reprinted by Augustus M. Kelley, New York, 1964.

Frank P. Ramsey (1928), A mathematical theory of saving, *Econ. J.* **38**, 543–559.

L. K. Raut (1986), Myopic topologies on general commodity spaces, *J. Econ. Theory* **39**, 358–367.

John Rawls (1971), *A Theory of Justice*, Harvard University Press, Cambridge, MA.

Debraj Ray and Peter A. Streufert (1993), Dynamic equilibria with unemployment due to undernourishment, *Econ. Theory* **3**, 61–85.

Sérgio Rebelo (1991), Long-run policy analysis and long-run growth, *J. Polit. Econ.* **99**, 500–521.

A. P. Robertson and Wendy Robertson (1973), *Topological Vector Spaces*, Cambridge University Press, Cambridge, UK.

Paul M. Romer (1986), Increasing returns and long-run growth, *J. Polit. Econ.* **94**, 1002–1037.

Paul M. Romer (1989), Capital accumulation in the theory of long run growth, *in Modern Business Cycle Theory* (Robert J. Barro, ed.), Cambridge University Press, Cambridge, UK.

Sheldon M. Ross (1983), *Introduction to Stochastic Dynamic Programming*, Academic Press, New York.

Stephen A. Ross (1976), The arbitrage theory of capital asset pricing, *J. Econ. Theory* **13**, 341–359.

Stephen A. Ross (1978), A simple approach to the valuation of risky streams, *J. Bus.* **51**, 453–475.

Ariel Rubinstein (1979), Equilibrium in supergames with the overtaking criterion, *J. Econ. Theory* **21**, 1–9.

Ariel Rubinstein (1994), Equilibrium in supergames, *in Essays in Game Theory in Honor of Michael Maschler* (Nimrod Meggido, ed.), Springer-Verlag, New York.

H. Sakai and H. Tokumaru (1980), Autocorrelations of a certain chaos, *IEEE Transactions on Acoustics, Speech and Signal Processing* (V.I ASSP-28), 588–590.

Paul A. Samuelson (1947), *Foundations of Economic Analysis*, Harvard University Press, Cambridge, MA.

Paul A. Samuelson (1966), Market mechanisms and maximization, *in The Collected Scientific Papers of Paul A. Samuelson, Volume I* (Joseph E. Stiglitz, ed.), (Chapter 33. Originally 3 RAND Corporation memoranda. Parts I and II, March 28, 1949; Part III, June 29, 1949), The MIT Press, Cambridge, MA.

Paul A. Samuelson (1973), Optimality of profit-including prices under ideal planning, *Proc. Nat. Acad. Sci.* **70**, 2109–2111.

Paul A. Samuelson (1974), Complementarities, *J. Econ. Lit.* **12**, 1255–1289.

Manuel S. Santos (1991), Smoothness of the policy function in discrete-time economic models, *Econometrica* **59**, 1365–1382.

Manuel S. Santos (1992), Differentiability and comparative analysis in discrete-time infinite-horizon optimization, *J. Econ. Theory* **57**, 222–229.

Thomas J. Sargent (1987), *Dynamic Macroeconomic Theory*, Harvard University Press, Cambridge, MA.

Carl Sawyer (1988), Stationary recursive preferences: myopia and impatience reconsidered—the many goods case, Working Paper, Southern Illinois University.

Herbert Scarf (1967), The core of an n-person game, *Econometrica* **35**, 50–69.

Helmut H. Schaefer (1966), *Topological Vector Spaces*, Springer-Verlag, New York.

Jose A. Scheinkman (1976), On optimal steady states of n-sector growth models when utility is discounted, *J. Econ. Theory* **12**, 11–30.

Jose A. Scheinkman (1977), A simple dynamic equilibrium model, unpublished notes, University of Chicago.

Chris Shannon (1995), Weak and strong monotone comparative statics, *Econ. Theory* **5**, 209–227.

Karl Shell and Joseph E. Stiglitz (1967), The allocation of investment in a dynamic economy, *Quart. J. Econ.* **81**, 592–609.

Tomoichi Shinotsuka (1990), *Choice and Equilibrium in Infinite Economies*, Ph.D. Dissertation, University of Rochester.

Tomoichi Shinotsuka (1997), Equity, continuity, and myopia: a generalization of Diamond's impossibility theorem, (forthcoming), *Social Choice and Welfare*.

George F. Simmons (1963), *Introduction to Topology and Modern Analysis*, McGraw-Hill, New York.

A. K. Skiba (1978), Optimal growth with a convex-concave production function, *Econometrica* **46**, 527–539.

Robert M. Solow (1956), A contribution to the theory of economic growth, *Quart. J. Econ.* **70**, 65–94.

Gerhard Sorger (1992a), *Minimum Impatience Theorems for Recursive Economic Models*, Springer-Verlag, New York.

Gerhard Sorger (1992b), On the minimum rate of impatience for complicated optimal growth paths, *J. Econ. Theory* **56**, 160–179.

Gerhard Sorger (1994a), On the structure of Ramsey equilibrium: cycles, indeterminacy, and sunspots, *Econ. Theory*, 745–764.

Gerhard Sorger (1994b), Period three implies heavy discounting, *Math. Oper. Res.* **19**, 1–16.

Gerhard Sorger (1995), Chaotic Ramsey equilibrium, *Internat. J. Bifurcation and Chaos* **2**, 373–380.

Joseph E. Stiglitz (1990), Symposium on bubbles, *J. Econ. Perspectives* **4**, 13–17.

B. P. Stigum (1973), Competitive equilibria with infinitely many commodities (II), *J. Econ. Theory* **6**, 415–445.

Nancy L. Stokey and Robert E. Lucas, Jr., with Edward C. Prescott (1989), *Recursive Methods in Economic Dynamics*, Harvard University Press, Cambridge, MA.

Peter A. Streufert (1990), Stationary recursive utility and dynamic programming under the assumption of biconvergence, *Rev. Econ. Studies* **57**, 79–97.

Peter A. Streufert (1992), An abstract topological approach to dynamic programming, *J. Math. Econ.* **21**, 59–88.

Peter A. Streufert (1995), A general theory of separability for preferences defined on a countably infinite product space, *J. Math. Econ.* **24**, 407–434.

Peter A. Streufert (1997), Recursive utility and dynamic programming, *in Handbook of Utility Theory* (Salvador Barbera, Peter J. Hammond, and Christian Seidl, eds.), forthcoming, Kluwer Academic Publishers, Dordrecht.

R. H. Strotz (1955), Myopia and inconsistency in dynamic utility maximization, *Rev. Econ. Studies* **23**, 165–180.

K. D. Stroyan (1983), Myopic utility functions on sequential economies, *J. Math. Econ.* **11**, 267–276.

Robert Summers and Alan Heston (1984), Improved international comparisons of real product and its composition, *Review of Income and Wealth* (June), 207–262.

Ning Sun and Sho-Ichiro Kusumoto (1996), Infinite horizon equilibria with convex production, Working Paper, Institute of Socio-Economic Planning, University of Tsukuba.

W. R. S. Sutherland (1970), On optimal development in a multi-sectoral economy: the discounted case, *Rev. Econ. Studies* **37**, 585–588.

Lars-Gunnar Svensson (1980), Equity among generations, *Econometrica* **48**, 1251–1256.

Donald M. Topkis (1976), The structure of sublattices of the product of *N* lattices, *Pacific J. Math.* **65**, 525–532.

Donald M. Topkis (1978), Minimizing a submodular function on a lattice, *Operations Research* **26**, 305–321.

Donald M. Topkis (1979), Equilibrium points in nonzero-sum *n*-person submodular games, *SIAM J. Control Optimization* **17**, 773–787.

Donald M. Topkis (1995), Comparative statics of the firm, *J. Econ. Theory* **67**, 370–401.

J. V. Uspensky (1948), *Theory of Equations*, McGraw-Hill, New York.

H. Uzawa (1968), Time preference, the consumption function, and optimum asset holdings, *in Value, Capital and Growth: Papers in Honour of Sir John Hicks* (J. N. Wolfe, ed.), Edinburgh University Press, Edinburgh.

Kirk Varnedoe (1990), *A Fine Disregard: What Makes Modern Art Modern*, Harry N. Abrams, NY.

Xavier Vives (1990), Nash equilibrium with strategic complementarities, *J. Math. Econ.* **19**, 305–321.

John von Neumann (1937), Über ein ökonomisches Gleichungssystem und eine Verallgemeinerung des Brouwerschen Fixpunktsatzes, *Ergeb. Math. Kolloq.* **8**, 73–83; (1945), A model of general equilibrium (translation), *Rev. Econ. Studies* **13**, 1–9.

Léon Walras (1954), *Elements of Pure Economics, Definitive Edition*, (translated by William Jaffé), Richard D. Irwin, Inc., Homewood, Illinois; (1926), *Eléments d'économie politique pure, Édition définitive*, R. Pichon et R. Durand-Ausias, Paris.

Martin L. Weitzman (1973), Duality theory for infinite horizon convex models, *Management Sci.* **19**, 783–789.

C. C. von Weizsäcker (1965), Existence of optimal programs of accumulation for an infinite time horizon, *Rev. Econ. Studies* **32**, 85–104.

Hermann Weyl (1952), *Symmetry*, Princeton University Press, Princeton, NJ.

Stephen Willard (1970), *General Topology*, Addison-Wesley, Reading, MA.

Nicholas C. Yannelis and W. R. Zame (1986), Equilibria in Banach lattices without ordered preferences, *J. Math. Econ.* **15**, 85–110.

Makoto Yano (1984a), Competitive equilibria on turnpikes in a McKenzie economy, I: a neighborhood turnpike theorem, *Internat. Econ. Rev.* **25**, 695–717.

Makoto Yano (1984b), The turnpike of dynamic general equilibrium paths and its insensitivity to initial conditions, *J. Math. Econ.* **13**, 235–254.

Makoto Yano (1985), Competitive equilibria on turnpikes in a McKenzie economy, II: an asymptotic turnpike theorem, *Internat. Econ. Rev.* **26**, 661–669.

Kôsaku Yosida (1974), *Functional Analysis*, Springer-Verlag, New York.

Kôsaku Yosida and Edwin Hewitt (1952), Finitely additive measures, *Trans. Amer. Math. Soc.* **72**, 46–66.

L. C. Young (1969), *Lectures on the Calculus of Variations and Optimal Control Theory*, Chelsea, New York.

W. R. Zame (1987), Competitive equilibria in production economies with an infinite dimensional commodity space, *Econometrica* **55**, 1075–1108.

Index